Barron's Review Course Series

Let's Review:

U.S. History and Government

Second Edition

John McGeehan
Teacher American History/Constitutional Law
 West Islip High School, New York
Member Connecticut and New York Bar
Writer and Consultant for Curriculum Revision
 in United States History and Government for
 State of New York.

Morris Gall
Teacher Social Studies
 New York City High Schools
Supervisor of Social Studies
 Norwalk, Connecticut, Public Schools
Professor of Education and Assistant Dean
 Yeshiva University Graduate School of Education,
 New York
Member New York Bar
Adjunct Professor of Education
 Indiana University
Fulbright Scholar, Japan

BARRON'S

ACKNOWLEDGMENTS

p. 26   Copyright William H. Sadlier, Inc. with permission of publisher. All rights reserved.

p. 58   Reprinted from *Gavel to Gavel, A Guide To The Televised Proceedings of Congress* with permission from the Benton Foundation, Washington, D.C.

p. 82, 105, 238   Mary Beth Norton, David M. Katzman, Paul D. Escott, Howard P. Chudacoff Thomas G. Patterson, William M. Tuttle, Jr. *A People And A Nation,* Fourth Edition © 1994 by Houghton Mifflin Company. Reprinted with permission.

p. 99   "The Kansas-Nebraska Act, 1854" from *The Americans: A Brief History to 1877.* Part One, Second Edition, by Henry F. Bedford and Trevor Colbourn, Copyright © 1976 by Harcourt Brace Jovanovich, Inc., reprinted by permission of the publisher.

p. 181   From ETHNIC AMERICANS: A HISTORY OF IMMIGRATION AND ASSIMILATION by Leonard Dinnerstein and David Reimers. Copyright © 1975 by Dodd, Mead & Co., Inc. Reprinted by permission of Harper and Row, Publishers, Inc.

p. 235   "The American Empire" from THE AMERICAN PAST: A SURVEY OF AMERICAN HISTORY by Joseph Conlin, Copyright © 1984 by Harcourt Brace Jovanovich, Inc., reprinted by permission of the publisher.

p. 256   Reprinted from June 1988 New York State Regents Examination.

p. 266   Reprinted from August 1988 New York State Regents Examination.

All inquiries should be addressed to:
Barron's Educational Series, Inc.
250 Wireless Boulevard, Hauppauge, New York 11788

International Standard Book No. 0-8120-1962-8

Library of Congress Catalog Card No. 94-29829

Library of Congress Cataloging-in-Publication Data
McGeehan, John.
　　Let's review: U.S. history and government / John McGeehan, Morris
Gall. — 2nd ed.
　　　　p. cm.—(Barron's review course series) Includes index.
　　ISBN 0-8120-1962-8
　　　　1. United States—History. 2. United States—History—Study and
teaching (Secondary) 3. United States—Constitutional history. 4. United
States—Constitutional history—Study and teaching (Secondary) I. Gall,
Morris, 1907– II. Title. III. Series
E178.1.M156　　1995
973—dc20　　　　　　　　　　　　　　　　94-29829
　　　　　　　　　　　　　　　　　　　　　　　CIP

PRINTED IN THE UNITED STATES OF AMERICA

567　　8800　　987654321

TABLE OF CONTENTS

UNIT 6 A World in Uncertain Times (1950–Present)   367

MAPS

CHARTS

PREFACE

For Which Course Was This Book Designed?

This book was designed as a review text for the New York State Regents course in U.S. History and Government. The material follows the revised syllabus in Regents Social Studies: U.S. History and Government (1987), which is used throughout New York State as the basis of a course of study in history on the secondary level. The new curriculum has incorporated the Thirteen Enduring Constitutional Issues as identified by Project '87, a joint project of the American Historical Association and American Political Science Association in celebration of the Bicentennial of the Constitution. These are the "thirteen enduring issues":

- National Power—limits and potential
- Federalism: the balance between nation and state
- The Judiciary: interpreter of the Constitution or shaper of public policy
- Civil Liberties: the balance between government and the individual
- Criminal Penalties—rights of the accused and protection of the community
- Equality: its definition as a Constitutional value
- The Rights of Women under the Constitution
- The Rights of Ethnic and Racial Groups under the Constitution
- Presidential Power in Wartime and in Foreign Affairs
- The Separation of Powers and the Capacity to Govern
- Avenues of Representation
- Property Rights and Economic Policy
- Constitutional Change and Flexibility

Although the material has been prepared to meet the needs of New York State students, this book can help students in any secondary-level U.S. History and Government course.

What Are the Special Features of This Book?

The arrangement of topical information parallels, for the most part, that of the New York State Regents syllabus in U.S. History and Government. Each of the six major units begins with a brief explanation of the key ideas in the unit and a list of unit goals that should remain major objectives as students progress through the course.*

* United States History and Government Syllabus, The University of the State of New York, The State Education Department, Bureau of Curriculum Development, Albany, New York 12234, 1988.

Each unit is broken down into several chapters that are consistent with the major divisions in the U.S. History and Government syllabus. At the end of each chapter are multiple-choice questions and essays that coincide with the style of question in Parts I, II, and III of the New York State Regents Examination. In some cases, past Regents Examination questions have been included. The questions range from recall-drill to complex thought questions. They may be used to start class discussion and to help students review important information.

Because of the intimidating amount and the complexity of information presented in a course on U.S. History and Government, it is necessary to provide order to the data. A comprehensive, overall **Chronology of Events in American History**, located at the end of the volume, should help the student with a visual order of important events and can show the cause and effect pattern of our country's story. This new and revised edition also contains a **Glossary of Terms** commonly used to discuss U.S. History and government, a section of short biographies of **Notable Americans**, a collection of **Historical Documents**, including the Declaration of Independence and the Constitution and Amendments, and a selection of significant **Quotations**, organized chronologically. These materials, located at the end of the volume, are intended both as reference aids and guides for study and review.

Complementing the text and questions are graphs, political cartoons, maps, and charts to help portray necessary information, express points of view, and allow the student to apply interpretive skills.

Finally, three complete Regents Examinations from the new curriculum have been reprinted for testing purposes.

Who May Use This Book?

Let's Review: United States History and Government provides a valuable supplement to a regular textbook in United States history. For teachers in New York State schools, this text offers an excellent source of review material to prepare students for the New York State Regents Examination in United States History and Government.

This book has been designed to meet the syllabus of the New York State course in American History and Government, but any student taking a course in American Studies will find it a helpful source for review and examination preparation.

Taking the Regents Examination

Although teachers and students alike find an "all or nothing" examination at the completion of a course distasteful, the Regents Examination in American History and Government in some ways, unfortunately, falls into this category. Without passing the Regents Examination, the student cannot obtain a Regents Diploma.

This brief passage does not claim to provide a comprehensive study guide for taking a Regents Examination. **Barron's Regents Exams and Answers** provides a complete, 70-page section on exam-taking tips and study techniques that will assist students in examination preparation. But here are a few tips to consider:

(1) Preparation for the Regents Examination begins the first day of class. Good study habits, effective note-taking, completion of all assignments, and a positive attitude throughout the year will make any exam easier at the completion of the course.

(2) Follow directions closely on the examination itself. Many students are not successful because they do not provide requested information, or they leave sections of the question out of their answer. The essays have repeatedly used a format like the following: *"Select **two** issues and for each one give **three** reasons which led to . . ."* It is imperative that the student provide the information requested. Graders have their "hands tied" by the directions; they must deduct points if information is missing.

(3) When answering the Part II and Part III essay question, be aware of the scoring breakdown. It will usually be indicated as follows: (5,5,5) or (10) and (5), etc. Keep in mind, especially if time grows short, that some areas are given greater credit than others and therefore should be answered first.

(4) Be aware of key terms in the questions, for example, *show, discuss, compare.* Underline key words in the directions to the questions.

(5) Budget your time. New York State allows three hours for completion of the exam. You have three parts: Part I (47–50 multiple-choice questions), Part II (one essay) and Part III (two essays). Wear a watch and plan your time while taking practice examinations.

(6) Answer all questions. In the Part I questions, use the process of elimination if necessary. In Parts II and III don't get lazy! You can be given credit only for information provided in your answers.

(7) Relax and be confident.

UNIT ONE _____

Constitutional Foundations of the United States

KEY IDEAS: Unit One explores both the formative stage of our Constitution and its implementation through the Civil War period. Chapters I and II illustrate the origins of the document, the actual structure and functions of its components, and the tests our constitutional system faced in its early development.

UNIT GOALS: By the end of the unit, the student should be able to demonstrate

1. A knowledge and understanding of the constitutional basis for our government and history during the nation's early years of development.

2. An appreciation and respect for the democratic values to which the United States is committed.

Chapter 1

THE CONSTITUTION FORMED

FOUNDATIONS, REVOLUTION, AND CONFEDERATION

> Let Americans disdain to be the instruments of European greatness. Let the thirteen states, bound together in a strict and indissoluble Union, concur in erecting one great American system, superior to the control of all transatlantic force or influence, and able to dictate the terms of the connection between the old and the new world!
> Alexander Hamilton, *The Federalist* (1787–1788), No. 11

Before the founding of the American republic, there were few examples in history of a successful republic that included more than a single city or a small confederation of a few cities and territories. The ancient city-state of Athens and the republic of Rome contributed many important concepts to the Western tradition of government, including direct and representative democracy, jury systems, and the development of legal systems. However, when Athens and Rome began to expand and took over new territories, their democratic governments eventually came to an end. They first became tyrannical empires and then either collapsed into anarchy or fell under the rule of military or oligarchic despotism.

Although the U.S. Constitution was not the first one in history, it is the oldest written constitution still in effect. The word **constitution** means the entire legal framework of a nation, or the nation's plan of government. A written constitution that specifically set forth a plan of government, established its institutions, and outlined the rights of citizens as the American Constitution does, is a relatively new development in history.

Foundations

Democratic Roots in the English Experience

During the colonial period (1607–1763) many of the political institutions of England were transmitted to the English colonies in America. Four major landmarks in English history provided a foundation for American constitutional government:

• *Magna Carta (1215).* Although this document was originally designed to protect the feudal nobles from the absolute rule of the king, it later came to apply to all English subjects and provided that (1) the king was subject to

3

the rule of law; (2) Parliament was responsible for the levying of taxes; and (3) all accused persons were guaranteed a trial by jury of peers, or equals.

• *English Bill of Rights (1689).* This document was truly revolutionary because, at a time when absolute monarchs ruled, it established the idea that there were limits on the powers of kings and queens. The English Bill of Rights, much of which was later incorporated into our own, provided that (1) the king could not interfere with parliamentary elections and debates; (2) the king could not suspend laws, levy taxes, or maintain an army without the consent of Parliament; and (3) the people were guaranteed basic rights to **petition the government**, to an **impartial and speedy trial**, to protection against **excessive fines and bails**, and to protection from **cruel and unusual punishment**.

• *Common Law.* In England, the verdicts of judges were written down, collected, and became the basis for future legal decisions. These common practices and legal decisions formed a body of law known as **common law**. Many of these legal precedents were later passed by Parliament and became **statute law**. Certain **fundamental rights** that developed from the English common law and later became part of statute law were designed to protect the citizen from tyrannical government.

• *A Bicameral Legislature.* By the 14th century, Parliament, the legislative body of English government, had divided into two houses or chambers: (1) the **House of Lords**, consisting of higher clergy and nobility; and (2) the **House of Commons**, representing the wealthy middle class.

Constitutional Development in Colonial America

Many of the democratic characteristics of American constitutional government can be traced back to the colonial experience. Two important precedents that influenced the development of government in the colonies concerned (1) the structure of government (primarily the distribution of power among its parts); and (2) the relationship of the individual to government. By the time the colonies were being settled, English subjects had already developed a theory of **limited government**, or the idea that government did not have absolute power, but was restricted by certain laws and procedures.

• *Colonial Charters.* During the early period of English settlement, the colonies in America were largely self-governing. This was due to the privileges granted by the colonial charters and because geographical distance and other conditions made it difficult for the Crown to tightly control the colonies during the 17th century. Each colony had a charter, or grant, of privileges from the king. There were three basic types of colonial government, the major difference being in the way the governor was chosen. In the **self governing** colonies, such as Connecticut and Rhode Island, the governor was chosen by the colonists. In the **proprietary** colonies, such as Pennsyl-

4

vania, Maryland, and Delaware, the governor was selected by the proprietor. In the **royal** colonies, such as New York, Virginia, and Georgia, the governor and other high officials were selected by the king. Later in the colonial period, most of the colonies were made royal colonies in order to bring them under direct control of the Crown.

• *Colonial Governing Instruments.* England did not send a governor and a council to each settlement in North America (as was the practice of the Spanish and the French). As a result, other methods of government were used in some of the English settlements in the early colonial period. Among these were the joint-stock corporation, the concept of government by compact, and the proprietorship.

Joint-Stock Principle. Some colonies were settled by a joint-stock company, a form of business organization. The company received a charter from the English Crown granting it a monopoly over trade and colonization for a period of years within a specific area. In return, the company was to give the Crown a share of profits earned and precious metals such as gold or silver that it acquired. Although the primary function of the joint-stock company was economic, the charter also gave it the authority to govern its territory. Consequently, in their early days as colonies, both Virginia and Massachusetts were governed by the company that founded them.

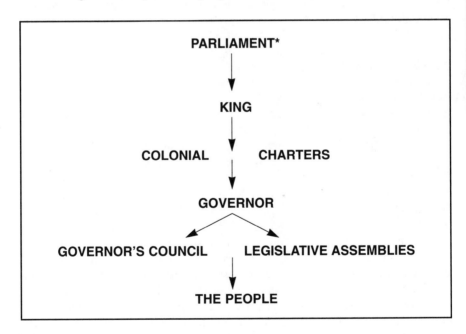

Figure 1.1 Colonial Government Structure

*The Supremacy of Parliament was established following the Glorious Revolution in 1688.

Virginia, the earliest successful English colony, was founded in 1607 by the Virginia Company of London under a grant from the Crown. In 1619 the governor allowed the eligible voters in the colony to elect a local representative assembly. This lawmaking body, called the **Virginia House of Burgesses,** was the first elected legislature in the colonies and marked the first step toward representative government in the colonies. It set an important precedent that eventually came to be accepted in the colonies: the people were the legitimate source of governmental authority. All the English colonies eventually established the same pattern of government. They all had a governor, a council, and a representative assembly.

The Massachusetts Bay Colony, which was also established by a joint-stock company, was founded by middle-class Puritans who wanted to establish a refuge for their religious beliefs in North America. Central to their world view was the idea of a covenant with God that made them a distinct people. This idea of a covenant carried over into the colony's government, which was based on a contract or agreement that existed between the rulers and the ruled. The government was still far from democratic, as only selected church members were allowed to become "freemen," and given the right to vote.

Government by Compact. Although the settlements of Plymouth, Rhode Island, Connecticut, and New Haven were never as politically important as Virginia and Massachusetts Bay, they were significant in that their governments were based on a **social contract**. In 1620, before they landed at Plymouth, the settlers on board the *Mayflower* realized that they had no recognized authoritative body and made plans for self-government. The adult males drew up and signed an agreement that later became known as the **Mayflower Compact**, in which they agreed to obey the laws that they would adopt. They agreed to consult each other about matters affecting the community and to abide by majority rule.

In 1636, after his banishment from Massachusetts Bay for advocating **separation of church and state**, **Roger Williams** and his followers founded the town of Providence in Rhode Island. They entered into a compact agreement very similar to that of the Plymouth settlers. In 1644 Williams obtained a charter for the colony of Rhode Island that did not require voters to be church members.

The settlements of New Haven and those along the Connecticut River were also settled by Puritan dissenters moving southward. Perhaps the most significant of all the early covenants was the **Fundamental Orders of Connecticut**, adopted in 1639, the first written constitution in America. The Fundamental Orders implied that government rested upon the **consent of the governed** and that it should express the will of the majority.

The significance of the written compacts of Plymouth, Rhode Island, and Connecticut, along with the corporation charters of the joint-stock companies, cannot be overemphasized in the study of the development and growth of self-government in North America. As the colonies constructed plans of government that defined the structure and powers of government, arbitrary rule by the Crown became less and less tolerable to them.

Proprietorship. The proprietary colonies were established by a feudal patent or a royal grant of land in the New World given by the Crown, usually to friends or relatives. Under this grant, the proprietor, or owner, was given the right to establish a colony and to rule it. However, a major restriction contained in the royal grant was that the laws for the colony must be made "by and with consent of the freemen," that is, a colonial legislature.

Such a royal grant was used in the founding of Maryland by George Calvert, the first Lord Baltimore, in 1632. James, the Duke of York, the younger brother of King Charles II, became the proprietor of New York after the Dutch surrendered what had been their colony of New Netherland to a British fleet stationed in the Hudson River in 1664.

Signs of Colonial Unity

Colonial unity, within the colonies and among them, evolved slowly. Although each colony maintained independent ties with England and in many ways acted independently, early attempts at achieving colonial union were made both by the colonies themselves and by England in order to gain greater control over its colonies.

• *The New England Confederation (1643–1684).* Massachusetts Bay, Plymouth, Connecticut, and New Haven made up the membership of this Puritan confederacy. Through representatives meeting together to face mutual problems, the colonists took important steps toward colonial cooperation. The New England Confederation was the first major step toward colonial unity.

• *Dominion of New England (1684–1688).* In 1686 King James II created the Dominion of New England, which joined the colonies of New York, New Jersey, and the New England colonies of Massachusetts Bay, Plymouth, New Hampshire, Maine, Rhode Island, and Connecticut under one government. He appointed Sir Edward Andros as governor-general of the Dominion and abolished the legislatures. **Town meetings**, the basic form of local government in New England, were restricted. James took these actions because the colonists refused to comply with the Navigation Acts, which were designed to regulate the trade of the colonies. As a storm of opposition rose from the colonists, the **Glorious Revolution** of 1688 in England brought about the overthrow of James II and confirmed the supremacy of Parliament over the king. As a result, the Dominion of New England collapsed.

• *The Albany Congress (1754).* In 1754 England called the Albany Congress to establish intercolonial cooperation in dealing with the growing French influence in the Ohio Valley and in lower Canada and to attempt to keep the Iroquois Indians loyal to the British. The **Albany Plan of Union**, drafted by **Benjamin Franklin**, who proposed that the colonies

Benjamin Franklin drafted a plan for a colonial union in 1754.

unite in a permanent union for defense, consisted of a governing body composed of a president-general, appointed and paid by the Crown, and a grand council, elected by the colonial assemblies. The plan was accepted by the delegates at the Albany Congress, but turned down by the colonies for not providing enough independence, and by England for providing too much colonial independence. Although the Albany Plan failed, it introduced the concept of a **federal** plan of representative government, with specific powers given to a central authority, which later served as a model for the United States Constitution.

• *The Iroquois Confederation.* The Iroquois Confederation, also called the **Haudenosaunee Union**, included the Six Nations—the Mohawk, Tuscarora, Cayuga, Seneca, Onondaga, and Oneida nations. Its purpose was to keep peace among the tribes and to provide for mutual defense. Based on a federal system, the individual nations maintained their independence while granting some powers to the Confederation. The central authority in the Confederation consisted of representatives from each Indian nation. It is likely that the union served as a model for colonial union and influenced the Albany Plan of Union and, later, the Articles of Confederation.

Problems of Control

By the middle of the 18th century, there were thirteen British colonies in North America. By 1750 most of the colonies had been made royal colonies, with governing structures reflecting those of the British government. A **governor's council,** made up mainly of conservative, wealthy colonists, sat as an upper house of the legislature. It could amend or reject legislation passed by the **popularly elected assembly**. This lower house of the legislature was chosen by the colonists who met the property qualifications for voting. The assembly could initiate tax bills, exercise administrative oversight concerning the expenditure of funds, and fix qualifications for their own membership. The governor, appointed by the Crown, had the power to veto legislation passed by the colonial assembly and to call or dissolve the assembly.

Frequent conflicts between the popularly elected assemblies and the royally appointed governors symbolized the struggle for colonial self-rule during the 18th century. An early example of this conflict was **Bacon's Rebellion** in Virginia. **Nathaniel Bacon**, a member of the Virginia House of Burgesses, led an uprising against the royal governor Berkeley that resulted in the burning of Jamestown in 1676. The governors gradually lost power to the colonial assemblies largely because the assemblies' control of finances allowed them to deny appropriations of money to governors who defied the popular will. The following five factors allowed the colonial legislatures to expand their powers and control over colonial government.

- *Expansion of Colonial Suffrage.* Although property ownership was a requirement for voting in the colonies, the abundance of inexpensive land made it possible for many colonists to own property and therefore to vote. By the time of the Revolution, about 75 percent of the adult white males in the colonies were able to vote.

- *Social and Economic Change.* Unlike England, the American colonies did not have a hereditary aristocracy. Consequently, the governor's council, which was the colonies' political equivalent of the House of Lords, was not made up of the nobility, but instead drew many of its members from the growing prosperous class of merchants, lawyers, and planters in the colonies. Representatives from this elite group not only served on the governor's council, but also frequently served as representatives in the colonial assemblies. As a result, the governor's council never had the political influence that the House of Lords had and the prosperous middle class provided the colonies with their leaders.

- *Actual Representation v. Virtual Representation.* **Virtual representation** was the belief that all English subjects were represented in Parliament simply by virtue of their status as citizens. However, the colonists came to believe in the concept of **actual representation,** the idea that to be properly represented in a legislature, citizens had to vote directly for delegates who represented their interests. By the time of the American Revolution, the American colonists formally rejected the British argument that they were "virtually represented" in Parliament.

- *Separation of Powers.* Rather than the overlapping of many powers between the executive and the legislature, such as existed between the British Crown and Parliament, the colonists believed that the powers of their legislatures ought to be free from executive (governor) control.

- *England's "Salutary Neglect."* Because of England's own problems— such as the Glorious Revolution of 1688 and wars with Holland, France, and Spain during the 17th century—the local governing bodies of the colonies were allowed to expand their powers and activities. During this period of so-called salutary neglect, the British allowed the colonies a great amount of self-government and economic freedom. When the British tried to tighten their control over the colonies after the French and Indian War (1756–1763), they met with opposition from the American colonists who saw the extension of royal authority as interfering with popularly accepted liberties. As this colonial opposition grew, it set the stage for the American Revolution.

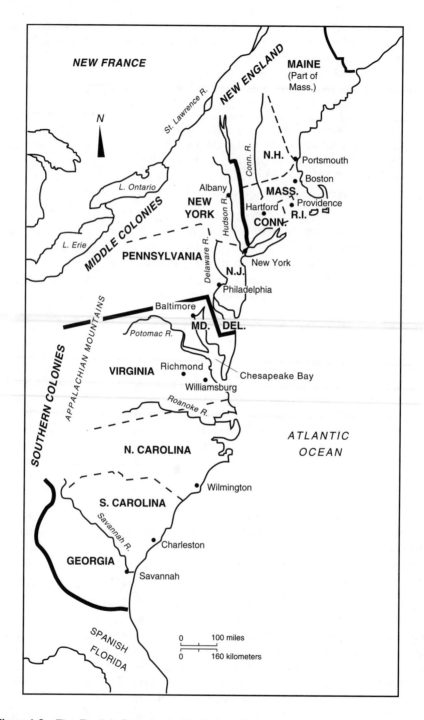

Figure 1.2 The English Colonies in North America

Revolution and Independence

Importance of Locke's Ideas

> The natural liberty of man is to be free from any superior power on earth, and not to be under the will or legislative authority of man, but to have only the law of nature as his rule. The liberty of man in society is to be under no other legislative power but that established in the commonwealth; nor under the dominion of any will or restraint of any law but what that legislative shall enact according to the trust put in it.
>
> John Locke, *The Second Treatise of Government* (1690)

In this quote the English philosopher and political thinker **John Locke** (1632–1704) refers to the law of nature. **Thomas Jefferson** later stated this idea in the Declaration of Independence:

> We hold these truths to be self-evident, that all men are created equal, that they are endowed by their Creator with certain inalienable rights, that among these are **life, liberty, and the pursuit of happiness**.
>
> *Declaration of Independence* (1776)

The second half of Locke's quote stresses the importance of self-rule and the responsibility of a government to those whom it governs. Again, Jefferson's reliance upon the thoughts of Locke becomes apparent when one examines the Declaration of Independence:

> That to secure these rights, governments are instituted among men, deriving their just powers from the consent of the governed. That whenever any form of government becomes destructive to these ends, it is the right of the people to alter or to abolish it, and to institute a new government . . .
>
> *Declaration of Independence* (1776)

An important distinction should be made between natural law and positive law. **Natural law**, as referred to in Locke's *The Second Treatise of Government,* includes those rights essential to the natural existence of humankind. Among these are the rights to life, liberty, and property and the belief that all people are equal in the possession of these rights. **Positive law**, on the other hand, includes the laws created by conventions, legislatures, and courts necessary for the proper operation of government.

The Fifth Amendment to the United States Constitution was prepared by **James Madison** as a necessary addition to the Constitution (along with the rest of the **Bill of Rights**) to place restrictions upon both the federal and state governments. The Fifth Amendment reads in part:

> No person shall . . . be deprived of life, liberty, or property, without due process of law.
>
> Fifth Amendment to the United States Constitution (1791)

The Amendment itself is an example of *positive law*, or law created to ensure the proper operation of government. However, the "life, liberty, and property" referred to within the Fifth Amendment are examples of natural rights of the governed being protected by the government. The Fifth Amendment provides an excellent example of the combination of natural and positive law.

Theory of Limited Government (Locke, Montesquieu, and Rousseau)

The period of English colonization came at a time when European political thinkers were setting forth the idea that governments should be structured on a foundation of law and that a contract existed between the government and the governed. It was not too great a step from that idea to the belief that revolution against those who abused the existing contract was justified. The makers of our own revolution and later the founders of our constitutional system of government were guided in their actions and beliefs by the theory of natural rights and the idea of representative government, as advocated by Locke, the idea of separation of the powers of government by dividing it into **executive**, **legislative**, and **judicial** branches, as outlined by Montesquieu, and finally, by the idea of **popular sovereignty**, as championed by Rousseau.

Although the common sentiment among the colonists on the eve of the Revolution was that the law of England prevailed, a transformation was taking place. The strong tendency toward political involvement among the colonists, combined with the evolution of a uniquely American form of representative government, made it difficult for the American colonists to find their place in the English parliamentary system.

British Mercantilism and American Capitalism

By the end of the French and Indian War in 1763, the American colonies had grown to be a strong and thriving part of the British Empire. This was a result of lax British regulation under the policy of salutary neglect, which allowed a considerable amount of manufacturing to develop within the colonies. It was also due to the "triangular trade" that involved Africa, the West Indies, and the colonies.

• *Mercantilism.* During the 17th and 18th centuries, England, as did most European countries, believed that power depended upon monetary wealth and that the colonies were a source of wealth in that they would (1) provide raw materials for the mother country; (2) import manufactured products of higher values from England; and (3) not compete with the mother country in economic activities.

English mercantile policy with the American colonies can be divided into two distinct periods, with 1763 as the dividing point. England's early mercantile policies were designed to make sure that the colonies produced raw materials and purchased manufactured goods from the mother country. It passed laws such as the **Woolen Act** (1699), the **Hat Act** (1732), and the **Iron Act** (1750), which prohibited manufacturing. Beginning in 1651 Parliament also passed a series of **Navigation Acts**, which required that (1) all commerce with the colonies had to be carried on in English-built and English-owned ships; (2) certain specific, or enumerated products, such as sugar, tobacco, indigo, and cotton could be exported only to England or English colonies; and (3) imports from Europe to the colonies had to be brought first to English ports for the payment of import duties before being sent to America.

Although the colonists resented these restrictions, they did benefit from them in some ways. These included (1) English (including colonial) goods had to be transported in English ships, resulting in the growth of a prosperous shipbuilding industry in the New England colonies; (2) certain goods could be sent only to England or the English colonies, giving the colonists a monopoly on those products in England and in some cases in the world market; and (3) colonial trade received the protection of the English navy.

After 1763 Britain decided to tighten its control over both the political and economic affairs of the colonies. To carry this out, Britain ended the policy of salutary neglect and began to enforce the mercantilist system. This new policy aroused strong colonial opposition for several reasons:

- *Salutary Neglect.* During the period of salutary neglect, Britain had allowed the colonies to develop in their own way, which resulted in the colonists viewing mercantilism differently from the British government. While the colonists thought of themselves as equal trading partners with England, the English government viewed them as subordinates, existing to benefit the mother country. After 1763 England attempted to vigorously enforce this viewpoint.

- *Mercantilism as an Answer to England's Economic Survival.* Because of the debts incurred from fighting the French and Indian War (1754–1763) and the need to protect the new territory acquired from France after the war, Britain found it necessary to create new sources of revenue. Since the British felt that the colonists should help pay for their defense, Britain decided to raise money by taxing the colonists.

- *Restrictions on Westward Expansion.* The colonists viewed the French and Indian War as a struggle to open the Mississippi valley and Ohio valley for settlement. After the war, many colonists began to migrate westward. This invasion of Indian land by white settlers resulted in **Pontiac's Rebellion** (May 1763), an uprising in which several Indian tribes joined together and attacked settlements and forts on the frontier. The British, who could not protect the frontier, and who wished to avoid further conflicts, issued the **Proclamation of 1763**. This forbade settlement west of the Appalachian Mountains. Encouraged by an adventurous and growing population, which had grown from a quarter of a million in 1700 to over two million in 1770, the colonists continued to settle in western Pennsylvania, Tennessee, and Kentucky.

The New Colonial System and the Formation of the American Resistance Movement

In its attempt to more closely supervise the colonies, Britain's "new" colonial policy had four main objectives: (1) to regulate western expansion and Indian affairs; (2) to keep a standing army in America; (3) to enforce the Navigation Acts; and (4) to raise money in the colonies through taxes including, for the first time, direct taxation of the colonists for the purpose of raising revenue rather than obtaining revenue through the regulation of trade.

• *The Grenville Ministry (1763–1765).* At the urging of George Grenville, the British Prime Minister from 1763 to 1765, Parliament set out to raise money to balance Britain's budget by strictly enforcing the existing mercantile laws and by passing new taxes for the colonies.

The Sugar Act (1764). Designed to replace the Molasses Act of 1733, the Sugar Act lowered the duty on imported molasses in an attempt to stop colonial smuggling. It also placed duties on sugar, indigo, coffee, wines, and linens. However, the stated purpose of the act was to raise money to help pay Britain's expenses of protecting the colonies. This was a revolutionary idea, for it turned the mercantile privilege of controlling trade into a method of directly raising revenue. It raised the question of Britain's right to tax the colonies without their actual representation in Parliament. Consequently, the colonists objected to the tax since the money collected from it was "revenue" to pay for colonial expenses, as opposed to a tax to regulate trade.

Currency Reform (1764). The Currency Act of 1764 forbade the colonies to issue paper money. This prohibition had been in effect in the New England colonies since the passage of the Currency Act of 1751, but it now applied to all the colonies. The act allowed only the use of "**hard money**" (silver and gold), which was scarce in the colonies, and required the colonists to pay taxes in gold or silver.

The Stamp Act (1765). Passed in February 1765, the Stamp Act was the second measure in Grenville's program that attempted to raise revenue to pay for Britain's costs in defending the colonies. It required that certain documents be written or printed on paper carrying a stamp from the British treasury office.

The tax, a constant reminder of Parliament's authority, affected nearly every aspect of commercial and industrial life in the colonies. Especially hard hit by the new tax were lawyers, merchants, and editors—those with the greatest ability to voice their objections to the revenue-raising measure. Those accused of violating its provisions could be tried in an admiralty court—without a jury.

Opposition to the Stamp Act. When news of the passage of the Stamp Act reached the colonies in March 1765, opposition exploded. Following a fiery speech by **Patrick Henry**, the Virginia House of Burgesses adopted the **Virginia Resolves**, which denied that Parliament had the right to tax the colonies without their consent, claiming that only the House of Burgesses could tax the Virginia colonists.

With Massachusetts in the lead, delegates from nine colonies met in New York in October 1765 to voice their opposition to the Stamp Act. The resolutions drafted by the **Stamp Act Congress** rejected the concept of "virtual representation" in the House of Commons. Parliament was to maintain responsibility for matters of a more general nature to the empire. Besides claiming that only the colonial legislatures in which the colonists were represented could levy taxes, they agreed to resist all taxes not consented to by the colonial legislatures.

Colonial opposition to the Stamp Act resulted in numerous nonimportation agreements, in which the colonists promised not to buy British goods. Early in 1766 Parliament repealed the Stamp Act, causing much celebration in the colonies.

The Declaratory Act. Early in 1766 Parliament also passed the **Declaratory Act**, which stated that Parliament had absolute authority over the colonies "in all cases whatsoever." This meant that Parliament had the authority to tax the colonies, in spite of colonial protests over the Stamp Act.

The Stamp Act crisis was significant in several ways. The Stamp Act Congress and the effectiveness of the widespread nonimportation agreements showed that the colonies could unite and work together. Resistance groups, such as the **Sons of Liberty**, coordinated opposition throughout the colonies. Secondly, the crisis helped bring into focus the primary issues that existed between Britain and the American colonies: the status of the colonists in the British Empire, and the taxation powers of Parliament over the American colonies.

- *The Townshend Acts (1767–1770).* Following the repeal of the Stamp Act, King George III appointed **William Pitt** as Prime Minister and **Charles Townshend** as Chancellor of the Exchequer. Under Townshend, Parliament once again tried to raise revenue in the colonies. Parliament decided to return to indirect taxes such as collecting duties on goods imported by the colonies. Such duties had long been accepted. The Townshend Acts included new taxes and stricter enforcement of the existing mercantile laws.

Import Duties on Glass, Lead, Paint, Paper, and Tea. These were passed to regulate trade and therefore were within the right of Parliament to create and enforce. However, their stated purpose was for "the support of civil government, in such provinces as it shall be found necessary." That is, they were to raise money to defend the colonies. Therefore, the colonists objected to the import duties because they were a tax measure to raise revenue, not a commercial regulation.

Board of Commissioners and Writs of Assistance. Under the Townshend Acts, Parliament established a special Board of Commissioners within the colonies to enforce the Navigation Acts and to make sure the duties were collected. The use of **writs of assistance**, or search warrants, by British customs officials to search colonists' businesses, homes, and ships for smuggled goods was approved.

Opposition to the Townshend Acts. Opposition to the Townshend Acts in the colonies was strong. In response to the new taxes, **John Dickinson**, a conservative Philadelphia lawyer, posed as a simple Pennsylvania farmer and published a series of unsigned newspaper articles entitled "Letters from a Farmer in Pennsylvania" (1767). Dickinson argued that although Parliament was the supreme legislature over the empire and had certain regulatory powers over the colonies, all other powers belonged to the colonies themselves. One of these rights was to control the raising of revenue by levying taxes.

Opposition to the writs of assistance was best expressed by **James Otis**, a Boston attorney. Using the principles of natural law, which included the freedom of one's "house" from unauthorized searches and seizures without **probable cause**, Otis argued that an act of Parliament against natural rights was void.

As colonial discontent and resistance grew, the difficulty of maintaining order increased. As a result, more British troops were sent to America. A period of greater disorder followed as customs agents were mobbed and tarred and feathered, and troops were harassed.

The Boston Massacre, in an engraving by Paul Revere.

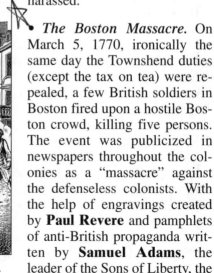

• *The Boston Massacre.* On March 5, 1770, ironically the same day the Townshend duties (except the tax on tea) were repealed, a few British soldiers in Boston fired upon a hostile Boston crowd, killing five persons. The event was publicized in newspapers throughout the colonies as a "massacre" against the defenseless colonists. With the help of engravings created by **Paul Revere** and pamphlets of anti-British propaganda written by **Samuel Adams**, the leader of the Sons of Liberty, the

American colonists became further inflamed in their resentment of British rule.

• *Period of Calm, 1770–1773.* This three-year period of relative tranquillity was due to the repeal of the Townshend duties and the reluctance of **Lord North**, who became Prime Minister in 1770, to impose new taxes. It was also due to the colonists' realization of potential hostilities with Britain that was made real by the deaths in Boston. Under the leadership of Samuel Adams in 1773, a system of **Committees of Correspondence** was developed in each colony to spread the word of any new crisis.

• *The Tea Act (1773).* To help the struggling **British East India Company**, Parliament decided to allow the direct shipment of tea from India to the colonies without having the tea go through London, thereby reducing the price of tea sold in the colonies. Parliament hoped that the lower-priced tea would end the boycott of British tea by the American colonists and end the large-scale smuggling of Dutch tea. The **Tea Act** meant that British tea could now be purchased in the colonies for about half the price of smuggled tea.

The colonists who smuggled and sold the tea took the lead in opposing the Tea Act. They claimed that the Tea Act was simply another tax on the colonies passed by Parliament. On the evening of December 16, 1773, approximately 60 men, thinly disguised as Mohawk Indians, boarded three ships in Boston harbor and threw 342 chests of tea worth approximately £10,000 ($15,000) into the sea.

• *The Coercive, or "Intolerable" Acts (1774).* In March 1774, in response to the Boston Tea Party, Britain retaliated with five acts that the colonies called the "**Intolerable**" **Acts**.

The Boston Port Act closed the port of Boston until the colonists paid the British East India Company for the destroyed tea.

The Massachusetts Government Act altered the Massachusetts charter of 1691, giving Britain greater control over the colony and severely limiting self-government. Colonists were restricted to holding one town meeting a year. The governor's council, which was the upper house of the legislature, was no longer to be elected by the colonial assembly, but was to be appointed by the Crown.

The Administration of Justice Act provided that, in the cases of crimes committed by officials of the Crown while enforcing British laws, the trial could be moved to Great Britain.

The Quartering Act, passed June 2, 1774, gave British officials within the colonies broad authority to quarter, or house, troops wherever they chose in a town, rather than in barracks provided by the colonies.

The Quebec Act was passed in an effort to maintain the allegiance of the French. It allowed Catholicism and French civil law in Canada and established the boundaries of Quebec as the Ohio River on the south, the Mississippi River on the west, and the Proclamation Line of 1763 on the east. The Quebec Act, though not passed to punish the colonists, outraged them for several reasons. First, it appeared to violate several colonial charters by destroying the claims of three colonies to lands west of the Appalachians. Secondly, it allowed religious freedom to the Roman Catholics, a religion strongly disliked by Protestant colonists.

Declaration and Revolution (1774–1783)

Most colonists strongly opposed the Intolerable Acts, and some came close to outright rebellion. The patriot organizations of Massachusetts responded to the acts by sending out appeals for aid from the other colonies and requested an immediate boycott of British goods. On a call from Virginia, all the colonies except Georgia sent delegates to a **Continental Congress**.

• *The First Continental Congress (1774).* It met at Carpenters Hall in Philadelphia on September 5, 1774. The delegates at the Congress were narrowly divided between those who favored resistance and those who advocated conciliation. Although illness kept **Thomas Jefferson** of Virginia away from the meeting, his *Summary View of the Rights of British America,* claiming Parliament to be only the "legislature of one part of the empire," was used as supportive argument by the more radical members at the Congress. Yet it must be understood that the Continental Congress opposed any "designs of separation from Great Britain and establishing independent states."

The Galloway Plan. Joseph Galloway proposed a plan for an intercolonial legislature composed of delegates chosen to serve for three years by the colonial assemblies. This legislature was to be presided over by a president-general appointed by the king. As the more radical group at the Continental Congress continued to gain influence, the Galloway plan was rejected by one vote.

The Suffolk Resolves. Samuel Adams presented these resolutions, which included an absolute disregard for the Coercive Acts and a demand for restoration of constitutional government in Massachusetts. They were unanimously adopted and set the tone for the statement drafted by Congress listing colonial grievances.

Declaration of Rights and Grievances. Adopted by Congress on October 14, 1774, the Declaration of Rights and Grievances held that: (1) obedience would be paid only to the king; (2) Parliament did not have the right to tax the colonies; and (3) the following rights were guaranteed to the colonists by

18

the laws of nature, principles of the English constitution, and the several charters or compacts: "life, liberty, and property"; "all rights, liberties, and immunities of free and natural-born subjects within the realm of England"; rights to the common law of England, benefits of English statutes, privileges and immunities of colonial charters; the right to assemble peacefully, petition the king, list their grievances, and to be free from a "standing army" in the colonies at a time of peace; and the right to popularly selected colonial councils.

The Continental Association. This measure called for an intercolonial effort to prohibit the importation of British goods after December 1774, and exportation of colonial goods to England after September 1775, unless the Coercive Acts were repealed by Parliament.

War in Massachusetts (1775). To enforce the boycott established by the Continental Association, committees of observation and inspection were elected in most counties, cities, and towns in the colonies. Nonimportation was enforced so effectively that trade between Britain and the colonies was almost at a standstill. As a result, colonial manufacturing was encouraged and "homespun" garments became symbols of patriotism. A few weeks later, Patrick Henry urged that the colonies prepare for war in a famous speech before the Virginia legislature that ended with the words, "Give me liberty or give me death." The idea of resistance was spreading through the colonies.

Resistance to British measures spread through the colonies in 1775.

• *Lexington, Concord, and Breed's Hill.* Colonial patriots began to train militia and to store military supplies. **General Thomas Gage**, the British commander in Boston, took the offensive against the rebellious colonists and sent British troops to Concord to seize colonial military supplies. Warned by Paul Revere, William Dawes, and Samuel Prescott, an undermanned and underarmed group of colonial minutemen were waiting for the British at **Lexington** on the morning of April 19th. Shots were fired, and the American Revolution began. After leaving eight Americans dead, the British troops moved to **Concord**, five miles away. The British were then driven out of Concord and retreated to Boston under heavy colonial fire. At day's end, the British had suffered over 250 casualties, including 73 fatalities. For the next eleven months, the British occupied the city of

Boston surrounded by American militia in a standoff. Only one battle occurred. On June 17 the British drove the colonial forces from **Breed's Hill** (misnamed **Battle of Bunker Hill**).

• *The Second Continental Congress (1775).* The Congress met on May 10, 1775, shortly after the outbreak of war in Massachusetts.

Declaration of the Causes and Necessity of Taking Up Arms (1775). The Congress transformed the colonial militia into a Continental Army and chose **George Washington** as its commander. He took command of the forces that were besieging the British in Boston. On July 6, 1775, deciding on continued resistance, the Congress issued the **Declaration of the Causes and Necessity of Taking Up Arms**. Prepared by Thomas Jefferson and John Dickinson, it promised armed resistance until the end of unconstitutional imperial control by England and the acknowledgement of the colonials' rights as British subjects.

Military Events. Between May 1775 and June 1776, continued military activity took place between British troops and the colonial forces. Canada was invaded by colonial forces that took Montreal in November 1775, but failed to capture Quebec the following month. General Washington's forces, strengthened by the cannon seized at Fort Ticonderoga, forced the British to evacuate Boston on March 17, 1776.

Breakdown of Diplomacy. On July 8, 1775, the Continental Congress adopted John Dickinson's **Olive Branch Petition**, an appeal to King George III to accept the offer of a "happy and permanent reconciliation." Any hopes for reconciliation ended when King George refused to receive the petition and, on August 23, declared the colonies to be in a state of rebellion. Parliament passed the **American Prohibitory Act** on December 22, 1775, which declared Americans to be outlaws and subjected their vessels to capture by the British navy "as if the same were the ships and effects of open enemies." Finally, in January 1776, Britain arranged for 18,000 German (Hessian) troops to be sent to America.

• **Common Sense** *(January 1776).* **Thomas Paine**, a 39-year-old political agitator and writer who had only one year earlier moved to the colonies from England, wrote a pamphlet entitled *Common Sense* that had tremendous influence. His 47-page document advocated the establishment of an independent American republic. Written in an emotional style in the language of the common people, it sold 120,000 copies in just three months and caused many colonists to favor independence.

Paine attacked the balance of monarchy, aristocracy, and democracy in the English system. Suggesting the abolition of the Crown and nobility, Thomas Paine advocated a republic that would derive its powers exclusively from the governed. Paine's advice would be remembered in one of the restrictions on

20

Congress included in Article II, Section 9, Paragraph 8 of the United States Constitution, which prohibits the granting of titles of nobility.

• *The Declaration of Independence (July 4, 1776).* By the late spring of 1776, independence had clearly become inevitable. The Second Continental Congress formally recommended to the colonies that they individually form governments of their own.

The Drafting. On June 7, 1776, **Richard Henry Lee**, representing the colony of Virginia, introduced into the Continental Congress the following resolution: "That these United Colonies are, and of right ought to be, free and independent states."

On June 11 the Congress referred the resolutions to an appointed committee consisting of Benjamin Franklin, John Adams, Robert R. Livingston, Roger Sherman, and Thomas Jefferson, and asked that they draft a "declaration of independence." The committee delegated the actual writing of the document to Jefferson, who submitted the draft to the Congress on June 28.

The resolution offered by Lee was adopted by the Congress on July 2 with the approval of twelve of the colonies (New York abstained). On July 4, 1776, the **Declaration of Independence** was formally adopted by all the colonies except New York, which finally granted approval on July 15. Congress ordered it printed and distributed to colonial officials, military units, and the press.

The Content. The Declaration of Independence had a profound effect on the political life of the United States. Authorities still disagree on the question of Jefferson's sources. Although there is no clear evidence that Jefferson had read Rousseau's *Social Contract* (1755), or Locke's *The Second Treatise of Government* (1690), Jefferson was familiar with the philosophies of the Enlightenment thinkers. It is also apparent that Jefferson was familiar with the writers of the Scottish Enlightenment, including Adam Smith, Thomas Reid, and David Hume. Following are explanations of the four sections and why they were included.

The **Preamble**, an opening statement or introduction, explains that separation has become necessary to preserve natural law and natural rights.

The paragraph following the Preamble contains a theory of democratic government and sets forth four fundamental political ideas: (1) the doctrine of "certain **unalienable Rights**," among them "Life, Liberty, and the pursuit of Happiness"; (2) the compact theory of government; (3) the doctrine of popular sovereignty in the form of governments "instituted among Men deriving their just powers from the consent of the governed"; and (4) the right of revolution to "throw off such Government" that is guilty of "a long train of abuses and usurpations."

The longest section of the Declaration is the list of complaints against King George III that are the reasons for separation. It should be noted that the entire Declaration of Independence is directed toward the king and not Parliament, because Americans claimed that Parliament had no authority over them and they did not want to alienate those members of Parliament who supported them.

The final section of the document is the actual declaration of independence and separation from England, resulting in "Free and Independent States." It is also a formal declaration of war.

The Effects. The Declaration of Independence's immediate effect was a revolution and the establishment of a new nation. However, its longer-lasting effect was to commit the new American nation to carry out the highest political ideals of the age. In Jefferson's own words, the document was "an expression of the American mind." Throughout our history, the Declaration's language of equality has continued to be important as American society becomes ever more sensitive to inequality in all its forms.

• *War and Peace (1776–1783).* About one third of the colonists who were called **Tories**, **Loyalists**, or sometimes **Friends of the King** remained loyal to Britain. The term "Tories" was generally used for the more conservative and disliked Loyalists. Although Loyalists came from many social classes, not primarily from the upper class, their prime objective was to have the government controlled by aristocracy.

Those Americans who supported the Revolution were called **Patriots**, **Yanks**, or even **Whigs**, a term used in the colonies since the early 1700s to refer to those who opposed various measures of the royal governors. Poorly trained and inadequately equipped, the Patriot army never numbered more than 18,000 soldiers at any one time.

British Advantages and Disadvantages. Among the advantages of the British were a unified effort, greater financial resources, better trained and disciplined troops, and, for most of the war, control of the seas. Disadvantages included the problems of supplying an army fighting 3,000 miles away from home, subduing an enemy that was thinly scattered over a vast area, adjusting to the "guerilla-type" warfare used by the colonists, fighting several enemies, including France, Holland, and Spain after 1778, and cutting off the flow of aid to the colonists from their European allies.

Colonial Advantages and Disadvantages. Colonial advantages included patriotic spirit spurred by defending their towns, homes, and families; superior officers, both native and foreign, including **Lafayette** of France, **von Steuben** of Prussia, and **Kosciusko** and **Pulaski** of Poland; and the extensive aid in money, supplies, troops, and naval support they received through a treaty of alliance with France in 1778. Major disadvantages of the colonists were problems associated with the lack of central governmental authority as the Continental Congress had little real authority, had not established a sound financial system, and did not have the power to tax; the Tories, who were hostile to independence and aided the British through subversive acts; and the constant struggle to raise and maintain the **Continental Army**.

The outnumbered Continental Army harassed the British forces.

• *Early Military Campaigns of the War (1776–1777).* After the signing of the Declaration of Independence, the British landed a large army of over 30,000 troops near New York to reinforce their military in America. General Washington fortified Brooklyn Heights, overlooking lower Manhattan, but was outflanked by **Sir William Howe** in August 1776 in the **Battle of Long Island**. Washington was forced to flee to Manhattan and then across New Jersey into Pennsylvania. This low point of the war for the Americans was reflected in Thomas Paine's *The Crisis,* which included the memorable line, "These are the times that try men's souls."

The British planned to end the war in 1777 with a three-pronged attack. **General John Burgoyne** planned to bring British troops from Montreal down the Hudson River, while **General St. Leger** was to lead an expedition from Lake Ontario to the Hudson River, and General Howe was to march from New York up the Hudson River. They planned to capture Albany, cut off New England from the rest of the colonies, and then advance southward to defeat the other colonies.

However, the plan did not work. St. Leger's troops were forced to retreat to Canada. Howe, who was supposed to march northward from New York City, moved his troops to Philadelphia instead. Although he eventually captured the city, General Washington's attempts to defend Philadelphia at Brandywine and Germantown in September 1777 stalled Howe's taking of Philadelphia long enough to make it impossible for his army to join with Burgoyne's troops at Albany. By the time Burgoyne's army reached Saratoga, just north of Albany, in October, he was surrounded by the American forces of **General Horatio Gates**. Burgoyne, knowing that he could receive no relief from General Howe's troops, had to surrender to the Americans on October 17, 1777.

• *Turning Point and the French Alliance.* The **Battle of Saratoga** was the turning point of the American Revolution. France, eager to avenge its defeat in the French and Indian War, saw an opportunity to split the British Empire apart by allying itself with the American colonies. After the American victory at Saratoga, France came into the war on the American side and signed two treaties with the Americans. The first of the treaties was a **commercial** treaty designed to extend trading and maritime agreements between the two countries. The second treaty was a **conditional** and **defensive** alliance. It provided that each party would not "lay down their arms until the

Independence of the United States shall have been formally or tacitly assured by the treaty or treaties that shall terminate the war." In addition, the alliance provided that if war broke out between France and Great Britain, the two allies (France and the United States) would fight the war together and neither would make peace with the enemy without the consent of the other.

• *Later Military Campaigns (1778–1781).* British plans for conquering the colonies were revised after the French entered the war. General Howe was replaced by **Sir Henry Clinton** in early 1778 and he moved his forces from Philadelphia to New York after an indecisive battle in June with Washington's troops at Monmouth, New Jersey. The same month, the British began to strike at the Southern states. Clinton sent a small expedition down the coast and seized Savannah and Atlanta with little difficulty. Charleston, South Carolina, fell to the British on May 12, 1780, and 5,500 American troops were forced to surrender to Clinton's army. Although the South appeared to be falling to British control, the growing presence of the French navy off the coast posed a constant threat to the British.

• *British Surrender at Yorktown.* In 1781 the Americans began to win battles against the British in the South. General Cornwallis withdrew his troops to Virginia, near the coast, where the British navy could support him. The British now held only New York City and a few Southern ports. When Cornwallis situated his army at Yorktown on the peninsula between the York and James Rivers, Washington moved overland from New York City with an army of about 7,000 troops. In Virginia, an army under **Lafayette**, about to be bolstered by 3,000 French regulars brought by the French fleet, made it impossible for Cornwallis to retreat back to the mainland. At the same time, the French fleet from the West Indies under **Admiral de Grasse** arrived. It brought additional troops and prevented an English naval force from aiding Cornwallis by providing British reinforcements or supplies and prevented any escape by sea. Trapped by the French fleet behind him and a superior combined force of American and French troops before him, Cornwallis was forced to surrender on October 19, 1781. Peace negotiations soon began in Paris.

• *Treaty of Paris (September 3, 1783).* Problems developed between the United States and France because of the Treaty of Alliance signed by the two nations in 1778. According to the terms of the treaty, the United States was obligated to continue fighting Britain until France stopped. France was obligated to Spain to continue fighting until Gibraltar was retrieved from the British.

Although the American diplomats **John Jay**, **John Adams**, and **Benjamin Franklin** were instructed by Congress not to enter into any separate peace agreements with Britain, and to be guided by France in the negotiations, they ignored these instructions. Negotiations were held with the British representative, **Richard Oswald**, and a preliminary treaty with very favorable terms was signed in September 1782. Its provisions included (1) the granting of unconditional independence to Americans; (2) the setting of boundaries of the new nation: to the north, the 45th parallel and the Great Lakes (approximately the current boundary with Canada), to the west, the Mississippi River, to the south the 31st parallel (the Florida-Georgia boundary of today), and on the east, the Atlantic Ocean including all islands twenty leagues out to sea; (3) the granting of unlimited fishing rights for the United States off the coast of Newfoundland and in the Gulf of St. Lawrence; (4) the freedom to both Great Britain and the United States to navigate the Mississippi River (somewhat presumptuous since Spain still controlled the lower part of the river); (5) the condition that debts owed to both British and American creditors were to be paid; (6) the recommendation by Congress that confiscated Loyalist properties were to be returned; and (7) the withdrawal of British troops "with all convenient speed" from the United States.

On January 30, 1783, France and Spain signed their own provisional treaties of peace with Britain. The final treaties were signed on September 3, 1783, and the United States Congress proclaimed the treaty of peace and independence, January 14, 1784.

The Revolution in Retrospect

Many historians have offered different interpretations about the American Revolution and its causes. Among them are

- a struggle between the tyrannical control of England and the liberty-loving Americans who saw an opportunity to carry out the beliefs of the **Enlightenment** thinkers;
- the impossibility of England's maintaining colonies 3,000 miles away as part of its empire;
- a struggle between the growing American free enterprise system and the English mercantile system;
- a conflict of religions—between the dissenting sects that settled America and the Church of England, the dominant religion of English officials and aristocrats;
- the development of a new class structure in the colonies primarily due to the ending of heredity, birthright status, and primogeniture, and the availability of land and the expansion of the franchise (vote) as leveling factors;
- the internal problems of English politics and the inconsistencies of English policy toward the colonies; and
- the fact that the revolution was actually no revolution at all, but a struggle to preserve a social and economic order rather than to change it.

When America freed itself from British control, it also eliminated a system of law and order that had to be replaced if the new republic was to have any chance of survival. There were many Americans who feared the consequences of democracy and the new social and political order that had been propagandized so effectively by many of the more radical patriots. The

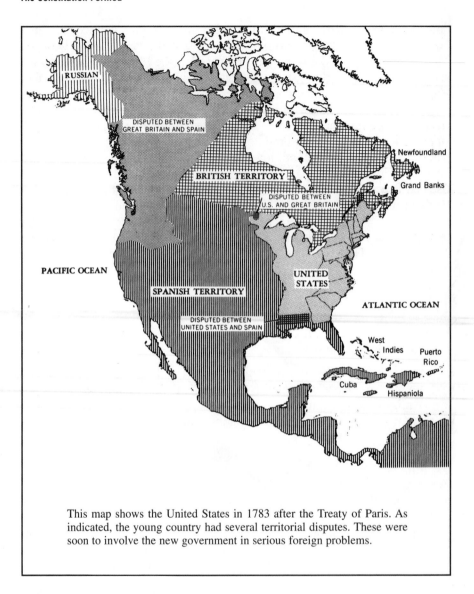

This map shows the United States in 1783 after the Treaty of Paris. As indicated, the young country had several territorial disputes. These were soon to involve the new government in serious foreign problems.

Figure 1.3 The United States in 1783

Articles of Confederation, the nation's first constitution, was a natural outcome of the revolutionary movement within the American colonies—a constitutional expression of the philosophy of the Declaration of Independence.

Problems of Confederation

> It has long been a grave question whether any government, not too strong for the liberties of its people, can be strong enough to maintain its existence in great emergencies.
>
> Abraham Lincoln, November 10, 1864

The winning of independence made necessary the establishment of a new government to replace British rule. How would the Americans meet the unprecedented task of establishing a government that was strong enough to govern and protect the nation, but restrained enough to preserve individual liberties?

The British surrender at Yorktown on October 19, 1781, and the Treaty of Paris in 1783 resulted in the establishment of the **sovereign state** known as the United States. The first years of the new nation under the Articles of Confederation from 1781 to 1789 are called the "critical period." Eventually, this first constitution was replaced by the one written at the **Constitutional Convention of 1787**. Yet, as the preceding quote from Abraham Lincoln during the depths of the Civil War indicates, even some 75 years after the ratification of the Constitution the balance between liberty and authority was a continuing challenge faced by the American republic.

The Nature of Revolution

> It is only after mature deliberation and thorough preparation that I have decided upon the Program of Revolution and defined the procedure of the revolution in three stages. The first is the period of military government; the second, *the period of political tutelage;* and the third, the period of constitutional government.
>
> Dr. Sun Yat-Sen, *The Three Phases of National Reconstruction* (1918)

In this quotation, Dr. Sun Yat-Sen, in reflecting on the Chinese Revolution of 1911–1912 that resulted in the overthrow of the Manchu Dynasty, presents a representative pattern of many revolutions.

If one reviews the history of revolutions, including those of the Americans, French, Chinese, and Russians, a pattern becomes apparent. In the case of the American Revolution, the Confederation Period from 1781 to 1789 can be studied as the period of convalescence, or, as Dr. Sun Yat-Sen termed it, a "period of political tutelage."

State Constitutions

Between May 1776—when the Continental Congress instructed the colonies to form local governments—and 1780, most of the colonies, which were now states, had written new state constitutions and established governments.

• *Characteristics.* A common characteristic of all these state governments was **constitutional republicanism**; that is, the source of political authority rested with the people. Another similarity was concern to control the abuses of political power; all of the states developed written constitutions that placed restraints upon the powers of government. All these documents provided for regular and frequent elections to keep the government close and accountable to its constituency. Some of the early constitutions included a list of principles that the government could not violate. Specific guarantees of civil liberties, including freedom of speech and press, protection from arbitrary arrest, the right to jury trial, liberty of conscience, and due process rights were also included in many of them.

Perhaps the most significant feature of these state constitutions was their treatment of the executive and legislative branches of government. The most feared branch, the **executive**, was kept comparatively weak. Most governors were elected for one-year terms by the legislature, stripped of veto power, and usually had only ceremonial functions. The **legislature**, the branch closest to the people, retained most of the governing power.

• *Separation of Powers.* During the colonial period the belief had developed that good government required the **separation of powers** between the three branches of government. The 1776 Virginia state constitution specified:

> The *legislative, executive,* and *judiciary* departments shall be separate and distinct, so that neither exercises the powers properly belonging to the other; nor shall any person exercise the powers of more than one of them at the same time.

The constitutions adopted by the American states used the idea of separation of powers as an organizing principle of government.

Figure 1.4 shows how the state constitutions established systems of government that used the concept of separation of powers.

Movement Toward Confederation

The need for a central government was recognized early in the Revolutionary War. In 1776 the Second Continental Congress appointed a committee under **John Dickinson** to draft a written constitution. The **Articles of Confederation** were accepted by the Continental Congress in 1777, but disputes over western land claims postponed their ratification by the thirteen states until March 1781. At this time, the new league of states came into being.

- *A "League of Friendship."* The most perplexing issue facing Americans during the Confederation Period may have been trying to define the term "United States." Articles 1 and 2 and the first sentence of Article 3 of the Articles of Confederation show the confusion that surrounded the concept of confederation. This confusion eventually made it necessary to redefine what the term "United States" actually meant and to write a new constitution for the nation.

The wording of the Articles of Confederation, especially Article 2, made it clear that state sovereignty was to be maintained and implies that the confederation consisted of independent states. If the states reserved for themselves such a high degree of independence from the central government, what then was the function of the national Congress?

- *Form of Government under the Articles.* The central government, consisting of a **unicameral** (one-house) Congress, acted as an administrative agency for the states. As the language of the document reveals, the Congress lacked any real power. According to the Articles, Congress could make resolutions, determinations, and regulations, whereas the states possessed the lawmaking legislatures, as well as executive and judicial branches. Nothing resembling such phrases as "supremacy of the laws," "necessary and proper" or "general welfare" was found within the Articles of Confederation. Unenumerated powers remained within the states. Although Congress was expressly granted the powers to control war and foreign affairs, regulate trade with the Indians, regulate the value of its coinage, maintain a post office, and standardize weights and measures, it could not infringe upon the right of a state to legislate upon matters within its own limits. In short, the central government was carefully subordinated to a union of states.

Powers of Congress. In the Congress established under the Confederation, each state had one vote. The votes of two-thirds of the states were required to pass legislation, and an **amendment** to the Articles required a unanimous vote by the states. Delegated powers included (1) the conduct of war, making treaties, and exchanging ambassadors with other nations; (2) the coining of money and regulating its value; (3) establishing and regulating post offices throughout the United States; (4) the appointment of military officers; (5) the regulation of Indian affairs; and (6) the settlement, on appeal, of disputes between states.

Powers of the States. Consistent with Article 2, the states retained all the powers (reserved powers) that were not expressly delegated to the central government. This left the states with such critical powers as (1) authority over commerce with other states and, in part, with other nations; and (2) the power to tax.

EXECUTIVE

Powers: Limited administrative appointments, enforcement of laws, limited veto power (New York and Massachusetts) usually reversible by simple majority of legislature.

LEGISLATIVE

Powers: Supreme lawmaker, election of governor in most states, impeachment powers, powers to establish own rules such as meeting frequency, procedures, and membership requirements.

JUDICIAL

Powers: Interpretation of laws (including bills of rights limiting government's authority over the people), life tenure during good behavior, beginning of judicial review (the right to declare acts of the legislature unconstitutional).

THE PEOPLE

Powers: Actual representation through the vote. Although restrictions on suffrage rights still existed (property qualifications, religious exclusions, lack of voting power among women, slaves, Indians), there were movements toward universal manhood suffrage. For example, limited substitution of a taxpayer qualification for property holding took place in Pennsylvania, New Hampshire, New Jersey, Georgia, and Maryland.

Figure 1.4 State Constitutions: Separation of Powers

Contributions of the Articles of Confederation

The ratification of the Articles of Confederation in 1781 legalized the measures carried out by the Continental Congress since 1775. Despite the severe limitations on its power, the Congress under the Articles of Confederation did make lasting contributions to the nation's well-being.

• *War and Diplomacy.* Under the leadership of the Continental Congress, and the Confederation Congress, the American Revolution was fought and won and a peace treaty concluded.

• *Establishment of a Federal System.* Federalism is the doctrine that advocates the division of powers between the national and state governments. Although the division of powers between the national government—the Congress—and the state governments under the Articles lacked the proper balance, the Articles did outline a federal system that provided a basis for establishment of a government at the Constitutional Convention of 1787.

• *Western Lands.* Perhaps the greatest contribution of the Articles of Confederation was the establishment of a policy for the settlement of western lands and the establishment of government in these new lands. These principles of settlement were used as Americans expanded across the continent throughout the 1800s.

Cessation of Western Land Claims. The United States had acquired the **Northwest Territory**, the land north of the Ohio River and west of the Appalachians, as a result of the Treaty of Paris of 1783 with Great Britain. Virginia claimed much of this area, a claim that was opposed by other states, especially neighboring Maryland. These states claimed that the territory had been acquired through the common efforts of all states in the Revolution. Maryland refused to ratify the Articles of Confederation until Virginia turned over its claims to this territory to Congress, which it finally did, with conditions, in 1781. Formal adoption of the Articles of Confederation came in March 1781 with Maryland's ratification.

Ordinance of 1785. With the passage of the Land Ordinance of 1785, the Congress established a pattern for the orderly division and settlement of the land north of the Ohio River. The Ordinance provided that (1) townships of six miles square would be divided into 36 subdivisions of 640 acres each (the minimal amount to be sold); (2) each section would be sold at auction for at least one dollar an acre with the revenue to be used to pay off the national debt; and (3) the revenue from the sale of one section from each township would be used to support public education—this provided a precedent for federal aid to education. Although some changes in the policy were made in later years, the Ordinance of 1785 remained the basis of public land policy until the **Homestead Act of 1862**.

There were two major drawbacks to the land ordinances: (1) few farmers could afford to pay $640, the amount necessary for a minimal purchase; as a result, land speculators purchased tracts and sold them to smaller farmers; and (2) the Indian tribes that occupied much of the Northwest Territory were disregarded. Confrontations between the Indians and land companies continued through the 1790s. Finally, in the **Treaty of Greenville of 1795**, the United States government accepted Indian sovereignty in specific areas and agreed to negotiate with the Indians rather than acquiring their land through negotiations with a European power.

The Northwest Ordinance of 1787. The Northwest Ordinance borrowed heavily from a plan of government for the new territories devised by Thomas Jefferson in 1784. It combined the concepts of **federalism**, **republicanism**, and **regard for civil liberties** in a plan of national development that ranks in significance with the Declaration of Independence and the Constitution. The Ordinance of 1787, passed by the Confederation Congress and later reaffirmed as federal law by the new United States Congress under the Constitution in 1789, provided for the government of the **Northwest Territory**, an area of more than 265,000 square miles. The two-stage plan by which territories could become states provided that (1) when an area had a population of more than 5,000 adult males, it could establish a territorial government consisting of an elected legislative house plus a legislative council, and a governor and judges appointed by Congress; and (2) as soon as the population of any territory reached 60,000 free inhabitants, the voters could elect delegates to write a state constitution, elect and appoint state government officials, and apply for statehood. When their constitution was approved by Congress, that territory became a state.

Between 1803 and 1848, Ohio (1803), Indiana (1816), Illinois (1818), Michigan (1837), and Wisconsin (1848) were admitted as states from the Northwest Territory.

The Articles of Compact. They included six guarantees of civil liberties and rights for the residents of the Northwest Territory and were as important as the provisions for government and statehood. The Compact provided for **freedom of religion**, the benefits of the **writ of habeas corpus**, **trial by jury**, **protection of property**, protection against **cruel and unusual punishment**, **sanctity of contracts**, the encouragement of **free public education**, and respect for the lands belonging to the **Indians**. Article Six provided that **slavery** would be prohibited in the territory. However, this was accepted at the Constitutional Convention by the Southern states only in return for the assurance that the **fugitive slave law** would be applied to the Northwest Territory and that slavery would be allowed to expand into the unorganized territory south of the Ohio River.

• *A Transitional Period.* The Articles reflected the fear on the part of Americans of centralized power. A government such as that established by the Constitution in 1789 would not have been acceptable to most Americans in 1776 or 1781. Perhaps most important of all, the Articles of Confederation provided the young nation with a temporary system of government through the critical period prior to the Constitutional Convention in 1787.

Weaknesses of the Articles of Confederation—Foreign Affairs

- *Foreign Occupation of the West.* Great Britain continued to occupy posts in the Northwest Territory, even though the Treaty of Paris of 1783 had provided that the British would leave this area "with all convenient speed." Among Britain's excuses for its slow withdrawal was that the United States Congress had failed to fulfill the provision of the Treaty of Paris that guaranteed payment of debts to British creditors and the return of confiscated property to the Loyalists. The inability of the Confederation Congress to compel the states to observe these treaty obligations, in addition to its lack of finances to patrol the frontier, prolonged this problem.

American problems with Spain included disputes over the boundaries established by the Treaty of Paris of 1783 and the navigation of the lower Mississippi River. Spain's decision to close the Mississippi to American shipping in 1784 led to negotiations between Secretary of Foreign Affairs **John Jay** and the Spanish minister. However, a bitter debate in Congress caused a breakdown in the negotiations.

- *Foreign Debts.* Between 1778 and 1783 the United States borrowed several million dollars from the French and the Dutch governments. Because of its failure to meet even the interest payments on these loans, the United States lost the respect of its former allies.

- *Barbary Pirates.* Commerce in the Mediterranean Sea had long been subject to attacks by coastal pirates unless financial tributes, or bribes, were paid. Since the United States was no longer protected by the British navy, and had no navy of its own, it could do little to prevent violations of its commercial rights by the Barbary pirates.

Weakness of Articles—Domestic Affairs

- *Problems of Commerce.* Under the Confederation, Congress lacked the power to control and regulate both domestic and foreign trade. As a result, this responsibility fell to the states, and the state legislatures were able to levy tariffs on imported goods. Since those states with lower tariffs received the most foreign trade, squabbles soon broke out among the states. As jealousies over trade developed between the states, they started to levy tariffs on each other's goods. This brought domestic trade almost to a standstill.

- *Need of Revenue.* Most of Congress's difficulties between 1776 and 1787 were related to its inability to raise money. Congressional income was dependent on the whims of the states, since Congress had no power to raise money on its own. As a result, Congress was unable to pay the national debt that totaled $40 million. The sale of public lands brought slight returns, and the request that the states assume the debts from the Revolutionary War met with only limited success.

• *Currency Problems.* A postwar depression led to a wide demand for the issuance of paper money by the state legislatures. In the states where debtors gained heavy influence over the legislatures, the amount of paper money became excessive. However, in the states in which the creditor classes controlled the legislatures, high taxes and a tight money system made it impossible for debtors to repay their debts. As a result, their property was repossessed, and, if foreclosure did not raise a sufficient amount to repay their obligations, debtors could be sent to jail.

Specie, or hard money, was scarce in the new nation.

During the fall of 1786, an incident in western Massachusetts helped to convince many Americans that changes in the national government were necessary. In Massachusetts, farmers who were crushed by demands for payment of debts and taxes joined together. They took matters into their own hands after the courts ordered that their homes and land be sold to pay their debts. Led by **Daniel Shays**, a captain during the Revolutionary War, some 1,200 armed followers gathered to attack the federal arsenal at Springfield. This attack was unsuccessful. A militia was raised and sent by the governor to put down the rebellion. It was completely suppressed by February 1787.

Shays' rebellion caused much fear among Americans and was used by conservative forces to bolster their demand for a stronger central government.

• *Political Structure.* It was with Shays' Rebellion and the weaknesses of the Confederation government in mind that the framers of the Constitution included Section 4 of Article IV:

> The United States shall guarantee to every State in this Union a Republican Form of Government, and shall protect each of them against Invasion; and on Application of the Legislature, or of the Executive (when the Legislature cannot be convened) against domestic violence.
>
> Article IV, Sec 4, United States Constitution

Although the foundations for a system of separation of powers can be found within the state governments during the Confederation period, abuses of legislative power were not uncommon. When asked by the secretary of the French legation in Philadelphia to comment on the government of Virginia, Thomas Jefferson made some insightful observations concerning the power of the legislature:

All the powers of government, legislative, executive, and judiciary, result to the legislative body. The concentrating these in the same hands is precisely the definition of despotic government . . . 173 despots would surely be as oppressive as one . . . An elective despotism was not the government we fought for.

Thomas Jefferson, *Notes on the State of Virginia* (1787)

What was needed at the state level was an effective system of checks and balances to maintain a true system of separation of powers. What was needed at the national level was the delegation by the states of some of the powers they currently held, primarily commerce and taxation.

Movement Toward a Constitutional Convention

The weaknesses of the Articles of Confederation, combined with the political, social, and economic difficulties faced by the nation at this time, led the states to consider revisions in the Confederation government.

* *The Alexandria Conference (1785).* Delegates from Virginia and Maryland met in Alexandria, Virginia, to discuss and consider ways of improving the navigability of the Potomac River and to settle a long-standing commercial dispute. The delegates from Virginia suggested extending invitations to all the states to meet at Annapolis the following year to discuss the problem of commerce on a national scale.

* *The Annapolis Conference (1786).* Although eight states named representatives to the September meeting, delegates from only five states arrived in time for the Annapolis Conference. In spite of the poor attendance, nationalist sentiment was strong. At the suggestion of **James Madison** and **Alexander Hamilton**, a convention was called to meet in Philadelphia in May of the following year to discuss revising the Articles of Confederation.

Alexander Hamilton encouraged the rewriting of the Articles of Confederation.

From Radicalism to Conservatism

There is evidence to support the idea that the American Revolution, although a concerted effort for independence, was fought by a population with distinct class lines. A conservative group, composed primarily of Northern lawyers, merchants, bankers, speculators, and wealthy Southern planters and merchants, sought independence from Britain's trade regulations and restrictions on capitalist growth. They had no desire to see the Revolution upset their positions in society, and were firm believers in a government that was controlled by the wellborn who were capable of maintaining the class structure. On the other hand, the small business owners, artisans, and farmers fought the Revolution in order to break America's political ties with England and to destroy the economic and social privileges of the colonial aristocracy. They regarded the principles of the Declaration of Independence as the guidelines for a new social order, as well as the political transformation of power to local representative bodies. The central issue between the conservative and the radical groups in America in the period of the 1780s was still the question of where supreme authority was to be located.

The Articles of Confederation represented the attempt to deny authority to any government superior to the legislative bodies of the states. A change in the balance of political power took place between 1776 and 1787. The movement to **centralize power**, which was assisted by the problems of the Confederation period, engineered a conservative counterrevolution and created a nationalistic government. Although this protected the interests of the conservative, propertied classes, it also preserved the system of republican government, the primary concern of all groups in the United States.

Excercise Set 1.1

1.   "In framing a government which is to be administered by men over men, the great difficulty lies in this; you must first enable the government to control the governed, and next, oblige it to control itself."
   James Madison, The Federalist, No. 51

   Which concept of government is being referred to in the quotation?
   A. unicameral legislature
   B. cabinet system
   C. popularly elected assemblies
   D. system of checks and balances

2. In most of the thirteen original colonies, the settlers gained experience in self-government by
   A. choosing governors to administer colonial affairs
   B. electing members of colonial assemblies
   C. regulating trade with England
   D. sending representatives to vote in Parliament

3. Which of the following democratic practices of the American heritage cannot be found in English history?
   A. a written constitution
   B. common law
   C. representative government
   D. the concept of limited government

4. As a result of the Albany Congress of 1754
   A. the Dominion of New England was eliminated
   B. an experiment in intercolonial union was proposed
   C. the colonies were granted limited tax power
   D. an intercolonial legislature was established

5. The most significant step toward intercolonial union was
   A. the New England Confederation
   B. the use of the town meeting in the New England colonies
   C. the drafting of the Mayflower Compact
   D. the formation of the Virginia Company of London

6. Colonial legislatures were often able to control royal governors by
   A. threatening impeachment
   B. controlling finances, including the governor's salary
   C. overruling the governor with authority granted by Parliament
   D. using the colonial militia

Base your answers to questions 7 and 8 on the following excerpt from the Declaration of Independence and your knowledge of social studies:

> "We hold these truths to be self-evident, that all men are created equal, that they are endowed by their creator with certain unalienable rights, that among these are life, liberty, and the pursuit of happiness. That to secure these rights, governments are instituted among men, deriving their just powers from the consent of the governed."

7. According to Jefferson's Declaration of Independence, governments receive their authority and power from
   A. only men
   B. military strength
   C. the people
   D. God

8. The ideas expressed in the preceding excerpt from the Declaration of Independence are consistent with the writings of which pair of Enlightenment thinkers?
   A. John Locke and Baron de Montesquieu
   B. Jean-Jacques Rousseau and John Locke
   C. Sir William Blackstone and Jean-Jacques Rousseau
   D. John Locke and Sir Henry Clinton

9. A review of the events that came before the American Revolution indicates that
   A. the Boston Massacre marked a point of no return toward independence
   B. after 1763 most Americans wanted nothing less than complete independence from England
   C. as late as February 1775, reconciliation was probably possible
   D. Parliament clearly welcomed the armed conflict in hopes of bringing the colonies back under control

10. According to the Declaration of Independence, the purpose of government is to
    A. equalize opportunities for all citizens
    B. provide for the common defense
    C. secure the people in their natural rights
    D. suppress the dangers of "raw democracy"

11. The original reason for adding bills of rights to early state constitutions was to
    A. prohibit state governments from depriving individuals of certain basic rights
    B. deprive the national government of any regulation of natural rights
    C. ensure the supremacy of the legislature over the executive in state governments
    D. provide an example for the eventual Bill of Rights added to the Constitution in 1791

12. The colonial branch of government that Americans had grown to suspect most during the period before the Revolution was the
    A. judicial branch
    B. executive branch
    C. legislative branch
    D. Continental Congress

13. Among the weaknesses of the Articles of Confederation was
    A. the need for a unanimous vote to amend the Articles
    B. the failure to establish a peace treaty at the conclusion of the American Revolution
    C. the abandonment of the principle of federalism
    D. the inability to deal with the western land problem

14. Which of the following best describes the "United States" under the Articles of Confederation?
    A. a confederation of colonies existing within an empire
    B. one nation, consisting of thirteen subordinate components
    C. free and independent states loosely held together by a Confederation Congress
    D. sovereign states with no cohesive element whatsoever

15. The Declaration of Independence
    A. contained a list of grievances against Parliament
    B. was written by Jefferson and adopted without change
    C. contained Jefferson's objections to slavery
    D. directed the grievances of the colonists against George III

CONSTITUTIONAL CONVENTION, RATIFICATION, AND A BILL OF RIGHTS

> The whole people declared the colonies in their united condition, of right, free and independent States .... But there still remained the last and Crowning act, by which the People of the Union alone were competent to perform the institution of civil government, for that compound nation, the United States of America.
>
> John Quincy Adams, *The Jubilee of the Constitution* (1839).

In 1786 James Madison described the Articles of Confederation as "nothing more than a treaty of amity and of alliance between independent and sovereign states." As attempts to amend the Articles failed, and the nation's problems, which stemmed from the lack of a central authority, increased, steps toward forming a new government began.

Constitutional Convention

The Delegates

The Convention met in Philadelphia on May 25, 1787 with 55 delegates from seven states in attendance. By July, twelve states were represented, Rhode Island choosing not to participate.

The delegates at the Constitutional Convention were as brilliant an assembly of statesmen as ever had met in America. The group included **George Washington**, who was selected as presiding officer of the Convention, **James Madison**, who kept a journal of the debates, **Benjamin Franklin**, **George Mason**, **Gouverneur Morris**, **James Wilson**, **Roger Sherman**, and

James Madison (1751–1836) 4th President of the United States. Madison was a key participant in the Constitutional Convention.

Elbridge Gerry. Notable absences included the more radical leaders of the Confederation period: **Samuel Adams**, **Patrick Henry**, and **Thomas Paine**. Also absent were **Thomas Jefferson** and **John Adams**, who were serving as ambassadors in Europe.

Most of the delgates to the Constitutional Convention were men of property, representing primarily the upper classes of American society. Their class status was reflected in their interest in a strong central government. Their goal was to form a government that would avoid the polar extremes of despotism and uncontrolled popular rule. Congress had authorized the Convention only for "the sole and express purpose of revising the Articles of Confederation." Few of them realized at the outset that their efforts would result in a new "constitution," rather than changes in the Articles of Confederation. In order to allow the delegates to debate freely without public pressure, sessions were secret and very little news leaked.

The Virginia, or Large States, Plan

Primarily the work of James Madison and Virginia **Governor Edmund Randolph,** the plan called for drafting a new document to organize a new form of government rather than for amending the Articles of Confederation. Introduced on May 29 by Edmund Randolph, the Virginia Plan proposed (1) **a bicameral legislature** representing the states proportionately (based on population), with the lower house elected by the people and the upper house to be chosen by the lower house. The powers of the Congress would be those that had existed under the Articles of Confederation, with the important addition of the right to "legislate in all cases in which the separate states are incompetent," a notable shift of power from the states to the central government; (2) **an executive** chosen by the legislature for an unspecified term and ineligible for reelection; (3) **a judiciary** consisting of one or more supreme courts and such inferior courts as the legislature might create.

The New Jersey, or "Small States," Plan

Presented to the Convention on June 15 by **William Paterson** of New Jersey, it called for changes in the Articles of Confederation rather than the drafting of a new document. The smaller states claimed that representation in Congress based upon population would allow the larger states to constantly outvote the smaller states. The larger states argued that equal representation of the states as had existed under the Articles resulted in the population of larger states being underrepresented. The New Jersey Plan proposed: (1) **a unicameral legislature** similar to that under the Articles with each state having one vote. The powers of Congress were to be enlarged to include taxation and regulation of foreign and interstate commerce, confirming the point that all states, both large and small, did not question the necessity of greater central authority; (2) a plural **executive branch** without veto power and subject to state control; (3) a **supreme court** with power to hear cases appealed from state courts.

The Great, or Connecticut, Compromise

On June 19 the convention decided to scrap the Articles of Confederation and write a new plan of government. The major area of debate concerned the method by which the states would be represented in the national Congress. On July 12, **Roger Sherman** of Connecticut offered a compromise plan, which provided for a Congress with two houses—a **Senate** and a **House of Representatives**. The lower house of Congress would be filled according to **proportional representation** (by population) with one member for every 40,000 residents. The upper house would be filled by **equal representation** of the states, each state having two members elected by the legislature of the individual states. The plan also recommended that all **appropriation bills** originate in the lower house, the chamber of direct representation. This followed the British example of all money bills originating in the lower house of Parliament, the House of Commons.

As debate continued over representation in Congress, early **sectional differences** began to surface, especially concerning the settlement of western lands and the issue of the extension of slavery. The **Northwest Ordinance**, which was approved by the Confederation Congress on July 13, 1787, banned slavery in the five states to be created out of the Northwest Territory. However, it made possible a plan for rapid statehood in other western lands where the South hoped to extend slavery. With the help of the Northwest Ordinance, the Great Compromise was approved by a slight majority on July 16, 1787. (Article I, Sections 2 and 3 of the Constitution, Amendment 17.)

The Three-Fifths Compromise

Three suggestions were made concerning how the population should be counted in order to determine the number of representatives each state was to have in the lower house. Each plan showed strong sectional biases. The first, supported primarily by the slave states, wanted all people (free and slave) counted for purposes of representation, but not for taxation. In the second, the nonslave-holding states of the North wanted only the free population counted. The third proposal, the method which was adopted by the members of the Convention, was to count three-fifths of the slave population for both representation and taxation. (Article I, Section 2, Clause 3. Overruled by Amendments 13 [1865] and 14 [1868].) It was also decided that the method for counting the population would be a census taken every ten years. (Article I, Section 2, Clause 3, Amendment 17.)

Prohibition on Banning of Slave Trade

Linked to the Three-Fifths Compromise, this provided that Congress would pass no law prohibiting the importation of slaves for twenty years. The importation of slaves became illegal after 1808. (Article I, Section 9, Clause 1.)

Fugitive Slave Clause

To placate the Southern states, this clause declared that slaves ("persons held to service or labor under the laws of a state") who escaped to a free state would be returned to their rightful owners. (Article IV, Section 2, Clause 3. Overruled in 1865 by Amendment 13.)

Tariffs

Again, sectional differences surfaced over the question of duties on trade. Southerners who exported agricultural products disapproved of granting power to the national government to impose taxes on exports. Northern business groups, however, wanted tariffs on imports to protect their interests from foreign competition. A **compromise** was reached and the delegates to the Convention granted Congress the authority to tax imports, but not exports. (Article I, Section 8, Clause 1 and Article I, Section 9, Clause 5.)

The Presidency

The small states desired a weak executive, chosen by and responsible to the legislature. The larger states supported a strong executive selected through direct election by the people. **James Wilson**'s compromise proposal, that the people of the states should choose **presidential electors** through their own methods who then should meet and choose the executive, was accepted as the method of election. (Article II, Sections 2 and 3, Amendment 12.)

Principles of the Document

Separation of Powers

The arrangement of Articles I, II, and III—the first devoted to the Congress, the second to the President, and the third to the federal judiciary— made it clear that Montesquieu's thoughts, and the experiences of the state governments, were well studied by the members of the Convention. The delegates established a government based on the idea of the separation of powers. However, the concept of separation of powers as used in American constitutional government does not mean absolute separation between the branches. For example, the President possesses some legislative functions, such as the power to veto acts of Congress and the right to recommend to Congress "such measures as he shall judge necessary and expedient." Congress approves the executive functions of approving appointments and treaties; and the Supreme Court, through its interpretive powers, intervenes in both legislative and executive functions.

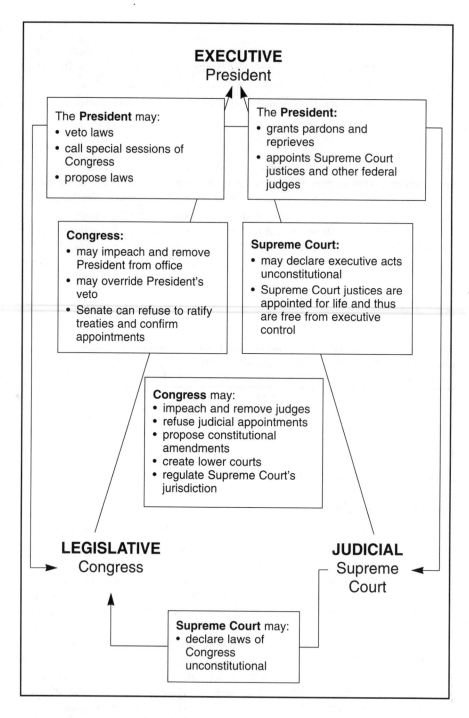

EXECUTIVE
President

The **President** may:
- veto laws
- call special sessions of Congress
- propose laws

The **President:**
- grants pardons and reprieves
- appoints Supreme Court justices and other federal judges

Congress:
- may impeach and remove President from office
- may override President's veto
- Senate can refuse to ratify treaties and confirm appointments

Supreme Court:
- may declare executive acts unconstitutional
- Supreme Court justices are appointed for life and thus are free from executive control

Congress may:
- impeach and remove judges
- refuse judicial appointments
- propose constitutional amendments
- create lower courts
- regulate Supreme Court's jurisdiction

LEGISLATIVE
Congress

JUDICIAL
Supreme Court

Supreme Court may:
- declare laws of Congress unconstitutional

Figure 1.5   Checks and Balances

Federal Government	Federal and State Governments	State Governments
Enumerated Powers:	*Concurrent ("Shared") Powers:*	*Reserved Powers:*
• Regulate interstate and foreign trade • Establish laws for citizenship • Coin money • Regulate patents and copyrights • Establish post offices • Establish federal courts • Declare war • Raise and support armed forces • Pass laws necessary and proper for carrying out preceding powers	• Lay and collect taxes • Charter banks • Take property for public use • Borrow money • Enforce the laws • Establish courts • Provide for the general welfare	• Determine qualifications of voters • Provide for education • Establish marriage and divorce laws • Regulate intrastate commerce • Conduct elections • Establish local governments • Incorporate businesses • Provide for public safety and morals

Prohibited Powers

Powers Denied Federal Government:	*Powers Denied Federal and State Governments:*	*Powers Denied State Government:*
• Suspend the writ of habeas corpus • Tax exports • Show preference to one state over another • Take money from treasury without right by law	• Pass bills of attainder • Pass ex post facto laws • Grant titles of nobility • Deprive persons of life, liberty, or property without due process of law	• Make treaties with other nations or states without consent of Congress • Coin money • Impair the obligations of contracts • Tax imports or exports • Keep troops or ships during peace without consent of Congress

Figure 1.6 The Federal System

Checks and Balances

The framers of the Constitution were concerned that the government should not act in a hasty or arbitrary manner. The system of checks and balances within our system requires an interaction between the three branches that prevents the abuse of power by any one of them. Figure 1.5 helps demonstrate some of the checks and balances among the three branches of government.

Federalism

This concept of distributing powers of government between one central or national government (usually called the "federal government") and the governments of the several states into which a country is divided was adopted by those at the Constitutional Convention.

It is now possible to compare three types of government structure, a **unitary** government such as Great Britain, a **confederational** government represented by the government of the United States during the period of the Articles of Confederation, and a **federal** government.

• *Unitary Government.* A system of government in which all political power rests with a central authority. The central government directly governs the people. This is the format of the British government.

• *Confederational Government.* An alliance of independent states. In a confederation, the states create a national government that has very limited powers. The national government does not directly govern the people and can do only what the states permit.

• *Federal Form of Government.* A form of government that combines characteristics of both **unitary** and **confederational** government. Figure 1.7 illustrates the three different formats of government and demonstrates the relationships between levels.

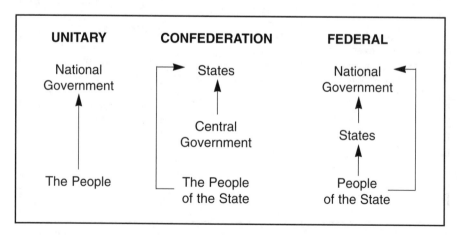

Figure 1.7 Types of Governments

Structure of the Document

The final document consisted of a preamble setting forth the reasons the Constitution was adopted and a main body of seven articles divided into sections and clauses. Shortly after ratification, an appendix of amendments to the Constitution was added.

Preamble

This opening paragraph of the Constitution establishes the people as the source of authority for the Constitution and sets forth six goals: (1) to set up a stronger government than had existed under the Articles of Confederation; (2) to improve the judicial system; (3) to guarantee peace within and among the states; (4) to provide protection for the country; (5) to provide for the general welfare; and (6) to maintain liberty for citizens, present and future.

Article I:	Legislative Branch
Article II:	Executive Branch
Article III:	Judicial Branch
Article IV:	Relations among the states
Article V:	Amending the Constitution
Article VI:	Supremacy Clause
Article VII:	Ratification Procedures

Articles I through VII

The first three articles of the Constitution describe the organization and functions of the three branches of the federal government: the **legislative**, **executive**, and **judicial**. Articles IV through VII set forth how the powers of the government are to be shared by the federal government, the states, and the people.

Amendments

Article V of the Constitution provides that the document may be changed when the need arises. Although there have been many attempts at amending the Constitution, there have been only 27 amendments added to the Constitution since 1789.

Ratification

Article VII provided that state conventions would be called and that, upon the approval of only nine states, the Constitution would go into effect. On

September 28, 1787, Congress directed the state legislatures to call ratification conventions in each state.

The ratification of the Constitution led to the formation of **political factions** and the nation's first organized political battle between the **Federalists** and the **antifederalists**.

Federalists

Those who supported the ratification of the Constitution called themselves **Federalists**. In favor of a stronger Union, the Federalists felt that anarchy could result without a stronger national government. Many of the Federalists came from the business and propertied classes and therefore had a personal economic interest in the establishment of a strong stable government. Alexander Hamilton and John Adams were early Federalist leaders.

Antifederalists

The **antifederalists** did not fear strong government as much as they feared a strong centralized government at the expense of local state governments. The antifederalists feared a conspiracy within government (especially between the President and the Senate) that would maintain itself with standing armies and military coercion. They were also afraid of the emergence of a dictator President with the right of veto over the legislature. Finally, they feared the loss of republican forms of government within the states. Another major concern of the antifederalists was the potential danger to individual liberties posed by the lack of a bill of rights.

The major weakness of the antifederalists, in addition to their lack of organization and control of the press, was their lack of a central principle. Though the antifederalists wanted the states to maintain a large degree of sovereignty, they also wanted Congress to act for the states in areas where the states could not act for themselves—notably foreign policy, western settlement, commerce, and disputes between the states. Among the early leaders of the antifederalists were **Richard Henry Lee** of Virginia, and **Thomas Jefferson**, to the extent that he insisted upon the addition of a bill of rights.

State Conventions

The debate over ratification took place in conventions within the individual states. The conventions of three states ratified the Constitution before the end of 1787 and two more did so in January 1788. By the time New Hampshire ratified in June 1788, the requirement of ratification by nine states had been satisfied. However, New York and Virginia had not yet voted, and most realized that the chances of the Constitution's succeeding without the support of those states were slim.

The Federalist Papers

The most serious criticism of the Constitution by the antifederalists was its lack of a bill of rights. In New York, **Governor George Clinton** expressed this and other fears in several published newspaper essays, while **Patrick Henry** and **James Monroe** led the opposition in Virginia. Between October 1787 and August 1788, **James Madison** of Virginia, and **Alexander Hamilton** and **John Jay**, both of New York, published 85 essays in New York newspapers above the signature "Publius" to answer the fears of the antifederalists. These essays came to be called *The Federalist* and stressed three major points: (1) the possibility of creating a political system strong enough to maintain itself while at the same time preserving a degree of autonomy for individual states in domestic affairs; (2) the concentration of authority in the hands of a single executive would not lead to tyranny because of the checks and balances working together with the system of separation of powers; and (3) the division of power between the federal government and the states would prevent a conspiracy by any faction.

Madison's leading role in the drafting of the Constitution has made *The Federalist* the most authoritative source for interpreting the Constitution.

A Bill of Rights

The first Congress under the new constitutional government met in April 1789. One of its first tasks was to respond to the calls of the state ratification conventions for amendments to the Constitution in the form of a bill of rights. In a number of states the Federalists had won ratification by promising a bill of rights.

As prepared by James Madison, nineteen proposed amendments were placed before the House of Representatives and the Senate for consideration; twelve of these were eventually sent to the states. Madison's original amendments were designed to restrict both the federal and state governments. However, those who favored states' rights prevailed and the amendments sent to the states for consideration applied only to the federal government. This leads to an interesting question: were the states more concerned with preserving civil liberties or restricting the powers of the federal government?

Of the twelve proposals sent to the states, ten were accepted and officially became part of the Constitution on December 15, 1791, when three-quarters of the states had ratified them. Article V of the Constitution provides for the amending process.

Throughout our nation's history, only Congress has proposed amendments for consideration by the states. The procedure allowing for two thirds of the states to petition Congress to call a constitutional convention has never been used. The scope and authority of such a convention are not defined or limited by the Constitution and therefore the method has prompted much debate.

PROPOSAL	RATIFICATION
Amendments to the Constitution may be proposed by a two thirds vote of Congress in both the House of Representatives and the Senate	The amendment must be ratified by at least three fourths of the state legislatures
or	or
when two thirds of the state legislatures request Congress to call a Constitutional Convention, which then proposes an amendment.	be ratified by a majority vote in three fourths of the state conventions called to vote on the amendment.

Figure 1.8 The Amending Process

Amendments	Provisions
I	1. The establishment clause of Amendment I states that Congress shall make no law that establishes religion in any manner. This has been referred to as the "wall of separation between church and state." 2. The second part of Amendment I prevents Congress from restricting the free practice of religion, freedom of speech, press, the right to assemble peacefully, or to petition the government.
II	Amendment II was designed to prevent Congress from denying states the right to have a militia of armed citizens. It is currently argued that the amendment guarantees people the right to own weapons, although states do have the right to restrict such ownership.
III	In peacetime, no citizen may be forced to quarter (house and feed) soldiers. In time of war, Congress may pass legislation allowing for such quartering. The quartering of troops in the colonists'·homes by the British government was well remembered by the residents of the states.
IV	Remembering the writs of assistance, supporters of the Fourth Amendment required that search warrants could be issued only under the following conditions: (a) the warrant must be issued by a judge; (b) there must be probable cause (good reason) for its issuance; and (c) the warrant must describe the place to be searched and the items to be seized.
V	1. Grand Juries: A person accused of a serious crime and tried in a federal court must first be indicted (charged) by a grand jury (jury of 12 to 23 persons). 2. Double Jeopardy: A person may not be tried twice for the same crime. 3. Self-Incrimination: A person may not be forced to say anything that would help convict himself or herself. This provision finds its origins in confessions that were obtained through forceful measure, i.e., torture. 4. Due Process: A person may not be deprived of life, liberty, or property (natural rights) except according to law. The Fourteenth Amendment applies this clause to the states as well as the federal government.

Figure 1.9 The Bill of Rights

Amendments	Provisions
V (cont.)	5. Eminent Domain: Congress may not (without paying a fair price) take private property for the benefit of the public, e.g., roads, hospitals, and airports.
VI	Amendment VI continues the rights of the accused started in Amendment V. The person accused of a crime must be given a prompt trial in public, and guilt or innocence must be decided by a jury chosen from the state and district where the crime was committed. The accused must be informed of the charges, be present when witnesses testify against him or her, and be provided with a lawyer if he or she cannot provide one. The Fourteenth Amendment has also applied these provisions to state courts.
VII	Amendment VII provides for a jury trial in federal civil cases (trials where one person sues another, usually for damages). The second part of the amendment limits the power of judges to interfere with a jury's decision.
VIII	If a person is accused of a crime and must await trial, he or she may be released from prison on bail—an amount of money that is put up to guarantee the accused will appear for trial; bail is forfeited if he or she fails to appear. Amendment VIII guarantees that a fine should be calculated according to the wrong done and that "cruel and unusual punishment" may not be inflicted on those convicted. The death penalty continues to be debated on the "cruel and unusual" punishment argument.
IX	Amendment IX was added out of fear that it might be dangerous to make only a partial listing of the basic rights guaranteed in the Constitution. This amendment makes it clear that the federal government may still do only what is authorized by the Constitution.
X	This amendment was added to reserve "all other powers" to the states and the people. The powers of the federal government are listed in Article I, Section 8. The powers denied to the states are listed in Article I, Section 10. All others are reserved to the states.
XIV*	Section 1 of Amendment XIV denied to the states the power to deprive any person of life, liberty, or property without due process of law. This due process clause protects individuals from unfair actions by state government, whereas, Amendment V protected individuals from unfair actions by the federal government.

*Note: The Bill of Rights was added to protect the people from the federal government. The Fourteenth Amendment, ratified in 1868, extended some of the original provisions of the Bill of Rights and applied them to the state governments. It protected individuals from actions by state governments.

Figure 1.9 continued The Bill of Rights

The only amendment to be ratified by popularly elected state constitutional conventions was the Twenty-first Amendment (1933) repealing Prohibition. All other amendments have been ratified by the state legislatures.

By studying the over 80 proposals from the state conventions for ratifying the Constitution, Madison was able to incorporate those he considered most important into his nineteen original proposals.

The **first ten amendments** to the United States Constitution gave formal recognition to certain traditionally accepted natural rights that had been included in the English tradition, colonial charters, and states' bills of rights. The wording of the first ten amendments makes it clear that those powers that are granted or denied to the federal government are powers that come directly from the people. Contrary to our provisions for individual liberties are those systems in which the government grants rights. For example: The First Amendment to the United States Constitution reads in part: *"Congress shall make no law* respecting the establishment of religion . . . or abridging the freedom of speech." Article 125 of the former Soviet Union's Fundamental Rights and Duties of Citizens reads in part: "In conformity with the interests of the working people, and in order to strengthen the socialist system, *the citizens are guaranteed* by law: freedom of speech, freedom of press . . .''

The important distinction is the source of authority in the two different systems of government, the first being the people, the second being the government.

Exercise Set 1.2

1. Arrested persons claiming they have already been acquitted of the charge for which they are now being tried are claiming the defense of
   A. ex post facto
   B. unreasonable search and seizure
   C. double jeopardy
   D. right to trial by jury

2. The right of government to take private property for public use, providing just compensation is made, is known as
   A. habeas corpus
   B. self-incrimination
   C. Federalism
   D. eminent domain

3. When a judge tells the accused person what he or she is charged with and that he or she may have legal counsel and a jury trial, the accused is being
   A. indicted by a grand jury
   B. denied due process of law
   C. informed of constitutional rights
   D. protected from cruel and unusual punishment

4. The principle of Federalism as established by the United States Constitution provides for the
   A. separation of powers of the three branches of government
   B. placement of ultimate sovereignty in the hands of the state governments
   C. division of power between the state governments and the national government
   D. creation of a republican form of government

5. The Great Compromise of the Constitutional Convention of 1787 concerned the
   A. issue of slavery
   B. representation of the states in Congress
   C. election of the President
   D. allocation of judicial power in the federal government

6. Which of the following compromises made at the Constitutional Convention was later changed by a constitutional amendment?
   A. the establishment of a bicameral legislature
   B. the Three-Fifths Compromise
   C. the tariff-commerce compromise
   D. representation in the House of Representatives

7. The Constitution differed most from the Articles of Confederation in that the Constitution
   A. gave greater power to the federal government
   B. gave greater power to the state governments
   C. made the amending process more difficult
   D. changed the method of admitting new states to the union

8. Which of the following is an illustration of the system of checks and balances?
   A. an individual pays income tax to both the federal government and the state government
   B. New York State requires at least 180 days of school per year
   C. the Senate must approve an appointment by the President to the Supreme Court
   D. Congress may pass no law establishing a state religion

9. The powers of Congress were limited by the Constitution, chiefly because
   A. representatives of the states feared too powerful a central government
   B. the Federalists desired strong, independent state governments
   C. the new government lacked a judiciary to check Congressional power
   D. supporters of a strong central government planned to carry out legislative powers through the executive branch

10. Within the first ten amendments to the United States Constitution is one providing
    A. that under no conditions shall soldiers be housed and fed by citizens at the request of the government
    B. that slavery will be banned
    C. for the right of the people to petition the government
    D. for women's suffrage

CONSTITUTIONAL STRUCTURE, FUNCTION, AND THIRTEEN ENDURING ISSUES

> Our Constitution is in actual operation; everything appears to promise
> that it will last, but in this world nothing is certain but death and taxes.
> Benjamin Franklin, letter to M. Leroy, 1789

Structure and Function

Article I, Congress

Congress has maintained its status as the most democratic branch of the federal government. The 535 members of the legislative branch are the only federal officials elected directly by the people.

In its early days, Congress met for only a few months each year. Today, Congress is in session nearly year round, and during a two-year session, lawmakers will consider more than 12,000 bills on diverse issues. On a typical day, a member of Congress will divide his or her time between committee meetings, sessions within the House or the Senate, meetings with constituents, lobbyists, and visiting dignitaries.

- *The Structure.* Congress is organized according to provisions in Article I of the Constitution.

- *Sessions of Congress.* Beginning with the first Congress of 1789–1790, each Congress serves for a two-year term. Each Congress meets in two sessions, each session convening, in accordance with the Twentieth Amendment, on or soon after January 3.

- *Powers of Congress.* The first 17 clauses of Article I, Section 8, detail the power of Congress. Some of the major **delegated** or **enumerated** powers of Congress include: the levying and collection of taxes, borrowing money, coining money and regulating its value, regulating interstate and foreign trade, granting patents and copyrights, declaring war, raising and supporting an army and navy, creating courts below the Supreme Court, using state militias to execute the laws of the nation, establishing post offices, controlling naturalization of aliens, and controlling federal property within the states. Powers shared by Congress and the states are referred to as **concurrent** powers.

	SENATE	HOUSE
Qualifications	• At least 30 years of age • U.S. citizen for nine years • Resident of state represented (Art. I, Section 3, Clause 3)	• At least 25 years of age • U.S. citizen for seven years • Resident of state represented (Art. I, Section 2, Clause 2)
Term of Office	• Six years • One-third of members elected every two years (Art. I, Section 3, Clauses 1 and 2)	• Two years • Full House is elected every two years (Art. I, Section 2, Clause 1)
Method of Election	• Originally by state legislatures (Art. I, Section 3, Clause 1) • Today, directly by voters of state (Amendment 17, 1913)	• Directly by voters of state and, district (Art. I, Section 2, Clause 1)
Membership	• Two Senators from each state (100) (Art. I, Section 3, Clause 1)	• Now set at 435 by law (1910). Determined by population of a state. Census taken every ten years. As of the 1990 census, each member of the House represented approximately 573,563 persons. (Art. I, Section 2, Clause 3)
Filling Vacancies	• Originally by Governor and state legislature. Today, Governor may appoint until a popular election within the state takes place (Amendment 17, 1913)	• Governor of state calls an election to fill vacancy. (Art. I, Section 2, Clause 4)
Presiding Officer	• Vice-President of the United States; Majority vote in case of tie vote. (Art. I, Section 3, Clause 4) • President Pro Tempore chosen by Senate as presiding officer to preside when Vice-President is absent (Art. I, Section 3, Clause 5)	• Chosen by members, usually represents majority party. (Art. I, Section 2, Clause 5)
Special Powers	• Chooses Vice-President if no majority in electoral vote (Amendment 12, 1913) • Sits as jury in impeachment trial (Art. I, Section 3, Clause 6) • Ratifies treaties with foreign nations by two-thirds vote (Art. II, Section 2, Clause 2) • Approves presidential appointments (Art. II, section 2, Clause 2)	• Chooses President if no majority in electoral vote (Amendment 12, 1913) • Brings impeachment charges (Art. I, Section 2, Clause 5) • All bills for raising revenue originate in the House of Representatives. (Art. I, Section 7, Clause 1)

Figure 1.10 Structure of House and Senate

- *Necessary and Proper Clause.* Clause 18 of Article I, Section 8 provides that Congress may "Make all laws necessary and proper for carrying into execution the foregoing powers . . ." This is commonly referred to as the **elastic clause**. The Supreme Court case of *McCullough* v. *Maryland* (1819) provided one of the earliest opportunities to test the use of the powers implied through the "necessary and proper clause." In this case the issue was whether Congress had the right to establish a national bank, even though the Constitution did not specifically grant it that power. Two groups with opposing views on how to interpret the Constitution developed as a result of the dispute:

Strict Constructionists. Those who felt that the Constitution should be read literally and that the elastic clause should be used only for expanding the powers of Congress in cases where the expansion is absolutely necessary.

Loose Constructionists. Those who held the belief that the Constitution, and specifically the elastic clause, should be read broadly and that the framers had intended the clause to mean that Congress should have the "proper" powers resulting from its other powers.

Taking a broad view of the elastic clause, the Supreme Court in *McCullough* v. *Maryland,* in an opinion written by **Chief Justice John Marshall**, held that the national bank was necessary and proper for carrying out Congress's powers of collecting taxes and coining and borrowing money.

The trend throughout our history has been toward loose construction. Examples include Congress's broadened definition of "commerce," increased government control over business practices, labor unions, minimum wages, and the establishment of a Social Security system and Medicare.

John Marshall (1755–1835). As Chief Justice of the Supreme Court, Marshall expanded federal power over the states.

- *How a Bill Becomes a Law.* The primary function of Congress is legislative—to make the laws that govern our nation. Article I, Section 7, provides for the lawmaking procedures of Congress. Except for **money bills**, which must originate in the House of Representatives, any bill may be intro-

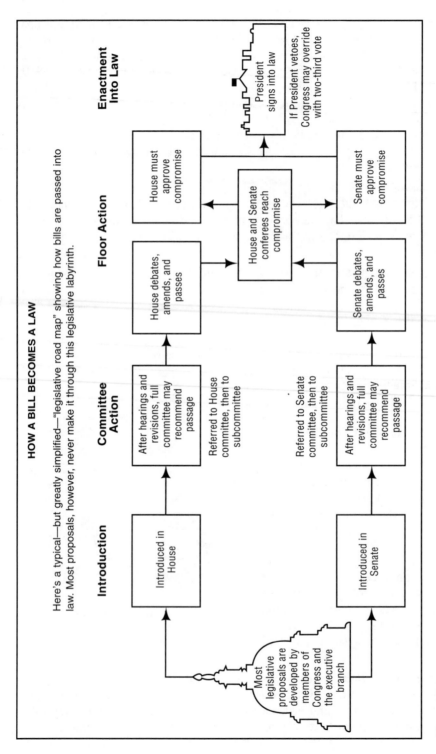

HOW A BILL BECOMES A LAW

Here's a typical—but greatly simplified—"legislative road map" showing how bills are passed into law. Most proposals, however, never make it through this legislative labyrinth.

Introduction

Introduced in House

Introduced in Senate

Most legislative proposals are developed by members of Congress and the executive branch

Committee Action

After hearings and revisions, full committee may recommend passage

Referred to House committee, then to subcommittee

Referred to Senate committee, then to subcommittee

After hearings and revisions, full committee may recommend passage

Floor Action

House debates, amends, and passes

House and Senate conferees reach compromise

Senate debates, amends, and passes

House must approve compromise

Senate must approve compromise

Enactment Into Law

President signs into law

If President vetoes, Congress may override with two-third vote

Figure 1.11

58

duced by any member of Congress. Of the thousands of bills introduced each year, only a small percentage actually become law. Much of the work of Congress occurs in committees of the House and the Senate, each with jurisdiction over certain areas of public policy. If the bill survives the debate of its committee, it will move on to consideration by the chamber of Congress in which it originated.

Article II, The Executive

Perhaps the most powerful political office in the world, the presidency of the United States combines the roles of chief of state, chief diplomat, Commander-in-Chief of the armed forces, chief executive, chief legislator, and head of his or her political party. Yet, in spite of the power which has grown with the office over time, the President has only those powers that the Constitution provides for, or implies.

• *Structure.* The office of the President and the executive branch are outlined in Article II, Sections 1 through 4, and in Amendments 12, 20, 22, 23, and 25.

• *Election of the President.* The election of the President actually involves two races: the first to be nominated by his or her political party and the second to win the national election for the office of the President.

The Nomination. Presidential candidates have not always been nominated by political parties. In the first two elections of George Washington, no nominations were necessary as Washington was unanimously chosen by the Electoral College. But as political parties formed and became better established, groups composed of individuals with common political, social, and economic interests competed to have their choice nominated for the presidency. John Adams, Thomas Jefferson, James Madison, and James Monroe were all nominated by party leaders in Congress in what was known as a **congressional caucus**. Change in the nominating process came when many Americans voiced their opposition to the selection of presidential candidates by a caucus of congressional leaders as a violation of the spirit of the Constitution and its provision for the separation of powers.

As part of the democratic reforms of the Jacksonian Era, the **national nominating convention**, a gathering of delegates from the different states to nominate a candidate, was developed. It allowed greater participation by citizens in the nomination of a party candidate. Today, delegates are chosen for the national convention either through the caucus method, or the **primary method** within the states.

National Election. Every four years, on the first Tuesday after the first Monday in November, Americans vote for electors pledged to one presidential candidate or another. The road to the presidency is described in Figure 1.13.

Article II, Section 1	Executive power shall be vested in the President, four-year term, electoral system (changed by Amendment 12), date of elections, qualifications for President, succession to the presidency, salary, and oath of office.
Article II, Section 2	Powers of the President: Military, treaties, appointments, powers over executive departments, pardon and reprieve, filling vacancies.
Article II, Section 3	State of the Union Address, calling special sessions of Congress, veto power, receiving ambassadors, execution of the laws.
Article II, Section 4	Impeachment and removal from office for treason, bribery, or other high crimes and misdemeanors.
Amendment 12 (1804)	Amendment 12 alters Article 2, Section 1, Clause 3. Prior to this amendment electors voted for two persons without designating who would become President and who would become Vice-President. Now, electors cast separate ballots for President and Vice-President.
Amendment 20 (1933)	Known as the "lame duck" amendment. Changed office-taking date for the presidency from March 4 to January 20 to shorten length of period a "lame duck" President would stay in office. Also provided that newly-elected members of Congress would take office January 3.
Amendment 22 (1951)	Although Presidents Washington and Jefferson set the two-term tradition, nothing in the Constitution limited a President to only two terms. After President Franklin Delano Roosevelt was elected to a third term in 1940 and then a fourth in 1944, the 22nd Amendment became law limiting a President to two terms or a maximum of ten years.
Amendment 23 (1961)	Gave the District of Columbia three electoral votes and enabled residents to vote for the President and Vice-President.
Amendment 25 (1967)	In an attempt to clarify Article 2, Section 1, Clause 6 dealing with disability and succession of the presidency, Amendment 25 became law.

Figure 1.12 The Presidency

• *Executive Branch.* The executive branch consists primarily of the **Cabinet**, the Executive Office of the President, and independent offices and agencies. Although the Constitution mentions only **executive departments** (Article II, Section 2, Clause 1) and does not mention a Cabinet (the first mention of the Cabinet came in 1967 with the adoption of the Twenty-Fifth Amendment), the group of presidential advisers was started by President Washington and has become an American governmental tradition. Over the years, the President's office has also assumed the responsibility of overseeing many agencies created by Congress to deal with domestic and world problems.

The entire executive branch has expanded greatly, especially in the past 50 years as the role of government has widened. A President today is aided by some 2.6 million civilian employees working within departments, agencies, boards, and commissions.

Article III, The Judicial Branch

> Watergate has taught us that our system is not invulnerable to the arrogance of power . . . (and) that our system of law is the most valuable asset in this land.
>
> Judge John J. Sirica, 1974

The Supreme Court is the only federal court specifically mentioned in the Constitution. Article III, Section I provides for a Supreme Court and gives Congress the power to establish inferior (lower) courts. Congress made use of this power with the passage of the **Judiciary Act of 1789**, which established thirteen **district courts** in principal cities, three **circuit courts**, and one **Supreme Court** with a **Chief Justice** and five **Associates**. Because the Constitution does not state the number of Justices to be appointed to the Supreme Court, Congress decides the number by law. Today the Supreme Court has nine Justices.

• *Structure.* The Constitutional provisions for the judicial branch are set out in Article III.

• *Original and Appellate Jurisdiction.* Article III grants the Supreme Court **original jurisdiction**, or the right to hear a case for the first time, and **appellate jurisdiction**, the right to accept and hear cases coming from lower federal courts and the highest state courts. When the Supreme Court agrees to hear a case on appeal from a lower court, it is said that the Court is granting **certiorari**.

• *Judicial Review.* The Court reviews the constitutionality of legislative acts. Like Federalism and separation of powers, the concept of judicial review is rooted in the principles of **limited government**. Although the framers of the Constitution refrained from specifically spelling out judicial review, they did state in Article III that "the judicial power of the United States, shall be vested in one Supreme Court..." Most of the delegates probably expected the Supreme Court to rule on the constitutionality of acts of Congress. Moreover, Hamilton supported the concept of judicial review in *Federalist No. 78* when he said that when the legislatures are in conflict with the Constitution, "the judges should be governed by the latter rather than the former."

The opinion of Chief Justice John Marshall in the Supreme Court case of *Marbury* v. *Madison* in 1803 established the precedent for judicial review. In this case, the Court held part of the Judiciary Act of 1789, an act of Congress, to be unconstitutional. Although the circuit courts had ruled on the constitutionality of state laws *(Ware* v. *Hylton* 1796), the Marbury case marked the first time the Supreme Court ruled an act of Congress to be contrary to the Constitution.

Primary Elections

In states not using caucuses or state conventions, primary elections are held in which voters pick either a candidate by name or delegates to the national convention who will support the particular candidate.

Caucuses and State Conventions

In states not having primaries, party members hold caucuses to pick delegates who then attend state conventions where the state's delegates to the national convention are chosen.

National Conventions

The delegates who have been selected in the state primaries and the state conventions attend the national convention of the party during the summer before the national election. At the convention the delegates vote for their choice for President and Vice-President and adopt a platform on which they run. The individuals selected become the candidates for the national election in November.

Election Day

After intense campaigning by the candidates of the major parties during the late summer and fall, American voters cast their ballots on the first Tuesday after the first Monday in November for electors pledged to one of the candidates. This is the popular vote.

Electoral Vote

In each state the electors of the party that won the greatest popular vote assemble in December and vote for the Presidential and Vice-Presidential candidates, usually of their own parties. Certified copies of these votes are sent to the President of the United States Senate. (Amendment 12)

Counting and Inauguration

The President of the Senate counts the electoral votes (538, the total number of members of Congress, plus 3 for the District of Columbia) in the presence of the House of Representatives and the Senate. The candidates with the majority of the electoral vote are elected and are sworn into office on January 20. (Amendment 20)

Figure 1.13 Election of the President

EXECUTIVE BRANCH

President's Cabinet

(In order of creation)

Department of State (1789)

Department of Treasury (1789)

Department of Justice (1789)

Department of the Interior (1849)

Department of Agriculture (1889)

Department of Commerce (1903)

Department of Labor (1913)

Department of Defense (1947)

Department of Health and
  Human Services (1953)

Department of Housing and
  Urban Development (1965)

Department of Transportation (1966)

Department of Energy (1977)

Department of Education (1979)

Department of Veterans Affairs (1988)

The Executive Office

(Partial Listing)

The White House Staff

Office of Management and Budget

Council on Economic Advisers

Council on Environmental Quality

Domestic Policy Staff

National Security Council

Central Intelligence Agency

Office of Administration

INDEPENDENT FEDERAL AGENCIES

(Partial Listing)

Federal Reserve System

Environmental Protection Agency

Equal Employment Opportunity
  Commission

Farm Credit Association

Federal Communications
  Commission

Federal Deposit Insurance
  Commission

Federal Election Commission

Federal Trade Commission

Interstate Commerce Commission

National Academy of Sciences

National Aeronautics and Space
  Administration (NASA)

National Foundation on the Arts and
  Humanities

National Labor Relations Board

Nuclear Regulatory Commission

Securities and Exchange
  Commission

Small Business Administration

Smithsonian Institution

Tennessee Valley Authority

United States Postal Service

Veterans Administration

Figure 1.14   The Executive Branch

Article III, Section 1	Establishment of the Supreme Court and the provision for Congress to establish inferior courts. Judges appointed for life assuming good behavior. Justices are appointed by the President and approved by the Senate (Article II, Section 2).
Article III, Section 2	The power of the federal courts extends to two types of cases: (1) those involving the interpretation of the Constitution, federal laws, treaties, and (2) those involving the United States government itself, foreign diplomatic officials, two or more state governments, citizens of different states, and states or citizens involved in disputes with foreign states. The Supreme Court has *original* jurisdiction in cases affecting ambassadors, public ministers, and in cases in which a state is a party. In all other cases, the jurisdiction of the Supreme Court is *appellate* with such exceptions as Congress shall make.
Article III, Section 3	Treason is the only crime to be defined in the Constitution. Article III, Section 3 provides for the definition and punishment of treason.

Figure 1.15   The Judicial Branch

THE MARSHALL COURT
EARLY SUPREME COURT CASES 1803–1824

CASE	ISSUE	DECISION
1803 *Marbury* v. *Madison*	Can the Supreme Court declare a federal law unconstitutional?	Declared the right of the Supreme Court to annul a law of Congress.
1810 *Fletcher* v. *Peck*	Can a state pass a law breaking a contract? Can the Supreme Court review a state law?	Established the right of the Supreme Court to declare state laws unconstitutional and protected private property.
1816 *Martin* v. *Hunters Lessee*	Can the Supreme Court review and reverse the decisions of the state courts?	Set the appellate jurisdiction of the Supreme Court over the state courts.
1819 *McCullough* v. *Maryland*	Has Congress power to create a bank? Can the states tax such a structure?	Accepted broad "implied" powers of Congress and sovereign power of the federal government.
1819 *Dartmouth College* v. *Woodward*	Is a charter to a corporation a contract, and is this beyond control of the state?	The Supreme Court limited state powers over individuals and companies and protected contracts.
1824 *Gibbons* v. *Ogden*	What is "commerce" and what is the extent of Congress's power to regulate "commerce"?	Enlarged rights of Congress to control commerce.

Figure 1.16

There have been efforts to curb judicial review by those who feel that the Supreme Court has abused its interpretive powers. Whenever judicial review is exercised in particularly sensitive areas, the Court is criticized for its actions and calls are made for restriction of its powers. This occurred after the desegregation decision in *Brown* v. *Board of Education* (1954), when cries for the impeachment of the Chief Justice and other members of the Court were heard. One of the more recent movements for restriction of the Court's jurisdiction has been in the area of religion in schools.

• *Federal Court System and Routes to the Supreme Court.* The United States is served by 12 regional federal judicial circuits. Each has its own

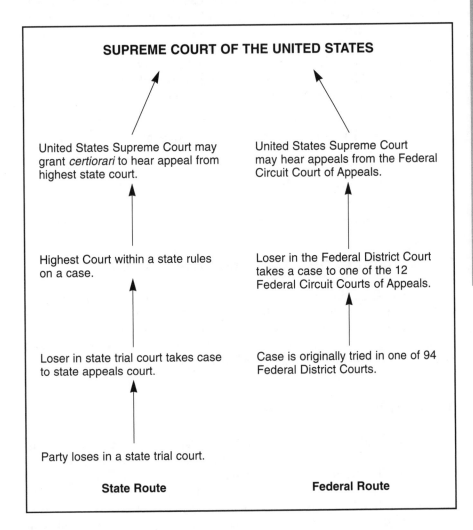

SUPREME COURT OF THE UNITED STATES

United States Supreme Court may grant *certiorari* to hear appeal from highest state court.

United States Supreme Court may hear appeals from the Federal Circuit Court of Appeals.

Highest Court within a state rules on a case.

Loser in the Federal District Court takes a case to one of the 12 Federal Circuit Courts of Appeals.

Loser in state trial court takes case to state appeals court.

Case is originally tried in one of 94 Federal District Courts.

Party loses in a state trial court.

State Route

Federal Route

Figure 1.17 Route to the Supreme Court

court of appeals and a varying number of district, or trial, courts— 94 in all. Each state has its own judicial structure with trial courts, courts of appeals, and a highest court of final state appeal. Cases reach the Supreme Court either through the federal court system or on appeal from the highest court within a state. Of the thousands of cases that seek Supreme Court review each year, only a small percentage are accepted by the Court.

The Federal Bureaucracy

The federal bureaucracy consists of more than 3 million civil servants performing a variety of tasks ranging from collecting taxes to investigating airplane crashes, from measuring air pollution to approving new medical devices. The size of government greatly increased during the administration of President Franklin Roosevelt and the New Deal years. It has continued to increase in size. Today the government's civilian payroll runs about $300 billion per year and is dispersed among 16.5 million employees.

Employees of the Federal Government	
Legislative Branch	40,000
Executive Branch	2,660,000
Judicial Branch	16,500

Comparison to New York State Government

Each of the 52 state governments has political structures similar to the federal government, including republican forms of representative government, division of powers, and a system of federalism between state and local governments. Figure 1.18 shows the similarities between the New York State governmental structure and that of the federal government.

Thirteen Enduring Issues

During the spring of 1983, **Project '87**, an undertaking of the American Historical Association and the American Political Science Association, designed to celebrate the bicentennial of the Constitution, set out to identify crucial constitutional issues of enduring concern. After polling numerous scholars and public officials and receiving a wide variety of issues for consideration, Project '87 compiled these thirteen issues that could be used to organize an examination of the Constitution, its evolution, and its meaning:

National Power—limits and potential
Federalism—the balance between nation and state
The Judiciary—interpreter of the Constitution or shaper of public policy
Civil Liberties—the balance between government and the individual
Criminal Penalties—rights of the accused and protection of the community
Equality—its definition as a constitutional value
The Rights of Women under the Constitution
The Rights of Ethnic and Racial Groups under the Constitution
Presidential Power in Wartime and in Foreign Affairs
The Separation of Powers and the Capacity to Govern
Avenues of Representation
Property Rights and Economic Policy
Constitutional Change and Flexibility

National Power—Limits and Potential

The framers of the Constitution carefully limited the power of the federal government by enumerating the delegated powers and, in the Bill of Rights, reserving all other powers to the states and people. Yet, over the years, as our society has become more complex, legislation, executive acts, and decisions by the courts have increased the power of the federal government enormously.

Federalism—the Balance between Nation and State

Our Constitution balances the powers between the federal government and the states by specifically delegating certain powers to the national government and reserving all others to the states or the people. Throughout the history of our nation, however, the flow of power has gone from the states to the national government.

EXECUTIVE BRANCH
Governor, elected by the people of New York for a four-year term
LEGISLATIVE BRANCH
Bicameral legislature consisting of a 50-member Senate and a 150-member Assembly.
JUDICIAL BRANCH
Court of Appeals: the highest appellate court in the state Appellate Divisions Supreme Courts: the lowest trial courts of the state system

Figure 1.18   New York State Government

The Judiciary—Interpreter of the Constitution or Shaper of Public Policy

Although the Supreme Court has been granted the judicial power of the United States by Article III of the Constitution, has it also become a second legislative body, establishing policy when Congress fails to do so?

Civil Liberties—the Balance between Government and the Individual

In the famous Supreme Court case of *Schenck* v. *United States* (1919) involving civil liberties during wartime, Justice Holmes wrote, "Free speech would not protect a man in falsely shouting fire in a theatre, and causing a panic." On a larger scale, when does national security require the restriction of civil liberties? How should the Court go about balancing the two forces?

Criminal Penalties—Rights of the Accused and Protection of the Community

How can our government protect the citizens of this country and yet uphold the rights of those who have been accused of committing crimes? If Amendments 4, 5, 6, and 8 protect the accused, what protects the victim of a crime?

Equality—Its Definition as a Constitutional Value

Are all men and women created equal as the Declation of Independence suggests? If our Constitution guarantees equality before the law, does it guarantee equality of opportunities for people, or equality of results?

The Rights of Women under the Constitution

Although the Constitution does not mention "women," it does make reference to "persons." Yet, the document prohibits only one form of sex-based discrimination, that no state may deny women the right to vote (Amendment 19). The proposed **Equal Rights Amendment**, which has not been approved, would prohibit discrimination on account of sex.

The Rights of Ethnic and Racial Groups under the Constitution

The trend during the 20th century has been toward much stronger guarantees of minority rights. However, can this go too far and begin to discriminate against the majority? Is it the obligation of society today to make up for the wrongs done to minorities in the past, as affirmative action suggests?

Presidential Power in Wartime

History shows that the President has exercised extraordinary powers during wartime both in restricting civil liberties at home and in sending troops into hostile environments without a declaration of war from Congress. Does the existence of the power of Congress to declare war and the President's power as Commander-in-Chief present an irreconcilable conflict that will be a continuing struggle between the executive and legislative branches?

The Separation of Powers and the Capacity to Govern

Through the system of checks and balances, combined with separation of powers, the framers of the Constitution tried to assure that no one branch would gain oppressive power over either of the other two. As a result, the federal government is often accused of being ineffective, too slow, or pitted against itself to the point of getting nothing done.

Avenues of Representation

Is our system truly a republic, government by the people representing the majority will, or have political parties, special interest groups, and political action committees helped create a government that may be for sale?

Property Rights and Economic Policy

Congress is delegated the power to provide for the general welfare of the United States. Through the enumerated powers and the "necessary and proper" clause, the federal government has assumed economic responsibilities in the areas of trade, taxation, and contracts, and has helped perpetuate a system of free enterprise. However, as Congress uses its powers to promote American business, it is also responsible for protecting Americans from abuses by businesses.

Constitutional Change and Flexibility

Although the Constitution has been amended only sixteen times since the addition of the Bill of Rights in 1791, in the last decade there have been numerous proposals for amending the document. How many times may the original document be amended without diluting its effectiveness? What are the assurances against insignificant changes to the document? Although the states have never made use of their constitutional power to call a constitutional convention, what would be the limits of such an exercise of power?

Exercise Set 1.3

1. Much of the authority of the United States Supreme Court is based on its power to
   A. propose legislation to Congress
   B. change the distribution of powers as outlined in the federal Constitution
   C. amend state and federal constitutions
   D. interpret the federal Constitution

2. The most serious threat to democracy resulting from high election campaign costs is that, once elected, candidates frequently
   A. owe money to friends and relatives
   B. plan to use public funds to pay their debts
   C. owe loyalty to a few major contributors
   D. have little of their own savings left

3. Base your answer to question 3 on the following headline and your knowledge of social studies.

THOMAS CONFIRMATION FIGHT CONTINUES FOR HIGH COURT

The confirmation fight referred to in the headline is one that would take place among
   A. Supreme Court Justices
   B. Senators
   C. Cabinet members
   D. members of the House Judiciary Committee

4. When Congress makes laws "necessary and proper for carrying into execution the foregoing powers," it is using
   A. enumerated powers
   B. implied powers
   C. concurrent powers
   D. general welfare powers

5. Which headline would be an example of judicial review?
   A. "Impeachment Charges Brought Against President"
   B. "Attorney General Advises Presidential Veto"
   C. "Judiciary Rules Law Unconstitutional"
   D. "Senate Rejects Nomination of Federal Judge"

6. "The Supreme Court is not so much a court of justice as America's ultimate lawmaking body."
This statement is most concerned with the power of the U.S. Supreme Court to
A. exercise judicial review
B. propose Constitutional amendments
C. exercise original jurisdiction
D. sit as a jury in impeachment proceedings

7. Which headline is the best example of the application of the system of checks and balances?
A. "President Truman Fires General MacArthur"
B. "Senate To Debate Abortion Funding Bill"
C. "Supreme Court Nominee Rejected by Senate"
D. "House of Representatives Votes To Discipline Its Own Member"

8. Base your answer to question 8 on the following headline and your knowledge of social studies.

President Bush Refuses to Finish
Term as a 'Lame Duck'

An assumption that may be drawn from the headline is that the President has
A. had numerous bills defeated by Congress
B. approached the end of his term of office
C. appointed ineffective staff members to the executive office
D. dismissed some of his Cabinet directors

LAUNCHING A NEW GOVERNMENT

All communities divide themselves into the few and the many. The first are the rich and the wellborn; the other, the mass of the people...Give therefore to the first class a distinct permanent share in the government. They will check the unsteadiness of the second...

Alexander Hamilton, 1787

Men...are naturally divided into two parties. Those who fear and distrust the people...and...those who identify themselves with the people.

I am not among those who fear the people. They, and not the rich, are our dependence for continued freedom.

Thomas Jefferson, 1824, 1816

On March 4, 1789, the first Congress under the new Constitution assembled in New York City. The members of Congress were supporters of the new Constitution and many of them had served as delegates in Philadelphia during the summer of 1787. Their primary intention was to carry out the purposes of the nationalists; to make the federal government a lasting institution and to create respect for the republic among the older nations of the world.

George Washington, who had been unanimously elected President, was inaugurated in New York City on April 30th, 1789. **John Adams** had been chosen Vice-President. Congress created three executive departments to which Washington appointed **Thomas Jefferson** as Secretary of State, **Alexander Hamilton** as Secretary of the Treasury, and **Henry Knox** as Secretary of War. The office of Attorney General was created by Congress as the government's chief law officer.

The Hamiltonian Program: Steps Toward Domestic Stability

Alexander Hamilton, as the first Secretary of the Treasury, formulated an economic program aimed at building the political support and respect necessary to assure the legitimacy of the new government. In a series of reports to Congress in 1790–1791, known as the "Reports of the Public Credit," Hamilton proposed the following financial plan.

Repayment of the Foreign Debt

The national government should repay approximately $12 million to foreign governments and investors, mostly to France.

Federal Assumption of the State Debts

Amounting to $25 million, this repayment was opposed primarily by Southern states such as Virginia, which had partially paid some of their debts. To win their support, Hamilton made a deal with Jefferson to give Northern support for a bill to locate the future national capital on the Potomac River, i.e., Washington, D.C.

Excise Taxes

To raise revenue to help repay both the foreign and domestic debt that Congress incurred during the Revolution and confederation period, a tax was placed on whiskey. In May 1792, alarmed by unrest on the frontier caused by the new tax, Congress passed a law authorizing the President to call out the militia in case of resistance to federal authority. Resentment to the tax on whiskey came to a head during the summer of 1794 with the "**Whiskey Rebellion**." President Washington called out 13,000 militiamen to put down the uprising, demonstrating that the new government possessed the power to enforce its authority—a power that had been absent under the Articles of Confederation.

Establishment of a National Bank

Hamilton asked Congress to establish a Bank of the United States that would be a depository of federal funds and able to issue sound paper money on the basis of the securities it held. In February 1791 the bank bill was passed by Congress, but President Washington was hesitant to sign it. First, he asked to hear the constitutional arguments of Jefferson and Hamilton on the issue:

• *Jefferson's arguments against the bank:* Using the "**strict constructionist**" view, Jefferson declared the proposed United States bank unconstitutional. He claimed that the power to create the bank was not listed in the enumerated powers (Article I, Section 8), nor could the power be implied from any other power through the use of the elastic clause. The word "necessary" in the "necessary and proper" clause of Article I, Section 8 did not mean "convenient."

• *Hamilton's arguments for the bank:* Using the "**loose**" or "**broad constructionist**" view, Hamilton held the bank to be constitutional. He claimed that the power to create the bank can be implied from the enumerated powers to coin money, borrow money, and raise money through taxation. The word "necessary" in the "necessary and proper" clause meant needful or useful. If the end (national financial stability) was necessary and proper, the means (creation of the bank) was constitutional. Since a national bank was necessary for carrying out the nation's financial functions, it was constitutional.

Passage of Hamilton's Program

After listening to the arguments of Jefferson and Hamilton, Washington was convinced that the Bank of the United States was constitutional and advisable. The bank proved to be a sound financial institution and the funding and

CONSTITUTIONAL FOUNDATIONS OF THE UNITED STATES

assumption of the state's debts helped to put the new nation on a solid economic footing.

The Unwritten Constitution (1789–1808)

The reason the United States Constitution has lasted for such a long time is that the document was written so that it could be changed and adapted to future conditions. The provisions that have allowed for adaptation include the elastic clause, the doctrine of implied powers, judicial interpretation, and the amendment process. Also, the language in the text is very general. The flexibility of our Constitution has also been made possible by the practice of custom and tradition, or what is sometimes referred to as the **unwritten Constitution**.

During the young nation's first three administrations, growth, experimentation, and necessity led to unwritten developments in our constitutional form of government. These included the development of a Cabinet, the formation of political parties, the establishment of judicial review, and a **two-term tradition** for the President. Later developments were the growth of the committee system within Congress, lobbying, and the practice of presidential electors pledging their votes for specific candidates. These elements were not provided for in the Constitution but developed over time through practice.

The Cabinet System

Article II, Section 2, Clause 1 of the Constitution provides that the President may "require the Opinion in writing, of the principal Officer in each of the executive Departments . . ." Functioning at the pleasure of the President, the purpose of the Cabinet is to advise the President on any matter. The evolution of the Cabinet is shown in Figure 1.19.

Political Parties

American political parties began as early as 1796 and the election of John Adams. Although Washington viewed his office as above partisan differences, it was impossible for him to remove himself from the political battles that developed in his government between Secretary of Treasury Alexander Hamilton and Secretary of State Thomas Jefferson. The followers of Hamilton came to be known as **Federalists** and the supporters of Jefferson as **Republicans**. By 1796 presidential candidates were assuming political party identification.

The two major political parties in the United States today are the **Republicans** and the **Democrats**. Although third parties have existed in our political structure many times, they have never won real political power. These parties were usually formed because of a single issue. Some of these third

74

ORIGINAL CABINET	ADDED, 1798–1913	ADDED, 1947–1979
State Dept., 1789 Treasury Dept.,1789 War Dept., 1789–1946 Attorney General, 1789 (Not head of Justice Dept. until 1870.)	Navy Dept., 1798–1946 Postmaster General, 1829–1970 Interior Dept., 1849 Agriculture Dept., 1889 Commerce and Labor, 1903 (divided in 1913) Commerce, 1913 Labor, 1913	Defense Dept., 1947 (combined War and Navy) Health, Education and Welfare, 1953 (divided in 1979) Housing and Urban Development Dept., 1965 Transportation Dept., 1966 Energy Dept., 1977 Health and Human Services, 1979 Education Dept., 1979 Veterans Affairs Dept.,1988

Figure 1.19 Evolution of the Cabinet

parties have included: the **Free Soil party**, which opposed the extension of slavery; the **Greenback Labor party** of the 1870s, which supported farmers and workers; the **Progressive party** in the early 20th century that worked for political and social reform; the **Socialist party** that advocated government ownership of the means of production in American industry; the **States Rights party** (Dixiecrats) of the 1940s, composed of Southern Democrats who opposed the more liberal wing of the Democratic party; the **Right to Life party** of the 1970s, 1980s and 1990s that opposed abortion; and Ross Perot's United We Stand party in the election of 1992. Third parties have often had their proposals adopted by the major parties and some have been passed into law.

In the United States, political parties perform the following functions: (1) provide qualified and responsible candidates; (2) establish public policy; (3) educate the electorate; (4) encourage voter participation; (5) finance political campaigns.

Judicial Review

The practice of judicial review by the Supreme Court, a power not specifically delegated in Article III of the Constitution, but implied by the Constitution and assumed by the Supreme Court itself, has broadened the authority of the national government. The primary basis of the judicial power in our system of government has been the practice of judicial review, that is, the practice by which courts can determine whether legislative acts, both federal and state, are constitutional.

Two-Term Tradition

Although Article II, Section 1, Clause 1 states that the President shall "hold his office during the Term of four Years," it does not say how many terms a President may serve. George Washington chose to leave office after two terms, and all Presidents followed that precedent until Franklin Delano Roosevelt was elected to four terms (1932–1945; dying during his fourth term). The two-term (or ten-year limit) custom became part of the written Constitution through the Twenty-second Amendment (1951).

Committee System of Congress

Because of the many complex issues that must be considered by the legislative branch, the Senate and the House of Representatives are divided into small legislative bodies called committees. The committee system, which is part of the unwritten Constitution, grew out of necessity and became custom.

Lobbying

The term describes attempts to influence elected representatives during the passage of legislation through Congress. Lobbying is an important part of the legislative process. Lobbyists present to legislators the opinion of various groups. They also provide legislators with information concerning issues and bills before Congress. Recently, much criticism has been directed against lobbyists' efforts to influence members of Congress and to purchase the First Amendment "right to petition" with large funds from special interest groups. Deriving somewhat from the concept of lobbying are **Political Action Committees** (PACS), special interest groups who contribute money to political candidates for their election campaigns. PACS now supply more than a third of funds raised by the House candidates and close to a fifth for the Senate.

Pledging of Electoral Votes

Although the Electoral College was designed because of the founders' distrust of the common citizen's capability to select a President, this undemocratic intent has been overcome. Today, political parties name the electors who are pledged in advance to vote for the party's presidential candidate. However, only some states legally bind electors to honor their pledges and, although it is uncommon, electors sometimes do break their pledges and change their vote.

The Birth of American Foreign Policy (1789–1824)

The Administration of George Washington (1789–1797)

- *The French Revolution (1789–1793).* Most Americans supported the French Revolution, until the executions under the Reign of Terror increased.

After this and the entrance of Great Britain and Spain into the war against the Revolutionists, opinion in the United States was mixed. It was divided along political lines, with the Federalists supporting England and the Republicans supporting the French. Other considerations included American economic ties to England, the Franco-American alliance of 1778, and the weak military power of the United States.

- *Proclamation of Neutrality (1793).* The French Revolution proved to be one of the most important events in the diplomatic history of the United States, because it established the principles of American neutrality concerning European affairs. Although President Washington recognized the French Republic, he issued a proclamation of neutrality that never used the word "neutral," but stated that the United States would adopt "a conduct friendly and impartial toward the belligerent powers."

- *Problems with England and Jay's Treaty (1794).* Although the United States tried to remain neutral as British hostilities with France continued, its economic ties and trade with both sides placed the nation in danger. The United States and Britain came close to war because of Britain's refusal to abide by rules of international law (primarily the right of neutral shipping), the impressment of American sailors by the British navy, and the failure of the British to evacuate forts in the American Northwest according to the provisions of the Treaty of Paris (1783). President Washington sent Chief Justice John Jay to England to settle differences between the two nations. Jay negotiated a treaty with the following provisions: (1) the British would evacuate the Northwest forts by June 1, 1796; (2) commissions would be set up to establish the amount due to American shippers for loss of goods and other controversies; (3) England's contention that food was contraband was accepted; and (4) direct commerce between the United States and the British East Indies was provided for.

Although the treaty was not popular in the United States, and passed the Senate by only one vote, it was a success because it avoided war with Britain at a time when the United States was weak and not ready to fight its former mother country. Much of the reason for its passage was the pressure from Federalist senators who threatened not to ratify Pinckney's Treaty, or the Treaty of San Lorenzo, with Spain granting free navigation of the Mississippi, unless the Jay Treaty was ratified. During the ratification controversy over the Jay Treaty, the precedent of **executive privilege** was set. When the House of Representatives requested all documents pertaining to the negotiations, President Washington refused to provide them, believing that the sensitive circumstances warranted his refusal.

- *Washington's Farewell Address (1796).* Before leaving office to be succeeded by Federalist **John Adams**, President Washington conveyed through the press on September 19 his "Farewell Address." Written mostly by Hamilton, Washington advised in the address that the United States should maintain commercial, but not political, ties to other nations, and not enter into any **"entangling,"** or **permanent alliances**. While not advocating isolationism, Washington laid out principles that would be followed in the making of American foreign policy until the 1940s and 1950s.

The Administration of John Adams (1797–1801)

• *Failure of Attempts at Neutrality.* Relations between France and the United States grew steadily worse after 1793. Hostile toward the treaties of the United States with England and Spain (the Jay and Pinckney treaties), and unhappy with the fact that the United States had abandoned the 1778 Franco-American Treaty, France ordered its vessels to start seizing American ships carrying British goods. Attempts by the United States to negotiate its differences with France were frustrated by the **XYZ Affair** of 1797 (request of bribes in exchange for negotiations by France) and by an undeclared naval war from 1798 to 1800. In 1800 **Napoleon**, who now ruled France and wanted to avoid war with the United States, agreed to the **Convention of 1800**, which established peace between the two nations and finally recognized an end to the Treaty of 1778.

The Administrations of Thomas Jefferson (1801–1809)

• *Tripolitan War (1801).* The problems of raids on American shipping by the Barbary pirates continued. In 1801 President Jefferson refused the demand of the Tripoli government for payments of "tribute," a form of extortion. Instead of payment, Jefferson sent a naval squadron to protect American shipping. One of the Barbary states, Tripoli, declared war on the United States in 1801, causing hostilities until 1805 when Tripoli was subdued.

• *Problems with England.* After a brief interlude, Britain and France were at war again in 1803. The neutrality of the American shipping was again threatened, as both England and France issued decrees ordering the seizure of ships carrying goods to the other. The British navy resumed its practice of impressing sailors aboard American vessels, claiming they were deserters from the British fleet.

• *The Louisiana Purchase (1803).* During Jefferson's first term, thousands of American farmers had moved west to the lands between the Appalachian Mountains and the Mississippi River. They used the port of New Orleans at the base of the Mississippi River to export much of their produce. New Orleans was part of the vast area known as Louisiana, which stretched from the Mississippi River west to the Rocky Mountains.

The Louisiana Territory had been given to Spain by France at the end of the French and Indian War. Americans became alarmed when it was learned that Spain had transferred the area back to France by the Treaty of San Ildefonso (1800) and that Spanish officials left in control of New Orleans had ended the right of American farmers to use the port (suspension of the "**right of deposit**.") Jefferson, fearful of a strong and aggressive France as a neighbor and concerned over conflicts concerning the use of New Orleans, sent **James Monroe** and **Robert Livingston** to France to try to buy New Orleans. Napoleon, burdened with problems in Europe, decided to sell the entire Louisiana Territory to the United States for $15,000,000.

Problems arose when the strict constructionist Jefferson realized that the Constitution did not authorize Congress to purchase territory. Jefferson was forced to modify his constitutional theories because of the importance of the purchase, and in 1803 the treaty was ratified authorizing the purchase, which nearly doubled the size of the United States.

- *The Embargo Act (1807).* Seeking to force England to respect American rights while avoiding war, Jefferson pushed through Congress the **Embargo Act**, which forbade all exports from the United States to any country. Although it caused some harm to England, the act hurt the American economy by causing a depression.

- *The Non-Intercourse Act (1809).* In his last days of office, President Jefferson replaced the disastrous Embargo Act with the **Non-Intercourse Act**, which opened trade with all nations except France and England.

The Administrations of James Madison (1809–1817)

- *Macon's Bill No. 2.* Congress allowed the Non-Intercourse Act to expire in 1810 and replaced it with **Macon's Bill No. 2**. This promised both England and France that the United States would resume trade with the first nation that stopped abusing American shipping rights. Macon's Bill No. 2 allowed Madison to resume trade with France and to forbid all trade with England in March 1811.

- *Sectional Politics.* Sentiment for war against England came from land-hungry Southerners and Westerners (**War Hawks**) led by **Henry Clay** of Kentucky and **John Calhoun** of South Carolina. The **commercial interests** of the New England states caused them to oppose war because they feared a complete shutdown of trade and continuing depression. Opposition from the New England states increased in 1814 as the British blockade strangled New England commercial interests. At the **Hartford Convention** (December 1814) Federalist representatives declared that a state had the right to oppose congressional action believed to violate the Constitution, thus supporting the doctrine of **states' rights**.

- *War of 1812.* Unable to resist the pressure by the War Hawks in Congress, President Madison recommended that Congress declare war on June 1, 1812. A close vote representing sectional divisions of the country resulted in the declaration of war on June 18, 1812.

- *Treaty of Ghent (December 1814).* For the most part, the peace settlement simply restored the prewar status. Provisions of the treaty included an end to hostilities and British influence in the Northwest Territory, restoration of conquered territory, and arbitration of boundary disputes. Perhaps the longest lasting result of the War of 1812 was the rise of American **nationalism** and the new impulse to expand the nation.

The Administrations of James Monroe (1817–1825)

James Monroe, Madison's Secretary of State, defeated the last Federalist candidate, **Rufus King**, to become the fifth President. Much of Monroe's success in foreign affairs can be credited to his Secretary of State, **John Quincy Adams**.

James Monroe (1758–1831), 5th President of the United States. The Monroe Doctrine discouraged European involvement in the Western Hemisphere.

• *Monroe Doctrine (1823).* As the stability of the Western Hemisphere was threatened by European events, the United States could ally with Great Britain in defending its close-to-home interests, or act independently. Russia was threatening to expand and was establishing trading posts on the West Coast. Moreover, the European alliance of France, Russia, Prussia, and Austria was considering an attempt to reclaim as colonies the Latin American states that had recently gained their independence in their war with Spain. With strong advice from Secretary of State Adams, President Monroe addressed Congress on December 2, 1823, with a statement of foreign policy that came to be known as the **Monroe Doctrine**. It declared: (1) the American continent was no longer open to colonization by European nations; (2) the United States would not interfere in European affairs; and (3) an act of intervention by a Euro-

John Quincy Adams (1767–1848), 6th President of the United States. As Secretary of State to President Monroe, Adams was the real author of the Monroe Doctrine.

pean power in the affairs of a country in the Western Hemisphere would be considered an act against the United States.

Manifest Destiny (1789–1853)

Although the term "manifest destiny" originated with newspaper editor **John L. Sullivan**'s comment on the **annexation** of Texas, the "fulfillment to overspread the continent" started long before. As nationalism grew, Americans came to believe that westward expansion would spread American freedom and democracy across the continent.

The acquisition of large tracts of territory during the 19th century increased sectional conflict, primarily over the extension of slavery. As the nation expanded rapidly from coast to coast, the American population with its varying social, political, and especially economic interests was able to find harmony only through compromise. However, in time, sectional differences made compromise impossible, and the final result was the Civil War.

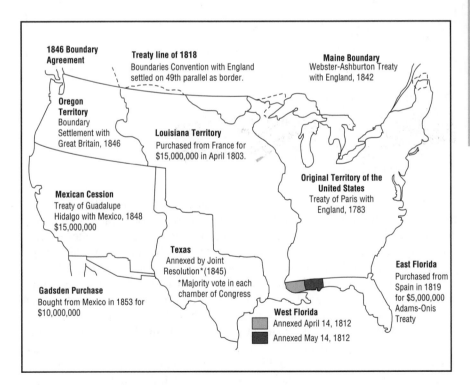

Figure 1.20 Territorial Growth of the United States, 1783–1853

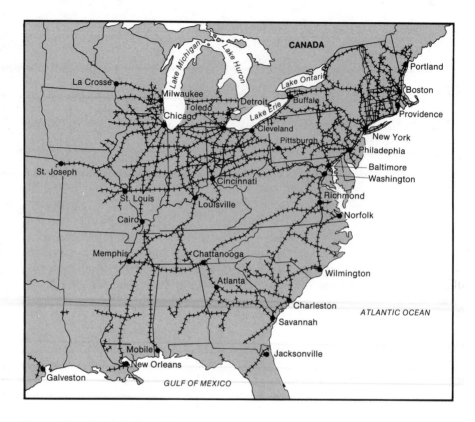

Figure 1.21 Major Railroads in 1860

Sectional Specialization and Improvements in Transportation

As the nation's economy developed, differences between the sections grew. In the North, industry advanced, helped by the decreased trade before and during the War of 1812, and because of the supply of adequate water power, a wealthy class with commercial capital to invest, and a plentiful labor supply. The South had an agricultural economy based on slave labor. After the invention of the **cotton gin** in 1793, the South had a one-crop economy based upon the cultivation of cotton. At the same time, the grains of the West were quickly transforming that area into the "breadbasket" of the nation.

The need to transport raw materials and manufactured goods between the sections and to ship products to their market created a demand for a better transportation system. Between 1800 and 1825 hundreds of turnpikes (privately built toll roads) and roads financed by the federal government were built to help transport people and products. In 1808, Secretary of the Treasury

Albert Gallatin proposed a system of internal improvements at federal expense, an issue that would eventually raise debate between states' righters and nationalists.

The years from 1820 to 1850 were the age of the steamboat and canal building to connect interior waterways, which resulted in over 3,300 miles of canals by 1840. In 1828 the first major railroad, the Baltimore and Ohio, was chartered, and by 1840 the nation's total railway mileage equaled that of its canals. At the beginning of the Civil War, railroads overshadowed all other forms of long-distance transportation in the country. Figure 1.22, showing the routes of the major railroads in 1860, helps to demonstrate the economic interdependency between the North and the West, a factor of great importance during the Civil War.

The growth of transportation brought with it legal questions. One of the earliest questions was who would regulate interstate commerce. The Supreme Court addressed this issue in the case of *Gibbons* v. *Ogden* (1824), when the Court held that, although Congress did not have the power to control trade within one state, its authority did extend to trade from one state to another and to the navigable rivers on which interstate or foreign commerce could be carried.

Excercise Set 1.4

1. The argument over the creation of the Bank of the United States concerned
   A. its effect on the funds kept in the state banks
   B. whether or not the country needed a central banking institution
   C. whether or not the Constitution provided for congressional authority to create a bank
   D. the creation of the Treasury Department by Congress

2. The Supreme Court under Chief Justice John Marshall influenced United States history in that the Court
   A. stimulated the states' rights movement by supporting the idea that states could reject acts of Congress
   B. helped to create a sense of national unity by strengthening the federal government
   C. weakened the judiciary by refusing to deal with controversial issues
   D. became heavily involved in foreign affairs

3. Which of the following practices has changed from custom and tradition to become part of the written Constitution?
   A. the pledging of electoral votes
   B. the existence of political parties
   C. limiting the number of terms for the presidency
   D. the committee system of Congress

Base your answers to questions 4 and 5 on the following quotation and your knowledge of social studies.

> "Now it appears . . . that this general principle is inherent in the very definition of government, and essential to every step of the progress to be made by that United States, namely: that every power vested in a government is in its nature sovereign, and includes, by force of the term, a right to employ all the means requisite and fairly applicable to the attainment of the ends of such power and which are not precluded by restrictions . . . in the Constitution, or not immoral, or not contrary to the essential ends of political society."

4. The quotation expresses the position on the Constitution advocated by
   A. a strict constructionist
   B. one in agreement with Thomas Jefferson
   C. a loose, or broad, constructionist
   D. a states' righter

5. The preceding quotation is most likely from
   A. Washington's Farewell Address
   B. Jefferson's opinions on the constitutionality of the National Bank
   C. Article III of the United States Constitution
   D. Hamilton's opinions on the constitutionality of the National Bank

6. All of the following are characteristic of the Embargo Act of 1807 EXCEPT
   A. it was initially destructive to the American economy
   B. it was generally recognized as a failure
   C. it was America's last attempt at economic pressure on warring European nations
   D. it was beneficial to American industry in the long run

7. The vote in favor of war in 1812 in the House of Representatives indicated that
   A. almost all Americans wanted war
   B. the country was divided over going to war with England
   C. when it came to an issue as serious as the consideration of war, Representatives put aside sectional differences
   D. most Americans desired war with France as opposed to England

8. The original Monroe Doctrine was part of
   A. a joint resolution of Congress
   B. a message to Congress
   C. a Supreme Court ruling
   D. an agreement between the United States and Latin America

9. The significance of the Supreme Court's decision in *Gibbons* v. *Ogden* (1803) was that it affirmed that
   A. intrastate trade fell within the jurisdiction of Congress
   B. tariffs on imported goods were prohibited by the Constitution
   C. the Bank of the United States was found to be permissible by the "necessary and proper" clause of the Constitution
   D. trade involving two or more states on the nation's internal waterways fell under the commerce clause of the Constitution and therefore was subject to congressional control

CHAPTER REVIEW QUESTIONS

1. Which of the reasons listed below was the most important for social and political mobility in the English colonies of North America during the 17th and 18th centuries?
   A. early emphasis on rapid industrialization
   B. existence of a strong cultural heritage
   C. absence of racial prejudice among the colonists
   D. availability of land

2. The best evidence that a nation is a democracy is its provisions for
   A. a system of civil and criminal courts
   B. a limited government responsible to the people
   C. the holding of periodic elections
   D. a two-house legislature

3. Which feature of the current day U.S. government is based upon the principles found in the Magna Carta (1215) and the English Bill of Rights (1689)?
   A. universal suffrage
   B. power of Congress to declare war
   C. power of the House of Representatives to originate all revenue bills
   D. presidential veto power

4. The Mayflower Compact was
   A. an early example of intercolonial unity
   B. a landmark in religious toleration
   C. an agreement to submit to the will of the majority
   D. an example of a successful proprietorship

5. The Dominion of New England was designed to
   A. promote self-government among the New England colonists
   B. enforce the Navigation Acts
   C. encourage fur trading with the French
   D. assist in the development of a Puritan confederation

6. Most English subjects came to America in the colonial period to
   A. enjoy religious freedom
   B. escape political oppression
   C. find economic opportunity
   D. join the forces of slave labor

7. "Direct democracy" is best illustrated by the
   A. New England town meeting
   B. British Parliament
   C. United States Congress
   D. Virginia House of Burgesses

8. The most troubling aspect of the Proclamation of 1763 for the colonists was that it
   A. increased the jurisdiction of the admiralty courts
   B. mandated the quartering of troops in the colonies
   C. discouraged settlement on western lands
   D. was another example of a revenue-raising tax

9. The American victory at Yorktown in 1781
   A. was assisted by French control of the sea
   B. ended fighting in America
   C. marked the end of the French Alliance
   D. convinced the Second Continental Congress to issue the Declaration of Independence

10. The Articles of Confederation
    A. created a supreme national government with subordinate state governments
    B. instituted a system of checks and balances between the executive, legislative, and judicial branches of government
    C. placed control over foreign and domestic trade at the national level
    D. created a national government that did not have adequate taxation powers

11. The convention in 1787 at Philadelphia was called for the purpose of
    A. completing the provisions of the Treaty of Paris (1783)
    B. drafting the Bill of Rights
    C. revising the Articles of Confederation
    D. writing a new Constitution

12. Under the original Constitution, the only government officials elected directly by qualified voters were
    A. Supreme Court Justices
    B. Representatives
    C. Senators
    D. the President and Vice-President

13. The provision that all powers not delegated to the national government are reserved to the states is included within
    A. Article I
    B. the Bill of Rights
    C. Article III
    D. the Preamble

14. In conflicts between the national Constitution and state constitutions, the national Constitution
    A. is silent
    B. states that it is the supreme law of the land and therefore takes precedence over state constitutions
    C. defers to the state constitutions
    D. is restricted by Amendment 10 of the Bill of Rights

15. Political parties were formed early during the country's history and were one of the earliest examples of
    A. the "necessary and proper" clause
    B. the unwritten constitution
    C. the use of the elastic clause
    D. separation of powers

16. Hamilton's arguments in support of a national bank included *all* the following EXCEPT
    A. the bank was among the listed, or enumerated, powers of Congress
    B. the bank would provide a stable currency for the nation
    C. in the use of the "necessary and proper" clause, the ends justified the means
    D. a national bank would benefit the commercial interests of the nation

17. Washington's Farewell Address
    A. favored political parties
    B. condemned all alliances
    C. advocated temporary, nonentangling alliances
    D. promoted economic and military alliance with all major European nations

18. In general, support for war against England in 1812 came from
    A. commercial interests in the East
    B. agrarian interests in the West and the South
    C. the Federalist party
    D. coastal shippers

19. The basis for federal control over interstate commerce was affirmed by the Supreme Court in
    A. *Marbury* v. *Madison*
    B. *Fletcher* v. *Peck*
    C. *Brown* v. *Board of Education*
    D. *Gibbons* v. *Ogden*

20. The Monroe Doctrine was
    A. basically a self-defense measure
    B. an example of an executive check on Congress
    C. soon abandoned for active United States involvement in European affairs
    D. inspired primarily for the defense of European colonies in the Western Hemisphere

ESSAYS

1. The U.S. Constitution has endured for 200 years in part because of its ability to adapt to changing times.
    a. One way in which the Constitution can be changed is through the use of the formal amending process. Following is an excerpt from the Constitution as originally written:

       Article I, Section 3: The Senate of the United States shall be composed of two Senators from each State, chosen by the Legislature thereof, for six Years; and each Senator shall have one vote.

    Discuss how this provision has been changed by amendment. Your discussion must include a clear description of the change and the reasons for the change. [5]

b. The Constitution has also been adapted to meet changing conditions through the use of the following methods:
- Judicial Review
- Custom and Usage
- Loose Interpretation

Choose *two* of these methods. Discuss one way each method has been used to adapt the United States Constitution to meet changing conditions. In your response, describe the specific condition that required constitutional change and describe the specific change that resulted. [5,5]

Regents Exam, June 1988

2. a. The political development of the American colonies demonstrated the ability to adapt English political heritage to their new settlements. Show in *one* way how colonial governments were influenced by English political practices in each of the following areas: [5]
- Structure of government
- Civil liberties
- Citizen participation

b. The United States broke its colonial ties with Great Britain and became a sovereign state after winning the American Revolution and subsequently establishing a constitutional government in the United States. Discuss *two* ways in which the Constitution changed the structure of power of government from that which existed within the British system. [5,5]

3. The concept of democracy has evolved over a long period of time. Throughout history, different societies have contributed to the development of democracy. Some of these societies are:
- Ancient Athens—5th century B.C.
- Roman Republic—509 B.C. to 31 B.C.
- Great Britain—1200 to 1920
- France—1780 to 1820
- United States—1770 to 1800

a. Choose *three* of the preceding societies. For each one chosen, show how a development in that society during the time period indicated contributed to the growth of the concept of democracy. [4,4,4]

b. Show how *one* of the democratic developments discussed in the answer to part a. is practiced in a society today. [3]

Regents Exam, June 1985

4. Since the U.S. Constitution was written, many generalizations have been made about it. Some of these generalizations are:
- The Constitution is a "bundle of compromises"
- The strength of the Constitution rests on its flexibility

- The Constitution is what the Supreme Court says it is
- The Constitution is basically an economic document
- The Constitution has both divided and limited the powers of government

Choose *three* of the preceding generalizations. For each one chosen, discuss the extent to which the generalization is accurate and use *two* specific examples to support your position. [5,5,5]

Regents Exam, June 1984

5. a. It has been said that the principles of the Declaration of Independence are part of America's debt to European thought. Select *two* principles of the Declaration of Independence, and for each *one* selected, describe how its origin would support the debt to European thought. [5,5]

   b. Select one principle of the Declaration of Independence and describe how that principle challenged previously held political views. [5]

6. Some historians have said that the Monroe Doctrine was America's first statement of foreign policy.

   a. State two provisions of the Monroe Doctrine and explain the reason for President Monroe's inclusion of the provision. [5,5]

   b. Describe how the Monroe Doctrine was designed to protect and preserve the national interest of the United States. [5]

Chapter 2

THE CONSTITUTION TESTED

CONSTITUTIONAL STRESS AND CRISIS

> When my eyes shall be turned to behold for the last time the sun in heaven, may I not see him shining on the broken and dishonored fragments of a once glorious Union . . .
>
> Daniel Webster, Speech on Foote's Resolution
> (January 26, 1830)

> I have heard something said about allegiance to the South. I know no South, no North, no East, no West, to which I owe my allegiance. The Union, sir, is my country.
>
> Henry Clay (1848)

Growth of Nationalism

With the end of the War of 1812, the United States experienced a period of nationalism, when westward expansion and internal improvements demanded much of the nation's attention.

Judicial Nationalism

The Supreme Court under Chief Justice John Marshall handed down a number of decisions that increased the power of the national government at the expense of the states, including the doctrine of judicial review.

Economic Nationalism

• *Rechartering of the National Bank (1816).* Under the direction of **John C. Calhoun** of South Carolina, the Second Bank of the United States was established with a twenty-year charter.

• *Tariff of 1816.* Supported by **Henry Clay** of Kentucky and John

Henry Clay (American statesman and orator, 1777–1852). Clay was a lifelong advocate of economic nationalism.

Calhoun, a 25 percent tariff was placed on imported goods as a protective measure.

* *Bonus Bill of 1816.* An attempt by Clay and Calhoun to have internal improvements (roads, canals) financed by the national government was vetoed by President Madison on constitutional grounds. Madison's claim that internal improvements for local benefit were in the province of states' rights was continued by his successor, James Monroe.

Era of Good Feelings

This term, dubbed by a Boston newspaper to describe the period's absence of political strife, was somewhat deceiving. The election of 1816 gave a victory to the Republicans, with Madison winning the electoral vote 183 to 34, painting a picture of national unity, and the Federalists disappeared as a political party. Yet, by 1819, postwar nationalism and economic stability were eroding, and sectionalism was beginning to become increasingly apparent.

Sectionalism

This term was used to describe the varying interests of the "sections" of the country, which were geographically different and had different economic enterprises suited to their environment. By 1824 three sections were emerging, each with its own concerns and therefore demands on the national government: the industrial Northeast, the cotton-producing South, and the agricultural West. Figure 1.23 lists some of the major issues facing the nation in 1828 and how each section stood on the issue

Federal-State Relations (1798–1835)

Central to many of the standoffs between the federal government and groups of states' righters was the **nullification doctrine**, which claimed that when the national government assumed rights or powers that had not been delegated to it, the states could nullify the act.

Virginia and Kentucky Resolutions (1798)

In response to the **Alien and Sedition Acts of 1798** (acts passed by Federalists that changed naturalization laws and suppressed criticism of the government to weaken political influence of the Republicans), the Republican-controlled legislatures of Virginia and Kentucky passed resolutions endorsing the doctrine that the Constitution was a compact between states and that the states could legitimately object when Congress exceeded the authority delegated to it by the states. This came to be known as the **doctrine of interposition**. The Kentucky Resolution, authored by Thomas Jefferson, went further and claimed that the states could refuse to obey the law, thereby **nullifying** legislation of Congress. The election of the Republicans in 1800 and the repeal of the acts postponed the question of nullification.

The Hartford Convention (1814)

The Embargo Act (1807) had been passed by Congress and was being vigorously enforced by President Jefferson, an enforcement that probably exceeded his powers. Resistance from the economically injured New England states climaxed in December 1814 when Federalists met and declared that a state had the right to oppose congressional action that it believed violated the Constitution. Thus, the doctrine of states' rights and interposition was being used by the Federalists as it had been used against them by the Republicans in 1798.

Issue	Northeast	South	West
Sale of inexpensive federal land (mostly in the West)	Opposed (early)	Favored	Favored
Internal improvement at federal expense	Favored	Opposed	Favored
Protective tariff	Favored	Opposed	Favored
Territorial expansion (new states)	Opposed (early)	Favored	Favored
Second Bank of the United States	Favored	Opposed	Opposed
Extension of slavery into the territories	Opposed	Favored	Opposed
Attitude toward European immigration	Favored	Opposed	Favored
Attitude toward use of implied powers (elastic clause)	Favored	Opposed	Favored

Figure 1.22 Sectionalism (1828)

Webster-Hayne Debate (1830)

The debate in Congress over the limitation of land sales inspired sharp debate. **Senator Robert Y. Hayne** of South Carolina defended the right of a state to nullify a federal law that "violated the sovereignty and independence of the states." In response to Hayne, Daniel Webster contended that it was the people, and not the states, who created the Constitution and that if the states could defy the laws of Congress at will, the Union would be a mere

Daniel Webster (American statesman, lawyer & orator, 1782–1852). Webster believed that the Union took precedence over the states.

"**rope of sand**." President Jackson, despite his sympathies to states' rights, was against nullification.

The Tariff Controversy (1832)

In 1828 Congress passed the so-called **Tariff of Abominations**, imposing high import duties that were opposed by the South. Although the Tariff of 1832 lowered some duties, South Carolina talked of nullification. Calhoun's **Exposition and Protest (1828)** claimed that state conventions had the power to declare laws passed by Congress unconstitutional and to nullify such laws. Calhoun went so far as to suggest **secession** as a last resort. South Carolina nullified the tariff in December 1832. The **Compromise Tariff of 1833**, sponsored by Henry Clay, caused South Carolina to withdraw its nullification and prevented a Jackson-Calhoun showdown on the constitutionality of the nullification doctrine. Although the doctrine of nullification is in direct conflict with the Supremacy Clause of the Constitution (Article VI, Section 2), even in recent times it has been threatened in heated debate. After the *Brown* v. *Board of Education* (1954) decision, Southern politicians threatened nullification of the Supreme Court's decree to end segregation "with all deliberate speed."

The Bank War (1832)

When a bill to recharter the Bank of the United States passed in 1832, Jackson vetoed the measure with an interesting constitutional argument. In addition to his dislike for the political power of the bank, Jackson claimed that, although the Supreme Court had affirmed the bank's constitutionality in *McCullough* v. *Maryland* (1819), the separate branches of the federal government were not bound by the judiciary's readings of the Constitution. The bank's charter was allowed to expire, federal deposits were placed in state banks, and control of the nation's banking system returned to the states.

Secessionists

Although actual secession did not take place until shortly after the election of Abraham Lincoln to the presidency in 1860, the theory had been discussed for some time. Those who supported the right of secession claimed that the Union was a league from which member states could withdraw.

The Age of Jackson

A Democratic party emblem from the 1840s.

Historians have long regarded the period that came to be known as that of **"Jacksonian Democracy"** as something unique, and have debated its significance in American history. The arguments range from those that suggest that Andrew Jackson was simply a product of the "Age of the Common Man" to those who consider the administrations of Jackson to be primarily responsible for a new wave of democracy in the American republic.

Extension of the Franchise

Popular participation in politics continued to increase during the first decades of the 19th century, and the right to vote was eventually extended to all white males over 21. Most of the new Western states ended property qualifications for voting, and the older states, concerned about loss of population to the West, followed their example. Whereas less than 4 percent of the population actually voted in 1824, over 14 percent voted by 1840, indicating extension of suffrage rights and participation in politics.

Modern Party Politics

From 1800 through 1820 the congressional caucus was the method used to select presidential nominees. However, democratic reforms during the early 1800s led to greater participation by the electorate. By 1824, 18 out of 24 states chose presidential electors by popular vote. The introduction of the convention system of nominating candidates for the presidency by the **Anti-Masonic Party** in 1831 offered a more democratic system that was quickly adopted by the Democrats and the National Republicans. Jackson and his running mate, **Martin Van Buren**, were nominated at the Democratic convention in 1832 and Jackson was reelected easily.

As the methods for selecting the candidates fell increasingly into the hands of the "common man," parties began building organizations at the local level and platforms at the national level became less clear-cut in order to appeal to larger groups of voters.

Reform Movements of the 1830s and 1840s

The reform movements of the 1830s–1840s centered around religion, temperance, health, antislavery, women's rights, education, and abolition.

- *Religion.* The **Second Great Awakening**, starting in the late 1790s and continuing through the 1840s, was a prime motivator of reform. Rapid changes, including industrialization, the growth of urban areas, and expansion, helped spark this religious movement to restore traditional community and family values.

- *Temperance.* Because the excessive consumption of alcohol was widespread among all classes of Americans, movements in the 1820s began demanding abstinence from liquor. The formation of the **United States Temperance Union** in 1833 led to demands for the legal prohibition of alcoholic beverages, and a dozen states passed such laws prior to the Civil War.

- *Health.* The movement to build asylums for the insane rather than housing them in prisons was spurred by the efforts of **Dorothea Dix**. Because of her work, prison reforms were also implemented in some states.

Elizabeth Cady Stanton (1815–1902), helped organize the first Women's Rights Convention.

- *Women's Rights.* Among the reform movements of the 1830s was the women's rights movement that sought to overcome the inferior status of women. Chief among the issues were women's lack of rights concerning property, voting, and education. In 1848, **Lucretia Mott** and **Elizabeth Cady Stanton** organized the **Women's Rights Convention** at Seneca Falls, New York. Minimal gains were made, and by the 1850s, women were focusing more and more on the issue of suffrage.

- *Education.* The demand for free public education grew out of the concern that only intelligent voters could support and perpetuate democracy; therefore, the state had the responsibility of financing education. The principal reformer in education was **Horace Mann** of Massachusetts. As Secretary of the State Board of Education, he helped establish public backing for tax-supported schools, lengthened the school year, increased the number of secondary schools, formalized the training of teachers, and broadened educational subjects beyond religious studies.

- *Abolition.* The Quakers led the earliest **antislavery** movement in the mid-1700s, preaching that it was a sin for Christians to keep people in bondage. By 1800 most states in the North had abandoned slavery. Many leading Southerners at this time disap proved of slavery and felt that it would soon end. However, as the South became increasingly dependent on cotton production after the invention of the cotton gin in 1793, slavery was viewed as an absolute necessity.

Frederick Douglass American abolitionist, (1817–1895) escaped from slavery to become a newspaper publisher and political organizer.

The abolitionist movement of the 1830s differed from earlier movements against slavery by emphasizing that slavery was morally wrong and that blacks were not inferior. This came into direct conflict with the beliefs of **"white supremacy"** in the South. By 1830 at least 50 antislavery societies had been formed and were reminding the nation that the ideals of the Declaration of Independence remained unrealized as long as slavery existed. Among the notable abolitionist leaders were **Frederick Douglass**, **Sojourner Truth**, **William Lloyd Garrison**, and **Harriet Tubman**. Garrison, founder of the abolitionist newspaper, *The Liberator* (1831), demanded immediate and complete **emancipation**, as opposed to the gradual emancipation supported by more moderate abolitionists. Tubman's efforts to assist the escape of Southern slaves to Canada by means of the **"underground railroad"** continued up to the eve of the Civil War.

The **slave rebellion** led by **Nat Turner** in Virginia in 1831, which resulted in the deaths of sixty whites, and the flow of radical Northern abolitionist literature into the South, turned Southerners from apologists for slavery into aggressive defenders of the institution. Attempts to halt the antislavery movement through restrictions on the freedom of the press and the right to petition involved important constitutional issues. In Southern states, abolitionist literature was suppressed by state officials, and in 1836 Congress adopted the **"gag rule,"** which automatically tabled abolitionist petitions, thus preventing debate on them.

As the Civil War approached, **free labor** and **slave labor** were pitted against each other. The North saw free labor as the key to a successful economy and realized that the free labor economic system had to be extended to the territories of the West if future generations were to prosper. Southerners, having built their fortunes and society on the institution of slavery, found it difficult to accept the moral arguments of abolitionists and felt that slavery was necessary to their way of life. They justified the institution of slavery as ordained by God (sanctioned in the Scriptures). Eessential to Southern economy, Southerners claimed slavery to be preferable to the "wage-slavery" of the North, and beneficial to blacks.

The Indian Removal Act

The reforms of the Jackson Age did not extend to **Native Americans**. The attempts of Native Americans to remain on their ancestral lands came into conflict with the government's aim to remove them from settled areas in the East and to resettle them in the West. This aim was facilitated by passage of the **Indian Removal Act of 1830**. When the Cherokees were ordered to leave their lands in Georgia, they refused and took the issue to the Supreme Court. In *Cherokee Nation* v. *Georgia* (1831), the Supreme Court ruled that the Cherokees could stay until they voluntarily ceded their lands to the United States. The Court went further in *Worcester* v. *Georgia* (1832) to state that the Cherokee Nation was a distinct political community in which the laws of Georgia had no force. President Jackson, having little sympathy for the Native Americans, refused to enforce the Court's decision.

The rulings of the Supreme Court had little effect on the destiny of the Indian tribes, and many groups, including the Seminole, Choctaw, Creek, Chickasaw, and Cherokee, were moved West. The so-called "**Trail of Tears**," in which thousands of Cherokees died on the forced journey westward, was repeated many times between 1831 and 1840. By 1840, the forced removal of 60,000 Native Americans had been carried out.

Constitutional Debates (1800–1860)

Although most constitutional debate during the first half of the 19th century involved the extension of slavery, the constant battle of state versus federal authority was involved in most issues. It was inevitable that the Supremacy Clause (Article VI) of the Constitution was going to come into conflict with the reserved powers provided for by the Tenth Amendment.

States' Rights v. Federal Supremacy

The early tests of state versus federal authority involved the battles over the **Sedition Act of 1800**, passed by the Federalists to suppress hostile criticism, the **Virginia and Kentucky Resolutions**, and the **Hartford Convention**.

The decisions of the Marshall Court enforced the sovereignty of the federal government and its right to exercise its constitutional powers. The **Louisiana Purchase**, which went against Jefferson's belief in strict construction of the Constitution, required that Congress use its implied powers to purchase the territory. It also demonstrated the need to shift constitutional positions when circumstances such as Napoleon's demands for quick action demanded such flexibility. This "flexibility" in constitutional positions has been used throughout our political history and has become part of our constitutional system.

Slavery and Struggle

The rising dispute over slavery coincided with the territorial expansion of the United States. Although the issue of extending slavery to the territories was solved by the **Missouri Compromise** in 1820, it was only a temporary solution. The controversy arose again after the acquisition of the **Mexican Cession (1848)** and the rapid growth of California's population. At the center of the slavery controversy was the delicate balance in the Senate, where the South was concerned about losing its equal footing with the North. (The larger population of the North had already given them control of the House of Representatives.)

After the Mexican War (1846–1848), Americans held four different views concerning slavery and the new territories: (1) barring slavery forever from the new territories; (2) extending the Missouri Compromise line to the Pacific Coast; (3) no federal interference with the extension of slavery; (4) popular sovereignty (allowing the people of the territory to decide whether or not to permit slavery).

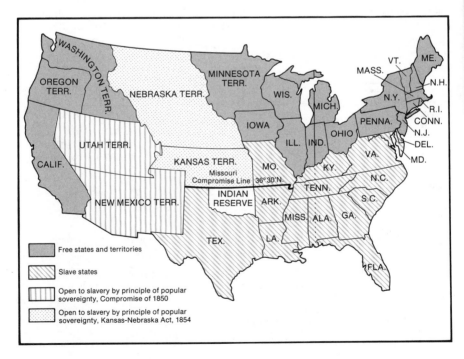

Figure 1.23   Status of Slavery (1854)

California's application to enter the Union as a free state brought up the slavery problem and marked the last of the great debates among **Daniel Webster**, **Henry Clay**, and **John Calhoun**. The result was the **Compromise of 1850**, which temporarily solved the problem and postponed the Civil War for ten years. The **Kansas-Nebraska Act** (1854), which divided the remainder of the Louisiana Territory into the territories of Kansas and Nebraska and provided for the admission of the territories as states according to the principle of popular sovereignty, resulted in the repeal of the Missouri Compromise. It also led antislavery elements among the Democrats and the Whigs to join with the antislavery third party Free Soilers to form the **Republican party** in 1854.

Dred Scott Decision (1857)

The Supreme Court decided that the Missouri Compromise was unconstitutional by virtue of the fact that a slave was property and that a slave owner who was protected by the Constitution could bring his or her property into a territory of the United States. It set the stage, in the Illinois senatorial campaign of 1858, for the **Lincoln-Douglas debates**, over the question of popular sovereignty. Although Stephen Douglas offered the **Freeport Doctrine**, stating that the legislature of a territory could still refuse to pass laws supporting slavery, the stand weakened Douglas in the South and cost him the presidential nomination from a united Democratic Party in 1860. Instead, it split the Democrats over the slavery issue and allowed the Republicans to elect Lincoln in 1860.

Event	Issue	Solution
Sedition Act of 1800	Freedom of speech and press	Virginia and Kentucky Resolutions suggesting interposition and nullification; election of 1800 and expiration of act.
Supreme Court decisions of the Marshall Court (1801–1835)	Federal-State relations	Expansion of federal powerand jurisdiction.
Louisiana Purchase (1803)	Power of Congress to purchase territory	Jefferson reads Constitution with "loose construction."
Embargo Act (1807)	Does commerce clause imply power to restrict commerce?	Yes; power to regulate includes power to control.
Hartford Convention (1814)	States' rights v. federal supremacy	Matter died down with end of War of 1812.

Figure 1.24 Constitutional Debates (1800–1860)

Event	Issue	Solution
Slavery	Constitutional or unconstitutional?	*Northern Argument:* Though not claiming that slavery was unconstitutional, provisions had been made in the Constitution for its gradual demise.
		Southern Argument: Slavery was recognized within the Constitution concerning representation (Article I, Section 2), and Fugitive Slave Law (Article IV, Section 2), and therefore legal.
Missouri Compromise (1820)	Power of Congress to prohibit slavery in territories and admit states with conditions	Congress could legislate against slavery in territories but not within states.
		Compromise: 1. Missouri admitted as a slave state. 2. Maine admitted as a free state. 3. No slavery in Louisiana Territory north of 36°30' line.
Wilmot Proviso (1846)	Could Congress ban slavery in territory acquired from Mexico?	*Northern Argument:* Congress could legally bar slavery acquired by virtue of Article IV, Section 3: "make all needful rules and regulations respecting the territory of the United States."
		Southern Argument: People had the right to take their property (slaves) into the territories.
		Debate over the Wilmot Proviso necessitated the Compromise of 1850.
Compromise of 1850	Extension of slavery into California, New Mexico Territory, and Utah Territory	*Compromise:* 1. California admitted as a free state. 2. Utah and New Mexico Territories admitted under popular sovereignty provision. 3. Slave trade in District of Columbia abolished. 4. Stricter Fugitive Slave Law enacted.

Figure 1.24 continued Constitutional Debates (1800–1860)

Event	Issue	Solution
Kansas-Nebraska Act (1854)	Status of slavery in remainder of Louisiana Territory	Kansas-Nebraska Act: Popular sovereignty in both territories.
Dred Scott Decision (1857)	Could a slave sue in federal court?	1. Slaves were not citizens and, therefore, could not sue in federal court.
	If a slave resided in free territory, did that end his or her status as a slave?	2. Congress could not prevent citizens from transporting their property (slaves) into a territory (Fifth Amendment protection of property). The Dred Scott decision declared the Missouri Compromise unconstitutional and the territories open to slavery.
Secession	Constitutional instrument?	*Argument of Calhoun and other secessionist theorists:* Yes. Union is a mere league from which states may withdraw at their pleasure. Constitution is a compact between states and a self-evident right.
		Argument of Lincoln and other antisecessionist theorists: No. Constitution is a compact between the people of the United States, not the states. Constitution is silent on the issue of secession and, finally, the very doing away with the confederation style of government is an argument against the league theory.

Figure 1.24 continued   Constitutional Debates (1800–1860)

Excercise Set 1.5

1. In the *Dred Scott* v. *Sandford* (1857) decision, the Supreme Court held that
   A. slavery could not be prohibited by any state
   B. the Fugitive Slave Law was unconstitutional
   C. Congress could not prohibit slavery in the territories
   D. the Missouri Compromise was valid

2. Chief Justice John Marshall is remembered most accurately for
   A. being a strict constructionist
   B. emphasizing states' rights in his decisions
   C. increasing the power and role of the Supreme Court
   D. frequently deferring to the opinions of state courts

3. The election of Andrew Jackson in 1828 indicated that
   A. political power was shifting to the Western states
   B. the Federalists were making a comeback
   C. Henry Clay was an incompetent opponent
   D. the Bank of the United States was a popular issue

4. All of the following were arguments of Southerners in their defense of slavery EXCEPT
   A. slavery had constitutional support
   B. the Bible justified slavery
   C. blacks were inherently inferior to whites
   D. most European nations still used slave labor

5. The most critical question facing the nation in the 1850s was
   A. what the status of states would be after secession
   B. the political balance between the North and South in the House of Representatives
   C. the extension of slavery into the territories
   D. the significance of a multi-party system in American politics

6. The history of the tariff between 1800 and 1860 shows that
   A. economic issues had little influence over political positions
   B. the North supported low protective tariffs
   C. the tariff issue contributed to the conflict between the North and South over states' rights
   D. higher tariff legislation received uniform support from all sections of the nation

7. The passage of the Wilmot Proviso would have resulted in
   A. the extension of the 36°30' line of the Missouri Compromise to the Pacific Ocean
   B. popular sovereignty as a means of deciding on slavery in the territory acquired from Mexico
   C. Southern domination of the Senate
   D. the banning of slavery in any territory received from Mexico

THE CONSTITUTION IN JEOPARDY: THE AMERICAN CIVIL WAR

> My paramount object in this struggle is to save the Union, and is not either to save or to destroy slavery. If I could save the Union without freeing any slave, I would do it; and if I could save it by freeing all the slaves, I would do it; and if I could do it by freeing some and leaving others alone, I would also do that.
>
> Abraham Lincoln, letter to Horace Greeley
> (August 22, 1862)

At the outset, the purpose of the Civil War from the northern point of view was to restore the Union and preserve the Constitution. Lincoln's goal of preserving the Union, even at the cost of tolerating slavery (as expressed in the preceding quote), was paramount. But as Congress became more determined to make emancipation a primary issue of the war, Lincoln drafted his own emancipation proclamation (July, 1862) and the South realized that what was at stake was their entire way of life.

Abraham Lincoln opposed slavery, but his first concern was to save the Union.

Just before the outbreak of the Civil War, two issues faced the nation. Slavery in the territories was the first issue. Although the Dred Scott decision had supposedly decided the matter, a new President had been elected (the "Party of the North") and the Supreme Court was in the process of turnover with **Chief Justice Taney**, the author of the Dred Scott decision, old and ill. Southerners believed that Lincoln's election spelled doom for the property protection reasoning of *Dred Scott* v. *Sandford* (1857).

The second issue was that of secession. As Calhoun had proposed during the 1820s–1830s, supporters of the right of secession held that the United States was merely a league of states, from which member states might withdraw at their pleasure. Secessionists supported the belief that the Constitution was a compact between the states, not between the people of the United States. President Lincoln, among others, argued that secession was not constitutional and that the constitutional system of government was a compact between the people of the United States.

A Nation Divided

Formation of the Confederacy

South Carolina led the way for the formation of the Confederacy when it adopted, through the use of a popularly elected convention, an "**Ordinance**

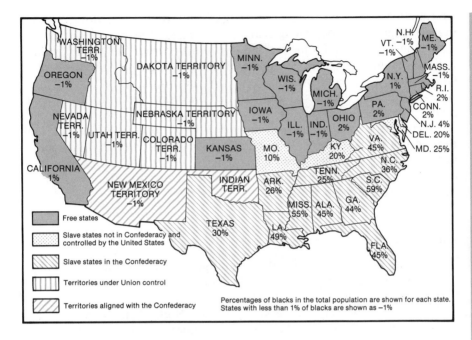

Free states

Slave states not in Confederacy and controlled by the United States

Slave states in the Confederacy

Territories under Union control

Territories aligned with the Confederacy

Percentages of blacks in the total population are shown for each state. States with less than 1% of blacks are shown as −1%

Figure 1.25 A Nation Divided

Jefferson Davis was U.S. Secretary of War before becoming President of the Confederacy.

of Secession" in December 1860. Ten additional states eventually followed South Carolina's example and the **Confederate States of America** was formed in February 1861, with **Jefferson Davis** of Mississippi as President.

In seceding from the Union, the Southern states affirmed the **compact theory** of the Constitution and claimed that it was the Northern states that had broken the compact by obstructing the constitutionally mandated return of fugitive slaves. The preamble of the Confederate Constitution read in part ". . . We, the people of the Confederate States, each State acting in its sovereign and independent character . . ."

Lincoln and Constitutional Issues of the War

The Civil War brought an unprecedented clash between the Executive and the Congress in their war power roles. Although minor differences had occurred during the War of 1812 and the Mexican War, the Civil War was about to spell out a new chapter in constitutional history. A reading of the

Constitution shows potential conflict between Article I, Section 8, which grants Congress the power to declare war, raise and support armies, maintain a navy, and to provide for the regulation of the land and naval forces, including militia, and Article II, Section 2, which provides that the President is Commander-in-Chief of the army and navy and Article II, Section 1, which states that the President is vested with full executive power of the government.

Lincoln believed that the oath he had taken to "**preserve, protect, and defend the Constitution**" obligated him to resort to practically any action necessary to maintain the **Union**. In doing so, he set a precedent for future expansion of the wartime powers of the President, and opportunity for future debate on the coexistence of Article I and Article II war powers.

Emancipation

At the outset of the Civil War, the federal government had been careful to insist that it was fighting to preserve the Union and not to free the slaves. In this way, proslavery forces, primarily in the border states, who were sympathetic to the Union cause were kept with the North. Yet, as the war progressed, Congress moved in the direction of **emancipation**. In the first half of 1862, Congress forbade military officers to return fugitive slaves, prohibited slavery in the territories, and abolished slavery in the District of Columbia. The **Confiscation Act of 1862** provided that slaves who had escaped from those who were still in rebellion would be "forever free of their servitude." On January 1, 1863, President Lincoln issued the **Emancipation Proclamation** declaring that "all slaves in those regions still in rebellion on that date would be free." Not applying to border states or the regions under Union control, but only to those under Confederate control, the Emancipation Proclamation did not immediately free any slaves. The actual end of slavery did not come until the passage of the **Thirteenth Amendment** in 1865.

Constitutional Significance of the Civil War

With the surrender by **Robert E. Lee** at Appomattox Court House on April 1, 1865, the Civil War came to an end. Perhaps the most important constitutional result of the Civil War was the repudiation of state sovereignty and the compact theory of union. The concepts of states' rights of secession and the United States as a "league" of states were ended and the nation emerged as a true sovereign entity. The Constitution had survived the war years. The emancipation of the slaves raised numerous issues to be addressed in the following decades, including the rights of states and the role of the federal government in relation to **civil rights**.

Actions by Lincoln	Constitutional Provisions	Justification
Labeled actions by South as "insurrection"	None	South could not legally secede.
Initiation of war by President	Art. I, Sec. 8: "Congress has power to declare war." "Congress has power to suppress insurrections."	President suppressing an insurrection; *Prize Cases* (1863), Art IV, Sec. 4.
Blockade of South	Art. I, Sec. 8: "Congress has power to declare war."	Approved by Congress (1861).
Increased size of army and navy	Art. I, Sec. 8: "Congress shall raise and support armies."	Approved by Congress (1861).
Appropriated funds from Treasury for war effort	Art. I, Sec. 8: "support armies."	Approved by Congress (1861).
Suspension of writ of habeas corpus; disregard for Supreme Court ruling in *Ex Parte Merryman* (1861)	Art. I, Sec. 9: "The privilege of the Writ of Habeas Corpus shall not be suspended, unless in Cases of Rebellion or Invasion the public Safety may require it."	First, none; Supreme Court rules against Lincoln in *Ex Parte Merryman* (1861); Congress later permits with passage of *Habeas Corpus Act.* (1863).
Use of military courts where civil courts still in operation	Amendments V, VI, and VII	Supreme Court in *Ex Parte Vallandigham* (1864) refused to hear case; claimed no jurisdiction; in *Ex Parte Milligan* (1866), Court held Lincoln's actions to be unconstitutional.
Suspension of freedom of speech and press	First Amendment	Permissible to a point during insurrection to prevent prolonged war and additional loss of life

Figure 1.26 Lincoln v. the Constitution

Exercise Set 1.6

1. The Dred Scott decision held that a slave
   A. could bring suit in a federal court
   B. was no longer a slave when he or she entered free territory
   C. was private property even in free territory
   D. could purchase his or her freedom when in a free territory

2. President Lincoln's interpretation and use of the Constitution was
   A. consistently supported by the Supreme Court
   B. influenced by his war aims
   C. never supported by Congress
   D. was typical of Presidents in wartime up to that point

3. The Emancipation Proclamation
   A. ended slavery in the United States
   B. freed slaves only in those areas where the North was not in control
   C. maintained slavery only in those areas that were still in rebellion
   D. was vetoed by Lincoln after passage in Congress

4. Many of Lincoln's actions during the Civil War would have been sup-
   ported by a
   A. believer in the compact doctrine of the national government
   B. strict constructionist of the Constitution
   C. proponent of the nullification doctrine
   D. loose constructionist of the Constitution

5. The greatest threat to civil liberties during the Civil War was the
   A. suspension of the writ of habeas corpus
   B. blockade of the South
   C. use of Treasury funds by the President without initial congressional
      approval
   D. identification of the South's actions as an "insurrection"

6. The Emancipation Proclamation was
   A. a law passed by Congress
   B. the result of a Supreme Court decision
   C. a use of the elastic clause
   D. a presidential order

7. The slaves were finally freed by the
   A. surrender of the Confederacy
   B. Emancipation Proclamation
   C. Thirteenth Amendment
   D. capture of Richmond

CHAPTER REVIEW QUESTIONS

1. The most serious problem facing the United States in the first half of the 19th century involved
   A. gaining territory for excess population
   B. the powers of the state governments and the national government
   C. gaining recognition as a sovereign nation
   D. unemployment

2. Sedition can best be described as
   A. preventing aliens from becoming citizens
   B. the illegal criticism of the government
   C. ignoring a law of Congress
   D. obstructing the war effort of a country

3. The Constitution, treaties made by the United States, and laws of Congress are to predominate when conflict arises with state or local laws. This concept, provided for in the Constitution, is called the
   A. reserved powers amendment
   B. elastic clause
   C. supremacy clause
   D. preamble

4. An analysis of the history of the presidency during wartime indicates that executive powers
   A. are usually curtailed severely by the judiciary
   B. operate through a strict construction approach to the Constitution
   C. are expanded and sometimes come into conflict with other branches of the federal government
   D. are unchecked

5. The event that caused the first Southern states to secede from the Union was
   A. the Dred Scott decision
   B. the Compromise of 1850
   C. the election of Lincoln as President
   D. the election of Jefferson Davis as President of the Confederacy

6. The West supported all of the following EXCEPT
   A. internal improvements at national expense
   B. sale of inexpensive government lands
   C. the Second Bank of the United States
   D. squatters' rights

7. In which of the following pairs was the second event a result of the first?
   A. the Mexican War—passage of the Missouri Compromise
   B. Indian land claims in Georgia—*Dred Scott* v. *Sandford*
   C. the application of California for statehood—Compromise of 1850
   D. the Thirteenth Amendment—Emancipation Proclamation

8. The doctrine that indicated that a state could object to a law of Congress if it was felt that Congress had abused its delegated authority was
   A. nullification
   B. sectionalism
   C. interposition
   D. secession

9. The basic cause of sectionalism in the United States during the first half of the 19th century was
   A. economic differences
   B. social differences
   C. political differences
   D. religious differences

10. Regarding the Native Americans, President Jackson favored
    A. upholding Cherokee rights
    B. removal to the trans-Mississippi area
    C. supporting the Supreme Court decision in the Georgia cases
    D. allowing Congressional control of the situation

ESSAYS

1. In the period 1815 to 1860, improvements in transportation and increased interregional trade should have united Americans, but instead produced sectional division and finally disunion.
   Discuss this statement with reference to the sectional impact of transportation and trade developments between the years given. [15]

2. The time period of the late 1820s to the 1840s has been described as the era of Jacksonian Democracy, or sometimes as the "Age of the Common Man." Andrew Jackson played an important role in the controversy concerning Indian removal, the Bank War, the Nullification Crisis of 1832, the spoils system, and the creation of the Democratic Party.

   Select *three* of these issues and discuss the following question in relation to the issue. "Was Jackson's role that of a 'man of the people' in the issue, or that of a demagogue?" [5,5,5]

3. Throughout United States history, there have been many instances where political, economic, or social difficulties led to demand for reform. In response to those demands, movements or programs have been developed. Referring to the abolitionist crusade (1820–1860) describe:
   - A specific problem that led to the movement or program. [5]
   - A specific reform advocated by the movement or program to deal with the program. [5]
   - Two individuals who were instrumental in the movement. [5]

   Regents Exam, June 1988

UNIT TWO _____

Industrialization of the United States

> **KEY IDEAS:** Unit Two first examines the restructuring of the Union following the Civil War, with emphasis on emancipation and the strengthening of the federal system of government. Chapters II and III review the growing diversity of the American population, the industrialization of the United States, and the new challenges to American society as a result of growth.

UNIT GOALS: By the end of this unit, the student should be able to demonstrate

1. An understanding of the changing nature of American society from 1865 to 1920.

2. Knowledge that while the Civil War kept the Union intact, it left deep social, political, and economic scars that have taken a long time to heal.

3. An understanding of immigration patterns as they related to the demands of an industrializing society.

4. An understanding of the shift from an agrarian-based society to an industrial society.

5. An understanding of the part that technological developments played in promoting the change to an industrial society.

6. An understanding of the emerging American culture and values in an industrial age.

Chapter 1

THE RECONSTRUCTED NATION

RECONSTRUCTION AND THE NATIONALIZATION OF CIVIL RIGHTS

The defeat of the Confederacy in 1865 settled the issues of disunion and states' rights that had troubled the nation since its beginning. Yet, during the period of Reconstruction, or the restoring of the South to the Union from 1865 to 1877, the nation had to answer two challenging questions: (1) How should the seceding states be dealt with and on what terms should they be readmitted to the Union? (2) What should be done about the newly freed slaves and what should be their political rights?

The political reconstruction of the South (as opposed to the social and physical rebuilding) can be divided into four stages: (1) the plans of President Lincoln; (2) the years 1865 and 1866 when President Andrew Johnson tried to carry out his policy; (3) Congressional Reconstruction between 1866 and 1868; and (4) the period of Southern reaction in the years after 1868.

Three Plans of Reconstruction

Lincoln's Plan

Lincoln's plan, which became the moderate approach to Reconstruction, was based on the belief that the war was a rebellion of individual citizens and that, since secession was not constitutionally permissible, the South had never legally left the Union. This view was endorsed by the Supreme Court in *Texas* v. *White (1869)* when the Court held that "the Constitution, in all its provisions, looks to an indestructible Union, composed of indestructible states." Lincoln also believed that Reconstruction should be lenient and carried out by the President. In his **Proclamation of Amnesty and Reconstruction** in December 1865, Lincoln set out his plan of Reconstruction: (1) all Southerners (except high-ranking Confederate political and military officials) would be pardoned and regain citizenship when they took an oath to support the Constitution and the emancipation of slaves; (2) when 10 percent of the voters in a state took this oath they could establish a legal government that would be recognized by the President.

• *Congressional Reaction.* The **"Radical" Republicans** in Congress did not agree with Lincoln's plan. They looked beyond emancipation to the problem of civil liberties of African Americans and felt that Congress should play a greater role in the assurance of such liberties. In the **Wade-Davis** bill

(July 1864) Congress set its own conditions for readmitting the Southern states. It required that: (1) 50 percent of the voters take the loyalty oath rather than 10 percent; (2) Confederate officials be disenfranchised; (3) Confederate debts be repudiated.

Lincoln killed the Wade-Davis bill with a **pocket veto** because it would have postponed the readmittance of the Southern states. Lincoln and Congress disagreed over Reconstruction, and hopes of compromise and the acceptance of Lincoln's moderate plan ended with his assassination on April 14, 1865.

Johnson's Plan

Southerners claimed that if secession was unconstitutional, then the Southern states were still in the Union and qualified to resume their place in Congress with no conditions attached. Andrew Johnson (who as Vice-President became President after Lincoln's assassination) took a slightly different view. Although he conceded the argument that the Southern states were still in the Union, he claimed that treason had temporarily disqualified them from resuming their place in the federal government. In May 1865 Johnson issued his plan of Reconstruction, which was similar to Lincoln's: (1) general pardon of all Southerners willing to take an oath upholding the Constitution, except military leaders and those whose wealth exceeded $20,000; (2) recognition of the governments of Virginia, Tennessee, Arkansas, and Louisiana, which had been established under Lincoln's Reconstruction Plan; (3) the remaining Southern states could reenter the Union when they repudiated war debts (bonds sold by the Confederate government to individuals to finance the war), disavowed their ordinances of secession, and ratified the Thirteenth Amendment, thereby abolishing slavery.

By December 1865, when Congress met, all the Southern states except Texas were ready to be readmitted to the Union. The **Thirteenth Amendment**, ending slavery, was ratified in December 1865, giving Congress the power to enforce the amendment with appropriate legislation.

Congressional Plan

The Republicans in Congress believed that the seceding states had reverted to territorial status and therefore required congressional legislation for readmission to the Union. They refused to seat in Congress the representatives and senators who had been elected by the new state governments in the Southern states. Under the influence of Radical Republican **Thaddeus Stevens**, Congress passed the following laws:

• *The Freedman's Bureau Act (1866).** This law extended the existence of a wartime bureau that had cared for freed slaves. It helped to provide the freed slaves with food, clothing, and shelter, helped them find jobs, and

*Note: The term *freedmen* was used in this period to refer to the freed slaves.

founded schools. Particularly troubling to Congress were the "**black codes**," laws passed by the Southern legislatures after the abolition of slavery, which were designed to keep freed blacks in a slavelike role. President Johnson vetoed the bill, questioning the constitutionality of its provisions, but it was passed over Johnson's veto in July 1866.

• *The Civil Rights Act of 1866.* This forbade states to discriminate against blacks, guaranteed persons of color equal protection of the laws, and placed jurisdiction of violations of the act in federal courts. President Johnson vetoed the bill, claiming unconstitutional violations of states' rights, but Congress overrode his veto.

• *The Fourteenth Amendment.* This amendment (ratified by Congress and the states) made blacks citizens of the United States. It: provided for national citizenship; forbade states from depriving citizens of equal protection of the law; provided penalties for not granting black Americans the vote; excluded Confederates from holding office unless pardoned by Congress; repudiated the Confederate war debt.

Military Reconstruction

The Congressional elections of 1866 gave the Radical Republicans the support necessary to put their Reconstruction plan into effect. On March 2, 1867, Congress took over Reconstruction with its passage of the **Military Reconstruction Act**, which (1) stated that no lawful governments existed in any of the Southern states except for Tennessee (which had accepted the Fourteenth Amendment); (2) divided the South into five military districts, each under a military governor with federal troops; (3) specified that no state could return to civilian rule and be readmitted to the Union until white and black voters framed a constitution that guaranteed suffrage to African Americans and ratified the Fourteenth Amendment.

Impeachment of Andrew Johnson

The struggle over how to reconstruct the Union provoked a clash between President Johnson and Congress. Johnson, intolerant of opposition and not able to compromise, failed to help his political cause. Although an advocate of the Democratic states' rights tradition, President Johnson was devoted to the Union. He wanted to restore the prewar federal system as quickly as possible with one change—that states no longer had the right to legalize slavery. Most Congressional Republicans, on the other hand, believed that sectional conflict would not be resolved until there were guarantees that the old Southern ruling class would not regain power and national influence. After two presidential vetoes and two congressional overrides, the Republicans in Congress took extreme steps to assure that the Military Reconstruction Act was carried out.

Denial of Supreme Court Authority

An act passed on March 7, 1868, denied the Supreme Court jurisdiction over the Reconstruction acts of Congress.

Denial of Presidential Authority

Beginning in March 1867, Congress adopted a series of acts intended to restrict the President's authority.

• *Tenure of Office Act.* Of greatest significance was the Tenure of Office Act (March 1867), which prohibited the President from removing any federal officials without the consent of the Senate. President Johnson, vetoed the act, asserting that the President possessed a separate right of removal without the Senate's consent, a right that had been recognized since the first Congress.

Impeachment

The Constitution provides in Article II, Section 4 that "The President . . . shall be removed from Office on Impeachment for and Conviction of, Treason, Bribery, or other high Crimes and Misdemeanors." The Radical Republicans in Congress were determined to limit the authority of President Johnson, with the goal that Congress would be the ultimate judge of its own powers. If Andrew Johnson were removed from the Presidency through impeachment, an added bonus would be that Radical Republican **Ben Wade**, President Pro Tem of the Senate, would succeed to his office and title. During the spring of 1867, the House of Representatives (responsible for bringing the initial charges, Article I, Section 2) searched for a possible charge against Johnson. The opportunity was finally found when Johnson violated the Tenure of Office Act in February 1868 by removing Secretary of War **Edwin M. Stanton**. Two days later, the House voted 128 to 47 to impeach the President. He was tried before the Senate with Chief Justice **Salmon Chase** presiding (Article I, Section 3) and was acquitted by only one vote short of the votes of two-thirds of the Senate needed for conviction. The incident appeared to indicate that the impeachment power could be used only for indictable crimes, not offenses resulting from political battles between two branches of government. The Tenure of Office Act was eventually repealed by Congress in 1887.

Reconstruction Comes to an End

Fifteenth Amendment (1870)

Suffrage had been indirectly granted to African Americans in the Fourteenth Amendment. The Fifteenth Amendment authorized the federal government to regulate voting in a limited sense. Although it prevented the denial of the vote based upon race, color, or previous condition of servitude, it did not stop the states from using **literacy** or **property tests** to restrict the vote.

End of Reconstruction

By 1872, Americans were tired of Reconstruction. Congress passed the **Amnesty Act**, which restored the franchise to almost all Confederates. As a result, white Democrats gradually regained control of the Southern states. Claiming that the Republican party was the party of corruption, the party of the black man, and responsible for the destruction of the South, the Democratic party became the majority party of the South until well into the 20th century, a phenomenon later referred to as the "Solid South." The withdrawal of the last federal troops took place following the election of 1876.

The Nationalization of Civil Rights

Perhaps with the sole exception of the New Deal era in the 1930s, the period of Reconstruction marked the greatest expansion of federal power in our country's history. The extension of national power over personal liberty and civil rights through the enactment of the Thirteenth, Fourteenth, and Fifteenth Amendments, the Civil Rights Act of 1866, and the Enforcement Acts of the 1870s was carried out at the expense of states' rights and resulted in a new balance of power in the federal Union. Although the states retained the responsibility of regulating civil rights, they did so under the watchful eye of the national government, which now had the right to step in when necessary. Although federal intervention in the South would all but cease by the 1880s, the federal government with greater powers and responsibilities would once again increase its supervisory role over state affairs during the second half of the 20th century.

Exercise Set 2.1

1. Lincoln's plan for Reconstruction was based on the theory that the Confederacy was
   A. to be considered a conquered nation
   B. to be divided into five states which would apply for statehood
   C. to be placed under congressional control
   D. to be considered as never having left the Union

2. By the 1890s Reconstruction had the effect of
   A. bringing complete civil rights to Southern blacks
   B. making the South solidly Democratic
   C. insuring the vote to all freedmen
   D. subduing all racist groups

3. The Reconstruction plan of the Radical Republicans (1867)
   A. established military control in the South
   B. was essentially the plan proposed by President Johnson
   C. was prompted by the South's acceptance of the Fourteenth Amendment
   D. included seating former Confederate military leaders in Congress

4. The most frequent basis for legislation expanding the role of the federal government in the guarantee of civil rights has been
   A. state court decisions
   B. the war powers of the President
   C. the Fourteenth Amendment
   D. the 18-year-old vote

5. The impeachment of President Johnson by the House of Representatives was based primarily on his
   A. creation of additional Cabinet positions
   B. attempts to exclude the South from the Union
   C. desire to run for a second term
   D. violation of the Tenure in Office Act

6. The "black codes" developed by the Southern states were designed to
   A. keep Southern blacks in the Democratic party
   B. keep freed slaves subordinate to whites
   C. help freed slaves adjust to their freedom through education
   D. divide old plantations and distribute land to former slaves

POST-CIVIL WAR ECONOMICS

In 1860 the United States was still primarily a producer of food and raw materials. However, in the half century that followed the Civil War, the United States became the world's leading industrial power. The statistics in Figure 2.1 demonstrate the extraordinary growth that took place during the 30 years following the Civil War.

Economic and Technological Stimuli

A number of factors were involved in the rapid transformation of American society in the years during and following the Civil War.

Population

Between 1860 and 1890 the country's population soared from 31.5 million to 62.6 million. Besides the high birthrate during this period, millions of immigrants came to the United States. They joined the large number of Americans moving from the farms to the cities. The population boom provided a source of cheap labor necessary during rapid economic growth.

	1860	1890	% of increase
Population	31,450,000	62,600,000	99
Number of factories	140,500	335,400	139
Value of factories	1,000,000,000	6,500,000,000	555
Value of manufactured goods	1,900,000,000	9,400,000,000	394
Industrial workers	1,300,000	4,200,000	223

Figure 2.1 Industrial Growth (1860–1890)

Raw Materials

The new industrial age was based upon steam power and heavy industry that made use of iron and steel. In addition to having about half the world's coal reserves, which were used for fuel, the United States also had abundant raw materials necessary for industrial growth. Iron ore and coal (the two raw materials used in the manufacture of steel with the use of the **Bessemer process** during the 1880s and afterward) were abundant, as were oil, copper, lead, silver, and gold.

Capital

In this period, capital from Americans and from Europe was abundant. As American industry became a lucrative investment opportunity, foreign capital financed many growing industries. By 1900, foreign investors owned approximately $3 billion in American securities. Domestic investment increased in American industry, especially after the decline of American shipping.

Technology

The demand for industrial goods during the Civil War acted as a catalyst to ingenuity and inventions, as American industry had to compete with foreign industry, which could employ labor at lower wages. However, techniques such as **interchangeable parts** and later the **assembly line** allowed cheaper production of goods. Inventions of the age included the **typewriter** (1868), **telephone** (1876), **incandescent light bulb** (1880), **linotype** (1886), and the **gasoline engine** in the 1890s.

Expanding Markets

Both the domestic and the foreign market for American goods expanded steadily during the second half of the 19th century. This was the result of increased demand by a growing domestic market with greater capability to consume and of increased demand by the foreign market made more accessible through the use of steam-driven iron ships.

Transportation

Before the Civil War, there were only about 30,000 miles of railroad track in the United States, and railroads barely existed west of the Mississippi River. After the war, railroad consolidation united many competing lines into a few giant systems that connected the many fragmented rail systems throughout the nation. By 1900, the New York Central System, created by **Cornelius Vanderbilt**, connected New York to Boston, Cleveland, Detroit, Chicago, St. Louis, Cincinnati, and Indianapolis. The federal government provided land grants to encourage the building of railroads in the sparsely populated West. Initially spurred by the California gold rush of 1849, Western railroad building increased again after the Civil War. The first **transcontinental railroad** was completed with the connection of the Union Pacific and the Central Pacific lines in Promontory, Utah, on May 10, 1869. By 1900, 200,000 miles of track existed in the United States, permitting the rapid transport of people and products.

The shift from wooden sailing vessels to steam-driven steel vessels made the transportation of goods less expensive and helped to expand the world market for American industrial and agricultural goods.

Labor

Before the Civil War, few Americans were wage earners. Most were self-employed in agriculture or small single-owner crafts. By 1900, however, about two-thirds of working adults were wage earners rather than self-employed. As the lives of workers were increasingly controlled by the employers who could hire and fire them at will, the struggle to combine and unionize became important in American labor history.

The Transformation of the South

The Civil War caused both the physical devastation and economic ruin of the South. The financial system based upon Confederate currency and bonds had collapsed, while the emancipation of the slaves stripped the propertied classes of their most valuable and productive assets.

Labor and Agriculture

- *The Freedmen.* Although the Civil War had emancipated the slaves, the adjustment for the freedmen proved to be difficult, since they did not have the means to become self-sufficient. Although Representative **Thaddeus Stevens** advocated the breaking up of large Southern plantations and the allocation of "forty acres and a mule" to each freedman, proposals for an effective program of land distribution failed to get through Congress. In most cases the freed slaves were forced to work for wages set by white landowners under the immediate supervision of a white overseer.

- *Sharecropping.* Black farmers and white landowners turned to a land and labor system known as **sharecropping**. The farmworker, often a freedman, farmed a tract of land belonging to a plantation owner and, in return for farming the land, was allowed to keep a percentage of the crop. The sharecropper system, however, was a poor substitute for landowning. Sharecroppers had little incentive to improve the land they farmed. Black sharecroppers lived in freedom, but they often became so indebted to the landowner and other creditors through the crop lien system, where farmers borrowed against their expected harvest, that the system virtually reenslaved the South's black population.

- *Land.* When Southerners returned to producing cotton after the Civil War, they discovered that the world demand for cotton had decreased. During the war, India, Brazil, and Egypt had supplied the cotton needs of the textile industries. The resulting depression in Southern agriculture affected white and black growers alike.

After the war, many large plantations were broken up. Between 1865 and 1880 the number of farms in the Southern states more than doubled, while the size of the average farm decreased. However, because of the sharecropping system, the number of landowners did not increase. As farmers continued to grow cotton and tobacco, overproduction caused prices to plunge, and constant growing exhausted the soil. In time, the necessity of crop diversification and scientific farming methods, including **crop rotation**, would be recognized.

Industrialization

One of the lessons of the Southern defeat in the Civil War was the realization that industrialization was necessary in the South. While Southern planters, shippers, and manufacturers depended heavily on capital from Northern banks and entrepreneurs, many Southern industries were mere subsidiaries of Northern firms. In the 1870s textile mills were built in the cotton states, and the South eventually replaced New England as the textile manufacturing center. The tobacco industry, aided by the invention of a cigarette-making machine in 1880, added to the industrialization of the South. Lumbering and iron and steel production increased, as did coal mining and railroad production.

Exercise Set 2.2

1. By the beginning of the 20th century, New England was being displaced as the leading textile center of the nation by
   A. the Canadian Provinces
   B. the South
   C. the Northwest
   D. the Southwest

2. Immediately following the Civil War, Southern agriculture
   A. was replaced by industrial output
   B. changed little from the time prior to the Civil War
   C. relied less on tobacco and cotton and became diversified
   D. returned to the plantation-slave labor system

3. The system whereby sharecroppers would borrow against their expected harvest, agreeing to pay a portion of their crops in return for credit, was called
   A. crop rotation
   B. homesteading
   C. nullification
   D. crop-lien

4. To encourage the building of railroads, the federal government
   A. provided land grants
   B. practiced a policy of laissez-faire
   C. increased tariffs on iron and steel products
   D. provided cheap immigrant labor for the railroad companies

Year	Total Value* Millions of Dollars	Cotton Millions of Dollars	Leaf Tobacco Millions of Dollars	Wheat Millions of Dollars
1850	101	72	10	1
1853	124	109	11	4
1855	151	88	15	1
1858	157	131	17	9
1860	270	192	16	4
1863	74	7	20	47
1865	154	7	42	19
1868	206	153	23	30
1870	359	227	21	47

* Selected Exports
SOURCE: U.S. Bureau of the Census, *Historical Statistics of the U.S., Colonial times to 1957.*

Figure 2.2 Value of Selected Exports from the United States

5. According to the information presented in the table on U.S. exports, all of the following are true EXCEPT
   A. the export of leaf tobacco was not affected by the Civil War as was the export of cotton
   B. the export of wheat grew rapidly during and after the Civil War
   C. the total value of United States exports rapidly recovered from the setback and disruption of the Civil War
   D. the total value of selected exports from the United States increased at a steady rate from 1850 to 1870

EMANCIPATION: AN UNSETTLED ISSUE

The freedmen were not really free in 1865, nor are most of their descendants really free in 1965. Slavery was but one aspect of a race and color problem that is still far from solution here, or anywhere. In America particularly, the grapes of wrath have not yet yielded all their bitter vintage.

Samuel Eliot Morison,
The Oxford History of the American People, 1965

Political

Although the Civil War and the post-war amendments had changed the legal status of the ex-slaves, in reality their social and economic status had changed very little. With the withdrawal of the last federal troops from the South in 1877, elements of white Southern society looked for methods to prevent blacks from voting.

Since the Fifteenth Amendment prohibited the denial of the vote due to "**race, color, or previous condition of servitude**," Southern state legislatures found other methods of denying the vote. **Poll taxes** and **literacy tests** were two methods used to disenfranchise black Americans. In some states, voters were asked to read and interpret the Constitution. By the late 1800s the **grandfather clause** became a widespread method of keeping blacks from the polls. This was a clause added to state constitutions giving the right to vote to all persons whose grandfathers could vote in 1867, even if the person could not pay the poll tax or pass the literacy test. Since blacks had been slaves and not able to vote in 1867, this clause disenfranchised them while giving the vote to poor illiterate whites. By the early 1900s African Americans had effectively lost their political rights in the South.

Social

The inferior social status of African Americans did not change after the Civil War. Although the Fourteenth Amendment prevented the states from discriminating against individuals, the Supreme Court ruled in 1876, in the case of *United States* v. *Cruikshank,* that the amendment "added nothing to the rights of one citizen against another." In other words, it had to be shown that the state was denying rights for the amendment to apply. The Court went further in the **Civil Rights Cases** (1883) when it invalidated the Civil Rights Act of 1875 that had prohibited **segregation** in public facilities. The Court held that the federal government could not regulate the behavior of private individuals. Later cases, primarily *Plessy* v. *Ferguson* (1896), held that blacks could be restricted to "separate but equal" facilities. This opened the door for the **Jim Crow** laws separating white and black Americans in Southern society.

Struggle for Political Control

As the Southern states followed the Reconstruction plan of Congress, they held conventions to draft new constitutions and established new state governments. Black voters exercised their newly acquired right to vote and elected black delegates to participate in these conventions and to the new state legislatures. Although black voters were in the majority in five states, only in South Carolina did they hold a majority in the lower house of the state legislature. Northerners known as **carpetbaggers**, who had recently arrived in the South, dominated the state governments in the early part of the Reconstruction period.

The "**Reconstruction governments**" passed much admirable legislation and introduced many overdue reforms in the South. The new constitutions were more democratic in that many eliminated property qualifications for voting and officeholding and made some former appointive positions now elective. Provisions for public schools, public works, and general rebuilding of the war-torn South were put through by the new governments.

Unfortunately, the Reconstruction governments under Republican rule were riddled with corruption. Some carpetbaggers and local Southern politicians were guilty of political graft. White resentment or "backlash" against the Reconstruction governments became widespread, and some secret societies such as the **Ku Klux Klan** were organized and turned to acts of terror. Such groups intimidated the freed slaves to prevent them from exercising their newly gained right to vote. Some relief came with the passage of federal laws, including the **Force Act** (1870) and the **Ku Klux Klan Act** (1871), allowing federal supervision of elections and the use of federal troops to control these white supremacy groups. However, the intimidation, including whippings, brandings, lynchings, and murder by these secret societies had already taken its toll.

The "**Solid South**" developed when white Democrats regained political control in the South. High taxes, corruption, a rising conservative class, and the tradition of white rule combined to end the temporary role of blacks in Southern politics.

The Supreme Court and the Fourteenth Amendment

The Fourteenth Amendment is perhaps the most important amendment ever added to the Constitution, and questions concerning its interpretation began to surface shortly after its ratification in 1868. Did the framers of the amendment intend to bar **discrimination**? If so, did this include private discrimination as well as public discrimination? Perhaps the most perplexing question to face the courts after its ratification: Did the framers intend to make the Bill of Rights applicable to the states as a result of the Fourteenth Amendment?

The wording of Section 1 of the Fourteenth Amendment is critical in understanding the amendment's history and changing interpretations:

> No **State** shall make or enforce any law which shall abridge the privileges or immunities of citizens of the United States; nor shall any **State** deprive any person of **life, liberty, or property**, without **due process of law**; nor deny any person within its jurisdiction the **equal protection** of the laws.

The Slaughter-House Cases

During the late 19th century, almost 600 cases involving the Fourteenth Amendment came to the Supreme Court, of which fewer than 30 dealt with ex-slaves. The first detailed discussion by the Supreme Court of the Fourteenth Amendment came in 1873 with the **Slaughter-House Cases**. When a group of butchers claimed that a monopoly on the slaughtering of livestock deprived them of equal protection of the laws as provided in Section 1 of the Fourteenth Amendment, the Supreme Court answered that the amendment was designed only to protect newly freed slaves. It also stated that the situation the butchers objected to was in the domain of the relationship between the state and its citizens, not the federal government, thus limiting the application of the amendment.

The Civil Rights Cases

In the **Civil Rights Cases** (1883), the Supreme Court voided the **Civil Rights Act of 1875**, which had forbidden hotels, restaurants, and public accommodations in general to discriminate based on race, color, or previous condition of servitude. The Court held that the Fourteenth Amendment prohibited discrimination only by state governments, not that in which individuals and private citizens engaged. With the *Plessy* case, the power of the Fourteenth Amendment to protect the civil rights of minority Americans reached its lowest point. As of 1896 the amendment was used to sanction "**separate but equal**" facilities and applied only to state actions.

Application of the Fourteenth Amendment to the States

Although the Fourteenth Amendment did not at first apply the Bill of Rights to the states, in time the Supreme Court, explaining the "due process" clause, made certain provisions of the Bill of Rights applicable to the states. The landmark case was *Gitlow* v. *New York* (1925), when the Supreme Court, in incorporating the First Amendment in the due process clause of the Fourteenth Amendment, declared that

For the present purposes, we may and do assume that freedom of speech and of the press—which are protected by the First Amendment from abridgement by Congress—are among the fundamental personal rights and 'liberties' protected by the due process clause of the Fourteenth Amendment from impairment by the states.

Since the *Gitlow* case, the following guarantees of the Bill of Rights have been applied to the states:

- prohibition against unreasonable searches and seizures (Fourth Amendment)
- privilege against self-incrimination (Fifth Amendment)
- guarantee against double jeopardy (Fifth Amendment)
- right to assistance of counsel (Sixth Amendment)
- right to a speedy trial (Sixth Amendment)
- right to jury trial (Sixth Amendment)
- right to confront opposing witnesses (Sixth Amendment)
- right to compulsory process for obtaining witnesses (Sixth Amendment)
- right to public trial (Sixth Amendment)
- right to notice as to the nature and cause of the accusation (Sixth Amendment)
- prohibition against cruel and unusual punishment (Eighth Amendment)

Role of Black Americans in Post-Civil War Society

In the postwar decades of Reconstruction and the rebuilding of the "New South," racial **segregation** in the form of Jim Crow laws, as well as poll taxes, grandfather clauses, literacy tests, lynchings, beatings, and other forms of violence by white supremacist groups were used to keep blacks in their "proper place." Between 1880 and 1930, three leading figures were instrumental in defining the position of blacks in American society: **Booker T. Washington**, **W.E.B. Du Bois**, and **Marcus Garvey**.

Booker T. Washington

Founder of the Normal and Industrial Institute at Tuskegee, Alabama (1881), and author of the autobiography *Up From Slavery*, Booker T. Washington stressed the importance of vocational education in preparing African Americans to earn a living and to gain equality. More militant groups and individuals criticized Washington's "willing to wait" methods as "practically accepting the alleged inferiority of the Negro race."

W.E.B. DuBois

DuBois's *The Souls of Black Folk* (1903) presented the black American's life to the white public in a series of essays. His **Niagara Movement** (1905), demanded immediate suffrage and civil rights for blacks. DuBois believed that a small group of educated, talented blacks, referred to as the "**Talented Tenth**," would save the race by setting an example to whites and other blacks. Du Bois and his associates, black and white, formed the **National Association for the Advancement of Colored People (NAACP)** in 1909 to pursue legal methods to end racial discrimination.

Marcus Garvey

Jamaican-born Marcus Garvey founded the **Universal Negro Improvement Association** (1916). Preaching racial pride, Garvey insisted that American blacks must return to Africa and create their own civilization in their homeland. Although Garvey's concept of black pride was hailed by many, few chose to leave America and return to Africa.

Exercise Set 2.3

1. All of the following were ways in which black Southerners were kept from voting EXCEPT
   A. literacy tests
   B. poll taxes
   C. "grandfather clauses"
   D. Force Acts

2. Laws requiring the separation of the races in public facilities were called
   A. equal protection provisions
   B. Amnesty Acts
   C. Jim Crow laws
   D. sharecropper statutes

3. The Supreme Court case of *Plessy* v. *Ferguson* (1896)
   A. mandated integration of public facilities
   B. found the poll tax to be unconstitutional
   C. gave legal support to segregation
   D. affirmed *Gitlow* v. *United States* in applying the Bill of Rights to the states

4. The legislatures established in the Southern states during Reconstruction
   A. excluded blacks
   B. were free from corruption and graft
   C. were primarily dominated by blacks
   D. were instrumental in passing necessary legislation

THE END OF RECONSTRUCTION

The Grant Era

> Let no guilty man escape, if it can be avoided. No personal considerations should stand in the way of performing a public duty.
>
> President Ulysses S. Grant,
> Endorsement of a letter relating to the **Whiskey Ring**,
> July 29, 1875

The Grant Administration (1869–1877)

Ulysses S. Grant, although a capable military leader, proved a failure at providing strong leadership in the White House. As the nation experienced tremendous economic expansion, incidents of widespread graft and corruption plagued American politics and reflected a low point in public morality.

- *Monetary Policy.* President Grant was not directly involved in the numerous scandals that plagued his administration, but he lacked good judgment concerning those he turned to for advice. During his first term he was influenced by two financial speculators, **Jay Gould** and **James Fisk**. Their attempts to "corner" the gold market and make huge profits were supported by treasury-department officials of Grant's administration. Gould and Fisk helped cause the ruin of many business people, financiers, and workers.

- *Crédit Mobilier.* A scandal involving the construction of the Union Pacific Railroad was revealed during Grant's second administration. The owners of the Union Pacific Railroad created the **Crédit Mobilier**, a construction company, to build the railroad. This company charged the railroad several times the actual amount of construction. To hide the fraud and prevent investigation they gave stock to several members of Congress and the Vice-President.

- *The Whiskey Ring Fraud.* This scandal involved a ring of liquor dealers in St. Louis who, with the assistance of treasury officials, defrauded the government of millions in unpaid taxes.

William Marcy "Boss" Tweed (1823–1878) controlled New York City from behind the scenes.

Urban Politics

Political corruption also existed at the local level. City political machines worked alongside the legal governments of a municipality. Led by a political "boss," their main goal—to obtain and keep political power—was achieved through graft and bribery. The infamous **Tweed Ring** of New York City's Tammany Hall stole some $100,000 from the taxpayers before being exposed by *The New York Times* and by the cartoons of **Thomas Nast** in *Harpers Weekly.*

The Solid South

As a result of Reconstruction and political upheaval in the South following the Civil War, the Democrats were able to convince many white voters that the Republican party was the party of corruption that had forced black rule on the South. The Democratic party was dominant in the South from 1876 until the 1970s.

Election of 1876 and the Compromise of 1877

As corruption became more widespread, reform-minded Republicans banded together in 1872 in a new wing of the party known as the "**Liberal Republicans**." They wanted to clean up politics and end military Reconstruction. In 1876, the Republican convention, realizing that the reputation of "Grantism" was hurting the party, nominated a compromise candidate, Governor **Rutherford B. Hayes** of Ohio. The Democratic nominee, Governor **Samuel J. Tilden** of New York, campaigned against Republican scandal and supported reform in the area of federal employment, or "civil service reform."

In the general election to choose the presidential electors who were to cast the Electoral College votes for the President, Tilden won a majority of the popular votes. However, neither candidate had enough undisputed electoral votes to win. Tilden was one electoral vote short of the necessary majority, while Hayes was twenty votes short. Charges arose of irregularities concerning vote-counting procedures in three Southern states: South Carolina, Florida, and Louisiana, where the election boards were under the control of Republican Reconstruction forces. After election board counts indicated that these three states had given Hayes the majority, Democrats charged that the vote in each state had actually gone for Tilden, a difference that would make Tilden the winner of the election. All three states sent two sets of returns to Congress, one Democrat and one Republican.

To resolve the unprecedented constitutional crisis, Congress established a fifteen-member electoral commission (**Electoral Count Act**). After lengthy discussion, the members of the commission agreed to accept the Republican returns, giving Hayes a one-vote electoral victory. In an informal compromise between the parties, the Democrats agreed that Hayes would take office in return for withdrawing troops from the two states where they remained, Louisiana and South Carolina, officially ending military Reconstruction in the South.

The Impact of the Civil War and Reconstruction

Political Alignments

During the Civil War and early Reconstruction era, the political parties exhibited clear-cut differences in ideology, primarily in the areas of race relations and civil rights. After the Civil War, however, sharp policy differences between the two parties faded, although they continued to differ on national issues such as the tariff and currency. The Democrats generally favored low tariffs and the silver standard, while the Republicans favored high tariffs and the gold standard. For the most part, the two major parties failed to develop any clear-cut program to deal with the major social and economic issues that faced the nation.

Nature of Citizenship

The Constitution was silent on the issue of citizenship. The Civil Rights Act of 1866 provided that "all persons born or naturalized in the United States...were citizens of the United States." The Fourteenth Amendment to the Constitution (1868) further defined citizenship on both the national and state level: "All persons born or naturalized in the United States, and subject to the jurisdiction thereof, are citizens of the United States and of the State wherein they reside." In addition to conferring citizenship on the freed slaves, the amendment prohibited the states from abridging their constitutional "**privileges and immunities**" and prohibited any state from taking a person's life, liberty, or property "without due process of law" and from denying "equal protection of the laws."

Federal-State Relations

With the nationalization of civil rights by virtue of the Civil Rights Act of 1866, the Thirteenth, Fourteenth, and Fifteenth Amendments, and the Civil Rights Act of 1875, the federal government came to play a far greater role in the preservation of civil rights. The increased jurisdiction of federal courts to hear civil rights cases also added to the expansion of federal power. As white rule returned to the South and attention to the rights of the freed slaves faded, the federal government turned its increased power to national economic issues that were a result of the industrial revolution of the late 19th century.

The North as an Industrial Power

While the Civil War marked a dividing point in American history, with the United States turning from an agrarian nation into an industrial power in a matter of decades, this development was sectional. As industrial development spread over the North, the South remained overwhelmingly rural. The second half of the 19th century saw industrial growth assisted by protective tariffs and corporate development nurtured by favorable Supreme Court decisions. The effect of industry and business would soon find its way into the lives of most Americans.

Exercise Set 2.4

1. In the disputed election of 1876, two different sets of electoral votes were received from
   A. South Carolina
   B. Florida
   C. Louisiana
   D. all of the above

2. By the Compromise of 1877
   A. the Fourteenth Amendment to the Constitution was ratified
   B. Tilden was selected as President of the United States
   C. military occupation of the South ended
   D. the Electoral College system was ended

3. The Crédit Mobilier scandal involved
   A. an increase in the salary of the President and members of Congress
   B. the transcontinental railroad
   C. whiskey and tax fraud
   D. different sets of electoral votes being sent to Congress

4. The section of the Fourteenth Amendment that had the greatest legal significance for the future dealt with
   A. equal protection of the laws guarantee
   B. the apportionment of representatives
   C. the repudiation of the Confederate war debt
   D. the disability clause

1. The Fifteenth Amendment to the U.S. Constitution does not prevent the denial of the vote based upon
   A. literacy
   B. race
   C. color
   D. previous condition of servitude

2. In the decades following the Civil War, the expression "Solid South" was used to refer to the
   A. return of the old plantation system based upon slave labor
   B. dominance by the Democratic party
   C. industrialization of the South
   D. changed attitude on the part of the Southern states toward black Americans

3. Which factor was *least* important in the industrialization of the United States in the 19th century?
   A. abundance of raw materials
   B. inventions
   C. supply of cheap labor
   D. foreign demand for American industrial goods

4. The Fourteenth Amendment is important because, in addition to awarding citizenship to former slaves, it
   A. guarantees women the right to vote
   B. abolishes the poll tax
   C. guarantees equal protection under the law
   D. provides protection against illegal search and seizure

5. The ability to amend the U.S. Constitution lends support to the belief that the document was designed to
   A. preserve the provisions of the original Constitution
   B. adapt to changing times and beliefs
   C. maintain the separation of powers in the national government
   D. accommodate the political party in power

6. Which of the following guarantees would today apply to the states through the "due process" and "equal protection" clauses of the Fourteenth Amendment?
   A. assistance of counsel in criminal prosecutions
   B. ownership of a gun
   C. consumption of alcohol at age eighteen
   D. privilege to drive an automobile at age sixteen

ESSAYS

1. The Fourteenth Amendment, ratified in 1868, came under the review of the Supreme Court shortly after ratification and has continued to be examined by the Court.

    Slaughter-House Cases (1873)
    United States v. Cruikshank (1876)
    Civil Rights Cases (1883)
    Plessy v. *Ferguson* (1896)
    Gitlow v. *New* York (1925)

    Select *three* of the Supreme Court decisions listed above. For each one chosen discuss the issue facing the Court and how the Court eventually ruled on the issue. [5,5,5]

2. Following the Civil War a number of prominent leaders proposed very different programs for the betterment of the black population in the United States.

    Booker T. Washington
    W.E.B. DuBois
    Marcus Garvey

    For *each* of the leaders listed above, discuss his significance in the drive for civil rights, including each leader's methods used to combat racial discrimination. [5,5,5]

3. The nature of the American presidency can be determined by such factors as

    The times in which the President serves
    Relationship with Congress
    Individuals chosen to advise the President

    Referring to the presidential administrations between 1860 and 1877, show how *each* of the factors listed above affected the nature of the presidency. A different President must be used for each factor. [5,5,5]

THE RISE OF AMERICAN BUSINESS AND LABOR (1865–1920)

TECHNOLOGY AND WORLD INDUSTRIALISM

> The fact is, that civilization requires slaves. The Greeks were quite right there. Unless there are slaves to do the uninteresting work, culture and contemplation become almost impossible. Human slavery is wrong, insecure, and demoralizing. On mechanical slavery, on the slavery of the machine, the future of the world depends.
>
> Oscar Wilde,
> *The Soul of Man Under Socialism* (1895)

The Industrial Revolution

"Industry" existed in the English colonies in North America from the time of colonization onward. The early manufacturers in the colonies were the goldsmiths, the silversmiths, the cobblers, the tanners, the cabinetmakers, and a host of other skilled artisans. As the colonial period ended and with it the stage of the rough struggle with nature, specialization in crafts developed and people started to depend on the "industries" of others.

The term "**Industrial Revolution**" refers to changes in the economic organization of society that include the factory system and machine-made goods. The Industrial Revolution began about 1750 in England with certain inventions in the textile industry and spread to many nations of the Western world, including the United States, during the next century. It involved the replacement on a massive scale of human and animal power with machine power. During the Industrial Revolution there was a shift from manufacturing in the home to the gathering of machines and workers to run them under a single roof (the factory). It also involved improved methods of transportation on land and water, and the growth of modern **capitalism** with the private ownership and control of the means of production.

England

The Industrial Revolution began in England because England possessed many of the elements necessary for industrial development. The wealth from its colonial empire in North America helped provide the capital to invest in new manufacturing enterprises. An ample labor supply provided workers for the factories. Natural resources including coal and iron were abundant, and a large merchant fleet enabled the import of raw materials and the export of industrial goods.

The following developments, most of which occurred in England between 1730 and 1870, contributed to early industrialization. Among the important inventions were:

- the **flying shuttle** (1733), which increased the speed of weaving
- the **spinning jenny** (1764), which increased the speed of spinning thread
- the **power loom** (1785), which greatly increased the speed of production of cloth
- the **cotton gin** (1793), invented by an American, **Eli Whitney**, which helped satisfy the demand for more cotton
- the **steam engine** (1769), introduced into factories to turn spinning and weaving machines
- the **blast furnace** (mid-1700s), used in iron products
- the **Bessemer process** (1856), used to remove the impurities from iron, to produce steel
- the **electric dynamo** (1831)
- the **vulcanization of rubber** (1839) by American Charles Goodyear

United States

The Industrial Revolution came to the United States somewhat later than to England. English **mercantilism** had stifled the development of some colonial industry. Moreover, after the Revolution, American capital was used primarily for agricultural development and the shipping industry. The difficulty of importing manufactured goods during the Napoleonic Wars and the War of 1812 provided a stimulus for the development of factories in the United States. The three decades following the Civil War brought economic and social transformation unmatched in the history of the United States. Rich in natural resources, human resources both in labor and scientific development, and capital, the United States approached the coming of the 20th century as a leader in industrial development. Large-scale immigration helped to provide the labor needed in the expanding factory system. By 1894 the United States was turning out more manufactured goods than any other country in the world. Of course, many problems accompanied the Industrial Revolution. Among them were problems between labor and management, uneven distribution of wealth, and harmful business combinations.

Germany

Although the effects of the Industrial Revolution were felt throughout western Europe, Germany's industrial development did not mature until after **unification** in 1871. The leadership of **Chancellor Otto von Bismarck**, large deposits of coal and iron, an excellent railway system, extensive technical training for workers, and the use of modern methods and machinery helped to accelerate the Industrial Revolution in Germany. High tariffs were used to protect new industries. Transportation was improved through the use of the state-owned railways and canal systems. By the beginning of the 20th century, Germany was competing with both Great Britain and the United States for leadership in world trade.

Japan

While **feudalism** prevailed in Japan through the middle of the 19th century, the adoption of Western ideas began by 1870. British experts were brought in to develop a strong navy, German military practices were studied, and American educational systems were studied to develop a national school system. Industrial methods were also copied from the West, and by 1900, Japan had built about 7,000 factories. Water power and an abundant supply of cheap labor helped Japan compete with the Western industrial nations. Banking, shipbuilding, mining, and utilities were encouraged by the government to grow, with an emphasis on military production. Following its victory in the Russo-Japanese War (1904–1905), Japan entered its own period of **imperialist** expansion and was soon recognized as a world power.

Impact of Industrial Development

On the surface, the Industrial Revolution appeared to benefit most Americans. Statistics suggest that the American standard of living improved in the decades following the Civil War, with prices declining, wage rates remaining consistent, and therefore **"real income"** increasing. Average working hours decreased and average life expectancy increased. Yet the new industrial age also brought many problems. As wage earners became more dependent on others, times of fluctuation in production resulted in prolonged periods of unemployment in the 1870s and again in the 1890s. The relationship between the factory owner and the workers was no longer personal, and there was little concern for injured or unemployed workers.

Collective bargaining made little progress by 1870 and there was no public welfare program to ease the hardships caused by injury, unemployment, or old age. As industrialism increased and capitalism thrived, the contrast between the rich and the poor increased. As the technology and business organizations of the industrial era generated unmatched powers for creating goods and services, a class of Americans was becoming "enslaved" by the factory system. The words of American social critic **Henry Demarest Lloyd** in his attack upon monopolies, *Wealth Against Commonwealth* (1894) appeared to be coming true: "Liberty produces wealth, and wealth destroys liberty."

Growth of Capitalism

Capitalism, a form of economic organization characterized by the factory system, private ownership, large-scale production, a free market and wage labor, became the dominant economic system in the industrial societies in the 19th century. Elements of capitalism include (1) **capital**, or the wealth used in producing more wealth; (2) **capitalists**, those who invest money in an enterprise from which a profit is expected; and (3) **labor**, or the working class employed by capitalists.

The leading critic of capitalism and its abuses in the 1800s was the German writer **Karl Marx** (1818–1883). According to Marx, all history involves the struggle between social classes. He saw modern society as divided between the **bourgeoisie** (upper class), which controlled the capital, and the **proletariat** (working class), which sold its labor for wages. Marx supported the organization of workers both as an economic force in **trade unions** and as a political force in a revolutionary movement to overthrow the bourgeoisie.

PRE-CIVIL WAR INDUSTRIAL GROWTH

Although the post-Civil War period has come to be identified with the rapid growth of the Industrial Revolution in the United States, manufacturing and industrial development can be traced back to colonial times. Colonists found that British goods cost nearly twice as much in America as they did in Britain. Moreover, the colonial trade imbalance created a serious shortage of currency for exchange with the mother country. This situation led the colonists to undertake small-scale manufacturing including the production of **textiles** (cloth), soap, candles, furniture, and crude tools and utensils. **Iron smelteries**, some subsidized by colonial legislatures, helped meet the need for farm tools and weapons. Although by 1800 manufacturing was still relatively unimportant to the American economy, soon after the War of 1812 the rise of merchant investors, wholesalers, retailers, and improved transportation marked the early beginnings of industrial transformation.

Textile Industry

Textile manufacturing became an important part of American industry shortly after independence was achieved. The first mill, built in Pawtucket, Rhode Island in 1790, used water-powered spinning machines constructed by **Samuel Slater**. The **Embargo Act (1807), Non-Intercourse Act (1809)**, and **War of 1812** stimulated manufacturing in the United States, and the number of textile mills increased. The first American power loom (1813) revolutionized textile manufacturing by increasing production and lowering the price of the finished product.

Originally, many industries, including the textile industry, used the "putting-out" or domestic system; workers received supplies at home where they finished the product and then returned it to a merchant who sold it. This system had problems of timing, shipping, and quality control. In 1813 **Francis Cabot Lowell** and other Boston merchants built the first textile factories in **Waltham, Massachusetts**, combining all the manufacturing operations at a single location. To satisfy the need for workers, the managers of the textile factories recruited young women from the New England countryside to work in the mills. They offered them appealing wages, boarding houses to live in, and cultural events. This came to be known as the **Lowell**, or **Waltham System** and was used in other mills in New England. The textile industry became the most important industry in the country before the Civil War, employing nearly 115,000 workers in 1860. However, the congenial worker-management relationship created in the New England mills ended as immigration increased and cheap labor became abundant.

Iron Production

The iron industry, like the textile industry, was stimulated by the **embargo** on trade before the War of 1812 and by its interruption during the war. A major breakthrough in the iron industry came with the discovery of how to produce **steel** inexpensively and in large quantities. The United States possessed the necessary elements, iron and coal, to produce steel, a mixture of iron, carbon, and other elements. Immense deposits of iron ore lay near the western shores of Lake Superior, and nearly one half of the world's coal reserves lay within our borders. In the 1850s **Henry Bessemer** of England and **William Kelly** of the United States independently discovered a revolutionary process for making large quantities of steel inexpensively by burning out the impurities in molten iron. With the use of the **Bessemer process**, steel production soared.

Exercise Set 2.5

1. The introduction of new textile machines in England at the start of the Industrial Revolution increased the employment of textile workers because
   A. the newly developed machinery was less efficient than the hand labor that it replaced
   B. the cost of machine-made textiles fell rapidly, leading to greater demand
   C. the division of labor that developed required more workers to produce the same amount of goods
   D. imported foreign textiles were superior to domestic textiles

2. The primary purpose of the colonies acquired by England during the 19th century was to provide
   A. raw materials and overseas markets
   B. a training ground for military forces
   C. labor for growing industries
   D. settlements for growing populations

3. Which of the following inventions had great influence in the 19th century?
   A. the steam engine
   B. the radio
   C. the automobile
   D. the flying shuttle

4. An important result of the War of 1812 was that it
    A. increased U.S. shipping
    B. encouraged immigration to the United States
    C. encouraged manufacturing in the United States
    D. increased investment in agriculture at the expense of industry

5. America's most important industry before the Civil War was the
    A. rubber industry
    B. machine tool industry
    C. automobile industry
    D. textile industry

BUSINESS AND ORGANIZATION: SIZE AND STRUCTURE

> They (corporations) cannot commit treason, nor be outlawed nor excommunicated, for they have no souls.
>
> Sir Edward Coke (1552–1634),
> *Case of Sutton's Hospital*

Proprietorships and Partnerships

Before the middle of the 19th century, most American businesses were either **single proprietorships**, with one owner, or **partnerships**, small businesses with two or more owners. In the years before the Industrial Revolution, the proprietorship and partnership were workable forms of business organizations. However, as American industry and business grew, facilitated by greater amounts of **capital**, improved transportation, greater demand for products, and an available working force, small organizations often proved to be inadequate. If a business wanted to expand, it was difficult for one or two persons to raise the necessary capital. If the organization faced financial difficulties, the owners who were financially responsible often lost their personal assets. Finally, the death of a proprietor or partner often meant the end of the business.

Incorporation

Following the Civil War, the **corporation** became the major form of business organization, gradually replacing proprietorships and partnerships. By selling part ownerships of the business to the public through the sale of **stocks** and **bonds**, the corporation was able to raise the necessary capital for operations and expansion. During the 1800s, to encourage industry and commerce, states passed general incorporation laws. These laws enabled almost anybody to start a company and raise money by selling stocks to investors, who in turn could share in profits while not being responsible for the company's debts (**limited liability**). The transferability of shares of stock allowed ownership to change hands without disrupting the operations of the business. The death of an owner did not affect the life of the corporation. During the 1880s and 1890s, corporations received important judicial protection when the Supreme Court ruled that corporations, like individuals, were protected by the **Fourteenth Amendment**. This extension of the Fourteenth Amendment meant that corporations could not be denied equal protection of the laws and could not be deprived of rights or property without due process of law. (*Chicago, Milwaukee, St. Paul Railway Co.* v. *Minnesota,* 1890)

Incorporation also had disadvantages. The corporation had to pay taxes on its profits and, in addition, individual stockholders had to pay taxes on their dividends. With the grant of a **charter** by the state in which the business was incorporated came regulations and procedures that the corporation had to follow.

Consolidation of Corporations

By 1900 corporations were responsible for nearly two-thirds of all the goods manufactured in the United States. As growth continued, corporate managers searched for ways to expand and increase stability. During the late 1800s, there was a trend toward business combination or consolidation, under new corporate forms such as **trusts** and holding companies that promoted growth and cut down on wasteful competition. Between 1889 and 1903 some 300 business combinations were formed. Perhaps the most spectacular was the **United States Steel Corporation,** the nation's first billion-dollar corporation, which controlled 60 percent of the nation's steel production, created by banker and international financier **J.P. Morgan**.

As investment opportunities increased, greater amounts of capital were necessary. In addition to domestic investments in American industry, foreign investment grew. Between 1870 and 1900 foreign investment in American companies increased from $1.5 billion to $3.5 billion.

Merchandising Changes and Retailing

In the early part of the 19th century, Americans purchased most goods from traveling peddlers or a local general store. The **barter system**, goods exchanged for other goods or services, was common, and prices of goods varied from town to town. In the years after the Civil War, as manufacturing grew, local retailers began to purchase goods from wholesalers located in larger cities. New kinds of **retail** outlets—chain stores, mail order houses, and department stores—drastically changed how goods were merchandised and purchased.

Department Stores

Early department stores, including those of A.T. Stewart of New York and John Wanamaker of Philadelphia, were able to purchase goods directly from the manufacturers and offer competitive prices, while providing many services that could not be duplicated by smaller general stores. Among the major early department stores were Macy's of New York, Gimbel's of Philadelphia, Jordan Marsh and Filene's of Boston, Lazarus of Columbus, and Abraham and Straus of Brooklyn, New York.

Chain Stores

Stores with branches in many cities were tied together by management and accounting. The Great Atlantic and Pacific Tea Company (A & P) and the Woolworth "five-and-ten-cent" stores were able to undercut general stores in prices and offer a wide range of goods. Like the department stores, they bought large quantities of goods at low prices.

Mail-Order Houses

Finally, the merchandising of goods to consumers was revolutionized by the mail-order house. Customers chose their purchases from catalogs and ordered by mail. Montgomery Ward and Sears Roebuck, assisted by faster and more dependable transportation services of the railroad, were the pioneers of the mail-order house.

TRANSPORTATION, COMMUNICATION, AND RESOURCES

Transportation

Railroads

During the first half of the 19th century, the nation's railroads were anything but a uniform system connecting the different sections of the country. There was little mileage beyond the Mississippi and virtually none beyond the Missouri River. Few tracks were connected; short stretches of lines using different gauges required the unloading and reloading of cargo for transport.

As settlement extended westward, it became apparent that the nation's rail system would have to expand into a uniform system. In 1850 the federal government transferred to promoters several million acres of public land for the purpose of railroad construction. This policy was continued by the government primarily in the construction of Western lines. The nation's first **transcontinental** railroad was completed in 1869 with the joining of the **Central Pacific Railroad** and the **Union Pacific Railroad** at Promontory

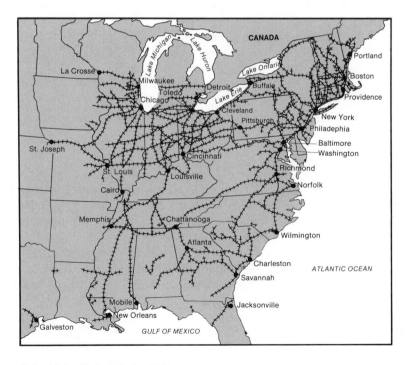

Figure 2.3 Major Railroads in 1860

147

Point, Utah. Between 1865 and 1890 the total mileage of track in the United States grew from 35,000 to 200,000, with the greatest growth taking place west of the Mississippi River. Technological advances, including uniform-gauge tracks, the automatic car coupler, the Pullman Sleeping Car, and the Westinghouse air brake, made rail transportation safer and more efficient. By 1910 the United States had a third of all the railroad track in the world. In the half-century following the Civil War, railroads enabled the growing nation to transport its enormous wealth in natural resources to factories, storehouses, marketplaces, and seaports.

Automobiles

Henry Ford, an electrical engineer with Detroit's Edison Company, developed and introduced the **mass production** of automobiles. Copying the meatpacking industry, Ford set up **assembly lines** to produce automobiles, which greatly reduced the time and expense of manufacturing cars. When the **Ford Motor Company** began production of the **Model T** in 1910, 10,000 cars were sold. By 1914, with the help of assembly-line production, 248,000 Fords, costing as little as $490 each, were sold. The production of automobiles also stimulated the growth of other industries, including steel, road building, service stations, rubber, etc. By the 1930s trucks and buses started to compete with railroads in hauling freight and passengers.

Automobile manufacturer Henry Ford (1863–1947) developed the assembly-line method of mass production.

Urban Transportation

The forces of industrialization and urbanization accompanied one another during the second half of the 19th century and into the 20th century. As American cities grew, mass transportation became an area of concern. Horse- and mule-drawn vehicles of the late 1800s were inefficient in urban areas. The first power-driven transportation used in the cities were **cable cars**. The increased production of electricity enabled electric-powered streetcars to be used by the 1890s; the amount of electrified track increased from 1,300 miles in 1890 to 22,000 miles by 1902. **Elevated tracks** and **subways** allowed mass transportation free movement through congested areas. As early as 1878, New York City had elevated railways on Third and Sixth Avenues. As suburbs spread out from the core of the city, tracks were constructed outward to bring commuters to and from their employment downtown.

Communication

Telegraph

The most revolutionary change in communications before the Civil War was the development of the long-distance telegraph by **Samuel F.B. Morse** in 1844. By 1853, 23,000 miles of telegraph wire spread across the United States, freeing the transport of messages from the human messenger. The first transatlantic cable was laid in 1858, making possible instantaneous communication with other continents.

Telephone

In 1876 **Alexander Graham Bell**, a teacher of the deaf in Boston, received a patent on a telephone he had invented. By 1885 the **American Telephone and Telegraph Company** was organized to put the new invention into widespread use.

Sources of Energy

New sources of energy have coincided with industrial development in the United States. During the late 1700s steam energy produced by wood and coal replaced earlier sources of power—humans animal, and water power. By the late 1800s two new sources of energy—oil and electricity—came into use.

Oil

In the early 1850s **kerosene** refined from petroleum was an efficient and inexpensive fuel used primarily in lamps. Discoveries of oil reserves in Pennsylvania, and later in California and Texas, provided a major source of fuel in the 20th century with the invention of the internal combustion engine. By 1920 the United States was producing about 65 percent of the world's petroleum, much of it controlled by **John D. Rockefeller's Standard Oil**.

Electricity

Harvard President **Charles W. Eliot** pointed out the enormous change electricity brought to American life, saying, "It is the carrier of light and power; devourer of time and space; bearer of human speech over land and sea; greatest servant of man."

In 1878 **Thomas Edison** formed the **Edison Electric Light Company** and developed the **incandescent light bulb** which, if not the first, was certainly the most practical light bulb of the time. Another invention of Edison's laboratories, the **dynamo,** solved some of the problems of power production and distribution, enabling the delivery of electrical power. Edison's work was improved upon by **George Westinghouse**. He used **alternating current** and transformers to reduce high-voltage power to lower voltage levels and was able to make the transmission of electrical power over long distances less expensive. During the 1890s Henry Villard and J.P. Morgan merged various electric companies to form **General Electric**.

Exercise Set 2.6

1. During the period 1860–1890, big business was characterized by
   A. the use of organizational methods to control prices and do away with competition
   B. support for union organization among workers
   C. attempts to curb immigration
   D. lack of adequate leadership in managerial positions

2. All of the following were objectives of merger movements in the late 1800s and early 1900s EXCEPT
   A. better working conditions for employees
   B. reduction of wasteful competition
   C. increased growth
   D. greater control of the market of a particular product

3. Introduction and improvement of the assembly line and mass production can be largely attributed to
   A. J.P. Morgan
   B. Thomas Edison
   C. George Westinghouse
   D. Henry Ford

4. Railroad building in the period after 1865 resulted in all of the following EXCEPT
   A. continued industrialization
   B. greater population growth west of the Mississippi
   C. formation of towns and cities along railroad routes
   D. a decrease in agricultural output

REPRESENTATIVE ENTREPRENEURS

> Upon the sacredness of property civilization itself depends—the right
> of the laborer to his hundred dollars in the savings bank, and equally
> the legal right of the millionaire to his millions.
>
> Andrew Carnegie, *Wealth* (1889)

A new group of business owners appeared during the middle of the 19th century who later became known as the **robber barons**. Through financial wizardry, stock manipulation, and fierce competition, these men built corporate dynasties that eventually threatened the free enterprise system in the United States. Yet their management of business and the nation's resources also lowered the cost of oil, steel, and other goods for America's consumers and helped create the modern corporation. Moreover, their willingness to reinvest profits in further business expansion contributed to the economic growth of the United States during the last half of the 19th century.

Captains of Industry

John Pierpont Morgan (1837–1913)

Born in Hartford, Connecticut, the son of a prominent international banker, J.P. Morgan built a reputation after the Civil War as a reorganizer of railroads. By the end of the 19th century, he controlled a vast transportation network. Morgan founded the **J.P. Morgan Company** in 1895 and in 1901 organized the first billion-dollar corporation, **United States Steel**.

Andrew Carnegie (1835–1919)

Born in Scotland the son of a poor weaver, Carnegie came to the United States in 1848 and worked in a Pittsburgh cotton factory for $1.20 per week. Later, working his way up through the Pennsylvania Railroad Company, Carnegie became rich investing in oil, ironmaking, and bridgebuilding. The **Carnegie Steel Company** became America's largest steel concern and was eventually bought by J.P. Morgan in the formation of United States Steel. Although he was a shrewd businessman, Carnegie's essay "**Gospel of Wealth**" (1889) demonstrated his belief in philanthropy, setting forth the idea that the rich are "trustees" of their wealth and should administer it unselfishly for the good of the public. The later part of his life was dedicated to putting his "gospel" into practice, with much of his money going toward foundations including the Carnegie Institute of Washington, the Carnegie Foundation for the Advancement of Teaching, and the Carnegie Endowment for International Peace.

John D. Rockefeller (1839–1937)

Rockefeller's fortune was made in oil, and in 1870 he formed the **Standard Oil Company** to consolidate his investments. By the 1880s his Standard Oil Trust controlled almost all the nation's oil refineries, refining 83.7 percent of all the oil produced in the country. A fierce competitor, Rockefeller explained his ruthlessness in business by comparing it to the American Beauty rose: "The American Beauty rose can be produced in all its splendor only by sacrificing the early buds that grow up around it." The Standard Oil Trust, ordered to dissolve by the Ohio Supreme Court, was reorganized as **Standard Oil of New Jersey**. It lasted for 12 years until the Supreme Court broke it up in 1911.

The Work Ethic

The American work ethic can be traced back to the Puritan settlements of the 1600s in New England. The **Puritans** believed that good luck and success during one's life on earth were evidence of the "elect status" necessary to gain entrance into heaven. Puritans, anxious about their spiritual state, devoted themselves to good works to help get to heaven, and to hard work, self-examination, and Bible study, looking upon laziness and idleness as sure signs of damnation.

Horatio Alger (1834–1899), A 19th-century American writer, dramatized the American dream of success through hard work in over 100 novels based on the idea that virtue is always rewarded. By leading an exemplary life entailing a valiant struggle with poverty and temptation, Alger's heroes all come to wealth and honor. His popular works, with titles like *Bound to Rise* and *Only an Irish Boy*, left a strong mark upon the character of a generation of American youth.

Public Good v. Private Gain

The principle of **laissez-faire** held that the way to obtain the greatest and cheapest productivity was to leave the individual employer and the individual worker to the free market. Those who favored the laissez-faire doctrine believed that interference by unions or government would upset the market and reduce total production. This would have a negative effect on workers, employers, and consumers. After 1870 the doctrine of laissez-faire received additional support from the principle of **Social Darwinism**, the belief that social progress depended upon competition among human beings resulting in the "survival of the fittest." Social Darwinism coexisted with the belief that individuals should be free to manage their property and should not be prevented from entering contracts of their own choosing, workers and employers alike.

The industrial age and the growth of business combinations brought many problems to American life, and concern developed over the abuses of industrialism. As Americans saw the suffering of the poor in city slums, the deteriorating working conditions and failing health of America's workers, the monopolistic practices of major businesses, the lack of consumer protection, the exploitation of the nation's resources, and the widening gap in the distribution of the nation's wealth, many realized that some government regulation was necessary. The **Progressive Movement** in the early 1900s was the culmination of a series of responses to the worst abuses of the new industrial age.

Exercise Set 2.7

1. Major industrial leaders contributed to economic growth during the last half of the 19th century by
   A. promoting further competition among businesses
   B. encouraging government to regulate unfair practices of the nation's businesses
   C. reinvesting profits in the expansion of business
   D. supporting the growth of labor organizations

2. John D. Rockefeller's most significant contribution to the growth of business enterprise in the United States was his
   A. support of labor unions and collective bargaining
   B. elimination of wasteful competitive practices
   C. introduction of assembly line techniques
   D. support of greater government intervention in business and an end to laissez-faire

3. Which of the following groups would have supported greater government intervention in business during the latter part of the 19th century?
   A. the robber barons
   B. supporters of laissez-faire and social Darwinism
   C. owners of the nation's major railroad lines
   D. the working classes

BUSINESS AND GOVERNMENT

> We accept and welcome . . . the concentration of business, industrial and commercial, in the hands of a few, and the law of competition between these as being not only beneficial, but essential for the future progress of the race.
>
> Andrew Carnegie, *The Gospel of Wealth* (1889)

Capitalism and Laissez-Faire

Capitalism

Capitalism can be defined as an economic system in which the means of production are privately owned, production and distribution of goods are determined in a free enterprise system by laws of supply and demand, and there is little government regulation of the economy. A characteristic of pure capitalism is the principle of **laissez-faire**.

Laissez-Faire

The economic policy known as laissez-faire can be traced to **Adam Smith**, whose *Wealth of Nations,* advocating free international trade, was published in 1776. The concept of laissez-faire was emphasized by Alexander Hamilton in 1791, when he claimed that "it can hardly ever be wise in a government to attempt to give a direction to the industry of its citizens . . . . To leave industry to itself, therefore, is, in almost every case, the soundest as well as the simplest policy." Thomas Jefferson, in his first message to Congress in 1801 reinforced the same doctrine, stating that "agriculture, manufactures, commerce, and navigation, the four pillars of our prosperity, are the most thriving when left free to individual enterprise."

• *Principles of Laissez-Faire.* By the middle of the 1800s three characteristics of laissez-faire were obvious in the American economy: (1) **Labor should find its price on the market.** In other words, an individual's wages were dependent on the price he or she could demand in the market. (2) **The value of money should be subject to an automatic mechanism.** There should be a uniform standard for currency among trading nations, such as the gold standard, that would stabilize currency among nations and allow greater ease of trade. (3) **Goods should be free to flow from country to country without restrictions.** Protectionist policies such as tariffs would only hurt trade among nations.

• *Movement away from Laissez-Faire.* Beginning in the latter part of the 1800s and continuing through the 1900s, the economic system in the United States moved away from the laissez-faire doctrine. Labor, represented by labor unions and protected by federal and state legislation, could no longer be considered simply a commodity; the country was no longer on a gold standard (ended in 1933), industry was subsidized, and international trade was not free from protective barriers. Today we have a system known as a **mixed economy**. Under this system, the government exercises some control over the nation's business, monetary system, and labor, while at the same time it allows the economy to regulate itself to a considerable extent.

The Supreme Court, Fourteenth Amendment, and Corporations

During the 1880s the Supreme Court began to change its direction concerning involvement in the economic matters within the states. As the social and political pressures of an emerging industrial nation increased, the Court demonstrated a greater willingness to exercise judicial review against state and federal regulation of industry. More specifically, it gave a new economic interpretation to the due process clause of the Fourteenth Amendment.

In the earlier cases testing the application of the due process clause of the Fourteenth Amendment to economic rights, the Supreme Court, demonstrating judicial restraint, upheld state regulations *(Slaughterhouse Cases,* 1873; *Mann* v. *Illinois* 1877; *Granger Cases,* 1877). The Court had accepted the idea in 1886 that the corporation was a person in the sense of the Fourteenth Amendment *(Santa Clara County* v. *Southern Pacific Railway* 1886). But it was the case of *Chicago, Milwaukee & St. Paul Railway Co.* v. *Minnesota* (1890) that marked the first time the Court declared a state law to be in violation of the due process clause of the Fourteenth Amendment, marking greater judicial protection of corporations.

Competition and Absorption: Mergers and Trusts

As competition among businesses during the second half of the 19th century cut prices and profits, business people sought ways to avoid price wars and increase profits. Combinations in business usually took two forms. Some were organized in a **horizontal fashion** so that an organization under one management controlled different producers of the same product. Others were organized in a **vertical fashion** so that an organization under one management controlled the different steps in the production of one commodity. An example of a vertical combination was the Ford Motor Company, which owned mines, shipping lines, railroads, and other businesses necessary for the production of the automobile. A number of business combinations resulted.

Pools

Agreements among business rivals sometimes managed to fix prices or divide profits and markets. During the 1870s and 1880s railroads made use of pooling agreements to fix prices. The pooling agreement lacked any legal way to guarantee its enforcement.

Trusts

A trust was a more formal and permanent agreement than the pooling arrangement. Stockholders of competing companies would turn their stocks and voting rights over to a central board of trustees who controlled the member companies to eliminate competition. The result of the trust agreement was a monopoly, or near total control, of an industry. **John D. Rockefeller**, in an attempt to reduce competition in the oil industry, was the first to employ the trust arrangement with the formation of the **Standard Oil Company**.

Holding Company

In their efforts to avoid combinations and mergers that had been declared illegal, businesspeople turned to the holding company. This arrangement included a central "holding company," which bought a sufficient number of voting stocks in different companies, resulting in the ability to control the "subsidiaries."

Interlocking Directorates

An arrangement in which the same individuals sit on the boards of directors of several companies; this serves many of the same purposes as a holding company.

Merger

A merger joins two or more companies, resulting in a single corporation. When a merger threatens to monopolize a particular industry, the courts may declare it illegal and a restraint on trade.

During the final decades of the 1800s, mergers and consolidations took place in many industries, including sugar, steel, machinery, tobacco, and copper. As combinations began to have an adverse effect on American society, however, the federal government began to consider intervention, moving away from its former laissez-faire policies.

Railroad Abuses and Government Regulation

Practices of the Railroads

The demand for government regulation of business first came from American farmers. Shortly after the Civil War, agricultural profits fell; some causes were overproduction, greater crop production in other nations, and high prices charged by middlemen. Farmers' grievances were directed against operators of grain elevators, manufacturers of farm machinery, bankers, and primarily, the railroads.

Complaints about the railroads included accusation of monopolistic practices. Railroads were absolutely necessary to the nation's farmers to transport their crops. However, in most farming areas there was only one railroad line. Because of the lack of competition, the railroad was able to charge "all that the traffic would bear" on the "**short haul**." For example, because of high freight rates, Pittsburgh, a large city served by only one railroad, paid 60 percent more for grain from Chicago than did New York, which was twice as far away. Railroads claimed that this was necessary to make up for the low rates charged on busier routes, or the "**long hauls**," because of fierce competition among the railroads.

Other unfair railroad practices included granting **rebates** to large shippers, giving free passes to politicians, bribing members of state legislatures, and entering into pooling agreements to control rates. During the 1870s and 1880s, demands for government regulation of the railroads came from farmers, small shippers, retailers, and reform politicians.

State Regulation

Regulation started at the state level with reform groups winning political control over state legislatures and passing legislation to control abuses. The **National Grange of the Patrons of Husbandry**, organized by **Oliver H. Kelley**, numbered 1,500,000 by 1874 and dominated the legislatures of Illinois, Wisconsin, Iowa, and Minnesota. Methods of control initiated by the Granger programs were rate regulation legislation, **cooperative buying** of farm supplies and machinery, and pressure for federal legislation.

State legislation was dealt a blow when the Supreme Court ruled in *Wabash, St. Louis and Pacific Railway* v. *Illinois* (1886) that states had no power to fix rates on shipments passing beyond their borders. **Interstate commerce** is under congressional control.

Federal Regulation

- *Interstate Commerce Act.* Congress responded in 1887 by passing the Interstate Commerce Act and establishing the **Interstate Commerce Commission**, which had the power to (1) require that railroads post their rates publicly; (2) require rates to be "reasonable and just"; (3) forbid practices such as pooling, rebates, and rate discrimination; (4) prohibit higher charges for short hauls than for longer hauls over the same line; and (5) investigate complaints against railroads and hand down rulings that could be enforced in courts.

- **Munn** *v.* **Illinois** *(1877).* The *Munn* case was one of the several so-called **Granger cases** that dealt with state regulation of railroads and grain warehouses. The Supreme Court, by allowing the Illinois statute fixing maximum charges for the storage of grain (grain that found its way into **interstate commerce** and was therefore under the control of Congress), held that "when one devotes his property to a use in which the public has an interest, he, in effect, grants to the public an interest in that use, and must submit to be controlled by the public for the common good."

In the opinion written by Chief Justice Waite, he referred back to the Massachusetts constitution and the idea of covenant and the body politic, stating that the establishment of laws requiring each citizen to . . . "so use his own property as not unnecessarily to injure another was a valid exercise of state police power."

- *Sherman Antitrust Act (1890).* In response to increasing pressure to halt the domination of the market by a small number of powerful corporations, Congress passed the Sherman Antitrust Act in 1890. The provisions of the Act included (1) that every contract, combination, or conspiracy in **restraint of trade** among the states or with foreign countries was illegal; and (2) that persons guilty of monopolizing trade or commerce were subject to fines and/or imprisonment.

The weaknesses of the Sherman Act soon became apparent. Although trusts were prohibited, holding companies soon started to replace them and were able to avoid the reaches of the law. The federal courts were hesitant to enforce the Act and continued to define the word "trade" narrowly. The Supreme Court made the law almost meaningless in the *United States* v. *Knight Company* (1895) case when it held that the sugar refining industry did not involve interstate commerce and therefore the Sherman Act did not apply to an almost complete monopoly that the American Sugar Refining Company had over the sugar industry. After the *Knight* case, few attempts were made to prosecute corporations in "restraint of trade." Only eighteen suits were brought between 1890 and 1900, some of which were against labor unions as "unreasonable restraints on trade."

Public Opinion

As the end of the century approached, more and more Americans were becoming concerned about the effects of large business combinations. This new social concern led to a mass of progressive social legislation in the 1900s.

Exercise Set 2.8

1. Of the following, the most important cause of agrarian discontent in the United States during the latter part of the 19th century was
   A. the belief that railroads and middlemen were exploiting the farmers
   B. the growth of population in the Eastern states
   C. the rise in prices of agricultural produce
   D. greater government control over public utilities

2. A major problem for businesses entering into a pooling agreement was
   A. falling profits
   B. lawsuits filed against members of pools who went against the agreement
   C. lack of a legal way to enforce the pooling agreement
   D. consumers turning to a company that did not participate in the pooling arrangement

3. Large business combinations of the late 1800s presented a threat to
   A. the currency system
   B. free enterprise
   C. the transportation system
   D. representative democracy

4. A present-day example of laissez-faire economics would be
   A. deregulation of the airline industry
   B. minimum wage laws
   C. farm subsidies
   D. breakup of American Telephone and Telegraph

LABOR ORGANIZATION AND STRUGGLE

> To protect the workers in their inalienable rights to a higher and better life; to protect them, not only as equals before the law, but also in their health, their homes, their firesides, their liberties as men, as workers, and as citizens . . . to this workers are entitled . . . The attainment of these is the glorious mission of the trade unions.
>
> Samuel Gompers, Speech (1898)

> Let us not destroy those wonderful machines that produce efficiently and cheaply. Let us control them. Let us profit by their efficiency and cheapness. Let us run them for ourselves. That, gentlemen, is socialisms . . . .
>
> Jack London, *The Iron Heel* (1906)

National Labor Unions

Organized labor in America can trace its roots to 1792 when the journeymen **cordwainers** (shoemakers) of Philadelphia organized a local union. Its successor, the Federal Society of Journeyman Cordwainers, operated until 1806 when, after a strike for better wages, the union was found guilty of conspiracy in a court of law. Although the strike and subsequent decision of the courts ended the small union, it marked the beginning of decades of struggle for the **bargaining power** of workers in the workplace.

Following the Cordwainers cases, confusion existed concerning the status of labor organizations. Although the courts recognized the right of labor to organize, they ruled that any "coercive action that harmed other businesses" was unlawful. In other words, strikes were against the law. In the case of *Commonwealth* v. *Hunt* (1842), the Massachusetts high court held that labor unions had a right to combine and strike "in such manner as best to subserve their own interests."

The modern labor movement is essentially a product of the Industrial Revolution. The development of the factory system made it impossible for individual workers to bargain on equal terms with a powerful employer. Only by organizing and presenting their demands as a group were the workers able to secure higher wages, shorter working days, improved working conditions, and protection against being discharged without just cause.

National Labor Union

Formed in 1866 under the leadership of **William Sylvis**, the National Labor Union helped to push legislation through Congress for an **8-hour workday** for laborers and mechanics employed by the federal government.

The Knights of Labor

Founded in 1869 by **Uriah S. Stephens**, the Knights of Labor started as a secret organization whose aim was to unite skilled and unskilled workers into one great national union. They advocated higher wages, 8-hour working days, equal pay for equal work by men and women, abolition of child labor (under 14 years), arbitration of labor disputes, prohibition of foreign contract labor, safety and health laws, workers' cooperative associations, a graduated income tax, and government ownership of railroads and other public utilities. Under the leadership of **Terence V. Powderly**, the Knights of Labor gained influence, and membership reached 700,000 by 1886. The union declined rapidly after 1886 for several reasons, including the failure of a strike against the Texas and Pacific Railroad and the blame attached to the Knights for the bombing at the **Haymarket Riot** in Chicago.

The American Federation of Labor

Samuel Gompers (1850–1924) founded the AFL in 1881.

Founded in 1881 by **Samuel Gompers**, the AFL was organized as a federation of many separate skilled craft unions rather than a general organization of workers. Each member craft union enjoyed a degree of autonomy in matters affecting its own trade. The goals of the AFL stressed "bread and butter" issues: higher wages, an 8-hour workday, improved working conditions, use of union-made products, and passage of state and federal legislation to benefit labor. The methods used by the AFL to obtain its goals included the **strike** (a work stoppage until goals are met) and the **boycott** (the practice of not purchasing the product of the employer). By 1900 the AFL claimed 500,000 members and eventually was successful in winning the **closed shop** (plants hiring only union workers) and the abolition of **yellow-dog contracts** (requirement by the employer that a newly hired employee sign an agreement not to join a labor union). Yet, as a union of skilled workers, the AFL excluded 90 percent of the American workers who did not have a craft or the skills to qualify for membership in one of its affiliated unions.

International Ladies Garment Workers Union

Of the 8 million female workers in 1910, only 125,000 were members of unions, primarily because most unions refused to accept women as members. A strike by thousands of women shirtwaist workers in New York in 1909 laid the foundation for the **International Ladies Garment Workers Union**. The ILGWU was instrumental in bringing relief to the families of the victims of the

Triangle Shirtwaist Factory fire in New York City in 1911. This tragedy claimed the lives of 146 workers and subsequently brought about a modern factory inspection system and laws to regulate the labor of women and children.

Attitudes of Labor Unions

For the most part, early labor unions opposed unrestricted immigration, because immigrants usually provided a source of cheap labor. They also refused to accept women as members, fearing that women represented competition for jobs and were willing to accept lower wages. African Americans were not accepted as members because of racial prejudice. Although the American Federation of Labor at first accepted black workers, stating that it looked "with disfavor upon trade unions having provisions that excluded from membership persons on account of race and color," the union's officials began to yield to member unions and their prejudices. Unions, for the most part, supported free compulsory education in order to remove child labor from the work force and to provide opportunities for the next generation.

Struggle and Conflict

Between 1881 and 1900 there were over 24,000 strikes in the United States that involved nearly 128,000 establishments. Many tried to blame labor unrest on the infiltration of socialists and anarchists into the work forces. However, the unrest among the American workers who faced great inequities in the late 1800s was typical of the activist undercurrent that flowed throughout American history.

Major Strikes

• *Railroad Strike of 1877.* Protesting wage cuts, railroad workers called a strike and attempted to stop the railroads from running. Federal troops were called in to settle riots in Pennsylvania, Maryland, West Virginia, and Illinois. Some $5,000,000 worth of property was destroyed before the strike was broken and the railroad workers eventually returned at the lower wages set by the railroads.

• *Haymarket Riot (1886).* Following a nationwide strike for an 8-hour day by the **Knights of Labor**, trouble broke out in Chicago as sympathetic **anarchists** addressed a protest meeting held by the strikers. After police entered the crowd to break up the meeting, a bomb was thrown, killing seven police and wounding sixty more. Because of this incident, the Knights of Labor became identified with anarchism and violence, and this led to the union's decline. It also helped to turn American public opinion against labor unions.

• *Homestead Strike (1892).* When the **Carnegie Steel Company** threatened to cut wages and crush the **Amalgamated Association of Iron** and **Steel Workers** in 1892, workers picketed the plant. Management called in Pinkerton guards to protect the plant, but they were attacked by the strikers and run out of town. An appeal to the governor of Pennsylvania brought in the militia. Although the workers struck for nine months, public opinion eventually turned against them and they went back to work, agreeing to the company's terms. The strike crushed the Amalgamated Union and left the steel industry unorganized for 40 years.

• *Pullman Strike (1894).* Workers at the **Pullman Palace Car Company** struck in protest over policies at the company town near Chicago and cuts in wages. The strike spread, bringing railroad traffic west of Chicago to a standstill when the **American Railway Union**, under the leadership of **Eugene V. Debs**, aided the strikers by calling a boycott in which union members refused to work on any train with a Pullman car. The railroads appealed to the federal government for protection. President **Cleveland** sent troops to Chicago to "protect the mails," but more probably to crush the strike. The federal government obtained a court **injunction** (order) that forbade the union to strike. Within a month the strike was ended, and Debs was imprisoned for failing to abide by the court injunction to end the strike. The Supreme Court upheld the conviction of Debs in the case of *In Re Debs*

Eugene Debs (1855–1926) led the American Railway Union in the strike against the Pullman Company.

(1895) on the grounds that an injunction was valid under the federal government's power to remove obstacles to **interstate commerce** as provided by the Sherman Antitrust Act. The injunction became a powerful weapon of employers to combat strikes.

• *Lawrence Textile Strike (1912).* Unskilled industrial workers ignored by the American Federation of Labor were organized by the **Industrial Workers of the World** (or **Wobblies**) formed in 1905 under the leadership of **"Big Bill" Haywood**. They advocated militant agitation, willful obstruction of industry, and damage to businesses. Although the IWW gained few victories, national attention was focused on the union in 1912 when 30,000 textile workers in Lawrence, Massachusetts, struck for better working conditions and higher wages. The **American Woolen Company** met nearly all of the union's demands. After America's entry into World War I, the federal government prosecuted various IWW leaders for their attempt to obstruct the draft.

Management's Position

Management (owners and managers of means of production) has been at odds with labor throughout modern industrial history. Management's position has usually included (1) conducting production and operations with as little interference from labor unions as possible; (2) increasing productivity and profits through efficiency and laborsaving techniques; (3) being free to increase and decrease work forces according to need; and (4) maintaining an **open shop** (the choice of the employer to hire both union and nonunion labor) as opposed to a **closed shop** (the employment of only union workers).

Tactics Employed in Disputes by Management and Labor

A strike by workers is usually the final means of attempting to gain demands and often hurts both labor and management. Very few disputes end in strikes because of the following techniques:

- *Collective Bargaining.* Representatives of management and labor meet, discuss issues and differences, and settle on a contract acceptable to both sides.

- *Mediation.* The **Federal Mediation and Conciliation Service** offers the services of mediators, or neutral third parties, who sit in on the negotiations between management and labor, offer suggestions of concessions to both sides, and encourage the two sides to reach an agreeable contract. The mediator's decision is not binding.

- *Arbitration.* Both management and labor agree to a neutral third party. That person hears the dispute and hands down a decision that will be accepted by both sides according to an agreement beforehand. In other words, the arbitrator's decision is binding.

- *Fact-Finding Board.* When a strike affects the welfare of the nation, the President may appoint a board to hear the dispute and hand down a decision.

Weapons Used by Labor and Management

When collective bargaining is not successful in settling labor-management disputes, more drastic means may be used:

- *Labor.* Workers may resort to a **strike**, **picketing** (demonstration by workers usually outside of the workplace), a **boycott**, and **publicity** to conince the public of the legitimacy of their demands and to seek support.

- *Management.* Employers may use **strikebreakers** (sometimes referred to as **scabs**), **lockouts**, in which the employer keeps the workers from their jobs until they accept management's terms, **injunctions** (court orders that say workers must return to work), and **publicity**, or appeal to the public for support.

Attitude and Role of Government

Beginning in the late 1900s government has played a crucial role in affecting the balance between labor and management. Examples of government intervention include:

- *Sherman Antitrust Act (1890).* This was used to restrain activities of unions, finding them to cause "unreasonable restraint of trade."

- *Clayton Antitrust Act (1914).* This act reversed some of the interpretations used under the Sherman Act and declared that legitimate union activities were not subject to antitrust laws. The Clayton Act also restricted the use of injunctions against unions in labor disputes.

- *Norris-LaGuardia Act (1932).* Federal courts were prohibited by this act from granting injunctions against workers who engaged in strikes, boycotts, or peaceful picketing. The Norris-LaGuardia Act also made unenforceable **yellow-dog contracts** (contracts that prevented a worker from joining a union after being employed).

Socialism, Communism, Anarchism

Marxist socialists in America at the end of the 19th century were primarily Germans who brought their political and economic theories with them from Europe. The **Marxist Workingmen's party** and the **Social Democratic party** attracted some support during the 1870s. In the early 1880s the **socialists** split into two groups: those who rejected capitalism and those who rejected both capitalism and organized government. The latter group was known as **anarchists**.

In 1900 the **Socialist party of America**, with **Eugene V. Debs** as its presidential candidate, won about 100,000 votes. In the next decade, after the arrival of many eastern Europeans and continued political interest among American workers, membership in the Socialist party grew. In 1912 its growth peaked and Debs received nearly one million votes as the Socialist presidential candidate. However, unlike labor in many European countries, American labor never established a major political party in the United States. Instead, it used its influence to seek its goals within the **"two-party" system**.

"Radicalism" was not restricted to politics and labor movements. The Socialist party's commitment to democratic gradualism attracted many members of the clergy, writers, and others who believed reform was not possible under the two major parties. Writers in the early 20th century who spoke for socialism and criticized the capitalist system included some of the most notable American literary figures, such as Upton Sinclair, Jack London, Theodore Dreiser, and Frank Norris.

Middle-Class Labor Support

Not all advocates of better working conditions and higher wages came from the "radical fringe" of politics and the labor movement. The **Women's Trade Union League** combined the forces of the wealthy elite with reformers, like **Jane Addams**, to aid working women in their efforts to organize. The

Consumers' Union was a "watchdog" organization formed to promote the purchase of only those goods produced in factories with approved working conditions.

Exercise Set 2.9

1. While the Knights of Labor included both skilled and unskilled workers, the American Federation of Labor consisted of
   A. only industrial workers
   B. the fringe element of radical labor
   C. craft unions of skilled workers
   D. primarily immigrant labor

2. An important reason for the growth of labor unions in the second half of the 19th century was
   A. the passage of the Clayton Antitrust Act
   B. a decrease in immigration to the United States
   C. the growth of a socialist movement in the United States
   D. the indifference of business to the welfare of employees

3. The primary reason for support of free compulsory public education by labor unions was to
   A. decrease the number of children in the work force
   B. educate youth for eventual union leadership
   C. provide day care for the children of union members
   D. train youth in different industrial skills

4. A powerful weapon used by employers to end strikes was
   A. the closed shop
   B. the injunction
   C. picketing
   D. the use of a mediator

CHAPTER REVIEW QUESTIONS

1. Which is a fundamental idea of laissez-faire capitalism?
   A. workers should own the means of production
   B. employers should provide social benefits for all workers
   C. government should control output and wages
   D. businesses should gain and lose according to their own efforts

2. In the United States, economic opportunities for women expanded during the last quarter of the 19th century primarily because of the growth of
   A. opportunities to buy farms in the West
   B. industry and technology
   C. big-city political machines
   D. organized labor

3. In which way did the joint-stock company help lay the foundation for the modern corporation?
   A. the major reason for forming a company was to produce industrial goods on a large scale
   B. the company made low-risk investments and thus could gurantee a profit
   C. the government sponsored and controlled the company
   D. the company was owned by more than one individual, each of whom received a share of any profits

4. Urbanization
   A. slowed the industrialization of the United States
   B. occurred primarily along the West Coast of the United States
   C. and industrialization stimulated one another
   D. would have progressed faster if industrialization had grown at a slower pace

5. In most of the major labor disputes that took place before 1900, the federal government
   A. supported organized labor
   B. maintained a completely laissez-faire attitude
   C. supported management
   D. claimed that strikes did not affect interstate trade and therefore did not become involved

6. Which was a major obstacle to the formation of labor unions in the United States during the period 1860–1900?
   A. prohibition of labor organizations by the Constitution
   B. general government support of management
   C. excellent working conditions in United States factories of the time
   D. status of factory workers as equal partners with management

7. A major reason for the passage of the Sherman Antitrust Act in 1890 was to
   A. encourage competition in business
   B. protect the rights and safety of workers
   C. promote free trade among nations
   D. raise protective tariffs in the United States

8. Methods used by management to combat the activities of unions included all of the following EXCEPT
   A. the lockout
   B. blacklisting
   C. the closed shop
   D. the injunction

9. An event that hurt unions and caused many Americans to associate labor with anarchism and socialism was the
   A. Triangle Shirtwaist fire
   B. candidacy of Eugene V. Debs for President in 1912
   C. formation of the National Women's Trade Union
   D. Haymarket Square incident

10. During the 20th century, labor unions in the United States were most strengthened by legislation that guaranteed workers
    A. the right to boycott
    B. the right to bargain collectively
    C. adequate retirement pensions
    D. a share of company profits

ESSAYS

1. Many aspects of United States society have been greatly affected by technological changes.

    Choose *three* of the aspects of United States society listed below. Explain how *each* one chosen has been affected by a specific technological development. (Use a different development for each aspect.) [5,5,5]
    Aspects of United States Society
    Urbanization
    Industrialization
    Agriculture
    Politics
    Environment
    Rights of the individual

    Regents Exam, June 1988

2. The position or status of workers in the United States has been influenced by a wide variety of factors.
    Factors
    Immigration
    Labor Unions
    Government Action
    Technology

Choose *three* factors from the list above. For *each* one chosen, show how that factor has influenced the economic and/or social and/or political position of workers in the United States. Use specific information to support your discussion of each factor. [5,5,5]

Regents Exam, January 1983

3. The concept of due process helps to guarantee that all "persons" receive justice before the law.
   a. Using the Supreme Court cases of *Santa Clara County* v. *Southern Pacific Railway* (1886) and *Chicago, Milwaukee & St. Paul Railway Co.* v. *Minnesota* (1890), show how the Supreme Court furthered the concept of due process in the legal system of the United States. [5,5]
   b. Discuss the impact of the two cases mentioned in part a. (*Santa Clara* and *Chicago, Milwaukee & St. Paul Railway*) have had on corporations and their development. [5]

Chapter 3

TRANSFORMATION OF AMERICAN SOCIETY

IMPACT OF INDUSTRIALISM

Urbanization and the Quality of Urban Life

Between the Civil War and 1910, the urban population increased dramatically. In addition to the general increase in the number of people living in cities—from about 6.2 million to 42 million—during the period from 1860–1910, there was also an extraordinary expansion in the size of large cities such as New York, Philadelphia, and Chicago.

Part of World Phenomenon

American cities soon rivaled the great European cities in size and population. By 1887 the United States had more large cities than any European country except Great Britain and Germany. The trend toward urbanization was a worldwide phenomenon, as the major cities of Europe also grew quickly in this period. This was a result of industrialization and the transfer of rural population to the city.

Attractions of the City

People moved to the cities because they offered opportunity. In the urban centers there were jobs in offices and factories, employment for both the skilled and the unskilled. American cities became marketplaces for people, resources, and ideas and centers of transportation, communication, and capital.

Cities also became centers of educational and cultural institutions. To reflect the needs of the industrial society, educational programs included "practical" subjects such as industrial arts, business, typing, home economics, and bookkeeping. In some instances, business leaders accepted the responsibility for using their wealth and resources to improve urban communities. During his lifetime, **Andrew Carnegie** gave $60 million to help cities establish free public libraries. Wealthy leaders of industry, including **John D. Rockefeller**, **Matthew Vassar**, and **Cornelius Vanderbilt**, founded or endowed colleges and universities. Others, including **Andrew Mellon** and **J.P. Morgan**, built extensive art collections, which were eventually opened to the public.

Problems of the Cities

As the American city grew, so did its problems, especially widespread poverty among city residents. Fast-spreading **slums** housed masses of low-income workers. In 1893 there were 702 people per acre in New York's Lower East Side. Poor workers lived in tenements and small apartments that lacked adequate space, safety, or sanitation.

Inadequate **sanitation** and the spread of disease became a by-product of rapid urban growth. By the 1870s few American cities had installed underground sewers, relying instead on cesspools. Cities including Baltimore, New Orleans, and Mobile allowed sewage to run through open gutters. The first sewer lines in Manhattan built of brick (some still in use today) were installed in the 1830s. Aqueducts carrying water to New York City were built in the 1840s and, during World War I, tunnels were constructed from reservoirs in the Catskill Mountains. Port cities dumped garbage into the sea with little awareness of **environmental** concerns.

Crime, though not exclusively an urban affliction, flourished in the slums of urban areas with their poverty and overcrowding. The fifty percent increase in the prison population between 1880 and 1890 reflected the fact that crime had become a way of life in American cities. In addition to crime generated by large concentrations of wealth existing next to extreme poverty, the cities were also centers of tension due to the mixing of races and nationalities. Police forces were still at an infant stage and in some cases easily corrupted by various interest groups.

City Architecture

Housing was a pressing problem in most rapidly growing urban centers. Many cities relied on row houses of brick that were two and three stories high and usually of adequate quality. Less desirable housing structures often typical of slum areas were the walkup tenements with narrow air shafts that often became receptacles for garbage. With the lack of adequate transportation, workers were forced to live near their jobs no matter how poor and congested the buildings were. The growth of tenements and the terrible sanitary conditions that caused outbreaks of disease eventually forced the passage of **Tenement House laws**.

The growth of structures in the downtown areas of the city was extraordinary. The concentration of business and professional offices along with the inflation of real estate value made tall buildings inevitable. The development of wrought iron, then steel, and finally the discovery that walls themselves could be supported on steel columns embedded in them allowed **skyscrapers** to grow in height. Finally, the development of the **elevator** allowed architects to overcome the problem of access to higher levels of the building.

Social Darwinism

The publication of *The Origin of Species* in 1859 by the Englishman **Charles Darwin** marked a major step in the **theory of evolution**. It proposed that many more individuals of each species are born than can possibly survive. As a consequence, there is a constant struggle for existence, and only the fittest survive. Darwin's theories were applied to American business by his friend, English philosopher **Herbert Spencer** in *Social Statics* (1865). He claimed that "**survival of the fittest**" applied to the "dog-eat-dog" competition of the American industrial age and that a policy of laissez-faire should keep government out of areas such as conditions of labor, public education, and welfare legislation. Spencer's thoughts became known as "**Social Darwinism**" and were preached in the United States by Yale professor **William Graham Sumner**. Social Darwinism affected American political thought by delaying legislation that required factory inspection, the limitation of work hours, and other protective measures.

- *Unequal Distribution of Wealth.* Along with industrial expansion and the growth of American cities came a growing gap between the rich and the poor. As the national wealth increased from $16 billion to $65 billion between 1860 and 1890, the distribution of wealth grew more uneven, with fewer Americans controlling more of the nation's wealth. By 1890 only 9 percent of the population owned 71 percent of the nation's money and 88 percent owned only fourteen percent. Yet those who advocated Social Darwinism held that the capable would rise to the top and that eventually the wealth would seep down to the masses in the form of greater employment opportunities.

- *Philanthropy.* The philanthropic activities of the wealthy were consistent with Social Darwinism. Adhering to the laissez-faire beliefs that government should not pass welfare legislation, some of the wealthy believed they had a social responsibility to assist those who were less fortunate.

- *Calls for Reform.* With the unequal balance of wealth and power, it seemed that the rich were growing richer and the poor, poorer. As the growing poverty of America's workers became increasingly apparent, many called for public and private relief that was not forthcoming. Movements for reform were spurred by the humanitarian concerns reflected in literature (*How the Other Half Lives,* Jacob Riis, 1890, *The Bitter Cry of Children,* John Spargo, 1906, *Progress and Poverty,* Henry George, 1879). Early efforts to help included the **Society for the Prevention of Cruelty to Children** (1874), settlement houses such as **Hull House** in Chicago, founded in 1889 by Jane Addams to offer social services, and the establishment of religious institutions such as the **Young Men's Christian Association** (1851), the **Salvation Army** (1879), and city missions.

Work and Workers

Peopling the Cities

Prior to 1870 relatively few Americans were wage earners. The United States was still primarily an agricultural nation, with most Americans owning farms. By 1900, as a result of the Industrial Revolution, the transfer of America's population to the cities and the growing employment in factories, about two thirds of the working population were selling their labor to employers for a daily or weekly wage.

The flow of workers to the cities came from two sources; first, the movement of large numbers of native-born Americans from the rural areas and second, the thousands of immigrants from Europe who settled in the cities where they found employment opportunities. The growth of American industry and the absence of restrictions on immigration drew a steady stream of immigrants, which reached its peak in 1907 when 1,285,000 immigrant entries were recorded. Quick to take advantage of the increased immigration were city **political machines** and **bosses** who helped immigrants become naturalized quickly. They also provided employment, social services, and housing in exchange for political support.

Working Conditions

Gone were the days when workers and employers maintained an intimate and caring relationship. The impersonal relationship between labor and management was a direct result of the urban factory system and led to deteriorating conditions for the average wage earner. Long hours, low wages, child labor, and dangerous working conditions were common during the 19th century when **collective bargaining** was nearly nonexistent and **unions** were looked upon as conspiracies. As the pool of workers increased with the flow of native-born Americans and immigrants to the cities, the plight of workers grew worse. Although the Thirteenth Amendment (1865) had ended "slavery and involuntary servitude except as punishment for a crime," the employees of the factory system were becoming "wage slaves" of industrial America.

A related problem was that of **child labor**. By 1870 many of the nation's industrial workers were children, under the age of twelve. Working in the factories brought problems for children including lack of education, emotional disruption, family breakdown, and physical abuse. Working from "dark to dark," children toiled six days a week earning little for 12- to 13-hour shifts.

The Working-Class Family

Industrialization also brought changes in the American family. The participation of family members in outside institutions, including schools, political organizations, social clubs, and places of employment replaced some of the companionship that had existed in the rural household. As mother and father each became wage earners, usually out of economic necessity, broken families were sometimes the result. Increasing numbers of women entering the work force lessened parental control over children. At the turn of the century, the majority of American households consisted of the **nuclear family**—a married couple with or without children, living with no other relatives. About 15 to 20 percent of households were made up of **extended families**—households with grandparents, grandchildren, aunts, uncles, cousins, or in-laws.

Ethnic and Racial Impact on Workers

American labor was affected by society's feelings concerning race and ethnic differences. Few labor leaders welcomed blacks into labor unions, the **Industrial Workers of the World** being the exception. Immigration, both early (consisting mostly of northern Europeans), and later (made up primarily of eastern and southern Europeans), provided labor competition that kept wages low and hampered unions' attempts to organize.

Women and the Industrial Age

With the new Industrial Age, the Victorian ideal of women as the pampered and weaker sex quickly disappeared in American society. In early colonial America, women worked as hard as their husbands to build families and homesteads on the frontier. Success in colonial life required a partnership between the sexes. Although life was hard and women did not have equal political rights, they had more equality with men during these times because of the common goal of survival. As conditions became more settled and life easier, women lost their equal status. By the early 1800s most women stayed home to tend to household chores and to raise the family, "protected" from the demands of education, politics, and business.

From Home to Factory

With the arrival of new inventions in the early part of the 19th century, some women began to work away from the home. **Textile mills** in New England provided the earliest industrial opportunities for women to enter the work force. Yet, factory work proved to be a mixed blessing, since women were often exploited and usually hired at wages far below those paid to men doing similar work. Throughout the 19th century the supply of women looking for work increased with the arrival of immigrants from Europe. Employers who had little trouble finding replacements for those women dissatisfied with pay and working conditions were able to impose wage cuts and work speedups. In 1870 women who worked in mills earned $5 to $6 for a 60-hour week, while those who did sewing piecework at home received about 6 cents per shirt and earned little more than $3 per week.

Technology and Women

In the late 1800s, business expansion and new inventions, including the typewriter and telephone, brought about an increasing need for office workers with special skills. Since these jobs were usually filled by women, education became more important; by 1890 twice as many young women were finishing high school as young men.

A profession that welcomed women throughout the 1800s was **teaching**. By the 1890s there were twice as many women teaching as men. Women teachers in city schools earned about $13 a week, while men teachers received two to three times that amount. Although women teachers worked shorter hours and had better working conditions than factory workers, they were expected to play the teacher's role at all times, being pious, socially discreet, and impeccable in conduct.

Religion in a Diversified Society

As poverty, urban overcrowding, and social disorder increased during this age of government laissez-faire, religious groups joined social reformers in attempting to ease society's problems. Emphasizing social responsibility as a means to salvation and service to fellow human beings as a Christian duty, religious reformers built churches in slum neighborhoods, provided community services, and joined drives to make businesses socially responsible.

The Growing Middle Class

Industrialism helped to create a growing middle class consisting of salaried workers, professionals, salespeople, government workers, and the like. A transformation was taking place in the lives of many Americans, in their homes, work, and leisure time.

Standards of Cultural Values

The buying power of the growing middle class fueled further industrial growth. Goods that had once been available only to a few were becoming available to many. American inventiveness, combined with technology, mass production, and mass marketing, provided goods such as ready-made clothes and home appliances—necessities rather than the luxury they had once been.

Middle-Class Materialism and Morality

As luxuries were being transformed into commonplace articles of everyday life, the difference between those who could afford such goods and services and those who could not became accentuated. As the turn of the century approached, incomes continued to rise. For example, the average yearly pay of a clerical worker rose from $848 a year in 1890 to $1,156 a year in 1910. But as wages increased, the cost of living also rose. For most ordinary workers, it was becoming harder to pay for even the necessities. As the concerns of the working class, middle class, and farmers—the group often referred to as the "common man," "taxpayer," or "man on the street,"—began to coincide, they joined to support the Progressive Movement that began in the 1900s.

Leisure Activities

Along with industrialism and the development of laborsaving devices in the factory and at home came a greater amount of leisure time for some Americans. The average work week for manufacturing workers decreased from 66 hours per week in 1860 to 51 hours per week in 1920. The most popular leisure activities were sports. By 1860 there were at least 50 baseball clubs in the country; football became the most popular collegiate sport; and cycling, tennis, golf, and basketball were also enjoyed. Of course it was the wealthy, with more free time and money to spend on sporting activities, who were able to take the greatest advantage of America's leisure-time revolution.

As they worked fewer hours, Americans had more time for leisure activities.

Art and Literature

Although critics have characterized the post-Civil War era as the "Gilded Age," suggesting crassness and lack of taste in a materialistic society, progress in art and literature was noteworthy.

Literature

As the degree of literacy in America increased, book reading by all levels of society increased. The popular press was reflected in the **"dime novels"** (low-priced, paperbound adventure novels about the wild West), detective stories, and science fiction, which became favorites of America's young people. Leading dime novels included stories of The Lone Ranger, Old Cap Collins, and Tom Swift.

"Local-color" writers produced regional literature, which depicted the people and environment of a particular region of the country. **Bret Harte** wrote about the West *(The Outcasts of Poker Flat),* Mark Twain wrote of the South *(The Adventures of Tom Sawyer, The Adventures of Huckleberry Finn),* and Jack London wrote of the West and Northwest *(The Call of the Wild).*

Art

The **Society of American Artists** was formed in 1877 to organize and popularize a new trend in American art: the breaking away from the romanticized works of the earlier generation. Among the new school of American artists were **George Inness**, a leading landscapist, **Winslow Homer**, whose art was best demonstrated in his bold paintings of the sea, and **James A. McNeill Whistler**, painter of realistic portraits. The development of **photography** helped to free the early American painters from realism and led to impressionism and abstract art.

Music

American music reached its greatest stage of development later in the 20th century. The later 19th century saw the spread of musical appreciation with the formation of the **New York Symphony Orchestra** in 1878 and the **Boston Symphony Orchestra** in 1881. A major discovery in the area of music was the reproduction of music by mechanical means. By 1900 over 150,000 American homes had a **phonograph**, an invention of Thomas Edison.

Role of Philanthropists

Cynically described as those who "stole privately and gave publicly," the "**robber barons**," including **John Rockefeller** and **Andrew Carnegie**, gave considerable amounts of money for the development of cultural centers promoting art, music, and education.

Exercise Set 2.10

1. All of the following indicate the growing emancipation of women in the late 19th century EXCEPT
   A. the greater numbers of women in the working population
   B. the women's movements demanding rights including women's suffrage
   C. the growing divorce rate
   D. the membership of political organizations

2. The trend toward urbanization involved
   A. the growth of rural America due to the unsafe conditions of the city
   B. the movement of people from rural areas into the cities
   C. decrease in metropolitan population
   D. a decrease in immigration

3. Urban political bosses and machines in the latter part of the 19th century
   A. took advantage of the needs of newly arrived immigrants
   B. contributed nothing to their cities
   C. were closely regulated by civil service organizations
   D. had little influence in urban politics

4. The belief concerning poverty that was consistent with Social Darwinism was that
   A. the poor were weak individuals
   B. the federal government had the responsibility of assuring economic equality
   C. systems of public welfare and relief had to be implemented to ease the hardships of the poor
   D. the problems of the poor were the fault of the wealthy

NATION OF IMMIGRANTS

> All of our people all over the country—except the pure-blooded Indians—are immigrants, including even those who came over here on the Mayflower.
>
> Franklin Delano Roosevelt,
> November 4, 1944

The heterogeneous nature of the American population throughout our history has been due to the continual influx of various immigrant groups. The American pluralistic societyconsists of many subdivisions known as **ethnic groups**, identified by race, religion, places of origin, culture, and history.

Old Immigration (1609–1860)

Motivations

Early immigration to North America came primarily from northern and western Europe. Settlers from the British Isles included English, Irish, Scots, and Welsh. Among the settlers from continental Europe were the Germans, Dutch, Swiss, Swedes, and French.

During the period of "colonial immigration" (1609–1789) most settlers came to the American colonies for one or more of the following reasons: desire for land, political strife at home, religious persecution, or economic opportunities. In the latter part of the old immigration period (1780–1860), motivations for immigration included the availability of land as the United States expanded westward, jobs provided by the early stages of the Industrial Revolution, and opportunities for social mobility that did not exist in Europe. Problems in Europe also encouraged emigration. Political and religious unrest in Germany, France, Austria, Hungary, Ireland, and Denmark during the middle of the 1600s increased rates of emigration. Between 1789 and 1815 Europe was ravaged by the French Revolution and Napoleonic Wars, while in the 1830s revolutions spread through Poland, France, and Belgium. Between 1845 and 1849 Ireland experienced a devastating famine. The European population doubled between 1750 and 1850 and emigration restrictions were relaxed in a number of nations. Improved transportation facilitated the movement of those who wanted to emigrate. Moreover, portions of our diverse population were acquired through conquest and annexation, including the French population of the lower Louisiana Territory and the Spanish population of the Southwest.

Indentured Servants and Forced African Immigration

In the English colonies labor was scarce and most newcomers were unwilling to work for others, because it was easy to acquire land and become independent farmers.

179

One answer to the labor shortage problem was the use of **indentured servants**. Europeans who lacked the funds to pay for their transportation to America (poor and landless farmers, unemployed and low-paid workers, debtors) were able to sign **indentures**, or contracts, in which they agreed to work from 4 to 7 years in exchange for their passage to America. Once they had fulfilled the terms of their indentures, they were free to find independent employment. Indentured servants accounted for nearly 80 percent of the 130,000 settlers in the Virginia and Maryland colonies in the 17th century.

Between 1492 and 1770 more **Africans** than Europeans came to the New World, most of them settling in the (Caribbean and in South America. However, they were brought in chains against their will. At first, most slaves were brought to the English colonies from the Caribbean islands, but as time passed, they were imported directly from Africa. The first black immigrants to the English colonies arrived in Virginia in 1619 aboard a Dutch privateer from the Spanish Caribbean and were offered as indentured servants. Nine years later, Africans were sold directly as slaves to Virginia settlers. By the 1660s most blacks in the colonies were legally held as slaves, numbering approximately 400,000 by 1775. The English settlers justified slavery, a tradition that did not exist in England, with the **ethnocentric** belief that fairskinned people like themselves were superior to darkskinned races, and with the economic need for labor in the colonies.

Early Nativism

In the early years of settlement, there was little opposition to immigration because labor was needed in the growing country. Moreover, most immigrants to the United States who came from northern and western Europe assimilated easily. One group, formed in the 1850s, that supported nativism, or favored native-born Americans and opposed immigration, was the **American party**, commonly known as the **"Know-Nothing" party**. Much of their opposition was directed at Irish and German immigrants who, they claimed, threatened native labor by taking jobs, were clannish, and failed to quickly assimilate. But the most important source of conflict between Protestant native-born Americans and immigrants was religion, specifically objections to Irish Catholics. Many feared that if the Catholics "took over" America, the Pope in Rome would rule, and religious and political liberty would be destroyed. Goals of the American party were the limitation of political officeholding to native-born Americans, a 21-year residency requirement for naturalization, and greater restrictions on immigration.

Ethnic Distribution (1820–1930)

Between 1820 and 1930 more than 37 million immigrants came to the United States, mostly from Europe. While most came from northern and western Europe prior to 1880, most came later from southern and eastern Europe. Figure 2.4 illustrates the geographic distribution of immigration to the United States during these years.

Decade	Germany	Ireland	England, Scotland, Wales	Scandinavia	Italy	Austro-Hungary	Russia & Baltic States	Totals
1820	968	3,614	2,410	23	30		14	7,059
1821–30	6,761	50,724	25,079	260	409		75	83,308
1831–40	152,454	207,654	75,810	2,264	2,253		277	440,712
1841–50	434,626	780,719	267,044	13,122	1,970		551	1,498,032
1851–60	951,657	914,119	423,929	24,680	9,231		457	2,324,073
1861–70	827,468	435,697	607,076	126,392	11,725	7,800	2,515	2,018,673
1871–80	718,182	436,871	548,043	242,934	55,795	72,969	39,287	2,114,081
1881–90	1,452,970	655,540	807,357	655,494	307,309	362,719	213,282	4,454,671
1891–1900	505,152	388,416	271,538	371,512	651,873	574,069	505,281	3,267,841
1901–10	341,498	339,065	525,950	505,324	2,045,877	2,145,266	1,597,308	7,500,288
1911–20	143,945	146,199	314,408	123,452	1,209,524	901,656	921,957	3,841,141
1921–30	412,202	220,564	330,168	98,210	455,315	214,806	89,423	1,920,688
Totals	5,947,883	4,579,182	4,198,812	2,343,667	4,751,311	4,279,285	3,370,427	

Figure 2.4 Immigration to America (1820–1930)

New Immigration (1870–1930)

New Sources

Emigration from southern and eastern Europe at the end of the 19th century affected cities worldwide. Although cities like Warsaw, Berlin, Vienna, Naples, and London received new immigrants, the United States, with its higher standard of living and reputation for being a land of opportunity, received the bulk of the new immigrants. Between 1880 and 1930 over 27 million immigrants came to the United States, many to Ellis Island in New York Harbor. The new immigration included Italians, Greeks, Jews, Poles, Rumanians, and those emigrating from the Austro-Hungarian Empire and Russia.

Reasons for Immigration

The "new immigrants" sought to escape the same economic problems that had caused many earlier immigrants to leave their homelands in northern and western Europe. Unemployment, high birth rates, overpopulation, and epidemics of malaria and cholera drove many southern Italians abroad, for example. The easing of immigration restrictions and faster, less expensive transportation made immigration into the United States a more viable option for many. The Jewish population of the United States grew from about 250,000 in 1877 to over 4 million in 1927, primarily because of the Russian pogroms (organized massacre of Jews) at the end of the 19th century. The Russo-Japanese War (1904–1905), the Balkan Wars (1912–1913), and World War I (1914–1919) motivated many others to come to the United States.

Attractions of the United States

America's greatest attraction was the opportunity for social mobility through economic opportunities not available in Europe and Asia. America's rapidly growing industries continually needed inexpensive labor, and the numerous foreign immigrants provided the necessary hands. As older immigrants were less likely to tolerate the deteriorating working conditions of unregulated industrial expansion, Slavs and Italians replaced British, Irish, and Germans in coal mines, while Portuguese, Greeks, and Italians found employment in New England textile mills. East European Jews took jobs formerly held by the Irish and Germans in New York City's garment factories, and the Japanese on the West Coast replaced many Chinese in agricultural and service tasks.

America's democratic and constitutional form of government, allowing for civil liberties and political freedoms not available in many European countries, was a strong attraction. Those persecuted in other countries, as the Jews were in Russia, were able to combat discrimination in their new home with the formation of constitutionally protected groups such as the **B'nai B'rith Anti-Defamation League**.

Urbanization and the Ghetto

As the decades following the Civil War saw increased immigration, many large cities developed a patchwork of ethnic neighborhoods. The new immigrants settled together in ghettos called "Little Germany," "Little Italy," and so on, where they clung to their own language and customs. Because immigrants felt more comfortable working and living among friends and relatives, ethnic groups concentrated in particular industries and locations.

Americanization Process

Most new Americans experienced stages of change as the "Americanization process" took place. The first stage, especially with the later immigrants from southern and eastern Europe, usually included discrimination by native-born Americans. Many times, these immigrants were excluded from better residential areas, received little protection in employment, and were belittled.

As immigrants began to adopt the ways of American society—the English language, an understanding of the legal system and government and its customs and traditions—they experienced the stage of acculturation, or the adaptation to the American culture.

A later stage of Americanization occurred when the immigrant was finally absorbed into American society. This is known as the stage of assimilation, which usually does not occur until the second or third generation of immigrant families.

Contributions of Immigrants to American Society

Most immigrants came to the United States seeking political, economic, and social freedom. As a result, they have continued to contribute to the American democratic heritage and its preservation. The rich cultural heritage that came to the United States with different groups of immigrants has continued to add to our heterogeneous society. Despite periods of discrimination, immigration has added to the American spirit of toleration and equal protection of the laws.

Notable immigrants:

Business Andrew Carnegie (Great Britain), James J. Hill (Canada), Eleuthere Irenee Du Pont (France)

Science John Audubon (Haiti), Alexander Graham Bell (Scotland), Albert Einstein (Germany), Enrico Fermi (Italy), Isador Rabi (Austria)

Government and Law Felix Frankfurter (Austria), Thomas Paine (Great Britain), John Peter Altgeld (Germany), Carl Schurz (Germany), Albert Gallatin (Switzerland)

Music Igor Stravinsky (Russia), Hans Kindler (Holland), Bruno Walter (Germany), Victor Herbert (Ireland), Arturo Toscanini (Italy), Artur Rodzinski (Yugoslavia)

Literature and Journalism Jacob Riis (Denmark), Joseph Pulitzer (Hungary), Thomas Nast (Germany), John Peter Zenger (Germany), Peter F. Collier (Ireland), Ole Rolvaag (Norway), Louis Adamic (Yugoslavia)

Reaction to the "New" Immigration

Cultural Pluralism

The long held concept of the "melting pot" suggested that all immigrants absorb the aspects of a uniform American culture and, as a result, become "Americanized." However, in reality, the patterns of acculturation and assimilation have not produced such homogeneous results. Although American society does have a homogeneous core including the English language, a democratic political system, and uniform economic institutions, our society is at the same time quite heterogeneous. Although different ethnic groups become Americanized, they also maintain a degree of their cultural heritage. This idea of "cultural pluralism," rather than a pure melting pot, was first expressed in 1915 by the Jewish-American philosopher Horace Kallen in his articles entitled "Democracy Versus the Melting Pot."

Nativist Reactions

Ironically, although the majority of the original settlers and immigrants to the English colonies and early United States came for economic opportunity, political freedom, and religious freedom, they lacked tolerance for anyone who deviated significantly from themselves. Americans of every generation have feared that newcomers would subvert established customs and undermine the traditions of society. Opposition to immigrants began toward the Scotch-Irish and Germans in the middle of the 19th century, followed by discrimination against Italians, Chinese, Jews, Poles, and Japanese at the turn of the century, and Mexicans, Puerto Ricans, Latin Americans, and Vietnamese in the 20th century. Native-born Americans have demonstrated "nativism" toward immigrants of minority groups who have deviated from the dominant culture. Stereotyping, or a fixed conception of groups, became a common form of discrimination.

Nativist groups discriminated against individuals because of race, religion, political beliefs, and economic fears. In 1887 the **American Protective Association** was founded, based on anti-Catholicism. The **Ku Klux Klan** originated as primarily an anti-black organization during the Civil War era and resurfaced as an anti-Semitic, anti-Catholic, anti-immigrant group in the 20th century. White workers in 1877 organized the **Workingmen's party** in California as an anti-Chinese organization based primarily on economic fears and racism. In 1894 a group of Bostonians formed the **Immigration Restriction League** to keep out foreign arrivals by imposing a literacy test. Pressures from nativists helped lead to legislation early in the 1920s designed to keep those with "radical" political beliefs from entering the country.

Nativist discrimination against minority groups, including black Americans, has had numerous effects, perhaps the greatest being economic. Although **affirmative action** legislation has attempted to remedy this trend, minority groups continue to remain at the lower end of the economic scale in the United States.

Legislation	Provisions	Causes
Chinese Exclusion Act (1882)	Restricted Chinese immigration for a 10-year period	Racism, economic fears
Gentlemen's Agreement (1907)	Japan persuaded to deny passports to those who wanted to emigrate	"Yellow Peril" racism, economic fears
Literacy Test (1917)	Immigrant required to pass literacy test in either English or another language	To keep out immigrants from eastern and southern Europe; most immigrants from northern and western Europe were literate
Immigration Act of 1921	Quota system set at 3% of total of that nationality in U.S. in 1910; general limit of 350,000 immigrants per year	Fear of Bolshevism (quota reduced immigration from eastern and southern Europe)
Immigration Act of 1924	Lowered quota set in 1921 to 2% and set base year at 1890	As nativisim grew, greater cutbacks desired
Immigration Act of 1927	Congress set limit to 150,000 immigrants per year with most from western and northern Europe and virtually no Asians	Continued nativism and desire for racial purity
National Origins System of 1929	No more annually than 150,000 from outside Western Hemisphere; quotas enacted based upon numbers in 1920; no restrictions on immigration from Western Hemisphere; prohibited all immigration from Asian countries	Extreme post World War I nativism
Refugee and Displaced Persons Acts (1940s–50s)	Provisions to admit immigrants (refugees) from Nazi Germany and later from eastern Europe	Exceptions made by Congress consistent with U.S. foreign policy

Figure 2.5 Immigration Restrictions (1882–1929)

Legislation	Provisions	Causes
McCarran-Walter Act of 1952	Annual total of 156,000 immigrants with quota on those from outside of the Western Hemisphere; 2,000 yearly from Far East; and screening for Communists	"McCarthy Era", fear of Communism
Immigration Act of 1965	Ended quota system; set annual number from outside Western Hemisphere at 170,000; 120,000 from within Western Hemisphere; preference for those with "special talents" and relatives	Improvement on earlier acts claimed to be racist and unfair

Figure 2.5 continued Immigration Restrictions (1882–1929)

Immigration Restrictions

On a number of occasions in our history, Congress has responded to nativist sentiments with the passage of restrictive legislation. Fig. 2.5 provides a listing of the major restrictive legislation passed by Congress during the 1800s and 1900s.

By changing the "base year" from 1910 (1921 Immigration Act) to 1890 (1927 Immigration Act), the 1927 act further limited the number of southern and eastern Europeans, since fewer of them lived in the United States in 1890 than in 1910. The immigration restriction acts of the 1920s, combined with the depression of the 1930s, drastically lowered the numbers of foreigners coming to American shores. Only 23,068 came in 1933, 28,470 in 1934, and 34,956 in 1935.

Exercise Set 2.11

1. Which is the main way that ethnic groups in the United States have helped to shape the national identity?
    A. most of the newer groups have blended in and adopted the ways of earlier immigrants
    B. each group kept cultural characteristics that became part of the general culture
    C. each group attempted to become the dominant force in society
    D. ethnic groups made large financial contributions in support of the arts in the United States

2. The immigration laws of the 1920s were noteworthy because they
   A. satisfied the Chinese and Japanese governments
   B. limited immigrants to 25,000 per year
   C. encouraged immigration from eastern and southern Europe
   D. established systems of quotas designating specific numbers of immigrants from different countries

3. All of the following groups of immigrants were distrusted by contemporaries for allegedly undermining or threatening important American institutions EXCEPT
   A. the Irish in 1850s
   B. the Chinese in 1880s
   C. the English in 1920s
   D. the Germans in 1840s

4. Which of the following statements is true about immigration to the United States during the last two decades of the 19th century?
   A. United States immigration laws sharply reduced the number of eligible immigrants
   B. nativist objection to immigration drastically reduced the numbers of foreigners coming to the United States
   C. quotas were placed on immigrant groups coming from the Western Hemisphere
   D. many immigrants of this period faced problems in assimilating into American society

5. The hostility of the Know-Nothing party was aimed primarily at
   A. slaveholders
   B. Protestants from northern Europe
   C. Irish and German Catholic immigrants
   D. labor unions

6. A major reason that no significant restrictions were placed on immigration to the United States before the end of the 19th century was that
   A. the American economy was in need of additional workers
   B. there were no signs of nativist objections to immigrants before the 20th century
   C. the numbers of immigrants coming to the United States continued to decrease as the 19th century came to a close
   D. European and Asian nations halted all emigration

THE LAST FRONTIER

> The result is that to the frontier the American intellect owes its strik-
> ing characteristics . . . that restless, nervous energy; that dominant
> individualism, working for good and evil, and with all that buoyancy
> and exuberance which comes from freedom—these are the traits of
> the frontier.
>
> Frederick Jackson Turner,
> *The Significance of the Frontier in American History* (1894)

The Significance of the Frontier in American History, an essay by University of Wisconsin professor **Frederick Jackson Turner**, was read to a confer- ence of historians in connection with the World's Fair in Chicago in 1893 and presented a new theory to the age-old question, "What is the American?" Professor Turner, contemplating the effects of the closing frontier, proposed that one of the major differences between European and American civiliza- tion was that the American was in part the product of the distinctive envi- ronment of the New World. The "free land" offered by a continuing westward moving frontier offered hopes of economic gain and adventure, changed the social stratification that typified European society, demanded new political institutions, changed traditional economic practices to meet the demands of self-sufficiency, and gradually produced an "Americanization" of the society that was making up the United States. Although the simplicity of Turner's thesis has been criticized over the years, the operation of the frontier process still remains a well-respected explanation of the develop- ment of the American character.

Land West of the Mississippi

By the early 1800s the "American West" continued to move as the white frontier advanced beyond the Mississippi River. The nation gained new ter- ritory with the purchase of the **Louisiana Territory** (1803), the annexation of Texas (1845), the acquisition of the **Oregon Country** through a treaty with Great Britain (1846), the **Mexican Cession** by treaty with Mexico (1848), and the **Gadsden Purchase** from Mexico (1853), fulfilling the emo- tional drive for expansion (**manifest destiny**). (See Figure 1.20 "Territorial Growth of the United States, 1783–1853")

Native Americans

As the white population continued to press westward, the original settlers, the American Indians, were ruthlessly forced onto poorer lands or onto **reservations**. The newcomers who desired land for railroads, farms, and speculation could not tolerate the nomadic Indian who recognized no individual ownership of land. By 1873, white settlers, with the assistance of federal troops, had subdued most of the native population.

The Homestead Act (1862)

Passed by Congress during the Civil War, the Homestead Act provided 160 acres of federal land for settlers who would inhabit plots of land for at least five years. Problems with the Homestead Act included the inadequacy of the small plots and abuse by mining and timber companies who gained considerable amounts of free federal land by having employees put in claims for homesteads.

The Impact of Industrialization

Transportation

During the 1820s and 1830s trade routes in the United States began to indicate greater **East-West economic interdependency**. The transportation improvements of the 19th century helped connect the agricultural interests of the West with the markets of the East, and the industrial centers of the East with the growing need for manufactured goods of the West. The building of canals, the steamboat, the railroad, and the telegraph helped to open up the frontier and brought many farmers into the market economy. Self-sufficient farmers who at one time produced many agricultural products began to specialize in one or two crops.

Immigration

Increased immigration during the 19th century increased the market for agricultural goods in the Eastern cities. Immigrants also contributed to the growing population of Western territories and states. Both public and private interests in the West encouraged the migration of immigrants westward to promote their economies.

Investment Opportunities

Public and private investment and a growing population stimulated economic growth during the 19th century. Lucrative investment opportunities in the nation's growth encouraged investment by banks, insurance companies, corporations, and private individuals.

Development of Urban Centers

As the population of the United States increased, the frontier moved steadily westward and rural settlements became towns and cities. Early cities grew along major river routes (Cincinnati, Louisville, Pittsburgh) and along the shores of the Great Lakes (Cleveland, Chicago, Detroit). With the continued growth of the railroad and telegraph, new cities grew along major lines (Omaha, Kansas City, Denver, Salt Lake City, El Paso, Sacramento, Los Angeles).

Native Americans

Advancing White Settlement

White settlement took its toll on the Native American population almost immediately. The greatest destruction of the American Indian population started long before the infamous wars of the 1800s between Western settlers and the Plains Indians. Diseases carried from Europe killed hundreds of thousands of Native Americans who had no natural immunity to these germs. Most deadly of the diseases was smallpox, which drastically reduced the Indian population in the Caribbean, Central America, the English colonies, and Canada.

Legal Status and Treaties

Early on, the British settlers viewed the American Indian as a type of "savage"—an inferior race, much the same as they viewed the black African. During the colonial period, British policy toward the Indians was to slowly push them westward and avoid conflict. The **Proclamation of 1763** (preventing settlement west of the Appalachians) was passed to prevent friction with the native populations, a problem the financially strained British government could ill afford.

Once independence was gained, the United States government found that conflict with the "red man" was "inevitable." The **Northwest Ordinance** of 1787 called for the Indians to be treated in "good faith," and the **Treaty of Greenville** (1795) accepted Indian tribal sovereignty by virtue of their residence in part of the Northwest Territory. However, both provisions were eventually violated.

The Indians, exempted from taxation and not counted in apportionment of representation and taxes, possessed an indefinite status under the Constitution. During the 1820s the federal government urged the removal of the tribes to the West, and several states took independent action to remove the Indians. Congress passed the **Indian Removal Act of 1830**, which appropriated $500,000 for treaties to remove tribes, primarily in the Southeast, west of the Mississippi.

In 1827, following attempts by the state of Georgia to have them removed, the Cherokees of Georgia adopted a written constitution and declared themselves an independent state. In *Cherokee Nation* v. *Georgia* (1831) the Supreme Court held that, although the Cherokee Indians could not bring a suit in federal court, they had a right to their own land until the time they chose to voluntarily cede it to the United States. In *Worcester* v. *Georgia* (1832), a case involving the conviction of two Protestant missionaries for residence on Indian lands, the Supreme Court went further in stating that citizens of Georgia had no right to enter Cherokee lands without the consent of the Indians. President **Andrew Jackson**, who, as a general, had led the expedition against the Seminoles in Florida in 1818, had little sympathy for the Indians. Jackson refused to implement the Supreme Court's decisions and, with support from Congress (**Removal Act of 1830**), he ordered the removal of Indians to lands west of the Mississippi, starting with the Choctaw in 1831. In 1835 a minority group of Cherokees signed a treaty agreeing to exchange their land in Georgia for Western land. In 1838, when many Cherokees refused to move, President **Martin Van Buren** sent federal troops to force the Indians from their land and march them to Oklahoma. Nearly one quarter died of disease and exhaustion on this forced move, which has come to be known as the **Trail of Tears**.

Indian Wars (1850–1900)

Although early policy toward the Indians called for their resettlement west of the Mississippi River, by the 1840s the movement of whites to the West forced a change in policy. Government policy now called for the establishment of **Indian reservations**. The legal status of the Indian under the reservation system was that of a **ward**, or one under the care of the federal government. However, this did not bring peace because whites entered reservation land and the Indians found the reservations too confining after their nomadic lifestyle. Battles continued throughout the 19th century with cruelties and brutalities committed by both sides. The last occurred in 1890 when unarmed Teton Sioux of South Dakota were massacred by federal troops armed with Gatling guns at **Wounded Knee**, South Dakota. The final "taming" of the American Indian came with the destruction of the **buffalo**, or bison. Depended upon by the Plains Indians for survival, the buffalo became the white man's source of food, sport (buffalo hunters such as "Buffalo Bill" Cody), and leather, and 9 million bison were killed between 1872 and 1874. By 1903 a known total of 34 buffalo survived. Fortunately, government protection allowed the buffalo population to increase and the species was preserved.

Legislating Indian Life

Reform movements in the late 1800s urged change in federal policy toward the Indians and organizations such as the **Indian Rights Association** awakened concern. The aim of most reformers was to **assimilate** the Indians into white society. The **Dawes Severalty Laws** of 1887, providing for the division of Indian lands among individual families and citizenship to those Indians who abandoned tribal allegiances, was passed in hopes of accelerating assimilation. Unfortunately, the Dawes Act failed. Attempts at assimilation violated Indian traditions and under the act nearly one half of the Indian lands was lost to white settlement.

Partially in recognition of those Indians who had served in World War I, Congress passed the **Snyder Indian Citizenship Act** in 1924, granting citizenship to all Indians born in the United States. In 1934 Congress passed **the Indian Reorganization Act**, a reform measure designed to stress tribal unity and autonomy. By returning surplus lands to the Indians, authorizing tribes to form corporations, and providing for elected tribal councils, the act attempted to restore the tribe as the center of Indian culture and life. In 1953 Congress began a policy of "**termination**," or the ending of federal responsibility and social services (education, health, welfare) in an attempt to assimilate the Indian into American society. The policy of termination ended in the 1960s and a new militancy surfaced among groups of American Indians in the 1960s and 1970s. The occupation of **Alcatraz Island** in San Francisco Bay in 1969 and the holding of hostages at Wounded Knee in 1973 by the **American Indian Movement** (AIM) are examples of attempts by the American Indians to regain lands that they felt were rightfully theirs.

The Mining Frontier

The **California Gold Rush** of 1849 brought nearly 100,000 new settlers. After gold was discovered near Denver in 1858, many settlers came to Colorado, and the discovery of the **Comstock Lode** in 1858 increased the population of the **Nevada Territory**, bringing statehood in 1864. Although few prospectors stayed on, a stable population formed around each mining camp and eventually resulted in territorial organization and statehood.

Discoveries of gold helped draw settlers to the West.

The Cattle Frontier

The grasslands of the Great Plains, east of the Rocky Mountains, were well suited for grazing and quickly became the cattleman's frontier, where large herds of cattle grazed on the "open range." The original market value of the Texas longhorn was for its hide, processed in the tanneries of the Northeast. However, after the Civil War there developed the "**long drive**," or the driving of cattle herds north to the nearest East-running railroad for the Eastern beef market. By the 1880s the long drive became less common as increased numbers of farms closed in the open range and the railroads were located closer to local ranches.

By the 1890s overproduction of cattle caused the prices in the Eastern markets to decline. Prices of steers dropped from $30 apiece to only $8. During the hot, dry summer of 1886 the grasses withered and the cattle starved. The winter of 1886–87 was so fierce that cattle were reported to have frozen upright in their tracks. Over the next few years the "open range" approach to cattle raising ended and, assisted by the invention of **barbed wire** by Joseph Glidden (1874), ranchers turned to smaller herds on fenced land.

Much cowboy dress was adopted from the Mexican *vaqueros*.

The West, sparsely populated and lacking law enforcement officers, lawyers, and judges, developed an unwritten body of customs sometimes known as the **Code of the West**. Under this code a man's word was his bond, rustling and horse stealing were evil, strangers were to be treated with hospitality as long as they did not outstay their welcome, a bargain sealed with a handshake was as good as any drawn up by lawyers, and shooting an unarmed man was contemptible. Justice on the frontier was carried out by federal district courts and United States marshals, who often employed hired guns to assist them. Some of the more notorious lawmen of the frontier were **Wyatt Earp**, **Bill Tilghman**, **Texas Ranger Ira Aten**, and **Judge Isaac C. Parker**. At times, when the legal system proved to be incapable of curbing gamblers, gunmen, and desperadoes, groups of self-proclaimed law enforcers formed **vigilante** committees to cope with lawbreakers.

The Farming Frontier

Farmer versus Nature

The frontier farmer found the turf of the Great Plains hard to manage, for the roots of the grasses extended deep and intermeshed to form sod up to twelve feet thick. Turning this hindrance into an advantage, the ingenious plains farmer used special plows to cut the sod into bricks ("Nebraska Marble"), which was then used to build homes. In an area lacking wood, rock, and brick clay, the **sod house** solved the problem of shelter for the plains farmer. It was cool in the summer, warm in the winter, and virtually bulletproof, fireproof, and windproof.

Perhaps the farmer's greatest foe was nature itself. Drought and wind combined to scorch the crops and lift the dry topsoil, creating swirls of dust that were deposited hundreds of miles away. Prairie fires raced across the plains in the fall when grass became dry. Winter blizzards and subzero weather froze farmers and livestock alike, and plagues of grasshoppers turned millions of acres into a wasteland.

Technology

New farming inventions allowed the plains farmer to cultivate the soil in spite of nature's resistance. **Barbed wire** enabled farmers to enclose the fields, keeping their own livestock in and the rancher's herds out. An improved prairie **plow** made of steel that did not break when it cut through the tough sod was devised in 1868. The **windmill** allowed the farmer to draw spring water from deep underground and cultivate the fields, while improved systems of irrigation made use of limited amounts of water. Laborsaving devices like the horse-drawn **reaper** and later the **combine** helped turn the plains into the "bread basket" of the nation, and later the world.

Government Policy

The railroads held tremendous amounts of land through federal grants and sold many acres to the farmers. The **Homestead Act** (1862) encouraged further settlement and about 600,000 homesteaders benefited. The **Morrill Land Grant Act** (1862) provided for the sale of federal land to finance agricultural colleges, promoting scientific agricultural development.

Life on the Great Plains Farm

Besides the hostile environment, the isolation and loneliness of the plains farm added to the challenge of survival. It was not uncommon for families to walk many miles to the nearest farm for simple conversation. Although the prairie towns consisted of just a few drab wooden buildings along a grass-centered, muddy street, a trip to town to sell produce and purchase provisions was an event long awaited by prairie families. Medical needs were met by self-proclaimed physicians who, with a mixture of folk remedy, medieval methods, and improvisation, served the needs of the prairie population. Frontier schools, usually an early priority in a prairie settlement, were financed by local districts, and the success of plains education was surprisingly high. By 1900, Nebraska, Kansas, and Iowa boasted the highest literacy rate in the nation.

Agrarian Protest

The Grange Movement

The transition of the American farmers from self-sufficiency to the market economy brought hardships that eventually caused them to form political organizations. During the 19th century, farmers found themselves at the mercy of forces—commodity prices, grain storage charges, interest rates, and shipping costs—that were beyond their control.

The **National Grange of the Patrons of Husbandry** was founded in 1867 to organize farmers into local chapters dedicated to education, culture, and socialization. However, in the 1870s its aims became less social and more political, with membership reaching 1.5 million by 1874. The Grange accused the railroads of discriminatory practices (long haul compared to short haul, rebates, monopolizing practices), the grain-elevator operators of monopoly practices, charging "all that the traffic would bear," and manufacturers of raising prices and the cost of credit so that farmers were unable to make a profit. On July 4, 1873, the Grange issued the **Farmers' Declaration of Independence** claiming that the farmers were suffering from "systems of oppression and abuse."

Legal Efforts; Court Cases

By the middle of the 1870s the Grangers held the political balance in several of the Midwestern states. In four states **Granger laws** were passed to regulate railroad rates and the practices of the owners of grain elevators. At first the Granger laws were challenged in the state courts as violations of private property rights. But the Supreme Court, in a series of landmark decisions, upheld the principle that government could regulate all those industries "affected with a public interest."

• **Munn v. Illinois** *(1877).* The Supreme Court upheld state regulation of grain elevators storage rates, declaring that "**the public has a direct and positive interest**" in private businesses "**clothed with a public interest.**" As a consequence, the rates and services of public utilities could be regulated, departing from the tradition of laissez-faire economics.

• **Wabash, St. Louis and Pacific Railway v. Minnesota** *(1886).* In this case, based on congressional **control over interstate commerce**, the Supreme Court restricted state control by holding that the states had no power to fix rates on shipments of goods passing beyond their borders.

• **Chicago, Milwaukee and St. Paul Railroad v. Minnesota** *(1889).* The Supreme Court ruled that **corporations could not be denied property rights** without being afforded equal protection of the laws and due process.

National Government Response: Interstate Commerce Commission

In response to the Supreme Court's decision in the *Wabash* case, Congress passed the **Interstate Commerce Act** (1887) establishing the **Interstate Commerce Commission**, which had among its powers the right to require that railroads post rates publicly, demand that rates be "reasonable and just," forbid pooling, rebates, and rate discrimination, prohibit "long haul vs. short haul discrimination," and investigate complaints against the railroads.

Populism

- *Farmers' Alliances.* As the agrarian crusade continued into the 1880s, farmers' alliances were formed to demand change concerning a number of issues. In 1887 the **Southern Farmers' Alliance** had a membership of 3 million. The **Northern Farmers' Alliance** attracted 2 million members by 1890. In 1889 delegates from both alliances met to discuss a common platform that included demand for free silver; graduated income tax (percent of tax rate increasing with amount earned); government ownership of the railroads; and the direct election of Senators. In the elections of 1890, members of the alliances were elected to many state positions and 53 members of Congress who were sympathetic to the desires of the farmers' alliances were sent to Washington, D.C.

- *Populist Party.* The **People's party**, or **Populist party**, was formed in 1891 through the efforts of the Farmers' Alliances. **James B. Weaver** ran for President on the Populist ticket in 1892 and received a million popular votes. The Populist platform, known as the **Omaha Platform**, included a graduated income tax, postal savings banks, government ownership of railroads and telegraph lines, the direct election of Senators, and the use of initiative (popular introduction of legislation) and referendum (the provision for the popular vote on laws rather than that of the legislatures). The Populist platform also continued to support an increased amount of currency in circulation, an issue endorsed by the **Greenback party** of the 1870s. Since most farmers were debtors, borrowing and buying on credit, the deflationary trends of the later 1800s proved to be devastating. They favored the inflation of the currency system because of its positive effect on the debtor and to meet the needs of a growing population. The Populist platform continued to be pushed by Progressives for a generation. As with many third-party movements in the nation's history, much of the Populist platform was later adopted by the major parties.

- *Election of 1896.* In the election of 1896, **William Jennings Bryan** ran on the Democratic ticket advocating increased coinage of silver. Speaking on the free-silver issue at the 1896 Democratic Convention, Bryan spoke his famous words, "You shall not press down upon the brow of labor this crown of thorns, you shall not crucify mankind upon a cross of gold." The platform of the Democrats was progressive and adopted much of the Populist platform, including reduced tariffs, antitrust legislation, and outlawing the injunction in labor disputes. The Populists also nominated Bryan, realizing that the nomination of their own Populist candidate would ensure a Republican victory by splitting the free silver votes. A vigorous Republican campaign, combined with rising farm prices due to overseas crop failures, resulted in a victory for the Republican candidate, **William McKinley**.

Exercise Set 2.12

1. The Dawes Severalty Act (1887) changed previous policy toward Native Americans by
   A. abolishing the reservation system
   B. granting them citizenship
   C. halting attempts at assimilation of the Indian
   D. dividing tribal lands among individual families

2. All of the following were true of farming on the Great Plains EXCEPT
   A. little threat from a hostile environment
   B. reliance on sod due to scarcity of lumber
   C. dependence upon the railroad
   D. an isolated lifestyle

3. Which of the following was true of the Grange Movement?
   A. it was primarily a southern agrarian movement
   B. it started as a social organization and became increasingly political in the 1880s
   C. it had little effect on future state and federal legislation
   D. it avoided politics

4. Cattle raising in the semi-arid lands of the West greatly increased as a result of the
   A. Homestead Act
   B. invention of the reaper
   C. extension of the nation's railroad network
   D. Morrill Land Grant Act

AMERICAN SOCIETY AT THE TURN OF THE CENTURY

In the late 1800s and early 1900s many changes were taking place that helped the nation become a world power. A once predominantly rural nation was becoming a nation of cities. A country whose economy was once based on agriculture was rapidly becoming an industrial giant. From 1860 to 1910 towns and cities developed and grew at a rate unmatched in modern times. While the rural population almost doubled during these years, the urban population multiplied nearly seven times.

Urbanization and Cultural Development

Urbanization stimulated cultural development by the mixing of many different types of people, the establishment of facilities including libraries, schools, museums, orchestras, and theaters, and the concentration of wealth that contributed to cultural growth. While public school systems and colleges received greater support from both government and private sources, curriculums broadened and specialized. The **American Library Association** was formed in 1876. Daily newspapers increased in number from 700 in 1870 to 2,500 in 1900, while circulation increased from 2.5 million to 15 million and magazines numbered 1,800 by the turn of the century. Museums began display the works of American painters and sculptors, The rise of the city contributed to cultural progress in the United States.

Growth of American Imperialism

American expansionism turned to **imperialism**, or the imposition of control over other peoples. **Manifest destiny** was completed by the turn of the century and the United States was continentally complete. **Imperialism** was beginning to play a role in American foreign policy. By 1900 the "American Empire" included Alaska, the Midway Islands, Samoa, the Philippines, Guam, Puerto Rico, Hawaii, and Wake Island.

Problems Caused by Industrialization

America's rise as an industrial power and its race to greatness brought many problems. With the coming of the new century, these problems started to be addressed. With the conquest of the continent had come reckless **abuse of the environment**—the soil, forest, and water. Rapid industrial growth had brought the **exploitation** of women, children, and workers. The belief in

"Social Darwinism" had led to disregard for the incompetent and the infirm. Wealth and power was concentrated among only a few, and **poverty** was becoming widespread. Although slavery had ended, **racism** plagued American society. Finally, corruption poisoned the political system. To remedy the nation's problems, it was necessary to cleanse politics and to regulate the business interests that controlled government.

The **"Progressive Era"** was an attempt to solve the many problems caused by an industrial society. In 1906 President Theodore Roosevelt labeled those individuals who were working to uncover corruption "**muck rakers.**" These philosophers, social scientists, and novelists included **Henry George** *(Progress and Poverty,* 1879), **Lester Ward** *(Dynamic Sociology,* 1883), **Edward Bellamy** *(Looking Backward: 2000–1887,* 1887). **Thorstein Veblen** *(The Theory of the Leisure Class,* 1899). They produced a literature of protest in the late 1800s. The common theme in most of their works was that laissez-faire had not worked and progress was possible only through social planning. The Progressive era was a reaction to laissez-faire and included greater governmental and legal control of big business and greater government accountability. It also led to a movement for greater social justice.

Chapter Review Questions

1. Between 1890 and 1914 most immigrants to the United States came from
   A. Latin America
   B. northern and western Europe
   C. southern and eastern Europe
   D. Southeast Asia

2. Which of the following accurately describes the Ku Klux Klan of the 1920s?
   A. its activities were limited to the South
   B. it favored immigration restrictions as well as white supremacy
   C. many of its members were elected to Congress
   D. it appeared for the first time during this decade

3. The destructive impact of white settlement on the Native American population was most strongly felt through
   A. the spread of disease unknown to Native Americans
   B. immediate elimination of the native population through warfare
   C. wholesale enslavement of the Indians
   D. immediate relocation of Indians to lands west of the Mississippi

4. All but which of the following major transportation developments affecting United States history took place in the period before the 20th century?
   A. the steamboat
   B. the airplane
   C. the stagecoach
   D. the railroad

5. In the 40 years following the Civil War, fundamental changes in the American system were brought about as a result of federal legislation in all of the following areas EXCEPT
   A. women's suffrage
   B. interstate commerce
   C. immigration
   D. civil rights

6. Which of the following American authors was least concerned with social criticism of America?
   A. Frank Norris
   B. Jacob Riis
   C. Upton Sinclair
   D. Horatio Alger

7. During the second half of the 19th century, an open immigration policy was generally opposed by
   A. factory owners
   B. land speculators
   C. sparsely populated Western territories
   D. labor unions

8. The Populist movement of the 1890s can best be described as a
   A. political coalition of farming interests directed against banking and railroad interests
   B. trade union movement located in major Eastern cities
   C. reform movement seeking to eliminate urban poverty and slums
   D. political interest group desiring war with Spain to protect United States interests in Cuba

ESSAYS

1. Throughout U.S. history, there have been many instances where political, economic, or social difficulties led to demands for reform. In response to those demands, movements such as those listed below developed.
   Agrarian Protest/1870–1900
   Movement for Immigration Restriction/1870–1930

For the *two* movements listed above:

- Describe a specific problem that led to the movement or program
- Describe a specific reform advocated by the movement or program to deal with this problem
- Discuss the extent to which this reform was successful in solving the problem (15 points)

Regents Exam, June 1988

2. During the second half of the 19th century, literary figures in the United States produced works critical of society and advocating change.

   Select *three* writers. For *each one* chosen, identify an issue that was addressed by the listed work and discuss the author's approach to the issue, including suggested change or reform. [5,5,5]

   Lester F. Ward, *Dynamic Sociology* (1883)
   Ida M. Tarbell, *History of the Standard Oil Company* (1902)
   Thorstein Veblen, *The Theory of the Leisure Class* (1899)
   Henry George, *Progress and Poverty* (1879)
   Edward Bellamy, *Looking Backward: 2000–1887* (1887)
   Jacob A. Riis, *How the Other Half Lives* (1890)

3. Throughout U.S. history, the development of democracy has been affected by a variety of actions. For the two statements listed below, discuss the extent to which the statement is accurate and use two specific examples to support your position. Use different specific examples for each statement. [5,5]

Statements

- Third-party movements have been an important factor in the democratic process.
- The legal process has been instrumental in regulating the nation's economy.

UNIT THREE _____

The Progressive Movement

KEY IDEAS: The rapid growth of the United States during the second half of the 19th century, and the problems that accompanied this development, resulted in a period of transition and reform. The age of laissez-faire was coming to an end as social conditions/governmental responsibilities for social conditions increased. As the United States entered the 20th century, expansionist desires, including economic imperialism, became a major component of its foreign policies.

UNIT GOAL: By the end of this unit, the student should be able to recognize and understand that changes in U.S. society caused by industrialization created the need to reexamine domestic and international goals and priorities.

Chapter 1

REFORM IN AMERICA

THE REFORM TRADITION

The American Republic was founded on the concept of equality. The founders of the nation held it to be a "self-evident truth" that all people are created equal, being endowed with the same basic rights to life, liberty, and the pursuit of happiness. Reform movements were started in various periods as a response to **changing social conditions** with the belief that the betterment of society was a possibility. Americans believed that in a democracy the people could create a better society through their own efforts.

American Revolution

The American Revolution was the first of a number of conflicts throughout the world that furthered the ideals of the **Enlightenment** thinkers. What distinguished the United States from other 18th century countries was that the American Revolution allowed the political theories of the Enlightenment to be put into practice. The United States based its government upon **Locke's** and **Rousseau's** idea of a "social contract." The purpose of government was to preserve people's natural rights to life, liberty, and property (Locke). The new Constitution, which proved to be an enduring plan of government, included **Montesquieu's** concept of separation of powers and checks and balances. Although the Confederation period was a time of experimentation and struggle, the result was a government strong enough to govern the nation and restrained enough not to imperil sacred civil liberties.

Abolition Movement

The movement to **abolish slavery** was a major reform movement during the first half of the 19th century. In the late 1700s many Southern planters realized that slavery was inconsistent with many of the principles upon which the nation was founded (especially the Declaration), and hoped that it would eventually disappear. But with the invention of the cotton gin in 1793 cotton exports rose from half a million pounds in that year to 83 million pounds in 1815. Increased demand for cotton intensified the South's dependency on the cotton-slave economy and slavery spread with great speed. The issue of slavery threatened the Union when it became entangled with problems raised by westward expansion.

The earliest reform movements opposing slavery originated with the **Quakers**. Before the American Revolution they freed their slaves, claiming it was a sin for Christians to hold people in bondage. By 1830 there were at least fifty black antislavery societies. However, in the 1840s, the movement became more widespread as many Americans came to believe that slavery was morally wrong. As whites became more involved in the movement, black abolitionists, including Sojourner Truth, Harriet Tubman, and Frederick Douglass, worked with white reformers to end slavery. **William Lloyd Garrison's** newspaper, *The Liberator,* launched a militant abolitionist movement in the North.

By the 1850s the question of slavery was dividing the country. A major setback to the abolitionist movement came with the Supreme Court's decision in *Dred Scott* v. *Sandford* (1857). The Court held that slaves were not protected by the Constitution. The Court said that Congress could not prevent citizens from transporting their slaves into a free territory because slaves were property, protected by the due process clause of the Fifth Amendment to the Constitution. Rather than settling the slavery question, however, the Dred Scott decision increased sectional conflict over the issue of slavery, especially over its expansion to western territory.

The end of slavery and the granting of citizenship and civil rights to black Americans did not come until after the Civil War and the passage of the Thirteenth, Fourteenth, and Fifteenth Amendments. Although the slavery question was finally resolved, reform movements for extension of civil rights to African Americans and other minorities have continued through the 20th century.

Women's Rights

Women in the 1800s were expected to keep house and raise children. Politics and work were the domains of men; women were the guardians of the home. The laws reinforced these perceptions. For example, married women in many states had no rights over property they inherited or wages they earned. They did not have legal control over their children, could not sue in their own name, and could not be a party to a contract.

Between 1820 and 1860, as other reforms began to sweep America, the women's movement began to develop. Women were active in all the reform movements in this period. Their involvement in these other reform movements made them realize that they were as oppressed as many of the groups they were attempting to assist.

As economic and social conditions changed with increased industrialization, equality slowly came to women. Early **industrialization** allowed women to develop some financial independence and opened new areas of employment. Women's colleges, including **Wellesley**, **Vassar**, and **Smith**, opened between 1865 and 1875. By 1900 about 70 percent of all colleges admitted women. The efforts to gain political equality by reformers such as

Elizabeth Cady Stanton, Lucretia Mott, and Susan B. Anthony, and groups such as the National American Woman Suffrage Association started to gain results during the second half of the 19th century. By 1895 sixteen states allowed women to vote, and in 1920 the Nineteenth Amendment was ratified, granting women throughout the nation the right to vote.

Susan Browell Anthony (1820–1906) was a leader in the women's suffrage movement.

Civil Service

The movement to appoint people to government jobs based on merit rather than through the **spoils system** aroused great interest following the Civil War. The scandals of the Grant era and later the assassination of President Garfield in 1881 by a "disappointed office seeker" focused attention on the need for civil service reform. The abuse of the spoils system led to the demand that certain offices be filled only by those who had performed adequately on a "**civil service**" examination. The **Pendleton Act** (1883), adopted during President Arthur's administration, authorized the President to appoint civil service commissioners to administer examinations for "classified" government positions. Although the number of classified areas were few at first, the list grew with later administrations. Today, most government jobs are filled through civil service exams.

The Mentally Ill

Before the 1840s the mentally ill had been treated either as criminals and placed in jails, or as social misfits placed in poorhouses. A pioneer in the reform movement for the mentally ill was a Massachusetts schoolteacher, **Dorothea Dix**. After reporting to the state legislature the shocking treatment of the mentally ill in Massachusetts—"confined . . . in cages, closets, cellars, stalls, pens! Chained, naked, beaten with rods, and lashed into obedience . . ."—legislation was passed to set up a state hospital for the insane. Dorothea Dix carried her crusade across the country, resulting in improved care for the mentally ill in many states.

PRESSURE FOR REFORM

> So long as all the increased wealth which modern progress brings
> goes but to build great fortunes, to increase luxury and make sharper
> the contrast between the House of Have and the House of Want,
> progress is not real and cannot be permanent.
>
> Henry George, *Progress and Poverty* (1879)

> In the face of the facts that modern man lives more wretchedly than
> the caveman, and that his producing power is a thousand times greater
> than that of the cave-man, no other conclusion is possible than that the
> capitalist class has mismanaged . . . criminally and selfishly misman-
> aged.
>
> Jack London, *The Iron Heel* (1906)

Struggle for Fair Standards

As industrialization continued to cause poverty for millions and an unequal
distribution of the nation's wealth, movements for change gained momentum. Reformers demanded that government begin to regulate industry,
finance, working conditions, and agriculture in the interest of the many
rather than the few. A new movement known as the **Progressive Movement**
resulted in the reform of the worst abuses in government and business.
Although Progressives attacked many of the same grievances as **Populists**
did in the 1890s, they received wider support from Americans, especially the
growing middle class, and from government leaders.

Increasing Inequities of Wealth and Poverty

By 1900 the unequal distribution of the nation's wealth was beginning to
threaten political democracy in America. Only one percent of the population
owned 50 percent of the nation's wealth, while the top 12 percent controlled
90 percent. With so much wealth concentrated in the hands of such a small
group, their influence over legislatures and candidates increased. Such class
inequities helped to spread **Marxist** thought in the United States. **Karl Marx**
predicted that discontent among the proletariat (working class) would result
in the overthrow of capitalism and the subsequent end of class struggle. However, change came in the United States through reform legislation passed
under the banner of the Progressive Movement rather than through revolution.

Rising Power and Influence of the Middle Class

An important result of industrialization in the United States was the rise of
the **middle class**, which included professionals, technicians, government

workers, salespeople, service employees, teachers, social workers, and clerical workers, among others. As the problems caused by business abuses and consolidation began to affect the middle class, they began to support the Progressive Movement and demand reform. Repelled by immorality in business, government, and human relations, the rising middle class set out to reform American society.

Communication of Progressive Thought

The Progressive Movement in the United States was assisted by a variety of nationwide organizations. Interest groups including the **National Consumers League**, **National Association for the Advancement of Colored People**, **National Child Labor Committee**, and **National Housing Administration**, joined with occupational groups such as the **American Bar Association** and the **American Health Association**, with nationwide membership. Technological improvements in communication—the telephone and telegraph—improved the availability of information and allowed progressivism to become a national movement.

The "Muckrakers" and Reform

> Men with the muckrake are often indispensable to the well-being of society, but only if they know when to stop raking the muck.
> President Theodore Roosevelt, April 14, 1906

The term "**Muckrakers**" was first used by President Theodore Roosevelt in referring to a character in John Bunyan's *Pilgrim's Progress* who rejected a crown for a muckrake (a rake used to gather dung into a pile). The term was applied to writers who investigated and attacked social, political, and economic wrongs. Books and magazine articles in *McClure's, Collier's,* and *Hampton's* exposed the worst abuses of the period and stirred public outcry against them.

The Authors

Magazine articles by **Ida Tarbell** exposed the abuses of the **Standard Oil Company. Lincoln Steffens** published stories of corruption in major American cities. These sensational accounts stirred popular concern. Novelists of the late 19th and early 20th centuries who spoke for socialism and criticized the capitalist system are among the most famous American literary figures. They include **Upton Sinclair**, **Jack London**, **Theodore Dreiser**, and **Frank Norris**. Sinclair's novel *The Jungle* (1906) brought the conditions in the meat-packing plants of Chicago to the attention of the nation and stimulated demand for laws regulating the meat industry. Jack London, a member of the Socialist party, wrote *The Iron Heel* (1906), warning of a Fascist America and idealizing a Socialist brotherhood of man. Theodore Dreiser's *The Financier* (1912) and *The Titan* (1914) exposed the ruthlessness of promoters and profiteers. Frank Norris's *The Octopus* (1901) showed the control of the railroads and corrupt politicians over California wheat-ranchers.

Legislation

The power to legislate for the health, safety, and welfare of the community belongs principally to the states, but during the early 20th century, Congress began to use its commerce and taxing powers to legislate for the "**general welfare**." Usually, such legislation followed revelations of corruption and immorality by muckraking publications. The **Pure Food and Drug Act** of 1906 barred adulterated and misbranded foods from interstate commerce. The **Meat Inspection Act** of the same year, passed shortly after the publication of Upton Sinclair's novel *The Jungle,* provided for local inspection services by the Department of Agriculture and banned from interstate commerce uninspected and rejected meat. The **Mann-Elkins Act** of 1910 extended the jurisdiction of the Interstate Commerce Commission over telephone and telegraph lines. The **Keating-Owen Act** of 1916 barred from interstate commerce any products made in factories, canneries, or similar workshops that employed children under fourteen. In *Hammer* v. *Dagenhart* (1918) the Supreme Court ruled that the Keating-Owen Act was unconstitutional because it was an illegal attempt to control the conditions of employment and manufacture within the states. In *United States* v. *Darby* (1941), the Supreme Court overruled the decision in *Hammer* v. *Dagenhart* (1918), claiming that goods manufactured in violation of the **Fair Labor Standards Act** of 1938 could be barred from interstate commerce.

Reasons for the Decline of Progressive Literature

The decline in Progressive literature was partly a result of the adoption of Progressive reforms by political parties. The **Progressive Republican League** (1911) organized by Senator Robert M. La Follette of Wisconsin was the result of a split within the Republican party between Conservatives and Progressives who advocated continued reform.

Contemporary "Muckraking"

Literature designed to make the public aware of problems and abuses in America did not end with the Progressive Era. Societal problems were the subject of many of **John Steinbeck's** novels during the Depression years. The Supreme Court ruled *(New York Times Co.* v. *United States,* 1971) that *The New York Times* could print the "**Pentagon Papers**," a secret document that revealed behind-the-scenes decision making during the Vietnam War.

The case provided a classic national security versus First Amendment confrontation, in which the Court ruled that

> paramount among the responsibilities of a free press is the duty to prevent any part of the government from deceiving the people and sending them off to distant lands to die of foreign fevers and foreign shot and shell.
>
> *New York Times* v. *U.S.* (1971)

Finally, investigative reporting by two writers on the *Washington Post* newspaper helped to uncover the **Watergate** scandal during the early 1970s and eventually led to the resignation of President **Richard Nixon**.

Other Areas of Concern

Problems of Poverty

As the imbalance in the distribution of wealth increased during the second half of the 19th century, poverty among the working class grew. The acute housing problems of the poor were described by reformer **Jacob Riis** in *How the Other Half Lives.* He advocated providing housing for low-income families in model tenements. Help for the urban poor also came from individuals like **Jane Addams**, who wanted to improve the lives of working class people by enabling them to obtain an education, better jobs, and better housing. **Hull House**, a settlement house established in Chicago in 1889 by Addams, served the needs of the city's urban poor.

Women's Rights and Efforts for Peace

The movement for women's suffrage rights, which continued throughout the 19th century, culminated in the adoption of the **Nineteenth Amendment** in 1920. The **Fifteenth Amendment** had given the right to vote to black men, but it had ignored women. Prominent women's leaders, such as **Elizabeth Cady Stanton** and **Susan B. Anthony**, led the movements to gain the vote and organized the **National American Woman Suffrage Association**.

The **birth control** movement was led by **Margaret Sanger**, who distributed information about contraceptives in the hopes of preventing unwanted pregnancies among poor women. Although most states still prohibited the sale of contraceptives in 1921, the formation of the **American Birth Control League** by Sanger enlisted physicians and social workers in the effort to convince the courts to allow the distribution of birth control information.

As the United States approached entry into World War I, **peace movements** developed in the nation. "Peace is a woman's job," Representative **Jeannette Rankin** believed, "because men have a natural fear of being classed as cowards if they oppose war." Representative Rankin was the first woman ever to be elected to Congress and she voted against the declaration of war in World War I and World War II.

The Black Movement

The **National Association for the Advancement of Colored People**, originally a predominantly white organization, was formed to battle discrimination by **W.E.B. Du Bois** and his supporters in 1909. The 1920s saw the emergence of a revised version of the **Ku Klux Klan**, determined to reach its goal of "native, white, Protestant supremacy." Using violence and political pressure, the Klan terrorized black Americans as well as Catholics, Jews, and immigrants. One response to discrimination was the formation of movements that advocated black independence, such as the **Universal Negro Improvement Association** (1914) headed by **Marcus Garvey**. Garvey's movement believed that blacks should separate themselves from the corrupt white society. Advocating the "uniting of all the Negro peoples of the world into one great body to establish a country and government absolutely their own," Garvey led a "**Back to Africa**" movement.

The Temperance Movement

During the Progressive Era the temperance movement made great gains and was supported by several organizations. The **Women's Christian Temperance Union** (1876) with **Frances E. Willard** as its leading spirit, preached that alcohol was the primary factor in crime, poverty, and vice. The **Anti-Saloon League** carried on a campaign against the evils of alcoholic beverages and saloons. Both organizations worked to outlaw the manufacture and sale of alcoholic beverages. However, they did not approve the methods of **Carrie Nation**, who invaded saloons with her hatchet and smashed bottles and bars. The temperance movement was assisted by the coming of World War I. The **Eighteenth Amendment** was passed in part to conserve grain that was to be used for feeding the armed forces and Europe instead of for alcohol production. It was ratified in 1919; in 1920 **Prohibition** began.

Anti-Defamation League (1913)

Pogroms in Russia brought attention to the plight of **Jews** abroad and encouraged the formation of the **American Jewish Committee**. The Committee pledged itself to protect the civil rights of all Jews throughout the world. In 1913 Jews organized the **B'nai B'rith Anti-Defamation League**, dedicated to combating prejudice in the United States.

Exercise Set 3.1

1. The Nineteenth Amendment to the U.S. Constitution provided for
   A. the direct election of senators
   B. voting rights for women
   C. a national income tax
   D. end of slavery

2. The Progressive Movement, on the whole, did not focus attention on
   A. impure food and harmful medicines
   B. poor living conditions in urban areas
   C. the unhealthy results of industrialization
   D. the plight of African Americans

3. Of the following pairs, the one that is not correctly matched is
   A. John Steinbeck—*Grapes of Wrath*
   B. Upton Sinclair—*The Jungle*
   C. Frank Norris—*Uncle Tom's Cabin*
   D. Jack London—*The Iron Heel*

4. Jane Addams worked to help people in city slums by establishing
   A. the American Red Cross
   B. the National Association for the Advancement of Colored People
   C. the Salvation Army
   D. Hull House

5. The National Association for the Advancement of Colored People
   A. subscribed to the beliefs of Marcus Garvey
   B. intended to fight discrimination through legal action
   C. was founded by William Lloyd Garrison
   D. attracted most of its members from the African American working class

6. All of the following reform movements were eventually successful in having an amendment added to the Constitution EXCEPT
   A. women's suffrage movement
   B. temperance movement
   C. advocates of better housing conditions
   D. abolition movement

PROGRESSIVISM AND GOVERNMENT ACTION

> We demand that big business give the people a square deal; in return
> we must insist that when anyone engaged in big business honestly
> endeavors to do right he shall himself be given a square deal.
>> President Theodore Roosevelt, *Autobiography* (1913)

Emerging Progressive Movement: Political Reform

The **Progressive Era**, which began about 1900 and came to an end with the
outbreak of World War I, was primarily a response to the industrial and urban
growth of the 1800s. In the late 1800s, labor unions, churches, Populists,
publicists, and utopian novelists called attention to the worst abuses of the
industrial age. Yet, by the turn of the century, class division was even more
obvious, the abuses of business had increased, and the poverty and squalor
of the cities had deepened.

Municipal Reform

A major aim or objective of the Progressive reform movement within the
cities was to "clean up" **municipal governments**. The attack on city
"bosses" and "machines" was led by civic-minded mayors and groups determined to abolish corruption. The concepts of the **city manager** (a specially
trained official in city government), **civil service reform**, **supervision of
public expenditures**, and **city commissions** (a commission of experts to
assist city government) were introduced. As cities rapidly expanded, pressure was put upon city governments to provide and maintain public utilities.
In some of the more progressive municipalities, there were movements for
public ownership of utilities such as gas, electric, telephone, and transportation systems. Settlement houses, similar to **Jane Addams' Hull House**,
were established in a number of cities. They provided education, health care,
child care, cultural events, and recreation.

State Reform

Reformers began to look to the state governments and the federal government for progressive legislation to address the nation's problems. Governors
became important figures in state reform, including **Braxton Bragg Comer**
of Alabama (business regulations), **Hiram Johnson** of California (railroad
regulation), **Woodrow Wilson** of New Jersey (administrative reforms),
Theodore Roosevelt of New York (improvement of urban tenements and
tax revision), and perhaps most outstanding, **Robert M. La Follette** of Wisconsin. La Follette, organizer of the **Progressive American League** in
1911, who was later elected to the Senate and was instrumental in guiding
progressive reform at the national level. With the help of other reformers, he

supported labor legislation, federal aid to farmers, and the continued government operation of federally owned utilities such as the hydroelectric dam at **Muscle Shoals**, Alabama.

Many cities and states adopted measures that provided for increased popular control of government. Among these were the **referendum**, which provided for a popular vote on laws rather than, or in addition to, that of the legislatures, **recall**, or popular removal of government officials, and **initiative**, the popular introduction of legislation. **Ballot reform** included the use of the secret ballot. The **Seventeenth Amendment** (1913) eventually provided for the direct election of senators, the **Nineteenth Amendment** (1920) gave the franchise to women, and **direct primaries** allowed more widespread participation in the selection of candidates by registered voters.

Theodore Roosevelt and the Square Deal

Progressivism emerged in full force during the presidency of Theodore Roosevelt between 1901 and 1909. In addition to calling for greater government intervention to protect the welfare of the American people from big business and the social evils of rapid industrialization, the Progressive Movement was marked by a change in the perception of executive leadership. Now reformers looked to the President to be both politically powerful and to demonstrate legislative leadership, while resisting the pressures from powerful business interests.

President **William McKinley** was assassinated in 1901 shortly after his inauguration for his second term. McKinley's successor, Vice-President **Theodore Roosevelt**, finished out the term and was reelected in 1904. Roosevelt's program of domestic reform was called the "**Square Deal**," a term developed from his promise to bring a "square deal" and "opportunity" to every citizen. Bringing a new definition of the office of the President, Theodore Roosevelt is considered the "first modern President."

The Stewardship Theory of Theodore Roosevelt

Roosevelt looked upon the presidency as a "**stewardship**" in whose care the common welfare and destiny of the American people were entrusted. Feeling that the safety, prosperity, and happiness of the American population were his responsibility, Roosevelt interpreted the duties of the presidency to be beyond those specifically listed in the Constitution. In this way, he revived the **Hamiltonian** doctrine that the President was not limited in authority by the exact functions listed in Article II. In other words, the President was restricted only by what the Constitution or acts of Congress specifically said he could not do. Roosevelt's use of the office of the President has come to be known as the "**bully pulpit**."

Theodore Roosevelt called the office of President a "bully pulpit."

Square Deal Legislation

The legislation passed during Roosevelt's administrations reflected his belief that the modern industrial era demanded government that was powerful enough to guide national affairs. Although Roosevelt has been termed a **"trust buster,"** his goal actually was government regulation of uncontrolled competition in order to eliminate unfair practices of bad trusts. Congressional legislation between 1901 and 1909 included (1) establishment of the **Department of Labor and Commerce** (1903) to regulate business and enforce economic regulations; (2) the **Elkins Act** (1903), which added strength to the Interstate Commerce Act by making the granting or acceptance of secret rebates illegal; (3) the **Hepburn Act** (1906), which increased the power of the Interstate Commerce Commission by giving it the power to reduce discriminatory rates of railroads and placing the burden on the railroad to show that the rates were not unreasonable, and forbidding most free passes; and (4) the **Pure Food and Drug Act** and **Meat Inspection Act** (1906), which responded to the efforts of "muckrakers," including Upton Sinclair's *The Jungle,* by giving the government greater power in the protection of the public from inferior and unhealthy foods and drugs.

President **Taft**, who succeeded Roosevelt, was as sympathetic to reform as Roosevelt was. He prosecuted twice as many trust cases in four years as Roosevelt had in eight years.

The Supreme Court and "Trust-Busting"

The regulation of trusts had been inefficient under the administrations of Grover Cleveland and William McKinley. Under Roosevelt and Taft many trusts were broken up. The Roosevelt administration initiated several federal government suits and won notable victories in two cases, *Northern Securities Co. v. United States* (1904) and *Swift and Co. v. United States* (1905). In *Northern Securities* the United States government brought a suit to break up the Northern Securities Company, a railroad holding company organized by James J. Hill and E. H. Harriman. The Supreme Court held that the company was an "**unlawful combination**" within the meaning of the Sherman Act. In the *Swift* case the Supreme Court affirmed the power of Congress to punish conspiracies in "**restraint of trade**." The Court found that livestock and packing houses were "commerce among the states" and therefore within the Article I, Section 8 powers of Congress.

In *Standard Oil Co. v. United States* (1911), the Supreme Court announced its "**rule of reason**" to be applied to the Sherman Antitrust Act. Ordering the dissolution of the Standard Oil Company of New Jersey, the Court held that the Sherman Act forbade only "**unreasonable combinations**" or "contracts" in restraint of trade. "Reasonable" monopolies, it held, were legal, and size alone was not to be a determinant.

Presidential Mediation

Roosevelt led the way for government's role as an **arbiter** (judge or umpire), in labor disputes affecting the **public interest**. In May 1902 the **United Mine Workers** walked out of the anthracite coal fields of Pennsylvania demanding a shorter work day, better wages, and union recognition. Forcing both sides to accept arbitration, Roosevelt appointed an arbitration board, which decided in favor of a 10 percent increase in wages and a nine-hour work day, but also declared that the owners did not have to recognize the union.

Conservation

President Roosevelt, a lover of the outdoors, was a determined **conservationist**. Before the beginning of the 20th century, Americans believed their nation's abundant natural resources could never be used up. This had resulted in considerable waste and lack of concern for the environment. However, Roosevelt was effective in pressuring both Congress and the states to pass conservation measures. Roosevelt added nearly 150 million acres to the national forests and was instrumental in protecting natural resources from private exploitation.

The **Newlands Reclamation Act** (1902) authorized, for irrigation purposes, the use of money obtained from land sales in the arid Western states. In 1908 the President called 44 governors and 500 natural resource experts to a **National Conservation Congress**, to plan nationwide resource management. Yet, in spite of his efforts, timber and mining companies continued to destroy the environment.

New York State's concern for its environment began in 1885 with the passage of the **New York State Forest Preserve Act** providing for the protection of much of the Adirondacks and the Catskills. The 1895 **New York State Constitution** provided that the forest preserves would be kept forever wild and not wastefully developed.

The Supreme Court and Labor

Progressive thought entered the legal field and did battle with traditional laissez-faire views. The Supreme Court interpreted the Fourteenth Amendment as protecting the sanctity and freedom of contract at the expense of reforms for workers. In *Lochner* v. *New York* (1905) the Court ruled that a New York law that limited working hours was an infringement upon the **contract rights** between "the master and his employees" and therefore unconstitutional. The Court continued the *Lochner* reasoning in *Adair* v. *United States* (1908) with the **Erdman Act** of 1898, which made it a crime for an interstate carrier to dismiss an employee for membership in a labor union, an unconstitutional interference with the employer's and employee's liberty of contract.

However, in *Muller* v. *Oregon* (1908) the Supreme Court modified its *Lochner* v. *New York* decision by upholding an Oregon statute that limited the length of the work day for women to ten hours.

Woodrow Wilson and the New Freedom

Progressivism was surging as the presidential election of 1912 approached. The victor, Democrat **Woodrow Wilson**, expressed his philosophy of Progressive government when he declared, "Freedom today is something more than being let alone. Without the watchful, resolute interference of the government, there can be no fair play between individuals and such powerful institutions as the trusts."

Election of 1912

The Republican party found itself split between the conservative followers of incumbent **William Howard Taft** and the Progressives, who themselves were split between **Theodore Roosevelt** and Senator **Robert M. La Follette** of Wisconsin. The Republican convention nominated Taft. Roosevelt and his followers formed the **Progressive party**, which nominated Roosevelt as the "**Bull Moose**" candidate on a platform embodying **New Nationalism**, the balancing of big business and big government through government's supervision of economic enterprise for the general welfare. The Socialist party nominated **Eugene V. Debs** as their candidate.

The Democrats, realizing the advantages of a race against the divided Republicans, nominated the Progressive governor of New Jersey, **Woodrow Wilson**. The Democrats' platform included the enforcement of the Sherman Act, better banking and currency laws, and tariff reform. The electoral outcome of the race was 435 votes for Wilson, 88 for Roosevelt, and 8 for Taft. The Socialist party received its greatest support in the election of 1912 with nearly a million popular votes cast for Debs. The Progressive measures supported by Wilson, Roosevelt, and Debs received the support of three fourths of the voters, demonstrating the strong national support for Progressivism.

The Underwood Tariff and the Graduated Income Tax

Upon entering office, President Wilson prepared for his attack on what he called the "**triple wall of privilege**": the tariff, the trusts, and the system of banking and currency.

Wilson saw the high rates of 40.8 percent established by the **Payne-Aldrich Tariff** (1909) as protecting the "special interests" of business while preventing consumers from benefiting from lower prices resulting from international competition. After Wilson's personal delivery of his message to Congress, a practice revived from the times of Washington and Adams, and the revelation of the pressures used by business lobbyists in Washington, the **Underwood Tariff** was finally approved in 1913. It lowered rates to 27 percent, the first significant tariff reduction since the Civil War.

Reformers during the administrations of Roosevelt and Taft introduced **income tax** legislation, which had been held unconstitutional by the Supreme Court in 1895 (*Pollock* v. *Farmer's Loan and Trust Company, 1895*). As a result, the **Sixteenth Amendment** was proposed and sent to the states for ratification in 1909 and, to the surprise of many, was passed and became part of the Constitution in 1913. Within a short time, the income tax became the principal source of federal revenue. The federal income tax is an example of a **progressive**, or graduated, tax. A person earning a greater income pays taxes at a higher rate. A **regressive** tax, such as a sales tax, is designed so that all people pay the same tax rate, no matter what their income.

Clayton Antitrust Act and the Federal Trade Commission

Wilson's battles against the trusts gained their greatest victories with the passage of the **Federal Trade Commission Act** and the **Clayton Antitrust**

Act. Wilson's special message to Congress during January 1914 asking for measures to break up monopolies was answered with the creation of the Federal Trade Commission. It was empowered to issue **"cease and desist"** orders to any business found guilty of unfair methods of competition.

The Clayton Antitrust Act, also passed by Congress in 1914, provided the following: (1) it expanded the definition of "unfair methods of competition" to include interlocking directorates, price discrimination, and purchase of a corporation's stock by a competing corporation; (2) it made officers of corporations liable for illegal acts of the corporation; and (3) it exempted labor unions and agricultural associations from antitrust acts and restricted the use of the labor injunction.

The Federal Reserve System

The third part of the "triple wall of privilege" identified by Wilson was the nation's **banking and currency system**. A major problem with the existing system, which was a product of the **Civil War National Banking Act**, was the inability of the amount of currency in circulation to adjust to the needs of the economy.

The **National Monetary Commission** (1908–1912) and the **Pujo Committee**, two investigations by Congress into the money problems of the country, both concluded that the nation's monetary system needed reform. The necessity for reform was also identified by Louis Brandeis' exposé *Other People's Money and How the Bankers Use It* (1914).

The **Federal Reserve Act** was passed in 1913 and it included (1) the division of the country into twelve districts, each having a Federal Reserve bank; (2) the use of the Federal Reserve banks as "bankers' banks" for deposits of cash reserves of national banks and of state banks who wished to join the system; (3) the issuance of Federal Reserve notes (nation's paper currency); (4) the provision for loans from the Federal Reserve banks to member banks in times of need (adding to currency "flexibility"); and (5) the establishment of a Federal Reserve Board.

Although viewed with suspicion at first, the Federal Reserve System helped bring the nation through the financial needs of World War I and proceeded to provide the nation with a working banking system.

Direct Election of Senators

The Constitution provided that the state legislatures would elect senators (Article I, Section 3). The Seventeenth Amendment (1913) provided for the direct election of senators by popular vote.

Women's Suffrage Amendment

The women's suffrage movement was part of the reform movement to improve the legal and social status of women in the second half of the 19th century. The franchise was granted to women by the Wyoming Territory in 1869, the state of Wyoming in 1890, and the state of Colorado in 1897. By 1914 twelve states, all of them Western, had granted women the right to vote. The increased role of women in business and industry during World War I finally led Congress to approve the women's suffrage amendment and to send it to the states for ratification. The Nineteenth Amendment was added to the Constitution in 1920.

World War I: Effect on Domestic Reform

The Progressive Era came to an end when the United States entered World War I. American reform efforts now turned to a "crusading zeal" to make the world "safe for democracy." The war left Americans disillusioned, and after the war they reverted to **conservatism** and **nationalism**, typical of postwar periods.

Exercise Set 3.2

1. Which of the following was not true of the Progressives?
   A. they believed that the age of laissez-faire should come to an end
   B. among their members were representatives of the growing middle class
   C. they did not like the boss-ridden, business-dominated political parties of the day
   D. they did not believe in a strong, responsible government

2. Which of the following reforms was not achieved during the Progressive Era, 1901–1914?
   A. tariff reform
   B. railroad legislation
   C. banking reform
   D. a national minimum wage law

3. The public's response to Upton Sinclair's novel *The Jungle* helped bring about
   A. passage of the Clayton Antitrust Act
   B. the Pure Food and Drug Act
   C. adoption of the Nineteenth Amendment
   D. America's entry into World War I

4. All of the following were considered legitimate functions of the federal government in the late 19th century EXCEPT
   A. guaranteeing the welfare of the poor and unemployed
   B. the regulation of trusts
   C. promoting industrial growth by means of a protective tarrif
   D. regulating immigration

CHAPTER REVIEW QUESTIONS

1. Reformers of the Progressive Era proposed all of the following changes in city government and politics at the turn of the century EXCEPT
   A. civil service
   B. city manager and commission governments
   C. increase in city "bossism" politics
   D. close supervision of elections

2. All of the following were major reforms of President Wilson's "New Freedom" program except
   A. tariff reform
   B. antitrust legislation
   C. social security
   D. banking and currency reforms

3. A Progressive measure used at the state and local level that permits voters to introduce legislation is referred to as
   A. initiative
   B. recall
   C. impeachment
   D. referendum

4. Wilson's first administration was characterized by all of the following EXCEPT
   A. personal appearances before Congress
   B. strengthening of antitrust legislation
   C. reforms in the country's banking and currency system
   D. increases in the tariff rate

5. The main objective of the Muckrakers was to
   A. establish communism
   B. cleanse capitalist society
   C. overthrow the existing form of government in the United States
   D. end government censorship of American literature

6. The Federal Trade Commission Act of 1914
   A. made all business combinations that resembled trusts illegal
   B. established the nation's first income tax
   C. established an investigatory board with the power to issue "cease and desist" orders
   D. replaced the Clayton Antitrust Act

7. All of the following could be considered leaders in the Progressive movement EXCEPT
A. Ida Tarbell
B. Theodore Roosevelt
C. Robert M. La Follette
D. Warren Harding

ESSAYS

1. In Andrew Jackson's day it seemed to be in the public interest for banking and government to be separated; in Woodrow Wilson's day it seemed to be in the public interest for them to be joined.
    a. Select *two* issues from the list below and explain how they may have contributed to the change in economic philosophies. [5,5]
        Issues
        Distribution of wealth
        Elasticity of currency
        Growth of industry
        Population increases
        Economic cycles
    b. *Explain* the economic philosophies for *both* Jackson's and Wilson's views concerning banking and government. [5]

2. "The ability of the Constitution to respond to changing conditions of society has been made possible in a large part by the amending provision." Assess the validity of this statement with reference to three of the issues listed below. [5,5,5]
        Issues
        Women's suffrage
        Tax revision
        Temperance
        Election of senators

3. Reform has been a continuing process in United States history.
    a. Listed below is a major reform movement with some of the problems it attempted to solve. For the reform movement provided, discuss why reform was needed in the problem areas listed. Show how the reform movement responded to that need. [5,5]
        Progressive Movement (1890–1920)
        Practices of big business
        Actions to make government more democratic
    b. Listed below are problem areas that many people believe are in need of reform today. Choose one of the areas and identify a specific prob-

lem related to it. Describe one proposal that has been made to deal with the problem. [5]

Areas in Need of Reform

Quality of education

Providing adequate housing

Dealing with crime

Regents Exam, June 1989

AMERICA REACHING OUT

THE INDUSTRIAL-COLONIAL CONNECTION

Economic Imperialism

In the 1870s and after, several developments combined to shift America's attention across the oceans. The end of the frontier, announced officially in the census report of 1890, an increase in American agricultural and industrial output, and fluctuations in the American economy fostered the belief that the fixture of the country's growth and prosperity lay outside its own continental borders.

United States Industrial Productivity

By the end of the 19th century, factories and farms in the United States produced more goods than the domestic market could consume. As American industry continued to grow, industrialists looked abroad for new sources of raw materials, additional markets for American goods, and places to invest surplus capital. Both farmers and industrialists were eager to enter new overseas markets, and the growing volume of exports began to change American trade relations. In 1870 United States exports totaled $451 million; in 1880, $853 million; and by 1900, $1.5 billion. In 1898 the United States exported more than it imported, a status known as a favorable balance of trade, beginning a trend that lasted through the 1960s. Although agricultural goods originally led industrial goods in American exports, by 1913, manufactured goods took the lead.

Theories of Expansionism

As overseas trade expansion continued to receive more attention, a school of thought developed that held that the only way to save and promote nationalism was through overseas territorial expansion.

President Lincoln's Secretary of State, **William Seward**, had envisioned an American empire that included Canada, Cuba, Central America, Hawaii, Iceland, and Greenland. Although his ambitious designs resulted only in the 1867 purchase from Russia of **Alaska** for $7.2 million, it was an important step toward American territorial expansion. **Josiah Strong**, a Congregational minister and strong advocate of expansionism, wrote a popular book, *Our country: Its Possible Future and Its Present Crisis* (1885), that called for overseas missionary work to "civilize the world under the Anglo-Saxon races." A growing popular belief was that Americans, the bearers of civil liberty and Christianity, were members of a God-favored race destined to lead the world. "As America goes, so goes the world," Strong claimed. Others in America who supported expansion drew on **Charles Darwin's** theories of evolution, applying them to human and social development and calling for the triumph of the fit and the elimination or subjugation of the unfit.

Naval Power

The importance of naval power became increasingly obvious toward the end of the 19th century. The American fleet had fallen into disrepair and by 1880 consisted of only 48 ships that were capable of even firing a gun. Big-navy proponents pointed to the growing fleets of Great Britain, France, and Germany, arguing that the United States needed a stronger fleet to protect its growing overseas interests, and Congress began to authorize new naval construction. One of the main forces behind naval expansion was Captain **Alfred T. Mahan**. After graduating from the Naval Academy in 1859, he devoted a lifetime to studying the influence of sea power in history and for over two decades he headed the Newport Naval War College. Mahan's beliefs were expressed in a number of his books: *The Influence of Sea Power Upon History, 1660–1783* (1890); *The Influence of Sea Power Upon the French Revolution and Empire, 1793–1812* (1892); and *The Interest of America in Sea Power* (1897).

Technological Advances

Technology continued to improve machinery, means of transportation, and methods of communication, as the "need" for expansionism grew. Exports to other countries included the inventions of **Thomas Edison** (electronics, communications) and **Alexander Graham Bell** (communications), **George Westinghouse** (air brakes), **Cyrus McCormick** (farm machinery), and **George Eastman** (photographic equipment). Improvements in transportation and communication accelerated America's involvement in world affairs with the speed and safety provided by **steam-powered ships** and the linking of the United States with other parts of the world through **underwater cables** to transmit **telegraph** communication. Finally, technological improvements in industry increased output and hastened the need for additional foreign markets.

European Imperialism

The last third of the 19th century was characterized by a worldwide scramble for empires. Great Britain, France, and Germany had established colonial claims in Africa and now looked to Asia for further gains. As imperialist expansionism grew throughout the world, Americans considered the acquisition of colonies necessary to attain a position of power in the world.

The Tariff Controversy: Free Trade vs. Protectionism

The tariff question, which was an issue throughout American history, continued to be raised during the expansionist period at the turn of the century. Through the mid-19th century, tariffs were continually raised to protect American manufacturing and agriculture. Those who advocated **protectionism** believed that a high tariff was necessary to allow continued economic growth at home. Those who claimed that tariffs were benefiting certain groups and were making prices artificially high for most consumers favored lowering the tariff rates to approach a system of **free trade** among nations.

The tariff question continues to be an issue today in international economics. Those who favor protectionism claim that the higher standard of living in the United States has resulted in a higher cost of production requiring protection from less expensive foreign goods. Advocates of free trade argue that the American consumer deserves a greater choice of goods at lower prices and that foreign competition would force an increase in the efficiency of American production.

The U.S. **trade deficit** (imports exceeding exports) has continued to increase during the 1980s. Reasons for the deficit include the lower production costs of foreign nations; the high value of the American dollar making imports less expensive while increasing the cost of exports; and the trade barriers (tariffs) established by countries with which the United States trades.

Exercise Set 3.3

1. Which of the following was not a reason for United States expansion between 1880 and 1914?
   A. the desire to extend Christianity
   B. the search for overseas markets
   C. the desire to maintain a position in the international race for power
   D. the search for outlets for surplus population

2. U.S. expansion abroad following the Civil War indicated that
   A. the demand for industrial and agricultural goods within the United States exceeded industry's ability to produce
   B. advocates of isolationism influenced national foreign policy
   C. economic expansion, nationalism, and cultural values worked together as reasons for overseas growth
   D. domestic growth and international growth were unrelated

3. Before 1898, possessions of the United States beyond its immediate boundaries
   A. included Alaska
   B. did not exist
   C. consisted of Alaska, Canada, and Mexico
   D. included most of Central America

4. A high protective tariff rate on imports into the United States may reflect
   A. an isolationist view of economic matters
   B. a desire for free trade
   C. the need to become more involved in the international market
   D. the desires of the average American consumer

AN EMERGING GLOBAL INVOLVEMENT

> Recent events—the navigation of the ocean by steam, the acquisition and rapid settlement by this country of a vast territory on the Pacific—have practically brought the countries of the east in closer proximity to our own. The intercourse between them has already greatly increased and no limits can be assigned to its future extension.
>
> Instructions by Secretary of State Conrad
> to Commodore Matthew Perry, 1852

Manifest Destiny and Expansion into the Pacific

The concept of "**Manifest Destiny**" was first expressed when journalist **John O'Sullivan**, responding to the question of the annexation of Texas, stated that "the fulfillment of our manifest destiny is to overspread the continent by Providence for the free development of our yearly multiplying millions." Implied in Sullivan's statement were the later components of American expansionism; the belief that the growth of America reflected the divinely ordained success of a chosen people, that the acquisition of new

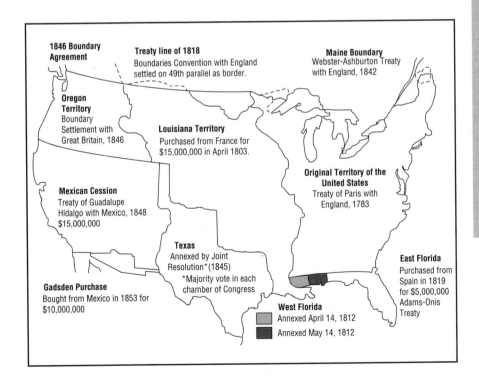

Figure 3.1 Territorial Growth of the United States (1783–1853)

territories would facilitate the extension of democracy and freedom, and that population growth would require the outlet that territorial gains would provide. With the additions of the **Mexican Cession** (1848), the **Oregon Country** (1846), the **Gadsden Purchase** (1853), and **Alaska** (1867), the continental boundaries of the United States were established.

The Opening of Japan

As European powers encroached on Chinese territory in the middle of the 19th century, warships of these powers also began to appear in Japanese harbors. From the middle of the 17th century until that time, Japan had been a feudal state, completely isolated from the rest of the world. In 1852 President **Millard Fillmore** sent **Commodore Matthew Perry** to end Japan's isolation and to convince the Japanese to open certain ports to American trade. In March 1854 Perry secured a treaty of friendship with Japan that granted some trading concessions. In 1857 **Townshend Harris**, the first American minister to Japan, negotiated treaties expanding the diplomatic and commercial relations between the two countries.

In the face of American and European imperialism, Japan quickly transformed itself from a medieval feudal state to a modern nation. By establishing a strong central government, creating a powerful army and navy, and encouraging industrialization, Japan soon became a leading trading and manufacturing nation. Japan's need for raw materials and markets for its manufactured goods turned the nation to active imperialism by the end of the 19th century.

Increased Japanese immigration into the United States by the beginning of the 20th century brought about considerable nativist opposition. Newspapers, state and local governments, and labor unions, among others, pressured for immigration restrictions, resulting in the **Gentlemen's Agreement** (1907), which curtailed the flow of Japanese laborers into the United States.

Early Relations with China

The United States had long been involved in trade with China, opening a small, but profitable, exchange of goods in 1784. In 1844 Commissioner to China **Caleb Cushing** secured the **Wang Hiya Treaty**, which opened five ports to American trade, established the principle of "**extraterritoriality**" (right of American citizens living in China to be tried in American courts), but annexed no territory and claimed no sphere of influence as other imperialistic nations had begun to do.

During the 1800s many Chinese immigrants came to the United States and settled on the West Coast. Nativists aroused widespread anti-Chinese feelings, claiming that the Chinese worked for low wages and were not able to assimilate into American society. The **Workingmen's party**, formed in 1877, included in its platform an anti-Chinese stance, and was instrumental in the passage of state and local laws discriminating against Chinese workers and shopkeepers. In 1882 Congress, responding to nativist pressures, passed the **Chinese Exclusion Act**, prohibiting Chinese immigration for ten years. A later law passed in 1902 excluded the Chinese completely. The Supreme Court addressed the problem of *Yick Ho* v. *Hopkins* (1886), in which the Court struck down a San Francisco ordinance on the grounds that it arbitrarily classified persons so as to discriminate against the Chinese.

Other Pacific Overtures

The Open-Door Policy

Following the **Spanish-American War** (1898–1899) and the **Philippine-American War** (1898–1902), which was a revolt against American rule, the United States annexed the Philippines and increased its Pacific trade. Anticipating increased trade with China, but realizing that the United States had entered the competition late and trade was threatened by the European spheres of influence, President McKinley's Secretary of State, **John Hay**, suggested an **Open Door Policy** in 1898. He proclaimed that "we do not seek advantages in the Orient which are not common to all. Asking only the open door for ourselves, we are ready to accord the open door to others." In 1899 Hay addressed identical diplomatic notes to Germany, England, and Russia, and later to France, Japan, and Italy, asking them to join the United States in respecting the preservation of China's independence and territory. However, the Open Door Policy failed to slow the pace of imperialism in China. The **Russo-Japanese War** (1904–1905) threatened the open door in China by making Japan the dominant power in the Far East. President Theodore Roosevelt persuaded both Japan and Russia to recognize the neutrality of all Chinese territory outside of Manchuria and brought the warring sides to Portsmouth, New Hampshire (September 1905) to draft a peace treaty.

The Boxer Rebellion

As their nation continued to fall into the hands of European and Asian imperialist nations, the **Boxers**, a Chinese society encouraged by **Manchu** leaders, vowed to drive the "foreign devils" out of China. In June 1900 members of the Boxers attacked the foreign holdings (concessions) in Peiping and massacred 300 people. A joint expeditionary force of European, Japanese, and American troops suppressed the rebellion. The Manchu Dynasty was overthrown in 1912 by the **Nationalists (Kuomintang)** under **Sun Yat-sen**, and China was proclaimed a republic.

The Acquisition of Hawaii

Possibly discovered by European navigators early in the 16th century, the Hawaiian Islands were visited by Captain Cook in 1778. During the early 19th century, American traders, missionaries, and whalers visited the Hawaiian Islands. In 1842 the State Department announced that the Hawaiian Islands would not be open to colonization by any other nation. In 1875 the **Reciprocity Treaty** granted commercial favors to the islands if the Hawaiian king assured the United States that he would not allow other powers to acquire territory. A treaty in 1887 between Hawaii and the United States provided for the leasing of **Pearl Harbor** as a naval station.

As American interests, represented primarily by sugar plantations and missionaries, grew in Hawaii, the white population of the islands became increasingly influential. When **Queen Liliuokalani** attempted to nationalize the sugar plantations and drive foreign investors out, American planters revolted (January 1893). They overthrew the queen, set up a provisional government establishing the **Republic of Hawaii**, and asked for annexation by the United States. President Cleveland withdrew the annexation treaty from the Senate, and arguments concerning the fate of Hawaii continued through the 1890s. After the victory in the Spanish-American War, annexation of the Philippine Islands, and emphasis on naval buildup heightened the expansionist excitement in the country, President McKinley obtained a joint resolution from Congress annexing the Hawaiian Islands on July 7, 1898. Hawaii remained a territory until it was admitted as the fiftieth state in 1959.

Samoa and Naval Bases

The Samoan Islands, some 3,000 miles to the southwest of Hawaii, provided strategic locations in the South Pacific shipping lanes. Like Hawaii, the

The expansion of American interests led to a need for overseas naval bases.

islands had been visited by American sailors and missionaries since the 1830s. In 1872 a United States naval officer negotiated an agreement granting the United States use of the harbor of **Pago Pago**, the site of a later naval station. Great Britain and Germany also secured treaty rights in Samoa and tensions between the three powers came to a showdown in 1889 when German threats of annexation brought fleets from the three countries face-to-face in the harbor at Pago Pago. A timely hurricane wrecked the fleets and subsequently the three nations established a **tripartite protectorate** over the islands.

Hesitant Colonialism

Review of the Monroe Doctrine (1823–1898)

On December 2, 1823, in a message to Congress, President James Monroe, influenced by Secretary of State John Quincy Adams, put forward an independent American foreign policy that later became known as the **Monroe Doctrine**. Claiming that the Western Hemisphere was no longer open to European colonization, the Doctrine proved to be of great importance to future foreign policy determinations of the United States.

The Monroe Doctrine received little attention during the administration of President Jackson, when Great Britain occupied the **Falkland Islands** of Argentina in 1833, and in later administrations, when Great Britain and France intervened in South America in 1838–1839 and 1845–1848. It was asserted as justification for U.S. foreign policy during the Polk administration, concerning Texas (1845) and California (1847). But it was not until after the Civil War that the United States was powerful enough to enforce the Monroe Doctrine throughout the Western Hemisphere.

Mexico's sovereignty was threatened in 1863 when the French took advantage of internal instabilities and created a puppet state under **Archduke Maximilian**. Secretary of State **William Seward** objected to French intervention by **Napoleon III**, emperor of France. In 1865, with the end of the Civil War, American troops were sent to the Mexican border. French troops were withdrawn in 1867, and Maximilian was executed by the Mexicans. The United States saw this as a victory for the Monroe Doctrine and a sign of growing American power in the Western Hemisphere. By the end of the 19th century, the United States had become powerful enough to enforce the Monroe Doctrine. With its growing economic and military power, the United States was ready to join the other world powers in the race for colonies in the 20th century.

The Spanish-American War (1898–1899)

American interests in Cuba increased with economic investments totaling over $50 million by 1895 and an annual trade worth $100 million, the strategic importance of the island, (especially as plans for a **canal** across Central America developed), and the growing spirit of manifest destiny. When Cuban Nationalists revolted against Spain in February 1895, American sympathy for an independent Cuba was encouraged by the sensational stories printed in the "**yellow press**"— **Joseph Pulitzer's** *New York World* and **William Randolph Hearst's** *New York Journal.* Newspaper accounts of Spanish oppression in Cuba, including thousands of deaths in concentration camps, were often exaggerated, but very effective in rallying American support for Cuba.

Following Cuba's refusal to accept President McKinley's plan for increased self-government under Spanish control, and the sinking of the American battleship *Maine* in Havana Harbor on February 15, 1898, popular support for war resulted in a declaration of war against Spain on April 17. At the same time, Congress adopted the **Teller Amendment**, pledging the United States to acquire no Cuban territory and to turn the island over to the Cuban people as soon as their independence was won.

Spain was defeated in Cuba after the battles of **El Caney** and **San Juan Hill**, and the fall of **Santiago** on July 13, 1898. A bloodless conquest of Spanish **Puerto Rico** was conducted by General **Nelson A. Miles**. While the war was being fought in Cuba, American Commodore **George Dewey** defeated the Spanish fleet in the Philippines and captured Manila on August 13.

Empire Building

The **Treaty of Paris** ending the Spanish-American War was signed December 10, 1898. The treaty provided that American troops would remain in Cuba until 1902 while the Cuban constitution was prepared. Included in the Cuban constitution was the **Platt Amendment**, which required that any treaties involving Cuba would have to be approved first by the United States; Cuba was to grant permission to the United States to intervene, if necessary, to preserve the island's independence, and a naval base at **Guantanamo** was to be leased to the United States. The Platt Amendment governed Cuban-American relations until 1934.

• *Puerto Rico.* As a result of the Treaty of Paris (1898), Puerto Rico was ceded to the United States. The **Foraker Act** of 1900 provided that the President of the United States would appoint Puerto Rico's governor and the executive council of its legislature. The **Jones Act** of 1917 granted Puerto Ricans American citizenship and the right to elect both houses of their legislature. In 1948 Puerto Ricans were granted the right to elect their own governor and in 1952 Puerto Rico voted in favor of **commonwealth** status.

• *Guam.* After it was annexed to the United States by Spain in 1898, the island of Guam, located east of the Philippines, was governed by the United States Navy. In 1950 Guam received limited self-government, American citizenship for its inhabitants, a governor appointed by the President of the United States, a popularly elected legislature, and a bill of rights.

• *The Philippines.* When the Treaty of Paris ending the war between Spain and the United States came before the Senate, the question of the annexation of the Philippines sparked heated debate. Anti-imperialists argued that annexation would violate the sacred concept of self-determination. Imperialists stressed the commercial and strategic advantages of ownership, along with the fact that Germany and Japan would most likely move into the Philippines if the United States were to pull out. The arguments of the imperialists triumphed, and the treaty was ratified on February 6, 1898, by a 57-to-27 vote.

When the Philippines did not receive independence following the Spanish-American War, a rebellion under the leadership of **Emilio Aguinaldo** broke out. This insurrection, known as the **Philippine-American War**, was a war of larger proportions than the Spanish-American War, and resulted in more American casualties. After the rebellion was suppressed, the United States imposed its regime on the Philippines. English was made the official language, public works were introduced, and sedition acts and political imprisonment silenced critics. Beginning in 1907 the Filipinos elected the lower house of their legislature. The **Jones Act** of 1916 granted the citizens of the Philippines the right to elect both houses of their legislature and promised eventual independence. During the administration of Franklin Roosevelt, the **Tydings-McDuffie Act** (1934) was passed, providing for eventual independence and allowing the Filipinos to write a constitution. In 1946 the islands formally received independence and the following year granted the United States military bases within their country.

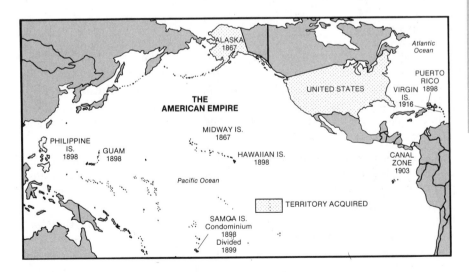

Figure 3.2 The American Empire (1903)

Constitutional Issues

America's new overseas territories raised a constitutional question concerning the status of alien peoples and whether constitutional protections of the United States were extended to them. In the so-called "insular cases," particularly *Downes* v. *Bidwell* (1901), the Supreme Court ruled on the question, "Does the Constitution follow the flag?" It concluded that the Constitution protected the basic civil rights of inhabitants of colonial possessions, but did not confer citizenship or political rights on them. Justice Brown, writing for the majority, held that there were "natural rights enforced in the Constitution," such as the right to personal liberty, property, religious freedom, and freedom of speech, which were beyond the power of Congress to deny.

Latin American Affairs

> There is a homely adage which runs, 'Speak softly and carry a big stick; you will go far.' If the American nation will speak softly and yet build and keep at a pitch of the highest training a thoroughly efficient navy, the Monroe Doctrine will go far.
>
> President Theodore Roosevelt, September 2, 1901

West Indies Protectorates

As American influence spread throughout the Caribbean following the Spanish-American War, the term **"American Lake"** was applied to the area. Between 1900 and 1917, American troops intervened in Cuba, Panama, the Dominican Republic, Mexico, Nicaragua, and Haiti.

Panama Canal

Following the acquisition of Oregon and California, the United States became interested in a canal across the **isthmus** (a narrow strip of land with water on both sides) in Central America. A treaty with **Colombia** in 1846 granted the United States the right to build either a canal or railroad across Panama (part of Colombia until 1903), and in 1850 the United States and Great Britain agreed to exercise joint control over a future canal.

• *Acquisition and Construction.* America's new possessions in the Caribbean and Pacific underscored the need for a means of faster transportation across Central America. Remembering the seventy-one days required for the battleship *Oregon* to sail from San Francisco around Cape Horn to its battle station in the Pacific at the outset of the Spanish-American War, President Roosevelt pushed for the construction of a canal. The **Hay-Pauncefote Treaty** (1901) with Great Britain gave the United States sole control over a future canal in return for the guarantee that the canal would be open equally to all nations. Colombia, seeking more money, rejected the **Hay-Herran Treaty** (1903), which was to give the United States a ninety-nine-year lease on a canal zone in the Colombian province of Panama. Frustrated by Colombia's lack of cooperation, President Roosevelt hinted at a Panamanian revolt and shortly thereafter (November 1903), Panamanians rose in revolt against Colombia for independence. Panama's independence was recognized immediately by the United States.

The **Hay-Bunau-Varilla Treaty** (1903) with Panama granted the United States perpetual control of a canal zone ten miles wide across the isthmus of Panama in return for a lump sum payment and an annual fee. On August 15, 1914, the first ocean steamer sailed through the completed canal, which had cost $275 million to build. The international bad feelings between Colombia and the United States were eased by a grant of $21 million in 1921.

• *Current Treaty.* During the 1960s and 1970s Panama demonstrated resentment over the presence of the United States and its sole control over the canal. In January 1964 Panama broke off diplomatic relations with the United States resulting in negotiations over the treaty between the two countries. President Lyndon Johnson announced in December 1964 that he would propose a renegotiation of the 1903 treaty. Although a new treaty granting Panama greater control over the canal was concluded, increased tensions between the countries prevented its ratification. In August 1977 the United States and Panama ended years of negotiations when President **Carter** and General **Torrijos Herrara** signed two treaties providing for the return of the Panama Canal Zone to Panama in the year 2000. The treaties were ratified by the Senate in 1978.

Interpretations of the Monroe Doctrine

As you read, the implementation of the Monroe Doctrine came years after its introduction in 1823. The Monroe Doctrine was tested in 1895 over a boundary dispute between **Venezuela** and the British colony of British **Guiana**. The United States demanded that Great Britain accept arbitration concerning the **Venezuelan boundary dispute**. President Cleveland's Secretary of State **Richard Olney** claimed that the Monroe Doctrine implied that the United States was justified in intervening in Western Hemisphere affairs because "the United States is practically sovereign on the continent." After military force was threatened, Great Britain agreed to arbitration, and Olney's stand became known as the **Olney Interpretation of the Monroe Doctrine**.

President Theodore Roosevelt's interventions in the **Venezuela debt dispute** (1902) and the **Dominican debt default** (1904–1905) illustrated his belief that the United States had to assume "international police power" in the Western hemisphere. This policy of United States intervention in Latin American affairs, excluding intervention by European nations, became known as the **Roosevelt Corollary** to the Monroe Doctrine. Latin American countries soon objected to the paternal and dominating role of the United States.

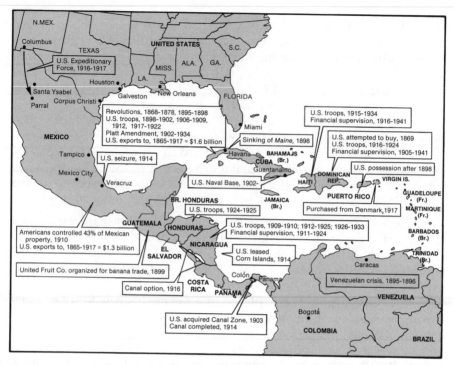

Figure 3.3 The United States and the Caribbean

President Taft and Dollar Diplomacy

United States influence continued to expand in Latin America during the administration of President **Taft** (1909–1913). Under a policy referred to as **"dollar diplomacy,"** United States bankers and businesspeople were encouraged to invest in areas of importance to the United States and were guaranteed full military and diplomatic support. In 1899 two of the largest banana importers merged to form the **United Fruit Company** which, by 1913, owned over one million acres and most of the railroad and steamship lines in Central America. Because of American investments in the countries of Honduras, Nicaragua, and Haiti, the United States felt able to justify military intervention to protect American interests. Intervention came when the United States Marines were ordered into **Nicaragua** in 1912, **Haiti** in 1915, and the **Dominican Republic** in 1916.

President Wilson and Mexico

Porfirio Diaz, the dictator of Mexico for 37 years, was overthrown by a revolution in 1911. After a period of constitutional government, General **Victo-**

riano Huerta seized power in 1913. President Wilson withheld recognition of his government during a time of "watchful waiting," because he considered Huerta a "butcher" whose regime was oppressing the Mexican people. Wilson stationed United States naval units off Mexico and seized the **Port of Vera Cruz** in 1914 to block a German arms shipment. In July 1914 Huerta resigned and Wilson recognized the new government under **Venustiano Carranza**.

In 1916 **Pancho Villa**, a rival Mexican leader, revolted and led raids into New Mexico, hoping to bring the United States into an action that would help him seize power. American forces under General **John Pershing** were ordered into Mexico to capture Villa. Objections from Carranza, and an elusive Pancho Villa, caused Wilson to recall Pershing. As Mexican objections to "**Yankee Imperialism**" continued, relations between the two countries worsened. As part of the **Good Neighbor** policy in the 1930s, Mexican control of its own resources was recognized, while compensation came to the United States in return for **nationalized oil properties**.

Good Neighbor Policy

The United States changed its policy toward Latin America in the 1930s. In 1933, under the "Good Neighbor" policy of President Franklin Roosevelt, the United States agreed that "no state had the right to intervene in the external or internal affairs of another," thus abandoning the (Theodore) Roosevelt Corollary. Some people feel that the 1980s has seen a resurgence of the Roosevelt Corollary to the Monroe Doctrine in the attempts of the United States to curb Communist influence in Nicaragua, El Salvador, and on the Island of Grenada.

Exercise Set 3.4

1. Which is the most valid conclusion that can be drawn concerning the territorial acquisitions of the United States?
   A. the use of a show of military force was always necessary
   B. the "fruits of war" rarely include territorial gains
   C. the addition of territorial gains increases a country's involvement in international affairs
   D. the territorial gains of the United States did not extend beyond the Western Hemisphere

2. The Platt Amendment provided for relations between the United States and
   A. Cuba
   B. Panama
   C. Hawaii
   D. Alaska

3. Which of the following is *not* an example of formal imperialism?
   A. annexation
   B. colonialism
   C. military occupation
   D. humanitarian aid

4. Which of the following did *not* become a United States possession as a result of the Spanish-American War?
   A. Puerto Rico
   B. Panama
   C. the Philippines
   D. Guam

5. The Roosevelt Corollary to the Monroe Doctrine
   A. was widely accepted by Latin America
   B. was reinforced by Franklin Roosevelt in the 1930s
   C. had been used since the introduction of the Monroe Doctrine in 1823
   D. made the United States the peace keeper in the Western Hemisphere

6. The right of American citizens living in China to be tried in American courts was called
   A. "following the flag"
   B. the Open Door Policy
   C. extraterritoriality
   D. dollar diplomacy

RESTRAINT AND INVOLVEMENT (1914–1920)

> The United States must be neutral in fact as well as in name.
> President Wilson, Message to U.S. Senate, 1914

> America cannot be an ostrich with its head in the sand.
> President Wilson, Address to U.S. Senate, 1916

> The world must be made safe for democracy.
> President Wilson, Address to Congress
> asking for declaration of war, April 2, 1917

On July 28, 1914, **Austria-Hungary** declared war on **Serbia** following the assassination of **Archduke Franz Ferdinand**, heir to the Austro-Hungarian throne, by a Serbian nationalist. Germany backed its ally Austria, while Russia mobilized to protect Serbia. Germany in turn declared war on Russia and France, Russia's ally. German troops marched through Belgium to crush France; Britain, honoring its pledge to defend Belgian neutrality, declared war on Germany. The Great War had begun with the Allies (Britain, France, Russia, Serbia, and Belgium) opposing the **Central Powers** (Germany and Austria). Later, the war would engulf most of the nations of the world.

European Background to World War I

Nationalist Rivalries and Alliance System

Following the French Revolution, the nations of Europe had created a "**balance of power**." However, after the unification of Germany in 1871, **Chancellor Otto Von Bismarck** first made an alliance with Austria-Hungary (**Dual Alliance**, 1879); later Italy joined, forming the **Triple Alliance** in 1882.

Seeing the Triple Alliance as a threat, France and Russia ratified a secret alliance in 1894. Although Great Britain did not immediately join the alliance with France and Russia, early in the 20th century an "understanding," which came to be known as the **Triple Entente**, developed between the three nations. Thus, by 1907 the chief European powers had organized themselves into two opposing camps—the Triple Alliance composed of Germany, Austria-Hungary, and Italy, and the Triple Entente, with France, Russia, and Great Britain.

Colonialism and the Spread of War

Underlying reasons for World War I included conflicting **territorial claims**, **imperialistic rivalries**, and **destructive nationalism**. Tension developed between Italy and France over French claims to the Turkish province of

Tunis in North Africa. Germany supported Austria in its rivalry with Russia over the Balkans.

As Germany attempted to secure its "place in the sun," its colonial ambitions turned toward North Africa (Morocco), where it came into conflict with France, and toward the Middle East (Turkey). Conflicts in the Balkans in 1908 and 1912–1913 increased the tensions in Europe and showed the possibility of potential conflict. Although the nations of Western Europe had not come into direct conflict, their armies and navies continued to grow in size and the "peace" that existed was an "armed peace," based upon a **balance of terror**."

Importance of Control of Sea Routes

Great Britain had long followed a policy of keeping its navy superior in strength to any other nation's naval fleet. Germany, realizing that a naval buildup was necessary to compete with Great Britain, began an effort to create a navy second to none. When war broke out in Europe, the fleets of the Allied Powers were effective in forcing German ships to seek the shelter of their home ports. Throughout the war the Allies maintained a **blockade** of Germany and Austria-Hungary that enabled the Allies to import food and raw materials, transport troops, and effectively destroy the commerce of their enemies.

Germany's power on the seas increased with the use of the submarine, or **U-boat**. Although first used to destroy enemy warships, the submarine was eventually used to destroy merchant ships as well. According to international law, a merchant ship was to be warned before attack. However, Germany began a policy of "**unrestricted submarine warfare**" that was so destructive it appeared to spell defeat for the Allies.

United States Involvement

Efforts at Neutrality

When war broke out in Europe in 1914, Americans reacted with horror and wanted to stay out of the hostilities. President Wilson declared American neutrality on August 4, 1914 and, in a message to the Senate, he proclaimed that the United States "must be neutral in fact as well as in name."

Neutrality proved to be a difficult policy as Americans became either pro-Ally, pro-German, or pro-neutral. Those who sympathized with the Allies felt a bond with England and remembered that France had come to the aid of the Americans during our Revolution. Leaders of the pro-Ally group tended to be college-educated and well-to-do people on the East and West coasts and in the South. The movement to enter the war on the side of the Allies was helped by propaganda describing Germany's militarism and unprovoked invasion of Belgium. A considerable part of the country was either pro-German, pro-neutral, or **pacifist** (anti-war). Irish-Americans were traditionally anti-British, and approximately 8 million Americans were of German descent. Among Progressives in the United States, war was seen as violating and interrupting the spirit of Progressive reform. In 1915, Progressives, including **Jane Addams**, **Florence Kelley**, and **Lillian Wald**, formed the **American Union Against Militarism** to stop the "machinery of war." Shortly thereafter, Addams and **Carrie Chapman Catt** formed the **Women's Peace Party** to organize women against the war. But on the whole American sympathies went out to Britain, France, and the other Allies, and against Germany, Austria, and the Central Powers. The memory of their Anglo-Saxon background and cultural heritage, along with the gross violations of Belgian neutrality by Germany, gave the Allied cause in the United States the momentum to quiet the dissenting opinions.

Neutrality became difficult to maintain as the United States continued to trade with both the Allies and the Central Powers. Violations of American neutrality came from both the British and the Germans. The British demanded that ships bound for Germany be first inspected in British ports for contraband (smuggled goods). Germany, to compensate for British naval superiority and to blockade Britain, turned to unrestricted submarine attacks in the war zone around the British Isles. The sinking of the British passenger liner *Lusitania* on May 7, 1915, resulting in the deaths of 128 Americans, outraged the American people. The **Sussex Pledge** (1916) by Germany halted unrestricted submarine warfare temporarily, but torpedo attacks began once again in January 1917. Although Woodrow Wilson had been reelected in 1916 on the slogan, "He kept us out of war," the situation in Europe continued to bring the United States closer to entry. After continued strikes against American ships in 1917, President Wilson asked Congress for a declaration of war against Germany. Congress declared war four days later on April 6, 1917.

Causes of United States Entry into War

Although Germany realized that the resumption of unrestricted submarine warfare might force the United States into the war, they felt that United States aid to the Allies would come too late to prevent a German victory. The publication of a telegram ("**Zimmermann Note**"), intercepted by the British in February 1917, turned American opinion against Germany. In the telegram, written by the German foreign minister to Mexico, Germany promised Texas, Arizona, and New Mexico to Mexico in return for its support in the war.

Economic ties with the Allies, including a profitable trade and numerous loans, was an added incentive for Americans to support the Allies. British propaganda, which represented Germany as a threat to democracy, helped convince many Americans that victory for the Allies meant victory for democracy. Finally, when the **Russian Revolution** (1917) resulted in the overthrow of the czar and the establishment of a temporary republican government, the war became more clearly a struggle between democracies and autocracies.

United States Role in the War

Besides American troops, the Allies desperately needed naval power, munitions, industrial goods, and food. The American fleet was primarily responsible for ending the U-boat threat and transporting troops and supplies. The **American Expeditionary Force** under the leadership of General **John J. Pershing** arrived in France in 1917, and in July 1918, along with French troops, drove the Germans back close to their border. Following major victories by the Allies, Germany agreed to consider a peace plan as provided for by Wilson's **Fourteen Points** (January 1918) and an **armistice** (cease-fire) was signed on November 11, 1918.

Communist Russia

Although the United States was initially pleased to see the overthrow of the czar in Russia, the seizure of power by the **Bolsheviks** and the establishment of communism caused concern. After the war, Europe was ravaged by poverty and chaos—conditions that made the area vulnerable to Communist propaganda and ideology.

Exercise Set 3.5

1. U.S. entry into both the War of 1812 and World War I was caused in part by
   A. foreign troops on American soil
   B. Presidents who encouraged entry into war
   C. interference with American shipping
   D. a foreign nation's threat to Mexico

2. The factor that was most significant in causing President Wilson to ask Congress for a declaration of War on Germany in April 1917 was
   A. the German invasion of Belgium
   B. the Russian Revolution of 1917
   C. the sinking of the *Sussex*
   D. the resumption of unrestricted submarine warfare by Germany

3. What was the primary focus of United States foreign policy in the decade after World War I?
   A. to defend the price of freedom of the seas
   B. to reduce United States commitments to other nations
   C. to contain the spread of communism in Eastern Europe
   D. to fulfill collective security agreements with Western European nations.

4. Wilson was reelected to the presidency in 1916 because of his claim that
   A. entry into World War I was inevitable
   B. he had kept the United States out of war
   C. he would immediately bring the United States into the war
   D. he would begin submarine attacks against the Germans

THE CONSTITUTION AND WORLD WAR I

> The question in each case is whether the words used are used in such circumstances and are of such nature to create a clear and present danger that they will bring about the substantive evils Congress has the right to prevent.
>
> Majority Opinion, *Schenck* v. *United States* (1919)

> Anarchy stands for the liberation of the human mind from the dominion of religion, the liberation of the human body from the dominion of poverty, liberation from the shackles and restraints of government.
>
> Emma Goldman, *Anarchism* (1910)

War Opposition and Patriotism, the Draft Issue

As America approached entry into war, public opinion was by no means unified. Heated debate continued between those who advocated military support for the Allies, supporters of neutrality, and antiwar critics.

Anti-German Feelings

Anti-German feelings were building before 1917, much the result of submarine warfare. After American entry into the war, preparation was encouraged by groups such as the **National Security League** and the **Navy League**, while public opinion was mobilized by George Creel's **Committee on Public Information (CPI)**. Recruiting the services of thousands of people in the arts, advertising, and film industries, the CPI effectively publicized the war. Films like *The Prussian Cur* and *The Kaiser, the Beast of Berlin* brought the message to the screen while the **Division of Industrial Relations** rallied labor around the war effort. As the anti-German sentiment increased, many schools stopped offering instruction in the German language, sauerkraut became "liberty cabbage," and orchestral works by German composers were not performed by American symphony orchestras. Extreme patriotism reached the point of vigilantism in some cases. Radical antiwar leader **Frank Little**, a member of the **Industrial Workers of the World**, was captured in Butte, Montana and hanged.

Antiwar Sentiment

Antiwar activists claimed that war was repressive to the progressive spirit, needlessly cost the lives of a nation's youth, violated Christian morality, and was a profit-making endeavor of the industrial-military leaders. Leaders in Congress including Senator **Robert La Follette** and House Majority Leader **Claude Kitchin** fought United States preparation for entry. Pacifist Progres-

246

sives such as **Jane Addams** and **Paul Kellogg** contributed to the efforts of the **American Union Against Militarism**. Addams helped found the **Women's Peace Party** and even **Andrew Carnegie** and **Henry Ford** helped to finance the peace movements.

The Draft

In 1917, after entry into the war, Congress passed the **Selective Service Act** establishing a system to **draft**, or **conscript**, men into the armed forces. All males between the ages of 18 and 45 were required to register. By the war's end, 24 million men had been registered by local draft boards, with over 4 million serving in the armed forces. In the *Selective Service Cases,* the Supreme Court decided in January 1918 that the draft was constitutional under Congress's power to "declare war and raise and support armies." **Chief Justice White** went on to state that power was derived from the very character of "just government" whose "duty to the citizen includes the reciprocal obligation of the citizen to render military service in case of need and the right to compel it."

Espionage and Sedition Acts

America's participation in World War I raised again, as it had earlier in the Civil War, the conflict between the Bill of Rights and the needs of war. Two laws passed by Congress in 1918, the **Espionage Act** and the **Sedition Act**, placed certain restrictions and limitations upon the freedoms of the press and speech. The Espionage Act outlawed any obstruction with military registration and enlistment and banned "treasonable and seditious" material from the nation's mails, at the discretion of the postmaster general. Publications seized for violation of the Espionage Act included *The New York Times* and the *Saturday Evening Post.* The Sedition Act, an amendment to the Espionage Act, was passed in reaction to activities of pacifists' groups, certain Labor leaders, and "Bolsheviks and radicals." Extending restrictions on interference with enlistment procedures, the act also made it a felony to "utter, print, or publish disloyal, profane, scurrilous, or abusive language about the form of government, the Constitution, soldiers and sailors, flag or uniform of the armed forces . . . ."

For the most part, the Supreme Court endorsed the repressive measures used against radical political activities during the war years. When Secretary **Schenck** of the **Socialist party** was convicted under the Espionage Act for distributing antidraft leaflets, the case (*Schenck* v. *United States,* 1919) was appealed to the Supreme Court on the grounds that the act violated the First Amendment and was therefore unconstitutional. **Justice Holmes**, writing for a unanimous court, upheld the constitutionality of the Espionage Act. Explaining that free speech was never an "absolute" right, he held that, during war, civil liberties could be restricted. "Free speech would not protect a man in falsely shouting fire in a theatre, causing a panic," was an example he provided for the court's reasoning that freedom of speech was not absolute. His approach in determining whether speech could be restricted became known as the "**clear and present danger**" rule. According to this, if words presented a "clear and present danger" of causing evils that Congress had the right to prevent, the speech could be curtailed. Holmes, in the later case of *Abrams* v. *United States* (1919), warned in a strong dissent that restriction of speech must be carefully applied so as not to stop the "**free trade in ideas**" so important in a democratic society.

Wartime Convictions

The decision in *Schenck* by the Supreme Court supported the government's prosecution of those who violated wartime security measures. The Espionage Act was upheld again in *Debs* v. *United States* (1919), an appeal from the conviction of Socialist party leader **Eugene V. Debs**. Debs was found guilty of felonious acts after delivering a speech denouncing capitalism and the war. "**Big Bill**" **Haywood**, leader of the **Industrial Workers of the World**, joined forces with 75-year-old **Mother Jones** and radical **Elizabeth Gurley Flynn** and appealed mostly to unskilled workers to join in destroying capitalism and stopping the war. Federal prosecutions during the war years sent Haywood and many radicals to prison. American anarchist **Emma Goldman**, imprisoned earlier for advocating birth control and pacifism, was deported to Russia in 1919.

The lower courts tried about 2,000 cases that involved the Espionage Act. Most of them, involving violations consisting of vague statements criticizing the war, government, or conscription, resulted in convictions.

The Red Scare 1918–1920

During the war, the **Bolshevik Revolution** in 1917 brought a Communist government to Russia. After the new Russian government under the leadership of **Lenin** withdrew from the war and made a separate peace with Germany, Americans felt betrayed. They were also frightened by the Bolsheviks' calls for workers everywhere to revolt. A "**Red Scare**" in the United States intensified as communism began to spread in Europe.

American Foreign Policy and Russia

American foreign policy also reflected hostile feelings toward Russia. In June 1918 President **Wilson**, without the consent of Congress, ordered American troops into Siberia to guard allied supplies and to observe Japanese influence in northern Russia. Wilson hoped to smash the Bolshevik government whose Communist influences were felt in short-term uprisings in both Germany and Hungary in early 1919. The American government refused to recognize the Bolshevik government, set up an economic blockade of Russia, sent arms to anti-Bolshevik forces, and later blocked Russian participation in the Paris Peace Conference.

Violations of Civil Rights

During the "Red Scare," extreme actions were taken against radicals. The civil liberties of "radicals," including many socialists and communists, were violated when Wilson's Attorney General, **A. Mitchell Palmer**, ordered the deportation of suspected radicals, raided homes of those suspected of being involved in "subversive" activities, and arrested hundreds whose economic and political views were unorthodox. The political implications of the trial and execution of anarchists **Nicola Sacco** and **Bartolomeo Vanzetti** for murder in 1920 brought worldwide attention to the "blind patriotism" of the Red Scare period.

Exercise Set 3.6

1. Where in the Constitution would you find the "freedom of speech" guarantee?
   A. the Preamble
   B. Article I
   C. the "elastic clause"
   D. the First Amendment

2. All of the following were found to be guilty of "subversive activities" before or during World War I EXCEPT
   A. Emma Goldman
   B. George Creel
   C. "Big Bill" Haywood
   D. Eugene V. Debs

3. A study of the Supreme Court's decision in the case of *Schenck* v. *United States* (1919) indicates that
   A. during times of war civil liberties may be restricted
   B. the First Amendment is absolute in nature
   C. all political speech is protected by the First Amendment
   D. the activities of subversive groups may be restricted without any review by the courts

4. The case of Sacco and Vanzetti aroused sympathy for them and criticism of government measures because they
   A. were executed immediately
   B. were found innocent of all charges against them
   C. probably did not receive a fair trial as a result of unsubstantiated fears
   D. were imprisoned without a trial

THE SEARCH FOR PEACE AND ARMS CONTROL (1914–1930)

> A general association of nations must be formed . . . for the purpose of affording mutual guarantees of political independence and territorial integrity to great and small states alike.
>
> President Woodrow Wilson
> Address to Congress, January 8, 1918

The Peace Movement

The movement that had objected to America's entry into World War I gained further support when the United States considered the peace settlement following the war that included membership in an international **League of Nations**. Americans were tired of war and were no longer receptive to President Wilson's justification of America's role in the Great War. Groups including Representative **Jeannette Rankin's American Women Opposed to the League of Nations** and the **Women's International League for Peace and Freedom** opposed American membership in the League of Nations. They viewed the League as a vehicle for bringing the United States into future international conflicts. Ironically, later in the 1920s and 1930s, some of these same groups, including the Women's International League for Peace and Freedom, advocated cooperation with the League of Nations and membership in the World Court as preventive measures to avoid war as a solution to international problems.

Wilson's Fourteen Points

President Wilson was able to transform the war, which was an ugly grinding struggle, into a noble crusade for liberty, democracy, and permanent peace. Wilson's peace aims were developed in a long series of speeches and public papers from 1914 to 1918. His **Fourteen Points** were listed in an address to Congress on January 8, 1918; a list would be circulated among the populations of Europe in millions of leaflets.

President Wilson's Fourteen Points included the following:

- the replacement of secret treaties with **open diplomacy** among nations
- **freedom of the seas**
- **removal of economic/trade barriers** between nations
- **reductions in armaments**
- **adjustment of colonial claims** with respect for native populations

251

- redrawing of European boundaries with a respect for nationalities and "**self-determination**"
- the formation of an **association of nations**

By the fall of 1918 the Allied Armies, with the assistance of American forces, were advancing toward the German border. Shortly thereafter, the German government opened negotiations with Wilson for a peace on the basis of the Fourteen Points.

The Versailles Treaty

Although President Wilson sailed for Paris in December 1918 with the intention of writing his Fourteen Points into the peace treaty, problems for his ambitious plans had already started. Worried about legislative support in the approaching peace negotiations, the President appealed to the American people for Democratic victories in the midterm elections of 1918. However, this appeal backfired. The Republicans captured both houses of Congress and they resented Wilson's partisan tactics. Wilson's second blunder was his failure to take any members of the House or the Senate with him to Paris, instead bringing with him a delegation he expected to dominate in the treaty-writing process.

The **Paris Peace Conference** began its work in January 1919 under the direction of Woodrow Wilson and Prime Ministers **Georges Clemenceau** of France, **David Lloyd George** of Great Britain, and **Vittorio Orlando** of Italy. Much of Wilson's plan for peace was negotiated away through compromise, much of it to preserve his League of Nations. The final **Treaty of Versailles**, signed by delegates from Germany on June 28, 1919 (separate peace treaties were drawn up with Germany's allies), provided for (1) an admission by Germany of its **war guilt**; (2) stripping Germany of its **colonies**; (3) **adjusting German borders**, taking away Alsace-Lorraine, Posen, the Saar Basin, parts of Schleswig and Silesia; and (4) stripping Germany of most of its **military** and **naval** forces.

Reluctantly, President Wilson agreed to a treaty that did not mention freedom of the seas, or reduced tariffs. Negotiations had been secretive and the reparations assigned to Germany were impossible to repay. Wilson's last hope was an effective association of nations in which the United States would have a major role.

The League of Nations and United States Rejection

The **Covenant** for the League of Nations was incorporated into the Versailles Treaty. It provided for an **Assembly** to represent all member nations, a **Secretariat**, permanently located in Geneva, Switzerland, a

Council controlled by the permanent members (United States, England, France, Italy, and Japan) and four other nations elected by the Assembly, and a separate **Permanent Court of International Justice** (known as the **World Court**). Under the Covenant the members of the League were pledged to seek disarmament, to arbitrate differences, and to act together against outside aggressors or covenant breakers in a system of "**collective security**."

The Struggle over Ratification

The struggle over American ratification of the Treaty of Versailles, including the League of Nations, became a bitter duel between Woodrow Wilson and the Republican Chairman of the Senate Committee on Foreign Relations, **Henry Cabot Lodge**. Much of the objection to the treaty was based on political jealousy, largely due to Wilson's refusal to consult Republican Senators in creating the treaty. However, many feared that participation in the League of Nations might draw the United States into European troubles.

As the Senate carried out its Constitutional role of "Advise and Consent" concerning foreign treaties (Article II, Section 2), three groups developed: Democratic followers of Wilson who favored immediate ratification; hard core "irreconcilables" (including **William Borah** of Idaho, **Robert La Follette** of Wisconsin, and **Hiram Johnson** of California) who opposed American membership in the international organization; and moderates who preferred a watered-down version of the League that would include certain "reservations" to protect American interests. While Lodge kept the treaty locked up in committee from July to September 1919, opponents of the League worked to turn public opinion against Wilson. Lodge proposed **fourteen amendments** to the League Covenant, the most important of which would require Congressional approval for the deployment of American troops. President Wilson decided to appeal directly to the American people, but in the midst of a speaking tour through the Middle West, he suffered a paralytic stroke and remained an invalid during the critical period of debate on the League.

Rejection of the Treaty

On November 19, 1919, Wilson's Democratic supporters and the "irreconcilables" combined to defeat the treaty with the Lodge reservations. The reservationists and the "irreconcilables" then voted down the treaty in its original form. Once again, in March 1920, the treaty failed to receive the necessary two-thirds approval of the Senate, although the vote was 49 to 35 in its favor. Finally, when the Republicans were victorious in the election of 1920, sending **Warren G. Harding** to the White House, they saw their victory as a mandate against the League of Nations. A joint resolution was adopted by Congress on August 25, 1921, declaring the war to be over.

Washington Naval Disarmament Conference

Although the United States did not formally join the League of Nations, it did cooperate on a limited basis. Gradually, the United States regularized its informal contacts at Geneva and joined some of the League's activities (**International Labor Organization**, efforts to wipe out disease, support of the League's efforts to settle the crisis in Manchuria in 1931).

President Harding sponsored the **Washington Disarmament Conference of 1921**, which led to the limitation of battleship construction among the chief naval powers (Britain, United States, Japan, France, and Italy) and stabilized the balance of power in the Far East. Temporarily, the Conference seemed to be a substantial step toward **arms control** and **economic rehabilitation**.

Reparation and War Debts

Following the war, the European nations owed debts that amounted to $26.5 billion, about half of which was owed to the United States. Ill feelings soon developed between Europe and the United States as a result of American demands for repayment. Europeans hoped that much of the debt would be forgiven in light of the fact that the loss of European lives had been so great.

Much of the ability of the Allies to repay the United States depended upon Germany's ability to pay its reparations (war debts) to the Allies. When Germany began to default on its debts, American investors loaned millions to Germany. In addition, the **Dawes Plan of 1924** reduced Germany's annual payments, extended the repayment period, and provided additional loans. Unfortunately, a **depression** in Europe contributed to the European nations' inability to repay their debts to the United States, and in 1931 President Hoover declared a **moratorium** on debt payments after the Allies had paid back only $2.6 billion.

Kellogg-Briand Pact (1928)

An agreement, eventually signed by 62 nations, and named for United States Secretary of State **Frank Kellogg** and French Foreign Minister **Aristede Briand**, was negotiated in 1928 "condemning recourse to war for the solution of international controversies, and renouncing it as an instrument of the national policy." The **Kellogg-Briand Pact** passed the Senate by a vote of 85 to 1, but was looked upon skeptically by many because it provided no means of enforcement.

The World Court

Periodic proposals for U.S. membership in the World Court (the League's judicial agency) were defeated in the Senate during the administrations of Presidents Harding and Coolidge. The Court itself rejected America's admission in 1926 when certain conditions were insisted upon by the United States. Attempts by Presidents Hoover and Franklin Roosevelt to gain America's membership were also frustrated by a Senate that was heavily influenced by isolationist forces and by those who feared that membership in the Court would involve the nation in League affairs and the problems of Europe.

Exercise Set 3.7

1. The major flaw of the Kellogg-Briand Pact (1928) was that it
   A. was signed by only four nations
   B. was discouraged by the League of Nations
   C. had no provisions for enforcement
   D. violated the provisions of the Washington Naval Disarmament Conference of 1921

2. The primary reason for the United States Senate's rejection of the Treaty of Versailles was
   A. the forced assumption by Germany of war guilt
   B. the fact that the war continued in the Western Hemisphere
   C. the inclusion of the League of Nations Covenant
   D. the refusal of the Allies to repay their war debts to the United States

3. At the Paris Peace Conference, President Wilson pushed for
   A. U.S. occupation of Western Europe
   B. the establishment of a League of Nations
   C. the immediate repayment of all war debts to the United States
   D. military occupation of Germany

4. European nations claimed they were having difficulty paying their war debts to the United States because
   A. the United States failed to join the League of Nations
   B. Germany had defaulted on its reparations to the Allies
   C. the United States lowered its tariffs
   D. American bankers were investing in Germany

CHAPTER REVIEW QUESTIONS

Base your answers to questions 1 and 2 on the cartoon and on your knowledge of social studies.

1. The main purpose of the cartoon is to express opposition to which President's action?
   A. Woodrow Wilson's support of the Treaty of Versailles
   B. Franklin Roosevelt's announcement of the Good Neighbor Policy
   C. Harry Truman's decision to send aid to Europe after World War II
   D. Ronald Reagan's 1985 summit meeting with Chairman Gorbachev of the Soviet Union.

2. According to the cartoon, the United States should follow a foreign policy of
   A. collective security
   B. noninvolvement
   C. detente
   D. imperialism

INTERRUPTING THE CEREMONY

McCUTCHEON, CHICAGO TRIBUNE-NEW YORK NEWS SYNDICATE, INC.

3. Supreme Court decisions in cases involving the First Amendment to the federal Constitution generally reflect the principle that
   A. if an action is based on a religious belief, it must be allowed
   B. only demonstrations that support the beliefs of the majority may be held
   C. freedoms of speech and press are absolute
   D. individual rights must be balanced against the needs of society at the time

4. An advantage of the United Nations that has contributed to its success when compared to the League of Nations is
   A. the provision that no armed forces are used to carry out its goals
   B. the membership of all the world's major powers
   C. the lack of a judicial body
   D. its complete prevention of war in the world

5. The most accurate statement concerning U.S. foreign policy is that the United States has generally
   A. used military confrontation to solve disputes
   B. reacted forcefully to imperialism around the world
   C. acted according to national self-interest
   D. formed entangling alliances with countries in need

6. The major foreign policy issue facing the Wilson administration between the outbreak of the First World War in 1914 and United States entry in 1917 was
   A. freedom of the seas
   B. German aggression in the Caribbean
   C. the future of United States overseas possessions
   D. tariff controversies with Japan

7. After the Spanish-American War Cuba was
   A. left completely independent
   B. restricted by the Platt Amendment
   C. admitted as a state to the United States
   D. reoccupied by the Spanish

ESSAYS

1. U.S. Supreme Court decisions in cases involving the First Amendment to the federal Constitution generally reflect the principle that individual rights are balanced against the demands of the time.

Select *one* of the Supreme Court cases listed below and discuss the significance of the statement above *and* its application to the Supreme Court case. [10]

Supreme Court Cases

Schenck v. *United States* (1919)
Abrams v. *United States* (1919)
Debs v. *United States* (1919)

Discuss why First Amendment speech and press protection during a period of national crisis may be necessary to protect a democratic form of government. [5]

2. Foreign policy actions by the United States, including American involvement in the Spanish-American War and World War I, have been based upon factors such as those listed below.

Factors

Ideology
Pressures from other countries
National self-interest
Domestic pressures
Geography

Select *three* factors from the list above and discuss their significance concerning the involvement of the United States in the Spanish-American War *or* World War I. [15 pts.]

Regents Exam, January 1985

3. Different individuals and governmental bodies have had roles in foreign policy determinations of the United States Government. Between the years 1898 and 1920, describe *one* way in which *three* of the following individuals or government body affected the direction of foreign policy of the United States. [5,5,5]

The President
Political parties
The Congress
Special interest groups/Lobbyists

Regents Exam, January 1984

UNIT FOUR _____

Prosperity and Depression (1917–1940)

> **KEY IDEAS:** The unit details the effect of World War I on the nation and the political, social, and cultural aspects of the decade of the 1920s. The second part of the unit examines the causes and effects of the Great Depression and the changing government role as it dealt with social and economic problems.

UNIT GOAL: By the end of this unit, the student should be able to explain the impact of war on a nation and its people, and the interaction of global, political, economic, and social issues.

UNIT FOUR

Prosperity and Depression (1917–1940)

WAR ECONOMY AND THE PROSPERITY OF THE TWENTIES

THE FIRST WORLD WAR AT HOME

> We are glad . . . to fight thus for the ultimate peace of the world and for the liberation of its peoples. . . . The world must be made safe for democracy.
>
> Woodrow Wilson, Address to Congress, April 2, 1917

> The highest and best form of efficiency is the spontaneous cooperation of a free people.
>
> Bernard M. Baruch, in *American Industry at War: A Report of the War Industries Board, March 1921.*

Selective Service

World War I, like all wars, brought about a dramatic change in people's lives. The **Selective Service Act** of May 28, 1917 required all men 18 to 45 years of age to register for military service. From the nearly 10 million who originally registered, some 700,000 names were drawn by lot for service. By the end of the war, Selective Service had registered 24 million names as a pool from which names could be drawn as needed for the armed services. Of these, close to 5 million were in uniform by the war's end, and more than 2 million were sent overseas. Women served in the Army and Navy Nurses Corps and in the auxiliary forces of the regular Navy.

Mobilizing American Industry

American industry was mobilized for the war. A **War Industries Board** was created, headed by the financier **Bernard M. Baruch**. The Board established priorities for the production of necessary war materiel. It supervised the purchase of supplies for the armed forces, and it allocated vital materials to ensure a steady flow of armaments to those at the front. Industry remained nominally independent, but under the direction of the War Industries Board it operated, as nearly as possible, as a unified production arm of the government's war effort.

In May 1918 President Wilson was given unprecedented powers by the **Overman Act**, which was to be in effect only during the war. It allowed him to create or abolish executive bureaus, agencies, and offices; to shift personnel from one to another; to reallocate funds from one to another, and in short, to do as he thought best for the conduct of the war. In retrospect, it is clear that the power of the President was enormously increased during the war not only in foreign affairs but in virtually every aspect of domestic life.

Providing Food and Fuel

Food and fuel were basic to the conduct of the war both for our troops and for our allies. **Herbert Hoover**, a mining engineer with a Quaker background, was put in charge of food distribution. His task was to see that adequate supplies of basic foods were produced and distributed as needed. He raised the price of wheat to $2.20 a bushel as an inducement to farmers to increase production. He instituted "wheatless" Mondays and "meatless" Tuesdays on a voluntary basis as a means of conserving these essential staples. People responded readily to his request that they plant "victory gardens."

Conservation of fuel was achieved under the direction of a fuel administration headed by **Harry A. Garfield**. Daylight savings time was introduced and motorists were urged to observe "gasless" days to aid the war effort.

Financing the War

The war was financed partly by increased taxes but primarily through borrowing from the American people, who bought **government bonds** in four "Liberty Loan" drives and one final "Victory Loan" drive. These drives yielded 22 billion dollars. Another 10 billion, approximately the amount lent to our allies, was raised through income taxes and by special taxes on liquor, tobacco, and theater tickets.

Transportation and Communication

To facilitate the transportation of troops and war supplies by rail, the railroads were placed under the direction of Secretary of the Treasury **William G. McAdoo**. Government control was later extended to the communication industries—telephone, telegraph, and cable. The Emergency Ship Corporation was created to produce a merchant fleet to transport troops and supplies to the war zone in the face of the threat of German submarines. Shipyards with barracks for 350,000 workers were constructed on an emergency basis at ports on the Atlantic and the Great Lakes. By the war's end more than 500 vessels were added to the carrying capacity of our merchant marine, most of them built in one year.

Labor and the War

The civilian labor force served as an essential underpinning of the war effort. The frequently heard slogan, "Labor will win the war," was both a spur and an expression of pride.

Support of the A.F.L.

Led by Samuel Gompers, the **American Federation of Labor (A.F.L.)**, which had two million members at the outbreak of the war, actively supported the war effort. As millions of men left their jobs to serve in the armed forces, the burgeoning war industries demanded more and more workers and a new labor force had to be formed.

Women in the Labor Force

The labor gap was filled, in part, by women who stepped in to "man" the factories, farms, mills, mines, and railroads in place of their brothers, sons, and husbands. The ranks of labor were filled also by a quarter of a million African Americans who moved from the South into the coal mines, steel mills, and railroads of the North.

Mobilizing the Arts for War

The arts, too, proved to be a mighty force in the war effort. Artists created posters to encourage enlistment and to sell war bonds. The classic "I Want You for the U.S. Army" by **Samuel Montgomery Flagg** and the Liberty Bonds poster by **Walter Whitehead** provided stirring visual war messages.

Song writers used their talents to support the war effort in music. The nation sang **George M. Cohan's** "Over There" with gusto. Another popular World War I song was **Irving Berlin's** "Oh How I Hate to Get Up in the Morning." With millions of American boys in France, the nation sang war-inspired songs such as "Hinky Dinky Parlay Voo" and "How 'Ya Gonna Keep 'em Down on the Farm after They've Seen Paree?"

Propaganda

Propaganda was also a war weapon. The Germans were "Huns" who committed terrible atrocities. The **Kaiser** was "The Beast of Berlin," and many schools discontinued teaching the German language.

Voices of Dissent

Yet, there were voices of dissent in the country despite the prevailing atmosphere of support for the war. Six members of the United States Senate and

57 members of the House of Representatives voted against Wilson's call for a declaration of war against Germany on April 6, 1917. The dissenting members included the first woman member of Congress, Republican **Jeanette Rankin** of Montana. In the Middle West, where many areas had large German-American settlements, sentiment against the war was strong. Republican Senator **Robert M. La Follette** of Wisconsin voted against the war resolution, asserting that "Germany has been patient with us," and Republican Senator **George W. Norris** of Nebraska charged that the United States was being manipulated into the war by financial and commercial interests that stood to profit from the war. Many parents were singing the popular 1915 anti-war song "I Didn't Raise my Boy to be a Soldier."

The "Return to Normalcy"

Reconversion and "Normalcy" (1918–1921)

A spirited demand for reconversion to a peacetime economy set in almost immediately after the war. Both the administration under President Wilson, and the Republican opposition, agreed that the dominance of government over industry must be reversed. The **Esch-Cummins Act** of 1920 provided for the return of the railroads to private control. The **Jones Merchant Marine Act** of the same year authorized the sale of government-built ships to private operators. The Republican campaign slogan in the election of 1920 was "back to normalcy," and the presidential candidate **Warren G. Harding** of Ohio declared, "We want a period in America with less government in business and more business in government."

The Fordney-McCumber Tariff

A month after his inauguration, Harding called Congress into special session and asked it to pass legislation for higher tariffs, reduction in taxes and spending, and a bonus for the veterans. Congress responded by passing the "protectionist" **Fordney-McCumber Tariff**, whose high rates were designed to keep foreign goods out of the United States. International trade was reduced when European nations retaliated with tariff restrictions of their own.

Tax Reduction

Congress approved Harding's tax proposals by reducing income taxes substantially. Government expenditures were to be brought under control by two newly created agencies—the **Bureau of the Budget** and the **General Accounting Office.** "Normalcy" had returned, but a rocky road lay ahead.

Exercise Set 4.1

1. "To protect the workers in their right . . . to be full sharers in the abundance which is the result of their brains and brawn . . . is the glorious mission of the trade unions."

Samuel Gompers, Speech, 1898

In pursuit of this goal during World War I, organized labor
A. resisted efforts to draft union members into the armed services
B. opposed the entrance of women and blacks into the labor market
C. engaged in a crippling general strike
D. essentially cooperated with and supported the U.S. war effort

2. Which of the following was *not* used during World War I as a means of securing an adequate food supply?
A. planting of "victory gardens" by people who were not farmers
B. raising the price of wheat to stimulate increased production
C. government restriction on the shipment of food to Europe
D. encouragement of voluntary reduction in the consumption of food through "wheatless" and "meatless" days during the week

3. Woodrow Wilson's doctrine of "strict accountability" had specific application to
A. submarine warfare
B. loans to belligerents
C. investment in foreign countries
D. treatment of prisoners of war

Base your answers to questions 4 through 6 on the cartoon below and on your knowledge of social studies.

4. Which economic concept is illustrated in the cartoon?
A. depression
B. protective tariff
C. supply and demand
D. government price controls

5. Cotton farmers in the South experienced the situation shown in the cartoon because of the region's reliance on
A. sharecropping
B. government subsidies
C. subsistence farming
D. a single-crop economy

6. Between 1914 and 1916, which factor helped bring about the change in the financial position of the cotton farmer as shown in the cartoon?
   A. the demand for cotton became high during World War I
   B. climatic changes in other cotton-growing nations greatly reduced their cotton crops
   C. American cotton became more resistant to destructive insect pests
   D. new styles of clothing required large amounts of cotton

   Regents Exam, August 1988

7. In World War I public opinion
   A. remained strictly neutral until Wilson asked for war
   B. remained disinterested in the war until the sinking of the Lusitania
   C. preponderantly favored the Allied nations
   D. was evenly divided between the two opposing sides

8. During World War I the United States financed the war effort by every means EXCEPT
   A. issuing "printing press" money
   B. selling bonds by high pressure campaigns
   C. levying excess profits taxes on corporations
   D. increasing excise taxes

9. The Republicans returned to power with the election of Warren G. Harding in 1920. The new President's call for a "return to normalcy" turned out to mean
   A. low tariffs and high taxes
   B. active participation in international affairs
   C. a huge increase in government expenditures
   D. isolationism and protectionism

THE TWENTIES: BUSINESS BOOM OR FALSE PROSPERITY?

> I have no fear for the future of our country. It is bright with hope.
> Herbert Hoover, Inaugural Address, March 4, 1929

> There is little question that in 1929 . . . the economy was fundamentally unsound.
> John Kenneth Galbraith in *The Great Crash, 1929*

The Election of 1920

The country entered a new era with the election of 1920. The Republicans chose Senator **Warren G. Harding** of Ohio as their presidential candidate, and Governor **Calvin Coolidge** of Massachusetts as his running mate. The Democrats nominated Governor **James M. Cox** of Ohio for President and Assistant Secretary of the Navy **Franklin Delano Roosevelt** for Vice-President.

Wilson called for a "solemn referendum" on the League of Nations as a key issue in the election. The Republicans accepted the challenge. The war-weary nation supported the Republicans in rejecting the League and the idealism of Woodrow Wilson. The Democratic party suffered from public disaffection with war measures—the draft, food shortages, restrictions on business. The "Red Scare" of 1920, resulting from the Bolshevik revolution in Russia, was another factor contributing to the overwhelming Republican victory—404 to 127 electoral votes and 61 percent of the popular vote—for Warren G. Harding.

The 19th Amendment to the Constitution, granting women the right to vote, was ratified by the required three fourths of the states on August 26, 1920, and, as a result, women were able to vote in a national election for the first time.

Economic Recession (1921–1922)

A severe economic recession, caused in part by the conversion of the industrial war machine to a peace economy, staggered the nation in 1921. A sharp deflation saw the consumer price index fall from 154.5 in 1920 to 97.6 in 1921. The market was glutted with heavy inventories of goods produced during the war. Exports dropped sharply. As 20,000 businesses failed in 1921, unemployment reached 4,750,000 or 11.5 percent of the labor force. As the war demand for food slackened, the American farmers experienced falling prices that resulted in mass bankruptcies and foreclosures. The war's end also brought on serious labor strife. Major strikes occurred in the coal, steel, and railroad industries.

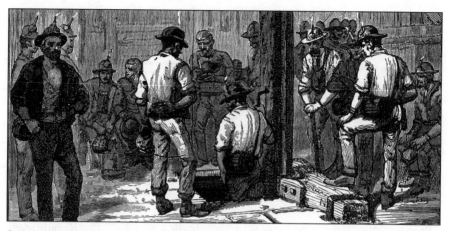

Coal miners struck for better working conditions following World War I.

The average work week of steel workers was 68.7 hours. Their demand for an eight-hour day and the right to unions of their own choosing was met with outright rejection by powerful corporations. Grievances of the coal miners included extremely dangerous working conditions, a work week often limited to two or three days, and company ownership of the miners' homes and of the markets in which they purchased food, clothing, and other necessities. Railway labor went on strike when wages were reduced by President Harding's Railway Labor Board. The textile industry, which had migrated to the South where labor conditions were more favorable to mill owners, witnessed strikes by employees, many of them young women, whose wages were generally 18 cents an hour for a 56-hour work week. Court injunctions, supported by public opinion, were used to break the strikes. Union membership declined steadily during the 1920s.

War Loans and Debts

When the United States entered the war, the Allies had been at war with Germany almost three years. Their financial resources were exhausted. Consequently, loans were extended by the U.S. government to enable them to pay for the food and war materiel supplied by the American farmers and manufacturers. The British war debt, including postwar loans (in money and goods) for rehabilitation, amounted to $4.3 billion; the French $3.5 billion; the Italian $1.6 billion, and smaller amounts were owed by Belgium, Greece, and other Allies. The Allies argued that these debts should be canceled because they had been incurred in a common cause, but the Harding administration insisted they be repaid. "Silent Cal" Coolidge summed it up in the terse remark, "They hired the money, didn't they?"

France and Britain presented Germany with a bill for $33 billion in **reparations** for damages caused by the war for which the Versailles Treaty had laid the blame on Germany. To enable Germany to pay, the United States adopted the **Dawes Plan of 1924** proposed by the Illinois financier **Charles G. Dawes**. Essentially, the plan scaled down reparations payments and provided for American loans to Germany. The entire war debts-reparations issue came to a halt with the **Great Depression** of the 1930s.

Scandals in the Harding Administration

President Harding died suddenly in San Francisco on August 2, 1923, and his Vice-President **Calvin Coolidge** was sworn in as President. Shortly before Harding's death rumors began to circulate about corruption in his administration. The villains included "friends" of the President, known as the "Ohio Gang," with whom he had surrounded himself in Washington.

Teapot Dome

A major scandal, but by no means the only one, centered around government oil resources at **Teapot Dome** in Wyoming and **Elk Hills** in California. About two months after Harding's death, a Senate committee under **Thomas Walsh** of Montana was formed to investigate oil leases made to private companies from these government oil reserves. The reserves had been set aside under Presidents Taft and Wilson for the use of the Navy.

Soon after his inauguration, President Harding transferred the Teapot Dome and Elk Hills oil reserves from the Navy Department (Secretary **Edwin C. Denby**) to the Interior Department (Secretary **Albert B. Fall**). Denby approved of this transfer. Fall then entered into a secret, illegal, and corrupt deal with two oil men, **Harry Sinclair** and **Edward Doheny**. Without competitive bidding and at a bargain price, Teapot Dome was leased to Sinclair, who had made a large contribution to the Republican campaign in 1920, and the Elk Hills reserve was leased to Doheny, a close friend of Fall. In March 1923, Fall resigned from the Cabinet.

The investigation committee discovered that Fall had received a "loan" of $100,000 from Doheny on which he was charged no interest, put up no security, and made no arrangement for repayment. Fall went to jail for accepting a bribe from Doheny. The Supreme Court declared the leases invalid because they were made by a "conspiracy" involving "fraud" and "corruption." Secretary of the Navy Denby resigned during the Senate investigation.

Fraud in the Veterans Bureau

The Senate disclosed that **Charles R. Forbes**, head of the Veterans Bureau, had defrauded the government of $200 million in connection with the building of veterans' hospitals and in conspiring to sell narcotics, liquor, and other government properties. He was sentenced to two years in prison. During the trial, **Charles F. Framer**, legal adviser to the Veterans Bureau, committed suicide.

Bribery in the Justice Department

The investigation also revealed that Harding's Attorney General, **Harry M. Daugherty**, another member of the "Ohio Gang," had been bribed by violators of the Prohibition amendment and had known of graft in the Veterans Bureau, but had taken no action. President Coolidge forced him to resign.

When it was disclosed that **Jesse Smith**, a close friend and aide to Attorney General Daugherty, had been taking bribes, Smith committed suicide. These scandals revealed what many, including Harding himself, had come to realize: the responsibilities of the presidency were too great for his capabilities.

Coolidge Prosperity Not For Everyone

> The Business of America is Business.
>
> Calvin Coolidge

In the election of 1924, the Republicans won an easy victory with President **Calvin Coolidge** triumphing over the Democratic challenger **John W. Davis**, a New York corporate lawyer. "Coolidge prosperity" was the keynote of the Republican campaign, which resulted in a popular vote of nearly 2 to 1 and an electoral vote of 382 for Coolidge and 136 for Davis.

Despite the conservative Republican victory, there were disquieting rumblings in their own party, indicating that the Coolidge prosperity was not for everyone. Charging that Coolidge "had literally turned his back on the farmers," Senator **Robert M. La Follette**, Republican of Wisconsin, ran for President on the newly formed **League for Progressive Political Action**. He received support not only from the farm belt but also from labor groups and Socialists. The Progressive program called for federal assistance, including low-interest credit to farmers, social legislation for the benefit of labor, and government ownership of railroads and water power. Despite the charge made by both Republicans and Democrats that La Follette was a dangerous radical, he received almost 5 million votes, about 16 percent of the total cast.

The election of 1924 was marked by a surge of women candidates in state elections. Two women, **Miriam A. "Ma" Ferguson** of Texas and **Nellie T. Ross** of Wyoming, were elected Governor of their states. Both were wives of former Governors. And 123 women were elected to state legislatures.

Slump in Agriculture

Agriculture, like other segments of the economy, had enjoyed economic prosperity during the war, heightened by greatly increased demand for food

Government support of farm prices was repeatedly vetoed by President Coolidge.

in the European war zone. As prices of wheat, meat, and other farm products rose rapidly, farmers borrowed money to buy farm machinery and to increase their acreage under cultivation. The **gasoline-engine tractor** could sow and cultivate more in an hour than the horse-driven plow could accomplish in a day. As farm hands returned from the war and European farms again entered the market, an over-abundance of farm produce caused a severe slump in farm prices. The wholesale price index of farm products (1910–1914 = 100) was at 211 in 1920 and dropped to 121 in 1921. Its high during the 1920s was 149 in 1928. In 1932 it was 68, lowest in 33 years. Farm mortgage debt rose from $7.8 billion in 1920 to $10.8 billion in 1923.

To help maintain farm prices, Senator **Charles L. McNary** of Oregon and Congressman **Gilbert N. Haugen** of Iowa introduced the **McNary-Haugen Bill** in 1924. It provided that the government would buy and store enough corn, wheat, and other staple crops to keep farm prices at a level that would yield a return comparable to that which prevailed prior to World War I. The government could either sell the surplus on the domestic market when farm prices rose above this "parity" level, or it could sell the surplus at any price in foreign markets. Congress passed the McNary-Haugen Bill in 1927 and again in 1928, but each time it was vetoed by President Coolidge, who thought it would cost the government too much money. "Farmers never made money," said Coolidge, "I don't believe we can do much about it."

The "Golden Twenties"

"Golden Twenties" was the name given to the period of economic prosperity for many, but not all, segments of the American economy. As we have seen, farmers generally were experiencing hard times. Coal and textiles remained in a slump after the recession of 1921. But most manufacturing, retail trades, transportation, the growing service industries, and other segments of the labor force were earning good wages and spending freely. Business was booming. Few doubted that good times would never end.

Speculation in the "Big Bull Market"

The stock market offered an almost irresistible temptation to make easy money. People from all walks of life began to "play the market" and watched the paper values of their investments soar. **Standard and Poor's Composite Index** of 500 stocks registered 67.7 in 1922. In 1929, just before the crash of stock prices, it stood at 190.3. The accelerating boom of the "Big Bull Market" led more and more people to risk their savings in the "get rich quick" orgy. Many were buying on margin, that is, putting as little as 10 percent of the purchase price down, which meant that if a stock dropped more than 10 percent and they were unable to "cover" their loss they would be wiped out. The bubble was soon to burst.

Exercise Set 4.2

1. The economic sector that benefited *least* from the Coolidge prosperity was
   A. agriculture
   B. labor
   C. large and small business
   D. banking and finance

2. Loans made by the United States during World War I to allied nations
   A. remained largely unrepaid by the debtor nations
   B. were payable in full under the Dawes Plan
   C. were repaid in full during the two decades following the war
   D. were voluntarily canceled during the Coolidge administration

3. In the 1920s the farmers demanded a change in the government's farm program in order to obtain
   A. a higher tariff barrier on agricultural goods
   B. a legislative program that would limit farm production and reduce farm indebtedness
   C. a farm program that included direct farm supports
   D. agricultural prices designed to give the farmer an equitable share of national income

4. Which of these was a general characteristic of the period 1920–1930 in the United States?
   A. strong executive leadership
   B. a retreat from a policy of laissez-faire
   C. apathy toward reform
   D. increase in federal tax rates

5. The main cause of the recession of 1921 was
   A. monetary policies
   B. a decline in American exports to Europe
   C. war scares
   D. greater use of machinery in industry

6. The prosperity of the 1920s was due to all of the following EXCEPT
   A. installment buying
   B. mass merchandising
   C. mass production
   D. higher prices for agricultural staples

OPTIMISM AND MATERIALISM

> The good old times were not good old times. Neither master nor servant was as well situated then as today.
>
> Andrew Carnegie, June 1889

Mass Consumption

Rapid Rise of the Automobile

A brief recession in the years between 1921 and 1922 was soon followed by seven years of phenomenal growth in the American economy. The **automobile**, which was driven by a gasoline engine and was invented as a result of experiments in Europe and America in the late 19th century, played a key role in this economic development. Passenger car registration in the United States reached 8,000 by 1900, jumped to 1.3 million by 1913, rose to 8.1 million by 1920, and catapulted to 26.5 million by 1930—one automobile for every five Americans.

Henry Ford

Industrialist **Henry Ford** was largely responsible for this phenomenon. Ford, of Dearborn, Michigan, built his first automobile in his shop in 1896. The famous **Model T**, first produced in 1909, began to be turned out on the Ford **assembly line** by **mass production** techniques at the rate of one car every 10 seconds by 1925. In 1914 Ford startled the industrial world by

Ford's assembly line turned out one Model T every ten seconds.

introducing the eight-hour day with a minimum daily wage of $5. The rising standard of living of the average American, coupled with an increase in leisure time, created a ready market for the sale of automobiles.

Economic and Social Developments Related to the Automobile

The transformation in the American way of life brought about by the automobile was accompanied by other significant economic and social developments. New road construction, required to accommodate the automobile, was also a spur to automobile production. By 1925 there were more than half a million miles of surfaced highways in the United States. Twenty years later the number had tripled. Other industries associated with the automobile came into being or grew to giant proportions—vulcanized rubber for tires, refined petroleum for fuel, steel, glass, batteries, paint, upholstery and other components of the automobile, as well as gas stations, repair shops, sales agencies, advertising, and insurance. Soon one in every nine American workers was earning a living directly or indirectly from the automobile.

Growth of Suburbia and the Middle Class

In other ways, too, the automobile transformed the character of American life. The movement of the urban middle class from the larger cities to their suburbs was due to automobiles that made it possible to commute to jobs. The growing middle class could afford to move to the suburbs where there was fresh air, space, better homes, and status, and to escape the congestion and the automobile fumes in the cities. This resulted in a real estate boom in suburbia and it accelerated the process of decay in the inner cities.

Decline of the Railroads

The construction of highways and superhighways marked the decline of interurban railroads and trolleys. Railroad mileage, which reached a high of 260,570 miles in 1929, declined to 231,494 thirty years later. Maintenance of the railroads was neglected while expenditures for road building soared.

Impact of Superhighways

Superhighways wrought havoc with planning as they intruded through tree-lined urban neighborhoods and gobbled up parkland. The popular trolley gave way to air-polluting buses. The toll of deaths, injuries, and property damage on the highways mounted steadily.

Life in Suburbia—New Political and Economic Growth

In the suburbs new regional political and economic units developed. Local boards of education, elected town officials, and neighborhood associations assumed added importance with the growth of suburbia. Highways began to be lined with shopping centers, gas stations, and chain restaurants.

Installment (Credit) Buying

Installment buying—buy now and make weekly or monthly payments later—enabled families to purchase durable goods on credit. Sales of automobiles, radios, refrigerators, vacuum cleaners, and other home appliances soared as consumers went deeper and deeper into debt. Chain stores and department stores promoted consumer credit by introducing charge accounts and time payments.

Advertising played a key role in promoting the business boom of the twenties. **Montgomery Ward** and **Sears Roebuck** issued massive illustrated order catalogs from which buyers nationwide could purchase by mail virtually every consumer item on the market. Ads for soap, cigarettes, and other products in daily use appeared in newspapers, magazines, on outdoor billboards, and over the radio. By 1929, American business was investing $3.5 billion annually to promote its products by advertising.

New Media

Both **radio** and **motion pictures**—destined to have profound influence on American culture-became important media in the 1920s. Regular radio broadcasting began in 1920 with station WWJ in Detroit. The results of the 1920 presidential election were the first to be broadcast over the radio by station KDKA in Pittsburgh. By the end of 1922, radios were broadcasting news reports over 69 stations. A year later more than 500 stations were providing news and music to millions of listeners. Sales of radio sets and parts which had already reached $60 million in 1922, skyrocketed to $400 million by 1929. In 1933 President Roosevelt was speaking to the entire nation in his radio "fireside chats."

Motion pictures, which first appeared early in the 20th century, became a major influence in American life during the 1920s. Large motion picture theaters were catering to 100 million viewers, to whom Charlie Chaplin, Mary Pickford, Douglas Fairbanks, Gloria Swanson, Greta Garbo, Harold Lloyd, and Rudolph Valentino became as familiar as their own neighbors. These stars of the silent screen faced a new challenge in 1927 when Al Jolson appeared in the first "talking picture," **The Jazz Singer**, released by Warner Brothers. Color films soon followed and Hollywood, California, became the center of the film industry.

With people all over the country listening to the same radio programs and viewing the same movies, a process of **homogenization** of American culture began. Colorful local speech patterns, dress, music, recreation, manners, and morals tended toward standardization as people took their cues from what they watched and heard on the radio and in the movie theater. This trend was greatly accelerated when television emerged two decades later.

Constitutional and Legal Issues

Attacks on Civil Liberties

In the years after World War I, there was a vigorous drive against Communists, anarchists, and Socialists by the federal government and state governments. The Espionage Act passed during the war remained in effect, and suspected revolutionists were arrested and fined under this law. This postwar concern over radicals in the United States was largely due to the Bolshevik Revolution.

- *The "Big Red Scare."* Toward the end of World War I, the revolutionary **Bolsheviks**, led by **Nikolai Lenin**, overthrew the czarist government of Russia and established a **Communist** regime. A wave of hysteria, the "**Big Red Scare**," swept through the United States. The country had experienced similar periods of fear and hate before. The Alien and Sedition Acts of John Adams' administration, the attacks on life and property of abolitionists in pre-Civil War days, and the rampaging violence of the post-Civil War Ku Klux Klan all had threatened the civil liberties guaranteed by the Constitution.

- *The Palmer Raids.* Between 1919 and 1920, during the Big Red Scare, **Attorney General A. Mitchell Palmer** conducted raids, arresting some 6,000 suspects, 500 of whom were deported as undesirable aliens with little regard for their constitutional rights. It was at this time that the **American Civil Liberties Union** was founded by a group of prominent citizens including **Roger Baldwin**, its director from 1920 to 1950, attorney **Clarence Darrow**, settlement house founder **Jane Addams**, philosopher **John Dewey**, and Harvard law professor, later Supreme Court Justice, **Felix Frankfurter**.

- *Repressive Legislation.* State legislatures passed "**criminal syndicalism**" laws which made the advocacy of violence illegal. In New York State five Socialists who were duly elected to the legislature were denied their seats because of their party affiliation. During World War I, Congress passed two espionage and sedition acts outlawing utterances detrimental to the war effort.

- *Supreme Court Decisions.* Cases involving the constitutionality of these acts came before the Supreme Court. These cases raised the question of freedom versus order—the need to balance the liberty of the individual with the peace and order of society. Justice **Oliver Wendell Holmes** expressed this balance in two classic opinions. Writing for the Court in *Schenck* v. *United States* (1919), he upheld the conviction of the defendant for distributing leaflets advocating refusal to enlist in the armed services and expressed the "**clear and present danger**" doctrine. Holmes said, "The most stringent protection of free speech would not protect a man in falsely shouting fire in a theatre and causing a panic." (The wartime Espionage Act was found not to have violated the First Amendment.)

In the case of *Abrams* v. *United States* (1919), where the defendant appealed his sentence of twenty years imprisonment for violating the 1918 Sedition Act by publishing and distributing leaflets alleged to bring the form of government of the United States into contempt, Holmes wrote, in a classic dissenting opinion, "In this case sentences of twenty years imprisonment have been imposed for the publishing of two leaflets that I believe the defendants have as much right to publish as the government has to publish the Constitution of the United States now vainly invoked by them."

• *The Case of Sacco and Vanzetti (1920–27).* On May 5, 1920 two Italian aliens, **Bartolomeo Vanzetti**, a fish peddler, and **Nicolo Sacco**, a shoe factory employee—both anarchists opposed to all organized government—were arrested and charged with the murder of a payroll official and his guard, at a factory in South Braintree, Massachusetts. The case was tried before Judge **Webster Thayer**. The defendants were found guilty and sentenced to death, but many believed they were convicted because of their beliefs and their Italian nationality. Harvard law professor **Felix Frankfurter**, in his book *The Case of Sacco and Vanzetti,* wrote of Judge Thayer's opinion, "His twenty-five thousand word document cannot accurately be described otherwise than as a farrago [mixture] of misquotations, misrepresentations, suppressions, and mutilations." Protest meetings were held throughout the world. Appeals to the U.S. Supreme Court were turned down. Protesting their innocence to the end, Sacco and Vanzetti died in the electric chair at Charlestown, Massachusetts, August 23, 1927.

• *The New Ku Klux Klan.* Another attack on civil liberties was mounted by a renewed Ku Klux Klan, which attained a membership of 5 million in the frightful postwar political climate. Targets of the Klan, which was especially strong in the Midwest and the South, were African Americans, Catholics, and Jews. The Klan spread terror by beating and lynching innocent people and by setting fire to homes and houses of worship. In a widely circulated article in 1926, "Imperial Wizard and Emperor" **Hiram Wesley Evans** wrote, "We have won the leadership in the movement for Americanism, except for a few lonesome voices, almost drowned by the clamor of the alien and the alien-minded 'Liberal,' the Klan alone faces the invader." The Klan declined after 1925, when the "Grand Dragon" of Indiana was convicted for the murder of his secretary. It turned out that the "Imperial Wizards" and "King Kleagles" were using the Klan treasury to line their own pockets.

Prohibition—the Eighteenth Amendment

I believe in liberty . . . . But I have never believed that democracy involved the liberty to guzzle when that liberty to guzzle was a menace . . . to the integrity of that society which constitutes the America we love together.

The Reverend John Haynes Holmes, 1924

The **Eighteenth Amendment**, which went into effect on January 16, 1920, outlawed the "manufacture, sale, or transportation of intoxicating liquors." For decades the **Anti-Saloon League** and the **Women's Christian Temperance Union (WCTU)** had been agitating for Prohibition. Several factors combined to make the period between 1917 and 1920 a favorable time for the adoption of this amendment. During the war many people thought it was wrong to use vast quantities of grain in the production of beer and liquor when food was needed for the Allies and armed forces overseas. The period of about two years when the amendment was before the states for ratification was the time when hundreds of thousands of Americans were in the armed forces and unable to exert political influence on the issue.

- *The Volstead Act.* The **Volstead Act**, or the **Prohibition Enforcement Act**, passed by Congress in 1919 over President Wilson's veto, defined "intoxicating" (as used in the Eighteenth Amendment) as any beverage containing over 1/2 of one percent alcohol. This made even beer and wine illegal. From the beginning, opposition to Prohibition was too strong and widespread to permit effective enforcement. Longtime habits, such as the workingman's pint of beer after a hard day's labor, could not easily be wiped out by law. Making "home brew" became a fad throughout the country. "**Speakeasies**," where patrons had to use passwords before the door was opened, flourished. "Bathtub gin" resulted in many cases of blindness and death. The sale of illicit "booze" gave rise to gang wars between "bootleggers," who killed each other to corner the market in the sale of illegal liquor. Some 500 gangsters were killed in Chicago in these wars. Racketeering spread to gambling, narcotics, prostitution, and "protection" of merchants whose property would be vandalized for failure to make the necessary payoffs. The limited facilities of law enforcement agencies could not cope with the widespread violation of Prohibition.

- *Repeal of the Eighteenth Amendment—the Twenty-first Amendment.* The movement to repeal the Eighteenth Amendment gained adherents when it became apparent that popular resistance can make a law virtually unenforceable. The Twenty-first Amendment to the Constitution, providing for the repeal of the Eighteenth, was proposed by two thirds of both houses of Congress on February 20, 1933, and was quickly approved by the necessary three quarters of the state legislatures, so that it was ratified December 21, 1933. The national experiment to end alcoholic beverages by law had ended.

Science, Religion, and Education

In the summer of 1925, the nation became absorbed in the **Scopes Trial**, or so-called "monkey trial," taking place in Dayton, Tennessee, where **John Scopes'** job was in jeopardy for teaching evolution to his high school biology class. Laws prohibiting the teaching of Darwin's theory had been passed in three Southern states, including Tennessee, in support of Fundamentalist theology.

The case attracted added attention because of distinguished counsel on both sides: **William Jennings Bryan** for the prosecution, and **Clarence Darrow** for the defense. Bryan, a gifted orator, had run for President three times as the Democratic party candidate. Darrow, a famous Chicago trial lawyer, had successfully defended more than 50 persons charged with crimes punishable by death. At the trial, Darrow mercilessly questioned Bryan who testified as an expert witness on the Bible. Bryan won the case and died of a stroke five days later. The law under which Scopes was convicted was ultimately repealed, but Fundamentalists continued to demand that "**creationism**" (the Bible account of creation) be taught in the schools on a par with the theory of evolution.

Native Americans

The legal status of Native Americans throughout our history is viewed by many as a test of our adherence to the Constitutional guarantees of civil liberties. From the earliest colonial times, the Indians were driven off their lands and forced to retreat westward by the guns of white settlers and their army units. Treaties with the Indians were repeatedly broken as valuable minerals—gold, silver, copper—were found on their territory or as white farmers and ranchers sought the western lands promised forever to the Indians by the treaties. The Indians were forced to live on reservations located in areas that were usually arid lands of little use to white settlers. Traditional tribal boundaries conflicted with those drawn by the federal government in the interest of white settlers, miners, hunters, and trappers. Government army units often suppressed Indian opposition with wanton cruelty at times amounting to genocide. The story is told by Helen Hunt Jackson in her book, published in 1881, aptly entitled *A Century of Dishonor*.

• *The Dawes Act (1887).* In an effort to make the Indians adopt white culture, the **Dawes Act** was passed in 1887. It attempted to substitute the single-family farm of 160 acres for the traditional Indian tribal way of life. After 25 years of "good behavior," the Indian would get title to the land plus American citizenship. The Dawes Act failed to achieve its purpose because most of the Indians preferred to remain on the reservation and retain their tribal ways, even though it meant that they continued to be wards of the federal government. In 1924, citizenship was extended to all Native Americans by an act of Congress. But their plight remained desperate as they continued to have the lowest standard of living of all Americans.

• *Indian Reorganization Act (Wheeler-Howard Act) 1934.* Failure of the policy adopted under the Dawes Act was finally recognized in 1934 by the **Indian Reorganization Act**, also known as the **Wheeler-Howard Act**. The former policy was reversed. Native Americans were no longer to be urged to adapt to the "individual" American norm. Traditional tribal life was to be preserved and encouraged. Self-government of the Indian tribes on the reservations was to be protected by law. Education was to receive a high priority. The Indian population began to increase. From a low of less than 250,000 in the 1920s, it rose to 800,000 in 1970.

• *Indian Policy from the 1950s to the 1970s.* In the 1950s the federal govenment adopted a new Indian policy whose goals were termination and relocation. Its intention was to end all federal responsibility to Indians, transferring responsibility to those states that had large Indian populations. A second goal was to assimilate Indians into the American culture by relocating them to cities. Relocation and termination proved to be a failure, and in 1970, termination was ended. It was replaced by a new policy of "**self-determination**," which encouraged Indians to develop their own tribal life on the reservations. In the 1960s and 1970s, under a new spirit of militancy, Native Americans began to assert their rights, sometimes by direct action. They turned to the courts for redress, as far as possible, for injustices of the past.

Immigration

Give me your tired, your poor,
Your huddled masses yearning to breathe free,
The wretched refuse of your teeming shore,
Send these, the homeless, tempest-tossed to me,
I lift my lamp beside the golden door!

Inscription on the Statue of Liberty in New York Harbor
From "The New Colossus" by Emma Lazarus

The Golden Door, which had beckoned millions of underprivileged and oppressed to seek refuge in America, was almost sealed after World War I. Prompted by the economic recession of 1920–1921 and the "Red Scare" with its fear of alien ideas, Congress enacted the **Emergency Quota Act of 1921**. This act limited the number of immigrants from any country annually to 3 percent of the number of persons from that country who were living in the United States according to the census of 1910. This was only the beginning. In a calculated decision to limit the number of immigrants from southern and eastern Europe, the immigration laws of 1924 limited the number of immigrants from any country to 2 percent of those living in the United States from that country as determined by the census of 1890 (instead of 1910). Total immigration was reduced to 164,000. The **National Origins Act of 1929** set the annual limit at 150,000 with quotas for each European nation. The Immigration Act of June 25, 1948, authorized the admission of 205,000 European displaced persons. The number was increased to 341,000 by the act of June 16, 1950. The **McCarran-Walter Act of 1952** included new measures designed to keep out "subversives" and gave the Attorney General the power to deport immigrants (even if they had become citizens) for belonging to "Communist or Communist-front" organizations.

The **Immigration Act of 1965** discontinued quotas based on national origin. Race, religion, and color are no longer factors in admission. Occupation and skills of the applicant are key considerations, as is having relatives already living in the United States. The act thus ended almost half a century of discriminatory immigration policy. The **Immigration and Control Act of 1986** (**Mazzoli-Simpson Act**) provides for legalizing the status of aliens who have been in the United States illegally since before January 1, 1981. Within six months, more than 300,000 aliens sought legal status under this provision. The 1986 law also imposes civil and criminal penalties on employers who knowingly hire, recruit, or refer aliens who are not authorized to work in the United States. The Refugee Act of 1980 provided for granting asylum in the United States to refugees who have good reason to fear persecution in their homeland. Under this act refugees have been admitted from Vietnam, Cambodia, Laos, Afghanistan, Poland, Czechoslovakia, and Central America.

Shifting Cultural Values

A Revolution in Morals and Manners

A revolution in morals and manners that began prior to World War I was greatly accelerated by the war and its aftermath. The psychoanalytic discoveries of **Sigmund Freud**, which opened the hither taboo field of sexual research, was interpreted as a warrant for rejecting the prevailing ethic of premarital chastity for women. The "flapper" of the 1920s "**lost generation**" took to smoking and drinking, wore short dresses, and found the automobile and movies a way to escape from the scrutiny of a chaperone. Women began to reject the double standard that permitted freedom for men but not for women. The Nineteenth Amendment, adopted in 1920, had finally guaranteed women's suffrage in national elections. By 1923, a **National Women's Party** was campaigning for the adoption of an **Equal Rights Amendment** to the Constitution.

Changing Role of Women

World War I had a dramatic effect on the status of women in American society. During the war, women served in the armed forces. They filled the gap in farms, factories, mills, and mines left by the men who were in military service. The new freedom gained during the war manifested itself in new moral and social behavior. Women were now openly drinking and smoking, and their clothing was more revealing.

The role of women in all aspects of life—economic, political, social, and cultural—was changing rapidly. A majority of women now lived in cities and they increasingly entered the work force. In 1920, one of every five employed people was a woman. By 1950, 18 million—nearly 30 percent of the work force—were women. Electric irons, washing machines, refrigerators, vacuum cleaners, canned goods, and ready-made clothing freed women from the relentless pressures traditionally associated with homemaking. Women began playing an active role in politics, civic affairs, the arts, and the pursuit of their individual interests and talents. Women in the work force began playing an equal role with their husbands in supporting the family. In response to these developments, Congress enacted the 1922 **Sheppard-Towner Act**, extending financial aid to the states for the welfare and health of pregnant women and newborn infants. The act authorized the appropriation of $1 million annually for maternity and infant care.

- *The Nineteenth Amendment (1920).* The Nineteenth Amendment, guaranteeing women the right to vote in state and national elections, was proposed by Congress on June 4, 1919, with little opposition. President Wilson urged its adoption, noting the part played by women during World War I. "The services of women during the supreme crisis have been of the most signal usefulness and distinction." The Amendment became the law of the land when it was ratified by the 36th state on August 26, 1920. It declared: "The right of citizens of the United States to vote shall not be denied or abridged by the United States or by any state on account of sex."

Literature and American Life

> And I wish American novelists would give up trying to make business romantically interesting. Nobody wants to read about it unless it's crooked business.
>
> F. Scott Fitzgerald, *This Side of Paradise* (1920)

> He serenely believed that the one purpose of the real-estate business was to make money for George F. Babbitt. True, it was a good advertisement at Boosters Club lunches . . . to speak sonorously of unselfish public service . . . and a thing called ethics . . . But they didn't imply that you were to be impractical and refuse to take twice the value of a house if a buyer was . . . an idiot. . . .
>
> Sinclair Lewis, *Babbitt* (1922)

The 1920s became known as "The Roaring Twenties," "The Gilded Age," and "The Jazz Age." Writers of the period, such as **Sinclair Lewis**, **F. Scott Fitzgerald**, **Theodore Dreiser**, **Ernest Hemingway**, and **John Dos Passos**, cast doubt on prevailing values and caused the participants in the giddy whirl to be dubbed "the lost generation."

- *The Search for Heroes.* It is doubtless significant that the period witnessed a frantic search for heroes. As a model, **Charles A. Lindbergh** was almost too good to be true. A tall, handsome, modest young man, Lindbergh startled the world by his solo, nonstop flight in his single-engine propeller-driven plane, "**The Spirit of St. Louis**," across the Atlantic from New York to Paris, May 20–21, 1927. The overnight flight took 33 hours, 39 minutes. On his return to New York, Lindbergh, the "Lone Eagle," was greeted with a triumphant parade up New York's Broadway. A year later, **Amelia Earhart**, a pioneer woman in aviation, made a similar trans-Atlantic nonstop flight.

In sports, the all-time baseball hero, **Babe Ruth**, came to the New York Yankees in 1920 as an outfielder after previously winning 24 games as a pitcher with the Boston Red Sox. He established a lifetime record of 714 home runs and led the great Yankee ball club to seven pennants and four world championships. Other sports heroes of the period included **Jack Johnson**, world heavyweight boxing champion (1910–1915); **Jack Dempsey**, who attracted the first million-dollar gate in 1921; **Bill Tilden**, who was ranked first in the world in tennis, throughout the 1920s; **"Red" Grange**, who scored 31 touchdowns for the University of Illinois; and **Gertrude Ederle**, the first woman to swim the English Channel and break the existing men's record on August 6, 1926. A member of the United States 1924 Olympic Team, Ederle helped win the gold medal in the 400-meter freestyle relay.

On the screen, the object of fascination was **Rudolph Valentino**. Born in Italy, Valentino came to the United States in 1913 and became a national idol for his performance in two 1921 blockbusters, *The Four Horsemen of the Apocalypse* and *The Sheik*.

• *The Black Renaissance.* The post-World War I period witnessed a great black renaissance in Harlem. Poets **Langston Hughes** and **Countee Cullen**, political activist **Marcus Garvey**, writer **Zora Neale Hurston**, scholar and nationalist leader **W.E.B. Du Bois**, as well as gifted painters and musicians, gathered in Harlem and made this part of New York, with its wide streets and classic buildings, an exciting place to live in the 1920s.

Exercise Set 4.3

1. Which of the following was a prime *cause* of the other three?
   A. imposition of immigration quotas
   B. the Big Red Scare
   C. raids conducted by Attorney General A. Mitchell Palmer
   D. rapid growth of the new Ku Klux Klan

2. Federal government policy toward Native Americans may properly be described as
   A. generally one of hostility to their best interest as fellow Americans
   B. a policy designed to destroy or basically alter their traditional culture patterns
   C. a series of changes in policy including making treaties with them, attempting to exterminate them, and treating them as wards of the government
   D. all of the above

3. Which of the following does *not* apply to the immigration policy of the United States during the 1920s?
   A. it sought to limit the number of immigrants
   B. it restored the traditional American immigration policy of keeping the Golden Door open
   C. it established the principle of selective immigration by favoring immigrants from some areas of the world over those from other areas
   D. it was enacted over the objection of a sizeable minority of public opinion

4. Between 1920 and 1930 passenger car registration in the United States leaped from 8.1 million to 26.5 million. This helped bring about all of the following EXCEPT
   A. a mass movement to the suburbs
   B. a stimulation of such related industries as advertising, insurance, and finance
   C. a gradual decline in railroads
   D. a spirited competition of foreign manufacturing for control of the American market

5. Which was *not* a characteristic of the economic life of the 1920s?
   A. new methods of production
   B. installment buying and borrowing to finance consumer growth
   C. a government tax policy that retarded accumulation of large personal fortunes
   D. investment by banks in real estate, mortgages, bonds, and stocks

6. A major effect of the new radio and motion picture industries was
   A. a steady decline in the circulation of newspapers and magazines
   B. a tendency toward homogenization of American culture
   C. a shift away from sports as a major source of recreation for both spectators and participants
   D. a decline in the influence of religion due to falling attendance at religious services

7. The rapid growth of the automobile industry was made possible by
   A. the introduction by Henry Ford of an eight-hour day and a minimum wage of $5 a day in 1914
   B. a ready market created by the rising standard of living and the increase of leisure time of the average American
   C. cooperation of labor and management in the trucking industry
   D. failure of trolleys and railroads to maintain a high standard in their facilities and operations

8. Which of the following pairs are associated with the Harlem Renaissance of the 1920s?
   A. Sigmund Freud and Ernest Hemingway
   B. Gertrude Ederle and Rudolph Valentino
   C. Sinclair Lewis and F. Scott Fitzgerald
   D. Langston Hughes and Countee Cullen

9. Which of the following was, at least in part, a cause of the other three?
   A. the changing role of women in economic, social, and cultural affairs
   B. the adoption of the Nineteenth Amendment
   C. the active participation of women in World War I
   D. the emerging emphasis on wife rather than mother

10. The adoption of the Nineteenth Amendment to the Constitution in 1920 was a result of
    A. the fact that many states had already extended suffrage to women before World War I
    B. the widespread belief that the time had come to stop classifying women with others most commonly denied the ballot: children, illiterates, the insane, and criminals
    C. the way women did "men's work" in war industries
    D. all of the above

CHAPTER REVIEW QUESTIONS

1. During the post-World War I period, civil liberties were under attack. Which of the following is *not* an example of this experience?
   A. the conviction of Sacco and Vanzetti
   B. the Scopes trial in Dayton, Tennessee
   C. the revival of the Ku Klux Klan
   D. the novels of Sinclair Lewis

2. An experience of the majority of immigrants to the United States was that they
   A. Frequently met resentment
   B. settled in rural areas where cheap land was available
   C. were rapidly assimilated into the predominant lifestyle
   D. joined radical parties to bring about economic reform

   Regents Exam, August 1988

3. President Calvin Coolidge once said, "The business of America is business." This slogan is most closely related to
   A. a laissez-faire attitude toward the economy
   B. government ownership of heavy industry
   C. the enactment of protective tariffs
   D. legislation benefiting organized labor
   Regents Exam, June 1983

4. At various times throughout history, racial and religious prejudices have been exploited for the purpose of
   A. expanding cultural diversity
   B. reenforcing nationalistic sentiments
   C. expanding international trade
   D. furthering the growth of fine arts
   Regents Exam, June 1984

5. All Native Americans achieved citizenship
   A. by the Dawes Act of 1887
   B. in 1968 as part of President Johnson's Great Society
   C. by an act of Congress in 1924
   D. by the Indian Reorganization Act of 1934

ESSAYS

1. During the period 1914–1929 (except for the years 1920–1921) the American economy made great advances, causing President Hoover to declare, "We are nearer today to the ideal of the abolition of poverty . . . than ever before in any land."
   a. Identify *three* factors that helped promote the growth of the economy during this period and discuss how each contributed to this growth. [4,4,4]
   b. Using specific historical information, discuss one impact that industrialization had on the United States during the period 1914–1921. [3]
   Regents Exam, August 1988

2. Many aspects of United States society have been greatly affected by technological changes. Choose *three* of the aspects of United States society listed below. Explain how each one chosen has been affected by a specific technological development. [Use a different development for each aspect.]
   Aspects of United States Society
   Urbanization
   Agriculture
   Cultural homogeneity

Rights of the individual
Politics
Environment

Regents Exam, June 1988

3. At various times, civil liberties have been seriously threatened in the United States. One such period was the decade following World War I. Give *three* examples of threats to civil liberties during this period. [3] For *each* one mentioned, describe the threat and indicate briefly the outcome. [4,4,4]

Chapter 2

THE GREAT DEPRESSION AND THE NEW DEAL (1933–1940)

FAILURE OF THE OLD ORDER: HOOVER AND THE CRASH

> Our immediate and paramount task as a people is to rout the forces of economic disruption and pessimism that have swept upon us.
> Herbert Hoover, June 16, 1931

> A glance at the situation today only too clearly indicates that equality of opportunity as we have known it no longer exists . . . . Our task now is . . . distributing wealth and products more equitably, of adapting existing economic organizations to the service of the people.
> Franklin D. Roosevelt, September 23, 1932

Cracks in the Economic Foundation

Overproduction and Maldistribution of Purchasing Power

The short-lived prosperity of the late 1920s was built on a fragile economic base. There were a number of serious cracks in the foundation. Technological advances, coupled with overexpansion of credit, brought about a vast increase in industrial production. At the same time the maldistribution of wealth—the concentration of money among wealthy individuals and surpluses in business corporations—meant that farmers and laborers were not able to purchase the goods produced. For a time the gap was made up by installment buying and other forms of credit. But the day of reckoning had to come.

Other factors, too, were involved in the troubled state of the economy. Both industry and agriculture were expanding and outproducing the purchasing power of consumers. Moreover, laborsaving machinery was causing technological unemployment while chronic agricultural depression was having a negative impact on the national economy.

Overexpansion of Credit

Overexpansion of credit was encouraging reckless gambling in the stock market. An investor could purchase shares of stock "on margin," that is, by putting up as little as 10 percent of the cost with the rest of the money on credit. This enabled people to buy much more than they could afford. Stock prices became overinflated. Should prices fall, margin buyers would have to put up more cash or lose all of their investments.

The Stock Market Crash

The Crash of 1929

Stock prices began to decline slowly in September 1929, and by October the decline gained momentum. The great crash came on **Black Tuesday**, October 29, 1929, when 16.5 million shares were traded in a precipitous decline that continued for the rest of the year. **U.S. Steel**, which sold for $262 a share in September, was quoted at $22 three months later. **Montgomery Ward** stock went from $138 to $4; **General Motors** from $73 to $8. Stockholders lost $40 billion.

Many investors went bankrupt in the crash of 1929.

Worldwide Economic Collapse

The economic crash and the resulting **depression** were worldwide. The banking systems of the world were interdependent. American banks had made large loans to their European affiliates. Banks on both sides of the Atlantic failed and caused others to fail. Between October 1, 1929, and August 31, 1932, 4,835 American banks failed. Their total deposits, representing the lifetime savings of millions of Americans, amounted to $3.25 billion. To make matters worse, the **Hawley-Smoot Tariff** of 1930, with its high protectionist rates, served only to dry up the sickly streams of international trade.

Hoover and the Depression

President Hoover did make efforts to revive the economy but he was stopped from taking drastic action by his own economic philosophy. He believed that direct government aid to the needy would destroy **"rugged individualism"** and might even lead to socialism. Moreover, he believed that the depression would soon end and that "prosperity [was] just around the corner." Finally, he attributed the depression to international factors, particularly the huge international debts.

Moratorium on War Debts

In 1931 Hoover recommended a one-year moratorium (postponement) on the payment of war debts and on reparations owed by Germany to the Allies.

Trickle-down Economics—the Reconstruction Finance Corporation

Hoover also believed in **"trickle-down economics,"** the idea that profits of big business would trickle down to average Americans. At Hoover's request, Congress established the **Reconstruction Finance Corporation** (1932). The RFC advanced some $2 billion in loans to state and local governments and to banks, railroads, farm mortgage associations, and large corporations in order to stimulate the economy. But the roots of the depression were too deep to be easily eradicated. Hoover's efforts to stem the tide proved to be inadequate, and the Republican party was swept out of office in the election of November 1932.

Misery and the Great Depression

Mass Unemployment and Its Effects

Mass unemployment was the hallmark of the Great Depression. Farms were abandoned, factories closed, and men and women stood on breadlines waiting for a handout. Youths rode the railroad lines in empty freight cars. Early in 1932, one fourth of the work force, some 10 million Americans, were unemployed. Some, like the fictional Joads in Steinbeck's *The Grapes of Wrath*, left their farms and drove West hoping for better times in California. In cities, men peddled apples on street corners. Women and children, helpless victims, perhaps suffered most, while minorities were hard hit by this unprecedented economic catastrophe.

Rundown shanty towns, their shacks put together with tin and paper collected in dumps, sprang up all over the country. They were named "Hoovervilles" in derision of an administration that was deemed inept, if not indeed lacking in compassion.

The Bonus Army in Washington

In the spring of 1932, about 15,000 veterans of World War I marched on Washington from all over the country to demand immediate payment of their bonus certificates, which were not due until 1945. They camped in shacks along the Anacostia River near the Capitol. When Congress failed to pass legislation to meet their demand, most of them departed. But some 2,000 remained, refusing the government's offer of funds to pay for their return home. Hoover ordered the Army to drive them out. Led by Chief-of-Staff

General **Douglas MacArthur**, army infantry and cavalry units attacked the veterans in force, scattering them with tear-gas bombs, sabers, and tanks, and burned their shacks. MacArthur and Hoover were severely criticized for this tactic, which they claimed was "necessary under the circumstances."

Exercise Set 4.4

1. From 1923 to early 1929 behavior of business cycles
   A. registered sharp fluctuations
   B. was indiscernible
   C. created the belief that a serious depression would never return
   D. created unrest and alarm

2. Hoover's policies in dealing with the Depression were criticized for all of the reasons below EXCEPT
   A. he postponed action in the belief that prosperity was just around the corner
   B. he minimized the domestic causes of the depression
   C. he depended too much on voluntary action
   D. he did less than earlier Presidents had done in similar crises

3. Which conditions are most characteristic of a depression?
   A. high production and high demand
   B. few jobs and little demand
   C. much money in circulation and high stock prices
   D. supply meeting demand and high unemployment
   Regents Exam, August 1988

4. Conditions that helped bring on the Great Depression included all of the following EXCEPT
   A. the fact that large-scale construction of new highways was undertaken to accommodate the rapid introduction of the automobile
   B. that increased industrial production was not matched by a corresponding increase in the purchasing power of consumers
   C. that newly introduced laborsaving devices were causing technological unemployment
   D. that overextension of credit was encouraging debt as well as speculation in the stock market

FRANKLIN D. ROOSEVELT: RELIEF, RECOVERY, AND REFORM

> In broad terms I assert that modern society, acting through its government, owes the definite obligation to prevent the starvation or the dire want of any of its fellow men and women who try to maintain themselves but cannot.
>
> Franklin D. Roosevelt, speech in campaign
> for reelection as Governor of New York, 1930

New York Serves as a Prototype for the New Deal

The "Little New Deal"

Soon after his reelection as Governor of New York in 1930, **Franklin D. Roosevelt** called a special session of the legislature to face the problem of mounting economic distress. New York became the first state to appropriate public funds for unemployment relief. The "**New Deal**" was foreshadowed in Roosevelt's governorship. It was, in effect, a "Little New Deal." A **State Power Authority** was created to control public utilities and establish the principle that the water power of the state belonged to the people. An **old-age Pension Law** became a forerunner of **Social Security**. **Reforestation** was undertaken despite serious opposition. Legislation was introduced to end the 54-hour work week, and to require an **8-hour day** and **48-hour week** for women and children. **Minimum-wage legislation** for women was also proposed.

Roosevelt met strong opposition, which he could not always overcome, for measures such as the reform of election laws, improvement of local government, the upgrading of state roads, and the reduction of rural taxation. State taxes were increased to provide funds for the alleviation of distress of the unemployed.

Mayor Fiorello LaGuardia

New York city had its own "Little New Deal," when it elected **Fiorello LaGuardia** (the "Little Flower") Mayor in 1933. Defeated in his bid for reelection to Congress in 1932, he formed the **Fusion party** and was elected Mayor of New York in 1933. He was reelected in 1937 and 1941. On first taking office he declared, "Our theory of municipal government is an experiment to try to show that a nonpartisan, nonpolitical local government is possible."

The LaGuardia administration found a sympathetic reception in Washington. During LaGuardia's first year in office, the federal government made significant commitments to New York City: $20 million for low-cost housing, $1.5 million toward completion of the **Triborough Bridge**, and $25 million to put 3,000 to work on subway construction. During LaGuardia's tenure, New York built 92 new schools and introduced the first inclusive health insurance plan in the nation for low-income city employees.

The New Deal in Washington

> I pledge you, I pledge myself, to a new deal for the American people.
> Franklin D. Roosevelt, accepting the Democratic
> nomination for the presidency, July 2, 1932

A Strong Cabinet

To help him tackle the problems facing the country and to bring relief, recovery, and reform to the beleaguered nation, Roosevelt surrounded himself with the best people he could find, regardless of their political affiliation. **Harold L. Ickes**, a former Republican, became Secretary of the Interior. **Henry Morgenthau, Jr.**, the President's close friend and Hyde Park neighbor, remained Secretary of the Treasury for twelve years. For Secretary of Labor, Roosevelt appointed **Frances Perkins**, the first woman to serve in a President's cabinet. Perkins, who had worked with Jane Addams at Hull House in Chicago, was to become a key figure in shaping New Deal labor legislation. **Henry A. Wallace**, a former Republican, who was to become Vice-President during Roosevelt's third term, was Secretary of Agriculture and later Secretary of Commerce.

A "Brain Trust"

In addition to his Cabinet, Roosevelt brought to Washington a number of brilliant unofficial advisers who came to be known as the "brain trust." Chief among these was **Harry Hopkins**, a former social worker, who had the President's complete confidence and was entrusted with sensitive missions. Also in the "brain trust" were **Rexford G. Tugwell**, **Adolphe A. Berle, Jr.**, and **Raymond Moley**, all members of the Columbia University faculty.

Relief of Human Suffering

> Let me assert my firm belief that the only thing we have to fear is fear itself.
> Franklin D. Roosevelt, First Inaugural Address,
> March 4, 1933

The first task set for the "New Deal" was relief of human suffering. Loss of people's life savings through bank failures had to be halted. The hungry had to be fed. The unemployed had to be put to work.

The Emergency Banking Relief Act

The day after his inauguration as President, Roosevelt summoned Congress into special session and proclaimed a **national bank holiday**, closing all the nation's banks for an indefinite period of time. Congress promptly passed the **Emergency Banking Relief Act** (March 9, 1933) granting extraordinary power to the President. Within a week the solvent banks reopened and deposits exceeded withdrawals. Swift action had restored public confidence in the banking system. Reform, to prevent future catastrophe, was to come later.

The Federal Emergency Relief Act

The **Federal Emergency Relief Act** (May 12, 1933) established a **Federal Emergency Relief Administration** (**FERA**) and authorized an appropriation of $500 million. The money was to be granted to states and municipalities for emergency relief. Harry L. Hopkins was appointed Administrator of the FERA. Ultimately, some $3 billion was spent under the act. A branch of the FERA was the **Civil Works Administration** (**CWA**), established in November 1933 to provide temporary jobs during the winter emergency. The CWA came under criticism because many of the jobs, such as leaf-raking, hastily created during the emergency, were called "boondoggling," useless or wasteful activities.

Dealing with Unemployment

A **Public Works Administration** (**PWA**) was established in June 1933 under the **National Industrial Recovery Act** (**NIRA**). It was directed by Secretary of the Interior **Harold L. Ickes**. The object of this legislation was called "pump priming," that is, the government pumps money into the economy to stimulate the economy. The belief is that an increase in employment will add to consumer purchasing and thus stimulate business. However, the PWA failed to achieve its objectives because Ickes, fearful of corruption, approved few projects and delayed others. A full-scale attack on unemployment came in the spring of 1935 with the creation of the **Works Progress Administration** (**WPA**). This act, administered by **Harry Hopkins**, provided 9 million useful jobs during the next eight years. Communities throughout the land were enriched by the construction of 6,000 school buildings, thousands of post-office and courthouse buildings, 128,000 miles of roads, and thousands of bridges. An effort was made to place people in jobs suitable to their education and experience. Unemployed architects designed buildings, engineers built dams, artists painted murals, authors, musicians, playwrights, and actors were enabled to work at their professions and contribute their talents as government employees during the Depression.

Aid to Youth

Agencies created specifically for the purpose of providing aid to needy youth were the **Civilian Conservation Corps (CCC)** and the **National Youth Administration (NYA)**. The CCC enrolled young men between the ages of 18 and 25 and assigned them to one of the 2,600 work camps throughout the country. There they cleared land for public parks, built dams for flood control planted trees, and cleared swamps. The CCC ultimately enlisted 2.5 million young men. In addition to food, clothing, and shelter, they received money payments that went in part to their needy families. The nation gained in two ways—outdoor resources were preserved and enhanced while young Americans were salvaged from the ravages of the depression. The **National Youth Administration (NYA)**, created in 1935, cooperated with schools and colleges in providing an income for needy students who performed tasks useful to their school or college. The NYA gave part-time employment to more than 600,000 college students and 1.5 million high school pupils. Aid was provided also to 2.6 million young Americans who were not in school. Some received vocational training; others were put to work renovating government buildings, repairing equipment, building playgrounds, and upgrading public parks.

Recovery for the American Economy

Besides trying to relieve human suffering caused by the Depression, the New Deal sought to restore the nation's economic health. The New Deal program for recovery set its sights on industry, agriculture, and housing.

Measures to Aid Industry

The **National Industrial Recovery Act (NIRA)**, which was signed into law June 16, 1933, created the **National Recovery Administration (NRA)** under General **Hugh S. Johnson**. Members of each industry were to establish "codes of fair competition" that, when approved by the President, were to be legally binding on the industry. In theory, the regulations adopted by each industry would revive that industry and reduce unemployment. The code of each industry was to prescribe wages, hours, and prices, provide for a minimum wage, and preserve labor's rights of collective bargaining. A blue eagle was adopted as a symbol that, when displayed, signified compliance with the code of that industry.

Helping Home Owners

The **Home Owners Loan Corporation (HOLC)** was established in June 1933 to help home owners save their homes. Every day 1,000 home owners were losing their homes to mortgage holders (banks) for failure to pay the mortgages. The HOLC loaned money at low interest to private home owners to pay off their old mortgages and new long-term mortgages were arranged at low interest rates. Within a year 300,000 loans amounting to almost $1 billion were made. During the three year period 1933–1936 the homes of more than a million families were saved by the HOLC. By insuring building loans made by banks, the **Federal Housing Authority (FHA)** created in 1934 encouraged banks to lend money for home repairs and for construction of homes and businesses.

Aid to Agriculture

To halt foreclosures on farms, a **Farm Credit Administration (FCA)** was established in June 1933. Farm mortgages were refinanced at low rates of interest for long terms, while farm debts were adjusted on favorable terms. In its first 18 months, the FCA refinanced the mortgages of nearly one fifth of America's family farms. To aid the poorest farmers—the tenant farmers and sharecroppers—a **Farm Security Administration (FSA)** was established in 1937. More than a billion dollars was extended in low-interest, long-term loans to enable tenants to buy farms. The FSA established camps for migrant farm laborers and helped launch medical care cooperatives in rural areas. It broke new ground in its scrupulously fair treatment of African American farmers.

- *The AAA (1933).* Major reform in agriculture was undertaken in two **Agricultural Adjustment Acts (AAA)**. The first AAA of May 1933 was designed to achieve "parity" between agriculture and industry by raising the prices of farm commodities, so that farm income would keep pace with non-farm income. This was to be attained by curtailing production. Farmers signed agreements to reduce their planting by one fourth to one half, since lower production would help to raise the market price of farm commodities. In return, the government made "benefit payments" to farmers for their crop reduction. The money was to come from a processing tax on meat packers, canners, millers, and other food processors. The AAA had an immediate effect on production and market prices of farm commodities. For example, with 10 million acres of cotton out of production, cotton prices rose from 5.5 to 9.5 cents per pound in the first year. The Supreme Court, by a 6 to 3 vote in January 1936, declared the AAA unconstitutional.

- *The SCDAA.* Congress then passed the **Soil Conservation and Domestic Allotment Act (SCDAA)** of 1936, which paid farmers for growing soil-conserving crops such as clover and soybeans and not growing soil-exhausting staples like cotton, corn, and tobacco.

- *Second AAA.* A second AAA in 1938 continued the soil conservation program of the 1936 act. With the approval of two thirds of the producers of a specific commodity, the government could decide the amount of corn, wheat, rice, cotton, or tobacco that could be marketed. Surpluses of each commodity were to be stored by the government and released when prices rose to the parity level. Despite all-out efforts at recovery, the level of unemployment and poverty remained above pre-Depression days well into Roosevelt's second term.

Reform Programs

> I see one-third of a nation ill-housed, ill-clad, ill-nourished.
> The test of our progress is not whether we add more to the abundance of those who have much; it is whether we provide enough for those who have too little.
>
> Franklin D. Roosevelt, Second Inaugural Address,
> January 20, 1937

The New Deal search for effective reform programs had a major impact on banking, stock market operations, social security and labor.

Banking Reform

The **Glass-Steagall Banking Act of 1933** was designed to protect depositors against bank failures. It separated commercial from investment banking and restricted the use of bank credit for financial speculation. Most significant was the provision creating a new agency, the **Federal Deposit Insurance Corporation** (**FDIC**), which insured savings bank deposits up to $2,500. The guarantee was raised to $5,000 the following year and proved a boon to the banks as well as to their depositors. The amount insured— $100,000 in 1994— was steadily increased as the purchasing power of the dollar increased.

Stock Market Reforms

To provide basic protection to investors in the stock markets, the **Securities Act of May 1933** required every new stock offering to contain specific information to enable prospective investors to judge the value of a share and the financial circumstances of the corporation. The **Securities and Exchange Commission** was established the following year to enforce the act.

Social Security

A landmark achievement of the New Deal was the **Social Security Act** of August 14, 1935. The act provided for (1) a fund for **unemployment insurance** to be derived from taxes on payrolls of employers having 8 or more employees. Each state was to administer its own system in conjunction with the federal government; (2) a fund for old-age and survivors insurance to be derived from taxes levied on employers and their employees. This fund was to be administered by the federal government and was to make monthly pension payments to retirees when reaching the age of 65; (3) money grants to states for pensions provided by state law; and (4) grants to states for relief of blind, handicapped, and other destitute dependents.

The act was to be administered by a three-member **Social Security Board**. The act, which President Roosevelt described as "a cornerstone in a structure which is being built" had an immediate impact. Two years after the Social Security program was passed into law, 21 million workers were covered by unemployment insurance and 36 million were entitled to old-age pensions.

Labor Legislation

• *The Wagner Act.* Through patient and effective persuasion, **Senator Robert F. Wagner** of New York gained enough support from the business community to make possible the passage of landmark labor legislation. The **National Labor Relations Act** of July 5, 1935, known as the **Wagner Act**, was designed to reduce tension in labor relations and thus avoid strikes and labor disaffection. It provided for an independent **National Labor Relations Board** (**NLRB**) that would conduct plant elections for employees to choose their agents for contract negotiations and grievance resolution. The Board could also issue "cease and desist" orders against "unfair labor practices" such as interference with the union in collective bargaining, refusal to bargain collectively, and discrimination against union members. Exclusive bargaining rights were granted to the union, that won a majority in the plant election as certified by the NLRB.

• *The Fair Labor Standards Act.* The **Fair Labor Standards Act (Wages and Hours Law)** of 1938 set minimum wages (40 cents an hour initially) and maximum hours (40 hours per week) and forbade the employment of children under 16 in business establishments engaged in interstate commerce.

• *Formation of the CIO.* In 1935, **John L. Lewis**, president of the **United Mine Workers** and vice-president of the **American Federation of Labor** (**AFL**), took his union out of the AFL and started a new organization to be known as the **Congress of Industrial Organization** (**CIO**). Lewis charged that the AFL, whose membership consisted essentially of craft unions, showed little interest in organizing the low-skilled workers in the mass production industries. For the first time, unions organized on an industry basis (automotive, electrical, steel, etc.), were successful in bargaining for all their employees with such industrial giants as General Motors, United States Steel, and General Electric. Among opponents of FDR's liberal labor initiative was the **American Liberty League**, one of whose leaders was **Alfred E. Smith** of New York, who had previously been a close ally of Roosevelt.

Exercise Set 4.5

1. In the early years of the New Deal, Roosevelt
   A. sought advice from very few others
   B. relied heavily on a "Brain Trust"
   C. consulted primarily business leaders
   D. sought advice only from politicians in his Cabinet

2. The policies of Franklin D. Roosevelt revealed
   A. a rejection of the capitalistic system
   B. a willingness to modify extensively American laissez-faire economic practices
   C. a Fascist philosophy of economic and political regimentation
   D. a timidity in dealing with the basic weaknesses of the free enterprise system

3. Franklin D. Roosevelt first gave his attention to what major problem?
   A. unemployment
   B. speculation in securities
   C. farm relief
   D. bank failures

4. Roosevelt did all of the following for agriculture EXCEPT
   A. increase the export market
   B. raise farm prices
   C. reduce the acreage in cultivation
   D. prevent farm mortgage foreclosure

5. A major difference between the New Deal and policies followed by earlier administrations was that the New Deal
   A. emphasized and encouraged rugged individualism
   B. advocated socialism as a solution to the problems of the times
   C. provided the government with a more active role in the economy
   D. was able to eliminate discrimination in employment
   Regents Exam, August 1988

6. On the political spectrum Roosevelt's domestic program for relief, recovery, and reform was
   A. at the far left between socialism and communism
   B. at the far right between conservatism and fascism
   C. right of center between moderate and conservative
   D. left of center between moderate and liberal

CONSTITUTIONAL ISSUES AND THE NEW DEAL

> When an act of Congress is appropriately challenged in the courts . . .
> the judicial branch of government has only one duty—to lay the arti-
> cle of the Constitution which is invoked beside the statute which is
> challenged and to decide whether the latter squares with the former.
> Justice Owen J. Roberts, writing for the majority of six in
> *United States* v. *Butler* et al. (1936) invalidating
> the Agricultural Adjustment Act.

> A tortured construction of the Constitution is not to be justified by
> recourse to extreme examples . . . .
> Justice Harlan F. Stone, dissenting for the minority of three

The Supreme Court and New Deal Legislation

The Schechter Poultry Case

Foes of the New Deal were heartened by several key decisions of the
Supreme Court. A major piece of legislation, passed early in the New Deal,
was the **National Industrial Recovery Act** (June 1933), which established
a **National Recovery Administration** (**NRA**) designed to revitalize
industry while protecting labor and consumers. The act was declared unconstitutional by the Supreme Court in the case of *Schechter Poultry Corp.* v.
United States (1935). Chief Justice **Charles Evans Hughes**, writing for a
unanimous court, ruled that the excessive delegation of legislative power to
the executive was unconstitutional. In addition, the application of the commerce clause to business only indirectly involved in interstate commerce
would undermine the authority of the states over their legitimate domestic
concerns.

United States v. *Butler*—the AAA

The following year, the Court invalidated another major piece of New Deal
legislation, the **Agricultural Adjustment Act** of 1933. In a 6 to 3 decision,
the Court, in the case of *United States* v. *Butler,* declared the act unconstitutional on the ground that the processing tax was an abuse of the taxing
power in regulating agricultural output. The action of the Supreme Court in
declaring these and other acts of the New Deal unconstitutional brought
about a storm of resentment. The controversy raised one of the enduring
issues in American history: Is the judiciary the interpreter of the Constitution
or a shaper of public policy?

The Tennessee Valley Authority (TVA)

Purpose and Extent of the Project

One major agency of the New Deal, established by legislation in 1933, survived attacks in the courts. It was the **Tennessee Valley Authority** (**TVA**), designed to revitalize one of the most economically depressed regions in the country. This region included parts of seven states—Virginia, North Carolina, Georgia, Alabama, Mississippi, Tennessee, and Kentucky. The TVA constructed 21 large dams on the Tennessee River to provide electric power for the region. The Roosevelt administration used the cost of producing this power as a "yardstick" to determine whether the private power company rates were fair to their consumers. The power companies, a $13 billion-dollar industry, fought the TVA, charging that the lower rates were made possible by the tax-exempt status of the government operation.

Additional Benefits to the Region

Besides supplying cheap power, TVA served the region in many ways. It provided thousands of jobs to residents in the area. Additional benefits included flood control made possible by the newly built dams, prevention of soil erosion by the planting of millions of trees, establishment of public parks, schools, libraries, and hospitals, and improvement in river and road transportation. TVA, probably the most revolutionary program of the New Deal, became a reality largely through the efforts of Republican Senator **George W. Norris** of Nebraska.

The Election of 1936

In 1936, Roosevelt, running for reelection, was pitted against Governor **Alfred M. Landon** of Kansas. In a campaign speech at Madison Square Garden in New York City, Roosevelt declared:

> I should like to have it said of my first administration that in it the forces of selfishness and of lust for power met their match. I should like to have it said of my second administration that in it these forces met their master.

In the presidential election of 1932, Franklin D. Roosevelt won over **Herbert Hoover** with an electoral vote of 472 to 59 and a popular vote of 23 million to 16 million. In 1936 Roosevelt's popular vote was 28 million against 17 million for Landon, but in the electoral college Roosevelt won every state but Maine and Vermont, giving him an electoral victory of 523 to 8. The New Dealers appropriately regarded this as a mandate, since they also won both houses of Congress and all but six governorships.

President Roosevelt and the Supreme Court

The "Court Packing" Proposal

Shortly after his reelection, Roosevelt asked Congress to give him authority to appoint one new Justice (not to exceed six) for every Supreme Court Justice who had reached the age of 70 and failed to retire. Since six of the nine Justices on the Court had reached the age of 70, this meant that, if Congress approved, Roosevelt could increase the Court to a membership of fifteen. This proposal was described by its critics as a "**court packing**" scheme and was seen as a threat to the separation of powers. It met with determined opposition, even among some liberal Democrats. Governor **Herbert H. Lehman** of New York, a close friend and political ally of the President, explained his opposition in a letter to Roosevelt: "I feel that the end which you desire to attain does not justify the means which you recommend." The Judiciary Committee of the Senate voted ten to eight to reject the measure, and the full Senate voted it down seventy to twenty.

Changes in the Court

After Roosevelt's attempt to reform the Court., the Court began to take a more liberal approach, giving rise to a popular saying: "a switch in time saves nine." Moreover, changes in the Court's membership came quickly. Conservative Justice **Willis Van Devanter** resigned in 1937, and Roosevelt appointed liberal Senator **Hugo Black** in his place. The following year Solicitor General **Stanley Reed** was sworn in after Justice **George Sutherland** left the Court. Before the end of his second term, Roosevelt had appointed three more Justices to the Court—Professor **Felix Frankfurter** of Harvard, **William O. Douglas**, formerly Professor of Law at Yale, and **Frank Murphy**, former Governor of Michigan. Within one term in office President Roosevelt had appointed a majority of the Court's members.

The Election of 1940

The election campaign of 1940 was waged during the dark days when Hitler's forces overran Western Europe and were poised to launch an all-out attack on Britain. The Republicans nominated the charismatic liberal corporation lawyer, **Wendell L. Willkie**, while the Democrats chose Franklin D. Roosevelt to run for a third term.

Third-Term Issue

If Roosevelt won the election, as seemed likely, it would upset the two-term tradition that George Washington had started. No President elected to two consecutive terms had ever sought a third. Despite public misgivings about violation of this tradition, Roosevelt won easily with 449 electoral votes to 82 for the Republicans. Opponents of aid to Britain had no real choice in 1940, for both major party candidates rejected isolationism in favor of opposition to the Nazi challenge. Roosevelt was to win a fourth term in 1944.

The Twenty-second Amendment

This reversal of the two-term tradition led to a reaction after the death of FDR. In 1951, the Twenty-second Amendment was added to the Constitution. It specifies: "No person shall be elected to the office of President more than twice . . . ."

Exercise Set 4.6

1. Which of the following New Deal acts or agencies was declared unconstitutional by the Supreme Court in *Schechter Poultry Corp.* v. *United States*?
   A. the AAA
   B. the NRA
   C. the TVA
   D. the WPA

2. Many Americans had misgivings about reelecting Roosevelt to a third term because
   A. it was a violation of precedent
   B. it was time to give someone else a chance since the problem of the Depression remained unsolved
   C. Roosevelt was an interventionist while his opponent was an isolationist
   D. Roosevelt was tampering with the Supreme Court

3. An argument advanced against the TVA by private power companies was that
   A. its lower rates would be subsidized by the taxpayers
   B. it would fail to provide cheap electric power for the people of the Tennessee Valley
   C. its activities would extend over too large an area
   D. it would eliminate jobs for residents of the area

4. Roosevelt's attempt to increase the number of Justices on the Supreme Court
   A. was acclaimed by most Americans as a brilliant solution to a Constitutional problem
   B. received solid support from the majority of both houses of Congress
   C. was narrowly defeated in the Senate Judiciary Committee
   D. was ridiculed in a popular book of the time entitled "Nine Old Men"

5. The election of 1936
    A. reflected grudging national support for the New Deal
    B. saw much debate over the Supreme Court issue
    C. may not be described as a landslide victory for the New Deal
    D. overwhelmingly endorsed the New Deal

6. FDR's attempt to reform the Supreme Court
    A. secured more decisions favorable to the New Deal
    B. was completely unsuccessful
    C. was the first attempt to change the number of members of the Supreme Court
    D. was endorsed by nearly all Democrats

THE HUMAN FACTOR

Franklin D. Roosevelt as Communicator

Franklin Delano Roosevelt had an extraordinary gift for communicating with the American people. From the very beginning of his first administration, he reached out to them in what he called "fireside chats." Within a week after his inauguration, as the banks reopened under the Emergency Banking Relief Act, he addressed his first nationwide radio audience of 35 million listeners, which included three out of four American families, and told them that it was now safer to keep their money in one of the reopened banks than "under the mattress." This was the first of what were to be some thirty "fireside chats," all calculated to communicate his message directly to the people. He was equally skillful in using press conferences to win public confidence. He met with members of the press twice a week. They enjoyed his friendly banter and gave him "a good press," an invaluable asset for a President engaged in making basic economic, social, and political reforms.

Eleanor Roosevelt, the Eyes and Ears of the President

Eleanor Roosevelt, wife of Franklin D. Roosevelt, played a major, if unofficial, role in his presidential administration, as she had done when he was Governor of New York. By keeping informed of public sentiment on vital issues, Eleanor Roosevelt served as the keen and reliable eyes and ears of the President. From her extensive travels, she brought him extremely useful firsthand information. A humanitarian, she was deeply concerned with the plight of the underdog, victims of the Dust Bowl, (the "Okies"), and especially, African Americans, who were denied opportunities open to other Americans. On behalf of the underprivileged, Eleanor Roosevelt did not hesitate to speak out to the President.

Ravages of the Dust Bowl

When the plow destroyed the protective grasses of the semiarid plains east of the Rockies, the defenseless soil was ready for catastrophe. It came in the hot drought-ridden spring and summer of 1934. A great dust storm ravaged parts of Oklahoma, Arkansas, Colorado, Kansas, New Mexico, and Texas. Howling winds drove the dust a thousand miles east, covering homes and farms, blackening the sky, disrupting railroad schedules, and spreading despair. In *The Grapes of Wrath* (1939), novelist **John Steinbeck** tells the tragic story of the Joads, a family driven from its Oklahoma farm by the ravages of the dust bowl. A quarter of a million farmers, who saw their cattle suffocate, their crops destroyed, and their few possessions menaced by relentless mountains of dust, left their farms and drove west in quest of a better life.

Women During the New Deal Era

The appointment in 1933 of **Frances Perkins** as Secretary of Labor, the first woman to serve as a member of the Cabinet, heralded a new era in the status of women. Perkins remained in the Cabinet during the twelve years of Roosevelt's presidency and then served for seven years under President **Truman** as a member of the **Civil Service Commission**. Outstanding women authors of the period included **Ellen Glasgow**, literary historian of the South, who won the Pulitzer Prize in 1941 for *In This Our Life,* and **Willa Cather**, whose novels depicted the struggles of pioneer women in frontier Nebraska.

Minorities and the New Deal

African Americans

African Americans found new hope in the relief, recovery, and reform measures of the New Deal. Traditionally Lincoln Republicans—in opposition to the dominant whites who exercised control through the southern Democratic party—African Americans began switching to the Democratic party in 1934, and contributed significantly to the New Deal landslide of 1936, especially in the cities of the North.

Native Americans

The Native American minority, too, saw new hope as the **Indian Reorganization Act** of 1934 reversed the antitribal policy of the **Dawes Act** of 1887 and recognized tribal life as the normal and viable Native American mode.

Culture of the Depression

Like wars and other catastrophes, the Great Depression brought forth sympathetic responses in the arts. John Steinbeck's *The Grapes of Wrath* is the quintessential literary portrayal of this disaster, particularly as it affected the poor farmers of the Dust Bowl. **Langston Hughes**, depicted the humiliation of African Americans in his semiautobiographical novel, *Not Without*

Laughter (1930) and in his short story, *The Way of White Folks* (1934). He won early recognition at the age of 24, when his first book of poetry was published in 1926.

Photography

The impact of the Depression is seen in the photographs of **Walker Evans**, who collaborated with the writer **James Agee** to produce the classic *Let Us Now Praise Famous Men*. In 1936 they lived with three families in Alabama for about six weeks and captured in photos and text the essence of the life of white tenant farmers in Alabama. Their book, published in 1941, is a unique documentary portrayal of American life. **Margaret Bourke-White**, a photographer with the **Resettlement Administration**, established in 1935 to help distraught farmers settle on better land, produced a series of black-and-white photographs that captured the essence of the time. Her photojournalism appeared in *Life* magazine, which, along with *Look* magazine, was created in 1930 to give readers a pictorial view of people and events.

Escaping Reality—Movies and Comics

Hollywood and comic books provided an escape from the harsh reality of the Depression. A special Academy Award went to **Walt Disney** in 1932 for **Mickey Mouse**; to MGM in 1935 for *Mutiny on the Bounty*; and to Selznick International in 1939 for the box-office favorite *Gone With The Wind*. Comic strips provided additional escape and became a regular feature of most newspapers. "Blondie" first appeared in 1930, "Dick Tracy" in 1931, "Li'l Abner" in 1934, and "Superman" in 1938. "Little Orphan Annie" dated back to 1924 and "Peanuts" had its debut in 1950.

The WPA and the Arts

The New Deal **WPA** provided funds for unemployed writers, actors, artists, and musicians. A series of WPA books on each of the states created an invaluable record of the period. Plays by **Clifford Odets** and music dramas like *Pins and Needles* entertained audiences that could not otherwise see a theater production, while it gave writers, actors, and directors a chance to practice their professions. In one WPA project, artists painted murals depicting historic scenes on the walls of public buildings, schools, libraries, and railroad centers. One of the finest collections of these works of art, painted a half-century ago by Alexander J. Rummler, has been carefully restored and is now displayed on the walls of the city hall in Norwalk, Connecticut.

Music

Music of the period evolved from **ragtime** developed by black orchestras in the South before World War I. A new form called **jazz** came into its own in the 1920s. Great performers and band leaders emerged, including the legendary cornetist **Bix Biederbeck** who died in 1931 at the age of 28, **Louis "Satchmo" Armstrong**, **Duke Ellington**, and the pianist and composer **"Fats" Wailer**. **Swing** bands led by **Paul Whiteman**, **Glen Gray**, **Tommy Dorsey**, **Glenn Miller**, **Benny Goodman**, and **Vincent Lopez** played as couples danced to their music on large dance floors, and millions listened on the radio and bought their records. Musicals, too, came into their own with long-run performances of *Oklahoma, Show Boat, Porgy and Bess,* and the music of **Irving Berlin**, **Richard Rodgers**, **George Gershwin**, **Cole Porter**, and **Jerome Kern**.

Opposition to the New Deal

As might be expected, there were those who felt the New Deal had gone too far and others who believed it had not gone far enough to correct the system that had led to the Great Depression.

On the Left

At the far left were the **Communists**, who nominated **Earl Browder** for President in 1936. He garnered 80,000 votes out of a total of some 46 million cast in the election. The **Socialist party**, with **Norman Thomas** again the candidate, polled 187,000.

• *Communist and Socialist Doctrines Differ.* The Communists, influenced by the doctrines of **Karl Marx** and the Russian Bolshevik **Lenin**, believed that justice for the working class (proletariat) would come only through the violent overthrow of capitalism. The Socialists, led by **Eugene V. Debs** and **Norman Thomas**, believed that democratic methods supported by education and legal agitation would bring about the necessary radical changes in the economic system.

On the Right

Those who attacked the New Deal from the right presented a united front by nominating the former Republican Congressman **William Lemke** of North Dakota for President. The Union party was endorsed by most of the major rightist organizations. Lemke received 891,858 votes, about 2 percent of the total cast.

• *Fascists Inspired by Mussolini and Hitler.* At the far right of the political spectrum were the **Fascists**, who drew their inspiration from the systems imposed by force in Italy under Mussolini, in Germany under Hitler, and in Spain under Franco. In the United States, these found their counterparts in the pro-Nazi German-American **Bund** and Italian Fascist "Black Shirts."

Homegrown Demagogues

"Homegrown" demagogues gained a considerable number of converts by denouncing the New Deal and offering their own solutions.

- *Huey P. Long.* A serious challenge was mounted by Senator **Huey P. ("Kingfish") Long** of Louisiana, who launched a "Share Our Wealth" program with the promise to make "every man a king" and to distribute $5,000 to every family. Long, a skillful rabble-rouser, was planning to take his campaign to New York in a huge parade when he was assassinated in the Louisiana State capitol in 1935.

- *Father Charles F. Coughlin.* A demagogue from Michigan who gained an army of followers through his weekly radio broadcast, which reached 40 million listeners. His call for "social justice" was accompanied by a steady stream of pro-Fascist, anti-Semitic messages that finally aroused his superiors in the church who in 1942 ordered him to discontinue his broadcasts.

- *Gerald L.K. Smith.* A pro-Fascist demagogue from Louisiana, the originator of the Share Our Wealth movement, and the successor to Long after the latter's assassination, Smith was described as "the greatest rabble-rouser on earth."

- *Dr. Francis E. Townsend.* A retired physician from California, his Townsend Plan promised federal payments of $200 a month to every person over 60, the money to be raised by a national sales tax. He is said to have attained a following of 5 million seniors.

Assessment of the New Deal

A brief assessment of the New Deal program suggests that it introduced at least one major new element in American life, the concept that the national government should assume responsibility for the welfare of the people. As Roosevelt expressed it: ". . . the government has the definite duty to use all its power and resources to meet new social problems with new social controls . . ." Roosevelt maintained that "it was this administration which saved the system of private profit and free enterprise after it had been dragged to the brink of ruin." The New Deal had saved the banking system, promoted the conservation of natural resources, and given new hope to the common people. Yet, on the eve of World War II, millions were still unemployed. It was World War II that finally revitalized the industrial machine and the national economy.

1. Which of the following was *not* a factor in bringing about the landslide victory of the Democratic party in the 1936 election?
   A. the black vote
   B. "fireside chats"
   C. solution of the unemployment problem
   D. press conferences

2. Prominent women of the (Franklin) Roosevelt era include all of the following EXCEPT
   A. Susan B. Anthony
   B. Ellen Glasgow
   C. Frances Perkins
   D. Eleanor Roosevelt

3. Which of the following was a cause of the others?
   A. departure of thousands of poor farmers from Oklahoma and Arkansas
   B. publication of the novel *The Grapes of Wrath*
   C. the great dust storm of 1934
   D. creation of a "dust bowl" in parts of Texas, New Mexico, and Kansas

4. The plight of black Americans during the Depression is depicted in
   A. the novels of Willa Cather
   B. the works of Langston Hughes
   C. the photography of Walker Evans
   D. the movie *Gone With The Wind*

CHAPTER REVIEW QUESTIONS

1. The major difference between Herbert Hoover and Franklin Roosevelt was
   A. their political philosophy
   B. their wealth
   C. the difficulty of the problems they faced
   D. the cooperation each received from his own party

2. The election of 1940
   A. showed fundamental foreign policy differences between the two major parties
   B. was unique in that no minor parties participated
   C. caused the later adoption of the Twenty-second Amendment
   D. helped perpetuate the two-term tradition

3. Which is a valid conclusion based upon a study of the New Deal?
   A. labor, but not business, was affected
   B. it resulted in a government budget surplus
   C. it forced individuals to accept responsibility for their own economic welfare
   D. it continued to influence United States economic policy for many years

   Regents Exam, August 1988

4. Although all segments of American society were affected by the Great Depression, those who suffered most severely were
   A. operators of small business
   B. the lower middle class
   C. senior citizens
   D. women and children

5. All of the following are true of the Twentieth Amendment to the Constitution EXCEPT
   A. it eliminated the unproductive "lame duck" Congress
   B. it changed the date of the President's inauguration
   C. it limited Presidents to two terms
   D. it specified that Congress would meet early in January of each year

6. The Civilian Conservation Corps did all of the following EXCEPT
   A. hire older men for leaf-raking jobs
   B. give useful work and some discipline to young men
   C. give most of the pay of enrollees to their parents
   D. promote development of natural resources

7. Private business opposed the Tennessee Valley Authority (TVA) because
   A. it was thought the lakes would soon be filled with silt
   B. the project did not provide satisfactory protection against floods
   C. electricity was produced and distributed by a government agency
   D. it called for regimentation of the farmers of the district

8. FDR's attempt to reform the Supreme Court
   A. secured more decisions favorable to New Deal laws
   B. was completely unsuccessful
   C. was the first attempt to change the number of members of the Court
   D. was endorsed by nearly all Democrats

9. As President, Franklin D. Roosevelt did all of the following EXCEPT
  A. continue several of the policies he had put into practice as Governor of New York
  B. cease relying on his wife Eleanor as his eyes and ears
  C. demonstrate the same capacity for vote-getting as he had in New York
  D. bring to Washington a number of key political and personal associates from New York

ESSAYS

1. In attempting to measure how successful a person has been as President of the United States, the following qualities have been identified as important:

> Communication skills
> Ability to interpret the mood of the country
> Ability to project a positive public image
> Willingness to initiate bold programs
> Firmness, yet willingness to compromise

  a. Select *two* qualities from the list which you think are the most important qualities necessary for success as a President. For *each* one selected, show how this quality contributed to the success of a specific United States President during his presidency. [You may use the same or a different President for each quality discussed.] [5,5]
  b. Explain how *one* of the qualities listed above was a significant factor in the 1940 presidential campaign. Include in your response references to a specific candidate. [5]

2. Cultural expression has at times been used as a form of social criticism. At other times, cultural expression has been used to promote or glorify the values of a society. From the list below, select three forms of cultural expression. For *each* one chosen, identify a specific example of that form of cultural expression and show how that example was used either to criticize or to support the values of American society in the period between World War I and World War II. [5,5]

Forms of Cultural Expression
Movies
Literature
Theater
Music
Painting or Sculpture

Regents Exam, January 1986

3. Periods of stress in American history have witnessed the emergence of antidemocratic forces either reacting to what they perceive as a reversal of traditional American values, or attempting to exploit stressful conditions in order to achieve their antidemocratic goals. Two such periods were the period immediately following World War I and the period of the Great Depression.

For *each* period describe the conditions that caused stress. [5] Explain how one antidemocratic group reacted to or attempted to exploit the stressful situation. [5] Discuss the outcome of the antidemocratic activities. [5]

UNIT FIVE _____

The United States in an Age of Global Crisis

KEY IDEAS: Unit Five explores the American policy of isolation in the 1920s and 1930s and American involvement in World War II. It describes the effects of the war on the United States and America's role in the postwar world, with emphasis on the Cold War.

UNIT GOAL: By the end of the Unit, the student should be able to explain how World War II forced the United States to make an increasingly heavy commitment to global involvement.

Chapter 1

DIPLOMACY AND WAR (1933–1945)

ISOLATION AND NEUTRALITY

Neutrality During the Eighteenth and Nineteenth Centuries

> 'Tis our true policy to steer clear of permanent alliances, with any portion of the foreign world.
>
> George Washington's Farewell Address,
> September 17, 1796

Washington's admonition against permanent alliances was still in the minds of America's leaders during the **Napoleonic Wars** of the early nineteenth century. There was pressure both on **Adams'** administration (1797–1801) and on that of his successor, **Jefferson** (1801–1809), to go to war against France as the Federalists urged, or against England as the Republicans demanded. But the sentiment for neutrality prevailed despite provocation by both warring nations. An undeclared naval war with France actually took place during two years of Adams' administration (1798–1800). Ultimately, the policy of noninvolvement failed and the United States became involved in the Napoleonic Wars in 1812. The **War of 1812** against Britain was fought to protect "neutral rights" on the high seas.

In the historic **Monroe Doctrine** (1823), President Monroe stated the policy of nonintervention in these words: ". . . our policy in regard to Europe . . . is not to interfere in the internal concerns of any of its powers." These sentiments prevailed and the United States avoided European conflicts for most of the rest of the 19th century, despite the efforts of the hawks during **Polk's** administration, who cried "Fifty-four forty or fight," calling for war with England unless our territory was extended to Russian Alaska (54° 40' north latitude).

Efforts to Remain Neutral in World War I

When Europe was engaged in World War I, Wilson, echoing the sentiments of the American people, declared, "The United States must be neutral in fact as well as in name . . . We must be impartial in thought as well as in action." This was in 1914, but three years later he called for war, and American troops were sent to Europe. The postwar reaction was dramatic. Popular disillusionment following World War I contributed to the strong sentiment for isolationism that caused the U.S. Senate to reject membership in the League of Nations. It was this sentiment, still strong in the 1930s, that confronted the Roosevelt administration while Hitler moved step by step toward realization of the Nazi boast, "Today we rule Germany; tomorrow the world."

Of course, total isolationism by a great world power is impossible. In the 20th century the United States had territorial possessions in the Pacific Ocean, the Caribbean, and Central America. Moreover, American business interests were engaged in commerce and industry throughout the world, and American capital was a major source of support for worldwide industrial development. It was inevitable that defense of these commitments would make complete isolationism a practical impossibility.

The World Disarmament Conference

When the **World Disarmament Conference** convened in Geneva, Switzerland, in February 1932, President Hoover, whose Quaker background predisposed him to peace efforts, sent an American delegation. It was understood, however, that prevailing isolationist sentiment in the United States would make any American commitment for participation in international action unlikely. The Conference, sponsored by the League of Nations and attended by representatives of the Soviet Union as well as the United States, adjourned in March 1933 and reconvened in October. It adjourned again when Germany, now led by Hitler, withdrew from the Conference and later, from the League of Nations. Efforts at international disarmament had failed.

Isolationism and the Nye Committee Hearings

In 1934, the U.S. Senate created a special committee to prepare legislation on government control of the munitions industry. The committee, headed by a confirmed isolationist, Senator **Gerald P. Nye** of North Dakota, held widely publicized hearings for the next three years. The hearings disclosed that munitions manufacturers had made huge profits from World War I. They also charged that arms manufacturers had successfully exerted pressure for U.S. involvement in the war. A frequently quoted book entitled *Merchants of Death* detailed the rapacious methods by which munitions dealers and their banking allies had enriched themselves from the war. Many who had supported America's participation in World War I now regarded it as a grave error. A spirit of pacifism, dominating college campuses, preached from pulpits, and bolstered on stage and in the cinema, reflected the prevailing national sentiment. The call for preparedness was answered with the phrase "never again."

318

United States Neutrality Legislation

It was in this atmosphere of isolationism that a series of **neutrality laws** were passed by Congress in the 1930s. In the summer of 1935, when Mussolini's troops were poised for the invasions of Ethiopia, Congress passed the **Neutrality Act of 1935**. The act required the President to place an **embargo** on arms to nations engaged in war and prohibited travel of U.S. citizens on belligerent vessels. It was designed to prevent any American armaments manufacturer, banker, or merchant from profiting from a foreign war or helping to embroil us in one. This meant that the United States had to remain neutral while Italy invaded and subjugated Ethiopia. Japan and Germany, of course, favored this American policy. Both had already embarked on programs leading to military conquest and expansion. In 1931 the Japanese invaded and occupied **Manchuria**, a large province of China, bordering on Korea, which Japan already controlled. The United States refused to recognize this conquest under the newly declared **Stimson Doctrine**. In 1936 Japan and Germany signed a military agreement called the **Anti-Comintern Treaty**. In the same year Germany and Italy formed an alliance called the **Rome-Berlin Axis**. With the addition of Japan in 1940, it became known as the **Rome-Berlin-Tokyo Axis**.

Civil War in Spain (1936–1939)

Events moved swiftly on the road to World War II. A "popular front" coalition of Liberals, Socialists, and Communists in Spain ousted the Conservative government in the 1936 national election. Five months later (July 1936) **Generalissimo Francisco Franco** led an uprising to overthrow the **Republican** government of Spain and replace it with a **Fascist** government. The **Spanish Civil War** that followed was a prelude to World War II. Germany and Italy openly aided Franco while England and France, following policies of nonintervention, looked on helplessly, and Russia, far from the scene, gave what help it could to the Spanish Republican government. The United States observed its own neutrality laws. A small contingent of American volunteers, which became known as the **Abraham Lincoln Brigade**, joined the forces of the Spanish Republic. Hitler's air force gained experience, valuable in the coming world war, by bombing Spanish cities and strafing their inhabitants. One such raid on **Guernica**, April 26, 1937, is depicted in a famous painting by the Spanish artist, **Pablo Picasso**. The war ended in March 1939 with the defeat of the **Loyalists** (those loyal to the Republic) and the establishment of a Fascist government under Franco.

American Isolationism and Axis Aggression

Meanwhile, in March 1936, Hitler's troops marched into the Rhineland in violation of the Treaty of Versailles. In 1937, Japan invaded China. In a speech in Chicago, President Roosevelt called on the democracies to "quarantine the aggressors," but his hands were tied by neutrality legislation and by the prevailing national sentiment of isolationism or, at least, nonintervention.

Neutrality Legislation of 1936 and 1937

The **Neutrality Act of 1935** was due to expire at the end of February 1936. Congress replaced it with the **Neutrality Act of 1936**, which extended the legislation for another year and added a provision prohibiting loans by Americans to nations engaged in war. A third neutrality law, with no time limit, was passed by Congress in 1937. The legislation banned shipment of munitions to either side in the Spanish Civil War and was particularly disadvantageous to the Republicans, since Franco was receiving supplies from Italy and Germany. In his "quarantine" speech, Roosevelt urged that the United States join the other powers to "quarantine," or check, the aggressor nations. He expressed a viewpoint most Americans were not ready to accept when he said, "It seems to be unfortunately true that the epidemic of world lawlessness is spreading. And mark this well! When an epidemic of physical disease starts to spread, the community approves and joins in a quarantine of the patients in order to protect the community against the spread of the disease." In an opinion poll taken shortly after the speech, only 31 percent of the public favored presidential action to check aggression, whereas the vast majority supported Congressional neutrality legislation. An amendment to the Constitution was proposed by Congressman **Louis Ludlow**, Democrat of Indiana. It would have required a national referendum for a declaration of war (except in case of armed invasion of U.S. territory), but it failed to pass the House of Representatives in January 1938 partly because of the opposition of Roosevelt's administration.

Exercise Set 5.1

1. The prevailing isolationist sentiment in the United States in the years prior to 1939 can be traced to each of the following EXCEPT
   A. the speech of President Roosevelt urging a "quarantine" of the aggressors
   B. the hearings held in the U.S. Senate committee presided over by Senator Gerald P. Nye
   C. a tradition first expressed by President Washington in his Farewell Address
   D. disillusionment of the American people with the consequences of World War I

2. Neutrality legislation of the 1930s was designed to
   A. prevent aggression by the Rome-Berlin-Tokyo Axis
   B. give the United States time to prepare for the coming war
   C. protect American lives and property in Europe and Asia
   D. keep the United States out of war by avoiding the mistakes of pre-World War I

3. A major foreign relations problem of the Roosevelt administration after 1935 was to
   A. negotiate a military alliance with Great Britain and the USSR
   B. persuade the American people of the need to abandon the policy of isolationism
   C. persuade the Axis powers to rejoin the League of Nations
   D. persuade the Congress to disband the Nye Committee investigating corrupt practices in the munitions industry

4. Which of the following was the most important reason for the rise of dictatorships in Europe in the two decades following World War I?
   A. general illiteracy of the working class
   B. stresses caused by the constant threat of renewed warfare
   C. destruction of homes and factories during World War I
   D. widespread economic disorder

FAILURE OF PEACE: TRIUMPH OF AGGRESSION

The Road to World War II (1933–1939)

In retrospect, it is clear that the aggressions of the Axis powers during the 1930s culminated in a world war because the democracies were not willing to go to war to protect the freedom of the nations that the Axis powers invaded. Hitler began rearming Germany in violation of the Treaty of Versailles in 1933 and occupied the Rhineland in 1936. Despite promises to make each demand his last, he annexed **Austria** in 1938, dismembered **Czechoslovakia** in 1938, and demanded the **Polish Corridor** in 1939. Another Axis member, Japan, invaded **Manchuria** in 1931 and the rest of China in 1937. The third Axis member, Italy, invaded **Ethiopia** in 1935 and **Albania** in 1939. With the help of Germany and Italy, the democratic government of **Spain** was overthrown (1936–1939) and replaced with a dictatorship friendly to the Axis. To protect his eastern flank Hitler made a "nonaggression" pact with Stalin on August 23, 1939. On September 1, 1939, Hitler's armies invaded Poland. Two days later France and England declared war on Germany.

The Policy of Appeasement—The Munich Conference (1938)

The policy of appeasement, exemplified in the **Munich Conference** of September 1938, had disastrous consequences. This policy, adopted by British Prime Minister **Neville Chamberlain**, relied on Hitlers Germany's becoming a friendly member of the family of nations once Hitler's demands were met. When Hitler insisted that the **Sudetenland** of **Czechoslovakia** be turned over to Germany, there was grave concern among opponents of Fascism. Czechoslovakia was a strong democratic country. The Sudetenland was heavily fortified and the Czechs were prepared to resist. However, Chamberlain decided to appease Hitler and he called a conference of four powers—Britain, France, Italy, and Germany—to meet in Munich, Germany. In Munich it was quickly decided to yield to Hitler's demands to occupy the Sudetenland. Hitler promised in return to make no more territorial demands. Chamberlain flew back to England and was greeted with wild acclaim when he said he brought "peace in our time." Six months after the Munich conference Hitler sent his troops to occupy all of Czechoslovakia. **Winston Churchill**, a leading member of Parliament who was opposed to appeasement, called the Munich agreement an unmitigated disaster. Less them a year after the Munich Conference, Britain was at war with Germany.

Changing Public Opinion in the United States

In January 1939 President Roosevelt tried to persuade Congress to revise the neutrality legislation. He saw a war coming between Germany and the democracies of Western Europe—France and Britain. Under the then existing law the United States could not sell war supplies to the democracies. Congress, reflecting public sentiment, refused to change the law. However, after the war started in Europe, public opinion began to shift. On September 21, 1939, three weeks after the beginning of World War II, President Roosevelt addressed a joint session of Congress and urged a change in the neutrality law. He said, ". . . by the repeal of the embargo the United States will more probably remain at peace than if the law remains as it stands today." Congress responded by passing the **Neutrality Act of 1939**, which contained a "cash and carry" provision. Belligerents (that is, Britain or France) could purchase any supplies, including armaments, provided they paid cash and carried the supplies from the United States in their own ships. This would keep American ships out of the war zone and would prevent American banks from making loans that American troops might later have to redeem.

Agreement on Western Hemisphere Defense

One policy on which Americans were in agreement was the defense of the Western Hemisphere against foreign aggression. An **Inter-American Conference** at which the United States was a participant issued the **Declaration of Panama** (October 3, 1939) a month after the outbreak of war. It designated sea safety zones in the Western Hemisphere south of Canada and warned belligerent powers against naval action within these zones. On July 30, 1940, the 21 republics of the **Pan-American Union**, meeting in Havana, signed the **Act of Havana**. It provided that the American republics, individually or collectively, might take over any European possession in the Western Hemisphere endangered by aggression. The purpose of this act was to ensure against the occupation or transfer of any of these possessions to Germany. The achievement of unity in Latin America for support of U.S. foreign policy was attributable in part to the "**good neighbor policy**" that President Roosevelt had proclaimed in his first inaugural address and to which he adhered throughout his presidency.

Victories of the German Armies in Western Europe

The war in Europe took an ominous turn in the spring of 1940 as Germany quickly occupied neutral Norway and Denmark. German troops also overran Holland, Belgium, and Luxembourg. Operating from Belgium, the German army was able to bypass the powerful line of fortifications (**Maginot Line**) on which France relied for its security. German troops poured into France and defeated the British and French defenders. Britain was able to evacuate troops trapped in France at **Dunkirk** on the English Channel by a sea flotilla of civilian ships. Italy invaded southern France, prompting Roosevelt's statement in an address that day at the University of Virginia, "On this tenth day of June 1940 the hand that held the dagger has stuck it in the back of its neighbor."

Moving Toward War

Aid to Britain

Winston Churchill replaced Chamberlain as Prime Minister of Britain after the fall of France. He promised his people only "blood, toil, tears, and sweat." In an appeal to America he said, "Give us the tools and we will finish the job." As Commander-in-Chief of the Armed Forces, Roosevelt took the unprecedented step of making a swap with Britain by transferring to Britain 50 World War I destroyers in exchange for 99-year leases on a number of British air and naval bases in the Atlantic and West Indies. This transfer took place in September 1940.

Peacetime Conscription

Public opinion changed enough in the same month to secure the passage of a peacetime conscription bill of men between the ages of 21 and 35.

Franklin D. Roosevelt's Four Freedoms Message

Shocked by events in Europe, the United States began to see its own defense in a new light. Only the armed forces of Britain stood between the United States and the Nazi military machine. On June 19 Roosevelt announced the appointment of two prominent Republicans to key posts in his cabinet—**Henry L. Stimson** as Secretary of War and **Frank Knox** as Secretary of the Navy. In a fireside chat on December 29, 1940, the month after defeating **Wendell Willkie**, his Republican opponent, for reelection to a third term, Roosevelt told the American people, "We must be the great arsenal of democracy." Public opinion was ready to accept this undertaking.

In his January 6, 1941, State of the Union message to Congress, the President proclaimed the "Four Freedoms":

> In the future days, which we seek to make secure, we look forward to a world founded upon four essential freedoms. The first is freedom of expression—everywhere in the world. The second is freedom of every person to worship God in his own way—everywhere in the world. The third is freedom from want . . . everywhere in the world. The fourth is freedom from fear . . . anywhere in the world.

Lend-Lease (February 1941)

The difficulty of serving as the **arsenal of democracy** was twofold. Britain could no longer pay cash for armaments, and the idea of extending credit raised the specter of old World War I debts that were never repaid. The solution was found in the **Lend-Lease Bill,** passed by Congress on March 11, 1941. Four days earlier, in his State of the Union message, the President had proposed to help Britain and other countries opposing Axis aggression by supplying "in ever-increasing numbers, ships, planes, tanks, guns." The lend-lease measure permitted the President to "sell, transfer, exchange, lease, or otherwise dispose of war equipment to any nation for use in the interests of the United States." The measure met fierce opposition from the **America First Committee** and its friends in Congress.

War Measures

With the passage of the Lend-Lease Act, the adoption of a draft, a vast increase in military appropriations, the repeal of the Neutrality Law of 1939, the use of American naval vessels to convoy supplies bound for Britain as far as Iceland, and the arming of American merchantmen to combat Nazi submarines, the United States was obviously moving toward war late in 1941. The move away from neutrality was accompanied throughout by unrestricted public debate followed by actions taken in Congress.

The Atlantic Charter

The moral dimension of the war became the focus of world attention when Roosevelt and Churchill held a conference aboard a warship off the coast of Newfoundland in August 1941 and issued the **Atlantic Charter**. It declared (1) no territorial gains are sought by the United States or Britain; (2) territorial adjustments must conform to the wishes of the people involved; (3) people have a right to choose their own government; (4) trade barriers should be lowered; (5) there must be disarmament; (6) there must be freedom from fear and want; (7) there must be freedom of the seas; (8) there must be an association of nations.

The Attack on Pearl Harbor, December 7, 1941

At the very time that the Atlantic Charter was being prepared, the Japanese war department was making plans to attack the United States. A surprise attack was to be made on **Pearl Harbor**, the U.S. naval base in Hawaii. On Sunday morning December 7, 1941, at 7:55 A.M., a wave of 189 Japanese war planes—dive-bombers and torpedo planes—roared over Pearl Harbor meeting little opposition from the completely surprised base. A second wave of attack planes followed. Ships and planes were bombed and torpedoed like sitting ducks. One hundred and seventy American planes were destroyed on the ground. Eight battleships—the pride of the Navy—were sunk or severely damaged. Nineteen fighting ships, including cruisers and destroyers, were incapacitated. Some 2,400 officers and enlisted men were killed, and 1,300 wounded. Japanese losses totaled 29 planes and 6 submarines. It was the greatest disaster in the history of the U.S. armed forces. The next day, December 8, 1941, in his war message to Congress, President Roosevelt said, "Yesterday, December 7, 1941—a date which will live in infamy—the United States of America was suddenly and deliberately attacked by naval and air forces of the Empire of Japan."

With but one dissenting vote, Congress declared war against Japan. On December 11, Italy and Germany declared war on the United States. On the same day, Congress passed a declaration of war on Germany and Italy.

Exercise Set 5.2

1. War measures adopted by the United States prior to the attack on Pearl Harbor included all of the following EXCEPT
   A. passage of the Lend-Lease Act
   B. assignment of African Americans to integrated army units
   C. repeal of the 1939 Neutrality Law
   D. arming of American merchant vessels to combat Nazi submarines

2. The policy of appeasement, pursued by the British government under Prime Minister Neville Chamberlain
   A. achieved the goal of securing "peace in our time"
   B. was disapproved by public opinion in the democracies
   C. encouraged the Axis powers to engage in aggression
   D. gained the support of Winston Churchill in England

3. The first peacetime draft in American history, passed into law September 6, 1940,
   A. showed that the United States was now ready to go to war
   B. had a significant effect on the national election held two months later
   C. was approved by both houses of Congress with little dissent
   D. was reluctantly accepted by the American people as an essential defense measure

4. Clear indications that the Roosevelt administration supported Britain in the war could be seen from all of the following EXCEPT
   A. the "lend-lease" law
   B. the exchange of destroyers for lease of bases
   C. the Declaration of Panama
   D. the Atlantic Charter

5. Hitler concluded a nonaggression pact with Stalin in August 1939 in order to
A. protect his eastern flank while he made war on the west
B. establish the supremacy of dictatorship over democracy
C. carry out the understanding reached with England and France at Munich
D. challenge the Atlantic Charter issued by Roosevelt and Churchill

HOME FRONT: THE HUMAN DIMENSIONS OF THE WAR

> We must be the great arsenal of democracy.
> Franklin Roosevelt, December 29, 1940

The United States, "Arsenal of Democracy"

With America's entry into the war, industry geared up rapidly to meet the challenge and soon performed incredible feats of productivity. By 1942 America's production of war materiel was equal to that of the three Axis powers combined. Two years later it had doubled. Before the war was over the United States had built 300,000 aircraft, 71,000 ships, and over 80,000 tanks. At war's end the fighting power of the Navy had been increased over that of 1941 by 6 more battleships, 21 more aircraft carriers, and 70 more destroyers, and America's merchant marine had become the largest in the world. Despite a decrease in farm labor brought about by military enlistments, agricultural production doubled during the war years. The Depression program of crop limitation gave way to an all-out war effort that produced bumper crops of cotton, corn, hogs, and other foods to supply our own needs as well as those of our allies.

Women, a Major Factor in the War Effort

America's capacity to produce was substantially increased by the addition of three million women—double the number previously employed—to the labor force. Women served in every industry, often performing tasks previously considered the exclusive province of men. They wore hard hats in making steel, operating cranes, and constructing barracks. They worked in shipyards, airplane plants, and munitions factories.

More than 250,000 women served in the armed forces wearing uniforms of the Army **WACS**, Navy **WAVES**, and Coast Guard **SPARS**. Of the 25,000 women who applied to the **Women's Air Force Service Pilots**, 1,074 of them risked their lives towing targets, testing aircraft after repair, and delivering planes to destinations in Canada and all over the United States. Of their number, 38 were killed in action. Women's Air Force Service Pilots were granted veterans' status in 1979. Women's contributions to the war effort were symbolized by Rosie the Riveter. She was thought to have been named after Rosena B. Bonavita, who, with her co-workers, reportedly put 3,345 rivets on the wing of a fighter plane in six hours.

Mobilizing the Armed Forces

In 1940, fifteen months before the attack on Pearl Harbor, Congress passed a **conscription** law—the first peacetime draft in American history—designed to secure 1.2 million troops and 800,000 reserves for the armed forces. When the war came, there were 1.6 million in the army. Recruitment and training proceeded rapidly after Pearl Harbor. All men between 18 and 45 were made eligible for military service, though many were rejected for failure to meet standards of physical fitness and intelligence. Over 15 million men and women served in the armed forces during World War II. This included 10 million in the Army, 4 million in the Navy and Coast Guard, and 600,000 in the Marine Corps.

Financing the War

Raising Funds for the War

For four years (1941–45) the United States was not only fighting a global war on land, sea, and in the air, but was serving as the "arsenal of democracy," supplying its allies with planes, tanks, guns, ships, and all the implements of warfare. It is not surprising, therefore, that the war cost $250 million a day. The national debt, which stood at $49 billion in 1941 (most of it incurred during World War I and the Depression of the '30s) zoomed to $258 billion in 1945.

Maintaining this giant enterprise required both taxing and borrowing, since it was impossible to operate on a "pay as you go" basis as President Roosevelt would have preferred. In seven massive **war bond drives**, the government borrowed $100 billion from its citizens. Despite a heavy increase in taxes, only 40 percent of the war's cost was paid as the funds were needed. For the first time, income taxes were collected by payroll deductions. Rates were raised substantially, running as high as 94 percent on the highest incomes.

Preventing Inflation

With full employment and high government expenditures, wages nearly doubled. It became necessary to take steps to prevent run-away inflation. An **Office of Price Administration** (**OPA**), headed by **Leon Henderson**, was established in August 1941. In April 1942 the OPA imposed a general **price freeze** including a freeze on rents. The OPA also distributed **ration booklets**, which limited civilian consumption of gasoline, meat, tires, and other commodities made scarce by the war.

Hollywood Goes to War

The movie industry gave its talents wholeheartedly to the war effort. War films depicted the bravery and skill of America's fighting forces, the cruelty and ineptness of the Axis forces, the sometimes exotic nature of war zones, and ultimately the goals for which we fought. Among outstanding war films were *Casablanca,* which portrayed the Free French in Africa standing firm against the Nazis; *Sahara,* which depicted soldiers of the allied nations gaining control of scarce water resources; *Air Force,* which pictured the exploits of a U.S. bomber "Flying Fortress"; and *A Walk in the Sun,* which presented U.S. Army units establishing a beachhead in Italy. Films that dealt with the war in Asia included *Bataan, Behind the Rising Sun,* and *Dragon Seed.* **Bob Hope**, one of Hollywood's best-known comedians, and many others went overseas to entertain the troops.

The War's Impact on Minorities

Impact on African Americans

World War II had a special impact on African Americans and on Japanese Americans. During the war, half a million African Americans moved from the deep South to seek employment in the defense industries in Northern cities. However, opportunities continued to be denied them despite the great need for labor in defense plants. A 1943 race riot in Detroit took the lives of 25 blacks and 9 whites. Membership in the NAACP leaped from 100,000 to half a million in the first three years of the war.

When the **United States Employment Service**, a federal agency, continued to fill defense contracts from employers stipulating "whites only," **A. Philip Randolph**, president of the **Brotherhood of Sleeping Car Porters**, proceeded to organize 50,000 people for a protest march on Washington. President Roosevelt met with Randolph at the White House on June 18, 1941. Randolph refused to call off the march until a satisfactory employment directive was issued by the President.

On June 25, 1941, President Roosevelt issued **Executive Order 8802**, declaring it the policy of the United States "that there shall be no discrimination in the employment of workers in defense industries or government because of race, creed, color, or national origin." The President appointed a **Fair Employment Practices Committee** to "receive and investigate complaints of discrimination" and to take "appropriate steps to redress grievances." Partly as a result of this order the number of black employees in the federal government increased from 40,000 to 300,000.

Impact on Japanese Americans

On the West Coast there was considerable apprehension about the part that Japanese Americans might play in the war. There was also latent prejudice and animosity toward Japanese Americans. On February 19, 1942, two months after the attack on Pearl Harbor, President Roosevelt issued **Executive Order 9066**, transferring authority for security to the Army. The Army commander of the West Coast, **Lt. General John DeWitt**, ordered the removal of 127,000 Japanese Americans, more than two thirds of whom were American citizens, from their homes in the western parts of Washington, Oregon, and California, and from southern Arizona. Without any charges or trials, they were forcibly "**relocated**" to dismal camps in the Western deserts and the Arkansas swamplands.

A suit to void the order as unconstitutional came to the U.S. Supreme Court and was decided on December 18, 1944. In *Korematsu* v. *United States* the Court was confronted with one of the enduring constitutional issues in American history—the balance between government security and the civil liberties of the individual. By a vote of 6 to 3, the Court upheld the government's action. Writing for the majority, **Justice Hugo Black**, whose overall record marks him as a staunch defender of the Bill of Rights, wrote, "He [Korematsu] was excluded because we are at war with the Japanese Empire, because the properly constituted military authorities feared an invasion of the West Coast, and felt constrained to take proper security measures . . ." In dissent, **Justice Owen J. Roberts** said the facts exhibited "a clear violation of constitutional rights," and **Justice Frank Murphy** said the exclusion went over "the brink of constitutional power" and fell "into the ugly abyss of racism."

On August 10, 1988, the United States finally admitted that the **internment** of Japanese Americans was a "mistake," agreed to issue apologies to each of the surviving internees, and to pay to each $20,000 tax-free over a ten-year period.

Segregation in the Armed Forces

When the draft went into effect in 1940, African American enlistments, proportional to their population, exceeded white enlistments by 60 percent. Yet African Americans were not accepted into the Air Corps or Marine Corps; the Army assigned them to segregated units as laborers and servants, and the Navy placed them as officers' cooks and stewards. African American combat troops served under white officers.

Pressure on the President from the African American community finally resulted in the organization of a few African American combat units, the commissioning of a limited number of African American officers in the Air Force, and the promotion of Colonel **Benjamin O. Davis** to Brigadier General. The numbers gradually increased during the war and more than 80 African American Air Force officers won the Distinguished Flying Cross. *The Crisis,* journal of the NAACP, contended that "a Jim Crow army cannot fight for a free world," but African Americans fought with distinction in every theater of the war. Complete integration in America's fighting forces did not come until the Korean War in the 1950s.

The Holocaust (1933–1945)

Early in the war, Hitler declared the Nazi policy concerning all the Jews under his control in Germany and the occupied countries. He called it "**the**

final solution." It consisted of the systematic murder of the entire Jewish people. The extermination of an ethnic group is called **genocide**. The Nazi "final solution," which resulted in the murder of six million Jews in Europe during the Third Reich (1933–1945), is known in history as the **Holocaust**. Major extermination centers were built at Auschwitz, Buchenwald, Treblinka, Bergen-Belsen, and Majdanek. There were a number of other such camps throughout Eastern Europe.

News of the Holocaust reached the West early in 1942, but the enormity of the crime was such that many found it unbelievable. The **U.S. War Refugee Board** produced radio programs on the Holocaust, but it could not persuade any radio stations to broadcast them because public opinion was not receptive.

When American armed forces entered the death camps in April 1945, they were horrified at what they found—massive starvation, unchecked disease, thousands of unburied corpses. General Eisenhower called the findings "almost unbelievable." Slowly the truth was impressed on the incredulous public. As the cry, "Never again" was raised, Holocaust studies became part of the school curriculum in New York State and throughout the United States. A widely used guide is *Teaching about the Holocaust and Genocide* (New York State Education Department, 1985).

Failure of the United States to act on the reports of the Holocaust is attributable to a number of causes—disbelief, reluctance of the media to report what they knew, Roosevelt's preoccupation with other war matters, calculated opposition by **Breckenridge Long** of the State Department, and disinterest of the American public.

In the spring of 1944, President Roosevelt approved a request of the War Refugee Board to admit 1,000 refugees to Fort Ontario at Oswego, New York. The refugees, at that time in southern Italy, were survivors of the death camps. They were to return to their homelands after the war. During the war, Sweden had welcomed 8,000 Jewish refugees from Denmark. But the admission of 1,000 to the United States under strict "security restrictions" met with bitter resistance from anti-Semites in the United States.

Exercise Set 5.3

1. During World War II the earnings of workers
   A. nearly doubled
   B. increased by 50 percent
   C. gained only slightly
   D. declined in terms of real wages

2. World War II was financed differently from World War I in that
   A. excess profits taxes were levied
   B. income taxes were levied
   C. more of the cost was raised by taxation
   D. the withholding tax was not used

3. Which statement best describes an important part of the experience of African Americans in the United States during the period between World War I and World War II?
  A. many African Americans moved back to the South in an attempt to recapture their roots
  B. interracial tensions increased because of the African American migration into Northern cities
  C. the influence of the Ku Klux Klan declined significantly
  D. the success of black soldiers in World War I led to equal treatment for African Americans

  Regents Exam, January 1986

4. Which is a valid conclusion based on a study of the Holocaust?
  A. world opinion is effective in stopping genocide
  B. savage acts can be committed by an advanced society
  C. people should not become involved in partisan politics
  D. military commanders cannot be held responsible for acts committed during wartime

  Regents Exam, June 1986

5. Agricultural policy during World War II
  A. favored the production of basic raw materials like cotton
  B. attempted to restrict production in order to enlist farm labor in the war production industries
  C. fostered bumper crops as a means of exchange for materials needed in defense industries
  D. was a reversal of New Deal agricultural policy

THE UNITED STATES IN WORLD WAR II

> More than any other war in history, this war has been an array of the forces of evil against those of righteousness . . . no matter what the cost, the war had to be won.
>
> Dwight D. Eisenhower, June 10, 1945

Allied Leadership and Strategy

Allied leadership and strategy were the key factors in attaining victory in World War II. The United States, under Commander-in-Chief **Franklin D. Roosevelt**, worked in close and harmonious cooperation with Britain, under the indomitable Prime Minister **Winston S. Churchill**. The military leaders of both nations, in a secret conference in March 1941, planned joint strategy. The primary effort was to be directed against Nazi Germany, because Germany, in control of the seacoast of western Europe, was using its **U-boats** to cut communications between Britain and the United States. Also, Germany had greater military power and resources than Japan, and there was great apprehension that Germany might develop the atom bomb or some other fearful weapon if given the time.

Marshall—the Architect of Victory

America's Chief of Staff **General George C. Marshall** was the leading architect of Allied strategy. Roosevelt turned down his request for a field command, asserting that Marshall's talents as an overall strategist were essential to victory.

The Joint Chiefs of Staff

Admiral Ernest J. King, Chief of Naval Operations and Commander-in-Chief of the fleet, was a key member of the joint chiefs, as was **General H.H. (Hap) Arnold**, head of the Army Air Force. **General Douglas MacArthur** was recalled to service in July 1941 as commander of United States forces in the Far East.

Planning the Attack on "Fortress Europe"

Leadership of Eisenhower

General Dwight D. Eisenhower was **Supreme Commander of Allied Expeditionary Forces** in Western Europe. He commanded the successful Allied invasion of North Africa and was then assigned the task of the invasion of Europe as commander of all Allied forces in Europe with headquarters near London.

From North Africa to Italy

In November 1942 General Eisenhower, in cooperation with the British, made landings in Africa and took Casablanca, Oran, and Algiers. On February 14, 1943, Eisenhower took command of the Allied forces in North Africa. Aided by **General George S. Patton** and British **General Bernard Montgomery**, he forced the surrender on May 13th of 250,000 Axis troops and brought the African campaign to a close. In September 1943 **General Mark Clark** led an American invasion of Italy at Salerno, south of Naples.

D-Day—June 6, 1944

In June 1944 General Eisenhower was made Supreme Commander of the Allied Expeditionary Forces with Supreme Headquarters, Allied Expeditionary Forces (**SHAEF**) in London. After months of careful planning, the invasion of Europe, called by the code name "**Operation Overlord**," was launched on "**D-Day**," **June 6, 1944**. The first few hours of Operation Overlord included heavy air bombardment all along the French coast; 4,000 troop ships crossing the Channel with 176,000 troops; air cover by 11,000 planes; glider planes with parachute troops being dropped behind enemy lines; and about 600 fighting ships escorting the fighting forces and shelling enemy batteries.

V. E. Day—May 8, 1945

By July 1944 one million troops were in France; by September that number exceeded two million. In September 1944, American troops entered Germany. On **May 8**, **1945** (**V. E. Day**), the German General Staff accepted the Allied terms of "unconditional surrender."

Turning Points in the War

At Sea—Midway

In the Pacific, the great air-naval battle of **Midway** (June 3–6, 1942) was a turning point in the war. Japan's attempt to take this strategic American base was repulsed with losses to the enemy of four carriers and about 275 planes.

In the Air—the Battle of Britain

A turning point in the air war in Europe came in the summer of 1940. Hitler's air force (**Luftwaffe**) bombed London and other British cities almost every night for three months. The **Royal Air Force** (**RAF**) downed 2,300 German planes during the **Battle of Britain**. Toward the end of August, the RAF gained control of the skies over Britain. They had won the battle and saved Britain. In the House of Commons on August 20, 1940, Churchill expressed

Britain's tribute to the RAF in the classic statement: "Never in the field of human conflict was so much owed by so many to so few."

On Land—Stalingrad

The turning point in the land war between the Nazi army and the Soviet forces came at **Stalingrad** in the fall of 1942, when the Russians broke the back of the German offensive by destroying or capturing more than twenty divisions, containing some 300,000 of Germany's elite troops.

The Atomic Bomb

In 1939, scientists in the field of theoretical physics were aware that **nuclear fission** could be used to make a bomb of incredible destructive power. There was evidence that Germany was working on the **atomic bomb**. In July 1939, **Albert Einstein**, a refugee from Nazi Germany then working at Princeton University, signed a letter to President Roosevelt urging that the U.S. government sponsor a program to harness atomic energy and stating: "This new phenomenon would lead also to the construction of bombs." Roosevelt considered the idea carefully and decided that he must pursue a project that was recommended by Einstein and other leading physicists, including **Enrico Fermi**, a Nobel Prize winner refugee from Italy, and **Niels Bohr**, another Nobel Laureate refugee from Denmark.

The Manhattan Project

On the morning of July 16, 1945, the first atomic bomb was detonated in the desert south of Los Alamos, New Mexico. Three weeks later, on August 6, 1945, a U.S. Army plane dropped a single atomic bomb over Hiroshima, Japan. The bomb had a force equal to 20,000 tons of TNT (dynamite). A blinding flash was followed by a "mushroom cloud" of debris and atomic radiation that reached skyward and spread over the city and its environs. It killed 260,000 people. When the Japanese refused to surrender, a second bomb was dropped three days later on Nagasaki.

Reason for Truman's Decision to Use the A-Bomb

President Truman's decision to use the bomb was justified in his mind by the need to end the war quickly and save American lives. The war in the Pacific had been bitterly fought with heavy losses. Fighting in the Philippines, Coral Sea, Midway, Guadalcanal, Tarawa, the Marshall Islands, Saipan, and Guam in the Marianas, and the reconquest of the Philippines had contributed substantially to the million American casualties. Now the fighting was on Japanese soil as the main islands of Japan were being approached. Capturing the small island of Iwo Jima took the lives of 5,000 American marines. The conquest of Okinawa, 360 miles from the main islands of Japan, resulted in 11,000 Americans killed and 34,000 wounded. It was estimated that the successful invasion of Japan would result in a million casualties.

The Japanese Surrender

On **August 14, 1945** (**V. J. Day**), five days after the bomb was dropped on Nagasaki, Japan surrendered and World War II ended.

Formal Surrender Ceremonies

Formal ceremonies of surrender and signing of surrender documents took place aboard the battleship *Missouri* in Tokyo Bay, September 2, 1945. The surrender was accepted by General Douglas MacArthur on condition that **Emperor Hirohito** be allowed to remain on the throne as emperor-figurehead. In a brief statement MacArthur concluded: "If we do not devise some . . . more equitable system than war, Armageddon will be at our door."

Occupation of Japan

General MacArthur was virtually the ruler of Japan during most of the period of Allied occupation (1945–1951). The Japanese cooperated in carrying out the reforms he instituted in decrees establishing a democratic, nonmilitary government, redistributing land, restricting the power of the industrial monopolies, establishing labor unions, reforming education, and granting women suffrage. A beginning was made in rebuilding the Japanese economy. These reforms, including provisions renouncing the making of nuclear arms and restricting the size and nature of Japan's armed forces, were included in the new Japanese Constitution, frequently referred to as "the MacArthur Constitution."

Exercise Set 5.4

1. Which of the following did *not* occur during the Allied occupation of Japan (1945–1951) after World War II?
   A. General MacArthur was not able to participate in the occupation because he was preoccupied with events in the Philippines
   B. The Japanese cooperated in carrying out the reforms requested by General MacArthur
   C. A new Japanese Constitution went into effect during the occupation
   D. The size of Japanese armed forces was substantially reduce

2. The first atomic bomb was developed in the United States with the help of a number of European scientists who were refugees from the Nazis. Which of the following was included in this group?
   A. Guglielmo Marconi
   B. Enrico Fermi
   C. Alessandro Volta
   D. Cyrus McCormick

3. The most accurate statement concerning U.S. foreign policy is that the United States has generally
   A. acted according to national self-interest
   B. reacted forcefully to imperialism around the world
   C. formed alliances with countries in need
   D. used military confrontation to solve disputes

   Regents Exam, June 1988

4. President Truman's justification for using the atom bomb on Hiroshima and Nagasaki was
   A. to vindicate the expenditure of $2 billion on solving the problem of nuclear fission
   B. to avenge the Japanese use of suicide bombing against American ships
   C. to demonstrate to Stalin that the United States was the strongest military power on earth
   D. to save perhaps as many as a million American lives

5. Which group of U.S. residents was subjected to the greatest loss of constitutional rights during a period of U.S. military involvement?
   A. Hispanic Americans during the Spanish-American War
   B. German Americans during World War I
   C. Japanese Americans during World War II
   D. Chinese Americans during the Korean conflict

   Regents Exam, June 1985

AFTERMATH OF WORLD WAR II

> The evidence relating to war crimes has been overwhelming in its volume and its detail . . . The truth remains that war crimes were committed on a vast scale, never before seen in the history of war.
>
> Report of the War Crimes Tribunal of the Nuremberg Trials, 1946

War Crimes Trials

The Nuremberg Trials

At the Nuremberg Trials (1945–1946) six German organizations and 24 top German civil, military, and naval leaders were charged with war crimes.The leaders included **Herman Wilhelm Goering**, the number two Nazi; **Joachim von Ribbentrop**, Nazi foreign minister; **Julius Streicher**, editor of *Der Sturmer*; **Rudolph Hess**, the number three Nazi; Generals **Wilhelm Keitel** and **Alfred Jodl**; and Admirals **Eric Raedler** and **Karl Doenitz**. (Hitler had committed suicide on April 30, 1945.) The charges included the killing of more than 10 million European civilians and captured war prisoners. Eleven of the defendants were sentenced to death by hanging, others to imprisonment for various terms.

War Crimes Trials in Japan

War crimes trials were also held in Japan at the direction of General MacArthur, who ordered the top Japanese war leaders to stand trial. General **Hideki Tojo,** the leading warmonger and former Premier, tried unsuccessfully to commit suicide. He and six of his colleagues were found guilty and hanged on December 23, 1948. The same fate overtook General **Tomoyuki Yamashita**, the Tiger of the Philippines. Sixteen others were given light sentences. Other trials were held throughout Japan before special courts; 4,200 were convicted of whom 720 were executed.

The Pursuit of Nazi War Criminals

Many Nazi criminals involved in the slaughter of Jews during the Holocaust escaped from Germany to countries as far away as Argentina.

• *Adolf Eichmann.* A case that stirred worldwide interest was that of Adolf Eichmann, who had been assigned the task of deporting all the Jews from Europe to the extermination camps in Eastern Europe. On March 14, 1945, shortly before the surrender of the Nazis, Eichmann proclaimed, "I'll happily die with the certainty of having killed almost six million Jews." Instead, he fled in disguise to Argentina. Eichmann's capture in Buenos Aires in 1960 by Israeli commandos and his deportation to Israel for trial was made possible by the efforts of one man, **Simon Wiesenthal**, who spent 4½ years in Nazi concentration camps. In 1947 he founded the Vienna Documentation Center for tracing the whereabouts of war criminals. He helped bring 1,100 criminals, including Eichmann, to justice. He also established the Wiesenthal Center for Holocaust Studies in Los Angeles.

• *Klaus Barbie.* The French Fascist Klaus Barbie was captured in La Paz, Bolivia, in 1983. Barbie, who earned the title "Butcher of Lyons," worked with the Nazis during their occupation of France and was responsible for the murder of thousands of French Jews and resistance fighters.

Conversion to Peace

Demobilization

When the war ended, President Truman wished to demobilize the armed forces slowly in order to have a strong military presence in Europe and Asia in case of emergency. But there was tremendous pressure at home for immediate return of the troops. In less than a year the armed forces were reduced from 12 million to 3 million; the Air Force went from 85,000 to 9,000 planes, and the Navy withdrew hundreds of ships from active service.

End of Price Controls

There was also heavy pressure on the President to remove wartime price controls on consumer goods. When the Democrats lost control of both houses of Congress in the 1946 elections, Truman yielded and withdrew controls on everything but rent.

Postwar Inflation

As might have been expected, runaway inflation was unleashed. People had earned good wages during the war, but consumer goods such as automobiles, refrigerators, and home appliances were not available because industry was engaged in making ships, tanks, and guns. Savings mounted until nearly $50 billion was available for consumer purchases. By the spring of 1947, prices were one third higher than they had been less than two years before.

Labor Unrest

With this surge in prices came a demand by labor for wage increases. A wave of strikes swept across the country. Major industries, including automobiles, steel, and railroads, were hit. The federal courts intervened in a strike of bituminous coal miners, led by **John L. Lewis**, who defied a court injunction in 1946. The strike was broken when a federal district court imposed heavy fines on Lewis and the union.

The Taft-Hartley Act

The Republican-controlled Congress passed the 1947 Taft-Hartley labor law over Truman's veto. The law forbade the "closed shop" and outlawed the "check off," which required employers to deduct union dues from paychecks and turn the money over directly to the union. It authorized the President to seek a court injunction calling for a 60-day "cooling off" period for strikes and authorized an 80-day injunction against strikes affecting public health or safety. The new law was denounced by labor as a "slave labor" law. However, supporters in Congress and among the citizenry felt that it restrained the excessive power that organized labor had gained from the Wagner Act of 1935.

The law also forbade unions from making political contributions and required labor leaders, but not management, to take a non-Communist oath. In the face of a threatened strike of steel unions, President Truman ordered **Charles Sawyer**, his Secretary of Commerce, to take possession of the steel mills and run them by authority of the federal government. The procedure was declared unconstitutional by a 6 to 3 decision of the Supreme Court in *Youngstown Sheet & Tube Co.* v. *Sawyer* (1952).

Congress Opposes Truman's Reforms

In Social Legislation

Congress and the President were at odds. The President's efforts to expand public housing, Social Security, and federal aid to education were rejected.

In Civil Rights

Africans Americans continued to find it difficult to obtain a fair deal in housing, employment, and education. When President Truman attempted to put an end to racial injustice, he met even greater resistance. His call for anti-lynching and anti-poll tax laws, stronger civil rights laws, and a permanent Fair Employment Practices Committee was stalled when Southern senators prepared to filibuster against these measures. In December 1946 the President appointed a **Committee on Civil Rights** in response to racial murders in the South. The committee issued a historic document entitled "To Secure These Rights" calling for enactment of the laws that Congress rejected. Truman did, however, begin the desegregation of the armed forces. He also appointed African American judges to the federal courts and issued an executive order banning discrimination in federal employment.

The G.I. Bill of Rights

An important series of laws, called the "**G.I. Bill of Rights**," was passed by Congress in anticipation of the return of 10 million veterans to civilian life.

One of the most far-reaching measures was the law providing subsidies for veterans who wished to continue their education. About 12 million veterans ultimately availed themselves of this opportunity for basic education as well as vocational education and the attainment of advanced professional diplomas and degrees. Other laws favorable to veterans provided reinstatement to their jobs with seniority rights, unemployment pay for up to one year, low-interest government loans for home building and for the purchase of farms or businesses, and provision for medical care.

The Election of 1948

As the election of 1948 approached, it seemed unlikely that President Truman would remain in office. There was even doubt that he would be nominated. The Democratic party split into three factions. Southern Democrats, called "**Dixiecrats**," alarmed by the President's civil rights agenda, organized a **States Rights** party and nominated Governor **J. Strom Thurmond** of South Carolina for President. Another wing of the Democratic party, led by former Vice-President **Henry A. Wallace**, opposed the President's "cold war" confrontation with the Soviet Union. Wallace was nominated for President by this faction under the name of the Progressive party.

Meanwhile the Republican party united behind Governor **Thomas E. Dewey** of New York. Dewey had lost to Roosevelt in 1944, when the war was still being fought. This time he was the strong favorite to win.

But the feisty President went around the country denouncing the "do-nothing, good-for-nothing" Republican-controlled Eightieth Congress. So certain were the Republicans of victory that the *Chicago Daily Tribune* published an early election edition with an eight-column front page headline: "Dewey Defeats Truman." Truman surprised the pollsters by winning 303 electoral votes to 189 for Dewey and 39 for Thurmond. The popular vote was 24.1 million to 21.9 million, with 1.17 million for Thurmond and 1.16 million for Wallace.

Truman's "Fair Deal" Program

In his State of the Union message (January 1949), Truman called for a **"Fair Deal"** for all Americans. The Democrats had gained majorities in both houses of Congress, and the President proposed to extend the social legislation of the New Deal. Most of his proposals met determined opposition by a conservative coalition of Republicans and Southern Democrats in Congress. But Truman did succeed with part of his "Fair Deal" program. Social Security benefits were extended to 10 million additional members; the minimum wage of the Fair Labor Standards Act of 1938 was raised from 40 cents to 75 cents an hour. The **National Housing Act** of 1949 provided for slum clearance and the construction of 810,000 housing units to be built during a six-year period for rental to low-income families. Proposals for strong civil rights measures, for repeal of sections of the Taft-Hartley Act, for a new farm subsidy program, for national health insurance, and for a comprehensive aid to public education program were rejected by Congress.

Exercise Set 5.5

1. An important outcome of The Nuremberg Trials held at the end of World War II was that they
   A. showed that many accounts of Nazi atrocities were exaggerated
   B. spread the blame for World War II among many nations
   C. held that moral and ethical considerations do not apply in wartime
   D. established that individuals are responsible for their actions
   Regents Exam, June 1988

2. The term "open shop" refers to a plant or business where
   A. only unionized workers are hired
   B. either union or non-union workers are hired
   C. employees must join a union after six months
   D. only non-union workers are hired

3. The Taft-Hartley Act
   A. imposed unusual restrictions on employers
   B. gave labor greater power than ever
   C. was opposed by the Republicans
   D. sought to curb the power of unions

4. The success of President Truman in the 1948 election was due to
   A. his direct and forthright statement of his position on public issues
   B. his calls for civil rights legislation
   C. his conservative position during the period of postwar reaction
   D. the intellectual quality of his television appearances

5. The "G.I. Bill of Rights" refers to
   A. an amendment to the Constitution adopted shortly after the end of World War II
   B. rights of veterans affirmed by the Supreme Court in a series of post-war decisions
   C. legislation passed by Congress pertaining to education, unemployment compensation, loans for home building, and provisions for medical care of veterans
   D. guarantees for employment of veterans in federal government departments and agencies

CHAPTER REVIEW QUESTIONS

1. Which statement best describes relations among the major powers during the period between World War I and World War II?
   A. major powers followed policies of international cooperation in order to insure peace
   B. major powers respected each other's territorial integrity
   C. the League of Nations was given the power to establish a strong multinational military force
   D. national interests took priority over international interests

   Regents Exam, January 1986

2. Evidence that the United States generally followed a policy of isolationism during the period 1919–1939 is that the United States
   A. condemned Fascist aggression
   B. rejected the policy of appeasement
   C. refused to join the League of Nations
   D. participated in disarmament conferences

   Regents Exam, June 1986

3. The neutrality legislation of 1935–1937 was based on the contention that one of the chief causes of American involvement in World War I was
   A. economic ties with the belligerents
   B. Wilson's failure to uphold American rights as a neutral
   C. creation by the press of hostile public opinion toward the Central Powers
   D. failure of the executive and legislative branches of the government to agree on foreign policy

4. The isolationist policies of the United States in the 1930s were broken down by the danger of
   A. a united Europe under the leadership of Soviet Russia
   B. a united Asia under the Chinese People's Republic
   C. a simultaneous two-ocean war against a united Europe and a united Asia
   D. the growth of British trade in Latin America and Canada

5. Roosevelt's decision to make the atom bomb was
   A. more difficult than Truman's decision to use it because there was greater opposition to it
   B. opposed by the leading scientists on both sides of the Atlantic
   C. based on reports that Germany was attempting to develop an atomic bomb or other decisive military invention
   D. not much of a risk since only a few million dollars were invested in the venture

ESSAYS

1. In the United States, the way of life is constantly changing. Listed below are some areas in which change has taken place in the 20th century.

    Areas of Change
    Global economic interdependence
    Role of government in everyday life
    Proportion of elderly in the population
    Population shifts
    Impact of technology on the work force

    Choose *three* of the areas listed. For *each* area chosen describe a change that has taken place during the 20th century and discuss how that change has affected life in the United States. [5,5,5]

    Regents Exam, August 1988

2. Discrimination has been a problem faced by many people throughout the world. Identify *two* specific groups that have experienced discrimination.

    For *each* group identified:
    • Show how the group has experienced discrimination. Include a specific time period and a description of the historical setting.
    • Describe specific actions taken by the group to overcome the discrimination.
    • Discuss the extent to which the group's actions have been successful in overcoming the discrimination. [15]

    Regents Exam, January 1987

3. Some historians view the history of U.S. foreign policy as a sequence consisting of the stages listed below.

    1776–1823/Protecting national independence
    1824–1897/Fulfilling Manifest Destiny
    1898–1918/Entering the world scene
    1919–1940/Limiting international involvement
    1941–present/Accepting world leadership

    Choose *three* of the time periods listed above. For *each* one chosen, identify a U.S. foreign policy development. Explain how this development was consistent with the foreign policy stage of that time period and show how this development reflected a domestic need of the United States at the time. [5,5,5]

    Regents Exam, January 1986

Chapter 2

PEACE WITH PROBLEMS (1945–1960)

INTERNATIONAL PEACE EFFORTS

We must cultivate the science of human relationships—the ability of
all peoples, of all kinds to live together and work together in the same
world of peace
> Franklin D. Roosevelt's last written words, April 11, 1945

Organizing the United Nations

The San Francisco Conference (1945)

Allied leaders met in August 1944 at Dumbarton Oaks, in Washington,
D.C.,where plans were laid for an international organization to be known as
the **United Nations**. On April 25, 1945, 13 days after the death of President
Roosevelt, delegates from 50 nations met in San Francisco to draft a charter
(constitution) for the United Nations. The United States sent a 5-member
delegation consisting of Secretary of State **Edward Stettinius**, two Republicans (Senator **Vandenberg** and Representative **Eaton**) and two Democrats
(Senator **Connally** and Congressman **Bloom**).

The UN came into formal existence on October 24, 1945. The charter was
ratified (approved) by the Senate on July 28, 1945, making the United States
a charter member of the UN.

The United Nations Organization

The charter of the United Nations provides for six major organs and numerous specialized agencies. The **General Assembly** is the major legislative
body, where each member has one vote. The **Security Council** is the peacekeeping authority. It consists of eleven members—five permanent and six
others elected for two-year terms. The five permanent members—the United
States, China, France, Russia, and Great Britain—each has the power to veto
any decision of the Council. The **Secretariat**, headed by a Secretary General, is the administrative body of the UN. The other three major UN organs
are the **Economic and Social Council**, the **Trusteeship Council** (to safeguard the interests of territories that were not self-governing), and the **International Court of Justice**. Headquarters of the United Nations are in New
York City.

The Universal Declaration of Human Rights

Eleanor Roosevelt's Role

The first U.S. delegation to the UN, appointed by President Truman, consisted of five members, one of whom was Mrs. Eleanor Roosevelt. At first she hesitated to accept the appointment, saying she had no experience in foreign affairs. But President Truman insisted and she agreed to serve.

The delegation assigned her to the **Human Rights Commission**, where it was believed she would engage in trivial activities. She worked with careful attention to every aspect of the task. Delegates from other lands soon came to recognize her leadership qualities, and she was chosen to head the committee drafting the Human Rights Declaration.

Adoption and Contents of the Universal Declaration of Human Rights

It took three years before the Universal Declaration of Human Rights was adopted (December 10, 1948)—a tribute to Eleanor Roosevelt's patient and effective leadership. The vote in the UN General Assembly was 48 in favor and 8 members abstaining. These included six members of the Soviet bloc, Saudi Arabia, and South Africa. The Declaration consists of 30 articles, many with subsections. Included in the Declaration are the following:

Art. 1: All human beings are born free and equal in dignity and rights . . .

Art. 2: Everyone is entitled to all the rights and freedoms set forth in this Declaration without distinction of any kind, such as race, color, sex, language, religion, political or other opinion, national or social origin, property, birth or other status . . .

Art. 3: Everyone has the right to life, liberty, and security of person.

Art. 5: No one shall be subjected to torture or to cruel, inhuman, or degrading treatment or punishment.

Art. 9: No one shall be subjected to arbitrary arrest, detention or exile.

Art. 11: (I) Everyone charged with a penal offense has the right to be presumed innocent until proven guilty.

Art. 13: (II) Everyone has the right to leave any country, including his own, and to return to his country.

Art. 16: (II) Marriage shall be entered into only with the true and full consent of the intending spouses.

Art. 18: Everyone has the right to freedom of thought, conscience, and religion; the right includes freedom to change his religion or belief . . .

Art. 21: (I) Everyone has the right to take part in the government of his country . . .

Art. 22: Everyone, as a member of society, has the right to social security . . .

Art. 23: (I) Everyone has the right to work, to free choice of employment, to just and favorable conditions of work and to protection against unemployment.

Art. 23: (II) Everyone, without any discrimination, has the right to equal pay for equal work.

Art. 23: (IV) Everyone has the right to form and to join trade unions for the protection of his interests.

Art. 25: (II) Motherhood and childhood are entitled to special care and assistance. All children, whether born in or out of wedlock, shall enjoy the same social protection.

Attacks on United States Participation in the UN

John Foster Dulles, a prominent international lawyer in Washington, served as a U.S. delegate to the UN (1946–1950). When Eisenhower became President in 1953, he appointed Dulles Secretary of State. A period of reaction was setting in, and attacks were being mounted against U.S. participation in the UN. The cry was heard, "Take the United States out of the UN and the UN out of the United States." In the Senate, the Secretariat of the UN was portrayed by Senator **Joseph R. McCarthy**, Republican of Wisconsin, as a nesting place of Communist spies.

In 1954 Senator **John W. Bricker**, Republican of Ohio, introduced an amendment to the Constitution to restrict the treaty-making powers of the President. In order to defeat the amendment, Secretary of State Dulles used his influence to have the Senate reject the conventions adopted by the United Nations Human Rights Commission. Mrs. Roosevelt resigned from the Human Rights Commission after the election of President Eisenhower. She then went to work as a volunteer for the **American Association for the United Nations**, an organization committed to educating the American public about the importance of America's role in the work of the UN.

Displaced Persons and Refugees After W.W. II

The post-World War II problem of displaced persons and refugees was of great magnitude. There were approximately one million such refugees in displaced-person camps, most of them from Eastern Europe. Mrs. Roosevelt observed, "A new type of political refugee is appearing, people who have been against the present governments and if they stay at home or go home will probably be killed." The United Nations established a **United Nations High Commission for Refugees** (**UNHCR**) on January 1, 1951. They were to provide "legal protection and, when needed, material assistance to refugees, and to seek permanent solutions to refugee problems on a purely social, humanitarian and nonpolitical basis." The Soviet Union's position was that the refugee problem should not be considered a matter of international concern. Mrs. Roosevelt opposed the Soviet delegate **Andrei Vishinsky**. She argued successfully that the rights of the refugees involved human rights, which took precedence over government rights.

Exercise Set 5.6

1. The charter of the United Nations provided for all of the following EXCEPT
   A. a Universal Declaration of Human Rights
   B. a General Assembly in which each member nation has one vote
   C. a Security Council in which each of the five permanent members has a veto power
   D. a Trusteeship Council to safeguard the interests of territories that were self-governing

2. The appointment of Eleanor Roosevelt as a member of the U.S. delegation to the United Nations
   A. was promptly accepted by Mrs. Roosevelt with great enthusiasm
   B. was considered by her colleagues as a good appointment from the very beginning
   C. was largely responsible for the creation of the Universal Declaration of Human Rights
   D. met with serious opposition in the U.S. Senate

3. The United Nations Universal Declaration of Human Rights was *not* approved by
   A. several African nations
   B. six member-states from Latin America
   C. China, Korea, and Indonesia
   D. Saudi Arabia, South Africa, and six members of the Soviet bloc

4. A factor that has strengthened the United Nations as compared with the League of Nations has been the U.S. policy of
   A. imperialism
   B. isolationism
   C. expansionism
   D. internationalism

   Regents Exam, January 1985

5. Which foreign policy approach would advocates of the balance-of-power concept most likely support?
   A. creation of military alliances
   B. unilateral disarmament
   C. abolition of foreign trade
   D. reliance on world peace organizations

   Regents Exam, June 1986

COMMUNIST EXPANSION AND CONTAINMENT IN EUROPE AND ASIA

I believe that it must be the policy of the United States to support free peoples who are resisting attempted subjugation by armed minorities or by outside pressures.

President Harry S. Truman, Message to Congress
(The Truman Doctrine), March 12, 1947

Yalta Conference, February 1945

At Yalta, a Black Sea port in southern Russia, the big three—**Roosevelt**, **Churchill**, and **Stalin**—met in February 1945 to plan the final blows against the Axis and to make postwar arrangements. Agreement was reached about the new international organization (the United Nations) that was to be established soon after the end of the war. Stalin agreed to hold free elections in Poland, Bulgaria, and Romania, but these were never carried out. Roosevelt was anxious to have Russia enter the war against Japan, because it was expected there would be heavy casualties before Japan surrendered. Stalin agreed to enter the war against Japan within two or three months after the defeat of Germany. In return, Russia was to get the southern half of Sakhalin Island (which Russia had lost to Japan in the 1905 war) as well as the Kurile Islands. The Soviet Union was also to have special rights in parts of China— the railroads in Manchuria and the ports of Dairen and Port Arthur. Russia entered the war against Japan on August 8, 1945, exactly three months after V.E. Day. At the time of Yalta, the atom bomb had not yet been developed. By August 8, the bomb had already been dropped on Hiroshima. Whether Roosevelt could have worked out a better deal at Yalta will never be known. The charge that he was too sick to negotiate was repudiated by Secretary of State Edward Stettinius, who reported in his memoirs that the President was "mentally alert" and in better health than he had been.

Potsdam Conference, July–August 1945

A final summit conference was held at Potsdam, Germany, from July 17 to August 2, 1945, before the end of the war in Asia. President Truman met there with Churchill and Stalin. Later in the negotiations, **Clement Atlee**, the Labor Prime Minister who had defeated Churchill at the polls, represented Britain. The conference issued a declaration calling for the "unconditional surrender" of Japan. A democratic government was to be set up in Germany, and war criminals were to be tried by an international court. A council of foreign ministers of the victors was to draft treaties with Italy, Austria, Hungary, Bulgaria, Romania, and Finland. Zones of occupation in

Germany were established, with East Germany assigned to the USSR, northwest Germany to Britain, southwest to the United States, and two small areas to France. Berlin, though located in the Russian zone, was to be divided into four zones, each to be occupied by one of the four powers.

Origins of the Cold War

The World War II alliance of Western democracies with the Soviet Union was really a "marriage of convenience or necessity." It broke up almost as soon as the war had been won. The hostility that developed, short of actual war, became known as the "**cold war**." Instead of allowing free elections in neighboring countries, Stalin established Communist regimes in Poland, Romania, Bulgaria, and Albania. The Communists threatened the governments of Greece and Turkey in 1947. Soviet troops were used to install a Communist regime in Hungary (1956). In 1968, the Soviet Union sent 200,000 troops into Czechoslovakia to ensure Communist control of that country.

In a speech at Fulton, Missouri in March 1946, Winston Churchill declared, "From Stettin in the Baltic to Trieste in the Adriatic, an **iron curtain** has descended across the continent." President Truman, who was present during this address, was fully in accord with this statement. The U.S. response to Communist aggression was the policy of **containment**. It sought to "contain" or limit Soviet expansion and prevent the spread of Communism. The first step in this policy was the **Truman Doctrine**, which was applied to Greece and Turkey.

The Truman Doctrine (March 1947)

In a dramatic appearance before a joint session of Congress on March 12, 1947, President Truman announced a historic new turn in American foreign policy that became known as the **Truman Doctrine**. "One aspect of the present situation," said the President, ". . . concerns Greece and Turkey." President Truman was gravely concerned because, late in 1946, about 13,000 Communist-led guerrillas entered northern Greece from Albania, Yugoslavia, and Bulgaria. Britain, with a strained economy, was terminating its traditional support, leaving Greece alone to deal with this Communist insurgency.

By 1947, Greek Communists, supported by the Soviet Union, threatened to seize control of the government. In his message, President Truman told Congress: ". . . assistance is imperative if Greece is to survive as a free nation." As for Turkey, it too was under pressure from Russia to give up control of the strategic Dardanelles. Soviet control of Greece and the Dardanelles would enable it to dominate the eastern Mediterranean and the Suez

Canal. President Truman told Congress, "As in the case of Greece, if Turkey is to have the assistance it needs, the United States must supply it." The heart of the message, the Truman Doctrine, was stated by President Truman in these words: "I believe it must be the policy of the United States to support free peoples who are resisting attempted subjugation by armed minorities or by outside pressures." Then the President made this request: "I therefore ask Congress to provide authority for assistance to Greece and Turkey in the amount of $400,000,000 for the period ending June 30, 1948." By 1950 the United States had invested nearly $1 billion to preserve the independence of Greece and Turkey.

The Marshall Plan (June 1947)

Europe lay in ruins and economic chaos following the war. The United States responded with a program of economic aid. The program for the rehabilitation of postwar Europe came to be known as the **Marshall Plan**. The plan was to give aid to 22 European countries including the Soviet Union, but the latter came to regard this plan as an anti-Soviet maneuver and refused to participate. In presenting his plan, Secretary of State **George Marshall** said, "The truth of the matter is that Europe's requirements, for the next 3 or 4 years, of foreign food and other essential products—principally from America—are so much greater than her present ability to pay that she must have substantial additional help, or face economic, social, and political deterioration of a very grave character. It is logical that the U.S. should do whatever it is able to do to assist in the return of normal economic health in the world, without which there can be no political stability and no assured peace." Sixteen European nations answered the call and formulated a four year "**European Recovery Plan**" calling for $16 to $24 billion in aid.

The plan met with mixed reactions in Congress. Opponents called the European Recovery Plan "operation rat-hole." However, after Russia overthrew the government of Czechoslovakia in March 1948 and established a Communist regime, Congress approved the Marshall Plan the following month.

Results of the Plan

Congress appropriated $6.8 billion for the European Recovery Plan for the first 15 months and prepared to extend further support. About $12 billion was spent during a four-year period. Britain, France, and West Germany made a remarkable economic recovery that may well have prevented serious political consequences. Interest of Eastern European nations in the plan was quickly quashed by the Soviet Union, which formed a feeble economic union (**Council of Mutual Economic Assistance**) with Poland, Czechoslovakia, Bulgaria, Hungary, and Romania.

The European Common Market

An outgrowth of the European Recovery Plan was the **European Common Market** (**European Economic Community** or **EEC**), organized in 1957 by France, West Germany, Italy, and the Benelux countries (Belgium, the Netherlands, and Luxembourg). Members reduced tariffs on each other's products and eased travel restrictions among members. Britain's efforts to join the Common Market during the 1960s were vetoed by France. In 1973 Britain, Ireland, and Denmark joined the Common Market. Greece was admitted in 1981. This economic union of 10 European nations stirred talk of political union. In the late 1980s a blueprint was drawn up for a European Parliament with a target date of 1992 for implementation. The nations of the Common Market have made significant progress towards economic cooperation, but political unity still seems far away.

The Berlin Crisis (1948–49)

A major test of will in the cold war between East and West occurred over Berlin. Deep in the Soviet zone of occupation, Berlin itself had been divided into four zones of occupation among the United States, Britain, France, and the USSR. In the spring of 1948, the Western democracies proposed elections for a new German Federal Republic. In response, the Soviets determined to oust the West from Berlin. On June 24, 1948, they set up a blockade around the city so that no food, fuel, or other supplies could reach the 2 million inhabitants of the western zones of Berlin. Short of trying to break the blockade by force, the Allies had only one means of entry to the city—by air. The Allies undertook an "airlift" to circumvent the blockade and bring food, fuel, and supplies to the 2 million people of Berlin. For almost a year, planes delivered essential supplies to the city. They flew more than 100 million miles and brought more than 2 million tons of food and other necessities to the city. With the face-saving intervention of the United Nations, the crisis was solved and the blockade withdrawn in May 1949.

The North Atlantic Treaty Organization (NATO)

A "hot war" was narrowly averted over Berlin, but steps had to be taken to prepare for future crises. On May 19, 1948, the Senate approved a resolution introduced by Senator **Arthur Vandenberg** of Michigan, the ranking Republican member, pledging American support for collective security among the Western democracies. In line with this resolution, President Truman proposed the **North Atlantic Pact**, setting up the **North Atlantic Treaty Organization** (**NATO**), which was signed on April 4, 1949.

The original parties, in addition to the United States and Canada, were Belgium, Denmark, France, Iceland, Italy, Luxembourg, the Netherlands, Norway, Portugal, and the United Kingdom (Great Britain). Article V of the treaty reads: "The parties agree that an armed attack against one or more of them in Europe or North America shall be considered an attack against them all." The treaty, overwhelmingly approved by the public, was ratified in the Senate by a vote of 82 to 13.

Expansion of NATO

In 1951 General Eisenhower took command of all military forces of NATO. Greece and Turkey joined NATO in 1952 and West Germany became a member in 1955. It had become the largest peacetime military alliance in history.

The Warsaw Pact

The Soviet Union countered with a military alliance of its own in 1955— the **Warsaw Pact**. This Pact united the Soviet Union with six allies in Eastern Europe: Poland, East Germany, Czechoslovakia, Hungary, Romania, and Bulgaria.

The USSR Explodes an A-Bomb (1949)

At the time NATO was organized (April 4, 1949), the Soviet Union did not yet have the atomic bomb, but Soviet scientists had been working frantically toward that end. On September 22, 1949, President Truman announced that the Soviet Union had successfully set off an atomic explosion. A huge buildup of armaments was in progress for NATO. The presence of American servicemen and women and U.S. armaments again became common throughout Western Europe. Before President Truman left office, $6 billion had been appropriated for NATO.

Truman's "Point Four" Program

In his inaugural address of January 1949, President Truman proposed a program of aid to the economically underdeveloped nations of the "Third World." This came to be known as the **Point Four Aid Program**. He spelled it out in detail in a special message to Congress on June 24, 1949:

> The grinding poverty and the lack of economic opportunity for many millions of people in the economically underdeveloped parts of Africa, the Near and Far East, and certain regions of Central and South America constitute one of the greatest challenges of the world today . . . I recommend the enactment of legislation to authorize an expanded program of technical assistance for such areas . . . To inaugurate such a program, I recommend a first-year appropriation not to exceed $45 million.

Congress approved the program and made an initial appropriation in 1950. This plan for underdeveloped nations was seen as both a means of defeating Communist encroachment in these areas and a spur to foreign trade by creating new markets for American industrial and agricultural products. During the period 1948–1960 the expenditures of the United States in foreign aid amounted to $72 billion.

Containment in Asia

Peace Treaty with Japan

On September 8, 1951, the United States signed a peace treaty with Japan bringing to an end the American occupation. No reparations were to be paid. Japan was to have the limited right to rearm. A security treaty, signed at the same time, gave the United States the right to maintain bases in Japan. In effect the United States was underwriting the security of Japan, a country now seen as an ally. The process of converting Japan to democracy had been undertaken during the occupation.

China Becomes Communist (1949)

China presented a different problem. For many years, the weakness of China was exploited by various powers. In 1927, **Chiang Kai-shek**, leader of the Chinese Nationalist government, sought to destroy the Chinese Communist forces under **Mao Zedong**. The latter fled deep into the interior of China. In 1931, Japanese forces invaded and overran Manchuria. In 1936, the Japanese invaded China. Faced with this crisis, the Chinese **Nationalists** and **Communists** fought the invader separately. But after the defeat of Japan in World War II, the fighting between the Chinese Communists and Nationalists resumed. The wily Mao had built a strong base of support among the Chinese peasants, while the arrogant Chiang became unpopular with the Chinese people. During 1948 and 1949 Mao's growing armies inflicted one defeat after another on the Nationalists. By December 1949 Chiang Kai-shek and his followers fled by air to the offshore island of Formosa, now called **Taiwan**, and established their government there. The Communist Chinese led by Mao Zedong now controlled all of mainland China. The United States, however, continued to recognize Chiang's government on Taiwan as the government of China.

The "Hot War" in Asia: Korea (1950–1953)

Korea Divided

Korea, formerly controlled by China, came under Japanese domination when Japan defeated China in 1894. At the end of World War II (as agreed at the

Potsdam Conference), Russian forces entered Korea from the north, and American from the south. Two Koreas were formed with a dividing line drawn at 38° north latitude, between Communist-dominated North Korea and democratic South Korea. Attempts to reunite the country were unsuccessful. The Republic of (South) Korea was proclaimed in August 1948 and the People's Republic (North) in September. The USSR and the United States withdrew their military forces from Korea by 1949.

North Korea Attacks South Korea

On June 25, 1950, North Korean troops, alleging an attack from the South, suddenly crossed the line in force and launched a full-scale attack on South Korea. President Truman brought the matter at once to the Security Council of the UN, which voted 9 to 0 (the Soviets had been boycotting the UN) for a resolution ordering North Korea to withdraw.

UN and American troops were dispatched to Korea to drive back the invaders in what President Truman characterized as a "police action," since Congress never declared war. General Douglas MacArthur was placed in command of the combined forces, which included troops from 15 UN nations, South Koreans, and American land, naval, and air forces. At first, South Korean armies were driven back, but MacArthur conducted a successful offensive and then invaded North Korea. As MacArthur's troops approached the border with China at the Yalu River, they were caught in a trap by Chinese armies (so-called "volunteers") that had crossed into North Korea in force.

MacArthur Attempts to Make Policy

When UN forces again counterattacked, MacArthur proposed to drive north and invade China. This was contrary to the limited war policy laid down by President Truman. General **Omar Bradley**, chairman of the Joint Chiefs of Staff, testifying before a Senate committee on May 15, 1951, said that MacArthur's proposal would "involve us in the wrong war, at the wrong place, at the wrong time, and with the wrong enemy." The statement implied that a land war in China would leave the way open for Soviet expansion in Europe and the Middle East and could lead to World War III. MacArthur refused to accept Truman's policy decision and appealed to Congress over the President's authority. He continued to press for intensive military operations against the Chinese and proposed to assist Chiang Kai-shek's Nationalist troops to return to the mainland of China.

Truman Removes MacArthur

MacArthur's failure to implement the policy laid down by the President raised the constitutional question of the superiority of the civilian authority over the military. On April 11, 1951, President Truman informed General

MacArthur that he was being relieved of his command in the Pacific and replaced by Lt. General **Matthew B. Ridgway**. President Truman explained his action by saying, "In the simplest terms, what we are doing in Korea is this: We are trying to prevent a third world war . . . By fighting a limited war in Korea we have prevented aggression from succeeding and bringing on a general war." Then he asked, "What would suit the ambitions of the Kremlin better than for our military forces to be committed to a full-scale war with Red China?" Although there was a roar of outrage in Congress and loud public acclaim for MacArthur, the public supported the President.

Armistice in Korea

On July 10, 1951, General Ridgway began armistice negotiations with the North Koreans and Chinese. The negotiations continued at Panmunjom for two years. On July 27, 1953, North Korea and the UN reached an armistice agreement; an actual peace treaty was never signed. According to the armistice, the ceasefire line was established just north of the **38th parallel**, the previous boundary of the two Koreas. In 1954 the United States and Korea entered into a treaty whereby the United States agreed to come to the aid of South Korea if attacked again. Under the terms of the treaty, American troops have been stationed in Korea continually since 1954.

Exercise Set 5.7

1. The formation of the North Atlantic Treaty Organization (NATO) in 1949 is a significant event in U.S. diplomatic history because it
    A. committed the United States to a peacetime military alliance
    B. strengthened United States influence in oil-producing nations
    C. eased tensions with the Soviet Union and its satellites
    D. created new patterns of international trade
    Regents Exam, August 1988

2. The term "iron curtain" used by Winston Churchill in a speech at Fulton, Missouri in 1946
    A. was a call for the use of the military to put an end to the Soviet dictatorship
    B. expressed a recognition of the existence of a "cold war" between the USSR and the Western democracies
    C. suggested that trade agreements between the United States and Britain could restore the prewar dominance of the West in steel production
    D. was a first step in restoring diplomatic relations between the Soviet Union and the West

3. The attempt by the Soviet Union to force the Western Allies out of Berlin (1948–1949) failed because
   A. the United Nations intervened by sending relief supplies to the people of West Berlin
   B. the blockade did not prevent the British-American airlift from bringing food and fuel to the people of West Berlin
   C. the Berlin wall had not yet been built
   D. the people of West Berlin were able to manage on their own despite great hardships

4. The Truman Doctrine, announced in 1947,
   A. was a reversal of the Monroe Doctrine
   B. was the first step in the American policy of giving military aid to help nations resist communism
   C. called for the unification of the occupied zones of West Germany
   D. required the nations saved from German aggression to adopt democracy

5. The Marshall Plan and the Point Four Program were similar in that
   A. both were intended to resist Communist aggression in Europe
   B. both were designed to help economically distressed peoples to help themselves
   C. both were seen as measures that would help the United States become a creditor nation
   D. the United States would assume leadership in the United Nations if these plans were implemented

6. MacArthur was recalled by President Truman because
   A. MacArthur committed acts of insubordination
   B. MacArthur was a Republican
   C. American allies demanded his recall
   D. America was losing the Korean War

INTERNAL SECURITY AND CONSTITUTIONALISM

Truman and Government Loyalty Checks

The increasingly dangerous international situation and the tension of the cold war had effects at home. Many Americans became concerned over internal security and Communist subversion within the United States.

Executive Order 9835 (1947)

On March 21, 1947, President Truman issued Executive Order 9835, designed to investigate the loyalty of government employees. The Attorney General was ordered to draw up a list of organizations that approved acts of violence to deny other persons their constitutional rights. Membership in such an organization might be considered evidence of disloyalty. Under this executive order some 3,000 persons were investigated, of whom 200 were dismissed. Though this was a small fraction of the 3 million government employees, the atmosphere in government service became poisoned. Many capable people who might otherwise have entered government service became reluctant to do so.

The National Security Act of 1947

In anticipation of the possible heating up of the cold war, the National Security Act of July 26, 1947, was passed after two years of wrangling between the army and navy. A new **Department of Defense** was established, headed by a **Secretary of Defense** of Cabinet rank. A separate air force was created. Each service—army, navy, and air force—was to have its own secretary below Cabinet rank. The uniformed head of each of the services, along with the President's chief of staff, were to constitute the **Joint Chiefs of Staff**, who would be the President's military advisers. To advise the President on security matters, a new agency, the **National Security Council**, was established, along with a new **National Security Adviser**. The Council was to include a new **Central Intelligence Agency** (**CIA**) to gather intelligence and conduct foreign activities associated with national security.

The McCarran Internal Security Act (1950)

The McCarran Internal Security Act required "Communist-front" organizations to register with the Attorney General. It authorized the government to arrest and detain anyone who might endanger the security of the United States by committing acts of espionage or sabotage. President Truman vetoed the act, calling it "a long step toward totalitarianism." But Congress passed it in 1950 over Truman's veto.

Earlier Attempts to Combat "Subversive Activities"

The Smith Act

In 1940, in the anxious days preceding the attack on Pearl Harbor, Congress had enacted the Alien Registration Act, commonly known as the **Smith Act** after its author, Senator **Howard Smith** of Virginia. The act made it illegal to advocate the overthrow of any government in the United States by force or violence or to become a member of any organization that adhered to this doctrine.

The House Committee to Investigate Un-American Activities (HUAC)

The **House Committee to Investigate Un-American Activities (HUAC)** was established in the House of Representatives in 1938, originally under the chairmanship of Congressman **Martin Dies**, Democrat of Texas. The committee held hearings, examined witnesses, issued reports and tarnished reputations over the years without ever defining "un-American" or disclosing anything not already known by the Justice Department.

The Supreme Court and Subversive Activities

Dennis v. *United States* (1951)

In 1949, under orders from President Truman, the Justice Department obtained the conviction of eleven high-ranking members of the U.S. Communist party for conspiring to advocate the violent overthrow of the U.S. government. The conviction (and imprisonment), based on the Smith Act of 1940, was appealed to the Supreme Court on the ground that the act was unconstitutional because it violated the freedom of speech provision of the First Amendment. The conviction was sustained by the Court in a 6 to 2 decision. Writing for the majority, **Chief Justice Frederick M. Vinson** declared that the defendants had conspired to teach and advocate the overthrow of the government of the United States and that this constituted a "clear and present danger" of an attempt to overthrow the government by force and violence. In dissent **Justice William O. Douglas** said, ". . . we deal here with speech alone, not with speech *plus* acts of sabotage or unlawful conduct." And **Justice Hugo L. Black** in his dissent said, "This is a virulent form of prior censorship of speech and press, which I believe the First Amendment forbids."

Yates v. *United States* (1957)

In the Yates case, the Supreme Court again considered an appeal from members of the Communist party charged with violating the Smith Act. The Court, speaking through **Justice Harlan**, overruled the conviction of the defendants. In his concurring opinion, **Justice Black** said, "I believe that the First Amendment forbids Congress to punish people for talking about public affairs, whether or not such discussion incites to action legal or illegal. As the Virginia Assembly said in 1785, in its Statute for Religious Liberty, written by Thomas Jefferson: "It is time enough for the rightful purposes of civil government, for its officers to interfere when principles break out into overt acts against peace and good order."

Watkins v. *United States* **(1957)**

John Watkins, a labor union official, was questioned by the House Un-American Activities Committee. Ile refused to name former Communist party members, stating that this question was not relevant to the work of the Committee. The Court (with only one dissent) reversed his conviction of contempt of Congress, denying the Committee the authority to punish uncooperative witnesses at will. Each of these cases involved the enduring constitutional issue of civil liberties—the balance between government security and individual rights.

The Alger Hiss Case (1948)

This case stirred great public interest because **Whitaker Chambers**, a former Communist, charged that **Alger Hiss**, a former official in the State Department, had given him classified government documents. Hiss testified before the House Un-American Activities Committee, denied the charges, and brought a libel suit against Chambers, who then produced microfilm to prove his charges against Hiss. Consequently, Hiss was convicted of perjury (lying under oath) and served a five-year term in prison. He continued to assert his innocence. The case was significant because Hiss had held important government positions. After graduating from Harvard Law School, Hiss served for a year as law clerk to Supreme Court Justice **Oliver Wendell Holmes**. An early New Dealer, Hiss had been a member of the delegation to the Yalta Conference, had helped plan the San Francisco Conference at which the UN was established, had been director of the State Department's Office of Special Political Affairs, and, at the time of his appearance before the HUAC, was president of the Carnegie Endowment for International Peace. At his trial, Supreme Court Justice **Felix Frankfurter** and Illinois Governor **Adlai E. Stevenson** testified that they considered Hiss to be a man of good character. His conviction for perjury helped set the stage for the most gruesome aspect of the "national security" drama.

McCarthyism

The Rise of Joseph R. McCarthy

Joseph R. McCarthy began his political career as a judge at the age of 32. After serving in the Marines in World War II, he entered the Wisconsin

Republican primary in 1946, unsuccessfully challenging Senator **Alexander Wiley** for the seat. In 1948 he challenged Senator **Robert La Follette, Jr.**, in the primary election for the Republican nomination. McCarthy won the Republican nomination and easily defeated his Democratic opponent in the 1948 Senatorial election in Wisconsin. He was now launched on his career in national politics.

In his quest for a popular cause, McCarthy proposed alerting America to the Red Menace. In a Lincoln's Day address in February 1950 to the Women's Republican Club in Wheeling, West Virginia, McCarthy waved a sheet of paper and declared, "I have in my hand a list of 205 card-carrying members of the Communist party who hold important positions in the State Department." The speech won instant attention throughout the country. McCarthy had found his cause. Thorough investigation later disclosed not one case of a Communist in the State Department and McCarthy never produced the names. McCarthy then charged that General George C. Marshall was a "traitor" and that he and his protege, General Eisenhower, were involved "in a conspiracy so immense and an infamy so black as to dwarf any previous such venture in the history of man."

By 1952, McCarthy had become the head of a Senate subcommittee on investigations. In this position, he investigated the State Department and other government agencies. Careers of many patriotic Americans in government, colleges, the arts, and the media were ruined by the "witch hunt" unleashed by McCarthy as he investigated and irresponsibly accused many individuals of having Communist affiliations.

The Army Hearings

Although some Americans were critical of McCarthy's unfair methods and accusations, many supported him. In 1954 he began to search for spies and Communists in the Army. Televised hearings were held April 22–June 17, 1954, investigating McCarthy's charges of subversion in the Army Signal Corps at Fort Monmouth, New Jersey. As chairman of the **Subcommittee of the Senate Committee on Government Operations**, McCarthy also brought charges against Army Secretary **Robert T. Stevens** and Brigadier General **Ralph W. Zwicker**. During these televised hearings McCarthy's bullying methods and his reckless, unproven accusations discredited him.

Censure of McCarthy

After the hearings, Senator **Ralph Flanders**, Republican of Vermont, filed a resolution calling upon the Senate to censure Senator McCarthy. Among the charges were the Senator's contemptuous behavior in refusing to appear before a Senate committee. His repeated offensive behavior to his colleagues was held to bring that august body into public disrespect. A special committee, headed by Senator **Arthur Watkins**, Republican of Utah, was appointed to investigate the charges. On December 2, 1954, by a vote of 67 to 22, the

United States Senate voted to censure Senator McCarthy. Thereafter, McCarthy was shunned by his colleagues and his statements ceased to be reported in the press.

McCarthyism, a New Word in the English Language

McCarthy's tactics added the word "**McCarthyism**" to the English language. The historian Samuel Eliot Morison called McCarthy "one of the most colossal liars in our history." Eisenhower, in his memoirs, says, "McCarthyism took its toll on many individuals and on the nation." Reckless, unsupported charges of treason and conspiracy destroyed government officials, teachers, scientists, ministers and scholars. McCarthy's methods are summed up in the word **McCarthyism**.

Loyalty and Dissent: The Case of J. Robert Oppenheimer

President Truman's loyalty order of March 22, 1947, had serious consequences for a number of government officials. The most celebrated case was that of **Dr. J. Robert Oppenheimer**, an American scientist who had played a key role in the development of the atomic bomb. As consultant to the post-war Atomic Energy Commission, Dr. Oppenheimer was declared to be a security risk by the Personnel Security Board. The Board's 2 to 1 decision was upheld by the Atomic Energy Commission on June 29, 1954, and Dr. Oppenheimer was denied further access to restricted data and suspended from his position as consultant to the Atomic Energy Commission. The Security Board, despite its vote to class Dr. Oppenheimer as a security risk, described him as devotedly loyal and unusually discreet. The decision of the Atomic Energy Commission against Dr. Oppenheimer was accompanied by the dissenting opinion of Commissioner **Henry DeWolf Smyth**, who pointed out that Oppenheimer had been under surveillance "for the past 11 years" and that there was "no indication in the entire record that Dr. Oppenheimer has ever divulged any secret information." After his association with the Atomic Energy Commission was severed, Dr. Oppenheimer was appointed Director of the Institute for Advanced Study at Princeton, New Jersey. In 1963 the Atomic Energy Commission admitted its error by designating Dr. Oppenheimer as the recipient of the $50,000 Enrico Fermi Award for his contributions to the field of nuclear science.

Exercise Set 5.8

1. Which of the following internal security measures was adopted prior to World War II?
   A. the McCarran Internal Security Act
   B. President Truman's Executive Order for the investigation of government employees' loyalty
   C. the establishment of the House Un-American Activities Committee
   D. the investigation of Senator Joseph McCarthy's subcommittee

2. The Alger Hiss case stirred great public interest because
   A. Hiss, charged with passing classified information to the Communists, had held high public office
   B. Whitaker Chambers, who accused Hiss, denied having been a Communist
   C. Supreme Court Justice Felix Frankfurter testified against Hiss
   D. Hiss refused to appear before the House Un-American Activities Committee

3. Dr. J. Robert Oppenheimer was denied access to restricted government data and suspended from his position as consultant to the Atomic Energy Commission because he
   A. played a major role in the development of the atomic bomb
   B. had access to data which included vital government secrets
   C. was classified as a security risk by a 2 to 1 vote of a special Personnel Security Board
   D. was being considered for the position of Director of the Institute of Advanced Study at Princeton University

4. The term "McCarthyism" generally means
   A. efforts to restrict the spread of communism
   B. effective use of the media to gain name recognition
   C. bringing false and reckless charges against people to secure publicity and political advantage for oneself
   D. the use of negative advertising during a political campaign

1. A major reason why a working system of international law has been difficult to achieve is that
   A. the many different languages in the world make communication difficult
   B. nations are unwilling to give up some of their sovereignty
   C. no precedent for international law exists
   D. many nations still lack even an internal system of law
   Regents Exam, January 1983

2. Which was a major cause of tension in Europe during the decade following World War II?
   A. formation of Soviet-dominated Communist governments in many Eastern European nations
   B. failure of non-Communist nations to support the United Nations
   C. cutbacks in fuel supplies by oil-producing nations
   D. return of United States military forces to pre-World War II levels
   Regents Exam, June 1983

3. Totalitarian societies in the 20th century could be most consistently identified by their
   A. unwillingness to allow free elections
   B. acceptance of a variety of political beliefs
   C. support for a state-controlled religion
   D. denial of public education to their citizens
   Regents Exams, January 1985

4. "The parties agree that an attack against one or more of them shall be considered an attack against all."
   This statement most clearly illustrates which foreign policy concept?
   A. détente
   B. appeasement
   C. balance of power
   D. collective security
   Regents Exam, June 1985

5. The relationship between the United States and Western European nations from 1945 to the present has most often been characterized by
   A. cooperation in efforts to gain political control of emerging nations
   B. division and resentment over competing economic systems
   C. continuance of military and economic interdependence
   D. economic conflict and military confrontation
   Regents Exam, June 1986

6. The United states sells manufactured products to Third World nations and purchases raw materials from these nations. This fact illustrates
   A. economic protectionism
   B. global interdependence
   C. pooling of resources
   D. finance capitalism

Regents Exam, August 1988

7. Evidence that civil liberties in the United States were under attack in the period preceding the cold war can be traced to
   A. the McCarthy speech at Wheeling, West Virginia
   B. the "iron curtain" speech of Winston Churchill
   C. the McCarran Internal Security Act
   D. the establishment of the House Un-American Activities Committee

ESSAYS

1. At various times, the United States has followed one or more of the foreign policies listed below.

   Foreign Policies
   Imperialism
   Isolationism
   Containment
   Nonrecognition
   Formation of military alliances
   Reliance upon international organizations

   Choose *three* of the policies listed above. For *each* one chosen, discuss a specific application of that policy by the United States. Include in your discussion one reason the United States applied that policy and one result of the application of that policy. [5,5,5]

Regents Exam, June 1988

2. Below is a list of violations of human rights that have occurred throughout history.

   Violations of Human Rights
   Repression of dissidents
   Genocide
   Destruction of cultural heritage
   Denial of civil and legal rights
   Forced relocation

   a. Select *three* of the violations of human rights from the list above. For *each* one chosen, describe a specific historic example of that violation, including approximate time period and place. Use a different example for each violation chosen. [4,4,4]

   b. Show how a specific group or organization, public or private, has promoted the cause of human rights. [3]

UNIT SIX ⎯⎯⎯⎯⎯⎯

A World in Uncertain Times (1950–Present)

> **KEY IDEAS:** Unit Six explores the global role of the United States in an increasingly interdependent world. It describes the social, political, and economic changes in American society in the period between the 1950s and 1990s as the United States entered the post-industrial era.

UNIT GOALS: By the end of the unit, the student should be able to

1. Recognize and understand the fact that the United States has moved from an industrially centered nation to one primarily concerned with commerce, finance, service, and communication.

2. Understand that the people of the United States have increasingly adjusted to the changes brought about by this shift in social, economic and political sectors—slowly in the 1950s, explosively in the 1960s, and more conservatively in the 1970s, 1980s, and 1990s.

3. Identify clearly the growing interdependent nature of the world and the role that the United States plays in global affairs.

Chapter 1

TECHNOLOGY AND INTERDEPENDENCE: LIVING IN A GLOBAL AGE

> Why does this magnificent applied science which saves work and makes life easier bring us so little happiness? The simple answer runs: Because we have not yet learned to make sensible use of it.
>
> Albert Einstein, in an address at the
> California Institute of Technology, February 1931

UNITED STATES AND POST-INDUSTRIALISM

Changing Energy Sources: Toward Nuclear Power

In the years after World War II, nuclear energy created by fission, or the splitting of atoms, seemed to offer a cheap and unlimited source of power.

The Atomic Energy Commission (AEC)

In 1946, Congress established the Atomic Energy Commission (now called the **Nuclear Regulatory Commission**), a civilian agency with authority to make policy decisions about the use of nuclear power. A program was launched in 1954 whereby private power companies could construct nuclear power plants and operate them under license by the **Atomic Energy Commission**. By 1989 there were over 100 operable **nuclear reactors** throughout the United States, generating 16.6 percent of domestic electricity. Nuclear research has resulted in beneficial applications of **radioactive isotopes** in medicine and has also made it possible to estimate the age of prehistoric objects by the process of **radiocarbon dating**. On the negative side, nuclear energy has caused disasters, near disasters, and widespread fear of possible nuclear calamities.

Problems of Nuclear Energy Plants

An accident in March 1979 at the **Three Mile Island** nuclear reactor near Harrisburg, Pennsylvania, caused grave concern about the danger of nuclear radiation escaping into the air and contaminating a wide area with cancer-causing by-products. On April 28, 1986, a major nuclear accident occurred at the Soviet Union's **Chernobyl** power station near the city of Kiev. The resultant cloud of radiation drifted over Europe as far north as Scandinavia. Twenty-three deaths were reported, along with an indeterminate number of injuries and illnesses that might later develop. Forty thousand people had to be evacuated from the contaminated area.

Nuclear plants located near large centers of population present a serious problem of how to evacuate nearby residents in case of a nuclear accident. The problem of safe disposal of **radioactive wastes** has not yet been solved. Failure to meet stringent safety regulations has led to long delays in licensing the operation of new plants.

In addition to concern about safety, other problems—financial, environmental, and operational—led in 1980 to the cancellation of all nuclear plants ordered after 1973.

Problems of Nuclear Arms Production

A report prepared for Congress in 1988 by the Energy Department indicated that three nuclear reactors used in making **tritium** for nuclear warheads at the government's **Savannah River** plant in South Carolina may never be able to produce enough tritium to meet the nation's nuclear weapons needs. The three reactors were shut down in the spring of 1988 because of structural and management flaws.

Changing Materials

Plastics and Nylon

The development of new materials, notably plastics and nylon, have had a major impact on our way of life. Plastics resulted from the inventive genius of **Leo H. Bakeland**, a Belgian chemist who came to the United States in 1889. He developed a material called **Bakelite**, which opened the entire field of modern plastics. A related product named nylon was produced in 1934 by Dr. **Wallace H. Carothers** in the Du Pont laboratories.

Light Metals

Light metals—**aluminum, beryllium, titanium**, and **magnesium**—have been introduced extensively in industrial production since World War II. Their special properties—light weight, high tensile strength, and resistance to corrosion—have made them prime materials in the aerospace, the biomedical, and the chemical industries. They are also used in the production of cans for liquid and solid foods, in aircraft, and in business machine parts, kitchen utensils, and many other products.

Changing Technology (Computers)

Advanced technology (hi-tech) is revolutionizing industry so rapidly that it is virtually impossible to keep abreast of developments. Extensive changes are occurring through the use of computers in business and industry, particularly in each of the following fields: missiles, spacecraft and aircraft, scientific instruments, drugs and medicines, electronics and telecommunications, and synthetic materials.

The computer is revolutionizing our lives in the fields of farming, manufacturing, management, business, education, banking, building and construction, entertainment, health, and other daily concerns and activities.

A computer is an electronic device that is able to store vast quantities of detailed information and retrieve specific items on demand. It can also be programmed to process information and make extremely complicated "decisions." Modern electronic computers first came into use during the 1940s in laboratory research, chiefly in universities. During the next two decades, the use of computers spread rapidly in the United States and throughout the industrialized world. By 1970 computers had become a major industry, with 100,000 manufactured in the United States for use in government agencies such as the Census Bureau and the Internal Revenue Service, and in the private sector.

Supercomputers entered the field in the late 1980s. Produced by Cray Research, Inc. in 1987, a supercomputer could make 2 billion complex multiplications in one second. Smaller **computer chips** are being designed as the speed and efficiency of electronic operations are steadily increased. **Transistors** will switch on and off in 2 trillionths of a second. **Artificial intelligence** (**AI**) and **robots** are still in their infancy but will doubtless bring further changes in our way of life.

Changing Corporate Structures

The **multinational corporation**—an organization that carries on its business through branches in more than one country—is nothing new in world commerce. But the trend toward multinational corporations has gained momentum since the end of World War II. American corporations open factories, sales offices, mining branches, or other operating units in one or more foreign countries. A percentage of the capital may be raised in the foreign country, making it a joint venture with the percentage of ownership specifically stated. Many American multinationals operate in Africa, Asia, and Latin America, as well as in Europe. Their fields of interest include all types of business and industry, as indicated by names such as Exxon, General Motors, and IBM. A major field for American multinationals is oil and petroleum products.

The Changing Nature of Employment

The total labor force in the United States has grown steadily, from 60 million at the end of World War II to 110 million by 1985. At the same time, there has been a dramatic change in the nature of employment.

Agriculture

The percentage of the labor force engaged in agriculture has declined rapidly since the 1930s. Of a total labor force of nearly 49 million in 1930, 10.5 million or 21.4 percent were engaged in farming. By 1970, the labor force had grown to 82 million, but the number of workers in agriculture had declined to 2.5 million or 3.1 percent of the labor force. A further decline continued during the 1970s and 1980s. By 1980, the percentage of workers employed in agriculture was 2.2 percent; in 1985 it was below 2 percent and estimates for the year 2000 show a continuing decline to below 1 percent.

Manufacturing and Service Industries

During the same period (1930–1970), the percentage of workers engaged in manufacturing increased steadily. Among their products were machinery, electrical equipment, textile products, processed foods, transportation equipment, printed materials, metal products, and many others. The percentage in the work force engaged in manufacturing rose from 20 percent in 1930 to 25 percent by 1970. However, the percentage of the work force engaged in manufacturing began to decline after 1970, with the astonishing growth of service occupations including retail sales, office workers, waiters/waitresses, medical services, advertising, and computer programming. By 1986, 75 percent of all employment was in service occupations. The Bureau of Labor Statistics predicted in 1986 that 20 million new jobs would be created by the year 2000. Nine of every ten new jobs will be in the service-producing industries, and nine tenths of those will be filled by women and minorities.

Exercise Set 6.1

1. The potential of nuclear generators to supply America's needs for energy has not been realized because
   A. investors have not been willing to supply the necessary capital
   B. most of the required resources have been devoted to the production of nuclear weapons
   C. plans for the construction of new plants ordered after 1973 have been on the increase
   D. problems of safety, environmental degradation, and plant operation have caused delays in licensing

2. Among the factors that have characterized the postindustrial society are changes in all of the following EXCEPT
   A. energy sources
   B. technology
   C. tariff and trade regulations
   D. corporate structures

3. During the past half century there has been a marked shift in occupations from
   A. agriculture to industry to service occupations
   B. service to agriculture to industry
   C. business to industry to professions
   D. manual to electrical to mechanical

4. The domestic need for electricity in the United States supplied by nuclear reactors is approximately
   A. 5 percent
   B. 15 percent
   C. 25 percent
   D. 50 percent

THE WORLD AND POST-INDUSTRIALISM

> It is futile to expect a hungry and squalid population to be anything but violent and gross.
>
> Thomas Huxley, 1874

Developed and Developing Nations

Contrasts in a Divided World

The **developed nations** of the world—those with a strong industrial base—are primarily located in North America and Europe, plus Japan in Asia. Most of Africa, the Middle East, Asia, and Latin America are classified as **third world** or **developing nations**. They differ from the developed nations— the democratic nations of western Europe and North America, and the former Soviet bloc—in their lower standard of living, lower educational standards, and lower health standards. The division is sometimes seen as one of North/ South, with the former being developed and the latter developing. Another point of reference uses the term East/ West, with the latter being the area of development and the former largely developing.

There was for many years an ongoing tension between the Soviet Union and the Western democracies in an effort to gain influence over or, at least, allegiance of the developing world. Areas of tension included Latin America (notably in Central America), in the Middle East, the Persian Gulf, Africa, and the third world generally. The developing nations, because they are poor and relatively weak, became a political battleground between the superpowers.

Third-World Debt

Efforts of third-world nations to make economic progress and raise the standard of living of their people have led to extensive borrowing of capital from banks in the developed world. But the money has not always been properly used, and living standards have generally not risen. Meanwhile the borrowers have gone deeper and deeper into debt, reaching a point where it is obvious to both debtors and creditors that repayment cannot be made. By 1992, the debt owed to foreign bankers by less developed nations amounted to more than one trillion (a thousand billion) dollars.

These debts are owed chiefly to American banks, although Japanese and European banks are also involved. Since debtors tend to have unfriendly feelings toward their creditors, particularly when they are unable to repay their debts, this world situation may have ominous overtones and repercussions.

Low Income, Hunger, and Life Expectancy

There is a clear relationship between the per capita income of a nation and its life expectancy. The developing nations with the lowest average national income are also at or near the bottom of the scale in life expectancy.

Even developed industrial nations, including the United States, may have millions living below the poverty level, and many, especially children, suffering hunger and malnutrition. The poverty level is adjusted each year according to the cost of living. In 1986 in the United States, it was set at an income of $11,203 for a family of four. In that year 13.6 percent of Americans were below the poverty level. Children were the worst off, with 19.8 percent living below the poverty level.

Economic and Social Problems

Agriculture

The developing nations have two thirds of the world's population but produce only one third of the world's agricultural output. The greater output of the developed nations is due to the use of farm machinery, fertilizers and chemicals, irrigation, and other technology applied to production, harvesting, and methods of preservation of agricultural produce. The average American farmer cares for about 15 acres, while the average for a farm worker in the developing world is about 3 acres. The great farm belts of the United States and Canada produce more basic food crops (wheat, rye, barley, oats, and corn) than the entire output of the third world.

• *The Malthusian theory.* The theory propounded by the English economist **Thomas Robert Malthus** in the late 18th century stated that poverty, hunger, and starvation would soon be the lot of humankind, since the population increases by geometric ratio (2 to 4 to 8 to 16), while the food supply increases by arithmetic ratio (2 to 4 to 6 to 8).

• *The "Green Revolution."* The Malthusian theory, so far as food production is concerned, was challenged by the "Green Revolution," a term first used in the 1960s to describe efforts to produce greater yields from farm acreage. New varieties of rice, wheat, and other grains were developed. These new strains were resistant to plant disease, better able to withstand prolonged drought and cold, and had a greater yield per cultivated acre. Better methods of harvesting, soil conservation, and farm management were introduced. New fertilizers and pesticides were developed. Agricultural output in many parts of the world increased dramatically, causing the term "Green Revolution" to be applied. Efforts to produce more and better crops from a given acreage continue to increase output. But environmental degradation, as we shall see, is having a contrary effect and threatening serious consequences.

World Population Growth

The graph below illustrates the trend in world population.

Prior to 1650, the world's population grew slowly. The graph shows the rapid increase in population growth since 1650. In the half-century from 1900 to 1950 the world's population increased by 50 percent. In the 38 years after 1950 it increased by 100 percent. More than half the world's people live in Asia. The continent showing the most rapid population growth is Africa, where the population catapulted from 199 million in 1950 to 677 million in 1993. Demographers (people who specialize in population studies) predict that the world population will be 6.5 billion by the year 2000. Most of this dramatic increase will be in the developing countries. The combined population of Europe, North America (excluding Mexico), and Australia has

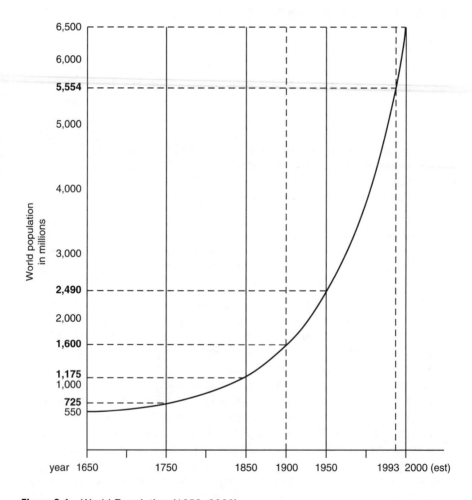

Figure 6.1 World Population (1650–2000)

remained relatively constant since the 1960s. While the population growth of the United States has not kept pace with that of world population, it has nevertheless been increasing steadily. (It is expected to reach 300 million, then begin to decline.) The total population figures for the United States are:

Census Data	U.S. Population
1960	179,323,175
1970	203,302,031
1980	226,545,518
1990	248,709,873

Figure 6.2   United States Population Increase

The astonishing momentum of world population growth is placing a heavy strain on the world's natural resources and contributing to grave environmental damage. The very survival of human life is in the balance.

Environmental Concerns

As crude a weapon as the cave man's club, a chemical barrage has been hurled against the fabric of life.

Rachel Carson, *Silent Spring,* 1962

Sooner or later, wittingly or unwittingly, we must pay for every intrusion on the natural environment.

Barry Commoner, *Science and Survival,* 1966

The Greenhouse Effect

The emissions into the atmosphere from the burning of fossil fuels (coal, oil, and natural gas) are causing a relentless global warming that has been named the **greenhouse effect**. The release of gases, especially carbon monoxide, into the atmosphere produces an artificial blanket that prevents heat from the sun from radiating back into space. This is thought to be the cause of a rise in the air temperature throughout the earth. Should this continue, it may cause not only heat waves, but also drought and floods.

Air Pollution

The air on which our lives depend has become a receptacle for the discharges from motor vehicles, factories, airplanes, space exploration refuse, nuclear research, electric power plants, cooking and heating chimneys, forest fires, incinerators, and exhausts and dust from construction and demolition projects.

Veteran air pilots recall that in the 1940s and 1950s they used their instruments to put them on a course to their destination. By the 1970s and 1980s this was no longer necessary because virtually every large city in the world was visible for 100 miles or more by its cover of a cloud of polluted air called **smog**. The **Clean Air Act of 1970** set national standards controlling six basic pollutants—notably carbon monoxide gas—but the act has not solved the air pollution problem.

Water Pollution

The first major **Federal Clean Water Act** was passed in 1965. The **Federal Water Pollution Control Act of 1972** was passed over President Nixon's veto. The **Federal Clean Water Act of 1987** was passed by an angry Congress over President Reagan's veto. Despite these laws, our limited supply of clean water is at risk. Not only the nation's rivers and lakes, but also its subterranean groundwater (the sources of our drinking water) are threatened by contamination. There are 5,000 types of wastes that have been released into the nation's ground water from homes, farms, factories, and other sources. In 1969 it was estimated that more than 40 million fish in 45 states were killed as a result of pollution—chemicals, overheating from discharge of nuclear plants, and leaching of farm pesticides. The closing of beaches because of the high bacteria count in the water is a common occurrence.

Lake Superior has absorbed over 400 million tons of metal tailings. These were dumped into the water daily for more than 16 years by mining and smelting operations. Hubert Humphrey denounced this procedure and lamented "the galloping deterioration of our Great Lakes—these magnificent inland seas that contain a third of all the fresh water on the world's surface."

The 20th-century phenomenon of water pollution is worldwide. On one of his exploratory voyages across the Atlantic Ocean, the scientist **Thor Heyerdahl** reported a 1,400-mile current of chemical contaminants. In Central Asia, the Aral Sea is reported to be a virtually lost body of water because of industrial pollution.

Nuclear weapons plants may be a prime source of water pollution. On October 15, 1988, *The New York Times* disclosed that United States government officials knew for years that a plant near Cincinnati was releasing thousands of tons of radioactive uranium waste into drinking water wells in the area. The plant also emitted radioactive particles into the air. The director of Ohio's Environmental Protection Agency testified that about 12.7 million pounds of uranium waste had been disposed of in pits since the plant opened in 1951.

Land Pollution

> Hurt not the earth, neither the sea, nor the trees. . .
>
> Revelation 7:3

The world's land is subject to a continuing barrage of environmental battering. The problem is international in scope. The rapid destruction of Brazil's rain forest for quick economic gain is threatening the extinction of rare and valuable plant and animal species. Discharge from the smokestacks of utilities and industries of our Middle West is poisoning the forests, lakes, and air of New York's magnificent Adirondack area and of New England as well, and is wreaking havoc on the Canadian side of the border. This daily chemical onslaught has been the subject of angry protests by the Canadian government. Despite several conferences, progress in solving this problem has been slow.

• *Destruction of Wetlands.* The destruction of wetlands has been particularly painful to environmentalists. Once these lands are paved over for condominiums, shopping malls, or other commercial use, their loss causes irreparable ecological damage. Not only is the habitat of wildlife destroyed, but the function of absorbing rainwater and of preventing pollutants from reaching groundwater is also lost. With this in mind, many communities have established "Save-the-Wetlands" associations.

• *Soil Erosion.* Soil erosion is another source of concern. According to a *New York Times* report in 1973, "the nation's farms still lose about two billion tons of soil each year." This topsoil was created through decay of animal and vegetable matter over many centuries. It is not easily replaced. In many lands, arid soil and deserts are the outcome in part of erosion accompanying soil abuse and neglect.

• *Oil Extraction.* Oil extraction in environmentally sensitive areas, both on land and offshore, have pitted environmentalists, led by the Wilderness Society, the Natural Resources Defense Council, the Sierra Club, and other environmental organizations, against the major oil corporations. The California coastal areas and the unsettled wilderness areas of Alaska have been key areas of contention in this controversy. Environmentalists point to the ecological damage caused by oil drilling. A 1969 blowout of **Union Oil's Platform A** in the Santa Barbara channel caused extensive damage to the California coast and to aquatic life.

The wreck of the oil supertanker **Exxon Valdez** in Alaska's Prince William Sound in the early hours of March 24, 1989, spilled 11 million gallons of oil along 730 miles of Alaska's spectacular coastline. The death toll to wildlife included 11,000 birds of 30 different species, 700 Pacific sea otters, and 20 bald eagles, according to a tally by the State Department of Environmental Conservation. Bears who feed on the oiled birds and fish are also victims of the spill, as are foxes and other species.

• *Hazardous Wastes.* Each day more than 200 million pounds of hazardous wastes are produced in the United States alone. A 1988 Air Force study disclosed the risk posed by the use of garbage incinerators. Antipollution devices capture dioxin, a highly toxic substance, which is then disposed of in landfills.

Serious health problems developed when the Army undertook a cleanup of the Rocky Mountain Arsenal near Denver, Colorado. A 93-acre cleanup site was one of several used as dumps for by-products of nerve gas made by the Army, as well as highly toxic pesticides made there later by the Shell Oil Company. Many of the 100 families living near the arsenal say that since work began to drain millions of gallons of sludge, they suffered from "coughing spells, severe headaches, chest pains, and nausea."

• *Radon.* In 1988 the Environmental Protection Agency (EPA) recommended checking every home in the nation for radon levels. The agency estimated that as many as 20,000 lung cancer deaths annually are linked to radon, a colorless, odorless radioactive gas emitted from decaying uranium. The gas seeps into homes from the ground.

Cities are running out of dumpsites for solid wastes—the millions of tons of garbage, automobiles, paper, plastics, and other refuse that are discarded annually by American consumers. Insecticides, herbicides, and chemical fertilizers used in farming are a major source of toxic pollution of soil and food supplies. In a *New York Times* op-ed article on October 15, 1988, the environmentalist **John B. Oakes** concludes, "The cumulative destruction and corruption of the earth's resources on land, in the seas, and throughout the atmosphere present as much of a challenge to the survival of the human race as nuclear war."

Exercise Set 6.2

1. A characteristic of third-world nations is that they
   A. are all located in Asia or Africa
   B. have a weak industrial base
   C. are all lacking in natural resources
   D. have governments controlled by the military

2. Geographically, the developed nations are chiefly found in the continents of
   A. Europe, North America, and Australia
   B. Europe, Asia, and North America
   C. Africa, South America, and Australia
   D. North America, South America, and Europe

3. The "Green Revolution" refers to the
   A. fluctuation of the dollar in international finance
   B. terrorist activities of the Irish Republican Army
   C. the radical program of a West German political group
   D. the dramatic increase in agricultural output

4. The fact that the agricultural output per acre in developed nations is many times that of developing nations may be explained chiefly by
   A. the difference in soil quality, climate, and other natural advantages
   B. more advanced agricultural technology
   C. a higher education and health level
   D. government support through favorable tariff and tax legislation

5. World population growth
   A. declined between 1650 and 1850, then began a rapid advance
   B. grew relatively slowly but steadily between 1650 and 1950 and then picked up momentum rapidly
   C. shows signs of leveling off at the current figure of about 5 billion people
   D. is proceeding at approximately the same rate on each of the six major continents

6. The continent with the highest percentage of population growth is
   A. Africa
   B. Asia
   C. Europe
   D. South America

CHAPTER REVIEW QUESTIONS

1. Since the establishment of the Atomic Energy Commission in 1946
   A. reliance on other sources of energy has gradually diminished
   B. the search for new sources of energy has been abandoned
   C. nuclear plants have become the major source of energy for home and industry
   D. the high expectations of the nuclear industry have failed to materialize

2. A drastic change in the categories of employment in the United States has come about primarily because of
   A. entrance of unprecedented numbers of women into the work force
   B. stringent state and federal regulation of employment of children
   C. technological developments in many fields of employment
   D. population shifts within the United States

3. Which of the following is *not* true of the third world?
   A. it has relatively little connection with multinational corporations
   B. it is a major factor in the world population explosion of the late 20th century
   C. it includes many of the nations that gained their independence after World War II
   D. its members are not politically affiliated with either the United States or the former Soviet Union

ESSAYS

1. Global interdependence has become an increasingly significant aspect of life in the second half of the 20th century. Listed below are several areas in which this development is clearly apparent.

    Areas of Global Interdependence
    Technological developments
    Environmental problems
    Rapid population growth
    Financial relationships
    Agricultural changes

    Choose *three* of the areas listed. For *each* area chosen, explain its impact on global interdependence indicating how the impact may be beneficial or detrimental. [5,5,5]

2. An interrelationship has been shown to exist between certain socio-economic factors. Below are listed a number of these interrelated factors.

    Socio-Economic Factors
    Life expectancy—per capita income
    Level of education—economic productivity
    Agricultural output—technological development
    Population explosion—financial dependency
    Political stability—multinational economy

    Choose *three* interrelated factors. For *each pair* chosen discuss the nature of the relationship and explain its effect on the nations involved. [5,5,5]

Chapter 2

CONTAINMENT AND CONSENSUS (1945–1960)

EISENHOWER POLICIES: FOREIGN AFFAIRS

There is no nook or cranny in all the world into which Communist influence does not penetrate.

John Foster Dulles, 1950

Threat of World Communism

Soviet Expansion In and After World War II

In 1940, while Germany was engaged in fighting France and Britain, the Soviets occupied and annexed the three Baltic States—Estonia, Latvia, and Lithuania. At the end of the war, Russia annexed eastern Poland and established a Communist government in the new Poland and in East Germany. Communist governments were also established in Czechoslovakia, Hungary, Romania, Bulgaria, Albania, and Yugoslavia.

Soviet efforts to overthrow the governments of Greece and Turkey were thwarted by American aid to these countries under the Truman Doctrine. In the Far East, the Soviets took from Japan the southern half of Sakhalin Island and the Kurile Islands. Communists dominated the northern half of Korea.

The Korean War

In 1950 North Korea attacked South Korea. In the ensuing Korean War, American and UN forces defeated Communist efforts to make all of Korea a Communist country. During the presidential campaign of 1952, Eisenhower promised to do all he could to bring the Korean War to an end. In a speech in October 1952, he said, "I shall go to Korea." After the election he kept his promise and in December 1952 went to Korea, where he conferred with American and UN leaders. Peace talks continued between negotiators for North and South Korea at Panmunjom, until finally an armistice agreement ending the war was signed on July 27, 1953. The boundary line between the two was set approximately where it had been before the war. A demilitarized zone was established between North and South Korea.

John Foster Dulles

> You have a row of dominoes set up, you knock over the first one, and
> what will happen to the last one is. . . that it will go over very quickly.
> Dwight D. Eisenhower, on the strategic importance of Indochina,
> in a press conference, April 7, 1954.

John Foster Dulles served as Secretary of State under Eisenhower from
1953 until Dulles died in 1959. During the Truman years, Dulles had contended that the Truman policy of **containment** of communism should be
replaced by a policy of attempted liberation of Communist-controlled countries. As the architect of American foreign policy, Dulles adhered to the
domino theory described in Eisenhower's statement, believing that if one
nation in an area fell to communism, the rest, like a row of dominoes, would
also fall to communism. This doctrine played an important role in the Vietnam War of the 1960s and 1970s. Dulles also spoke of a rollback in Soviet
influence in eastern Europe.

Massive Retaliation

A Department of State bulletin issued by Secretary of State John Foster
Dulles in January 1954 made two important changes in the nation's military
policy. First, there was to be a cutback in the use of conventional military
weapons. Second, there was to be greater reliance on atomic weapons. In
1952 the nation had successfully tested a new weapon, the **hydrogen** or **H-
bomb**. This bomb had 500 times the destructive power of the A-bomb that
had destroyed Hiroshima seven years before.

In the 1954 bulletin Dulles declared, "We want, for ourselves and the
other free nations, a maximum deterrent at a bearable cost . . . Local defenses
must be reinforced by the deterrent of massive retaliatory power." This came
to be known as the policy of "**massive retaliation**" dependent on a prepon-
derance of nuclear weaponry. Under this policy both the Soviet Union and
the United States became involved in an arms race, each trying to build up a
stockpile of nuclear weapons in order to show it could still destroy the other
side, even if attacked first.

Brinkmanship

The Dulles conduct of relations with the Soviets came to be known as
"brinkmanship." Dulles believed that the United States had to show the
Communists it was willing to use force and to go to the brink of war in order
to keep the peace. In an address in 1956, Dulles explained his policy in these
words: " You have to take chances for peace just as you take chances in war
. . . the ability to get to the verge without getting into the war is the necessary art. If you try to run away from it, if you are scared to go to the brink,
you are lost."

The H-Bomb; Atoms for Peace

> The United States pledges... its determination to help solve the fearful atomic dilemma—to devote its entire heart and mind to find the way by which the miraculous inventiveness of man shall not be dedicated to his death, but consecrated to his life.
>
> Address by President Eisenhower
> to the United Nations General Assembly, December 8, 1953

The explosion of an H-bomb by the United States in 1952 was followed by the successful explosion of a similar bomb in 1953 by the Soviet Union. In his address, Eisenhower summarized the developments in atomic weaponry, predicted the spreading of these weapons of destruction to other nations, and urged that steps be taken to reverse the trend immediately. He offered to cooperate toward that end in implementing the UN resolution of November 1953. He proposed that ". . . this fissionable material would be used to serve the peaceful pursuits of mankind. Experts would be mobilized to apply atomic energy to the needs of agriculture, medicine, and other peaceful activities."

This atoms-for-peace proposal did not reverse the confrontational trend that was nourished by the cold-war atmosphere of suspicion and fear.

The Southeast Asia Treaty Organization (SEATO)

On September 8, 1954, a treaty negotiated by Secretary of State John Foster Dulles was signed in Manila. It had the same purpose and design for Southeast Asia as NATO did for the North Atlantic, namely, **collective security** measures against Communist aggression. The nations that signed the SEATO agreement were: Australia, France, New Zealand, Pakistan, the Republic of the Philippines, Great Britain, and the United States.

The SEATO agreement specified: "Each Party recognizes that aggression by means of armed attack against any of the Parties . . . would endanger its own peace and safety, and that it will in the event act to meet the common danger in accordance with its constitutional processes." The agreement came on the heels of the defeat, earlier in the year, of French military forces at the hands of the Vietnam Communists in the North, led by **Ho Chi Minh**. The struggle for control of Vietnam ultimately involved the United States in the disastrous Vietnam War.

Aswan Dam and the Suez Canal

In 1956 a crisis developed over the Suez Canal. Egypt, led by **Gamal Abdel Nasser**, who had led a successful army coup against **King Farouk**, entered into an arms deal with the Soviets, who agreed to supply Egyptian armies for their military action against the new state of Israel on Egypt's eastern border. Afterwards, Nasser approached the United States for help in building a huge dam at **Aswan** on the Nile River for irrigation and flood control. The United States turned Nasser down because of Egypt's arms deal with the Soviets. In response, Nasser seized the Suez Canal, which had been run by a joint Anglo-French company. He declared that the Canal was the property of Egypt and that revenues collected from its use would be applied to the building of the Aswan Dam. Great Britain and France were especially alarmed by Nasser's takeover of the canal, fearing it would interrupt the flow of oil from the Middle East to Europe.

On October 29, 1956, Israel attacked Egypt. Two days later, France and Britain joined Israel, and the three succeeded in gaining control of the Suez Canal. To avoid a military confrontation, both the United States and the Soviet Union supported Egypt and approved a UN resolution ordering a cease-fire and withdrawal from Egyptian territory. Troops of the three occupying powers were withdrawn and replaced by a United Nations peacekeeping force.

Polish and Hungarian Uprisings

In 1956, three years after Stalin's death, the new Soviet premier, **Nikita S. Khrushchev**, denounced Stalin as a tyrant who had committed grave crimes against his own people. This soon led to movements for more freedom in Poland and Hungary, two Communist-dominated Soviet satellite states. Polish workers rioted, demanding better working conditions. A new Polish Premier granted bargaining rights to labor. Khrushchev threatened to intervene but refrained when Poland continued its support of Soviet foreign policy.

In Hungary, the new premier, **Imre Nagy**, attempted to institute a democratic government and prepared to withdraw Hungary from the Warsaw Pact. An uprising in Hungary in 1956 was suppressed by Soviet troops. Thousands of "freedom fighters" in the Hungarian resistance lost their lives. Many fled to the United States, England, and France. Nagy was seized in the Yugoslav embassy and executed. Hungary remained under Communist control.

The Eisenhower Doctrine—Intervention in Lebanon

Pressure from the United States resulted in the withdrawal of British, French, and Israeli troops from Egypt after the Suez Canal crisis. But the fear of Soviet infiltration and influence in the Middle East led President Eisenhower in 1957 to request authority from Congress to extend military and financial aid to any country in the Middle East threatened by Communist aggression. Congress responded in March 1957 with legislation that became known as the **Eisenhower Doctrine**. The doctrine applied specifically to "the general area of the Middle East" and authorized economic and military assistance, including the use of "armed force to assist any such nation or group of nations requesting assistance against armed aggression from any country controlled by international communism."

A crisis occurred in the spring of 1958 when Syria and Egypt attempted to overthrow the pro-Western government of Lebanon. When the President of Lebanon asked the United States for help, Eisenhower—in accordance with authority granted by Congress to implement the Eisenhower Doctrine—sent the Sixth Fleet into the Mediterranean and ordered 14,000 United States Marines to Lebanon. U.S. armed forces were withdrawn when Egypt and Syria agreed to refrain from intervention in Lebanon.

China Policy

When the **Nationalist** forces of **Chiang Kai-shek** fled from the mainland of China to the island of **Formosa** (**Taiwan**) in 1948, they also occupied the two offshore islands of **Quemoy** and **Matsu**. In the summer of 1958, the Chinese Communists began artillery fire against these islands, seemingly intending to occupy them by force. In a nationwide broadcast, Eisenhower warned that the United States would not "retreat in the face of armed aggression" and deployed the Seventh Fleet in the area as evidence of his determination. Meanwhile, Secretary Dulles flew to Formosa and prevailed on Chiang Kai-shek to give up his idea of invading mainland China. The shelling ceased, but in November the Chinese foreign minister issued this challenge: "The Americans must pull away their hand from the Taiwan Strait . . . We are determined to liberate Formosa and the offshore islands . . ." The issue remained unsettled, and in the 1960 election campaign, Kennedy and Nixon debated as to who would most effectively protect American interests in these islands off the coast of Communist China.

Summits and U-2's

In the fall of 1959, Premier **Nikita S. Khrushchev** of the Soviet Union toured the United States and had private talks with President Eisenhower at Camp David. Another summit meeting was planned to take place in Paris in May 1960. But on May 5, 1960, Khrushchev announced that the Russians had brought down an American **U-2 reconnaissance** (**spy**) **plane** four days earlier, 1,200 miles inside the Soviet Union. Two days later Khrushchev announced that the pilot, **Francis Gary Powers**, was alive and had confessed to spying. Powers was tried in the Soviet Union for espionage and was sentenced to ten years imprisonment but was released less than two years later.

A State Department bulletin of May 1960 stated that unarmed reconnaissance flights were common practice by many nations and admitted that the United States had been engaged in this activity over the Soviet Union for four years. The bulletin claimed that these flights would have been unnecessary if the Soviet Union had not rejected President Eisenhower's "open skies" proposal made in 1955.

In a subsequent statement, issued May 25, 1960, President Eisenhower declared that he had ordered that the U-2 reconnaissance flights be stopped. He refused Khrushchev's demand for a public apology, whereupon the Soviet leader canceled the summit conference scheduled for May.

Sputnik: The Space Missile Race

Experiments with rockets that could project missiles into outer space had been carried on long before World War II. In the last year of the war, the German army launched V-2 rockets, each carrying a ton of explosives, into cities in England, bringing death and destruction in their wake. There was no defense against this dreaded menace. After the war, Russia and the United States raced to perfect this new device, which would make it possible to send vehicles into orbit around the earth, reach out into space, and even land on the moon.

On October 4, 1957, the Russians launched the first successful earth satellite, which circled the earth and was called *Sputnik*, meaning "fellow traveler" (of the earth). A month later they launched *Sputnik II* with a dog on board to find out if an earth creature could live in space beyond the earth's atmosphere. It could!

The United States, stunned by the seeming superiority of Soviet science, quickly reacted to the challenge. The implications were ominous. Rocket-launched vehicles could soon carry the new H-bomb to pinpointed targets anywhere in the world. The first successful U.S. satellite, *Explorer I*, was launched in February 1958. Shortly thereafter, Congress passed the **National Defense Education Act**, appropriating $1 billion for science education. The defense budget for research, was increased by $4 billion, and the **National Aeronautics and Space Administration** (**NASA**) was established to carry out a program of space exploration and related defense applications.

Exercise Set 6.3

1. The Suez Crisis of 1956 was settled by
   A. the United States acting unilaterally
   B. Russia and the United States acting through the UN
   C. British and French voluntary withdrawal
   D. the defeat of Israeli military and naval forces

2. The Eisenhower foreign policy as conducted by Secretary of State Dulles was dominated by all of the following doctrines EXCEPT
   A. the domino theory
   B massive retaliation
   C. brinkmanship
   D. economic nationalism

3. A scheduled 1959 summit meeting between Eisenhower and Krushchev was canceled because of
   A. the Soviet testing of an H-bomb
   B. the U-2 incident
   C. U.S. intervention in the suppression of uprisings in Poland and Hungary
   D. U.S. launching of *Explorer I*

4. By the time Eisenhower took office as President in 1953, the Communists were in control of all of the following EXCEPT
   A. Estonia, Latvia, and Lithuania
   B. Poland, East Germany, and Hungary
   C. Afghanistan, Greece, and Turkey
   D. North Korea, the Kurile Islands, and half of Sakhalin

5. The Dulles policy of "massive retaliation" was dependent on the use of
   A. nuclear weapons
   B. conventional forces
   C. joint action with our allies
   D. the overwhelming weight of public opinion

EISENHOWER DOMESTIC DEVELOPMENTS

> In the councils of government, we must guard against the acquisition of unwarranted influence, whether sought or unsought, by the military-industrial complex. The potential for the disastrous rise of misplaced power exists and will persist.
>
> Dwight D. Eisenhower,
> Farewell Address, January 17, 1961

Return to Peacetime Economy

> What is good for the country is good for General Motors, and vice versa.
>
> Charles E. Wilson, President of General Motors, nominated by
> President Eisenhower to be Secretary of Defense,
> testifying before the Senate Armed Services Committee
> at his confirmation hearings, 1952.

Relaxing Government Controls

The new Eisenhower administration that came to office in 1953 removed the wage and price controls that had been imposed on business and labor during the Korean War. With the approval of Congress, the government sold to private industry the government-owned factories that had produced synthetic rubber for the war effort. Private power companies were given increased authority to conduct atomic research and provide atomic power for civilian use. More than 100,000 government jobs were left unfilled when vacancies occurred by resignation, retirement, or death.

Budget Problems

Still, efforts to balance the budget were unsuccessful. Military expenditures remained high, and foreign aid was extended to combat Communist influence. Veterans Administration costs had to be met, and the government purchase of surplus grain to help maintain farm income was essential to avoid total collapse of farm prices. A $27 billion federal interstate highway program was approved by Congress and signed into law by President Eisenhower in 1956. The federal government was to assume 90 percent of the cost.

Social Programs

A new department of Cabinet rank, the **Department of Health, Education and Welfare (HEW)**, was established in April 1953. It was responsible for administering the **National Institutes of Health**, food and drug laws, education, Social Security, and welfare programs.

President Eisenhower appealed to Congress to pass social welfare legislation. Congress passed legislation extending Social Security to an additional 10.5 million individuals and increasing Social Security benefits. Additional money was appropriated for construction of hospitals, medical research, slum clearance, and urban renewal. The President's request for appropriation of federal funds for public elementary and secondary education was narrowly defeated in Congress because aid to private and religious schools was not included and because there was concern about federal control of education.

Labor Unrest

A strike in 1959 by the 500,000 member **United Steel Workers of America** halted production of steel from July 15 into November with no prospect of settlement. The steel workers were demanding wage increases based on rising living costs and high profits in the steel industry. President Eisenhower, using his authority under the Taft-Hartley Act, secured an injunction on November 7, ending the work stoppage for an 80-day cooling-off period. The strike was settled by an agreement reached on January 4, 1960, calling for moderate wage increases over a 30-month period.

Offshore Oil; Natural Gas

Vast deposits of oil were known to exist below the water of the Pacific coast, the Gulf of Mexico, and possibly the waters adjoining other states. Measures giving title to this rich oil reserve to the states were passed by Congress in 1946 and 1952. President Truman vetoed this attempt by Congress to turn over to the states resources that, he said, belonged to all the people of the country.

During his campaign for the presidency, Eisenhower had promised to yield claims to this oil resource to the states. The **Submerged Lands Act** was signed by Eisenhower in May 1953. It provided that control of the so-called tideland oil should pass to the states, which could permit private oil companies to drill for oil in the tidelands and pay royalties to the states involved. In May 1960 the Supreme Court ruled that the historic boundaries of the states extended three miles offshore except for Florida and Texas, whose historic boundaries were declared to extend 10.5 miles.

A proposal to exempt natural gas in interstate pipelines from regulation by the Federal Power Commission was strongly advocated by oil and gas interests and was about to be passed into law in 1956 with the approval of the Eisenhower administration. But Senator **Francis P. Case**, Republican of South Dakota, disclosed that he had received an unsolicited pre-election contribution of $2,500 (which he had returned) from an oil company that expected him to vote for the natural gas exemption. The bill was passed by

Congress despite the disclosure, but was vetoed by President Eisenhower, who was responding to the national reaction against the methods used to gain its adoption.

Public and Private Power

Intense rivalry developed between advocates of public ownership and private power interests over the construction of dams on the Snake River in Idaho for the development of hydroelectric power. The dams were ultimately constructed and operated by private power companies with approval of the Eisenhower administration.

In the case of the TVA, Eisenhower conceded that he could not sell this "socialist" enterprise to private operators because there were too many ramifications involved. He did, however, try to limit its scope by encouraging a private power company to begin operations in the area.

Exercise Set 6.4

1. In his farewell address, President Eisenhower warned against the growing power of the "military-industrial complex." He was referring to
   A. the arms race between the United States and the Soviet Union
   B. the confrontation between the members of NATO and the Warsaw Pact nations
   C. the alliance of the Pentagon and American arms manufacturers
   D. the growing power of the scientific community in American defense planning

2. Under President Eisenhower, social programs for health, education, and welfare were
   A. turned back from the federal government to state, local, and private control
   B. maintained but not expanded
   C. expanded by Congress at the request of the President
   D. passed by Congress over the President's veto

3. The Submerged Lands Act, advocated by President Eisenhower and signed into law by him in 1953, provided
   A. that control of the tideland (offshore) oil should pass to the states
   B. for joint exploitation of the tideland oil by state and federal agencies
   C. for sale of the offshore properties by the federal government to private interests
   D. that the potential oil resources be reserved to be available in case of national emergency

THE WARREN COURT AND CIVIL RIGHTS

It is the spirit and not the form of law that keeps justice alive.

Earl Warren, 1955

In 1953, President Eisenhower appointed **Earl Warren**, Republican three-term Governor of California, as Chief Justice of the United States. Warren held this high office until 1969. This 16-year period was to witness many changes, particularly in the area of civil rights.

Jackie Robinson

For a half century prior to World War II, professional baseball was completely segregated. No African American was signed by any major league club after 1884, though it was well known that there were many well-qualified players in the black leagues.

In 1947, the **Brooklyn Dodgers** took the first step by signing second baseman **Jackie Robinson**. Robinson's professional and personal qualities soon led to his acceptance by his teammates. It was not long before other African American players such as Roy Campanella, Willie Mays, Hank Aaron, Roberto Clemente from Puerto Rico, and many others were enriching the sport with their talents and underlining the all-American aspect of professional baseball.

Brown v. *Board of Education of Topeka* (1954)

In 1896, the Supreme Court, with only Justice **John Marshall Harlan** in dissent, ruled in the case of *Plessy* v. *Ferguson*, that segregation of the races was legal under the Fourteenth Amendment as long as the facilities provided the races were equal. This "separate but equal" doctrine was reversed by unanimous decision of the Warren Court in 1954 in the case of *Brown* v. *Board of Education of Topeka*. Writing for the Court, Chief Justice Warren said, "To separate them [African American children] from others of similar age and qualifications solely because of their race generates a feeling of inferiority as to their status in the community that may affect their hearts and minds in a way unlikely ever to be undone . . . . We conclude that in the field of public education the doctrine of 'separate but equal' has no place. Separate educational facilities are inherently unequal."

In a subsequent ruling on May 31, 1955 (*Brown* v. *Board of Education*), the Supreme Court instructed federal district courts to require local school authorities to move "with all deliberate speed" toward full compliance with this decision. But resistance to the Court's order was intense in the Southern states and in parts of the North as well. Delaware and the District of Columbia integrated their schools promptly. But a dozen years after the Brown decision thousands of public schools in the South still had 100 percent black student bodies.

Beginning of the Civil Rights Movement

Little Rock (1957): School Desegregation

An attempt was made at the beginning of the 1957 school year to integrate Little Rock's Central High School by enrolling nine African American students. Governor **Orval Faubus**, alleging that violence was about to erupt, sent units of the Arkansas National Guard to the school and ordered them to turn away the black students. When the guard was withdrawn on orders of a federal court, the black students entered the school through a back door, but a mob rushed the building and was barely restrained by the local police. Reporters and photographers on the scene were beaten.

• *President Eisenhower Takes Action.* At this point, President Eisenhower decided to act. In an address to the nation on September 24, 1957, he declared; "In that city [Little Rock, Arkansas] under the leadership of demagogic extremists, disorderly mobs have deliberately prevented the carrying out of proper orders from a federal court. . . . the President's responsibility is inescapable. In accordance with that responsibility, I have today issued an Executive Order directing the use of troops under federal authority to aid in the execution of federal law at Little Rock, Arkansas."

• *A Constitutional Challenge.* The challenge of the Arkansas governor and legislature to the validity of the Supreme Court's decision in the Brown case was not yet put to rest. The Court had to dispose of the claim by the Governor and legislature of Arkansas that they were under no duty as state officials to obey federal court orders. The case—*Cooper* v. *Aaron* (1958)—came to the Court in the form of a petition, presented by the Little Rock School Board and School Superintendent, asking to be relieved from implementing their desegregation program because of the "extreme hostility" of the Governor and Legislature of Arkansas.

The decision of the Court in *Cooper* v. *Aaron* was unusual because it was signed by each of the nine justices, implying joint authorship. After reviewing the Constitutional challenge, the Court stated: "It follows that the interpretation of the Fourteenth Amendment enunciated by this Court in the Brown case [1954] is the Supreme law of the land . . ."

Rosa Parks and the Montgomery Bus Boycott

On December 1, 1955, **Rosa Parks**, an African American seamstress in Montgomery, Alabama, boarded a crowded public bus on her way home from work. She sat down in a seat in the front part of the bus reserved for white passengers. The bus driver told her to give up her seat to a white passenger and move to the back of the bus. She refused to do so and was arrested for violating a Montgomery ordinance.

At that time **Dr. Martin Luther King, Jr.** was a 26-year-old pastor in a Baptist church in Montgomery. The black community was outraged by the injustice of segregation and were ready to take violent action, but Dr. King urged **nonviolent resistance** and organized a **bus boycott**. Blacks refused to ride the buses of Montgomery until all riders were treated alike.

The boycott went on for 381 days. Many walked long distances to and from work, while others organized car pools. A number of white people in Montgomery cooperated in the boycott, which attracted national attention. The Montgomery boycott achieved its purpose peaceably when the bus company gave up its practice of segregated seating.

Segregation in Interstate Transportation Unconstitutional

In *NAACP* v. *St. Louis-San Francisco Railway Company* (1955), the Interstate Commerce Commission ruled that segregation in interstate transportation was unconstitutional and ordered desegregation on all interstate transportation facilities.

Sit-ins, Civil Disobedience

The next step was to challenge local laws throughout the South requiring separate restaurants, lunch counters, or other public food and drink establishments for whites and blacks. This also included drinking fountains and restrooms, which were marked either "white" or "colored." The non-violent method used by blacks (aided by some whites) was the **sit-in**. A group entered a white restaurant or diner and sat down at the counter until they were served or forcibly removed. There were many arrests for violation of local ordinances. In May 1963 the Supreme Court ruled that the arrests were illegal because the segregation laws on which they were based were in violation of the Fourteenth Amendment's "privileges or immunities" clause.

First Civil Rights Legislation

In 1957, in a bipartisan effort supported by the Eisenhower administration, Congress passed the first **Civil Rights Act** since the Civil War. It addressed the key issue of **voting rights**, since blacks in the South were systematically disenfranchised by "literacy tests," poll taxes, and intimidation. The act created a **Civil Rights Commission** composed of members of both the Democratic and Republican parties and authorized the **Justice Department** to bring suits against persons interfering with anyone's right to vote.

When voting rights continued to be denied to blacks, a second and much stronger **Civil Rights Act** was passed in 1960. The act provided for the appointment of **federal referees** with power to issue voting certificates. It declared obstruction of voting rights by "threats or force" a federal crime. The number of black voters increased slowly but there was still a long way to go.

Exercise Set 6.5

1. In the landmark 1954 decision, *Brown* v. *Board of Education of Topeka*, the United States Supreme Court
   A. confirmed the earlier decision of *Plessy* v. *Ferguson*
   B. established the principle that "separate educational facilities are inherently unequal"
   C. ordered immediate integration of all public educational facilities
   D. divided 5 to 4 in favor of the plaintiffs

2. Implementation of the Supreme Court's school integration decision in Little Rock, Arkansas led to
   A. reluctant but prompt compliance by state authorities
   B. a subsequent reversal of the Court's decision
   C. an Executive Order by President Eisenhower directing the use of federal troops to enforce the Court's order
   D. disclosure of corruption in the local educational establishment

3. Throughout the year 1956, public attention in the nation was centered on Montgomery, Alabama, because
   A. the outcome of a nonviolent bus boycott could put an end to segregation on local public transportation facilities
   B. violence had erupted in connection with the bus boycott
   C. Rosa Parks had attempted to integrate the schools of Montgomery
   D. Dr. Martin Luther King, Jr. was a minister in Montgomery

4. The Warren Court is generally associated with
   A. a more liberal approach to the rights of minorities
   B. adherence to conservative principles of criminal justice
   C. split decisions representing divergent opinions of the justices on basic civil rights issues
   D. overwhelming public support of the Court's decisions

THE AFFLUENT SOCIETY

Postwar Consumption

Homes

A troublesome housing shortage developed as World War II came to an end and American soldiers returned by the millions, because there had been virtually no construction of residences during the war. In October 1945, when only 3 million of the 16 million had returned home, more than a million newlyweds could find no place to live and had to move in with parents or in-laws.

The postwar economic boom, stimulated in part by the demand for housing, witnessed a vast building expansion, especially in the **suburbs**. The **Housing Act of 1955** provided for 45,000 new public housing units a year for four years. This obviously fell far short of the nation's needs.

By 1960, average real income in the United States had risen nearly 20 percent since the end of World War II, and 15 million new housing units had been constructed. By 1972, the Bureau of the Census reported that 45 million housing units (of a total of 70 million) were owned by their occupants. Ninety-four percent of all homes had plumbing, hot and cold piped water, flush toilets, bath and/or shower.

Automobiles

The family car was a symbol of the affluent society. A few years after the end of World War II, when production of civilian goods had returned to high gear, 45 percent of American families owned an automobile. By 1970 it was 75 percent. The percentage increased to 80 in the next five years and, in addition, 30 percent of all American families now had at least two cars. Factory sales of passenger cars exceeded 8 million in 1985, with an additional 3.3 million trucks and buses. Over 189 million cars, trucks, and buses were registered in the United States in 1992.

Television

Television, with only a few thousand sets in use in the United States at the outbreak of World War II, became an important medium after the war. By 1960, nine of every ten American homes had television sets. A decade later TV had become the universal mass medium for communicating with the American public. By 1965 live TV broadcasts were being sent from Europe and other continents via satellite. People all over the world watched their TV screens in awe as the two American astronauts, Armstrong and Aldrin, walked on the moon in July 1969. As of January 1, 1988, 98 percent of the

90 million American homes had at least one TV set and more than 53 million had two or more sets. During Sunday prime time (7–11 P.M.) there are an estimated 105.8 million TV viewers. The average household usage of TV is more than 7 hours per day!

New Educational Opportunities

In response to the Soviet challenge posed by the launching of *Sputnik* in October 1957, Congress passed the **National Defense Education Act** (**NDEA**) of September 2, 1958, stating that "the national interest requires that the federal government give assistance to education for programs which are important to our defense." The act (1) authorized the expenditure of $300 million for loans to college students who were preparing to teach or who showed a superior capacity in science, mathematics, engineering, or modern foreign languages; (2) provided assistance to strengthening instruction in these curriculum areas; (3) provided for national defense fellowships; and (4) provided for the appropriating of $15 million annually to the states to identify and encourage able students. The act was extended in 1961, 1963, and 1964 and broadened to include additional curriculum areas, notably English and the social sciences.

Baby Boom

The post-World War II baby boom helped cause a marked increase in the population, which rose from 132 million in 1940 to 151 million in 1950. At the peak of the boom, the average number of children per family was 3.8. (It was below 2 in 1992) The population boom continued in the 1950s with the total nearing 180 million by 1960. The number was swelled, in part, by the admission of 2.5 million refugees from war-torn regions. Although the boom slowed down during the 1960s and came to a halt in 1972, the population of the United States continues to increase. It was 226 million in 1980 and 249 million in 1990.

Year	Population	Year	Population	Year	Population
1990	248,709	1920	106,021	1850	23,191
1980	226,545	1910	92,228	1840	17,069
1970	203,302	1900	76,212	1830	12,866
1960	179,323	1890	62,979	1820	9,638
1950	151,325	1880	50,198	1810	7,239
1940	132,164	1870	38,558	1800	5,308
1930	123,202	1860	31,443	1790	3,929

Figure 6.3 U.S. Population (in thousands)

Migration and Immigration

Americans on the Move

About 3 percent of the population moves annually from one state to another. Special circumstances affect migration. For example, the figure was much higher during the Great Depression of the 1930s when people lost their jobs, their farms, and their savings, and many pulled up roots and went West looking for a new life.

The war years of the 1940s were another era of large-scale migration. This time the move tended to be from South to North and from rural to urban areas where there were better economic opportunities in the new war industries. An estimated 15 million people, or more than 10 percent of the population, were involved in this migration. Another 15 million or more in the military were moved from place to place before going overseas.

The momentum of westward migration was accelerated after World War II. The population of Arizona was half a million in 1940. By 1990 it was more than 7 times as great at 3.6 million. California grew from 7 million to 29 million in the same period. By 1964, California had surpassed New York as the most populous state in the nation. In the 1960s the previous migration trend (chiefly blacks) from South to North was sharply reversed by the new trend (chiefly whites) from North to South. The population of Houston, now the fourth largest city in the United States, leaped from half a million to 1.75 million since 1950. Dallas, the eighth largest city, more than doubled in population (434,000 to over 1 million) in the same period, and San Antonio went from 408,000 to 900,000. The "sunbelt" states of the South and Southwest became the fastest growing section of the country.

Suburbanization

A major postwar trend was the exodus of the middle class from the cities to the suburbs. Long Island, New York, long famous for its potato farms, was suddenly transformed into a strip of bedroom communities reaching eastward 100 miles from Manhattan.

The ingenious builder, **William J. Levitt**, secured large tracts of land, laid out plans approved by local authorities, and rapidly constructed thousands of reasonably priced homes on small plots of land. **Levittowns** sprang up within commuting distance of New York and Philadelphia. Other builders soon adopted this pattern to meet the almost insatiable appetite of migrants from the cities. When President Eisenhower delivered his farewell address in January 1961, the population of the suburbs already exceeded that of the cities. Eighty-five percent of the homes built during the 1950s were located in the suburbs.

Declining Cities

As the relatively affluent middle class left the cities, the older or "inner" sections began to erode. Factories, shopping centers, educational facilities, research and cultural foundations moved to the suburbs. A declining tax base made it impossible for cities to keep their infrastructure (streets, transportation facilities, public utilities, schools, public buildings, subsurface pipelines) in good condition. A visit to the inner city became a discouraging experience with empty buildings, boarded-up store fronts, broken windows, graffiti, piled up garbage, and an air of despair. Cities all over the land were in decline.

New Immigration Patterns

The pattern of immigration (legal and illegal) has been changing. The new immigration stems from Mexico and other lands south of the border, from the Caribbean, and from Asia.

In an attempt to solve the problem of the vast number of immigrants who entered the United States illegally and had to remain "underground," the **Immigration and Naturalization Service**, as provided in the **Immigration and Control Act of 1986**, offered amnesty to those who could prove they had resided in the United States since January 1, 1982. By the deadline date of May 4, 1988, the Service had received applications for amnesty from 1.4 million illegal immigrants, 71 percent of whom had entered from Mexico and more than half of whom were living in California.

Immigration to the United States is limited to 270,000 annually, but additional provision is made under the **Refugee Act of 1980** for the admission of persons for humanitarian reasons who would be subjected to political persecution if they were returned to their country of last residence.

During the decade 1970–1980 a total of 1,588,200 immigrants were admitted from Asia, chiefly from the Philippines, Korea, and India. During the same period, nearly 2 million were admitted from countries south of the border—600,000 from Mexico, 271,000 from the West Indies, 265,000 from Cuba, and 170,000 from Colombia. In the 1980s the numbers increased. Some 2 million were admitted from Asia by the end of 1990, and about 3.5 million from Latin America.

Exercise Set 6.6

1. During the decade following World War II, the United States experienced
   A. a recession similar to the one that followed World War I
   B. an economic boom stimulated in part by a vast building expansion
   C. a slow but steady rise in income keeping pace with inflation
   D. rapid fluctuations in stock and bond prices

2. In the post-World War II period, transportation trends were characterized by
   A. expansion in the use of canals, lakes, and rivers for moving heavy freight
   B. a rapid development of the railroads
   C. a leveling off of international air traffic
   D. the extensive use of the family car

3. In the affluent American society of the post-World War II period
   A. unemployment was virtually abolished
   B. television had become a standard source of entertainment and information in 90 percent of homes
   C. labor strife was a relatively rare occurrence
   D. the national budget showed a surplus in most years

4. Which has *not* been responsible for major migrations within the United States?
   A. loss of economic security brought on by the Great Depression
   B. dislocations resulting from World War II
   C. attraction of the wide open spaces of the Great Plains
   D. a movement to the so-called Sun Belt

5. A major cause of the movement to the suburbs in the decades following World War II was
   A. the growth of the middle class during the post-World War II period
   B. greater economic opportunities found in the suburbs
   C. the availability of comfortable and efficient railroad transportation from suburban to urban centers
   D. opportunities for minorities to find jobs and homes in the suburbs

CHAPTER REVIEW QUESTIONS

1. In the case of *Brown* v. *Board of Education* (1954), the United States Supreme Court decided that
   A. busing children to overcome segregation is unconstitutional
   B. closing public schools to avoid integration is unconstitutional
   C. separate educational facilities are inherently unequal and unconstitutional
   D. the use of civil disobedience to achieve legal rights is constitutional

Regents Exam, August 1988

2. The development and operation of the Tennessee Valley Authority by the U.S. government is an example of
   A. a return to laissez-faire economics
   B. government's attempt to earn maximum profits in business
   C. experimentation with nuclear technology
   D. federal intervention to meet regional needs

   Regents Exam, August 1988

3. An experience of the majority of immigrants to the United States was that they
   A. settled in rural areas where cheap land was available
   B. frequently met resentment
   C. joined radical political parties to bring about economic reform
   D. were rapidly assimilated into the predominant lifestyle

4. Which is a major difference between immigration to the United States during the period 1860–1920 and immigration since 1970?
   A. immigrants today are not likely to experience discrimination
   B. there is a greater need for unskilled labor today
   C. the primary areas of origin have changed dramatically
   D. today's immigrants tend to be members of the middle class

   Regents Exam, January 1987

5. "A just society is one that treats fairly the most disadvantaged members of its society." Which government action would best illustrate this principle?
   A. creating "separate but equal" schools for minority groups
   B. shifting governmental funds from public schools to private schools
   C. establishing programs to train unskilled workers
   D. passing legislation making ownership of property a requirement for voting

   Regents Exam, January 1986

ESSAYS

1. Many aspects of U.S. society have been greatly affected by technological changes. Choose *three* of the aspects of U.S. society listed below. Explain how *each* one chosen has been affected by a specific technological development. [Use a different development for each aspect.] [5,5,5]

   Aspects of U.S. Society
   Urbanization
   Agriculture
   Cultural homogeneity
   Rights of the individual
   Politics
   Environment

   Regents Exam, June 1988

2. American foreign policy has often been influenced by events or developments abroad. Following are terms used to describe foreign policies adopted by the United States:

- the Truman doctrine
- massive retaliation
- the Eisenhower doctrine
- collective security
- joint action with the UN

Choose *three* of the above policies adopted by the United States. For *each* policy chosen describe the events or developments that led to the policy and discuss the application of the policy in a specific international crisis. [5,5,5]

Chapter 3

DECADE OF CHANGE (THE 1960s)

THE KENNEDY YEARS: THE NEW FRONTIER

> We stand today on the edge of a New Frontier—the frontier of the
> 1960s—a frontier of unknown opportunities and perils—a frontier of
> unfulfilled hopes and threats.
>> John F. Kennedy accepting nomination for President
>> at Democratic National Convention, 1960

The 1960 Election

The election of 1960 pitted **John F. Kennedy**, Senator from Massachusetts,
against **Richard M. Nixon**, Vice-President. In this election, television
played a key role for the first time. The two candidates faced the nation in
four one-hour televised debates. An estimated 70 million Americans viewed
each debate. Kennedy, at 43, was the youngest candidate ever elected to the
presidency. In addition, he was a Roman Catholic, and no one of his religion
had ever been President. Kennedy faced the religious question head-on when
he said, "I believe in an America where the separation of church and state is
absolute . . ."

The 1960 election was one of the closest in American history. Of the total
votes cast—68.8 million—Kennedy's margin over Nixon was 119,450 votes
or 3/10ths of 1 percent. In the electoral college, Kennedy received 303 votes
to 219 for Nixon.

Domestic Policies and Programs

> Let the word go forth from this time and place, to friend and foe alike,
> that the torch has been passed to a new generation—born in this cen-
> tury, tempered by war, disciplined by a hard and bitter peace, proud
> of our ancient heritage, and unwilling to witness or permit the slow
> undoing of those human rights to which this nation has always been
> committed . . .

> And so, my fellow Americans—ask not what your country can do for
> you—ask what you can do for your country.
>> John F. Kennedy, Inaugural Address, January 20, 1961

Domestic Policy Initiatives Stalled in Congress

On taking office, Kennedy, despite Democratic majorities in both houses of Congress, faced a coalition of Republican and Conservative Southern Democrats steadfastly opposed to social reform. Congress turned down his proposals for support of mass transportation, for health care legislation, for the establishment of a Department of Housing and Urban Affairs, and, most vexing of all, for federal aid to elementary and secondary education.

Domestic Gains

Despite these reversals, Kennedy did secure from Congress approval of a number of social programs—the minimum wage was raised, Social Security benefits were extended, unemployment compensation was increased, additional funds were appropriated for housing, mental health, and public works, and a Federal Water Pollution Control Act was approved. The President responded to an increase in steel prices by calling the steel magnates to his office and forcing them to rescind the price increases. He initiated a multi-billion-dollar program to put a man on the moon, which eventually bore fruit in July 1969.

Kennedy and Civil Rights

Appointments

Kennedy appointed members of the black community to key positions in the federal government. His appointment of **Thurgood Marshall** to the U.S. Circuit Court of Appeals later led to the elevation of Marshall to the Supreme Court by President Johnson in 1967. Marshall had been general counsel of the National Association for the Advancement of Colored People (NAACP) when he argued the case of *Brown* v. *Board of Education of Topeka* before the Supreme Court in 1954. Kennedy also appointed a number of African Americans to the federal bench as U.S. district court judges.

In the executive branch, he tried to establish a Cabinet post Department of Urban Affairs, but the bill was defeated in Congress by a conservative bipartisan coalition. The cabinet post would have gone to **Robert Weaver** who was appointed instead to head the **Housing and Home Finance Agency**. **Carl Rowan** was appointed U.S. Ambassador to Finland.

Attorney General Robert F. Kennedy

President Kennedy appointed his brother, Robert F. Kennedy, to the sensitive post of Attorney General in a time of turmoil over civil rights and other constitutional issues. "Bobby" Kennedy proved to be a firm advocate of civil rights. While he held office, the **Justice Department** brought over 50 suits to secure voting rights for African Americans in states where they were virtually disenfranchised. The suits were brought under the Civil Rights Act of

1960, which empowered the federal courts to appoint referees to investigate claims that citizens' voting rights had been violated by state voting regulations. The act authorized federal courts to levy heavy penalties on anyone who infringed on the civil rights of others.

James H. Meredith

In the fall of 1962 **James H. Meredith**, an African American Air Force veteran of the Korean War, attempted to enroll in the all-white University of Mississippi in his home state. The governor of the state took charge of the university and ordered that Meredith, who had met all necessary qualifications, be denied admission because he was black. When federal marshals escorted him to the university, a white mob touched off violence in which two people were killed and many were seriously injured. President Kennedy dispatched 5,000 federal troops to Mississippi and Meredith was registered in the University.

Medgar Evers

On June 11, 1963, President Kennedy, who was trying to get Congress to pass stronger civil rights legislation, delivered a stirring appeal to the nation on television. He asked his audience, "Are we to say . . . that this is a land of the free except for Negroes . . . that we have no class or caste system, no ghettos, no master race, except with respect to Negroes?"

That night, **Medgar Evers**, head of the NAACP of Mississippi, and a war veteran, was murdered outside his home by a white racist. Despite President Kennedy's best efforts, stronger civil rights legislation had to wait until the administration of Lyndon Johnson.

Martin Luther King, Jr.

> I have a dream that one day on the red hills of Georgia the sons of former slaves and the sons of former slave owners will be able to sit down together at the table of brotherhood. . .
>
> I have a dream that my four little children will one day live in a nation where they will not be judged by the color of their skin but by the content of their character.
>
> Martin Luther King, Jr.
> at the Lincoln Memorial on the occasion of the Civil Rights March
> in Washington, D.C., August 28, 1963.

Rise to Leadership

Martin Luther King, Jr. was born in Atlanta, Georgia, January 15, 1929, and died in Memphis, Tennessee, April 4, 1968, the victim of an assassin's bullet. Like his father and his maternal grandfather, he was a Baptist minister in Alabama.

King's rise to leadership in the civil rights movement began when he led the bus boycott in Montgomery, which began on December 1, 1955. Although he was arrested in January 1956 and his parsonage was bombed, his leadership succeeded in integrating Mongomery's buses. In February 1957, he became president of a new antisegregation organization known as the **Southern Christian Leadership Conference (SCLC)**. The organization sponsored nonviolent sit-ins at lunch counters and other nonviolent protests.

Dr. Martin Luther King, Jr. (1929–1968) led the civil rights movement in the 1950s and 1960s.

Birmingham Protest

Like Gandhi in India, King preached that racism and social injustice should be fought by disobedience but not by violence. King urged **civil disobedience** of Birmingham's segregation laws as a means of bringing injustice out where all could see it. He and his followers persisted despite violence against them instigated by Birmingham's police commissioner. King was arrested and put in solitary confinement in the jail, where he wrote his famous "Letter from a Birmingham Jail," giving the rationale for nonviolent disobedience to unjust laws. He treated the subject more fully in his 1964 book, *Why We Can't Wait*.

March on Washington and Later Activities

In 1963 King led the famous march on Washington where, on August 28, he delivered the classic "I have a dream" speech. He continued to campaign for civil rights and for equal treatment of African Americans. In 1964 he was awarded the **Nobel Prize** for peace. In 1966 he led a campaign for slum clearance in Chicago. In 1968 he was in Memphis helping to coordinate a strike of sanitation workers. He was making plans to lead a Poor People's Crusade on Washington and had taken a public stand against the Vietnam War. King's life was cut short in Memphis on April 4, 1968, by a bullet that struck him in the head as he stood on the balcony of his hotel room. He received recognition as one of America's great leaders when his birthday was designated a national holiday by an act of Congress in 1983.

Exercise Set 6.7

1. Which would be most in accord with the ideals of Dr. Martin Luther King, Jr.?
   A. underpaid workers sabotage the machinery at their factory
   B. a minority worker assaults a bigot
   C. an 18-year-old pacifist accepts a jail term rather than register for military service
   D. radical leaders advocate black separatism if their group's demands are not met

   Regents Exam, June 1988

2. "Under a government which imprisons any unjustly, the true place for a just man is also a prison."

   Henry David Thoreau

   Which idea does this quotation most strongly support?
   A. social control
   B. conformity
   C. suspension of civil liberties
   D. civil disobedience

   Regents Exam, June 1988

3. President Kennedy's inability to secure passage of many of his legislative recommendations was due to
   A. a combination of Republicans and Conservative Democrats
   B. a lack of legislative experience on the part of the President
   C. distractions of foreign problems
   D. a Republican majority in one or both houses of Congress

4. During the Kennedy administration up to 1963, tactics employed to end discrimination included all of the following EXCEPT
   A. "sit-ins" at public lunch counters
   B. violence by African Americans
   C. use of federal troops
   D. "freedom riders" on public transportation

ACTION IN FOREIGN POLICIES

Latin American Policies

Review of Earlier Policies

> The American continents are henceforth not to be considered as sub-
> jects for future colonization by any European Power. We should con-
> sider any attempt on their part to extend their system to any portion of
> this Hemisphere as dangerous to our peace and safety.
>
> President James Monroe, 1823

The principles established by the Monroe Doctrine became basic to American foreign policy and were followed throughout the 1800s. Concern in the
United States over the ruthless conduct of the Spanish government against
internal Cuban opposition came to a head in 1898 when the U.S. battleship
Maine was blown up in Havana harbor and the United States declared war
against Spain.

The years between the Spanish-American War and the New Deal era
beginning in 1933 have been described as a period of "**dollar diplomacy**" in
American foreign policy. American business invested heavily in economic
exploitation of resources in Latin America. When the safety of these investments was threatened by local violence, the American response generally
was to send in detachments of U.S. Marines "to restore order" and protect
the investments. Under this policy during the 35-year period after the
Spanish-American War, troops were deployed at various times in Cuba,
Haiti, the Dominican Republic, Nicaragua, Honduras, and Panama.

In 1933 President Franklin D. Roosevelt changed American policy toward
Latin America and declared, "I would dedicate this nation to the policy of the
good neighbor." With the outbreak of World War II, the republics of the
Western Hemisphere held an Inter-American Conference in 1939 and issued
the Declaration of Panama, warning the combatants to keep armed vessels
clear of a 300-mile zone surrounding the United States and Latin America.

The Alliance for Progress

On March 31, 1961, Kennedy announced a new inter-American program
designed to help the countries of Latin America raise their standard of living
and establish strong democratic governments. He spoke of "a vast new ten-
year plan for the Americas" and "called to all people of the hemisphere to
join in a new Alliance for Progress to satisfy the basic needs of the American people for homes, work and land, health and schools."

This 10-year plan envisaged the expenditure of $20 billion by the United
States, of which about $1 billion was spent during the first year. But the

Alliance failed to materialize. The economic and political power structure of the Latin American countries was opposed to extending economic advantages and political control to the emergent middle class. There was also the cynical belief that Kennedy's Alliance was more concerned with preventing the spread of communism than with raising living standards. Support for the program faltered in Latin America. Without this support it was doomed.

The Bay of Pigs

Shortly after President Kennedy took office, he was informed that under the previous (Eisenhower) administration the **Central Intelligence Agency (CIA)** had been training, arming, and financing thousands of Cuban refugees in Florida and Guatemala for an attempt to overthrow the anti-American Castro dictatorship in Cuba. Kennedy met with his advisers and reluctantly agreed to let the plans go forward on condition that no U.S. military or naval forces be used in the invasion of Cuba. He was assured that the anti-Castro Cubans could accomplish the task on their own, with strong internal support.

On the morning of April 17, 1961, about 1,400 Cuban exiles who had embarked from Florida and Guatemala landed at the **Bay of Pigs** on the southern coast of Cuba. They were met by a force of some 14,000 well-armed defenders who, in three days of fighting, killed or captured almost all of the anti-Castro invaders. With the invasion a total failure, President Kennedy admitted that it was a mistake and accepted full responsibility for the outcome.

The Cuban Missile Crisis

Following the Bay of Pigs fiasco, **Fidel Castro** invited the Soviets to install intermediate-range ballistic missiles on Cuban soil. Installation of these missiles was under way when they were discovered by a **U-2 plane** taking photographs from high altitude on October 14, 1962. Careful analysis of the photographs revealed that launching pads were being installed and that nuclear warheads would soon be capable of striking as far north as Hudson Bay in Canada and as far south as Lima, Peru.

Kennedy convened top advisers from the Defense and State Departments, the CIA, the Cabinet, and his personal staff. They met daily and considered all possible responses for turning back this grave threat. Two possible courses emerged—a lightning air strike to destroy the installations, or a **blockade** to prevent offensive weapons from being delivered to Cuba. The latter course was agreed upon. The gravity of the crisis was clearly understood. "The worst course of all," said the President, "would be for us to do nothing." In a television address to the nation on Monday evening, October 22, he explained the threat contained in the installations and said, "A strict quarantine of all offensive military equipment under shipment to Cuba is being initiated . . . Let no one doubt that this is a difficult and dangerous effort on which we have set out."

Meanwhile, contact with the Soviets was maintained and every effort was made to enable Khrushchev to retreat gracefully without loss of face. Kennedy accepted Khrushchev's offer to remove the missiles in return for his public promise not to invade Cuba. Kennedy also agreed privately to withdraw American missiles from Turkey. Soviet ships bound for Cuba turned back and the tension was relieved. The missiles were subsequently removed and the launching pads dismantled under the eyes of UN observers. The Cuban missile crisis was resolved.

The Vienna Summit (Berlin Wall)

On January 6, 1961, two weeks before Kennedy's inauguration, Soviet Premier Nikita Khrushchev made a threatening speech about the city of Berlin. Located in East Germany, the city was divided into East Berlin, the Communist part, and West Berlin, the free part. Khrushchev threatened to end free access by the Western nations to West Berlin.

Khrushchev invited Kennedy to meet with him for a friendly talk in Vienna in June 1961. Khrushchev again threatened to close off West Berlin. Kennedy responded that our national security was involved in Berlin and that our abandoning it would mean abandoning our commitments not only to our allies but to all of Europe. Afterward, Kennedy made plans to defend Berlin, and he increased the military budget and the size of the armed forces.

In mid-August the Communists sealed off West Berlin by erecting the **Berlin Wall**, a wall of concrete and barbed wire between the two sectors. But access to Berlin from the West was not cut off and the crisis subsided.

In June 1963 Kennedy visited West Berlin and made the memorable statement: "All free men, wherever they may live, are citizens of Berlin, and therefore, as a free man, I take pride in the words 'Ich bin ein Berliner.' "

In November 1989 tremendous changes took place in East Germany as a result of demands and demonstrations by the people. The Berlin Wall was opened and East Germans were allowed to travel freely to West Berlin and all of West Germany for the first time in 28 years. In 1990 East and West Germany were reunited to form one nation.

The Peace Corps

In 1961, President Kennedy recommended to Congress the establishment of a permanent **Peace Corps**, which he had set in motion on an experimental basis by executive order. He described the Peace Corps as "an organization which will recruit and train American volunteers, sending them abroad to work with the people of other nations." Peace Corps members could help the people in the developing nations with their day-to-day problems. They could teach English in primary and secondary schools, help establish and operate public health and sanitation projects, aid in village development, and increase agricultural productivity by assisting local farmers to use modern implements and techniques.

Membership in the Peace Corps was to be open to men and women of all ages. Length of service was to be generally from 2 to 3 years. There was to be no salary, only an allowance sufficient to meet basic needs and maintain health. Service in the Peace Corps would not exempt volunteers from selective service in the military.

The Peace Corps was approved by Congress on September 22, 1961 with an appropriation of $40 million. **Sargent Shriver**, who had proposed the idea, was appointed first director of the Peace Corps. At home, the Peace Corps was received with enthusiasm, and abroad, in the emerging nations of Asia, Africa and Latin America, it helped to replace the negative image of the "Ugly American" with one of American idealism and altruism.

The Race to the Moon

In April 1961 the Soviet astronaut **Yuri Gagarin** became the first human to orbit the earth. A month later, President Kennedy declared, "This nation should commit itself to achieving the goal, before this decade is out, of landing a man on the moon and returning him safely to earth." There was an immediate enthusiastic response from the nation and from Congress, and a $25 billion program was launched.

The Nuclear Test Ban Treaty

In August 1961, after the Berlin Wall was built, Khrushchev announced that the Soviet Union would again begin nuclear testing, in violation of a 1958 agreement between the United States, Great Britain, and the Soviet Union to suspend tests for three years. The Soviets began tests in the fall of 1961 and after they refused a **test ban treaty**, the United States agreed to set up a "**hot line**" telephone between Washington and Moscow, to be installed August 30, 1963. President Kennedy said the purpose of the line was "to avoid on each side the dangerous delays, misunderstandings, and misreadings of the other's actions which might occur at a time of crisis."

Finally, three-power talks between the United States, Great Britain, and the Soviet Union began in Moscow in July 1963. A treaty banning nuclear tests in the atmosphere, in outer space, and under water (but not under ground) was concluded on July 25. It was signed by the three powers in Moscow on August 5 and was ratified by the U.S. Senate on September 24. Two weeks later, President Kennedy approved the sale of $250 million of wheat to the Soviet Union. The nuclear test ban treaty was soon signed by more than 100 nations.

Assassination in Dallas

In November 1963 President Kennedy traveled to Texas to help heal a rift in the state Democratic party. On Friday, November 22, 1963, during the visit, President Kennedy was riding in an open car, sitting next to Governor **John B. Connally** of Texas, in a motorcade along the main street of Dallas, Texas. Suddenly he was hit in the head and neck by two rifle bullets. Governor Connally was wounded but recovered. The President died within an hour. The shots that killed the President were fired from a building adjoining the route of the motorcade. The suspected killer, **Lee Harvey Oswald**, was apprehended an hour and a half later.

Lyndon B. Johnson Sworn in as President

Vice-President Lyndon B. Johnson, who was also riding in the motorcade, was unharmed. He was sworn in as President on a plane returning that day to Washington. The day after the assassination, Oswald was being moved by police from the city jail to a more secure county jail when he was shot and killed by **Jack Ruby**, a Dallas night club operator.

The Warren Commission

President Johnson appointed a special commission to investigate the assassination of President Kennedy. The Commission was headed by **Earl Warren**, Chief Justice of the United States, and included leaders in the Senate and House of Representatives. The Commission conducted an exhaustive inquiry and presented its report on September 24, 1964. The report concluded that there was no conspiracy to assassinate the President and that "the shots which killed President Kennedy and wounded Governor Connally were fired by Lee Harvey Oswald." Warren asserted that "no one has produced any facts that are contrary to the commission's conclusion." But allegations continue to be made that the evidence is inconclusive and that there may have been a conspiracy to assassinate the President.

Exercise Set 6.8

1. The most serious crisis in foreign affairs under Kennedy before the midterm elections in 1962 was
   A. in Berlin
   B. in Cuba
   C. in Vietnam
   D. with Britain

2. In space exploration the idea of placing astronauts on the moon and bringing them back safely to earth was
   A. first undertaken by the Soviet Union
   B. at first rejected by the National Aeronautic and Space Administration
   C. considered too costly by Congress
   D. advocated by President Kennedy within a few months after his inauguration

3. Kennedy's foreign policy was effective in all of the following EXCEPT
   A. the Bay of Pigs affair
   B. controversy over Berlin
   C. the Cuban missile crisis
   D. Peace Corps operations

4. The Warren Commission concluded that the assassination of President Kennedy
   A. had been planned for 1,000 days
   B. was planned and executed by conspirators
   C. was accomplished by Lee Harvey Oswald
   D. had no precedent in American history

5. The nuclear test ban treaty of 1963 was
   A. rejected by the U.S. Senate
   B. negotiated by representatives of more than 100 nations
   C. designed to prohibit testing of nuclear weapons in the atmosphere, in outer space, and under water, but not underground
   D. approved at a time when the United States and the Soviet Union were engaged in frantic testing of nuclear weapons

MOVEMENT FOR THE RIGHTS OF THE DISABLED

> I walked down to the basement where the lunatics were housed in cells about ten feet square, made as strong as a prison . . . A door opens into each of them; in each door is a hole, large enough to give them food, etc., which is closed with a little door secured with strong bolts."
>
> Description by a late 18th-century visitor to the section of a hospital in Pennsylvania, where mentally ill and mentally handicapped people resided.

Background

Historic Attitude Toward the Disabled

Until the 19th century, the mentally ill were frequently confined in prisons along with common criminals. The views of the prominent 18th-century Philadelphia physician **Benjamin Rush**, who held that insanity was an illness, not a scourge of the devil, did not gain acceptance during his lifetime.

Prior to the 19th century it was generally believed that mentally handicapped children could not be taught. The idea that this constituted discrimination developed very slowly. Public acceptance of responsibility for the education of the handicapped came first in the area of deafness and blindness, then in mental retardation. As late as the year 1919, in the case of *Beattie* v. *State Board of Education*, the Wisconsin Supreme Court ruled that a child with cerebral palsy could be denied a public school education because of his depressing and nauseating effect on the teacher and school children and . . . [because] he required an undue portion of the teacher's time."

Emergence of Humanitarian View

Thomas H. Gallaudet founded the first school for the deaf (now the American School for the Deaf) at Hartford, Connecticut, in 1817. **Louis Braille** established the first school for the blind (now the Perkins School) in 1829 at Watertown, Massachusetts.

Dorothea Dix, who in 1841 taught a Sunday school class for women convicts in an East Cambridge prison, discovered that the inmates included mentally ill women living in unheated, dirty rooms. Dix began a crusade that resulted in the improvement of the treatment of mentally ill people in 32 states. In 1848 she presented to Congress testimony relating to mistreatment of the mentally ill, based on extensive research. She requested an appropriation, in the form of a land trust, to help mentally ill people and those with serious auditory or visual impairment. Congress passed the legislation in

415

1854, but it was vetoed by President Franklin Pierce. However, the work of Dorothea Dix had important results in many of the states.

The nation's first residential school for the mentally handicapped opened in Boston in 1859. It was named the Massachusetts School for Idiotic and Feebleminded Youth. The first public day school classes for mentally handicapped pupils were started at Providence, Rhode Island, in 1896.

In 1865 President Lincoln signed legislation establishing **Gallaudet College** in Washington, D.C., for the education of the hearing impaired, the only college of its kind in the world.

Twentieth-Century Organizations and Educational Programs

In 1922 the **Council of Exceptional Children** was founded, and nine years later, the U.S. Office of Education added a section on exceptional children. This became the **Bureau for the Education of the Handicapped** in the U.S. Office of Education in 1966. The **National Association for Retarded Citizens** was organized in 1950.

Progress During the Kennedy Administration

> We as a nation have long neglected the mentally ill and the mentally retarded. This neglect must end, if our nation is to live up to its own standards of compassion and dignity and achieve the maximum use of its manpower.
>
> John F. Kennedy, Address to Congress, February 5, 1963

President Kennedy's humanitarian interest in the mentally handicapped—one of his sisters was mentally handicapped—was reflected in substantial advances during the 1960s. On October 11, 1961, he appointed a 26-member **Presidential Panel on Mental Retardation**. Members of the Panel visited Scandinavia to observe advances in educating the handicapped in the mainstream along with the nonhandicapped.

The panel issued a final report in 1962 that included a comprehensive list of recommendations for research, preventive health measures, strengthened educational programs for the mentally handicapped and for public awareness, improved clinical and social services, and a new legal approach to the mentally handicapped.

Based on the panel's report, President Kennedy made specific demands on Congress that included: "to retain in and return to the community the mentally ill and mentally retarded, and there to restore and revitalize their lives through better health programs and strengthened educational and rehabilitation services . . ." The thrust of the President's request, based on the panel's report, was concern for the special needs of the mentally handicapped: physical and mental health; shelter and protection; mental and social development; recreation; work and economic security.

Litigation and Legislation

Important Law Cases

Beginning in the 1960s and 1970s, parents and advocates began to use the legal system to bring about changes in the treatment of the mentally handicapped.

- **Buck v. Bell** *(1927)*. In the early years of the 20th century, **sterilization** of the mentally handicapped had become common practice sanctioned by law in many of the states. The question of the constitutionality of these state laws reached the U.S. Supreme Court in 1926 in the case of *Buck* v. *Bell*, on appeal from the decision of the high court of Virginia sustaining the state sterilization statute. The Supreme Court upheld the right of Virginia to sterilize Carrie Buck, an 18-year-old mentally handicapped woman who was the daughter of a mentally handicapped woman and the mother of a mentally handicapped child. The language of the Court is indicative of the prevailing attitude toward the mentally handicapped at that time. In his opinion, Justice Oliver Wendell Holmes wrote:

> It is better for all the world, if instead of waiting to execute degenerate offspring for crime or to let them starve from their imbecility, society can prevent those who are manifestly unfit from continuing their kind.
>
> The principle that sustains compulsory vaccination is broad enough to cover cutting the Fallopian tubes. Three generations of imbeciles are enough.

- **PARC v. Pennsylvania** *(1971)*. In the leading case of *Pennsylvania Association for Retarded Citizens (PARC)* v. *Commonwealth of Pennsylvania,* a federal circuit court in Pennsylvania established the right of all children, no matter how deviant from the norm, to an education. The right was broadly described to include all aspects of individual growth and development. The Court also sustained the parents' right to participate in decisions affecting the welfare of their children. The decision of the Court had wide repercussions in the education of mentally handicapped children, including a recognition that "the least restrictive alternative" meant at least partial if not total mainstreaming.

- **Mills v. Board of Education** *(1972)*. In this case a federal court in Washington, D.C., confirmed and extended the rights proclaimed in the PARC case. The ruling laid down the principle that all children, regardless of the severity of their handicap, had the right to public education. All public schools are required to provide alternative educational programs. Lack of resources does not exempt school districts from providing appropriate education to the disabled.

- **Goss v. Lopez** *(1975)*. In this case the Supreme Court held, that school authorities acted at their peril in suspending or excluding students from public schools. Due process protected children, no matter what their disabilities, from being denied an education unless the most careful legal procedures were meticulously applied.

Legislation

In the 1970s, laws began to be passed to eliminate discrimination against the handicapped especially in the area of education.

• *Rehabilitation Act of 1973.* This act constituted an expression by Congress of a national commitment to eliminate discrimination against the disabled. The law mandated that educational services for children with disabilities be equal in every possible way to those provided for children who are not disabled. A building that does not have access for disabled children is not an acceptable legal excuse for failing to provide equal educational services. The act also guarantees equal rights to the handicapped in employment and in educational institutions that are funded by the Federal government.

• *The Education for All Handicapped Children Act of 1975.* This landmark federal legislation pertained to the rights of handicapped children and was passed largely through the lobbying efforts of parent groups. The law required states to make available to all handicapped children an appropriate free public education from ages five to eighteen; also to children ages three to five and eighteen to twenty-one unless specifically enjoined by state law or court order.

The law requires the school district to make a comprehensive evaluation of the abilities of the disabled child to guard against discrimination based on the disabling conditions or on cultural or racial factors. An **Individualized Education Program** (**IEP**) must be developed for children who are disabled. The requirement that the handicapped child be educated in the "least restrictive environment" is based on the premise that it is to the advantage of the handicapped child to educate the child, as far as sound education practice warrants, in the regular educational program of the school. Under the law, opportunities for parental participation in arrangements for, or alternatives in, the handicapped child's educational program must be provided.

• *State Implementation (New York).* Since education is primarily a state function, the implementation of federal legislative mandates becomes a responsibility of the state's educational program.

An example of this implementation may be found in the regulations pertaining to the education of handicapped children promulgated July 1, 1982, by the New York State Commissioner of Education. The detailed regulations are contained in a printed 50-page booklet, and include the following: (1) each local Board of Education is required to locate and identify all children with handicapping conditions who reside in the district and who are entitled to attend public school during the next school year; (2) specific procedures are described for "referral, evaluation, individualized education programs

418

(IEP), development, placement, and review; and (3) detailed legal provisions are stated for meeting the requirements of "procedural due process."

Dependence to Independence

The history of the treatment of the handicapped in the United States shows a slow progression from total dependence toward total independence. The battle has been fought in the courts, the legislatures, public meetings, voluntary organizations, the media, and sometimes by militant direct action. Foremost in the progression has been the part played by public education and by research in the behavioral sciences. The 1988 *Bulletin of the Association for Supervision and Curriculum Development* (*ASCD*) reports: "According to the U.S. Department of Education the number of children receiving special education through federal programs rose from 3.7 million in 1976–77 to 4.4 million in 1986–87, a 19 percent increase."

A 1987 survey by the U.S. Bureau of the Census disclosed that 37 million Americans, close to one sixth of the population, have a disability. Of these, 13.5 million could not perform a basic physical activity, or needed help to do so. Some 12.8 million had trouble seeing words in newsprint even with glasses, and 7.7 million had trouble hearing a normal conversation.

The U.S. Department of Education's "Tenth Annual Report [1988] to Congress on the Implementation of the Education of the Handicapped Act" indicates that 41 percent of special education services take place in a "resource room." Most significant is the disclosure that 26 percent—more than one fourth—of the handicapped child's school time is spent in the regular classroom (see chart).

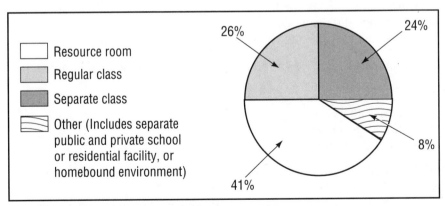

(Note: Figures do not total 100% because of rounding)

Source: "Tenth Annual Report to Congress on the Implementation of the Education of the Handicapped Act," U.S. Department of Education, 1988.

Figure 6.4 Where Students Receive Special Education Services

Special Provisions for the Handicapped

The 1973 **Rehabilitation Act** declared it to be public policy to end discrimination against the physically handicapped in any program or facility supported by federal funds. Regulations implementing this act required public sidewalks to accommodate wheelchairs and public buildings to be accessible to the handicapped. Special toilets were to be provided; new buses were to be equipped with special boarding devices; signs had to be installed in elevators to enable the blind to read the raised letters; and signs had to be provided for the deaf as a supplement to sirens or warning signals for the hearing. Society has come a long way, if not yet all the way, to make available to the physically, emotionally, socially, and mentally handicapped the educational, economic, social, and cultural opportunities enjoyed by the nonhandicapped majority.

Exercise Set 6.9

1. The 19th century treatment of mentally ill and mentally handicapped people was based on all of the following EXCEPT
   A. the feeling that the mentally handicapped were not educable
   B. the idea that the handicap was the work of the devil
   C. the theory that society was responsible for protecting the handicapped for their own welfare
   D. the theory that society must be protected from the potentially dangerous acts of the mentally ill or mentally handicapped

2. Public acceptance of responsibility for education of handicapped people came first in the area of the
   A. physically handicapped
   B. mentally handicapped
   C. emotionally disturbed
   D. socially maladjusted

3. Dorothea Dix helped introduce reforms in treatment of handicapped people in the
   A. early 19th century
   B. mid-19th century
   C. late 19th century
   D. early 20th century

4. The rights of handicapped people were upheld or advanced by each of the following EXCEPT
   A. federal legislation signed by President Pierce at the request of Dorothea Dix
   B. the decision in *Pennsylvania Association for Retarded Children (PARC)* v. *Commonwealth of Pennsylvania*
   C. the Rehabilitation Act of 1973
   D. the Supreme Court decision in *Goss* v. *Lopez*

JOHNSON AND THE GREAT SOCIETY

> This nation, this generation, in this hour has man's first chance to
> build a Great Society, a place where the meaning of man's life
> matches the marvels of man's labors.
>
> Lyndon B. Johnson,
> Democratic National Convention, August 1964

Expanding the Kennedy Social Programs

Soon after he was sworn in as President on the day of Kennedy's assassination, November 22, 1963, **Lyndon B. Johnson** moved to implement and expand Kennedy's program of domestic civil rights and social legislation.

The War on Poverty

President Johnson prevailed on Congress to give him the key measure in his war on poverty, the billion-dollar **Economic Opportunity Act** (1964) creating the **Office of Economic Opportunity (OEO)**. The act set up job- and work-training programs and provided for loans to college students and to small businesses for hiring the unemployed. The appropriation was doubled the following year with appropriations for rehabilitation in poverty-stricken Appalachia and for granting aid directly to needy elementary and secondary school students in public and nonpublic schools.

One agency in OEO was called **Volunteers in Service to America (VISTA)**. It was organized in 1965 as the domestic counterpart to the Peace Corps. Volunteers receive training in working with children, the elderly, Native Americans, agricultural migrant workers, and the mentally ill. VISTA operated chiefly in pockets of poverty in rural areas.

Other programs of OEO included **Operation Head Start** for aid to preschoolers from underprivileged homes, a **Job Corps** for school dropouts, a **Neighborhood Youth Corps** for unemployed teenagers, and a **Community Action Program** whereby inner-city neighborhoods get financial aid for planning and executing programs of self-help.

Congress approved a rent-supplement program for poor families and established a **Department of Housing and Urban Development (HUD)** with Cabinet rank. The appointment of **Robert C. Weaver** as head of HUD made him the first Cabinet member from the African American Community.

Medicare and Medicaid

The **Health Insurance Act for the Aged**, passed in 1965 as an amendment to the Social Security Act, provided federally funded hospital insurance for people over 65. It also included limited nursing home care and home visits by nurses and health care workers other than physicians. Those covered by

Social Security could also secure medical care other than hospitalization by paying a small monthly fee. These fees were sharply increased during the 1980s. The plan called **Medicare** (for seniors) was accompanied by a plan called **Medicaid** for the needy of all ages. It required the states to administer financially aided programs of care for people below the poverty level as well as for needy families with dependent children, the blind, and the totally disabled.

Aid to Education

In a speech at the University of Michigan in May 1964, President Johnson declared, "The Great Society is a place where every child can find knowledge to enrich his mind and to enlarge his talents." This precept was advanced by the **Elementary and Secondary Education Act of 1965**. The act provided federal aid in the amount of $1.3 billion directly to pupils in school districts. To promote school integration as required by law the U.S. Office of Education now required proof as a condition of federal aid, that beginning with the 1966–1967 school year, desegregation had been undertaken in good faith.

The Moon Landing

Kennedy's prophetic vision to land a man on the moon was realized on July 20, 1969, when **Neil Armstrong** and Colonel **Edwin E. Aldrin, Jr.**, walked on the moon and returned safely to earth. Their spaceship, *Apollo 11*, carried a four-legged landing module, the *Eagle*, which placed them on the moon. When Armstrong descended from the *Eagle* and set foot on the moon he said, that's one small step for man, one giant leap for mankind." Colonel Aldrin joined him later while **Michael Collins**, the third astronaut on the mission, guided *Apollo 11's* command module, the *Columbia*, in orbit around the moon. The world watched this historic event on television.

A year later a Soviet spaceship left a robot on the moon to perform some of the same operations the astronauts had done.

The *Apollo 11* voyage was followed by six additional moon landings during which ten other American astronauts walked on the moon. The program was phased out after the last landing in December 1972.

The Struggle for Equal Rights

A Review: From Slavery to Equality Under the Law

A contingent of 20 blacks arrived in Jamestown, Virginia, in 1619, before the *Mayflower* landed at Plymouth Rock. These 20 Africans came as indentured servants, as did many thousands of whites prior to the American Revolution. However, by the 1640s, blacks were enslaved to work in the sugar, rice, and tobacco fields on Southern plantations as well as to serve as domestics in the homes of their masters. With the invention of the cotton gin in 1793, cotton became the basis of the economy of the South and slavery spread. Since slaves were considered property, they had no legal rights and could be bought and sold according to the owner's whim.

Meanwhile the evils inherent in slavery caused thoughtful people in both the North and the South to seek its end. Jefferson, contemplating slavery in 1784, wrote: "I tremble for my country when I reflect that God is just." By the mid 1800s, many Northerners came to believe that slavery was morally wrong. In the North, **William Lloyd Garrison**, a leading abolitionist, began publishing *The Liberator* in 1831. Anti-slavery societies with nearly a quarter of a million members sprang up in the North and the "**underground railroad**" was established to help slaves escape to freedom.

At the outbreak of the Civil War, there were more than 4 million slaves in the United States. In the free states of the North there were close to half a million free blacks, many of them former slaves or descendants of slaves. With emancipation and the passage of the Fourteenth Amendment it was thought that equality for blacks would be secure. But this was not to be the case. Blacks were disenfranchised through the use of the poll tax, Grandfather clause, and intimidation. **Jim Crow laws** were passed in the South to separate the races. In *Plessy* v. *Ferguson* (1896) the Supreme Court's doctrine of "**separate but equal**" institutionalized the inferior status of the African Americans in American society. The reversal of this doctrine in *Brown* v. *Board of Education* (1954) opened the way for equality. But its complete attainment remained elusive.

Black Protest, Pride, and Power

With the passage of Jim Crow laws and disenfranchisement in the late 1800s, African Americans sought various means to gain equality. Over the years, they formed various organizations to struggle for their civil rights.

• *The National Association for the Advancement of Colored People (NAACP).* This organization was founded in 1909 by a group of black and white leaders, including **W.E.B. Du Bois**, the black scholar and activist, **Jane Addams**, a white social reformer, and **John Dewey**, a white philosopher-educator. The NAACP provided leadership in the early 20th century in the struggle for civil rights and voting rights for African Americans. One of its main methods was to bring cases to court. In the 1938 Supreme Court case of *Missouri ex rel. Gaines* v. *Canada,* the NAACP helped the black plaintiff Gaines win the right to attend the all-white law school of the University of Missouri. It was the NAACP chief counsel, **Thurgood Marshall**, who successfully argued for school integration in *Brown* v. *Board of Education* (1954). Under the leadership of **Roy Wilkins**, who joined the national staff of NAACP in 1931 and rose to the top position in 1955, the membership grew to over 400,000 by 1977. Its methods also became more militant, supplementing education, lobbying, and court action with demonstrations, sit-ins, and boycotts.

• *The National Urban League.* This organization was founded in 1910 and its efforts first concentrated on helping blacks who had migrated from the South to Northern cities find homes, jobs, and training programs in their new environment.

• *Congress of Racial Equality (CORE).* Another civil rights organization, the **Congress of Racial Equality**, founded in 1942, was committed to nonviolent, direct action to end racial discrimination. Many of its members were recruited on college campuses. Sit-ins and freedom rides were adopted as means to dramatize demands of equal treatment for blacks.

• *Southern Christian Leadership Conference (SCLC).* In 1957, **Dr. Martin Luther King, Jr.** organized the **Southern Christian Leadership Conference** (**SCLC**). This organization provided the leadership for the 1963 **March on Washington**, where a quarter of a million people heard Dr. King deliver the memorable "I have a dream" speech at the Lincoln Memorial. The SCLC worked primarily in the South to attain "full citizenship rights, equality, and the integration of the Negro in all aspects of American life. " The Reverend **Ralph David Abernathy** became the leader of SCLC after the assassination of Dr. King in 1968.

• *Student Nonviolent Coordinating Committee (SNCC).* Founded in 1960 to eliminate segregation through nonviolent means, it was later led by **Stokely Carmichael** and other more militant leaders who favored "black power." SNCC had a substantial following on college campuses. One technique used by SNCC was to have buses with black and white "freedom riders" tour the South, stopping in various cities to demonstrate against discrimination. One of their main targets was Jackson, Mississippi, a bastion of segregation. Another technique used by SNCC was the sit-in. College students sat at segregated lunch counters until they were served or evicted. In 1964 over 500 SNCC volunteers, blacks and whites, went to Mississippi to work on voter registration.

By 1967, under leader **H. Rap Brown**, SNCC began to resort to violence and discourage white membership. The term "black power" was first used in a march into Jackson, Mississippi, led by **James Meredith**, the first member of the black community to be admitted to the University of Mississippi. "Black power" became a rallying cry for militants but was rejected by Roy Wilkins, head of the NAACP, who called it "the father of hatred and the mother of violence." Carmichael answered that "black power" did not mean violence but instead referred to voting power and meant, "Look, buddy, we're not laying a vote on you unless you lay so many schools, hospitals, playgrounds, and jobs on us."

- *Black Muslims.* Elijah Muhammad's **Nation of Islam** (sometimes called the **Black Muslims**) rejected integration and sought to establish a separate African American government in one or more of the United States. Its best known member was **Malcolm X**, who later broke with the Black Muslims and formed his own organization. His followers used "X" as a surname to designate their rejection of names acquired under slavery. A gifted speaker and writer, Malcolm X conveyed a message of hatred against white injustice, which he describes in his widely read *Autobiography*. He had begun to change and speak of alliances with white radicals before he was assassinated in 1965.

- *Civil Unrest.* In August 1965, **Watts**, the black ghetto district of Los Angeles, erupted in a week of terrible rioting. Shooting, burning, and looting resulted in 34 deaths and over 100 wounded. Violence during the "long hot summer" of 1965 was followed by more racial violence the following summer. The unrest reached its peak in the summer of 1967. In Detroit, 38 people died and property damage exceeded $200 million. Newark, New Jersey, and other cities also experienced racial violence. More than 100 riots raged in American cities in the 1960s. The racial violence, following on the heels of the Civil Rights Act of 1964 and the Voting Rights Act of 1965, caused disillusionment and even a backlash. President Johnson, a strong advocate of civil rights, understood the frustration of the African American people and said, "God knows how little we've really moved on this issue despite all the fanfare. As I see it, I've moved the Negro from D+ to C−. He's still nowhere and he knows it. That's why he's out in the streets."

In 1967 Johnson appointed a **National Commission on Civil Disorders** headed by Governor **Otto Kerner** of Illinois. The **Kerner Commission** issued a report that blamed the race riots primarily on white racism and concluded with the oft-quoted finding: "Our nation is moving toward two societies, one black, one white—separate and unequal."

Assassinations of the 1960s

President Kennedy once said, "Those who make peaceful revolution impossible will make violent revolution inevitable." He was assassinated in Dallas in 1963; Dr. Martin Luther King, Jr. was shot to death in Memphis, Tennessee in 1968; and Robert F. Kennedy, whose campaign for the presidency was gaining momentum, was fatally wounded by an assassin's bullet at the Ambassador Hotel in Los Angeles on the night of June 5, 1968. No one can assess the loss to the nation, indeed to the world, brought about by these violent acts.

Exercise Set 6.10

1. Which was *not* included in the Equal Opportunity Act sponsored by President Johnson?
   A. Volunteers in Service to America (VISTA)
   B. a new Department of Housing and Urban Development (HUD)
   C. loans to college students and to small business
   D. job- and work-training programs

2. Which was *not* part of President Johnson's program for aid to under-privileged inner-city residents?
   A. Operation Head Start
   B. Medicare and Medicaid
   C. a rent-supplement program
   D. the Alliance for Progress

3. In *Plessy* v. *Ferguson* (1896) the Supreme Court decided that
   A. the Dred Scott Decision was unconstitutional
   B. the "separate but equal" doctrine was not a violation of the Four-teenth Amendment
   C. blacks were full-fledged citizens of the United States and of the state wherein they resided
   D. the Court lacked jurisdiction in that case

4. The chief counsel of NAACP who argued *Brown* v. *Board of Education* before the Supreme Court was
   A. W.E.B. Du Bois
   B. Robert C. Weaver
   C. Thurgood Marshall
   D. Roy Wilkins

THE MOVEMENT FOR EQUAL RIGHTS

> The fight must go on. The cause of civil liberty must not be surrendered at the end of one or even one hundred defeats.
>
> Abraham Lincoln, November 19, 1858

> The core of the civil rights problem is the matter of achieving equal opportunity for Negroes in the labor market. For it stands to reason that all our other civil rights depend on that one for fulfillment. We cannot afford better education for our children, better housing or medical care unless we have jobs.
>
> Whitney M. Young, Director of the National Urban League, 1968

Truman and Civil Rights

In 1946, President Harry Truman appointed a **President's Committee on Civil Rights**. The Committee issued its report in 1947 in a document entitled "To Secure These Rights" and, based on this report, Truman called on Congress to pass a **Fair Employment Practices** law, to establish a **Civil Rights Commission**, to prohibit poll taxes, and to protect the right to vote. This blueprint for civil rights paved the way for a comprehensive civil rights program. Truman did all he could in the face of congressional resistance. He moved toward integration of the armed forces and issued an executive order prohibiting discrimination in employment in federal agencies.

The leading Supreme Court segregation case, *Brown* v. *Board of Education of Topeka* (1954), along with similar cases from South Carolina, Virginia and Delaware, moved through the lower federal courts during the Truman administration. The Supreme Court took jurisdiction and heard arguments in 1952, the last year that Truman was in office, and rendered its unanimous decision two years later.

Civil Rights Legislation

Beginning in the 1950s, laws were passed to ensure equal civil rights for all Americans.

Civil Rights Act of 1957

In 1957, Congress passed the first civil rights law in the 20th century. It established a bipartisan **Civil Rights Commission** with authority to investigate denial of voting rights and/or denial of equal protection as provided in the Fourteenth Amendment. It authorized federal courts to issue injunctions to prevent interference with voting rights.

Civil Rights Act of 1960

The act authorized federal courts to appoint referees with power to evaluate state voting qualifications. Suits could be brought against states, and heavy penalties could be imposed for violations of civil rights.

Civil Rights Act of 1964

This comprehensive civil rights legislation (1) prohibited discrimination in places of public accommodation (hotels and motels); (2) established an **Equal Opportunity Commission** to end job discrimination; (3) strengthened voting rights statutes; and (4) allowed federal funds to be withheld from school districts that violated integration orders.

Voting Rights Act of 1965

This landmark law was designed to end the denial of voting rights to blacks in the South. The act authorized the "appointment of federal examiners . . . to enforce the guarantees of the Fifteenth Amendment." It outlawed literacy tests and other voter-qualification tests in states or counties where fewer than half of those of voting age had registered or voted in 1964. It authorized the use of federal examiners to register voters in counties that practiced voter discrimination.

The act substantially increased the number of African American voters, particularly in the deep South. More than 150,000 black voters were registered in the three years following its passage. In Mississippi, where fewer than 7 percent of voting-age blacks were registered prior to the 1965 law, close to 60 percent were on the voting rolls in 1968.

Civil Rights Act of 1968

The last of the civil rights legislation passed during the Johnson administration contained a strong open-housing provision that prohibited discrimination in the sale or rental of housing. It also provided penalties for persons who intimidated or injured civil rights workers and for those who traveled from one state to another to "incite, organize, promote, encourage, participate in, or carry on a riot."

Twenty-fourth Amendment

The twenty-fourth Amendment to the Constitution, ratified in January 1964, abolished the poll tax in federal elections.

Court Decisions

Besides legislation to end discrimination and ensure equal civil rights, African Americans also received support for equal rights from the courts.

- **Smith *v.* Allwright** *(1944).* The Democratic party in Texas adopted a resolution in 1944 that made only white citizens eligible to vote in the Democratic party primaries. The plaintiff, **Lonnie E. Smith**, brought suit in the District Court of Texas, contending that his exclusion from voting in the primary election was an abridgment of his right to vote, in violation of the Fifteenth Amendment. The Supreme Court struck down the Texas law.

- **NAACP *v.* St. Louis-San Francisco Railway Company.** In this 1955 case the Interstate Commerce Commission ruled that segregation on interstate trains and buses was illegal.

- **Brown *v.* Board of Education of Topeka** *(1954).* This case struck down racial segregation in the public schools.

- **Baker *v.* Carr** *(1962).* This case involved the apportionment of legislative districts. Those who brought the case contended that failure by the state of Tennessee to redraw and reapportion districts for election to the state legislature for 60 years constituted a denial of "the equal protection of the laws accorded them by the Fourteenth Amendment by virtue of the debasement of their votes." The Court's ruling in this case, frequently referred to as "one man, one vote," was a major victory for equal representation in the state legislatures. This was particularly significant in crowded areas where blacks and poor people generally were underrepresented.

The Drive for Equal Rights for Women

The Women's Rights Movement from 1607 to the Present

The colonial patriarchal tradition, derived from Europe, established the principle of the father's primary authority in the home, in the world of work, in politics, and in the church. Women in the 17th and 18th centuries had no political rights and were generally considered inferior.

- *The 19th Century.* During the period of reform between 1820 and the 1840s, the women's rights movement began. The first women's rights convention was held at **Seneca Falls**, New York, in 1848. The delegates adopted a Declaration of Sentiments that said, "All men and women are created equal" and listed demands for political, social, and economic equality with men. The earliest victories came in education as some schools were gradually opened to women, starting in the 1840s and 1850s.

Prominent 19th-century feminist leaders included **Susan B. Anthony**, a relentless advocate of women's suffrage; **Lucy Stone**, who was both a women's rights advocate and an abolitionist; **Elizabeth Cady Stanton**, the philosopher of the 19th century feminist movement; and **Lucretia Mott**, feminist, abolitionist, and a founder of Swarthmore College. **Harriet Tubman** and **Sojourner Truth**, better known for their efforts to free their people from slavery, were also ardent advocates of women's suffrage. **Carrie Chapman Catt**, in the early 20th century, carried forward the effort for women's suffrage.

The Modern Women's Movement

We can no longer ignore that voice within women that says: "I want something more than my husband and my children and my home ."
Betty Friedan, in *The Feminine Mystique* (1963)

• *Kennedy Commission and the 1964 Civil Rights Act.* In 1963 President Kennedy appointed a **Commission on the Status of Women** headed by **Eleanor Roosevelt**. The Commission report disclosed that discrimination against women was rampant in virtually every aspect of American life. The following year, Congress passed the **Civil Rights Act** of 1964, designed to protect the civil rights of blacks. However, it also contained a provision pertaining to women's rights. The provision was introduced as an amendment to **Title VII** of the act banning discrimination on the basis of sex as well as race and made discrimination in employment on the basis of sex a violation of federal law.

• *NOW, 1966 to Present.* The **National Organization for Women** (**NOW**) was founded by **Betty Friedan** in 1966. NOW resorted to strikes, boycotts, and demonstrations to attain equality with men in all aspects of life in the 1960s and 1970s.

As the "**women's liberation**" movement gained momentum, women sought equal pay for equal work, equal opportunity for promotion, the right to maternity leave without loss of job or seniority, advancement to positions of responsibility and authority in government, industry, and in the professions, recognition of the value of work in the home, participation of men in the duties and responsibilities traditionally performed by women, recognition in textbooks of women's role in history, and a more positive image in the media than the traditional one of sex symbol.

NOW has continued to agitate for women's rights, particularly for the adoption of the **Equal Rights Amendment**. The organization includes both women and men in its membership. Its agenda comprises a broad spectrum of social reforms, including affordable child care, lesbian and gay rights, pay equity, keeping abortion and birth control legal, greater research on women's diseases such as breast cancer, and reducing military expenditures.

• *Shifting Roles and Images.* The roles and images of male and female in our society have undergone radical transformation in one generation. The idea of the wife as homemaker and the husband as breadwinner has given way to one of equal responsibility for home and work. In the one area—childbearing—where roles are not reversible, many women have opted for fewer children or none at all. In many marriages today both partners have jobs, both do housework, and both care for the children. With women no longer confined to the home, child-rearing becomes increasingly the function of day-care centers.

With divorce on the increase, child custody and child support have assumed new importance and spawned new laws and procedures. Paying child support is no longer the sole responsibility of the father, and child custody is now often sought by, and sometimes awarded to, the father.

The national divorce rate was 10 percent in 1915, climbed to 25 percent by 1945, then catapulted to 50 percent by 1985. A total of 1.2 million couples were divorced in the United States during 1992. In 1987 there were 46 million children under 18 living with both parents; 13.5 million living with the mother alone (4 million of these with a mother who had never married); and 1.7 million living with a father alone (300,000 with a father who had never married).

• *The Equal Rights Amendment (ERA).* The recognition that women often received the poorest paying jobs in the work force and that they were generally paid lower wages (sometimes as little as one-half those paid to men for the same work), led to a demand by the **National Women's Party** in 1923 for the adoption of an **Equal Rights Amendment to the Constitution**. This would force states and cities to change laws and end practices that discriminated against women.

An Equal Rights Amendment was introduced in Congress in 1923 and every year thereafter until 1948, but failed to pass. During the ensuing years the measure was bottled up in the Judiciary Committee of the House of Representatives. It was finally forced out of Committee in 1970 and passed with an overwhelming vote in the House. Two years later it was approved by the necessary two-thirds vote in the Senate and sent to the states for ratification by the state legislatures. Approval by three fourths of the states, as required by Article V of the Constitution for ratification of amendments, proved difficult to attain.

The original time limit for ratification was set at March 22, 1979 (seven years after it was submitted by Congress to the states). The deadline was extended to June 30, 1982, but it failed to be ratified, by that date since only 35 of the necessary 38 (three fourths of the fifty states) had voted approval.

• **Roe v. Wade** *(1973).* In a 7 to 2 decision, written for the Court by Justice **Harry Blackmun**, the constitutional right of a woman to have an abortion was recognized. The Court held that this was part of the right to privacy implied by the **Bill of Rights**. The decision gave unqualified abortion rights to the pregnant woman during the first trimester (3 months), permitted the states to place limitations during the second trimester, and affirmed the right of the state to prohibit abortion during the final trimester except when the mother's life was in jeopardy.

With the appointment of three new justices by President Reagan and the elevation of Justice **William H. Rehnquist** to the position of Chief Justice, it was widely believed that the decision might be overturned. The Court agreed to hear challenges to the decision during its 1988–1989 term. On July 3, 1989, in *Webster* v. *Reproductive Health Services*, the Court upheld a restrictive Missouri abortion law, stopping just short of overturning *Roe* v. *Wade*. By a 5 to 4 vote, in an opinion written by Chief Justice William H. Rehnquist, the Court indicated that it no longer considered abortion to be a woman's fundamental right. The determination was left up to the individual states.

• *Equality in the Workplace.* During the 1970s and 1980s women entered the work force in ever-increasing numbers. Barriers fell as prestigious colleges became coeducational, women entered the professions on a par with men, and engaged in work such as mining, construction, heavy industry, transportation, police, and other arduous and dangerous jobs previously regarded as exclusively male occupations.

Admission of women to the service academies—West Point, Annapolis, and the Air Force Academy—began in 1976. By 1980 there were 19,000 women officers in the armed forces including a number of generals and admirals. Women were governors of states, members of the Senate, and judges on both the federal and state benches. Thousands of women held legislative and judicial offices in the states. **Sandra Day O'Connor** became the first woman member of the Supreme Court in 1981 as the first Reagan appointee to the Court. In 1984 **Geraldine Ferraro** was the Democratic vice-presidential candidate.

Despite obvious progress, the attainment of equality in the job market remained elusive. Widespread disparity in wages and salaries for equal work continued to exist in the labor market. Most top positions in business and industry continued to be held by men.

• *Affirmative Action.* In 1965 President Johnson signed an executive order requiring employers on federal contracts to take "affirmative action" to bring the number of women, African Americans, Hispanics, Native Americans, and Asians into better balance with the number of men and whites employed. The rationale was to correct past injustices done to these groups by giving preferences in employment, college admissions, and appointments to members of the disadvantaged categories who were equally qualified. The implementation of this directive aroused resentment and anger as some white men contended they were the victims of "reverse discrimination" based on past injustices to which they were not a party. Particularly rankling was the use of quotas that tended to give preference to less qualified applicants on the basis of race or sex.

The Supreme Court faced this issue in two cases during the 1970s. In the case of *Regents of the University of California* v. *Bakke* (1978), the Court ruled 5 to 4 that the University of California at Davis, which was receiving federal funds, had acted unconstitutionally in setting up a 16 percent admission quota for minority students in its medical school, thus denying admission to **Allan Bakke**, a white applicant who was better qualified than some minority applicants admitted under their quota.

But in a 1979 case, *Kaiser Aluminum Co.* v. *Weber* (1979), **Brian Weber** sued the Kaiser Aluminum and Chemical Corporation when he was denied a place in a training program for advancement because less qualified black applicants were admitted under the 50 percent quota. The Court ruled 5 to 4 that this private company was within its constitutional right to adopt this quota system in an attempt to overcome past "patterns of social segregation and hierarchy."

Under a 1972 directive of the Department of Labor, companies that held federal government contracts were ordered to set goals and timetables for hiring women and members of minorities. The **Equal Employment Opportunity Act** of 1972 required employers to operate on the principle of equal pay for equal work.

Rising Consciousness of Hispanic Americans

Background

Spanish-speaking Americans (Hispanics or Latinos) have a cultural background reaching back to Columbus and before. Settlers from Spain have been in the Americas since 1492. Texas, New Mexico, Arizona, Utah, Nevada, California, and part of Colorado were part of Spanish-speaking Mexico until the middle of the 19th century. Puerto Ricans, whose culture is Hispanic, came under American rule about a century ago (1898), and became American citizens even more recently (1917). Cuba was part of the Spanish empire for four centuries before the Spanish-American War (1898).

Immigration

The term "**Chicanos**" designates Mexican-Americans, while the Mexicans refer to Americans as "Anglos." By the early 1990s there were more than 15 million Chicanos in the United States, though the actual number is certainly much larger because of illegal immigration. Many came during the Mexican Revolution, which caused turmoil in Mexico from 1910 until the end of World War I. Immigration was spurred by the demand for migrant labor to pick fruits and vegetables in California, Arizona, New Mexico, and Texas. Those who chose to remain, often without legal status, settled in the "**barrios**" (inner city neighborhoods—generally slums) of Los Angeles and other cities of the Southwest. As economic conditions worsened in Mexico, illegal immigration skyrocketed. These immigrants became the poorest-paid workers in the textile industry, in restaurants, as domestics, on farms, factories, ranches, and estates.

Migration from Puerto Rico to the United States on a permanent basis became legal after 1917, when Puerto Ricans became American citizens. By the early 1990s there were about 2 million Puerto Ricans living in the United States, chiefly in New York and other cities of the Northeast.

Immigration of Cubans to the United States dates from the overthrow of the **Batista** regime in Cuba in 1959 by revolutionary forces led by **Fidel Castro**. About 1 million Cubans fled to the United States, and most settled in the Miami, Florida, area.

After the attempt to overthrow the Castro regime failed at the Bay of Pigs (1961), the United States imposed an economic blockade. Despite the hardships suffered by the people of Cuba, Castro remained in power with considerable help from his communist ally, the Soviet Union. This aid vanished in 1989 with the demise of the Soviets. As economic conditions became intolerable, many Cubans attempted to escape to the United States. In 1994, the trickle became a deluge as Cubans began to arrive on rafts and by other hastily improvised means. Many were picked up at sea by the U.S. Coast Guard and taken to "temporary" quarters at the U.S. naval base at Guantanamo Bay in Cuba. By October 1994, there were over 15,000 Cubans at Guantanamo.

During the 1980s the Hispanic population of the United States grew four times as fast as the total population, reaching nearly 24 million or about 10 percent of the U.S. population.

César Chavez

In 1963, César Chavez, a Chicano who had been a migrant farm worker, emerged as a leader of the exploited Mexican workers. He established the **United Farm Workers Organizing Committee** and led the union in a strike against the powerful grape growers of California. After a five-year struggle, during which he went on a 25-day fast to prevail upon his members to renounce violence, the union won contracts providing for an increase in pay and better working conditions.

Luis Muñoz Marin

Marin, a charismatic public figure, led Puerto Rico to "Commonwealth" status—partway between independence and statehood—within the United States. He was elected Governor of Puerto Rico in 1952. To raise the standard of living, he instituted a program called "Operation Bootstrap," whereby the resources of the Commonwealth—people, capital, and natural endowments—were marshaled to increase per capita income. The income level did rise, but it remained far below that of the United States, so, despite language problems, many Puerto Ricans chose to come to or remain in the United States. The people of Puerto Rico are divided about their political relationship with the United States. The majority prefer Commonwealth status, which gives them U.S. citizenship without requiring them to pay federal taxes on money earned in Puerto Rico. As a self-governing Commonwealth, they do not vote in U.S. national elections for President and Vice-President, nor do they elect members to the

Senate or House of Representatives. They do have representation in Congress by a resident commissioner, who can speak but does not have a vote.

Hispanic Power

With growing numbers in the United States and a rising ethnic consciousness, Hispanics have become more aggressive in seeking recognition in economic, political, and cultural aspects of American life.

In 1974 **Jerry Apodaca** was elected Governor of New Mexico while **Joseph Montoya**, also Hispanic, was serving as U.S. Senator. **Henry Cisneros** was elected Mayor of San Antonio, Texas and later was appointed Secretary of the Department of Housing and Urban Development.

The time when the use of Spanish in the public schools was forbidden, as it was for a time in Texas, is long gone. Indeed in a number of states, English is now taught as a second language to Spanish-speaking immigrant children, who are instructed in Spanish in public schools until they become proficient in English. In many cities, election laws mandate the printing of ballots and other election instructions in both English and Spanish. Spanish has become the number one foreign language taught in the public schools of the United States. Fear that Spanish might force the United States to become a bilingual country, as French did in Canada, has caused a severe backlash and a strong movement for legislation to establish English legally as the sole official language of the United States.

Equality for Native Americans: American Indian Movement (AIM)

The relationship between the U.S. government and Native Americans is, for the most part, a shameful page in American history. In his book, *Custer Died for Your Sins*, **Vine Deloria, Jr.**, who is a Standing Rock Sioux and former Executive Director of the **National Congress of American Indians**, writes: "America has yet to keep one Indian treaty or agreement despite the fact that the United States government signed four hundred such treaties and agreements with Indian tribes."

When whites arrived in America, there were an estimated 850,000 Indians in what is now the lower 48 states. By 1890 that population had declined to 250,000. Since then, it has come back and surpassed the original number, but the economic status of Native Americans remains severely depressed. An Indian is three times as likely to be unemployed as is a non-Indian living in the United States.

Alcatraz

In the 1960s Native Americans began to show a new militancy as they witnessed the developing counterculture of other disaffected Americans. In

1969, 78 Native Americans seized and held **Alcatraz Island**, a former federal prison, in San Francisco Bay. They were finally ousted by federal marshals, but not before nationwide publicity had brought their cause to the attention of the American public.

Wounded Knee (1973)

Indian Power manifested itself in surprising acts of defiance. In 1972, militant members of **AIM** (the **American Indian Movement**) occupied the Washington, D.C., offices of the Bureau of Indian Affairs, demanding that the Bureau be put in the hands of Indians and that treaty promises made to Indians be honored. They remained in control of the building for a week while talks were held with officials of the Department of the Interior.

A year later, about 200 armed members of AIM took control of the village of **Wounded Knee** on the Oglala Sioux Pine Ridge Reservation in South Dakota. They remained in the village for two months, during which violence broke out repeatedly in fighting with government agents. Major buildings were destroyed by the occupants and two Indians were killed in the fighting. The decision to occupy Wounded Knee was symbolic: it was near there that the last Indian resistance was broken when the U.S. 7th cavalry killed **Sitting Bull** and massacred 200 men, women, and children in 1890.

Example of Treaty Violation

The building of **Kinzua Dam** in western New York in the early 1960s inundated a large part of the Seneca reservation. Flooding the Indians out of their ancestral homeland was a violation of the **Pickering Treaty** of 1794, negotiated between the United States and the Seneca tribe of the Iroquois Nation and signed by George Washington as President of the United States.

Exercise Set 6.11

1. Of the five major civil rights acts passed during the period 1957–1968, the Voting Rights Act of 1965 is often regarded as the most far-reaching because
   A. prior to 1965 there was no legal guarantee of the right to vote for African Americans
   B. protection of the right to vote was regarded as a means whereby other basic rights could be secured
   C. voting rights would put an end to riots and racial violence
   D. Martin Luther King, Jr. was a strong advocate of the Voting Rights Act of 1965

2. The Supreme Court decision in *Baker* v. *Carr* (1962), involving reapportionment of state legislative districts, was a necessary complement to the 1965 Voting Rights Act because
   A. it protected voting rights in state elections
   B. the decision established the supremacy of federal over state voting regulations
   C. voting rights were reduced in practice by voting districts that were substantially unequal
   D. the appeal came from Tennessee, a state not directly involved in voting rights

3. The National Organization for Women (NOW)
   A. was founded in 1948 by Eleanor Roosevelt
   B. took the lead in support of the Civil Rights Act of 1964
   C. receives overt or tacit support from virtually all women
   D. includes in its membership both women and men

4. An Equal Rights Amendment to the Constitution
   A. was first proposed in 1970
   B. was declared unconstitutional by the Supreme Court
   C. failed to be approved by two thirds of each house of Congress
   D. failed to be ratified by the necessary three fourths of state legislatures

5. Women's organizations, for example—the National Organization of Women (NOW)—favored an Equal Rights Amendment (ERA) primarily because
   A. there is only one woman on the Supreme Court
   B. women in many jobs still receive lower pay than men for the same work
   C. educational opportunities for women are limited
   D. recent gains may be lost without a constitutional amendment

6. Hispanics, people with a Spanish-speaking cultural background, have come to the United States for all of the following reasons EXCEPT
   A. to experience the superior Anglo-American culture
   B. as an escape from the turmoil of violence and revolution
   C. to improve their economic conditions
   D. for better education and better opportunities for advancement for their children

7. In the last decades of the 20th century, Native Americans
   A. are ceasing to be a recognizable ethnic group because of intermarriage
   B. have been steadily declining in population since the arrival of Europeans
   C. are demanding a return of territory taken from them in violation of treaties with the American government
   D. no longer live on reservations

CHAPTER REVIEW QUESTIONS

1. Each of the following court cases was concerned with the struggle for equal rights in the 1960s and 1970s EXCEPT
   A. *Pennsylvania Association for Retarded Children (PARC)* v. *Commonwealth of Pennsylvania*
   B. *Baker* v. *Carr*
   C. *Plessy* v. *Ferguson*
   D. *Regents of the University of California* v. *Bakke*

2. African Americans realized they could not escape from the ghetto unless
   A. the right to vote was guaranteed
   B. open housing was assured
   C. children could be bused to integrated schools
   D. Black Power succeeded in establishing businesses owned and operated by blacks

3. The President responsible for beginning the program to land astronauts on the moon was
   A. Truman
   B. Eisenhower
   C. Kennedy
   D. Johnson

4. Which is a valid generalization about U.S. relationships with Latin America in the last 100 years?
   A. the success of democracy in Latin America is due largely to United States intervention
   B. Latin American resentment of the United States is due to Communist influence
   C. the United States has gradually realized that events in Latin America have little bearing on United States security
   D. economic interests have generally influenced United States policy toward Latin America

   Regents Exam, June 1988

5. Which of the following describes the program of the Kennedy Administration?
   A. Great Society
   B. New Deal
   C. New Freedom
   D. New Frontier

6. The Kerner Commission reported: "Our nation is moving toward two societies, one black, one white—separate and unequal." The major reason for the failure to solve the race problem is
A. failure of the black community to agree on a proper course of action
B. preoccupation of administrations in Washington with foreign affairs
C. lack of concern coupled with racism in the white society
D. unfavorable Supreme Court decisions

ESSAYS

1. During the 19th and 20th centuries, women in the United States have worked to bring about change.
   a. Several women are listed according to the century in which they worked to bring about change. Select *one* woman from *each* list. For *each* woman chosen, identify an issue in which she was involved, describe her involvement in that issue, and discuss the impact of her involvement. [5,5]

19th Century	20th Century
Harriet Tubman	Margaret Sanger
Elizabeth Cady Stanton	Eleanor Roosevelt
Susan B. Anthony	Gloria Steinem
	Geraldine Ferraro

   b. Many social issues of special concern to women are subjects of controversy today. Listed below are three such issues. Select *one* of these issues and discuss *two* conflicting viewpoints concerning that issue. [5]

Issues
Government funding of day-care centers
Guarantee of comparable worth
Elimination of media exploitation of women
Strengthening of affirmative action programs

Regents Exam, June 1988

2. Throughout U.S. history, the development of democracy has been affected by a variety of actions. Select *three* of the statements listed below. For *each* one chosen, discuss the extent to which the statement is accurate and use *two* specific examples from U.S. history to support your position. Use different specific examples for each statement. [5,5,5]

Statements
Court decisions have been an important factor in the democratic process.
Amendments to the U.S. Constitution have increased the rights of citizens.
Citizen groups have had an impact on making government policies more democratic.

Civil disobedience has been an effective way of achieving changes in society.

Ethnic and racial groups have made gains in achieving political equality.

Regents Exam, January 1986

THE LIMITS OF POWER: TURMOIL AT HOME AND ABROAD

THE VIETNAM WAR

United States Historic Involvement in Asia

Prior to the Nineteenth Century

United States involvement in Asia is not a recent development.

• *The China Trade.* In 1787 the Boston ship *Columbia*, loaded with ginseng, made a historic voyage from Boston to Oregon, where it picked up furs, and sailed across the Pacific Ocean to China, where it traded its cargo for tea and silk. The *Columbia* returned home in 1790, beginning a regular and profitable trade between the United States and China. From the late 1790s on, the China trade increased, and by 1850 the swift American clipper ships carried on most of the trade. After the **Opium War** with Britain (1839–1842), China opened more of its ports to trade. Prior to this, only Canton had been open to trade. In 1844, the American diplomat **Caleb Cushing** traveled to China with four warships and received generous trade arrangements for the United States. In the 1840s the first Chinese immigrants began to arrive in San Francisco. Chinese laborers were brought to California to help build the transcontinental railroads.

Nineteenth Century

The 19th century saw increased United States involvement in Asia.

• *Opening of Japan.* President **Millard Fillmore**, seeking trade with Japan, sent a special mission headed by **Commodore Matthew C. Perry**, that arrived in Tokyo Bay in 1853. He returned the following year with a fleet of seven warships and negotiated the **Treaty of Kanagawa**, a treaty of peace, friendship, and commerce. The Japanese, confronted with superior American power, agreed to open several ports to United States trade.

• *19th-Century Imperialism in Asia.* The United States became an imperial power in Asia toward the end of the 19th century by acquiring the Hawaiian Islands and Samoa in 1898 and the Philippine Islands from Spain at the conclusion of the Spanish-American War. Events in China at the close of the 19th century prompted Secretary of State **John Hay** to propose in

1899 the "**Open Door Policy**" for trade with China. This policy declared that China should be open to all nations on an equal basis. Hay announced (March 20, 1900) that the acceptance of the Open Door Policy by the major powers (Germany, Russia, Britain, France, Italy, and Japan) was "final and definitive." The United States returned to China part of the money awarded for damages resulting from the **Boxer Rebellion** of the same year.

Twentieth Century

By the 20th century, the United States had become a major power, and its contacts with all areas of the world, including Asia, increased.

* *Theodore Roosevelt and the Russo-Japanese War.* In 1905, President Theodore Roosevelt helped bring to an end the war in Asia between Japan and Russia when he met with the envoys of the warring powers at Portsmouth, New Hampshire. He was awarded the Nobel Peace Prize for this act.

* *World War I (1914–1918).* While the war was fought primarily in Europe, there were repercussions in Asia. Japan joined the war against Germany in 1914. At the peace negotiations at Versailles, Japan acquired several islands in the Pacific previously held by Germany and was made a permanent member of the Council of the League of Nations.

* *World War II (1939–1945).* Asia was a major battleground of World War II. At the conclusion of the war, the United States had become the leading world power and a great power in Asia. The challenge was now perceived to be from the Soviet Union, itself a major power in Asia, the Middle East, and Europe.

* *The Korean War (1950–1953).* By prompt action, the United States and the UN prevented all of Korea from becoming a Communist outpost in Asia.

The French-Indochina War

The French in Indochina

Vietnam was part of a French colonial empire in Indochina that also included **Cambodia** and **Laos**. During World War II the Japanese took control of Indochina from the French and made it part of their "greater East Asia co-prosperity sphere." When the war ended, France attempted to reestablish its control over Vietnam. However, in 1946 the **Viet Minh**, a group of revolutionary nationalists and Communists led by **Ho Chi Minh**, began a war to drive out the French and their anti-Communist allies led by **Bao Dai**. In 1950, after it was found that Communist China was aiding the Viet Minh, President Truman sent military equipment and economic aid to the Vietnamese and French armies. Although President Eisenhower believed that a

French defeat might lead to the Communist domination of Southeast Asia, he did not involve the United States in the war. He did continue to send military equipment, and the United States paid for much of the cost of the war. The civil war went on for eight years until a decisive battle at **Dien Bien Phu** in May 1954 resulted in the defeat of the French. After the fall of Dien Bien Phu to the Communists, the French withdrew from Indochina and the Communist Viet Minh took over North Vietnam.

An international conference was held at Geneva, Switzerland, attended by representatives of both Vietnams, France, Great Britain, the Soviet Union, the People's Republic of China, and the United States. At the Geneva conference, the independence of Cambodia, Laos, and Vietnam was recognized. Vietnam was divided along the 17th parallel into North Vietnam and South Vietnam. North Vietnam became a Communist state under the leadership of Ho Chi Minh. South Vietnam became a republic and was led by **Ngo Dinh Diem**. Provision was made for elections to be held in 1956 to reunite Vietnam, but the elections were never held. Neither South Vietnam nor the United States signed these accords. When the time for the election to unify Vietnam arrived (July 1956), Ngo Dinh Diem, with approval of the United States, refused to participate in the election. He was convinced that he would lose to Communist North Vietnam, and American intelligence sources agreed with this conclusion.

The United States and the War in Vietnam

The Domino Theory

The American attempt to prevent a Communist victory in Vietnam was based primarily on the fear that such a victory would result in the spread of communism in Asia. According to President Eisenhower's domino theory, ". . . you knock over the first one [domino—in this case, Vietnam] and . . . the last one . . . will go over very quickly." Americans feared that the dominoes in Southeast Asia might include not only Indochina but also Thailand, Malaysia, Indonesia, the Philippines, and Burma, since each of these countries was also facing problems with Communist insurgencies.

Early American Involvement in Vietnam

As you have read, President Truman sent military equipment and economic aid to Vietnam. Both the People's Republic of China and the USSR extended diplomatic recognition to the Democratic Republic of Vietnam in 1950. This indicated their support for the North Vietnamese Communists whom they also provided with military aid.

• *Under Eisenhower.* President Eisenhower offered economic aid to South Vietnam soon after the Geneva Conference in 1954. Communist guerrilla forces in South Vietnam called **Viet Minh** (later called **Viet Cong**) were putting the government of South Vietnam under strong military pressure. President Eisenhower also began sending **military advisers** to Vietnam. There were several hundred American advisers in Vietnam when John F. Kennedy became President.

* *Under Kennedy and Johnson.* The war in South Vietnam carried on by the **Viet Cong**, Communist guerrilla forces aided by the North Vietnamese, was going badly for the South Vietnamese government. Consequently, President Kennedy, who also believed in the domino theory, increased the number of American military advisers.

In 1954 the United States had helped to install **Ngo Dinh Diem** in power in Saigon. In May 1963, Diem's troops killed nine Buddhists taking part in an anti-Diem demonstration in Hué. The demonstrators were protesting a government order barring the flying of flags and processions on Buddha's birthday. On June 11 the first of seven monks committed suicide by burning himself to death in Saigon to dramatize protest of government policies toward Buddhists. On November 1, 1963, a military coup deposed and assassinated Diem. The United States welcomed the coup but denied direct involvement.

When Lyndon Johnson became President (November 22, 1963) there were 15,000 American troops, including "Green Beret" special forces, in Vietnam. By January 1965, when Johnson began his full four-year term, there were 23,000 American troops in Vietnam.

Johnson and the Escalation of the War

In August 1964, two United States destroyers were reportedly fired upon by North Vietnamese patrol boats in the **Gulf of Tonkin**, off the coast of North Vietnam. At the time it was not known that these U.S. naval vessels, with President Johnson's approval, were cooperating with the South Vietnamese in raids on the North Vietnamese coastal areas. Johnson called these incidents "unprovoked attacks" and ordered retaliatory air raids on North Vietnam. He asked Congress for wider authority to take military action. On August 7, 1964, Congress overwhelmingly passed the **Gulf of Tonkin Resolution** authorizing the President to "take all necessary measures to repel any armed attack against the forces of the United States and to prevent further aggression."

The Gulf of Tonkin Resolution marked a turning point in the war and led to the beginning of large-scale American involvement. In February 1965 Johnson began the bombing of North Vietnam, which continued until 1968. More American troops were sent to Vietnam and committed to combat. Before this, Americans had served as military advisers. As American involvement increased, so too did North Vietnamese involvement. Supplies were sent from the north, and for the first time troops from North Vietnam went south to fight with the Viet Cong. Before this the fighting had been between the Viet Cong and the South Vietnamese army.

Prior to the November 1964 election Johnson said, "We will seek no wider war." He also told the voters, "We are not going to send American boys nine or ten thousand miles away from home to do what Asian boys ought to be doing for themselves." His Republican opponent, **Barry Goldwater**, called for more intensive bombing of North Vietnam. In the presidential election, the voters gave Johnson an overwhelming victory—more than 60 percent of the popular vote and a 486 to 52 triumph in the electoral college. It was clear that the people wanted no wider war in Asia, and Johnson was their "peace candidate." However, soon after the election Johnson proceeded to widen the war. In February 1965 after an attack on an American base in South Vietnam, Johnson ordered an escalation in the war. American planes began to bomb North Vietnam, and in June 1965 U.S. field commanders were authorized to send American troops into combat. By November 1966 the U.S. had 358,000 troops in Vietnam. By the middle of 1968, the number exceeded half a million.

Opposition to the Vietnam War

Early Opposition

From the very beginning, a few well-placed voices spoke out against the war. In 1965 Senator **Wayne Morse** of Oregon advocated American withdrawal. Some senators opposed the war because Americans were being drafted and sent into combat without a declaration of war by Congress. Heavy casualties were being incurred. The bombardment and the overwhelming fire power of the American forces were proving ineffective in the jungle against the hit-and-run guerrilla tactics of the Viet Cong. There was no real battlefront, and it was difficult to fight an invisible enemy who moved by night and hid by day in the jungles and villages.

Draft Resistance

At home the war was brought into people's living rooms on television screens. As they watched the horrors of war, Americans began to oppose the war, because there was no consensus as to what we were fighting for in Vietnam. Many young men sought to avoid the draft by failing to register or by seeking exemptions. Some fled to Canada, Sweden, and other foreign sanctuaries. Quotas were filled quickly in the National Guard and Coast Guard, two branches of the service not generally assigned to overseas duty.

Intensified Opposition

By 1967 many leading senators were openly demanding U.S. withdrawal from Vietnam. In an effort to answer the opposition, President Johnson addressed the nation on September 29, 1967, and once again used the domino theory to support the war.

But the nation did not accept the President's explanation. **Peace marches** and **protest meetings** throughout the United States showed the deep disaffection. Others were frustrated over the way the war was being fought, and many Americans believed that "hold back" tactics were being used. By March 1968, polls showed that only 36 percent of the people approved of Johnson's presidency. Except at military bases, it was becoming impossible for the President to speak in public without facing antipathy.

Reports from the front fueled the discontent with the war. The nation learned of a massacre by American troops at **My Lai** village in March 1968. Frustrated American troops under the command of Lieutenant **William Calley** entered the village and murdered its inhabitants (old men, women, and infants). Many villages were destroyed in indiscriminate bombing. **Agent Orange**, a powerful chemical with long-lasting, serious health effects on people, was used extensively as a defoliant. Land mines took life and limb from countless civilians. In a war against guerrillas, it was impossible to distinguish combatants from noncombatants. Despite assurances from General **William Westmoreland**, Commander of American forces in Vietnam, that the war was being won, there was growing skepticism in Congress.

The Tet Offensive

In January 1968, during the Vietnamese New Year's holiday called "Tet," the Viet Cong and North Vietnamese launched a powerful offensive. Virtually all of South Vietnam, including the U.S. embassy in Saigon, was suddenly besieged. The attack was over in a few days and the North Vietnamese suffered tremendous losses. But the offensive demonstrated the Vietnamese will to continue to engage the U.S. military forces. Reports of the attack profoundly affected public opinion and the political situation in the United States. Opposition to the war intensified, and candidates in the Democratic party challenged President Johnson in the primaries for the November 1968 election.

On March 31, 1968, President Johnson delivered an address to the nation. He stated, "Tonight I renew the offer I made last August—to stop the bombardment of North Vietnam We ask that [peace] talks begin promptly . . ." He then startled the nation by declaring that he would not run for another term as President.

President Nixon and the Vietnam War

"Vietnamization" of the War

During the election campaign of 1968, **Richard Nixon** delared that he had a "secret plan" to end the war. Although President Johnson had tried to induce peace talks by halting bombing raids for short periods and offering economic aid, North Vietnam insisted that the United States leave Vietnam before talks could begin. In November 1969 Nixon unveiled his plan, which was later termed Vietnamization, of shifting the responsibility of fighting the war to South Vietnamese forces. He said, "We shall furnish military and economic assistance when requested in accordance with our treaty commitments. But we shall look to the nation directly threatened to assume the primary responsibility of providing the manpower for its defenses."

However, the fighting in Vietnam, including heavy bombing raids, continued. With the lack of success of peace negotiations being held in Paris, Nixon widened the war. In April 1970 he ordered American and South Vietnamese forces to invade **Cambodia**, a neutral nation neighboring Vietnam where the North Vietnamese and Viet Cong had bases. This action set off a chain of fierce protests, particularly on college campuses. To many, Nixon's credibility was minimal, and his assertion that the invasion was designed to facilitate the withdrawal of American troops from Vietnam was widely rejected. However, at the same time as the Cambodia invasion, Nixon began to withdraw American troops from the war. By the end of 1972, Nixon withdrew 500,000 American soldiers, leaving only about 24,000 in Vietnam Under the policy of Vietnamization, the United States armed and trained the South Vietnamese. Heavy bombing of Communist-controlled areas was undertaken.

Negotiations for a Cease-Fire

During this period the war continued while negotiations for a cease-fire, first begun under President Johnson in April 1968, were carried on in Paris by Nixon's foreign policy adviser (later Secretary of State) **Henry A. Kissinger**. On March 30, 1972, North Vietnamese forces launched a sustained offensive into South Vietnam. Heavy American bombing of North Vietnam was resumed, and on May 8, 1972, Nixon ordered the mining of North Vietnam's ports. Although United States participation in the ground war terminated in August 1972, aerial bombardment continued.

Shortly before the 1972 election, Kissinger announced from Paris that "peace is at hand." In November, Nixon was reelected in an overwhelming victory, defeating **George McGovern**, the Democratic anti-war candidate, by an electoral vote of 520 to 17. However, by December, no agreement had been reached and Nixon authorized the "carpet bombing" of North Vietnam declaring "I will show them no mercy." Hospitals, schools, and residences, were indiscriminately destroyed.

This attack caused peace talks to resume, and the long-awaited cease-fire agreement was finally reached on January 27, 1973, in the Paris negotiations between Henry Kissinger and **Le Duc Tho**, chief of the Vietnam mission. The United States agreed to respect the independence, unity, and territorial integrity of Vietnam and to withdraw all forces within 60 days. The Communist government of North Vietnam agreed to release all prisoners and to account for all soldiers missing in action. The final U.S. troops left Indochina on March 29, 1973. To achieve "peace with honor," the United States retained the right to recognize the government of **President Thieu** as the sole legitimate government of South Vietnam. But it was obvious to all that the Thieu government could not endure long against the forces of North Vietnam The end came in April 1975, when North Vietnam mounted a major offensive and gained control of all of Vietnam. As Communist troops from the north besieged Saigon, President Thieu and his followers fled the country. Thousands of refugees fled to Thailand. The people of Cambodia and Laos were also tragic victims of the war.

The Vietnam Veterans Memorial in Washington is engraved with the names of 58,156 Americans who died in Vietnam; 300,000 more were wounded. The monetary cost of the war was over $150 billion. The intangible costs are still being assessed and the lessons pondered. Nearly 5,000 American servicemen were missing in action (MIA's) at the end of the war. The United States continued to press Vietnam to abide by its agreement to account for the MIA's.

The Pentagon Papers

Background

In June 1967 **Robert S. McNamara**, President Johnson's Secretary of Defense, authorized a comprehensive study to review the policy-making procedures whereby the United States became so deeply involved in Vietnam. After a year and a half of intensive study, a 47-volume report known as the **Pentagon Papers** was compiled. Only 15 copies were issued. They were classified as top secret and were given only to McNamara, former President Johnson, President Nixon, the State Department, and the Pentagon files. The *Papers* revealed new facts about the Tonkin Gulf incident of 1964, which President Johnson used to gain a free hand in Vietnam It appeared that the North Vietnamese attack on American destroyers in the Tonkin Gulf (if indeed, it ever *had* occurred) had been deliberately provoked by attacks on North Vietnamese territory carried out by South Vietnam and supported by U.S. destroyers in order to gain Congressional approval for the free hand sought by the President.

Publication of the Papers

One of the authors who compiled the *Pentagon Papers* was **Daniel Ellsberg**. Ellsberg had volunteered for service in Vietnam and spent two years in combat with the marines. He felt strongly that the American people should be informed of the contents of the *Pentagon Papers*. Considering it to be an act of the highest patriotism, he decided to release the report to the press. On June 13, 1971, *The New York Times* startled the nation with its front-page installment of the secret government report. The Justice Department indicted Ellsberg for theft, conspiracy, and espionage.

While Ellsberg awaited trial, the Nixon administration, via **John D. Ehrlichman**, assistant to the President for domestic affairs, sounded out the presiding judge on becoming the new director of the FBI. He also authorized a special secret contingent called "the plumbers" (leak stoppers) to break into the California office of Ellsberg's psychiatrist and steal whatever data they could find (they found none) about Ellsberg's personal affairs or problems. They also carried out other illegal activities, including wiretaps. When it was revealed that an illegal FBI wiretap had been in operation on Ellsberg's telephone from late 1969 to early 1970, the judge in the case dismissed the charges against Ellsberg, stating, "The conduct of the government has placed the case in such a posture that it precludes the fair, dispassionate resolution of these issues by a jury."

The New York Times Co. **v.** *United States*

When *The New York Times* began publication of the *Pentagon Papers*, the Justice Department obtained a court order enjoining the newspaper from further publication of any material contained in the confidential report. The *New York Times* sought an order from the Supreme Court vacating the injunction, on the grounds that prior restraint was a violation of the free press guarantee of the First Amendment. The government contended that disclosure of the contents would work "irreparable injury" to the "national security." The Court was asked to order prior censorship against a newspaper for the first time in American history.

The Court, in a 6 to 3 decision, rejected the government's request and vacated the injunction. Nine opinions, totaling over 11,000 words, were issued. The arguments against prior restraint were strongly stated by Justice Black with whom Justice Douglas joined in concurrence.

> Now for the first time in 182 years since the founding of the Republic, the federal courts are asked to hold that the First Amendment does not mean what it says . . .
>
> In revealing the workings of government that led to the Vietnam War, the newspapers nobly did that which the Founding Fathers hoped and trusted they would do . . .
>
> To find that the President has "inherent power" to halt the publication of news by resort to the courts would wipe out the First Amendment and destroy the fundamental liberty and security of the very people the government hopes to make "secure."

Exercise Set 6.12

1. Which of the following did *not* involve U.S. relations with China prior to 1901?
   A. John Hay's "Open-Door Policy"
   B. building of the transcontinental railroads
   C. acquisition of the Philippine Islands
   D. the "Boxer Rebellion"

2. President Johnson's use of American troops to save the independence of South Vietnam was
   A. unpopular in Congress almost from the beginning
   B. a logical development of the policies pursued by Presidents Truman, Eisenhower, and Kennedy
   C. contrary to the advice of the Joint Chiefs of Staff of the Armed Forces
   D. tacitly approved by China, Japan, and Russia

3. The decision of the Supreme Court in the *New York Times Company* v. *United States* (1971) [the *Pentagon Papers* case] is important because
   A. it involved important officials in the U.S. government
   B. it was widely reported in newspapers throughout the country
   C. the government's attorneys lost the case in a 6 to 3 decision
   D. the Court ruled that the First Amendment prevented "prior restraint" of publication, even against a charge that such publication would jeopardize national security

4. U.S. actions in the Vietnam War demonstrated that
   A. the domino theory is an effective military tactic
   B. military policy in a democracy is affected by popular opinion
   C. advanced technology ensures victory
   D. limited use of tactical nuclear weapons can be successful
   Regents Exam, January 1989

5. The executive branch of the U.S. government has traditionally gained power during periods when
   A. the presidency has been occupied by a high-ranking military officer
   B. the Republican party was in the majority in Congress and the President was a Democrat
   C. there has been a serious domestic or international problem facing the United States
   D. the Supreme Court and Congress have been in conflict over constitutional issues
   Regents Exam, January 1989

PROTEST AND THE COUNTERCULTURE

Sources of Discontent

The decade of the 1960s was a period of rapid social change in American life. The traditional family underwent radical transformation. Divorce increased sharply. The authority of parents, teachers, churches, leaders in business, industry, the professions, and government was questioned, challenged, and attacked. By 1967 half of America's 200 million people had been born after the Great Depression and had no memory of the economic problems of that period.

Young people, impatient to correct injustice, found two areas for discontent: the unequal treatment of minorities and the war in Vietnam The **Kerner Commission** had found that the nation's two societies—one black and one white—were becoming increasingly "separate and unequal." Senator **Eugene McCarthy** of Minnesota described the war in Vietnam in his 1967 book *The Limits of Power*: "Vietnam is a military problem. Vietnam is a political problem; and as the war goes on it has become more clearly a moral problem."

Vexing social problems were associated with these sources of injustice— one was that a disproportionate share of fighting was being borne by young black Americans. For African Americans and other minorities and the poor, lack of opportunity, unequal education and health care, unemployment, hunger, and slum living produced a permanent underclass, alien to the tradition of the "American dream."

The Counterculture

The rejection of traditional American society, because of its many injustices, by many young Americans created a **counterculture**. Many young people rejected the norms and values of people "over 30."

The baby boom of the 1950s had produced a generation of 36 million Americans between the ages of 15 and 24 in 1970. In the 1960s many of these young people seriously questioned the injustice in American society and the unexplained war for which they were expected to risk their lives. They felt alienated from American society. The counterculture was one way of showing their rejection of their parents', teachers', and the older generation's values. Many wore long hear, beads, and bizarre clothing, and went barefoot. "Flower children" handed flowers to police officers. Many tried drugs, most commonly marijuana and LSD. Some followed Oriental gurus and went to live in communes. The "rock music" of groups such as the **Beatles** expressed their yearnings and feelings. In 1969, near **Woodstock**, New York, 400,000 gathered for an outdoor concert that became a symbol of the togetherness of this generation. Some young Americans rejected the quest for economic advancement, turning to part-time occupations or crafts such as making furniture, pottery, or jewelry. They rejected ideas of personal achievement, material gain, and, above all, conformity. Rebellious youths referred to themselves as "**hippies**." (They were "hip" or wise to what was going on.)

The counterculture mood of rejection and rebellion was strongly reflected in the behavior of the military in Vietnam. "Fragging" of officers and high-ranking sergeants was a sign of the rejection of authority of the times—a source of the serious crisis in discipline in Vietnam.

The Election of 1968

In 1968 a sharply divided Democratic party faced a united Republican party that chose **Richard Nixon** as its candidate. Nixon picked Governor **Spiro T. Agnew** of Maryland as his running mate.

The contest for the Democratic presidential nomination began in the New Hampshire primary on March 12, 1968. Senator **Eugene McCarthy** of Minnesota, virtually unknown outside his own state, ran as an "end the war" candidate and challenged President Johnson. To everyone's surprise, he received 42 percent of the vote and showed how vulnerable the President was in his own party. Four days later, Senator **Robert F. Kennedy** of New York announced his candidacy for the presidential nomination. And on March 31, in an address to the nation, President Johnson announced, "I shall not seek, and I will not accept the nomination of my party for a second term as your President." The way was now clear for Vice-President **Hubert Humphrey** to seek the Democratic party nomination. The assassination of Robert F. Kennedy in Los Angeles on June 5 made the selection of Humphrey a virtual certainty, and it was confirmed at the Democratic convention in Chicago in August.

A third candidate, **George C. Wallace**, Democratic Governor of Alabama, ran as the Independent party candidate espousing segregation, hoping to garner enough electoral votes in the South to throw the election into the House of Representatives.

The Democratic convention was marred by a bitter battle over the party platform on Vietnam. The followers of Eugene McCarthy (and the Kennedy delegates) sought a quick withdrawal from Vietnam. However, the Humphrey delegates wrote a platform calling for stopping the bombing of Vietnam only when "it would not endanger the lives of our troops." But the greatest damage to the Humphrey candidacy was caused by what the voters saw on television. Outside the Chicago convention, fierce fighting broke out in the streets between antiwar demonstrators and the police, who were under orders from Chicago Mayor **Richard J. Daley** to preserve order, if necessary with their clubs. Among the demonstrators were the "**Yippies**" (**Youth**

International Party), who ridiculed the convention and nominated a pig named "Pigasus" for President.

During the campaign, which hinged on the issue of our involvement in the Vietnam War, Nixon said he had a secret plan to bring the war to a successful end. In the weeks before the November election, Humphrey gained steadily but failed to overcome the Republican lead. Nixon won in a close race by half a million votes of 73 million cast. Wallace received nearly 10 million votes. In the electoral college Nixon took 301 votes against 191 for Humphrey and 46 for Wallace.

Rallies, Protests, and Demonstrations

College Students on the Offensive

Many young Americans, especially college students, expressed their resentment against the Vietnam War and other adult institutions and practices. Even before the war, students had begun to show a new militancy. At the University of California in Berkeley they had organized **a Free Speech Movement** and attempted to disrupt a San Francisco hearing conducted by the **House Un-American Activities Committee.** Some 800 members of Berkeley's Free Speech Movement staged a violent sit-in at the administration building and heard their spokesman, **Mario Savio**, claim, "There's a time when the operations of the machine become so odious . . . you've got to put your bodies on the gears . . . and make it stop."

At Greensboro, North Carolina, African American students from the nearby state university staged a sit-in in February 1960 at a segregated lunch counter in Woolworth's and started the process that brought integration to the nation's restaurants.

At Columbia University, students occupied and barricaded key sections of the institution in a confrontation with the administration. Issues, summed up in the term "student power," included the proposal to build a gymnasium in Morningside Park used chiefly by the neighboring black community, the University's connection with **IDA** (the **Institute for Defense Analysis**), and the university ban on indoor demonstrations.

In colleges and universities around the country, indeed around the world, students were occupying and barricading buildings, holding vigils, and disrupting university procedures. During the first six months of 1968 there were major demonstrations in 101 American colleges and universities.

In Washington in November 1969, a quarter of a million people converged on the nation's capital to demand an end to the Vietnam War. The following May, the nation was shocked at President Nixon's announcement of the "incursion" of United States troops into Cambodia. A rally opposing this action was quickly organized, bringing 100,000 people to the capital.

Kent State and Jackson State

Meanwhile at colleges and universities, demonstrations against the widening of the war in Indochina were common occurrences. In April 1971 an "end the war" demonstration resulted in the arrest and imprisonment of some 10,000 protesters and spectators, who were held without trial in the Washington Redskins' stadium. Participating in the demonstration were the **VVAW (Vietnam Veterans Against the War)**, who took the dramatic action of throwing their medals over a fence at the Capitol.

The extension of the war into Cambodia brought on a massive student demonstration at **Kent State University**. The Governor of Ohio sent 600 armed National Guard troops to the University to suppress the violence. The guardsmen fired a volley into the crowd, killing four of the demonstrators and wounding nine others. At **Jackson State College** in Mississippi, an institution with a predominantly black student body, protests against the invasion of Cambodia were broken up when the state highway patrol fired into a dormitory, killing two students.

The school year 1969–1970 saw nearly 1,800 student demonstrations, including some 250 cases of arson on college campuses. Many faculty members, parents, and prominent adults sympathized with the students.

Opposition to the War in Congress

After the invasion of Cambodia (April 29, 1970) a measure was introduced in the U.S. Senate by **Mark Hatfield** of Oregon and **George McGovern** of South Dakota, that would have required all U.S. troops to be recalled from Vietnam by the end of 1971. It was defeated 55 to 39. In June 1969 the Senate had approved by a vote of 76 to 10 a "sense of the Senate" resolution requiring the President to refrain from committing men or funds to any country without the express approval of Congress. And on June 24, 1970, the Senate voted 81 to 10 to repeal the Tonkin Gulf Resolution of 1964. On April 2, 1970, Massachusetts passed a law attempting to exempt its citizens from serving in combat overseas "unless such hostilities were initially authorized or subsequently ratified by a congressional declaration of war according to the constitutionally established procedures in Article I, Section 8, of the Constitution of the United States." The act underscored the fact that Congress had not declared war. The Supreme Court refused to hear arguments on the constitutionality of this Massachusetts act. But. the principle involved continued to surface.

The efforts of Congress to regain its constitutional war power, which was eroded during the Vietnam War era, culminated in November 1973 when Congress passed the **War Powers Act** over President Nixon's veto. The act provided that the President, within 48 hours of sending troops where they might be involved in combat in a foreign country, must fully explain his action to Congress. Unless Congress gave its approval, the troops were to be brought home within 60 days.

1. The candidate running against Richard Nixon on the Democratic ticket in the election of 1968 was
   A. Robert Kennedy
   B. Adlai Stevenson
   C. Edmund Muskie
   D. Hubert Humphrey

2. The most important protest movements during President Nixon's first term were against
   A. war in Vietnam
   B. broken treaties with Native Americans
   C. discrimination against Native Americans
   D. pollution of the environment

3. Since World War II, African Americans in the United States have made the greatest gains in the area of
   A. equal economic opportunity
   B. major corporate leadership
   C. voting rights
   D. desegregation of social life

4. Which was *not* true of the election of 1968?
   A. the Democrats were badly divided
   B. Nixon won by a close vote in the electoral college
   C. Democrats retained control of both houses of Congress
   D. Humphrey lost overwhelmingly in the popular vote

5. U.S. participation in the undeclared war in Vietnam during the 1960s and 1970s raised a serious question in the United States about the
   A. loyalty of U.S. military commanders
   B. authority of the President to make war
   C. intervention of the Supreme Court in matters of national security
   D. ability of Congress to finance a war

   Regents Exam, June 1987

6. The War Powers Act of 1973 was passed in order to
   A. strengthen the hand of President Nixon in pursuing the elusive victory on the battlefields of Vietnam
   B. modify the constitutional provisions pertaining to presidential power in wartime
   C. reassert the constitutional war-making power of Congress
   D. reassert the authority of the Supreme Court as an arbiter between the executive and legislative branches of government

CHAPTER REVIEW QUESTIONS

1. Which of the following is *not* true about support for the Vietnam War effort? It
   A. was maintained in Congress along partisan lines
   B. showed a steady buildup from the Eisenhower Administration well into the Johnson Administration
   C. was rejected by many of our traditional democratic allies abroad
   D. divided the American people into two groups generally described as "doves" and "hawks"

2. "We shall look to the nation directly threatened to assume the primary responsibility of providing the manpower for its defense." This statement represents
   A. President Johnson's strategy for successful prosecution of the war in Vietnam
   B. Senator Goldwater's position as candidate for President in 1964
   C. Senator McGovern's position as candidate for President in 1972
   D. Richard Nixon's "secret plan" to win the war as revealed after his election in 1968

3. Which of the following is not connected directly with the war in Vietnam?
   A. The Free Speech Movement at the University of California in Berkeley
   B. A rally in 1969 at which a quarter of a million people converged in Washington
   C. A demonstration which resulted in the arrest of some 10,000 people who were held without bail in the Washington Redskin's stadium
   D. The killing of two students at Jackson State College in Mississippi by members of the state highway patrol

4. All of the following legislative actions were taken during the Vietnam War EXCEPT
   A. a measure introduced in the Senate requiring all U.S. troops to be recalled from Vietnam by the end of 1971
   B. a resolution introduced in the Senate in 1970 to repeal the 1964 Gulf of Tonkin resolution
   C. an act of the Massachusetts legislature exempting its citizens from serving in combat unless Congress passed a declaration of war
   D. an act of Congress calling for sanctions against any foreign nations giving sanctuary to American draft evaders

ESSAYS

1. The period of the 1960s and 1970s was one of severe social and political upheaval in the United States.
   a. Choose *one* example of extreme social turmoil and *one* example of historic political upheaval. For *each* of these examples describe the unusual events that occurred and explain their significance. [5,5]
   b. Choose *one* of the examples from "a" above and discuss its relationship to national developments of the period. [5]

2. During the turbulent period of the Vietnam War, government policies and practices were greatly influenced by *nonelected* groups or individuals. Select *three* of the groups listed below and for *each* one chosen, show how that group or an individual within that group had an influence on the policies and practices of the United States government. Use specific historical examples to support your answer. [5,5,5]

   Groups

   President's Cabinet
   The military
   Presidential advisers
   The mass media
   Interest/lobbying groups
   Public opinion consultants (pollsters)

Chapter 5

THE TREND TOWARD CONSERVATISM (1972–1992)

NIXON AND THE IMPERIAL PRESIDENCY (1969–1974)

> The truth is America's most potent weapon. We cannot enlarge upon the truth. But we can and must intensify our efforts to make the truth more shining.
>
> Richard M. Nixon, *The Challenge We Face,* 1960

> Nixon is a shifty-eyed...liar... He's one of the few in the history of this country to run for high office talking out of both sides of his mouth at the same time and lying out of both sides.
>
> Harry S. Truman, from Leo Rosten, *Infinite Riches* (1978)

In the election campaign of 1968, Richard Nixon ran against Hubert Humphrey. The three main issues in the campaign were the Vietnam War, violence and disorder at home, and racial strife. Nixon promised to end the war and to restore "law and order" in the United States. The election was very close, with Nixon winning by 260,000 votes. When he became President, the Vietnam War was the most pressing problem facing the nation. President Nixon began "**Vietnamization**" and increased bombing. American troops were withdrawn gradually and finally, in 1973, a cease-fire agreement was reached.

During the Nixon presidency some Americans realized that the President had grown increasingly powerful in the American political system. This power was largely the result of World War II and the Cold War, as the President took control of foreign affairs in a world situation of ever-increasing danger. Some Americans, alarmed by presidential power, began to speak of an "**imperial presidency**."

Foreign Affairs

President Nixon took charge of foreign affairs himself and used **Henry Kissinger** as his adviser. Kissinger served first as a member of the National Security Council and in 1973 became Secretary of State. Nixon's foreign policies, except for the Vietnam War, were widely approved by the American people. Especially popular was the policy of **détente**, or easing tensions, between the United States and the Communist nations.

Détente with the Soviet Union

Closer relations between the United States and the two Communist super-powers—the Soviet Union and the People's Republic of China—during the Nixon presidency could hardly have been foreseen from his adamant anti-Communist record at home. Shortly after he became President, Nixon began exploratory talks with the Soviets on a number of issues that concerned both powers, particularly the reduction or limitation of nuclear arms. In May 1972 Nixon arrived in Moscow for talks with the leaders of the Soviet Union. He was the first President to visit Moscow. Discussions proceeded over a wide range of subjects. Most important were the **Strategic Arms Limitation Talks** (**SALT**). Agreements were reached on arms limitation, particularly **antiballistic missile systems** (subject to ratification by the U.S. Senate) and a treaty was signed May 26, 1972. Under the treaty each party agreed "not to develop, test, or deploy ABM systems or components which are sea-based, air-based, space-based, or mobile land-based." Interpretation of this provision later caused controversy over President Reagan's proposal to develop the **Strategic Defense Initiative** (**SDI**), often called "**Star Wars**," in the 1980s. The treaty also provided that "ABM systems in excess of those prohibited by this treaty shall be destroyed or dismantled within the shortest possible agreed period of time."

Shortly after the signing of the ABM treaty, the United States sold $750 million worth of wheat, corn, and other cereals to the Soviet Union. The huge surplus of grains produced by American farms went to help relieve food shortages in the Soviet Union.

Détente with the People's Republic of China

When Nixon took office in 1969, the Communist government had ruled China for almost 20 years. Yet diplomatic relations between China and the United States had never been established because the United States still recognized the **Nationalist** (**Chiang Kai-shek**) government in Taiwan as the legitimate government of China.

In a television address to the nation, delivered July 15, 1971, President Nixon made a startling declaration: "The announcement I shall now read is being issued simultaneously in Peking and in the United States... Premier Chou En-lai and Dr. Henry Kissinger [President Nixon's Assistant for National Security Affairs] held talks in Peking from July 9 to 11, 1971... the government of the People's Republic of China has extended an invitation to President Nixon to visit China... President Nixon has accepted the invitation with pleasure."

On October 25, 1971, the People's Republic of China, with the acquiescence of the United States, was admitted to the United Nations. The UN General Assembly then recommended that the permanent seat on the Security Council held by the Nationalist government on Taiwan be turned over to the government of the People's Republic of China.

The historic visit of President Nixon and his wife to China took place in February 1972. Nixon met with Chairman **Mao Zedong** and Premier **Zhou En-lai**. The visit culminated in a joint communiqué issued at Shanghai February 27, 1972, stating: "…that Taiwan is a part of China. The U.S. government does not challenge that position… it affirms the ultimate objective of the withdrawal of all U.S. forces and military installations from Taiwan."

The Arab-Israeli War of October 1973

On the eve of Yom Kippur, the holiest day of the Jewish year, Israel was suddenly attacked by the armed forces of Egypt and Syria. At first the Israelis were driven back. The attackers had the initiative and were armed with Soviet military equipment. But, despite heavy losses, the Israelis, supplied with American equipment, drove the invaders back beyond their borders and occupied the Golan Heights previously held by Syria. Sporadic fighting continued until a cease-fire was urged on the Arabs and the Israelis by the United States and the Soviet Union and negotiated by May 31, 1974. But the uneasy peace was regarded on all sides as merely temporary.

The Arab nations were angered by the American support for Israel and several halted oil shipments to the United States. This **oil embargo** resulted in long lines at gas stations and calls for conservation measures.

Domestic Policies and Developments

Many pressing problems faced President Nixon when he took office. The Vietnam War divided American society as protests continued across the nation, while **inflation**, also largely a result of the war, caused problems at home.

Dismantling the Great Society

The Great Society of President Johnson was based on the idea that the federal government had a major responsibility to provide for the health, education, and welfare of the American people. Nixon rejected this idea and, instead, proceeded to shift the burden of responsibility to the states in what he called "**the new federalism**." Through **revenue sharing**, the federal government would aid the states in providing minimum levels of social benefits. The idea was that each state could decide its own needs and how to meet them. However, over the years, the diminishing share of federal funds left the states in a position of reducing these services or raising taxes. In 1969, with inflation mounting, 10 million Americans were on welfare. Unemployment among young people, especially African American teenagers, was at a post-World War II high. Also, as American troops left Vietnam, Americans in war industries were becoming unemployed. A **recession** was in progress and new economic measures had to be undertaken.

Economic Initiatives

Although he had previously rejected a Democratic proposal to freeze wages and prices in order to stem inflation, in August 1971, Nixon yielded and ordered a 90-day wage-price freeze (the first in peacetime). A special pay board and a price commission were authorized to grant or deny wage and price increases when the freeze expired.

To improve America's position in world trade, Nixon freed the dollar from its tie to gold, permitting the dollar to decline in relation to the currency of other nations. This gave American-made goods an advantage in foreign markets, because foreigners could pay for the goods with cheaper American dollars. Nixon also imposed a 10 percent surcharge on foreign imports. Improvements in the economy helped set the stage for Nixon's reelection in 1972.

Moon Landings

On Sunday, July 20, 1969, while **Michael Collins** guided the command module of *Apollo 11,* **Neil Armstrong** and **Edwin E. Aldrin, Jr.** landed on the moon. As the world watched on TV, the two astronauts walked on the surface of the moon, set up scientific apparatus, collected rocks, and planted the American flag. The mission, planned eight years earlier by the Kennedy administration, was a 20th-century miracle.

In all, six Apollo missions landed twelve American astronauts on the moon, the last one in 1972.

The Environment

Congress took a strong stand on the environment by passing the **Water Quality Improvement Act of 1970**. The act created the **Office of Environmental Quality** and made oil companies responsible for cleaning up oil spills. It limited the use of pesticides and water pollutants and restricted thermal pollution of waters by discharges from power plants.

An oil spill that caused severe damage to the Santa Barbara coastline resulted in an order from Nixon's Secretary of the Interior **Walter J. Hickel** stopping undersea oil drilling in the area. Hickel also delayed the construction of an 800-mile oil pipeline in Alaska because of the potential damage to the flora, fauna, and other natural elements in the area. However, Nixon ordered work on the pipeline to be completed.

The Supreme Court

The Supreme Court under Chief Justice **Earl Warren** (1953–1969), former Republican Governor of California, who had been appointed by President Eisenhower, often came under attack during the 1950s and 1960s as being too "activist." Its liberal approach to civil rights, criminal procedures, church and state, and other social issues, was opposed by conservative Americans.

They were especially critical of the Court's decisions concerning criminal procedures. In *Gideon* v. *Wainright* (1963) the Court set aside a state court verdict in a felony criminal case because the state had failed to furnish counsel for the defendant, an indigent person, at his request. In *Escobedo* v. *Illinois* (1964) and *Miranda* v. *Arizona* (1966) the Court set aside verdicts against the defendants because the police had failed to notify them of their right to remain silent and to be represented by counsel during questioning.

In 1962, in *Engle* v. *Vitale*, the Court ruled that a New York State decision permitting the reading of a "nonsectarian" prayer in the public schools was a violation of the First Amendment. The following year the Court prohibited Bible reading in public school assemblies or classrooms for the same reason.

In his 1968 campaign for election to the presidency, Nixon promised to reverse these trends by appointing "**strict constructionalist**" judges to the Supreme Court. Nixon's opportunity to reform the Court was not long in coming. In 1969 Chief Justice Earl Warren retired, and the President nominated **Warren E. Burger** of Minnesota to be Chief Justice. Burger, who was on the District of Columbia Federal Court of Appeals, was quickly confirmed by the Senate.

Difficulties arose in attempting to fill the next vacancy, the resignation of Justice **Abe Fortas** in 1969. Nixon nominated **Clement F. Haynesworth, Jr.**, Chief Judge of the Fourth Circuit Court of Appeals. Disclosures of questionable ethics (conflict of interest) resulted in rejection of the nomination by the Senate. Nixon then appointed Judge **G. Harrold Carswell** of the Federal District Court of Florida to fill the vacancy on the Supreme Court. But Carswell's professional stature was poorly received by the American Bar Association and the Senate again turned down Nixon's nominee. Nixon then nominated **Harry A. Blackmun** of Minnesota, a judge on the Federal Eighth Circuit Court of Appeals, who was quickly confirmed in a unanimous Senate vote.

In September 1971 two additional vacancies on the Supreme Court came about with the resignations of Justices **Hugo LaFayette Black** and **John Marshall Harlan**. Nixon's nomination of **Lewis F. Powell, Jr.**, of Richmond, Virginia, was quickly approved by the Senate, as was the nomination of the conservative **William H. Rehnquist** of Arizona. Nixon had now appointed the Chief Justice and three associate Justices, or four out of the nine members.

Twenty-Sixth Amendment

In 1971, during Nixon's first term as President, the Twenty-Sixth Amendment was added to the Constitution. Proposed by Congress in March 1971, it was ratified by the required 38 states by June 30, partly because it granted voting rights to many young Americans who served in Vietnam. The amendment provided: "The right of citizens of the United States, who are eighteen years of age or older, to vote shall not be denied or abridged by the United States or by any state on account of age."

The Election of 1972

Both parties held their national nominating conventions at the Miami Beach convention hall in Florida—the Democrats in July and the Republicans in August. The Republicans again nominated Nixon and Agnew. The chief contender for the Democratic nomination was Senator **George McGovern** of South Dakota, a liberal and an advocate of withdrawing American troops from Vietnam. Another contender was Governor **George Wallace** of Alabama, who had run as a third party candidate in 1968. His campaign was virtually ended when he was shot and paralyzed from the waist down while delivering a campaign speech at Laurel, Maryland. A third contender, **Edmund Muskie** of Maine, was the early Democratic front-runner.

New voting procedures at the Democratic convention gave the liberal delegates—young people, civil rights activists, and advocates of women's liberation—an advantage over the professional politicians. McGovern was nominated on the first ballot. He chose Senator **Thomas F. Eagleton** of Missouri as his running mate. It was soon disclosed that Eagleton had been twice hospitalized for mental depression, and he withdrew as a candidate. **Sargent Shriver**, the first director of the Peace Corps, and later administrator of the OEO (Office of Economic Opportunity), became the vice-presidential candidate.

During the election campaign, McGovern promised to end the war in Vietnam and to introduce basic economic and social reforms at home. Nixon was the "law and order" candidate and pointed to his impressive foreign affairs achievements in improving relations with the Soviet Union and the People's Republic of China. In October, shortly before the election, Nixon's campaign received a crucial boost when Henry Kissinger, who was then negotiating with the North Vietnamese, announced "peace is at hand."

The results of the 1972 election gave Nixon and Agnew an almost clean sweep in the electoral college. The vote was 521 to 17, with Nixon winning the entire country except for Massachusetts and the District of Columbia. The popular vote gave Nixon 46,631,189 votes to McGovern's 28,422,015.

The Resignation of Spiro Agnew

Vice-President Agnew, a hard-line conservative, stood for "law and order." His vitriolic comments on the opponents of the war in Vietnam were frequently quoted in the press. He attacked "permissiveness" in the courts and the "coddling" of criminals. But after the 1972 election it was discovered that Agnew was himself a lawbreaker. While serving as Governor of Maryland, he had taken bribes from contractors and was still receiving "kickbacks" while Vice-President of the United States. He was charged with extortion and income tax evasion. He was permitted to plead "nolo contendere" (no contest), which constituted an admission of guilt. He resigned as Vice-President, was fined $10,000, and was placed on three years probation. He was also disbarred as a lawyer.

With the resignation of Vice-President Agnew, the Twenty-Fifth Amendment to the Constitution, adopted in February 1967, came into effect. It provides: "Whenever there is a vacancy in the office of the Vice-President, the President shall nominate a Vice-President who shall take office upon confirmation by a majority vote of both houses of Congress." The choice in 1973 was of crucial importance because of the growing concern over the **Watergate** scandal. Nixon nominated **Gerald R. Ford** of Michigan, a twelve-term member and minority leader of the House of Representatives. Congress promptly confirmed the nomination, and Ford took the oath of office as Vice-President on December 6, 1973.

Watergate: The Imperial Presidency in Trouble

> When the President does it, that means that it is not illegal.
> Richard M. Nixon, in a television interview, May 20, 1977

Nixon's second term was overshadowed by the **Watergate** affair, which included both the break-in at Democratic headquarters at Watergate and other political scandals in the Nixon Administration, drawing up a list of enemies (those who opposed Nixon's policies) to be harassed by every means available to the administration, including the CIA, the FBI, and even the IRS. Many members of the press were on the enemies list, as were the leaders of the opposition to the Vietnam War. To discover who was "leaking" information to the press, Nixon also had illegal wiretaps placed on the telephones of suspects. He formed a special secret unit in the White House whose mission was to stop the leaks. The unit became known as "**the plumbers**," and they carried out a number of illegal activities.

The Break-in

On June 17, 1972, at the Watergate apartment complex in Washington, a burglary in progress was discovered in the Democratic National Headquarters. The burglars, who were rummaging through files, taking photographs, and installing bugging equipment, were arrested and pleaded guilty. It was discovered that some of them were connected to Nixon's "**Committee to Reelect the President**" (**CREEP**), including **James W. McCord, Jr.**, a former CIA wiretap expert; **G. Gordon Liddy**, a former FBI agent and White House consultant; and **E. Howard Hunt, Jr.**, a former CIA agent and a White House aide.

The Cover-up

Five days after the break-in, President Nixon said the matter was "under investigation...by the proper legal authorities" and that "the White House had no involvement whatever in this particular incident." At a news conference on August 29, 1972, the President said that, under his direction, his counsel **John Dean** had "conducted a complete investigation which disclosed that "no one on the White House staff, no one in this administration, presently employed, was involved in this bizarre incident." Dean later testified under oath that he had had a series of meetings about Watergate with the President, that he had warned him that Watergate was "a cancer growing on the presidency" and that the President had taken part in the cover-up for eight months.

At first the President's cover-up statements were successful. The press seemingly lost interest in the case. However, two investigative reporters on the *Washington Post*—**Robert Woodward** and **Carl Bernstein**—pursued every lead and kept the story alive in the press.

The Watergate Hearings

With pressure for a thorough investigation mounting, the U.S. Senate, in February 1973, adopted a resolution establishing the **Senate Select Committee on Presidential Campaign Activities**, headed by **Senator Sam J. Ervin, Jr.** The Committee was directed to conduct an investigation into the extent to which illegal, improper, or unethical activities were involved in the 1972 presidential election. Televised hearings began in May 1973, and interrogation of witnesses continued for seventeen months.

Along with the establishment of the investigating committee, **Archibald Cox** of the Harvard Law School and former Solicitor General of the United States, was appointed as special prosecutor (counsel) the day after the hearings began. He was to collect evidence that would eventually lead to the indictments, trial, and conviction of those who had committed crimes.

In April 1973, **H.R. Haldemen**, Nixon's Chief of Staff, and **John D. Ehrlichman**, his Chief Assistant for Domestic Affairs, resigned. Both were deeply involved in the matters, under investigation. The same day, Nixon fired his counsel, **John Dean**, who had revealed damaging information in testimony before the Senate committee. On May 22, Nixon declared, "It its clear that unethical, as well as illegal surveillance activities took place in the course of the campaign. None of these took place with my specific approval or knowledge."

The Tapes

During testimony before the Senate committee, it was revealed that President Nixon had ordered the Secret Service to install listening devices in the White House Oval Office and other locations. Tapes of all conversations were made and stored "as a historical record."

These tapes could be used to corroborate or disprove testimony that had been given by key witnesses. Senator Ervin asked the President to make the tapes available to the committee, but Nixon refused. Special prosecutor Archibald Cox also requested the tapes and was also turned down. Judge

John J. Sirica of the Federal District Court in Washington ordered the President to deliver the tapes. The President offered to make a summary of the tapes and deliver it to Cox and to the Senate Committee. Cox demanded the original tapes and refused to accept Nixon's "compromise." On Saturday, October 20, 1973, Nixon ordered Attorney General **Elliot Richardson** to fire Cox. Richardson refused and resigned. Nixon then ordered Deputy Attorney General **William Ruckelshaus** to fire Cox. Ruckelshaus also refused and resigned. Next in line in the Department of Justice was Solicitor General **Robert Bork**, who carried out the President's order and fired special prosecutor Cox. This series of events became known as "the Saturday Night Massacre." **Leon Jaworski**, a distinguished attorney practicing in Houston, Texas, was appointed special prosecutor, and Senator **William Saxbe** of Ohio became Attorney General.

When Nixon produced the tapes as ordered by the Federal District Court, it turned out that two of the key tapes were "missing" and that there was a "gap" of 18½ minutes in an important taped conversation that Nixon had with Haldeman, his Chief of Staff, three days after the Watergate break-in.

Special prosecutor Leon Jaworski demanded that the President release more of the relevant tapes. The Judiciary Committee of the House of Representatives also wanted the tapes to help them decide whether there were grounds for **impeachment**. In response, Nixon furnished edited tapes sprinkled with omissions and deletions. The President insisted that he had "**executive privilege**" to refuse Judge Sirica's subpoena to produce unedited tapes. Jaworski appealed to the Supreme Court, and in June 1974 the Supreme Court decided that the President was legally obligated to deliver the requested tapes to the Special Prosecutor. Nixon conceded that the tapes, which he was now required to release, were "at variance with my previous statements." In other words, he had lied in order to cover up illegal acts.

Impeachment Proceedings

Article I Section 2: The House of Representatives… shall have the Sole Power of Impeachment.

Article I Section 3: The Senate shall have the sole power to try all impeachments. When sitting for that purpose, they shall take an oath or affirmation. When the President of the United States is tried, the Chief Justice shall preside: and no person shall be convicted without the concurrence of two thirds of the members present.

Judgment in cases of impeachment shall not extend further than the removal from office, and disqualification to hold and enjoy any office of honor, trust, or profit under the United States: but the party convicted shall nevertheless be liable and subject to indictment, trial, judgment, and punishment, according to law.

> Article II Section 4: The President, Vice-President and all civil offi-
> cers of the United States shall be removed from office on impeach-
> ment for, and conviction of, treason, bribery, or other high crimes and
> misdemeanors.

The Judiciary Committee of the House of Representatives began conducting an inquiry and gathering data to prepare **Articles of Impeachment**. It had become clear that the President had engaged in "high crimes and misdemeanors" sufficient to warrant his impeachment.

On June 30, 1974, the Judiciary Committee of the House of Representatives voted for, and sent to the full House, three Articles of Impeachment: (1) the President was charged with obstruction of justice; (2) he was charged with abusing his authority and violating his oath of office; and (3) he was charged with subverting the Constitution by defying eight subpoenas for tapes in order to block impeachment. There was little doubt that the House would vote these charges and that President Nixon would stand trial in the Senate. On August 8, 1974, President Nixon announced his resignation of the office of President of the United States to take effect the following day.

Indictments, Trials, and Convictions

Several important members of the Nixon administration were indicted for illegal activities. In March 1974, indictments were handed down against Mitchell, Haldeman, Ehrlichman, and four others connected with the Committee to Reelect the President, for crimes including obstruction of justice, conspiring to obstruct justice, and perjury. They were found guilty and were sentenced to prison terms of from two and a half to eight years. In all, 40 officials of the Nixon administration, including Vice-President Agnew and four cabinet officers, were indicted for various crimes including fraud, extortion, burglary, perjury, and destruction of evidence.

Watergate was a blot on the American political record comparable to the scandals of the Harding and Grant administrations. On the positive side, it demonstrated the effectiveness of our democratic institutions. Freedom of the press and our two-party system worked in a crisis. The Constitution, with its carefully crafted procedures for checks and balances, provided the resilience necessary to meet the severe challenges presented by Watergate.

Exercise Set 6.14

1. Which of the following is generally regarded as *the* major accomplishment of the Nixon administration?
   A. economic reforms
   B. environmental regulations
   C. détente with the Soviet Union and China
   D. Supreme Court appointments

2. The Watergate crimes were undertaken in order to
   A. assure success in the 1972 election
   B. secure approval for Nixon's domestic programs
   C. support continued prosecution of the war in Vietnam
   D. provide funds for "the plumbers"

3. Which of the following did *not* occur during Nixon's presidency?
   A. the Arab-Israeli War of 1973
   B. an attempt to cut back on the Great Society
   C. a 90-day freeze on wages and prices
   D. conviction of President Nixon of "high crimes and misdemeanors" by the Senate

4. In the United States, informing suspects in custody of their legal rights before they are questioned by a government official is required as a result of
   A. customs adopted from English common law
   B. state legislation
   C. decisions of the U.S. Supreme Court
   D. laws passed by Congress

   Regents Exam, June 1987

5. Which description best characterizes the decisions of the U.S. Supreme Court of the 1950s and 1960s under Chief Justice Earl Warren?
   A. activist, with a liberal approach to interpreting the Constitution
   B. cautious, with a philosophy of strict construction
   C. traditional, with a stress on states' rights
   D. conservative, with a strong emphasis on "cracking down" on war criminals

6. Since World War II, a major goal of U.S. foreign policy in the Middle East has been to bring about
   A. permanent United Nations control of disputed territories
   B. a peaceful settlement of Arab-Israeli issues
   C. ownership of oil resources by Western nations
   D. an end to U.S. cooperation with Arab nations

THE FORD AND CARTER PRESIDENCIES (AUGUST 1974–JANUARY 1981)

> I am a Ford, not a Lincoln.
>> Gerald R. Ford of Michigan upon being sworn in as Vice-President,
>>> Dec. 6, 1973

> To me the presidency and the vice-presidency were not prizes to be
> won but a duty to be done.
>> Gerald R. Ford in *A Time to Heal*, 1979

Gerald R. Ford served in the House of Representatives for 25 years (1949–1973), and was minority (Republican) leader from 1965 to 1973, when President Nixon appointed him Vice-President to replace Spiro Agnew. Upon the resignation of Nixon, Ford became President on August 9, 1974. No other person has ever served in this high office without having been elected on a national ticket.

Domestic Developments Under President Ford

Vice-President Rockefeller

To fill the vacancy in the vice-presidency created by his elevation to the presidency, Ford followed the provisions of the Twenty-fifth Amendment to the Constitution. He nominated **Nelson A. Rockefeller**, Governor of New York from 1958 to 1973. Congress confirmed the nomination in December 1974. For the first time in history, the United States had an appointed President and Vice-President, neither having been elected to office. Ford retained Henry A. Kissinger as Secretary of State along with most of the remaining members of the Nixon cabinet. The nation felt relieved at the transition from the Nixon administration to the frank, open, and amiable administration of the new President.

The Pardon

In September 1974, a month after taking office, Ford declared, "By virtue of the authority vested in me by the Constitution of the United States, I hereby grant to Richard M. Nixon a full, free and absolute pardon… for all offenses against the United States which he… has committed or may have committed or taken part in during his presidency." The pardon was designed "to end the nightmare" and avoid the rancor of a public trial of the ex-President with its unpleasant consequences. Many Americans protested the pardon, claiming it was unfair to grant immunity to Nixon while those who had carried out his orders had served prison terms. It also raised the question of whether there had been a "deal" between Nixon and Ford.

The pardon was followed by a presidential announcement of **clemency** (but not amnesty) for draft evaders and deserters during the Vietnam War. To avoid punishment, deserters and draft evaders were required to take an oath of allegiance to the United States and then serve periods of up to two years in jobs to promote the national health, safety, or interest. Only about 25,000 of the 125,000 eligible accepted the offer. The others were later pardoned by President Carter.

Economic Difficulties

Within a year of Ford's assuming the presidency, the nation faced the worst **economic recession** since the 1930s. Unemployment reached an alarming level of nearly 10 percent in 1975, while annual inflation reached a high of 12 percent. The combination gave rise to a new term "**stagflation**," an economic anomaly. The economic situation improved slowly, but hard times continued throughout Ford's presidency and worked against his election in 1976.

Rising oil prices played a large part in the inflation of the 1970s. As the nation cut back on coal (an air pollutant) and nuclear energy (a safety hazard) and as the number of motor vehicles on the highways steadily increased, the use of oil (for gasoline) began to exceed the national production. The United States, traditionally an oil exporter, began to import oil in the early 1970s. **Libya**, a key source of oil, raised its prices, and other foreign producers did likewise. By 1973 world oil prices had quintupled.

Led by **Venezuela**, oil producers in the Middle East, Asia, Africa, and Latin America formed a **cartel** (monopoly) named **Organization of Petroleum Exporting Countries** (**OPEC**). American motorists began paying five times what they had paid for gasoline only a few months earlier. Gas that sold for 16 cents a gallon in 1972 was now priced at $1.00, and oil companies made "windfall" profits. The crisis created by the oil embargo after the Arab-Israeli War of 1973 occurred before Ford became President, but it contributed greatly to the hard times of his administration.

Political Aspects

• *Supreme Court Appointment and Rulings.* In 1975, Justice **William O. Douglas** retired after 36 years on the Supreme Court. President Ford nominated **John Paul Stevens** of Illinois, a judge of the Seventh Circuit Court of Appeals, and the Senate confirmed the appointment. The following year the Supreme Court handed down two important decisions. It ruled that African Americans and other minorities are entitled to retroactive job seniority and that capital punishment is not a violation of the constitutional prohibition of cruel and unusual punishment.

• *The CIA and the FBI.* Charges of illegal activities by the **CIA** and the **FBI** under previous administrations led to investigations. Soon after he took office, President Ford appointed a commission, headed by Vice-President Rockefeller, to examine and report on CIA abuses. The report, issued in June 1975, disclosed that the CIA, which was authorized to conduct foreign operations only, had been involved in clandestine domestic activities almost since its beginning in 1947. It had infiltrated and attempted to disrupt antiwar, civil rights, and other legal organizations. It had compiled intelligence files on 300,000 American citizens, including members of Congress who opposed the Vietnam War. It had intercepted mail, participated in illegal wiretaps and engaged in break-ins.

An earlier study had revealed that the **Federal Bureau of Investigation** under **J. Edgar Hoover** had likewise attempted to disrupt organizations engaged in legal activities.

• *Freedom of Information Acts; Privacy Act.* The **Freedom of Information Act of 1966** was strengthened by Congress in 1974 as a reaction to secret illegal dossiers compiled by the Nixon administration against his "enemies" and those who openly opposed his policies. Government agencies were required to open their files (except for national defense and foreign policy matters) and permit photocopying of contents by interested persons. The **Privacy Act of 1974** gave citizens the right to examine files compiled about them by government agencies.

• *Federal Election Campaign Finance Reform Act.* The act, passed in 1974 and revised in 1976, gave the President power to appoint a six-member **Federal Election Commission**. Candidates for President and Vice-President in primary and national elections are required to file detailed accounts of sources of moneys received for their campaigns. Limitations are imposed on the amounts that **Political Action Committees** (**PACs**) of unions, corporations, or other organizations may contribute. Individuals who contribute over $100 must certify that the contribution was made without communicating with the candidate or the campaign committee. Violators are subject to severe civil and criminal penalties. The main source of presidential campaign funds was designed to be the $1.00 checkoff allotted to election campaigns from income tax return forms. This $100 million source plus small individual contributions takes the presidential election, to some extent, out of the control of large corporations, unions, and special interest political organizations. Efforts to impose similar restrictions on the election campaigns of members of Congress have proved unsuccessful.

• *Budget and Impoundment Act of 1974.* Funds appropriated by Congress for social purposes (health, welfare, education, legal aid, etc.) over presidential vetoes were regularly "impounded," that is, not used by the government at President Nixon's direction. The **Budget and Impoundment Act of 1974** specifically declared that the President was required by law to expend all funds appropriated by Congress. The act created a **Congressional Budget Office**, whereby Congress could maintain its own records of federal income and expenditures in order to monitor presidential compliance with the law.

- *Space Explorations. Viking 1*, launched in August 1975, landed on Mars in July 1976, and relayed back to earth detailed scientific research including photographs of the planet. It was designed for 90 days of operations but continued to function for almost 6½ years, until it ceased operating in November 1982. *Viking 2*, launched in September 1975, landed on Mars in September 1976, and continued to report its findings for 3½ years. Other launching and explorations (*Voyagers 1* and *2* of September 1977) explored the planets Jupiter, Saturn, and Uranus. *Voyager 2* passed Neptune in 1989 and sent back important new information on this planet. The Hubble Space Telescope was placed in orbit by the space shuttle *Discovery* in 1990. Problems with faulty equipment were repaired by astronauts in 1993.

- *Conrail (1976) and Amtrak (1971).* The **Consolidated Rail Corporation** (**Conrail**) was established in 1976 by combining seven freight lines in the Northeast. Conrail was granted a $2.1 million government loan to maintain the railroads, which were all in financial difficulties. The railroads would then be able to continue operating without a government takeover. Conrail handles about one fourth of the nation's freight and serves a population of 100 million.

Amtrak, a national passenger traffic combine, was organized in 1971 with federal subsidies to help maintain a viable system of national passenger transportation as an alternative to automobiles, buses, and airline transportation. Government subsidies were cut back during the Reagan administration. Yet Amtrak, despite its enforced elimination of many trains, has shown steady growth in the number of passengers served, particularly in the Northeast corridor (Boston–Washington), the Chicago area, and the West Coast. Because of motor vehicle highway gluts, air pollution, and accidents, it is expected that rail transportation will continue to increase in proportion to total passenger traffic.

Foreign Relations Under President Ford

Gerald Ford kept Henry Kissinger as Secretary of State and continued the policy of détente.

President Ford in the Soviet Union and Asia

In November 1974, three months after he took the oath of office as President, Ford met with Premier **Leonid Brezhnev** of the Soviet Union at a health resort near Vladivostok, the chief Soviet port on the Pacific Ocean. They agreed to place a ceiling on the number of **ICBMs** (intercontinental ballistic missiles) launched from submarines, of **MIRVs** (multiple independently targeted reentry vehicles), and bombers. The meeting, a signal that both sides sought détente, was a tacit recognition of the need to avoid a nuclear holocaust.

From the Soviet Union, Ford went to Japan for a four-day goodwill visit. His last stop in Asia was a one-day visit to South Korea that symbolized the continuing friendship of the two nations.

Angola

This former Portuguese colony in East Africa was one of the last colonies to gain its independence. A revolution in 1974 led Portugal to grant Angola its independence in 1975. American interest in Angola was based on the intervention by the Soviets, bolstered by Cuban troops. President Ford had Secretary of State Kissinger use his diplomatic skill to prevent a full-scale war or a Communist takeover. The problem was complicated by South Africa's control of **Namibia**, south of Angola. Namibia, the former German colony of Southwest Africa, became a trust territory of South Africa after World War I. Despite pressure from the UN, South Africa retained a dominant influence in Namibia, and was deeply involved in developments in Angola.

Capture of the *Mayaguez*

In May 1975, the United States merchant ship *Mayaguez*, with a crew of 39, was seized in the Gulf of Siam by Cambodian forces. After brief negotiations failed to free the crew, President Ford sent American forces to rescue the ship and crew. The Americans were freed, but 15 marines were killed in the battle, 23 died in a helicopter crash, 50 were wounded, and 3 missing.

South Vietnam

With the collapse of the Thieu government of South Vietnam in April 1975, Congress appropriated $405 million to aid refugees fleeing from the North Vietnamese Communists. President Ford admitted 140,000 South Vietnamese refugees to the United States after Congress rejected his appeal for military aid. Most of the refugees later became American citizens.

Helsinki Accords

In July 1975 President Ford attended a conference of representatives of 35 nations in Helsinki, Finland. Boundaries drawn in Eastern Europe at the end of World War II were officially legitimized. In return, the Soviet Union and its satellites signed a "human rights" guarantee, which included a provision for the right to emigrate. The hopes raised by these agreements did not materialize when the Soviets failed to implement them.

President Jimmy Carter (1977–1981)

> As President I will not be able to provide everything that every one of
> you might like. I am sure to make many mistakes. But I can promise
> you that you will never have the feeling that your needs are being
> ignored, or that we have forgotten who put us in office.
> Jimmy Carter, in a televised address to the nation, February 1, 1977

The Election of 1976

In the 1976 election, the incumbent President Ford (Republican) ran against
the little known challenger, **James Earl (Jimmy) Carter** (Democrat), former Governor of Georgia. To gain the nomination, each overcame strong
competition from contenders in their respective parties. Ford was challenged
by **Ronald Reagan**, the former Governor of California, who appealed to the
conservative wing of the Republican party. Ford won the nomination on the
first ballot by a close vote—1187 to 1070.

On the Democratic side there were a number of logical contenders for the
nomination but no clear favorite. Among them were former Vice-President
Hubert Humphrey, Senator **Henry "Scoop" Jackson** of Washington,
Congressman **Morris Udall** of Arizona, and Governor **George C. Wallace**
of Alabama. However, it was Jimmy Carter who won the nomination by conducting a well-planned campaign. He entered his name in every primary and
appealed to grassroots partisans willing to support an "outsider" who could
bring a breath of fresh air to the stale politics-as-usual atmosphere.

Both parties adopted middle-of-the-road platforms. Ford, the more conservative candidate, defended his record of honesty in government and fiscal
restraint. Carter ran against the Washington "establishment" and pledged full
employment and support for necessary social programs along with a promise
to balance the budget.

In the November election, Carter and the Democratic party won a hard-
fought victory. It was the first time since 1932 that an incumbent President
was defeated in his bid for reelection. Only 53 percent of the eligible voters
bothered to cast their ballots, The Democrats also retained control of the
House and Senate and won nearly three fourths of the state governorships.

Domestic Policies of President Carter

Carter relied on his former Georgia associates when he took command in
Washington. He and they had little experience with how the federal government worked. Moreover, Carter did not know many members of Congress,
and he did not consult with them on his legislative program. As a result, Congress blocked many of Carter's programs.

President Carter did win the approval of Congress to add two new Cabinet-
level departments to the executive branch—a **Department of Energy** in
1977 and a **Department of Education** in 1979.

Soon after he took office, Carter sought to end the Vietnam trauma. President Ford had offered clemency to draft evaders and deserters. Carter went further and pardoned some 100,000 Americans who were still subject to punishment.

• *The Economy.* Inflation plagued the Carter administration as it had Ford's. Led by rising oil prices, inflation reached 13 percent in 1979, while the economy remained in a slump. Mounting unemployment and skyrocketing interest rates (which reached more than 20 percent by 1980) added to the national economic malaise, while a budget deficit of $60 billion in 1980 called for new measures to turn the economy around. The proposal to raise taxes was rejected in favor of the alternative of reducing taxes in order to stimulate the economy. By 1980 the economy was suffering a recession. The same year, the Carter administration moved to bail out the **Chrysler Corporation**, which was facing bankruptcy, by supporting loan assurances of $1.5 billion.

The nation's economic problems were exacerbated by an energy crisis in 1979. Another oil shortage causing long gas lines was largely the result of a revolution in Iran, a major oil producer. The **Shah**, ruler of Iran, was forced to flee and was replaced by a fundamentalist Moslem religious regime headed by the **Ayatollah Ruhollah Khomeini**. As the Iranian oil supply temporarily stopped flowing into world markets, oil shortages developed and gasoline prices rose rapidly. Carter proposed a program to deal with the energy crisis. His proposals for making the nation independent of the OPEC oil included the development of synthetic fuels and other sources of energy such as solar, thermal, and nuclear, and a concerted national program of **energy conservation**. His aim was to cut oil imports in half by 1990. He called the proposed national effort to conserve energy "the moral equivalent of war." At first, the public and Congress did not support his proposals. His request for a tax on imported oil and for standby gas rationing authority was turned down by Congress. He did manage to lift the controls on domestic oil production and get approval of a "windfall profits tax" on the huge profits of oil companies.

• *The Environment.* President Carter secured Congressional approval of the **Alaska National Interest Lands Conservation Act** of 1980. This act set aside 103 million acres (an area larger than California) of unspoiled wilderness in Alaska. It was part of a compromise whereby other undeveloped areas in Alaska were opened for exploitation by oil, mining, and timber interests.

Concern developed over environmental damage caused by **strip mining**, **acid rain**, and **water pollution**. Strip mining, or mining coal near the earth's surface, is an inexpensive process that scars the earth's surface. Erosion, destruction of wildlife and natural habitat, flooding, and water pollution are among the undesirable side effects of this process. A partial solution is to restore the surface after removing the coal, but this adds to the cost of the coal. President Carter advocated laws to require restoration of the landscape.

Acid rain destroys lakes and forests and is caused by chemicals in the smoke from factories. Winds carry the chemicals from America's industrial

Midwest to the lakes and forests of the northeastern United States and Canada. The damage is irreversible. The solution is to "scrub" the exhausts and capture the harmful chemicals before they are released into the air. However, the cost would have to be passed on to the consumer. It is argued that unless factories in other countries take similar steps to prevent acid rain, the United States would be at a competitive disadvantage.

• *Judicial appointments.* President Carter made 265 appointments to the federal judiciary. His choice of a number of minority persons and women for the federal bench was widely hailed. No vacancies on the Supreme Court occurred during his term.

Foreign Affairs

Concern for human rights throughout the world was a key aspect of President Carter's foreign policy. He criticized the Soviet Union for failing to live up to the 1975 Helsinki Accords and denying dissidents and Jews the right to emigrate. His crusade for human rights was also directed against dictatorial regimes in Latin America and Africa. He denounced South Africa's practice of **apartheid** and castigated Cuba and Uganda for oppression. He cut off foreign aid to dictatorships in Argentina, Brazil, Ethiopia, and Uruguay. But he approved massive arms sales to Iran's dictatorial Shah because his government was serving as "a bastion against communism."

• *Panama Canal Treaties (1978).* By the Hay-Bunau-Varilla Treaty of 1903, a 99-year renewable lease to the Canal Zone in the newly established Republic of Panama was granted by Panama to the United States for the payment of an annual fee. In 1978 the lease still had 25 years to run, but discussions over the future of the Canal had been going on with Panama since the Eisenhower administration. Rising nationalist sentiment in Latin America and resentment in Panama against United States control of their territory led to negotiations to turn over the Canal Zone. President Carter felt it was in the best interest of the United States to return the land to Panama and strengthen America's position throughout Latin America.

Two treaties were drawn up in 1977. One provided for the return of the Canal Zone and its operation to Panama by December 31, 1999. The other treaty provided that: "If operations [of the canal] are interfered with, the United States of America shall have the right to the use of force in the Republic of Panama."

• *Camp David Accord.* When Carter became President in 1977, three wars had already been fought between Israel and the neighboring Arab nations, which were determined to destroy the Jewish state. In 1977, President **Anwar el-Sadat** of Egypt surprised the world by accepting an invitation to visit Israel. He delivered a long, emotional plea for peace in an address to the Israeli **Knesset** (Parliament). President Carter promptly invited Sadat and Israeli Prime Minister **Menachem Begin** to join him at his

Camp David retreat in the mountains of Maryland. In the ensuing dialogue, Carter acted to bring the positions of the two leaders closer together.

Finally, on September 17, 1978, a tentative agreement between Egypt and Israel was reached. President Carter went to Egypt and Israel in 1979 to facilitate peace negotiations and the peace treaty was signed in March 1979. Israel returned the **Sinai** peninsula to Egypt in return for guarantees of normal relations between the two countries. Exchange of ambassadors and the establishment of travel and trade relations raised hopes for an expanding good-neighbor relationship. The Arab world outside of Egypt refused to accept the new era of friendly relations with Israel.

Shortly after this diplomatic success, President Carter took another significant move in foreign affairs by establishing full diplomatic relations with the People's Republic of China.

- *SALT II.* The **Strategic Arms Limitation Treaty of 1972 (SALT I)**, between the United States and the Soviet Union, was scheduled to expire in December 1977. However, both sides continued to observe the terms of the treaty and a **SALT II** agreement was signed by President Carter and Soviet Premier Leonid Brezhnev in Vienna in June 1979. If ratified by the U.S. Senate, it would have extended arms limitations until December 1985. But it ran into strong opposition in the Senate and was tabled when Soviet troops invaded Afghanistan in December 1979.

- *Nicaragua.* Nicaragua, the largest country in Central America, was governed by the **Somoza** family from the 1920s until rebel forces known as **Sandinistas** succeeded in overthrowing the dictatorship of **Anastasio Somoza** in July 1979. The United States quickly recognized the new government, hoping to assist in the establishment of a democratic republic. But the Sandinistas proceeded to establish a Socialist regime modeled on Marxist economic principles.

- *Afghanistan.* In December 1979 the Soviet army launched a full-scale invasion of Afghanistan. This attempt to strengthen the faltering pro-Soviet government in Kabul met with unexpectedly strong resistance from guerrilla forces. The Brezhnev government's justification for the invasion was its claim that China and Pakistan were attempting to overthrow Afghanistan's pro-Soviet government. But the United States regarded the move as a thrust at the Persian Gulf and its oil resources.

President Carter responded energetically to this challenge. He sent naval forces into the Persian Gulf, declaring that the area was "vital" to American interests. He ordered an embargo on the shipment of grain and high-technology machinery to the Soviet Union, called for a boycott of the 1980 Olympic Games in Moscow, and requested Congress to pass legislation requiring young men and women to register for a possible military draft.

Aid to Afghanistani rebel forces resisting the Soviet troops was stepped up throughout 1980 and reached a climax during the second term of the

Reagan presidency. American military supplies flowed to the anti-Soviet forces. The Soviet air force was neutralized by sophisticated American Stinger missiles. The invasion turned out to be a disaster for the Soviets and in February 1986, the new Soviet leader, **Mikhail S. Gorbachev**, announced the withdrawal of Soviet forces "in the nearest future." Peace talks were held in Geneva under UN auspices, and accords providing for Soviet withdrawal were signed in April 1988. The last of 100,000 Soviet troops left Afghanistan in February 1989. The war cost the Soviets at least 15,000 dead, an indeterminate number of wounded and missing, and billions of rubles. It underscored the difficulty of defeating armed guerrillas fighting on their own terrain in defense of their country.

• *American Hostages in Iran.* The **Shah of Iran** was overthrown early in 1979 and replaced by a fanatical religious leader, the **Ayatollah Ruhollah Khomeini**. Fierce hatred of the United States by Muslim fanatics erupted in an unprecedented act of international terrorism. On November 4, 1979, a mob surrounded the American embassy in Teheran and seized its occupants, 52 members of the American diplomatic corps. The Iranian government alleged that it exercised no control over the militant "students" who occupied the American embassy. The failure of a nation to protect foreign embassy personnel is a flagrant violation of international law. Efforts by President Carter and the UN to secure release of the hostages failed. As the weeks passed there was growing concern in the United States over the condition of the hostages. In desperation, President Carter approved a military plan to rescue the hostages. However, conditions for the rescue plan proved unfavorable and the attempt was abandoned. On January 20, 1981, after a 444-day ordeal in captivity, the 52 hostages were released. They were freed minutes after **Ronald Reagan** took the oath of office as 40th President of the United States.

Exercise Set 6.15

1. Nelson Rockefeller became Vice-President in the Ford administration as a result of
   A. his election to the office in 1974
   B. the decision of the Republican National Committee
   C. his nomination by President Ford and confirmation by both houses of Congress
   D. a decision by the U.S. Supreme Court

2. The Federal Election Campaign Finance Reform Act of 1974 as amended in 1976 provides for all of the following EXCEPT
   A. a limit on the amount that candidates for the Senate or House of Representatives may spend on their election campaigns
   B. a voluntary contribution to presidential campaigns by a $1.00 checkoff on federal income tax returns
   C. limitations on the amount that political action committees may contribute to candidates for national office
   D. candidates in primary elections and regular national elections must file detailed accounts with the Federal Election Commission specifying the amounts and sources of contributions to their campaigns

3. Least known among the early contenders for the presidential nomination in 1976 was
   A. George Wallace
   B. Edward Kennedy
   C. Henry Jackson
   D. Jimmy Carter

4. The largest contributor to the high rate of inflation during the Ford and Carter administrations was
   A. imports of oil
   B. high farm commodity prices
   C. high building costs
   D. budget deficits

THE REAGAN ERA (1981–1989)

The Election of 1980

> The Republican party is sharply different under Reagan from what it was under Gerald Ford and Presidents all the way back to Eisenhower.
>
> Jimmy Carter, Sept. 2, 1980

> In this present crisis, government is not the solution to our problems. Government is the problem.
>
> Ronald Reagan, first inaugural address, Jan. 20, 1981

As the 1980 election approached, the nation was plagued by unemployment, inflation, high interest rates, and frustration over the captivity of 52 American hostages in Iran. The apparent inability of the Carter administration to resolve these problems caused Senator **Edward M. (Ted) Kennedy** to challenge President Carter for the Democratic presidential nomination. Many members of the Democratic party feared that Carter would not be reelected. A public opinion poll in the summer of 1980 revealed that only 21 percent of the American people approved of President Carter's performance in office. This was an all-time low. Carter turned back Kennedy's challenge and won the nomination. He was opposed in the election by **Ronald Reagan**, who was nominated by the Republican party. Some voters turned to a third party, the Independent party, led by Representative **John Anderson** from Illinois, who won more than 5.5 million votes. A fourth-party candidate, the environmentalist **Barry Commoner** of California, was supported by nearly one million voters.

During the campaign, Reagan stressed the nation's military weakness and Carter's failure to solve the nation's problems. Carter pointed to his foreign policy achievements.

In the popular vote, Reagan received 51.6 percent against Carter's 41.7 percent, with 6.7 percent going to Anderson. But Reagan won an overwhelming majority of votes in the electoral college, 489 to 49.

In addition to winning the presidency, the Republicans gained control of the Senate for the first time in 28 years and picked up 33 seats in the House of Representatives. It was a stunning victory for conservatives and a shocking defeat for the liberal "New Deal" Democrats.

Reagan Policies

Ronald Reagan had long been a leader of the conservative movement in the United States. He favored limited federal government, lower taxes, and reduced federal regulation of business. Although Reagan favored a more limited role for the federal government, in social issues he supported constitutional amendments to ban abortion and to permit prayer in public schools. He also favored a return to traditional values and family roles.

Attempt to Assassinate the President

On March 30, 1981, President Reagan was shot by **John W. Hinckley, Jr.**, a deranged young man. A bullet caused the collapse of the President's left lung, but after twelve days in the hospital, he returned to work. By April 28 he was able to deliver an address to Congress. His resiliency won public admiration.

Domestic Programs

President Reagan felt that he had a mandate from the electorate to carry out his programs for the nation. He immediately turned his attention to the nation's economic crisis.

Supply-side Economics

To bring down inflation, President Reagan adopted a policy known as **"supply-side" economics**, based on the belief that cuts in income taxes, especially on higher incomes, would result in business investment and act as a stimulus to business. Cuts in corporation taxes would promote business expansion, resulting in greater production of goods and bringing about full employment. The emphasis would be on supply of goods, rather than on demand, to revive the economy. During the presidential primaries, Vice-President Bush had expressed doubts about the effectiveness of this approach, as did many economists. Bush called it **"voodoo economics."** Reagan prevailed on Congress to cut taxes on high incomes, corporations, and investors, and in July 1981, Congress passed the largest tax cut in the nation's history. American taxpayers received tax benefits of $750 billion over a five-year period.

The Federal Budget; Cuts and Priorities

To help him carry out his budgetary program, Reagan chose **David Stockman** as his director of the **Office of Management and Budget**. The goal of a balanced budget was to be attained through sharp cuts in federal expenditures. The one exception was the defense budget, which was expanded. Although the Reagan administration believed supply-side economics and cuts in the budget would painlessly decrease inflation, the economy did not respond as expected. Inflation came down, but within a year the nation was in a severe **recession**. In November 1982, unemployment reached 10.8 percent, with 11 million unemployed. By 1983, the economy began to recover and the twin demons— inflation and high interest rates—were brought under control. But the national budget remained unbalanced. By 1986, budget deficits, mounting annually, exceeded $200 billion. By 1989 the national debt was $3 trillion ($3 thousand billion). To remedy this, President Reagan called for an amendment to the Constitution requiring a balanced budget. If it were passed, its primary impact would be felt by succeeding administrations. In December 1985, Congress passed the **Gramm-Rudman-Hollings Act**, designed to achieve a balanced budget by 1991. On July 7, 1986, the Supreme Court invalidated the provision of the law that authorized the controller general to institute the "automatic" cuts because it vested executive branch authority in a legislative branch officer (the controller general was removable by Congress) and thus violated the constitutional principle of separation of powers. However, the basic provision of the law requiring that federal income and expenditures be brought into balance by 1991 remained intact. The law set annual targets for reducing the deficit by across-the-board cuts in federal spending.

The first Reagan budget called for drastic cuts in social programs. The budget proposed a cut of $1.1 billion in aid to education with no provision for aid to handicapped or gifted students. Direct financial aid to college and university students (programs in existence since 1965) was phased out. Support for the National Science Foundation, basic research, the National Endowment for the Arts, the National Endowment for the Humanities, and educational television was drastically reduced.

As for the poor, President Reagan spoke of a national "safety net," but this budget called for a reduction of $1.6 billion in school lunch programs for needy children, extinction of the Legal Services Corporation, reduction in Medicaid by nearly $1 billion, sharp cuts in federal aid to low-income housing, and a $2.3 billion cut in the food stamp program.

The "new federalism" of the Reagan administration offered grants to the states to help them assume responsibility for funding these programs.

Social Issues

The Reagan administration supported the position of conservatives on social issues, favoring organized prayer in the schools, support for nonpublic education, and less emphasis on civil rights. It opposed the Equal Rights Amendment, abortion, and sex education in the schools. In opposition to this agenda, funds began to pour into long-established liberal organizations— the American Civil Liberties Union, Planned Parenthood, Common Cause, Public Citizen, the National Organization for Women, the Natural Resources Defense Council, and new ones like People for the American Way.

Supreme Court Appointments

With the retirement of Justice **Potter Stewart** from the Supreme Court in 1981, President Reagan nominated **Sandra Day O'Connor** of the Arizona Supreme Court. She was confirmed by the Senate and sworn in September 25, 1981, the first woman to serve on the Supreme Court. This was to be Reagan's only appointment to the Supreme Court during his first term. Five years later additional openings came. Chief Justice **Warren E. Burger** retired in 1986 and President Reagan's nominee for the chief justiceship, Justice **William H. Rehnquist**, was confirmed by the Senate. The vacancy brought about by Justice Rehnquist's move to the chief justiceship was filled when the Reagan nominee, Judge **Antonin Scalia** of Virginia, was confirmed.

After the retirement of Justice **Lewis F. Powell, Jr.**, in 1987, President Reagan nominated Judge **Robert Bork** of the United States Court of Appeals for the District of Columbia to fill the vacancy. Judge Bork, a former law professor at Yale Law School and Solicitor General in the Nixon administration, was a conservative whom Reagan described as "a powerful advocate of judicial restraint." He was opposed by many groups, and after hearings on the nomination the Senate Committee on the Judiciary recommended to the Senate that the nomination be rejected. Reagan's next nominee, **Douglas Ginsberg**, met with opposition because he admitted having once used marijuana. He asked to have his name withdrawn. Judge **Anthony M. Kennedy** of California was then nominated and promptly confirmed.

Meanwhile President Reagan nominated judges to fill vacancies on the lower federal courts—District Courts and Circuit Courts of Appeals—throughout the country. In selecting appointees, he was advised by his Attorney General, **Edwin Meese**, who sought candidates that satisfied the ideological criteria of conservative Republicans. During his eight years in office, Reagan appointed nearly 50 percent of all the judges on the federal bench. Elevation to the federal bench carries lifetime tenure, signaling the awesome responsibility of the President in nominating, and the Senate in confirming, appointees to federal courts.

The Environment

The assault on the environment caused by budget cuts for enforcement agencies such as the Environmental Protection Agency (EPA), the Food and Drug Administration (FDA), and the Occupational Safety and Health Administration (OSHA), was a source of concern for conservationists, environmentalists, and public health agencies. Public lands in the West, under Secretary of the Interior **James Watt**, were offered for sale at low prices, often as little as pennies an acre. Charges of mismanagement and favoritism in the EPA led to the appointment of **William Ruckelshaus**, an environmentalist and skilled administrator, to head the agency that he had led when it was first established in 1970.

Acid rain, pollution of air and water, and safe disposal of nuclear wastes constitute major unsolved environmental problems. Negotiations with Canada for control of acid rain were stalled while investigations were conducted to determine the source of the destruction of forests and lakes in eastern Canada and northeastern United States.

In November 1986 President Reagan vetoed a clean water bill passed by Congress. The bill called for expenditure of $20 billion for facilities to treat sewage and water poisoned by toxic dumps. The bill was resubmitted and passed over the President's veto by the (new) 100th Congress in February 1987.

- *Depletion of Ozone.* In March 1989 the 12 European Community countries agreed to eliminate, by the end of the century, the production and use of chemicals that destroy the earth's protective **ozone** shield. The action was endorsed by **William K. Reilly**, head of the Environmental Protection Agency in the Bush administration. Ozone, the natural shield that gives protection from the sun's direct ultraviolet radiation, is declining steadily due to chemicals released into the air. These industrial chemicals used in refrigeration, solvents, and aerosol propellants are destroying ozone molecules.

- *Waste Disposal.* Waste disposal is a major environmental concern. **Nuclear wastes** pose a special problem because they remain radioactive for centuries and must be buried in sealed containers. It is difficult, if not impossible, to guarantee against leakage, and acceptable sites are becoming difficult to find. **Hospital wastes** are another hazardous source, particularly wastes potentially containing material infected with the AIDS virus. Cities find it difficult to make long-range plans for garbage disposal, because they are running out of dumpsites. Dumping at sea is poisoning fish. The commercial importance of ocean fishing has lead to legislation banning disposal of sewage and other wastes at sea.

- *Greenhouse Effect.* The earth's temperature is slowly rising because of the "**greenhouse effect**." Gases in the air, especially carbon dioxide released in automobile exhausts and industrial smoke stacks, prevent heat from the sun from radiating back into space. The rising temperature will have serious adverse effects on humans. Many scientists believe the glacial ice at the polar regions will melt, bringing about a disastrous rise in the ocean level.

The Election of 1984

As the election of 1984 approached, the nation was in an economic upswing. The recession of 1981–1982 was over, inflation and interest rates were down, and employment was up. In January 1984 President Reagan sounded his campaign theme, declaring "America is back, standing tall, looking to the '80s with courage, confidence and hope." Despite a doubling of the national debt during his first term, the President stood firm on his economic program of tax reduction. He was equally consistent on social issues: opposing abortion, the Equal Rights Amendment, affirmative action, and busing for school desegregation.

The front-runner for the Democratic nomination, former Vice-President **Walter Mondale**, was strongly challenged by Senator **Gary Hart** of Colorado and Reverend **Jesse Jackson** of Chicago. However, Mondale secured enough delegates to clinch the nomination before the convention. For Vice-President he chose Representative **Geraldine Ferraro** of New York, the first woman candidate for the vice-presidency nominated by a major party. Of the 92 million votes cast, 53,354,037 (59 percent) went for Reagan and 36,884,260 (41 percent) for Mondale. In the electoral college, the Republicans won 525 to 13. Only Minnesota (Mondale's home state) and the District of Columbia (perennially in the Democratic column) went to Mondale-Ferraro. In the land-slide victory, the Republicans retained control of the Senate.

Foreign Affairs

Cold War Resumed

During the 1980 election campaign, Ronald Reagan denounced SALT II, the Strategic Arms Limitation Treaty negotiated with the Soviets in 1979 by the Carter administration. The treaty, which was to run until 1985, was never acted on by the Senate because of the Soviet invasion of Afghanistan, but both sides observed its terms. In a press conference soon after his inauguration, President Reagan censured the Soviets, saying they were "prepared to commit any crime, to lie, to cheat" in order to achieve world conquest. Reagan's insistence on a hard-line approach toward the Soviet Union, as well as increased military spending and the placement of nuclear weapons in Europe, alarmed many. Fear of a global nuclear war increased throughout Europe and America. In New York's Central Park in June 1982, a peaceful demonstration against nuclear arms brought out more than 500,000 people. Antinuclear demonstrations took place in the major cities of our NATO allies. In 1985, a new leader, **Mikhail Gorbachev**, came to power in the Soviet Union. Reagan agreed to meet with him in Geneva in November.

Lebanon

On October 23, 1983, a truck carrying explosives drove into the marine barracks in Beirut, Lebanon, and blew up, killing 241 marines. The following year pro-Iranian terrorists took three American hostages in Beirut, including the CIA station chief, **William Buckley**, who died while being held captive.

Bitburg

In May 1985 Reagan paid a prearranged visit to a cemetery in West Germany where members of the Waffen SS, Hitler's elite troops, were buried. Reagan was urged to cancel the visit, because the Waffen SS oversaw the death camps where millions of victims of the Nazis were murdered. These elite Nazi troops were also known to have executed American troops taken prisoner during the Battle of the Bulge. But Reagan rejected the pleas and visited the Bitburg cemetery.

Grenada

In October 1983 President Reagan made a surprise announcement of an invasion of the tiny eastern Caribbean nation on the island of **Grenada** by 6,000 U.S. marines and paratroopers. The leftist government of Grenada, supported by Cuba and the Soviet Union, was overthrown and replaced by a pro-American government. Protection of the 700 American medical students in Grenada was a factor in the invasion.

Nicaragua

In Central America, the Reagan administration found a more serious challenge. The **Somoza** dictatorship, which had governed Nicaragua since 1933, was overthrown in 1979 by the pro-Marxist revolutionists, called **Sandinistas**. Leftist guerrillas were also attempting to overthrow the government of neighboring **El Salvador**. The Reagan administration decided to support the opponents of the Sandinistas, called **Contras**, who operated from bases in Honduras. The United States financed and supplied the Contras with arms. Economic pressure was applied to Nicaragua. To prevent Soviet arms and supplies from entering Nicaragua, that country's harbors were mined by the CIA in violation of international law. Congress was divided, as were the American people, almost 50-50 as to whether this policy or a policy of seeking a political solution was preferable. The countries of Latin America, as well as some Americans, feared that force could lead to a wider war.

In 1982 a defense appropriation bill signed by President Reagan included an amendment introduced by Representative **Edward Boland**, Democrat of Massachusetts, prohibiting the CIA and the Pentagon from providing military equipment, training, or advice to any group "for the purpose of overthrowing the government of Nicaragua." A defense appropriation bill in 1983 appropriated not more than $24 million for the Contras. Another Boland amendment passed in 1984 prohibited the expenditure of any funds for the Contras between October 1 and December 3, 1985. In 1986 Congress approved an appropriation of $100 million in Contra aid. In November 1986 a new Congress was elected with Democratic majorities in both houses and the outlook for more Contra aid was dim. Four Latin American nations—Mexico, Venezuela, Panama, and Colombia, named the **Contadora** countries after the island on which they met, started a process that they hoped would prevent war and lead to a negotiated settlement. A startling development came in late 1986 with disclosure of covert aid to the Contras. (See **Iran-Contra**.)

Reagan-Gorbachev Summit Meetings

In March 1985 Mikhail Gorbachev became the new General Secretary of the Soviet Communist party. His ideas began a new phase in both domestic and foreign policy in the Soviet Union. On the home front he called for "**glasnost**" (openness) and "**perestroika**" (restructuring). In foreign policy, he called for détente with the United States.

• *Geneva: November 1985.* President Reagan and Gorbachev held their first summit meeting in Geneva, where they met face-to-face for five hours. A stumbling block was Reagan's insistence on proceeding with the Strategic Defense Initiative (SDI), commonly called "Star Wars," which the Soviets regarded as destabilizing. Though no formal agreement was reached, the two leaders approved plans for arms control talks to make 50 percent reductions in strategic weapons their longterm goals. Provisions for cultural and educational exchanges were a concrete result of the talks.

• *Reykjavik.* The second meeting between Reagan and Gorbachev took place in October 1986 in Reykjavik, Iceland. On the American side, there was little planning for the hastily arranged meeting. The President made the astonishing proposal that all ballistic missiles—airborne, landbased, and seaborne—be eliminated by 1996. It fell apart when Reagan refused to agree to an interpretation of the 1972 ABM treaty that would restrict the Strategic Defense Initiative to laboratory research.

• *Washington—the INF (Intermediate Nuclear Forces) Treaty.* President Reagan and Soviet leader Gorbachev held their third summit meeting in Washington in December 1987. They signed a major arms limitation treaty providing for the dismantling of all short-range and intermediate-range (300–3,400 miles) missiles. This applied specifically to 1,752 American missiles in Europe, and 859 Soviet missiles in Europe facing them. The removal of these Soviet missiles was hailed by America's NATO allies as a long step toward ultimate security. After a four-month debate, the Senate, by a vote of 93 to 5, ratified the INF treaty for eliminating medium- and shorter-range land-based nuclear missiles. It was perhaps the most historic accomplishment of the Reagan presidency. In 1988, Reagan visited Moscow. Discussions were held regarding Soviet dissidents and the promotion of human rights.

Middle East

Constant turmoil in the Middle East marked the region as one of the danger areas requiring the constant attention of the United States.

• *Israel.* The Reagan administration's support for America's ally, Israel, was matched by Soviet support for Syria. In June 1981, Israeli war planes demolished an Iraqi atomic installation near Baghdad, charging that the plant was nearing completion for the production of atomic weapons. In June 1982 Israeli armed forces invaded southern Lebanon and advanced to Beirut. The area harbored **PLO** terrorist brigades that repeatedly attempted to infiltrate Israel. The immediate mission was accomplished, but the Israelis suffered losses and withdrew from Lebanon in 1985 without achieving any lasting results. An uprising ("**intifada**") of the Palestinians in areas occupied by Israel resulted in violence and was met by harsh repressive measures on the part of Israeli armed forces. In late 1988, **Yassir Arafat**, leader of the major PLO faction, seemed to renounce terrorism when he addressed the UN. The Bush administration hoped to work toward a political solution to the Israeli-Palestinian impasse as a step toward a comprehensive Middle East peace.

• *Libya.* A center of Middle East terrorism was Libya under the leadership of Colonel **Muammar Qaddafi**. Qaddafi, in power since 1969 and violently anti-American, trained and supplied international terrorists, using the profits of his oil-rich land to finance terrorist operations. In August 1981 Soviet-built Libyan fighter planes attacked American navy planes on maneuvers in the Mediterranean. In 1982 the United States placed restrictions on trade with Libya and in January 1986 all Libyan assets in the United States were frozen. In April 1986 American planes bombed Libyan military bases in retaliation for terrorist acts. In January 1989 two U.S. Navy F-14 fighter planes shot down two MIG-23 fighters off the coast of Libya.

• *The Persian Gulf.* A border dispute between Iraq and Iran, major oil-producing countries, precipitated a war in 1980. Oil tankers in the Persian Gulf came under attack from both Iraq and Iran. U.S. naval vessels were deployed in the Gulf to protect American shipping. Kuwait, a major oil-producing country on the Gulf, was supporting Iraq in the war. In March 1987 Kuwait asked the United States to protect its oil tankers in the Persian Gulf. In May 1987, an Iraqi aircraft, mistaking the *U.S.S. Stark* for an Iranian merchant vessel, fired two missiles killing 37 sailors and wounding 21 on the *Stark*. On the same day the United States agreed to replace the Kuwaiti flag with the American flag (called reflagging) on eleven Kuwaiti oil tankers and to provide naval escort for these ships in the Gulf. By the end of 1987, twelve major American warships were deployed in the Gulf to insure an uninterrupted flow of oil to America and its allies. In October 1987 one of the reflagged tankers was successfully attacked in Kuwaiti waters by Iranian *Silkworm* (Chinese-built) missiles. Other nations also sent ships to protect their countrys' oil tankers and to keep the Gulf shipping lanes open. In 1988, an Iranian civilian airliner was destroyed over the Persian Gulf by gunfire from the *U.S.S. Vincennes*, which mistook the plane for a fighter jet. All 290 persons on the plane died in the attack. The destruction by a terrorist of a Pan

Am flight bound from London to New York on December 21, 1988, was believed to be in retaliation for the *Vincennes* action. All 259 people on board the plane died, as well as 11 people on the ground, as the plane went down over Lockerbie, Scotland.

Reagan's Second Term

Income Tax Reform

The 1986 **Income Tax Reform Act**, which the President signed on October 22, completed a long overdue process. The tax code had become unwieldy, with patchwork changes and revisions introduced over the years. The 1986 act simplified the code, exempted millions of low-income families from federal income taxes, reduced the highest bracket to 28 percent, and closed numerous loopholes. The act was supposed to be revenue neutral; that is, no income group would bear more or less of the tax burden than it bore prior to the passage of the new tax code. The new law was phased in over a two-year period.

The federal budget deficit continued to demand attention. For the fiscal year ending September 30, 1988 the deficit was $155 billion, up $5.4 billion over the previous year.

The Election of 1986

Attention focused on the Senate, where the Republicans had held a majority since the election of 1980. President Reagan toured the country to help elect Republicans to the Senate, but the voters gave the Democrats a resounding victory. They picked up eight seats, giving them a majority of 55 to 45.

Wall Street Crash

On Monday, October 19, 1987, the New York Stock Exchange registered its largest point decline in history when the Dow-Jones industrial average plummeted 508.32 points in a day of frenetic trading, as 604 million shares (by far the greatest number ever) changed hands. The Dow made a quick recovery and regained almost 300 points in the next two days.

The Balance of Trade

A worrisome aspect of the American economy was the persistent negative balance of trade which, during the Reagan years, had seen the United States change from a creditor to a debtor nation in international trade. The annual negative balance was running at $170 billion. The dollar, which was worth 360 yen during the first quarter century following World War II, was now trading at about 120 yen—one third its previous value. Americans were buying automobiles, cameras, computers, radio and television sets, even steel from Japan, while the Japanese were buying only unprocessed raw materials such as timber, oil, metals, grains, and fiber from the United States. A similar imbalance, though not as steep, prevailed in trade with West Germany, Taiwan, and Korea. Pressure was mounting in Congress for tariff and trade legislation—resisted by the Reagan administration—to attempt to bring about a balance in international trade. The imbalance was causing the closing of factories and the displacement of labor in American industry.

In July 1988 Congress passed a plant-closing bill, which required management to give workers 60 days notice of an impending plant closing. In May, President Reagan vetoed a trade bill because it contained a plant-closing provision, but the vote in July was one-sided enough to assure overriding a presidential veto. In August, the bill became a law without the President's signature.

The Iran-Contra Affair

On November 3, 1986, the Lebanese newspaper, *Al-Shiraa* reported that the United States had sold arms to Iran after a secret visit by National Security Adviser **Robert McFarlane**. Less than 24 hours earlier, the U.S. hostage, **David P. Jacobsen**, who was kidnapped in May 1985, was released. Six hostages remained in Beirut. It was apparent that an "arms for hostages" deal had been made.

In an effort to win the release of the hostages, the Reagan administration secretly sold arms to Iran. The money paid by Iran for these arms was then used to fund the Contra rebels in Nicaragua. This secret and illegal diversion of funds was carried out by Lt. Colonel **Oliver North** with the knowledge of his superiors (Robert McFarlane and **John Poindexter**) on the National Security Council. It was an attempt by the Reagan administration to bypass Congress, which had passed the **Boland Amendment** outlawing aid to the Contras. Revelation of these activities caused a furor in the nation.

Investigation of the Iran-Contra Affair

Both the House and the Senate established select committees to investigate the Iran-Contra scandal. It was decided that the committees would meet jointly and conduct televised hearings. The hearings before the joint congressional committee opened in May 1987 and terminated three months later in August 1987. The committee's final report was submitted in November 1987. Criminal prosecution was assigned to an independent counsel, **Lawrence E. Walsh**.

Conclusion

Testimony at the hearing disclosed that high U.S. government officials provided the Contras with private and international sources of funds for conducting military operations against the Nicaraguan government. President Reagan was aware that **Robert C. (Bud) McFarlane**, his National Security Adviser, from October 1983 to December 1985, had solicited and received monthly contributions of $1 million from **King Fahd** of Saudi Arabia. **Elliot Abrams**, Assistant Secretary of State for Inter-American Affairs, obtained a $10 million contribution from the oil-rich Sultan of Brunei.

In its final report, the majority concluded: "It was the President's policy— not an isolated decision by (Oliver) North or Poindexter—to sell arms secretly to Iran and to maintain the Contras, 'body and soul,' the Boland amendment notwithstanding . . ."

On Wednesday, March 16, 1988, a federal grand jury in Washington, D.C. charged Oliver North, John Poindexter, **Richard Secord**, and **Albert Hakin** with conspiracy to defraud the United States, theft of government property, and other crimes. Poindexter, a Vice-Admiral in the U.S. Navy, was National Security Adviser from December 1985 to November 1986. The four defendants pleaded not guilty. McFarlane had previously pleaded guilty to four counts of withholding information from Congress.

Independent counsel **Lawrence Walsh** secured indictment of **Oliver North** on twelve counts. North, a Lt. Colonel in the U.S. Marines, played a key role in the illegal Contra aid operations when he served as Assistant Director of the National Security Council from 1981 to 1986. He was tried in Federal District Court presided over by Judge **Gerhard Gesell**. The trial ended in a verdict of not guilty on nine counts and guilty on three counts: (1) aiding and abetting obstruction of Congress; (2) destroying government documents; and (3) receiving an illegal gratuity in the form of a security system for his home. North was fined $150,000 and given a three-year suspended sentence, but his conviction was later overturned on technical grounds. In 1994, North ran unsuccessfully for the U.S. Senate in Virginia.

Decline of President Reagan's Popularity

A "Special Review Board" was appointed by President Reagan on December 1, 1986 to investigate the Iran-Contra affair. **John Tower** was named chairman and the other two members were **Edmund Muskie** and **Brent Scowcroft**.

The Tower Commission report of February 26, 1987 stated "The President did not seem to be aware of the way in which the operation (arms for hostages) was implemented and the full consequences of U.S. participation . . . At no time did he insist on accountability."

In a nationally televised speech on March 4, 1987, President Reagan said, "I told the American people I did not trade arms for hostages. My heart and my best intentions still tell me that's true. But the facts and the evidence tell me it's not. . . . what began as a strategic opening to Iran deteriorated in its implementation into trading arms for hostages. It was a mistake." Disclosure of the arms deals had a dramatic impact on Reagan's standing in the polls. In *The New York Times*-CBS News poll reported December 1, 1986, his approval rating dropped from 67 percent a month earlier to 46 percent.

The decline in Reagan's popularity was reflected in his difficulty in gaining congressional support for his agenda. Congress overrode his veto of a transportation bill for spending $87.5 billion on highway and mass transit and allowing states to increase the speed limit to 65 m.p.h. The Senate rejected his nomination of Judge Robert H. Bork for the Supreme Court. In February 1988, the House voted against military aid to the Contras and the Contra forces went into decline.

But Ronald Reagan was flexible enough to ride out the storm. Moreover, his success at the Moscow summit with the Soviet leader Mikhail Gorbachev that produced a nuclear arms agreement helped to restore his popularity. In Moscow the President and Gorbachev signed the historic **Intermediate Nuclear Forces (INF)** treaty.

Exercise Set 6.16

1. President Reagan's "supply-side" economic program was characterized by
   A. a budget brought into balance by income equal to expenditures
   B. a budget evenly balanced between spending for defense and spending for social programs
   C. an effort to maintain a favorable balance of trade
   D. a tax program designed to bring about an increase in the supply of consumer goods

2. Which of the following was *not* an aspect of the 1984 elections?
   A. Ronald Reagan scored a landslide victory
   B. television debates were held between the presidential and vice-presidential candidates
   C. Democrats failed to gain control of the U.S. Senate
   D. there was a growing movement in favor of modifying the method of electing a President

3. Which of the following was *not* a foreign policy objective of the Reagan administration?
   A. cessation of violence and armed conflict between Arabs and Israelis in the Middle East
   B. immediate end of the apartheid policy of the South African government
   C. overthrow of the Marxist government of Nicaragua
   D. economic and diplomatic cooperation with the government and people of Japan

4. Which of the following was *not* a sign of President Reagan's declining influence during his second term?
   A. appointment of a congressional committee to investigate the Iran-Contra affair
   B. Democrats regain control of the Senate in the 1986 election
   C. Congress passes the 1986 Tax Reform Act
   D. Congress passes the Clean Water Act of 1987 over President Reagan's veto

5. Which of the following did *not* occur during President Reagan's second term?
   A. the trade deficits were brought back approximately into balance
   B. a severe crash occurred on the New York Stock Exchange
   C. Reagan and Gorbachev negotiated the Intermediate Nuclear Forces (INF) treaty
   D. Congress passed the Gramm-Rudman-Hollings Balanced Budget Act

PRESIDENT GEORGE BUSH (1989–1993)

The Election of 1988

The Primaries

Major contestants for the Republican nomination were Vice-President **George Bush**, Senator **Robert Dole** of Kansas, minority leader of the Senate, television evangelist **Pat Robertson**, and Representative **Jack Kemp** of New York.

On the Democratic side there were more contestants. Former Senator **Gary Hart** was an early casualty of the media when he was caught in a liaison with a woman other than his wife. Others actively seeking the nomination were Governor **Michael Dukakis** of Massachusetts, the Reverend **Jesse Jackson** of Chicago, Senator **Albert Gore** of Tennessee, Representative **Richard Gephardt** of Missouri, Senator **Paul Simon** of Illinois, and Senator **Joseph R. Biden, Jr.**, of Delaware.

In the first Republican primaries, Dole made a strong showing, but Bush fought back, gained the lead, and pulled ahead, clinching the nomination in April, four months before the Republican convention. The Democratic race narrowed down to a contest between Dukakis and Jackson, with the former steadily increasing his lead. Dukakis was nominated at the Democratic convention in July and chose Senator **Lloyd Bentsen** of Texas for Vice-President.

In August, Bush won the nomination at the Republican convention. He made a controversial choice for a running mate, the young and relatively inexperienced Senator **Dan Quayle** of Indiana.

The Campaign and Election

Neither candidate evoked enthusiasm from the electorate, and the campaign seemed lackluster. It was fought chiefly on television and in the press. Bush was accused of using negative campaigning for calling Dukakis a "card-carrying liberal" and for running the controversial and racist "Willie Horton" TV ad campaign.

Two nationally televised debates were held between the presidential candidates and one between the vice-presidential candidates. In the first debate, Dukakis had a slight edge, while in the second, Bush came out ahead. As the election approached, the polls correctly indicated an impending victory for the Bush-Quayle ticket.

	Popular Vote	Percent	Electoral Vote
Bush	47,917,341	54	426
Dukakis	41,013,030	46	112

494

In Congress the Democrats gained strength in both houses while failing to win the presidency. The voters evidently determined to divide governmental power between the two parties. In the Senate, the Democrats gained one seat, giving them a majority of 55 to 45. In the House, they added 5 seats to give them a majority of 262 to 173.

The Bush Program and Promises

In a 20-minute inaugural address on January 20, 1989, President Bush singled out major problems that his administration would address. Referring to the national deficit he said, "We have more will than wallet; but will is what we need." He called the national epidemic of drug abuse a scourge and said, "Take my word, this scourge will stop." He called on the Democratic Congress, whom he referred to as his "friends" in the "loyal opposition," to join him in a bipartisan effort to solve the social problems of homelessness, poverty, and "the rough crime of the streets." Bush had earlier expressed the hope that he could lead "a kinder, gentler nation."

In a nationally televised address to Congress in February 1989, Bush outlined his budget proposals, encompassing broad outlines for the future. "We must make a very substantial cut in the federal budget deficit." In addition to the immediate goal of "meeting the targets set forth in the Gramm-Rudman-Hollings law," he asked for enactment of two-year budgets, a line-item veto provision, and the passing of a constitutional amendment requiring a balanced budget. He repeated his pledge of no new taxes.

Specific proposals included $2.2 billion for the National Science Foundation; a permanent tax credit law to promote basic research; a cut in the maximum tax rate on capital gains; and incentive awards for educational excellence. He said, "I'd like to be the Education President." President Bush asked for an increase of almost a billion dollars in budget outlays to escalate the war against drugs. Additional outlays were proposed for a new attack on organized crime; for education to prevent AIDS and research to find a cure; for upgrading and protecting the environment through a new Clean Air Act, and enforcement of laws against toxic wastes.

He called for a new child-care tax credit adjustment and guaranteed full funding of Social Security, including a full cost-of-living increase. He asserted his support for restoring the integrity of the failing savings and loan industry. He asked for a one-year freeze in the military budget, and overhauling of the defense procurement process.

On plans for world peace he would carefully assess the changes taking place in the Soviet Union and added, "I have personally assured General Secretary Gorbachev that . . . we will be ready to move forward."

Domestic Events

Savings and Loan Scandal

Savings and loan institutions (S&Ls or "thrifts") boomed following World War II, primarily by financing veterans' guaranteed home-mortgage loans at low interest rates. The S&Ls were legally restricted from matching the higher interest rates charged by other financial institutions, like commercial banks. In the early 1980s Congress and the Reagan administration **deregulated** the S&L industry, eliminated interest ceilings, and allowed the banks to make commercial loans. Although the S&Ls were still regulated, and their deposits insured by the **Federal Savings and Loan Insurance Corporation (FSLIC)**, a laissez-faire attitude prevailed, and following deregulation many of the S&Ls began to make high-risk loans and unsound investments, often in commercial real estate.

When the nation's economy faltered, many of the S&Ls' borrowers were unable to repay their loans, and the savings and loan institutions began to collapse. The FSLIC soon ran out of funds to back up the failing S&Ls, and the **Federal Deposit Insurance Corporation (FDIC)** had to assume the responsibility. The eventual cost to taxpayers over the next 40 years is estimated at $500 billion.

In 1989, Congress created the **Resolution Trust Corporation (RTC)** to handle the bailout and to dispose of property and assets held by the bankrupt thrifts. Federal investigations into the operating practices of some of the failed S&Ls led to the indictment of hundreds of bank directors and officers. On May 20, 1992, the FDIC limited the rates that the S&Ls could offer.

Census of 1990

Article I, Section 2, of the Constitution provides that a census be taken every ten years to determine the number of representatives a state shall have in Congress. According to the 1990 census, the nation's population in 1990 was approximately 249,500,000, an increase of about 23 million over the 1980 count. Adjustments in Congress, where the total number of Representatives remains at 435, included losses in New York (3 seats), Pennsylvania, Michigan, Ohio, and Illinois (2 seats each), and the loss of one seat in each of eight other states. Gains in congressional representation came in California (7 seats), Florida (4 seats), Texas (3 seats), and gains of one seat in each of five other states.

Americans With Disabilities Act (1990)

Passed by Congress July 13, 1990, and taking effect on January 26, 1992, the Americans With Disabilities Act has been considered the most significant antidiscrimination legislation since the **Civil Rights Acts** of the 1960s. The law bans discrimination against the handicapped (physical and mental) in employment, transportation, public accommodations, and communications services.

Nomination and Confirmation of Clarence Thomas to the Supreme Court

President Bush selected Judge **Clarence Thomas** of the District of Columbia Circuit Court, a conservative Republican African American, to replace the retiring Justice **Thurgood Marshall**, an African American liberal and longtime proponent of civil rights. This nomination created some of the most heated Senate confirmation proceedings in the history of the nation. Major points of debate during the early hearings of the Senate Judiciary Committee were Thomas's opposition to **affirmative action** for minorities and women and questions about his stance on the *Roe* v. *Wade* decision on abortion rights.

In the course of the hearings, Democratic committee members raised allegations of sexual harassment, supported by testimony from law professor Anita Hill of the University of Oklahoma, who had worked for Judge Thomas at the Equal Employment Opportunity Commission during the Reagan administration. Judge Thomas reappeared before the committee to deny Professor Hill's charges and called the hearings a "high-tech lynching." After heated and partisan debate, the Senate confirmed his appointment on October 15, 1991, in a very close 52 to 48 vote, with 11 Democrats crossing party lines to vote with the Republicans.

Foreign Affairs

Invasion of Panama (December 20, 1989–January 3, 1990)

In April 1989 a report of the narcotics subcommittee of the Senate Foreign Relations Committee charged that the head of the Panamanian Defense Forces (PDF), **General Manuel Noriega**, "controlled all elements of the Panamanian government essential to the protection of drug trafficking and money laundering." Federal grand juries in Miami and Tampa, Florida, indicted Noriega on charges of drug trafficking. President Bush appealed for his overthrow, but Noriega survived economic sanctions and several coup attempts and annulled a May 1989 election in which he had been defeated.

On December 16, 1989, an off-duty American marine was shot to death by members of the PDF. With fairly wide approval, both in the United States and Panama, President Bush sent 10,000 American troops into Panama on December 20, 1989, to protect American lives and interests and to capture General Noriega and bring him to the United States to stand trial.

Noriega surrendered on January 3, 1990, and was taken to Miami, where he was tried and found guilty of cocaine trafficking, racketeering, and money laundering; he was sentenced to a 40-year jail term. The invasion was condemned by the United Nations, but President Bush found legal support for the military action in a clause of the **1977 Panama Canal Treaty**, which allowed the United States to take action to protect the Panama Canal.

Operation Desert Storm

After unsuccessful talks about oil production and debt repayment between Iraq and its neighbor Kuwait, Iraqi president **Saddam Hussein** invaded and annexed Kuwait on August 2, 1990, declaring it to be a province of Iraq. Fearing that Iraq's next target might be Saudi Arabia, President Bush ordered 430,000 U.S. troops to Saudi Arabia to protect the world's largest oil reserves. "Operation Desert Shield," as this first phase was known, began on August 6, 1990, and its purpose was to "draw a line in the sand" (between Kuwait and Iraq) behind which Iraq's large army would have to retreat. On November 8, 1990, a United Nations Security Council resolution set a January 15, 1991, deadline for Iraq to withdraw from Kuwait.

The Iraqi withdrawal from Kuwait did not take place, and President Bush ordered a devastating air assault against military targets in Iraq and Kuwait. The phase of bombing and ground offensive by the allied powers was known as "Operation Desert Storm." The U.S. and allied forces carried out a massive bombing campaign for five weeks. On February 24, 1991, they began a ground campaign, directed by **General Norman Schwartzkopf**, that smashed through Hussein's armies, retaking Kuwait and occupying most of southern Iraq in only four days of combat. The retreating Iraqi forces set fire to over 500 of Kuwait's oil wells, causing a widespread environmental disaster. Iraq launched a number of Soviet-designed SCUD missiles against targets in Saudi Arabia and Israel with only limited success. Allied forces were sometimes able to intercept and destroy the SCUDs with Patriot anti missile missiles, but many of the Iraqi missiles disintegrated or blew up in flight on their own. There were widespread fears that the Iraqis would resort to chemical and biological warfare, as they had previously done in their war with Iran and in campaigns against the Kurdish minorities. There has been no evidence that the Iraqis used any such weapons, although traces of nerve gas and mustard gas were detected, possibly from stockpiles destroyed by U.S. bombings.

On February 27, 1991, President Bush ordered a unilateral cease-fire, and on March 3, 1991, Iraq agreed to abide by the UN resolutions. An official cease-fire agreement was signed April 6, 1991.

Exercise Set 6.17

1. In the United States, most new jobs created during the 1980s were jobs that
   A. were classified as managerial
   B. provided services rather than goods
   C. depended on heavy manufacturing
   D. were farm related
   Regents Exam, January 1994

2. Both the Bay of Pigs invasion of Cuba (1961) and the invasion of Panama (1989) are examples of the U.S.' attempt to
   A. eliminate unfriendly governments geographically close to the United States
   B. cultivate good relations with Latin American nations
   C. stop the drug trade
   D. end the cold war
   Regents Exam, January 1994

3. Under curent federal laws, Americans with disabilities must be
   A. placed in federally funded institutions near their homes
   B. guaranteed access to public transportation and facilities
   C. educated and supported by their families without governmental help
   D. educated only until they complete the eighth grade
   Regents Exam, June 1993

4. Which demographic trend has occurred in the United States during the past ten years?
   A. The average age of the population has decreased
   B. The birthrate has rapidly increased
   C. Life expectancy has decreased
   D. The proportion of the population over age 65 has grown
   Regents Exam, January 1993

5. Which of the following was the result of a congressional declaration of war?
   A. the 1989 invasion of Panama
   B. Operation Desert Storm
   C. World War II
   D. Vietnam War

6. Presidential nominations of the Supreme Court Justices can lead to controversy because
   A. Congress consistently refuses to approve candidates who are not members of the majority parties
   B. Congress claims it has the sole right to nominate justices
   C. Presidents most often nominate their friends rather than persons with judicial experience
   D. The President and Congress sometimes have different views on the judicial philosophy that a proposed justice should hold

   Regents Exam, June 1992

7. The results of the national census taken every ten years most directly affects which of the following?
   A. Number of justices on the Supreme Court
   B. Total electoral votes
   C. Composition of the House of Representatives
   D. President's Cabinet

CHAPTER REVIEW QUESTIONS

1. President Ronald Reagan's federal budget proposals came under sharp criticism because they
   A. lowered interest rates and decreased inflation
   B. increased social welfare spending
   C. included very large deficits
   D. advocated raising the income tax

   Regents Exam, August 1988

2. In the United States in the 1980s, negotiations between labor and management frequently resulted in labor's acceptance of lower wages and greater automation in return for management's guarantees of job security for workers. This trend best indicates that
   A. labor and management are responding to the threats posed by foreign competition
   B. management is becoming more interested in strengthening labor unions
   C. legislation has required changes in labor contracts
   D. labor unions are becoming more powerful

   Regents Exam, June 1988

Base your answer to question 3 on the cartoon below and on your knowledge of social studies.

3. The main idea of the cartoon is that
   A. regulation of the savings-and-loan industry is more important than campaign reform
   B. some problems cannot be solved by congressional action
   C. Congress cannot agree on spending priorities
   D. members of Congress sometimes avoid legislative actions that might limit their political careers

Regents Exam, January 1994

4. In the United States, large corporations would most likely support a congressional plan to
   A. require corporation-funded pension plans to workers
   B. grant capital investment tax credits
   C. mandate union shops in all corporations
   D. increase the minimum wage

Regents Exam, June 1987

5. In the 1980s, the reason that the federal government aided certain cor-
   porations that were on the verge of bankruptcy was that the government
   A. used the opportunity to break up monopolies
   B. pursued a trend toward public ownership of key industries
   C. sought to minimize the economic harm from collapse of these corpo-
   rations
   D. wished to have more influence on the kinds of products made for sale
   to American consumers.
   Regents Exam, January 1987

6. A major reason for the ending of the Cold War Era was that
   A. the Soviet Union was seriously weakened by internal conflict and
   economic difficulties
   B. the United States and the Soviet Union were unable to destroy one
   another
   C. the Berlin Wall fell and Germany was reunited
   D. a recession forced the United States to cut military spending
   Regents Exam, June 1993

ESSAYS

1. In the United States, situations frequently occur in which the interests of
   individuals have come into conflict with the perceived needs of society.
   Listed below are several issues that may lead to conflict.
   Issues
   Gun control
   Affirmative action
   Abortion
   Death penalty
   Prayer in public schools
   Testing of individuals for drug use
   a. Choose *three* of the issues listed. For *each* one chosen, describe a per-
   ceived need of society related to the issue and show how the interests
   of individuals have come into conflict with this need [3,3,3]
   b. For *two* of the issues discussed in answer to "a", explain how a leg-
   islative or a judicial body has dealt with the conflict [6]
   Regents Exam, August 1988

2. U.S. Presidents have used the power of their office to address a number
   of national and international issues. Each issue in the list below is paired
   with a specific President who addressed that issue.
   Issues/Presidents
   Reconstruction/Andrew Johnson
   Environmental destruction/Theodore Roosevelt
   Isolationism/Woodrow Wilson

Civil rights violations/Lyndon Johnson
Arab-Israeli tensions/Jimmy Carter
International aggression/George Bush

Choose *three* pairs from the list and for *each* one chosen:
- Describe conditions that let to the issue faced by the President
- Discuss how the President exercised a power of his office to deal with the issue
- Evaluate the success of the President's response in dealing with the issue [5,5,5]

Regents Exam, January 1994

3. In the United States today, people hold different viewpoints concerning controversial issues. Some of these areas of controversy are listed below.

Areas of Controversy
Capital punishment
Right to die
Affirmative action
Censorship
Health care funding
Homelessness

Choose *three* of the areas of controversy listed and for *each* one chosen:
- State an issue involved in the controversy
- Discuss *two* different points of view concerning the issue
- Describe a specific action taken by government or a group to deal with the issue [5,5,5]

Regents Exam, June 1992

Chapter 6

THE CLINTON ADMINISTRATION

THE ELECTION OF 1992

> Political campaigns are designedly made into emotional orgies which
> endeavor to distract attention from the real issues involved.
>> James Harvey Robinson, *The Human Comedy* (1937)

The national elections, besides ending 12 years of Republican control of the
executive branch, had several interesting features.

The Primaries

Democrats

The major contestants for the Democratic presidential nomination were
Governor Bill Clinton of Arkansas, former Governor Jerry Brown of California, former Senator Paul Tsongas of Massachusetts, Senator Robert Kerry
of Nebraska, and Senator Thomas Harkin of Iowa. Tsongas, Kerry, and
Harkin left the field early after poor showings in the early primaries and caucuses, and the Democratic race came down to Governor Clinton and former
Governor Brown.

By June, Clinton had gained the support of enough delegates to assure
him the nomination. At the Democratic National Convention in New York
City in July the party's delegates selected Clinton to be the Democratic nominee for President. The delegates also approved Clinton's choice of Senator
Albert Gore of Tennessee as the vice-presidential candidate.

Republicans

The two main candidates for the Republican nomination were the incumbent President George Bush and conservative newspaper and television
commentator Pat Buchanan. At the Republican National Convention in
Houston in August, the party's delegates renominated George Bush for
President and Dan Quayle for Vice-President. The convention and the campaign were influenced, however, by conservative and religious elements
within the Republican party who wanted stronger efforts to ban abortion
and permit school prayer. Bush's efforts to accommodate the right-wing
Republicans may have hindered his ability to appeal to more middle-of-the-
road voters.

Independent

Ross Perot, a self-made Texas billionaire, entered the presidential race, withdrew, and then reentered. Perot's platform consisted mainly of a businessman's approach to economic reform. With the help of his "Volunteers," Perot succeeded in getting his name on the ballot in all 50 states, and in the November elections he polled 19% (19,236,411) of the popular vote, an unusually high showing for a third-party candidate.

The Campaign and the Election

Bush's popularity, based on his successes in foreign affairs (the Persian Gulf War, the end of Communism in the Soviet Union and Eastern Europe), appeared to assure him of an easy victory, but the realities of economic problems at home soon increased the electorate's demand for change. The recession of 1990 lingered on through 1992, and the unemployment rate remained at about 7.5%. Further reflecting a weak economy, the government reported that the poverty rate had risen again for the second consecutive year, to 14.2% of the population.

Governor Clinton's campaign concentrated on the economic issues, and his platform included raising taxes on the wealthy and trimming tax breaks for corporations. President Bush criticized the Democratic platform as a "tax and spend" program and blamed the nation's economic troubles on the Democrat-controlled Congress. Perot's platform attacked federal government bureaucracy and promised to address the nation's economic problems through a business management approach.

Clinton Becomes the Nation's 42nd President

The total turnout of voters (101,129,210) for the presidential election represented about 55% of all those eligible to vote, an increase of about 5% over the 1988 election. Perot's showing in the election was the strongest for a third-party candidate since Theodore Roosevelt ran on the progressive Bull Moose ticket in 1912. Democrats maintained control of Congress, and four women were elected to the Senate (bringing the number of women Senators to six), including Carol Mosely Braun of Illinois, the first African-American woman ever elected. The Senate gained its first Native American member when Ben Nighthorse Campbell, a Democrat, was elected from Colorado.

	Popular Vote	Percent	Electoral Vote
Clinton	43,727,625	43	370
Bush	38,165,180	38	168
Perot	19,236,411	19	0

PRESIDENT BILL CLINTON (1993–)

"All progress has resulted from people who took unpopular positions."
Adlai E. Stevenson, Speech at Princeton University, New Jersey,
March 22, 1954.

Clinton Policies and Programs

President William Jefferson ("Bill") Clinton took the oath of office as the nation's 42nd President on January 20, 1993. Born in Hope, Arkansas, August 19, 1946, he is the first President born after World War II. In contrast to the laissez-faire policies of his immediate predecessors, Clinton immediately proposed a series of far-reaching domestic reforms. Focusing on the economy and health care, his agenda included a North American Free Trade Agreement (NAFTA), anticrime legislation—which he characterized by the phrase "three strikes and you're out"—welfare reform designed to put people to work, and a national service program whereby federal education loans could be repaid through community service.

Family Leave

One of President Clinton's first initiatives was the signing of a family leave bill, which had been vetoed by the previous Republican administrations. The law permits employees up to 12 weeks of unpaid leave without loss of seniority in order to respond to family needs, such as the birth of a child or the illness of a parent.

Economic Stimulus

An early casualty of Clinton's economic program to get the economy moving was his economic stimulus package designed to reduce unemployment particularly among recent graduates. The bill was defeated in the Senate by the repeated filibustering of Republican Senators, who contended that the bill would do little for the economy. Clinton's main economic legislation, the overall federal budget bill containing many compromises, finally squeaked through Congress by a vote of 218 to 216 in the House of Representatives and with a tie vote of 50 to 50 in the Senate, where Vice- President Al Gore cast the tie-breaking vote in favor.

Health Care

A key element in Clinton's agenda was health-care reform. He proposed to provide health care for every American adult and child, which would extend health care to 37 million uninsured Americans.

North American Free Trade Agreement (NAFTA)

The pact was negotiated among Canada, the United States, and Mexico to stimulate trade among them by removing trade barriers, particularly tariffs. The international agreement was successfully negotiated with the support of a number of Republican members of Congress, despite opposition from the AFL-CIO, which feared that American labor would suffer in competing with low-paid workers in Mexico. Ross Perot contributed to the opposition by his widely repeated comment about the "sucking sound" of American jobs being siphoned off to Mexico, where labor received very low hourly wages. The agreement as finally signed included provisions for tighter enforcement of labor laws and environmental standards.

Foreign Affairs—New Challenges in the Post-World War II World

Somalia

A UN-sanctioned force entered Somalia December 10, 1992. Led by 1,800 American marines, it included also French and Italian troops. The military mission was to ensure delivery of food to starving people. Under President Bush, as many as 28,000 American troops were involved in this effort. Some 5,000 still remained in October 1993, when a number of American troops were killed or taken hostage. President Clinton declared that all American troops would be withdrawn by April 1994.

Bosnia

With the breakup of Yugoslavia following the demise of the Soviet Union, century-old ethnic and religious hatreds flared up in violence. In 1992, Serbian forces began a campaign of territorial expansion against their Croat and Muslim neighbors, completely removing them from villages where they had lived for centuries, in a campaign that took on many aspects of genocide. President Clinton condemned the actions of the aggressors but resisted pressure for American military intervention that would run counter to the wishes of a majority of Americans.

Haiti

After the election as president of Father Jean-Bertrand Aristide, a Catholic priest, in September 1991, Haitian military commanders took control of the government and forced him to flee. The new dictatorship caused more than 50,000 Haitians to seek refuge abroad, many losing their lives at sea in fragile boats that sank or capsized.

With some 3,500 Americans remaining in Haiti, there was considerable pressure on President Clinton to use American military forces to liberate Haiti and restore Father Aristide to power. The military junta in Haiti signed an agreement in 1992 promising to step down, but it did not carry it out. The United States then enforced an economic embargo sanctioned by the UN. In 1994, when the military still refused to cede power, President Clinton threatened military action. At that point an eleventh hour compromise was reached. President Clinton then sent 20,000 U.S. troops to Haiti to oversee the transition to democracy.

The Middle East

In 1993, a major break-through for peace in the Middle East occurred during secret talks held in Norway between Israel and the Palestinian Liberation Organization (PLO). In September, Yasir Arafat, the chairman of the PLO, publicly stated that the PLO recognized Israel's right to exist, while Yitzhak Rabin, the Prime Minister of Israel, stated that Israel recognized the PLO as the representative of the Palestinian people.

At the White House on September 13, 1993, before a large gathering of international dignitaries organized by President Clinton, Israel and the PLO signed an interim accord providing for Palestinian self-rule in the Gaza Strip and the West-Bank town of Jericho. The accord was the initial step in the peaceful resolution of the long-standing Israeli-Palestinian confrontation.

Nominations and Appointments

Supreme Court Justices

The retirement of Supreme Court Justice Byron H. White made Clinton the first Democratic president in 25 years to make a nomination for the Supreme Court. After two tentative choices, he nominated **Ruth Bader Ginsburg** of the U.S. Court of Appeals for the District of Columbia. The nomination was easily confirmed by the Senate, making Ginsburg the second woman on the high court, after Sandra Day O'Connor of Arizona, who was appointed in 1981 under President Reagan. In 1994, President Clinton nominated **Stephen G. Breyer**, Chief Judge of the U.S. Court of Appeals for the First Circuit in Boston, who was then confirmed by the Senate to sit on the Supreme Court.

The Cabinet

Clinton's main Cabinet advisers included **Warren Christopher**, Secretary of State; **Lloyd Bentsen**, Secretary of the Treasury; **Les Aspin**, Secretary of Defense, succeeded by **William J. Perry** in 1994; **Janet Reno**, Attorney

General; **Bruce Babbit**, Secretary of the Interior; **Ron Brown**, Secretary of Commerce; **Mike Espy**, Secretary of Agriculture; **Robert B. Reich**, Secretary of Labor; **Donna E. Shalala**, Secretary of Health and Human Services; **Henry A. Cisneros**, Secretary of Housing and Urban Development; **Frederico F. Pena**, Secretary of Transportation; **Hazel R. O'Leary**, Secretary of Energy; **Richard W. Riley**, Secretary of Education; **Jesse Brown**, Secretary of Veterans Affairs.

The White House

Clinton's staff included **Thomas F. McLarty**, **3rd**, Chief of Staff, succeeded by **Leon Panetta** in 1994; **David Gergen**, Counselor to the President; and **George Stephanopoulos**, Adviser on Policy and Strategy.

HISTORICAL DOCUMENTS

On the following pages are the complete texts of the Declaration of Independence and the Constitution and Amendments in their official published form at the time they were enacted or ratified. Parts of the documents follow 18th-century conventions of writing and printing, such as the capitalization of all nouns, and some words, such as "chuse," are spelled in ways no longer considered standard. But the documents are plain and straightforward in style and are not difficult to understand, even after 200 years.

Portions of the Constitution and Amendments that have been changed by subsequent amendments are printed in *italics*.

The outline of the Constitution and Amendments is intended as a guide to its various articles, sections, and clauses, some of which are known by specific names, such as the "elastic clause" or the "three-fifths clause."

THE DECLARATION OF INDEPENDENCE

In CONGRESS, July 4, 1776.
The unanimous Declaration
of the thirteen united States of America,

When in the Course of human events, it becomes necessary for one people to dissolve the political bands which have connected them with another, and to assume among the powers of the earth, the separate and equal station to which the Laws of Nature and of Nature's God entitle them, a decent respect to the opinions of mankind requires that they should declare the causes which impel them to the separation.—We hold these truths to be self-evident, that all men are created equal, that they are endowed by their Creator with certain unalienable Rights, that among these are Life, Liberty, and the pursuit of Happiness.—That to secure these rights, Governments are instituted among Men, deriving their just powers from the consent of the governed,—That whenever any Form of Government becomes destructive of these ends, it is the Right of the People to alter or to abolish it; and to institute new Government, laying its foundation on such principles and organizing its powers in such form, as to them shall seem most likely to effect their Safety and Happiness. Prudence, indeed, will dictate that Governments long established should not be changed for light and transient causes; and accordingly all experience hath shewn, that mankind are more disposed to suffer, while evils are sufferable, than to right themselves by abolishing the forms to which they are accustomed. But when a long train of abuses and usurpations, pursuing invariably the same Object evinces a design to reduce them under absolute Despotism, it is their right, it is their duty, to throw off such Government, and to provide new Guards for their future security.—Such has been the patient sufferance of these Colonies; and such is now the necessity which constrains them to alter their former Systems of Government. The history of the present King of Great Britain is a history of repeated injuries and usurpations, all having in direct object the establishment of an absolute Tyranny over these States. To prove this, let Facts be submitted to a candid world.—He has refused his Assent to Laws, the most wholesome and necessary for the public good.—He has forbidden his Governors to pass Laws of immediate and pressing importance, unless suspended in their operation till his Assent should be obtained; and when so suspended, he has utterly neglected to attend to them.—He has refused to pass other Laws for the accommodation of large districts of people, unless those people would relinquish the right of Representation in the Legislature, a right inestimable to them and formidable to tyrants only.—He has called together legislative bodies at places unusual, uncomfortable, and distant from the depository of their public

Records, for the sole purpose of fatiguing them into compliance with his measures.—He has dissolved Representative Houses repeatedly, for opposing with manly firmness his invasions on the rights of the people.—He has refused for a long time, after such dissolutions, to cause others to be elected; whereby the Legislative powers, incapable of Annihilation, have returned to the People at large for their exercise; the State remaining in the mean time exposed to all the dangers of invasion from without, and convulsions within.—He has endeavoured to prevent the population of these States; for that purpose obstructing the Laws for Naturalization of Foreigners; refusing to pass others to encourage their migrations hither, and raising the conditions of new Appropriations of Lands.—He has obstructed the Administration of Justice, by refusing his Assent to Laws for establishing Judiciary powers—He has made Judges dependent on his Will alone, for the tenure of their offices, and the amount and payment of their salaries.—He has erected a multitude of New Offices, and sent hither swarms of Officers to harass our people, and eat out their substance.—He has kept among us, in times of peace, Standing Armies without the Consent of our legislatures.—He has affected to render the Military independent of and superior to the Civil power.—He has combined with others to subject us to a jurisdiction foreign to our constitution, and unacknowledged by our laws; giving his Assent to their Acts of pretended Legislation:—For Quartering large bodies of armed troops among us:—For protecting them, by a mock Trial, from punishment for any Murders which they should commit on the Inhabitants of these States:—For cutting off our Trade with all parts of the world:—For imposing Taxes on us without our Consent:—For depriving us in many cases, of the benefits of Trial by Jury:—For transporting us beyond Seas to be tried for pretended offences—For abolishing the free System of English Laws in a neighbouring Province, establishing therein an Arbitrary government, and enlarging its Boundaries so as to render it at once an example and fit instrument for introducing the same absolute rule into these Colonies:—For taking away our Charters, abolishing our most valuable Laws and altering fundamentally the Forms of our Governments:—For suspending our own Legislatures, and declaring themselves invested with power to legislate for us in all cases whatsoever.—He has abdicated Government here, by declaring us out of his Protection and waging War against us.—He has plundered our seas, ravaged our Coasts, burnt our towns, and destroyed the Lives of our people.—He is at this time, transporting large Armies of foreign Mercenaries to compleat the works of death, desolation and tyranny, already begun with circumstances of Cruelty & perfidy scarcely paralleled in the most barbarous ages, and totally unworthy the Head of a civilized nation.—He has constrained our fellow Citizens taken Captive on the high Seas, to bear Arms against their Country, to become the executioners of their friends and Brethren, or to fall themselves by their Hands.—He has excited domestic insurrections amongst us, and has endeavoured to bring on the inhabitants of our frontiers, the merciless Indian Savages, whose known rule of warfare, is an undistinguished destruction of all ages, sexes and conditions. In every stage of these Oppressions We have Petitioned for Redress in the most humble terms: Our repeated Petitions have been answered only by repeated injury. A Prince, whose character is thus marked by every act which may define a Tyrant, is unfit to be the ruler of a free people. Nor have We been wanting in attentions to our British brethren. We have warned them from time to time of attempts made by their legislature to extend an unwarrantable jurisdiction over us. We have reminded them of the circumstances of our emigration and settlement here. We have appealed to their native justice and magnanimity, and we have conjured them by the ties of our common kindred to disavow these usurpations, which, would inevitably interrupt our connections and correspondence. They too have been deaf to the voice of justice and of consanguinity. We must, therefore, acquiesce in the necessity, which denounces our Separation, and hold them, as we hold the rest of mankind, Enemies in War, in Peace Friends.—

We, therefore, the Representatives of the united States of America, in General Congress, Assembled, appealing to the Supreme Judge of the world for the rectitude of our intentions, do, in the Name, and by Authority of the good People of these Colonies, solemnly publish and declare, That these United Colonies are, and of Right ought to be Free and Independent States; that they are Absolved from all Allegiance to the British Crown, and that all political connection between them and the State of Great Britain, is and ought to be totally dissolved; and that as Free and Independent States, they have full Power to levy War, conclude Peace, contract Alliances, establish Commerce, and to do all other Acts and Things which Independent States may of right do.—And for the support of this Declaration, with a firm reliance on the protection of divine Providence, we mutually pledge to each other our Lives, our Fortunes and our sacred Honor.

John Hancock

Josiah Bartlett	Fra^s. Hopkinson	George Wythe
Wm Whipple	John Hart	Richard Henry Lee
Saml Adams	Abra Clark	Th Jefferson
John Adams	Robt Morris	Benj Harrison
Robt Treat Paine	Benjamin Rush	Th^s Nelson Jr.
Elbridge Gerry	Benj. Franklin	Francis Lightfoot Lee
Step. Hopkins	John Morton	Carter Braxton
William Ellery	Geo. Clymer	Wm Hooper
Roger Sherman	Ja^s. Smith	Joseph Hewes
Saml Huntington	Geo. Taylor	John Penn
Wm Williams	James Wilson	Edward Rutledge
Oliver Wolcott	Geo. Ross	Thos Heyward Junr
Matthew Thornton	Cæsar Rodney	Thomas Lynch Junr.
Wm Floyd	Geo Read	Arthur Middleton

Phil. Livingston
Fran^s. Lewis
Lewis Morris
Richd Stockton
Jno Witherspoon

Tho M:Kean
Samuel Chase
W^m. Paca
Thos. Stone
Charles Carroll
  of Carrollton

Button Gwinnett
Lyman Hall
Geo Walton

OUTLINE OF THE CONSTITUTION OF THE UNITED STATES:

Preamble

Article I: The Legislative Branch and Its Powers

Section 1: The two houses of Congress

Section 2: The House of Representatives; its elections and qualifications; apportionment; the **three-fifths clause**; Speaker and officers; power to impeach

Section 3: The Senate; its election and qualifications; the Vice President as presiding officer; power to try impeachments

Section 4: Elections and sessions

Section 5: Each house to judge elections and qualifications of its members; definition of quorum; adjournments; powers to compel attendance, make rules of proceedings, and expel members; journal of proceedings; reports of votes

Section 6: Compensation; freedom from arrest; protection from lawsuits for slander or libel; prohibition against holding other offices simultaneously

Section 7: Revenue bills originate in House of Representatives; bills must pass both houses; President's power to veto; overriding a veto; a bill may become law without President's approval; the "pocket veto"

Section 8: The **enumerated powers** of Congress:
1. To impose taxes
2. To borrow money
3. To regulate commerce between states and with foreign nations
4. To make laws for naturalization and bankruptcy
5. To coin money and establish weights and measures
6. To punish counterfeiters
7. To establish post offices and roads
8. To establish copyrights and patents
9. To establish lower courts
10. To punish piracy and violations of international law
11. To declare war
12. To raise and support armies
13. To maintain a navy
14. To make regulations for the army and navy
15. To call out the militia
16. To organize and arm the militia
17. To govern federal districts and buildings
18. To make all laws necessary and proper to execute the other powers (the **elastic clause** or **necessary and proper clause**)

Section 9: Importation of slaves until 1808; guarantee of habeas corpus; prohibition of bills of attainder, ex post facto laws, direct taxes, taxes on exports, spending money without a public accounting, granting titles of nobility, accepting titles or presents from foreign nations

Section 10: Limits on powers of the states: states may not make treaties, coin money, pass bills of attainder or ex post facto laws, impair contracts, grant titles of nobility, tax imports or exports, keep armies or navies in peacetime, make compacts with other states, or engage in war

Article II: The Executive Branch and Its Powers

Section 1: The President and Vice President; their term of office; manner of election; the electoral college; qualifications; succession of Vice President; compensation; the oath of office

Section 2: President as Commander in Chief of army and navy; power to pardon; power to make treaties and appoint ambassadors

Section 3: State of the Union message; power to convene special sessions of Congress

Section 4: Civil officers can be impeached and removed only for treason, bribery, or high crimes and misdemeanors

Article III: The Judicial Branch and Its Powers

Section 1: The Supreme Court; federal judges serve for life

Section 2: Federal jurisdiction includes all cases involving the Constitution, federal laws, treaties, ambassadors and consuls, admiralty and maritime cases, cases with the United States as a party, cases between states, cases between a state and citizen of a different state, cases between citizens of different states, cases between foreign nations and states or citizens; Supreme Court's original and appellate Jurisdiction; guarantee of trial by jury

Section 3: Treason—definition, proofs, and punishment

Article IV: State and Federal Relations

Section 1: Each state must give full faith and credit to public laws and proceedings of other states

Section 2: Citizens of each state have full rights in other states; extradition of fugitives from justice; the **fugitive slave clause**

Section 3: Admission and formation of new states; Congress governs federal territories

Section 4: States guaranteed a republican form of government and protection against invasion and domestic violence

Article V: Amending the Constitution

Methods of proposing and ratifying amendments by Congress, state legislatures, and special state conventions

Article VI: The Federal Government

All debts and engagements of the Confederation are valid un
tution
The Constitution and federal treaties are the supreme law of t
riding state laws or constitutions (the **supremacy clause**)
Federal officers are bound by oath to uphold Constitution; no religious test
may be applied to officeholders

Article VII: Ratification

Ratification by nine states will establish the Constitution

Amendments to the Constitution

1st Amendment: Guarantees freedom of religion, freedom of speech, freedom of the press, freedom of assembly, freedom to petition the government

2nd Amendment: Guarantees the right to keep and bear arms

3rd Amendment: Prohibits quartering of soldiers in peacetime

4th Amendment: Guarantees protection against unreasonable searches and
seizures; search warrants can be issued only for probable cause

5th Amendment: Criminal indictments only by grand jury; prohibition of
double jeopardy; protection against self-incrimination; guarantee of due
process (**due process clause**); compensation for private property taken for
public use (**takings clause**)

6th Amendment: Rights of accused to have a public trial in local district,
to be informed of accusations, to confront witnesses, to subpoena witnesses, and to have assistance of counsel

7th Amendment: Right to trial by jury; rules of common law

8th Amendment: Prohibition of excessive bail, excessive fines, and cruel
and unusual punishments

9th Amendment: Any rights not mentioned are retained by the people

10th Amendment: Powers not delegated to federal government are retained
by the states or by the people

The 1st through 10th Amendments are known as the **Bill of Rights**.
They were ratified in 1791 and took effect in 1792.

11th Amendment (1798): Federal judicial power does not extend to cases
between states and citizens of other states or foreign nations

12th Amendment (1804): Election of the President and Vice President by
the electoral college or by the House of Representatives

5th Amendment (1865):   Abolition of slavery in the United States and territories

14th Amendment (1868):   Section 1:   U.S. and state citizenship extended to all persons born or naturalized in the United States (the freed slaves); states barred from infringing on rights of citizens or depriving them of life, liberty, or property without due process of law (**due process clause**); states prohibited from denying citizens equal protection of the laws (**equal protection clause**)

Section 2:   Representation in Congress; repeal of the **three-fifths clause**

Section 3:   Former officials of government who violated their oath to uphold the Constitution by supporting rebellion are barred from holding federal or state offices

Section 4:   Debts incurred by federal government during the Civil War are reaffirmed; debts incurred by the Confederate states are illegal and void

15th Amendment (1870):   Right to vote shall not be denied on account of race, color, or previous condition of servitude

16th Amendment (1913):   Congress shall have power to impose and collect income tax, without regard to apportionment among the states

17th Amendment (1913):   Senators to be directly elected by people of the state they represent, rather than by state legislatures

18th Amendment (1919):   Prohibition of the manufacture, sale, or transportation of alcoholic beverages

19th Amendment (1920):   Right to vote shall not be denied on account of sex

20th Amendment (1933):   Section 1:   President's inauguration moved from March 4 to January 20 following election; initial meeting of Congress moved from December to January 3; provisions for succession if President-elect dies before assuming office

21st Amendment (1933):   Repeals the 18th Amendment, which had prohibited manufacture and sale of alcoholic beverages

22nd Amendment (1951):   Prohibits President from serving more than two terms

23rd Amendment (1961):   Provides for presidential electors from the District of Columbia

24th Amendment (1964):   Right to vote in federal elections cannot be restricted by required payment of poll tax

25th Amendment (1967):   Succession in case of death or removal from office of the President

26th Amendment (1971):   Right to vote extended to all citizens 18 years old or older

27th Amendment (1992):   Congressional pay raises cannot take effect until after a new Congress is elected

THE CONSTITUTION

We the People of the United States, in Order to form a more perfect Union, establish Justice, insure domestic Tranquility, provide for the common defence, promote the general Welfare, and secure the Blessings of Liberty to ourselves and our Posterity, do ordain and establish this Constitution for the United States of America.

Article. I.

Section 1.   All legislative Powers herein granted shall be vested in a Congress of the United States, which shall consist of a Senate and House of Representatives.

Section 2.   The House of Representatives shall be composed of Members chosen every second Year by the People of the several States, and the Electors in each State shall have the Qualifications requisite for Electors of the most numerous Branch of the State Legislature.

No person shall be a representative who shall not have attained to the Age of twenty five Years, and been seven Years a Citizen of the United States, and who shall not, when elected, be an Inhabitant of that State in which he shall be chosen.

Representatives *and direct Taxes*[1] shall be apportioned among the several States which may be included within this Union, according to their respective Numbers, *which shall be determined by adding to the whole Number of free Persons, including those bound to Service for a Term of Years, and excluding Indians not taxed, three fifths of all other Persons.*[2] The actual Enumeration shall be made within three Years after the first Meeting of the Congress of the United States, and within every subsequent Term of ten Years, in such Manner as they shall by Law direct. The Number of Representatives shall not exceed one for every thirty Thousand, but each State shall have at Least one Representative; and until such enumeration shall be made, the State of New Hampshire shall be entitled to chuse three, Massachusetts eight, Rhode-Island and Providence Plantations one, Connecticut five, New-York six, New Jersey four, Pennsylvania eight, Delaware one, Maryland six, Virginia ten, North Carolina five, South Carolina five, and Georgia three.

When vacancies happen in the Representation from any State, the Executive Authority thereof shall issue Writs of Election to fill such Vacancies.

The House of Representatives shall chuse their Speaker and other Officers; and shall have the sole Power of Impeachment.

[1] See the 16th Amendment.
[2] See the 17th Amendment.

Section 3. The Senate of the United States shall be composed of two Senators from each State, *chosen by the Legislature thereof,*[1] for six Years; and each senator shall have one Vote.

Immediately after they shall be assembled in Consequence of the first Election, they shall be divided as equally as may be into three Classes. The Seats of the Senators of the first Class shall be vacated at the Expiration of the second Year, of the second Class at the Expiration of the fourth Year, and of the third Class at the Expiration of the sixth Year, so that one third may be chosen every second Year; *and if Vacancies happen by Resignation, or otherwise, during the Recess of the Legislature of any State, the Executive thereof may make temporary Appointments until the next Meeting of the Legislature, which shall then fill such Vacancies.*[2]

No Person shall be a Senator who shall not have attained to the Age of thirty Years, and been nine Years a Citizen of the United States, and who shall not, when elected, be an Inhabitant of that State for which he shall be chosen.

The Vice President of the United States shall be President of the Senate, but shall have no Vote, unless they be equally divided.

The Senate shall chuse their other Officers, and also a President pro tempore, in the Absence of the Vice President, or when he shall exercise the Office of President of the United States.

The Senate shall have the sole Power to try all Impeachments. When sitting for that Purpose, they shall be on Oath or Affirmation. When the President of the United States is tried, the Chief Justice shall preside: And no Person shall be convicted without the Concurrence of two thirds of the Members present.

Judgment in Cases of Impeachment shall not extend further than to removal from Office, and disqualification to hold and enjoy any Office of honor, Trust or Profit under the United States: but the Party convicted shall nevertheless be liable and subject to Indictment, Trial, Judgment and Punishment, according to Law.

Section 4. The Times, Places and Manner of holding Elections for Senators and Representatives, shall be prescribed in each State by the Legislature thereof; but the Congress may at any time by Law make or alter such Regulations, except as to the Places of chusing Senators.

The Congress shall assemble at least once in every Year, and such Meeting shall be *on the first Monday in December,*[3] unless they shall by Law appoint a different Day.

Section 5. Each House shall be the Judge of the Elections, Returns and Qualifications of its own Members, and a Majority of each shall constitute a Quorum to do Business; but a smaller Number may adjourn from day to day,

[1] See the 17th Amendment.
[2] See the 17th Amendment.
[3] See the 20th Amendment.

and may be authorized to compel the Attendance of absent Members, in such Manner, and under such Penalties as each House may provide.

Each House may determine the Rules of its Proceedings, punish its Members for disorderly Behaviour, and, with the Concurrence of two thirds, expel a Member.

Each House shall keep a Journal of its Proceedings, and from time to time publish the same, excepting such Parts as may in their Judgment require Secrecy; and the Yeas and Nays of the Members of either House on any question shall, at the Desire of one fifth of those Present, be entered on the Journal.

Neither House, during the Session of Congress, shall, without the Consent of the other, adjourn for more than three days, nor to any other Place than that in which the two Houses shall be sitting.

Section 6. The Senators and Representatives shall receive a Compensation for their Services, to be ascertained by Law, and paid out of the Treasury of the United States. They shall in all Cases, except Treason, Felony and Breach of the Peace, be privileged from Arrest during their Attendance at the Session of their respective Houses, and in going to and returning from the same; and for any Speech or Debate in either House, they shall not be questioned in any other Place.

No Senator or Representative shall, during the Time for which he was elected, be appointed to any civil Office under the Authority of the United States, which shall have been created, or the Emoluments whereof shall have been encreased during such time; and no Person holding any Office under the United States, shall be a Member of either House during his Continuance in Office.

Section 7. All Bills for raising Revenue shall originate in the House of Representatives; but the Senate may propose or concur with Amendments as on other Bills.

Every Bill which shall have passed the House of Representatives and the Senate, shall, before it becomes a Law, be presented to the President of the United States; If he approve he shall sign it, but if not he shall return it, with his Objections to that House in which it shall have originated, who shall enter the Objections at large on their Journal, and proceed to reconsider it. If after such Reconsideration two thirds of that House shall agree to pass the Bill, it shall be sent, together with the Objections, to the other House, by which it shall likewise be reconsidered, and if approved by two thirds of that House, it shall become a Law. But in all such Cases the Votes of both Houses shall be determined by yeas and Nays, and the Names of the Persons voting for and against the Bill shall be entered on the Journal of each House respectively. If any Bill shall not be returned by the President within ten Days (Sundays excepted) after it shall have been presented to him, the Same shall be a Law, in like Manner as if he had signed it, unless the Congress by their Adjournment prevent its Return, in which Case it shall not be a Law.

Every Order, Resolution, or Vote to which the Concurrence of the Senate and House of Representatives may be necessary (except on a question of Adjournment) shall be presented to the President of the United States; and before the Same shall take Effect, shall be approved by him, or being disapproved by him, shall be repassed by two thirds of the Senate and House of Representatives, according to the Rules and Limitations prescribed in the Case of a Bill.

Section 8. The Congress shall have Power To lay and collect Taxes, Duties, Imposts and Excises, to pay the Debts and provide for the common Defence and general Welfare of the United States; but all Duties, Imposts and Excises shall be uniform throughout the United States;

To borrow Money on the credit of the United States;

To regulate Commerce with foreign Nations, and among the several States, and with the Indian Tribes;

To establish an uniform Rule of Naturalization, and uniform Laws on the subject of Bankruptcies throughout the United States;

To coin Money, regulate the Value thereof, and of foreign Coin, and fix the Standard of Weights and Measures;

To provide for the Punishment of counterfeiting the Securities and current Coin of the United States;

To establish Post Offices and post Roads;

To promote the Progress of Science and useful Arts, by securing for limited Times to Authors and Inventors the exclusive Right to their respective Writings and Discoveries;

To constitute Tribunals inferior to the supreme Court;

To define and punish Piracies and Felonies committed on the high Seas, and Offences against the Law of Nations;

To declare War, grant Letters of Marque and Reprisal, and make Rules concerning Captures on Land and Water;

To raise and support Armies, but no Appropriation of Money to that Use shall be for a longer Term than two Years;

To provide and maintain a Navy;

To make Rules for the Government and Regulation of the land and naval Forces;

To provide for calling forth the Militia to execute the Laws of the Union, suppress Insurrections and repel Invasions;

To provide for organizing, arming, and disciplining the Militia and for governing such Part of them as may be employed in the Service of the United States, reserving to the States respectively, the Appointment of the Officers, and the Authority of training the Militia according to the discipline prescribed by Congress;

To exercise exclusive Legislation in all Cases whatsoever, over such District (not exceeding ten Miles square) as may, by Cession of particular States, and the Acceptance of Congress, become the Seat of the Government of the

United States, and to exercise like Authority over all Places purchased by the Consent of the Legislature of the State in which the Same shall be, for the Erection of Forts, Magazines, Arsenals, dock-Yards, and other needful Buildings,—And

To make all Laws which shall be necessary and proper for carrying into Execution the foregoing Powers, and all other Powers vested by this Constitution in the Government of the United States, or in any Department or Officer thereof.

Section 9.   The Migration or Importation of such Persons as any of the States now existing shall think proper to admit, shall not be prohibited by the Congress prior to the Year one thousand eight hundred and eight, but a Tax or duty may be imposed on such Importation, not exceeding ten dollars for each Person.

The Privilege of the Writ of Habeas Corpus shall not be suspended, unless when in Cases of Rebellion or Invasion the public Safety may require it.

No Bill of Attainder or ex post facto Law shall be passed.

No Capitation, or other direct, Tax shall be laid, unless in Proportion to the Census or Enumeration herein before directed to be taken.[1]

No Tax or Duty shall be laid on Articles exported from any State.

No Preference shall be given by any Regulation of Commerce or Revenue to the Ports of one State over those of another: nor shall Vessels bound to, or from, one State be obliged to enter, clear, or pay Duties in another.

No Money shall be drawn from the Treasury, but in Consequence of Appropriations made by Law; and a regular Statement and Account of the Receipts and Expenditures of all public Money shall be published from time to time.

No Title of Nobility shall be granted by the United States: And no Person holding any Office of Profit or Trust under them, shall, without the Consent of the Congress, accept of any present, Emolument, Office, or Title, of any kind whatever, from any King, Prince, or foreign State.

Section 10.   No State shall enter into any Treaty, Alliance, or Confederation; grant Letters of Marque and Reprisal, coin Money, emit Bills of Credit; make any Thing but gold and silver Coin a Tender in Payment of Debts; pass any Bill of Attainder, ex post facto Law, or Law impairing the Obligation of Contracts, or grant any Title of Nobility.

No State shall, without the Consent of the Congress, lay any Imposts or Duties on Imports or Exports, except what may be absolutely necessary for executing it's inspection Laws: and the net Produce of all Duties and Imposts, laid by any State on Imports or Exports, shall be for the Use of the Treasury of the United States; and all such Laws shall be subject to the Revision and Controul of the Congress.

[1] See the 16th Amendment.

No State shall, without the Consent of Congress, lay any Duty of Tonnage, keep Troops, or Ships of War in time of Peace, enter into any Agreement or Compact with another State, or with a foreign Power, or engage in War, unless actually invaded, or in such imminent Danger as will not admit of delay.

Article. II.

Section 1.   The executive Power shall be vested in a President of the United States of America. He shall hold his Office during the Term of four Years, and, together with the Vice President, chosen for the same Term, be elected as follows

Each State shall appoint, in such Manner as the Legislature thereof may direct, a Number of Electors, equal to the whole Number of Senators and Representatives to which the State may be entitled in the Congress: but no Senator or Representative, or Person holding an Office of Trust or Profit under the United States, shall be appointed an Elector.

The Electors shall meet in their respective States, and vote by Ballot for two Persons, of whom one at least shall not be an Inhabitant of the same State with themselves. And they shall make a List of all the Persons voted for, and of the Number of Votes for each; which List they shall sign and certify, and transmit sealed to the Seat of the Government of the United States, directed to the President of the Senate. The President of the Senate shall, in the Presence of the Senate and House of Representatives, open all the Certificates, and the Votes shall then be counted. The Person having the greatest Number of Votes shall be the President, if such Number be a Majority of the whole Number of Electors appointed; and if there be more than one who have such Majority, and have an equal Number of Votes, then the House of Representatives shall immediately chuse by Ballot one of them for President; and if no Person have a Majority, then from the five highest on the List the said House shall in like Manner chuse the President. But in chusing the President, the Votes shall be taken by States, the Representation from each State having one Vote; A quorum for this Purpose shall consist of a Member or Members from two thirds of the States, and a Majority of all the States shall be necessary to a Choice. In every Case, after the Choice of the President, the Person having the greatest Number of Votes of the Electors shall be the Vice President. But if there should remain two or more who have equal Votes, the Senate shall chuse from them by Ballot the Vice President.[1]

The Congress may determine the Time of chusing the Electors, and the Day on which they shall give their Votes; which Day shall be the same throughout the United States.

---

[1] See the 12th Amendment.

No Persons except a natural born Citizen, or a Citizen of the United States, at the time of the Adoption of this Constitution, shall be eligible to the Office of President; neither shall any Person be eligible to that Office who shall not have attained to the Age of thirty five Years, and been fourteen Years a Resident within the United States.

In Case of the Removal of the President from Office, or of his Death, Resignation, or Inability to discharge the Powers and Duties of the said Office, the Same shall devolve on the Vice President, and the Congress may by law provide for the Case of Removal, Death, Resignation or Inability, both of the President and Vice President declaring what Officer shall then act as President, and such Officer shall act accordingly, until the Disability be removed, or a President shall be elected. [1]

The President shall, at stated Times, receive for his Services, a Compensation, which shall neither be encreased nor diminished during the Period for which he shall have been elected, and he shall not receive within that Period any other Emolument from the United States, or any of them.

Before he enter on the Execution of his Office, he shall take the following Oath or Affirmation: "I do solemnly swear (or affirm) that I will faithfully execute the Office of President of the United States, and will to the best of my Ability, preserve, protect and defend the Constitution of the United States."

Section 2.   The President shall be Commander in Chief of the Army and Navy of the United States, and of the Militia of the several States, when called into the actual Service of the United States; he may require the Opinion, in writing, of the principal Officer in each of the executive Departments, upon any Subject relating to the Duties of their respective Offices, and he shall have Power to grant Reprieves and Pardons for Offences against the United States, except in Cases of Impeachment.

He shall have Power, by and with the Advice and Consent of the Senate, to make Treaties, provided two thirds of the Senators present concur; and he shall nominate, and by and with the Advice and Consent of the Senate, shall appoint Ambassadors, other public Ministers and Consuls, Judges of the supreme Court, and all other Officers of the United States, whose Appointments are not herein otherwise provided for, and which shall be established by Law: but the Congress may by Law vest the Appointment of such inferior Officers, as they think proper, in the President alone, in the Courts of Law, or in the Heads of Departments.

The President shall have Power to fill up all Vacancies that may happen during the Recess of the Senate, by granting Commissions which shall expire at the End of their next Session.

---

[1] See the 25th Amendment.

Section 3.   He shall from time to time give to the Congress Information of the State of the Union, and recommend to their Consideration such Measures as he shall judge necessary and expedient; he may, on extraordinary Occasions, convene both Houses, or either of them, and in Case of Disagreement between them, with Respect to the Time of Adjournment, he may adjourn them to such Time as he shall think proper; he shall receive Ambassadors and other public Ministers; he shall take Care that the Laws be faithfully executed, and shall Commission all the Officers of the United States.

Section 4.   The President, Vice President and all civil Officers of the United States, shall be removed from Office on Impeachment for, and Conviction of, Treason, Bribery, or other high Crimes and Misdemeanors.

Article. III.

Section 1.   The judicial Power of the United States, shall be vested in one supreme Court, and in such inferior Courts as the Congress may from time to time ordain and establish. The Judges, both of the supreme and inferior Courts, shall hold their Offices during good Behaviour, and shall, at stated Times, receive for their Services, a Compensation, which shall not be diminished during their Continuance in Office.

Section 2.   The judicial Power shall extend to all Cases, in Law and Equity, arising under this Constitution, the Laws of the United States; and Treaties made, or which shall be made, under their Authority;—to all Cases affecting Ambassadors, other public Ministers and Consuls;—to all Cases of admiralty and maritime Jurisdiction;—to Controversies to which the United States shall be a Party;—to Controversies between two or more States;—*between a State and Citizens of another State;—between Citizens of different States—between Citizens of the same State claiming Lands under Grants of different States, and between a State, or the Citizens thereof, and foreign States, Citizens or Subjects.*[1]

In all Cases affecting Ambassadors, other public Ministers and Consuls, and those in which a State shall be Party, the supreme Court shall have original Jurisdiction. In all the other Cases before mentioned, the supreme Court shall have appellate Jurisdiction, both as to Law and Fact, with such Exceptions, and under such Regulations as the Congress shall make.

The Trial of all Crimes, except in Cases of Impeachment, shall be by Jury; and such Trial shall be held in the State where the said Crimes shall have been committed; but when not committed within any State, the Trial shall be at such Place or Places as the Congress may by Law have directed.

Section 3.   Treason against the United States, shall consist only in levying War against them, or in adhering to their Enemies, giving them Aid and

[1] See the 11th Amendment.

Comfort. No Person shall be convicted of Treason unless on the Testimony of two Witnesses to the same overt Act, or on Confession in open Court.

The Congress shall have Power to declare the Punishment of Treason, but no Attainder of Treason shall work Corruption of Blood, or Forfeiture except during the Life of the Person attainted.

Article. IV.

Section 1.   Full Faith and Credit shall be given in each State to the public Acts, Records, and judicial Proceedings of every other State. And the Congress may by general Laws prescribe the Manner in which such Acts, Records and Proceedings shall be proved, and the Effect thereof.

Section 2.   The Citizens of each State shall be entitled to all privileges and Immunities of Citizens in the several States.

A Person charged in any State with Treason, Felony, or other Crime, who shall flee from Justice, and be found in another State, shall on Demand of the executive Authority of the State from which he fled, be delivered up, to be removed to the State having Jurisdiction of the Crime.

No Person held to Service or Labour in one State, under the Laws thereof, escaping into another, shall, in Consequence of any Law or Regulation therein, be discharged from such Service or Labour but shall be delivered up on Claim of the Party to whom such Service or Labour may be due.[1]

Section 3.   New States may be admitted by Congress into this Union; but no new State shall be formed or erected within the Jurisdiction of any other State; nor any State be formed by the Junction of two or more States, or Parts of States, without the Consent of the Legislatures of the States concerned as well as the Congress.

The Congress shall have Power to dispose of and make all needful Rules and Regulations respecting the Territory or other Property belonging to the United States; and nothing in this Constitution shall be so construed as to Prejudice any Claims of the United States, or of any particular State.

Section 4.   The United States shall guarantee to every State in this Union a Republican Form of Government, and shall protect each of them against Invasion; and on Application of the Legislature, or of the Executive (when the Legislature cannot be convened) against domestic Violence.

[1] See the 13th Amendment.

Article. V.

The Congress, whenever two thirds of both Houses shall deem it necessary, shall propose Amendments to this Constitution, or, on the Application of the Legislatures of two thirds of the several States, shall call a Convention for proposing Amendments, which, in either Case, shall be valid to all Intents and Purposes, as Part of this Constitution, when ratified by the Legislatures of three fourths of the several States, or by Conventions in three fourths thereof, as the one or the other Mode of Ratification may be proposed by the Congress: Provided, that no Amendment which may be made prior to the Year One thousand eight hundred and eight shall in any Manner affect the first and fourth Clauses in the Ninth Section of the first Article; and that no State, without its Consent, shall be deprived of its equal Suffrage in the Senate.

Article. VI.

All Debts contracted and Engagements entered into, before the Adoption of this Constitution, shall be as valid against the United States under this Constitution, as under the Confederation.

This Constitution, and the Laws of the United States which shall be made in Pursuance thereof; and all Treaties made, or which shall be made, under the Authority of the United States, shall be the supreme Law of the Land; and the Judges in every State shall be bound thereby, any Thing in the Constitution or Laws of any State to the Contrary notwithstanding.

The Senators and Representatives before mentioned, and the Members of the several State Legislatures, and all executive and judicial Officers, both of the United States and of the several States, shall be bound by Oath or Affirmation, to support this Constitution; but no religious Test shall ever be required as a Qualification to any Office or public Trust under the United States.

Article. VII.

The Ratification of the Conventions of nine States, shall be sufficient for the Establishment of this Constitution between the States so ratifying the Same.

DONE in convention by the Unanimous Consent of the States present the Seventeenth Day of September in the Year of our Lord one thousand seven hundred and Eighty seven and of the Independence of the United States of America the Twelfth In Witness whereof We have hereto subscribed our Names,

Attest—William Jackson, Secretary

Go: Washington—Presidt.
and deputy from Virginia

Delaware
Geo: Read
Gunning Bedford junr
John Dickinson
Richard Bassett
Jaco: Broom

Maryland
James McHenry
Dan of St. Thos. Jenifer
Danl Carroll

Virginia
John Blair—
James Madison Jr.

North Carolina
Wm. Blount
Richd. Dobbs Spaight.
Hu Williamson

South Carolina
J. Rutledge
Charles Cotesworth Pinckney
Charles Pinckney
Pierce Butler

Georgia
William Few
Abr Baldwin

New Hampshire
John Langdon
Nicholas Gilman

Massachusetts
Nathaniel Gorham
Rufus King

Connecticut
Wm: Saml. Johnson
Roger Sherman

New York
Alexander Hamilton

New Jersey
Wil: Livingston
David Brearley
Wm. Paterson.
Jona: Dayton

Pennsylvania
B Franklin
Thomas Mifflin
Robt Morris
Geo. Clymer
Thos. FitzSimons
Jared Ingersoll
James Wilson
Gouv. Morris

ARTICLES in Addition to, and Amendment of, the Constitution of the United States of America, proposed by Congress, and ratified by the Legislatures of the several States pursuant to the fifth Article of the Original Constitution

Article I.

Congress shall make no law respecting an establishment of religion, or prohibiting the free exercise thereof; or abridging the freedom of speech, or of the press; or the right of the people peaceably to assemble, and to petition the Government for a redress of grievances.

Article II.

A well regulated Militia, being necessary to the security of a free State, the right of the people to keep and bear Arms, shall not be infringed.

Article III.

No Soldier shall, in time of peace be quartered in any house, without the consent of the Owner, nor in time of war, but in a manner to be prescribed by law.

Article IV.

The right of the people to be secure in their persons, houses, papers, and effects, against unreasonable searches and seizures, shall not be violated, and no Warrants shall issue, but upon probable cause, supported by Oath or affirmation, and particularly describing the place to be searched, and the persons or things to be seized.

Article V.

No person shall be held to answer for a capital, or otherwise infamous crime, unless on a presentment or indictment of a Grand Jury, except in cases arising in the land or naval forces, or in the Militia, when in actual service in time of War or public danger; nor shall any person be subject for the same offence to be twice put in jeopardy of life or limb; nor shall be compelled in any criminal case to be a witness against himself, nor be deprived of life, liberty, or property, without due process of law; nor shall private property be taken for public use, without just compensation.

Article VI.

In all criminal prosecutions, the accused shall enjoy the right to a speedy and public trial, by an impartial jury of the State and district wherein the crime shall have been committed, which district shall have been previously ascertained by law, and to be informed of the nature and cause of the accusation; to be confronted with the witnesses against him; to have compulsory process for obtaining witnesses in his favor, and to have the Assistance of Counsel for his defence.

Article VII.

In Suits at common law, where the value in controversy shall exceed twenty dollars, the right of trial by jury shall be preserved, and no fact tried by a jury, shall be otherwise re-examined in any Court of the United States, than according to the rules of the common law.

Article VIII.

Excessive bail shall not be required, nor excessive fines imposed, nor cruel and unusual punishments inflicted.

Article IX.

The enumeration in the Constitution, of certain rights, shall not be construed to deny or disparage others retained by the people.

Article X.

The powers not delegated to the United States by the Constitution nor prohibited by it to the States, are reserved to the States respectively, or to the people.

Articles I.–X. ratified 1792

Article XI.

The Judicial power of the United States shall not be construed to extend to any suit in law or equity, commenced or prosecuted against one of the United States by Citizens of another State, or by Citizens or Subjects of any Foreign State.

Ratified 1798

Article XII.

The Electors shall meet in their respective states, and vote by ballot for President and Vice-President, one of whom, at least, shall not be an inhabitant of the same state with themselves; they shall name in their ballots the person voted for as President, and in distinct ballots the person voted for as Vice-President, and they shall make distinct lists of all persons voted for as

President, and of all persons voted for as Vice-President, and of the number of votes for each, which lists they shall sign and certify, and transmit sealed to the seat of the government of the United States, directed to the President of the Senate;—The President of the Senate shall, in the presence of the Senate and House of Representatives, open all the certificates and the votes shall then be counted;—The person having the greatest number of votes for President, shall be the President, if such number be a majority of the whole number of Electors appointed; and if no person have such majority, then from the persons having the highest numbers not exceeding three on the list of those voted for as President, the House of Representatives shall choose immediately, by ballot, the President. But in choosing the President, the votes shall be taken by states, the representation from each state having one vote; a quorum for this purpose shall consist of a member or members from two-thirds of the states, and a majority of all the states shall be necessary to a choice. *And if the House of Representatives shall not choose a President whenever the right of choice shall devolve upon them, before the fourth day of March next following, then the Vice-President shall act as President, as in the case of the death or other constitutional disability of the President.*[1]—The person having the greatest number of votes as Vice-President, shall be the Vice-President, if such number be a majority of the whole number of Electors appointed, and if no person have a majority, then from the two highest numbers on the list, the Senate shall choose the Vice-President; a quorum for the purpose shall consist of two-thirds of the whole number of Senators, and a majority of the whole number shall be necessary to a choice. But no person constitutionally ineligible to the office of President shall be eligible to that of Vice-President of the United States.

Ratified 1804

Article XIII.

SECTION 1.   Neither slavery nor involuntary servitude, except as a punishment for crime whereof the party shall have been duly convicted, shall exist within the United States, or any place subject to their jurisdiction.

SECTION 2.   Congress shall have power to enforce this article by appropriate legislation.

Ratified 1865

Article XIV.

SECTION 1.   All persons born or naturalized in the United States, and subject to the jurisdiction thereof, are citizens of the United States and of the State wherein they reside. No State shall make or enforce any law which shall abridge the privileges or immunities of citizens of the United States; nor shall any State deprive any person of life, liberty, or property, without

[1] See the 20th Amendment.

due process of law; nor deny to any person within its jurisdiction the equal protection of the laws.

SECTION 2.   Representatives shall be apportioned among the several States according to their respective numbers, counting the whole number of persons in each State, excluding Indians not taxed. But when the right to vote at any election for the choice of electors for President and Vice President of the United States, Representatives in Congress, the Executive and Judicial officers of a State, or the members of the Legislature thereof, is denied to any of the *male*[1] inhabitants of such State, *being twenty-one years of age,*[2] and citizens of the United States, or in any way abridged, except for participation in rebellion, or other crime, the basis of representation therein shall be reduced in the proportion which the number of such *male* citizens shall bear to the whole number of *male* citizens *twenty-one years of age* in such State.

SECTION 3.   No person shall be a Senator or Representative in Congress, or elector of President and Vice President, or hold any office, civil or military, under the United States, or under any State, who, having previously taken an oath, as a member of Congress, or as an officer of the United States, or as a member of any State legislature, or as an executive or judicial officer of any State, to support the Constitution of the United States, shall have engaged in insurrection or rebellion against the same, or given aid or comfort to the enemies thereof. But Congress may by a vote of two-thirds of each House, remove such disability.

SECTION 4.   The validity of the public debt of the United States, authorized by law, including debts incurred for payment of pensions and bounties for services in suppressing insurrection or rebellion, shall not be questioned. But neither the United States nor any State shall assume or pay any debt or obligation incurred in aid of insurrection or rebellion against the United States, or any claim for the loss of emancipation of any slave; but all such debts, obligations and claims shall be held illegal and void.

SECTION 5.   The Congress shall have power to enforce, by appropriate legislation, the provisions of this article.

Ratified 1868

Article XV.

SECTION 1.   The right of citizens of the United States to vote shall not be denied or abridged by the United States or by any State on account of race, color, or previous condition of servitude.

SECTION 2.   The Congress shall have power to enforce this article by appropriate legislation.

Ratified 1870

---

[1] See the 19th Amendment.
[2] See the 26th Amendment.

Article XVI.

The Congress shall have power to lay and collect taxes on incomes, from whatever source derived, without apportionment among the several States, and without regard to any census or enumeration.

Ratified 1913

Article XVII.

The Senate of the United States shall be composed of two Senators from each state, elected by the people thereof, for six years; and each Senator shall have one vote. The electors in each State shall have the qualifications requisite for electors of the most numerous branch of the State legislatures.

When vacancies happen in the representation of any State in the Senate, the executive authority of such State shall issue writs of election to fill such vacancies: Provided, That the legislature of any State may empower the executive thereof to make temporary appointments until the people fill the vacancies by election as the legislature may direct.

This amendment shall not be so construed as to affect the election or term of any Senator chosen before it becomes valid as part of the Constitution.

Ratified 1913

Article XVIII.

SECTION 1.   After one year from the ratification of this article the manufacture, sale, or transportation of intoxicating liquors within, the importation thereof into, or the exportation thereof from the United States and all territory subject to the jurisdiction thereof for beverage purposes is hereby prohibited.

SEC. 2.   The Congress and the several States shall have concurrent power to enforce this article by appropriate legislation.

SEC. 3.   This article shall be inoperative unless it shall have been ratified as an amendment to the Constitution by the legislatures of the several States, as provided in the Constitution, within seven years from the date of the submission hereof to the States by the Congress.[1]

Ratified 1919

Article XIX.

The right of citizens of the United States to vote shall not be denied or abridged by the United States or by any State on account of sex.

Congress shall have power to enforce this article by appropriate legislation.

Ratified 1920

---

[1] See the 21st Amendment.

Article XX.

SECTION 1. The terms of the President and Vice President shall end at noon on the 20th day of January, and the terms of Senators and Representatives at noon on the 3d day of January, of the years in which such terms would have ended if this article had not been ratified; and the terms of their successors shall then begin.

SEC. 2. The Congress shall assemble at least once in every year, and such meeting shall begin at noon on the 3d day of January, unless they shall by law appoint a different day.

SEC. 3. If, at the time fixed for the beginning of the term of the President, the President elect shall have died, the Vice President elect shall become President. If a President shall not have been chosen before the time fixed for the beginning of his term, or if the President elect shall have failed to qualify, then the Vice President elect shall act as President until a President shall have qualified; and the Congress may by law provide for the case wherein neither a President elect nor a Vice President elect shall have qualified, declaring who shall then act as President, or the manner in which one who is to act shall be selected, and such person shall act accordingly until a President or Vice President shall have qualified.

SEC. 4. The Congress may by law provide for the case of the death of any of the persons from whom the House of Representatives may choose a President whenever the right of choice shall have devolved upon them, and for the case of the death of any of the persons from whom the Senate may choose a Vice President whenever the right of choice shall have devolved upon them.

SEC. 5. Sections 1 and 2 shall take effect on the 15th day of October following the ratification of this article.

SEC. 6. This article shall be inoperative unless it shall have been ratified as an amendment to the Constitution by the legislatures of three-fourths of the several States within seven years from the date of its submission.

Ratified 1933

Article XXI.

SECTION 1. The eighteenth article of amendment to the Constitution of the United States is hereby repealed.

SECTION 2. The transportation or importation into any State, Territory, or possession of the United States for delivery or use therein of intoxicating liquors, in violation of the laws thereof, is hereby prohibited.

SECTION 3. This article shall be inoperative unless it shall have been ratified as an amendment to the Constitution by conventions in the several States, as provided in the Constitution, within seven years from the date of the submission hereof to the States by the Congress.

Ratified 1933

Article XXII.

SECTION 1.   No person shall be elected to the office of the President more than twice and no person who has held the office of President, or acted as President, for more than two years of a term to which some other person was elected President shall be elected to the office of the President more than once. But this Article shall not apply to any person holding the office of President when this Article was proposed by the Congress, and shall not prevent any person who may be holding the office of President, or acting as President, during the term within which this Article becomes operative from holding the office of President or acting as President during the remainder of such term.

SEC. 2.   This article shall be inoperative unless it shall have been ratified as an amendment to the Constitution by the legislatures of three-fourths of the several States within seven years from the date of its submission to the States by the Congress.

Ratified 1951

Article XXIII.

SECTION 1.   The District constituting the seat of Government of the United States shall appoint in such manner as the Congress may direct:

A number of electors of President and Vice President equal to the whole number of Senators and Representatives in Congress to which the District would be entitled if it were a State, but in no event more than the least populous State; they shall be in addition to those appointed by the States, but they shall be considered, for the purposes of the election of President and Vice President, to be electors appointed by a State; and they shall meet in the District and perform such duties as provided by the twelfth article of amendment.

SEC. 2.   The Congress shall have power to enforce this article by appropriate legislation.

Ratified 1961

Article XXIV.

SECTION 1.   The right of citizens of the United States to vote in any primary or other election for President or Vice President, for electors for President or Vice President, or for Senator or Representative in Congress, shall not be denied or abridged by the United States or any State by reason of failure to pay any poll tax or other tax.

SEC. 2.   The Congress shall have power to enforce this article by appropriate legislation.

Ratified 1964

Article XXV.

SECTION 1.   In case of the removal of the President from office or of his death or resignation, the Vice President shall become President.

SEC. 2.   Whenever there is a vacancy in the office of the Vice President, the President shall nominate a Vice President who shall take office upon confirmation by a majority vote of both Houses of Congress.

SEC. 3.   Whenever the President transmits to the President pro tempore of the Senate and the Speaker of the House of Representatives his written declaration that he is unable to discharge the powers and duties of his office, and until he transmits to them a written declaration to the contrary, such powers and duties shall be discharged by the Vice President as Acting President.

SEC. 4.   Whenever the Vice President and a majority of either the principal officers of the executive departments or of such other body as Congress may by law provide, transmit to the President pro tempore of the Senate and the Speaker of the House of Representatives their written declaration that the President is unable to discharge the powers and duties of his office, the Vice President shall immediately assume the powers and duties of the office as Acting President.

Thereafter, when the President transmits to the President pro tempore of the Senate and the Speaker of the House of Representatives his written declaration that no inability exists, he shall resume the powers and duties of his office unless the Vice President and a majority of either the principal officers of the executive department or of such other body as Congress may by law provide, transmit within four days to the President pro tempore of the Senate and the Speaker of the House of Representatives their written declaration that the President is unable to discharge the powers and duties of his office. Thereupon Congress shall decide the issue, assembling within forty-eight hours for that purpose if not in session. If the Congress, within twenty-one days after receipt of the latter written declaration, or, if Congress is not in session, within twenty-one days after Congress is required to assemble, determines by two-thirds vote of both Houses that the President is unable to discharge the powers and duties of his office, the Vice President shall continue to discharge the same as Acting President; otherwise, the President shall resume the powers and duties of his office.

Ratified 1967

Article XXVI.

SECTION 1.   The right of citizens of the United States, who are eighteen years of age or older, to vote shall not be denied or abridged by the United States or by any State on account of age.

SEC. 2.   The Congress shall have power to enforce this article by appropriate legislation.

Ratified 1971

Article XXVII.

No law varying the compensation for the services of the Senators and Representatives, shall take effect until an election of Representatives shall have intervened.

Ratified 1992

CHRONOLOGY OF MAJOR EVENTS IN AMERICAN HISTORY

1607	Founding of Jamestown in Virginia
1619	Virginia House of Burgesses formed. First Africans brought to Virginia.
1620	Mayflower Compact
1676	Bacon's Rebellion in Virginia
1688	Glorious Revolution in England
1754	Albany Congress proposes Plan of Union drafted by Benjamin Franklin for defense against Indians and French. Plan is rejected by the colonies.
1763	Treaty of Paris ending Seven Years War (French and Indian War) gives Canada to Great Britain and ends French threat to colonies.
1765	Stamp Act Congress (delegates from nine colonies) meets in New York to oppose Stamp Act and other British taxes.
1770	Boston Massacre
1773	Boston Tea Party
1774	Parliament passes Coercive Acts and Quebec Act. First Continental Congress meets in Philadelphia.
1775	Battles of Lexington and Concord (April 19). Second Continental Congress meets in Philadelphia.
1776	Thomas Paine publishes *Common Sense*. Congress adopts Declaration of Independence, July 4; begins drafting Articles of Confederation.
1778	Treaties with France bring important military supplies and naval support.
1781	Maryland is thirteenth and last state to ratify Articles of Confederation. British commander Cornwallis surrenders to Washington at Yorktown, Virginia, October 19, ending major fighting in the Revolutionary War.
1782	Preliminary peace treaty with Great Britain recognizes independent United States with borders of Great Lakes in the north, the Mississippi River on the west, and the 31st parallel to the south.
1783	British evacuate New York City Nov. 25, but continue to hold forts in Northwest territories.
1786	Annapolis Convention discusses interstate cooperation and recommends a convention to revise the Articles of Confederation. Shays' Rebellion in Massachusetts suppressed.
1787	Constitutional Convention meets in Philadelphia, May–Sept. Continental Congress adopts Northwest Ordinance. The Constitution submitted to Congress, Sept. 20, and to the people in special state conventions, Sept. 28.
1788	Eleven states (all but Rhode Island and North Carolina) ratify Constitution, putting new federal government into effect.
1789	New federal Congress convenes in New York City. George Washington receives all 69 electoral votes for President; nominates Thomas Jefferson as Secretary of State, Alexander Hamilton as Secretary of the Treasury, and John Jay as Chief Justice of the Supreme Court. Congress passes Judiciary Act creating federal court system. Proposed amendments to the Constitution approved by Congress and submitted to the states. North Carolina ratifies Constitution.

1790   Rhode Island ratifies Constitution. First American textile mill built in Pawtucket, R.I.

1791   Bank of the United States chartered. Vermont admitted to the Union.

1792   Washington reelected President, receiving all 132 electoral votes; vetoes first bill and veto is sustained by House. First ten amendments ("The Bill of Rights") officially ratified, March 1. Kentucky admitted to the Union.

1793   Supreme Court decision in *Chisolm* v. *Georgia* permits citizen of South Carolina to sue state of Georgia in federal court. Washington issues Proclamation of Neutrality in war between the new French Republic and Great Britain. Cotton gin invented by Eli Whitney.

1794   Whiskey Rebellion in Pennsylvania suppressed.

1795   Jay Treaty with England and Pinckney Treaty with Spain approved by Senate. 11th Amendment ratified, barring citizens of one state from suing another state in federal court.

1796   Washington refuses to furnish House of Representatives with documents about negotiation of Jay Treaty, establishing precedent for executive privilege; announces he will not seek a third term and publishes "Farewell Address." Oliver Ellsworth becomes Chief Justice. Tennessee admitted. John Adams elected President with 71 electoral votes, to 68 for Thomas Jefferson.

1798   Congress passes Alien and Sedition Acts. Adams administration hampered by interference from Alexander Hamilton. Undeclared naval war with France; creation of Navy Department. Kentucky and Virginia Resolutions, passed by state legislatures, assert the Alien and Sedition Acts are unconstitutional and claim that states have the power to declare them void.

1800   Congress meets for the first time in Washington, D.C. Republican presidential and vice-presidential candidates, Thomas Jefferson and Aaron Burr, receive 73 votes each in Electoral College (incumbent President John Adams receives 65), throwing election into House of Representatives. After 36 ballots over six days, Jefferson is elected President.

1801   Outgoing Secretary of State John Marshall becomes Chief Justice. Judiciary Act passed by lame-duck Congress. President Jefferson sends naval squadron to Mediterranean to protect American shipping from Barbary pirates in Tripoli.

1802   Congress repeals Judiciary Act of 1801.

1803   Louisiana Territory purchased from France for $15 million; treaty approved by Senate. Supreme Court decision in *Marbury* v. *Madison* declares the Judiciary Act of 1789 unconstitutional; decision establishes principle of judicial review of acts of Congress. Ohio admitted.

1804   12th Amendment allows separate balloting for President and Vice-President. Jefferson sends Meriwether Lewis and William Clark to explore and map Louisiana Territory. Vice-President Aaron Burr kills Alexander Hamilton in a duel. Jefferson reelected President; George Clinton elected Vice-President.

1807   Embargo Act prohibits exports to foreign nations.

1808   James Madison elected President. Importation of slaves prohibited.

1809   Non-Intercourse Act reopens trade with all nations except France and England.

1810   Supreme Court decision in *Fletcher* v. *Peck* establishes Court's power to declare state laws unconstitutional.

1811   Macon's Bill No. 2 allows trade with France and forbids trade with England.

1812   Madison reelected President. Louisiana admitted. War declared on Great Britain.

1814   British military expedition burns Washington, D.C. Hartford Convention of New England federalists declares states' right to oppose federal actions. Treaty of Ghent approved by Senate.

1816   Congress charters Second Bank of the United States; passes Tariff of 1816 and Bonus Bill for internal improvements (vetoed). Indiana admitted. Supreme Court decision in *Martin* v. *Hunters Lessee* sets appellate jurisdiction over state courts. James Monroe elected President.

1817   Mississippi admitted. Thomas Gallaudet founds first school for the deaf at Hartford, Ct.

1818   Illinois admitted.

1819   Supreme Court decision in *McCullough* v. *Maryland* accepts broad implied powers of Congress, including power to create a bank, and asserts that states cannot tax federal agencies; in *Dartmouth College* v. *Woodward*, Court holds that states cannot interfere with contracts. Alabama admitted.

1820   Monroe reelected President. Maine admitted. Missouri Compromise bars slavery north of 36° 30' in Louisiana Purchase.

1821   Missouri admitted.

1823   James Monroe sets forth Monroe Doctrine to Congress, barring intervention by European powers in Western Hemisphere.

1824   Supreme Court decision in *Gibbons* v. *Ogden* asserts federal power to control interstate commerce. John Quincy Adams elected President in House of Representatives.

1825   Erie Canal completed; first American steam locomotive built in Hoboken, N.J.

1828   Tariff of Abominations. Andrew Jackson elected President.

1829   David Walker publishes *Appeal to the Colored Citizens of The United States* in Wilmington, N.C.

1830   Indian Removal Act

Andrew Jackson (1767–1845), 7th President of the U.S., had the most popular and electoral votes for President in 1824, but was short of a majority. The House of Representatives decided the election in favor of John Quincy Adams.

542

1831   Nat Turner's Rebellion in Virginia. William Lloyd Garrison begins to publish *The Liberator*. Cyrus McCormick invents mechanical reaper. First regularly scheduled railroad service.

1832   Congress recharters Second Bank of the United States (vetoed). South Carolina nullifies Tariff of Abominations. Jackson reelected President.

1833   Congress passes Compromise Tariff. American Anti-Slavery Society founded.

1836   Roger B. Taney becomes Chief Justice. American settlers in Mexico revolt and declare Texas an independent nation. Martin Van Buren elected President.

1837   Michigan admitted. John Deere develops steel plow.

1838   Van Buren sends troops to force Cherokee removals to Oklahoma Territory, known as Trail of Tears. Frederick Douglass escapes from slavery in Maryland to Massachusetts.

1839   Vulcanized rubber developed by Charles Goodyear.

1840   William Henry Harrison ("Tippecanoe") elected President.

1841   Harrison dies; John Tyler becomes President.

1844   James K. Polk elected President. Telegraph developed by Samuel F.B. Morse.

1845   Florida and Texas admitted.

1846   Oregon Territory purchased from Great Britain. War declared on Mexico. Iowa admitted.

1848   Treaty ending Mexican War acquires territory from Texas to Pacific Ocean. Wisconsin admitted. Women's Rights Convention at Seneca Falls, N.Y., organized by Lucretia Mott and Elizabeth Cady Stanton. Zachary Taylor elected President.

1849   California Gold Rush

1850   Taylor dies; Millard Fillmore becomes President. Compromise of 1850, including Fugitive Slave Law, passed by Congress. First land grants for development of railroads. California admitted.

James K. Polk (1795–1849), 11th President of the U.S., used the Monroe Doctrine to justify annexing Texas and California.

1851   Indian Appropriations Act

1852   Harriet Beecher Stowe publishes *Uncle Tom's Cabin*. Franklin Pierce elected President.

1853   Gadsden Treaty purchases parts of Arizona and New Mexico from Mexico.

1854   Kansas-Nebraska Act

1856   Mass production of steel developed by Henry Bessemer and William Kelly. John Brown and followers kill five proslavery settlers at

Pottawatomie Creek, Kansas. S.C. Representative Preston Brooks assaults Sen. Charles Sumner of Massachusetts with cane in Senate chamber. James Buchanan elected President.

1857   Supreme Court decision in *Dred Scott* v. *Sandford* denies slaves right to sue, declares Missouri Compromise unconstitutional, and opens territories to slavery.

1858   Minnesota admitted.

1859   Oregon admitted; John Brown leads attack on federal arsenal at Harper's Ferry, Va., hoping to begin popular insurrection.

1860   Abraham Lincoln elected President, winning 180 of 303 electoral votes in four-way race. South Carolina secedes.

1861   Virginia, North Carolina, Georgia, Florida, Alabama, Mississippi, Louisiana, Texas, Arkansas, and Tennessee secede. Lincoln attempts to resupply federal Fort Sumter in Charleston, S.C., harbor. Confederate forces attack fort April 12, and it surrenders April 15. Lincoln calls out 75,000 militia, orders blockade of Southern ports, and suspends habeas corpus in some areas. Kansas admitted.

1862   Lincoln abolishes slavery in District of Columbia. Congress passes Homestead Act, Morrill Land Grant Act, and Confiscation Act, granting freedom to slaves escaped from persons in rebellion. Lincoln issues Emancipation Proclamation Sept. 22, to take effect Jan. 1, 1863.

1863   Confederate invasion of North halted at Gettysburg July 3; Grant takes Vicksburg, Miss., July 4, securing federal control of Southwest. West Virginia, created from Virginia counties loyal to Union, admitted.

1864   Salmon P. Chase becomes Chief Justice. Nevada admitted. Lincoln reelected, with 212 of 233 electoral votes; Sherman marches from Chattanooga, Tenn., through Atlanta, Ga., to the sea.

1865   Confederate army surrenders to Grant. Lincoln assassinated April 14 by actor John Wilkes Booth; Andrew Johnson, a Tennessee Democrat, becomes President. 13th Amendment abolishes slavery. John D. Rockefeller buys oil-refining company.

1866   National Labor Union founded. Ku Klux Klan founded. Congress passes Civil Rights Act of 1866 and Freedman's Bureau Act.

1867   Congress passes Military Reconstruction Act and Tenure of Office Act. Senate ratifies treaty with Russia acquiring Alaska. Nebraska admitted. National Grange of the Patrons of Husbandry founded. Andrew Carnegie adopts Bessemer steel-making process.

1868   Johnson impeached but avoids removal by single vote. 14th Amendment assures citizenship, equal rights, and due process to freed slaves, repeals "three-fifths clause," and repudiates debts of Confederate states. Ulysses Grant elected President.

1869   Knights of Labor founded. First transcontinental railroad completed. Wyoming Territory grants voting rights to women. First professional baseball team organized in Cincinnati. Black Friday financial panic on Wall Street, Sept. 24.

1870   15th Amendment guarantees voting rights. Congress passes Force Act (federal supervision of elections). Department of Justice established. Standard Oil Co. founded by John D. Rockefeller.

1871   Congress passes Ku Klux Klan Act. Tweed Ring in New York City exposed.

1872   Amnesty Act restores suffrage to former Confederates. Yellowstone Park established. Grant reelected.

1874   Morrison R. Waite becomes Chief Justice. Women's Christian Temperance Union founded. Invention of barbed wire.

1875   Congress passes Specie Resumption Act, returning dollar to gold standard. Whiskey Ring in St. Louis exposed.

1876   Colorado admitted. Alexander Graham Bell patents telephone. Gen. George A. Custer's forces wiped out by Sioux and Cheyenne at Little Big Horn, Montana. Disputed returns in close presidential race between Rutherford B. Hayes and Samuel Tilden are decided by Congress in favor of Hayes, leading to his election by single electoral vote.

Rutherford B. Hayes (1822–93), 19th President of the U.S., a Republican, narrowly won the disputed election of 1876 and then ended Reconstruction in the South.

1877   Hayes withdraws last federal troops from South, ending Reconstruction. National railroad strike; Nez Perce Indian uprising.

1878   Thomas Edison forms Edison Electric Light Co.

1880   James Garfield elected President.

1881   Garfield assassinated; Chester Arthur becomes President. American Federation of Labor founded. Normal and Industrial Institute at Tuskegee, Alabama, founded by Booker T. Washington. Helen Hunt Jackson publishes *A Century of Dishonor.*

1882   Congress passes Chinese Exclusion Act.

1883   Congress passes Pendleton Act establishing Civil Service. Supreme Court decision invalidates Civil Rights Act of 1875 and allows segregation in public facilities.

1884   First skyscraper built in Chicago. Linotype machine patented. Grover Cleveland elected President.

1886   Haymarket Riot in Chicago. American Federation of Labor formed.

1887   Congress passes Interstate Commerce Act and Dawes Act.

1888   Melville Fuller becomes Chief Justice. Benjamin Harrison elected President.

1889   South Dakota, North Dakota, Montana, and Washington admitted. Andrew Carnegie publishes *The Gospel of Wealth.*

1890   Congress passes Sherman Antitrust Act. Army troops massacre 300 Sioux at Wounded Knee, S.D. Populist party founded. Wyoming and Idaho admitted.

1892	Homestead Strike against Carnegie Steel Co. Grover Cleveland elected President.
1894	Pullman Strike in Chicago. Congress repeals Force Acts of 1870–1875.
1895	J.P. Morgan Co. founded.
1896	Supreme Court decision in *Plessy* v. *Ferguson* sets "separate but equal" standard for segregation. Utah admitted. William McKinley elected President.
1898	Congress declares war on Spain, April 25. Senate approves treaty annexing Hawaii.
1899	Thorstein Veblen publishes *The Theory of the Leisure Class.* McKinley sends troops to Philippines to put down uprising. Open-Door Policy in China.
1900	McKinley sends troops to China to help suppress Boxer Rebellion. Congress passes Gold Standard Act. McKinley reelected.

Grover Cleveland (1837–1908), 22nd & 24th President of the U.S., sent troops to Chicago to "protect the mails" during the 1894 Pullman strike.

1901   Platt Amendment to Cuban constitution allows U.S. intervention. McKinley assassinated; Theodore Roosevelt becomes President. U.S. Steel Co. organized.

1902   Newlands Reclamation Act for Western irrigation.

1903   Elkins Anti-Rebate Act passed by Congress. Department of Labor and Commerce established. W.E.B. DuBois publishes *The Souls of Black Folk.* First baseball World Series. Panama Revolt; Hay-Bunau-Varilla Treaty.

1904   Roosevelt reelected.

1905   Niagara Movement demands suffrage and civil rights for blacks. Industrial Workers of the World (IWW) founded.

1906   Upton Sinclair publishes *The Jungle.* Congress passes Pure Food and Drug Act, Meat Inspection Act, and Hepburn Act controlling railroads.

1907   Inland Waterways Act. Oklahoma admitted.

1908   William H. Taft elected President.

1909   International Ladies Garment Workers Union founded. National Association for the Advancement of Colored People (NAACP) founded. Congress passes Payne-Aldrich Tariff Act.

1910   Congress passes Mann-Elkins Act, extending control over telephone and telegraph systems. Edward White becomes Chief Justice. Ford Motor Co. begins production of Model T. National Urban League founded.

1911   Triangle Shirtwaist Factory fire in New York City kills 146 workers. U.S. troops sent to Nicaragua.

1912   New Mexico and Arizona admitted. Lawrence Textile strike by IWW. Woodrow Wilson elected President, defeating Republican William H. Taft and Bull Moose Theodore Roosevelt.

1913   Jewish Anti-Defamation League organized. Underwood Tariff Act and Federal Reserve Act passed by Congress. 16th Amendment allows federal income tax; 17th Amendment provides for direct election of senators.

1914   Congress passes Clayton Antitrust Act and Federal Trade Commission Act.

1915   Wilson sends U.S. marines to Haiti.

1916   Marcus Garvey founds Universal Negro Improvement Association. Wilson reelected. Congress passes Keating-Owen Act limiting child labor (ruled unconstitutional in 1918).

1917   Congress passes Selective Service Act, Espionage Act, and Jones Act (citizenship for Puerto Ricans). Wilson sends marines to Dominican Republic. War declared on Germany.

1918   Overman Act (presidential war powers) and Sedition Act passed by Congress. Wilson announces Fourteen Points.

1919   18th Amendment prohibits manufacture, sale, and transport of alcoholic beverages (Prohibition). Supreme Court decision in *Schenck* v. *United States* establishes "clear and present danger" standard for limiting free speech. Senate rejects Treaty of Versailles. Volstead Act (Prohibition enforcement) passed.

1920   19th Amendment extends voting rights to women. Republican Warren G. Harding elected President.

1921   Conviction of Sacco and Vanzetti in Massachusetts; Emergency Quota Immigration Act; William Howard Taft becomes Chief Justice.

1922   Dyer Anti-Lynching Bill defeated by Senate filibuster.

1923   President Harding dies; Calvin Coolidge becomes President.

1924   Congress passes Snyder Indian Citizenship Act and Immigration Act. Coolidge elected President.

1925   Trial of John Scopes in Tennessee. Supreme Court decision in *Gitlow* v. *New York* applies guarantees of Bill of Rights to the states.

1927   Congress passes Immigration Act of 1927. *The Jazz Singer* first talking movie. Charles Lindbergh first to fly across Atlantic.

1928   Herbert Hoover elected President.

1929   National Origins Act passed by Congress. Stock market crash on Oct. 29 sets off Great Depression.

1930   Congress passes Hawley-Smoot Tariff Act. Charles Hughes becomes Chief Justice.

1932   Congress passes Norris-LaGuardia Act (labor). Drought turns much of Midwest into Dust Bowl. Hoover orders troops to disperse "Bonus Army" of WWI veterans in Washington. Franklin D. Roosevelt elected President defeating incumbent Hoover.

1933   Frances Perkins named Secretary of Labor, first woman to serve in Cabinet. Congress passes Emergency Banking Relief Act, Federal Emergency Relief Act, National Industrial Recovery Act, Glass-Steagall Banking Act, Tennessee Valley Authority, Civilian Conservation Corps, and First Agricultural Adjustment Act. 20th Amendment reduces "lame-duck" period by moving inauguration of President and beginning of Congressional term to January. 21st Amendment repeals Prohibition.

1934   Congress establishes Federal Housing Authority, Home Owners Loan Corporation, and Securities and Exchange Commission, and passes Indian Reorganization Act.

1935   Supreme Court decision in *Schecter* v. *United States* declares National
        Recovery Act of 1933 unconstitutional. Congress passes National
        Labor Relations Act (Wagner Act), Neutrality Act, Social Security Act,
        and Works Progress Administration.

1936   Neutrality Act and Soil Conservation and Domestic Allotment Act passed
        by Congress. Roosevelt reelected President.

1937   Congress establishes Farm Security Administration.

1938   Congress passes Second Agricultural Adjustment Act, Fair Labor
        Standards Act, and Foreign Agents Registration Act.

1939   Congress passes Neutrality Act. John Steinbeck publishes *The Grapes of
        Wrath*.

1940   Smith Alien Registration Act passed. Harlan Stone becomes Chief Justice.
        Roosevelt reelected to third term.

1941   Congress on Racial Equality founded. Congress passes Lend-Lease Act
        and declares war on Japan and Germany following attack on Pearl
        Harbor, Hawaii, December 7.

1942   Naval battle at Midway, June 3–6, halts Japanese advance in Pacific.
        Military relocates 125,000 Japanese-Americans from West Coast to
        interior for security reasons.

1944   Supreme Court decision in *Korematsu* v. *United States* upholds
        internment of American citizens of Japanese descent. Allied forces
        invade Europe on D-Day, June 6. Roosevelt reelected to fourth term.

1945   Roosevelt meets with Stalin and Churchill in Yalta. Harry Truman
        becomes President when Roosevelt dies April 12. Germany surrenders
        on V-E Day, May 8. United Nations chartered. Truman at Potsdam
        Conference with Stalin and new British Prime Minister Clement Atlee.
        First atomic bomb exploded on Hiroshima, Japan. Japan surrenders on
        V-J Day, August 14.

1946   Congress passes Regulation of Lobbying Act and G.I. Bill of Rights.
        Frederick Vinson becomes Chief Justice.

1947   Truman announces Truman Doctrine and proposes Marshall Plan.
        Congress passes Taft-Hartley Act and National Security Act. Brooklyn
        Dodgers integrate Major League baseball by signing Jackie Robinson.

1948   Berlin airlift. Former State Department official Alger Hiss convicted of
        perjury before House Committee to Investigate Un-American
        Activities. Congress passes Displaced Persons Act. W.E.B. DuBois
        dismissed from NAACP staff for criticising American foreign policy.
        Truman reelected, defeating Republican Thomas Dewey.

1949   Congress passes National Housing Act. North Atlantic Treaty
        Organization (NATO) formed.

1950   North Korean armies invade South Korea; United Nations and American
        troops committed. Congress passes McCarran Internal Security Act.

1951   Truman relieves Gen. MacArthur of command in Korea for attempting to
        broaden the war and invade China. 22nd Amendment sets two-term
        limit for President. Julius and Ethel Rosenberg convicted of espionage
        for passing atomic secrets to Soviet Union (executed 1953). W.E.B.
        DuBois arrested, tried, and acquitted of being a foreign agent.

1952   Congress passes McCarran-Walter Act, allowing deportation of subversives.
        Dwight D. Eisenhower elected President, defeating Adlai Stevenson.

1953   Secretary of State John Foster Dulles practices brinkmanship and declares policy of massive retaliation against Soviets. Earl Warren becomes Chief Justice. Submerged Lands Act gives oil drilling rights to states. Department of Health, Education and Welfare established.

1954   J. Robert Oppenheimer deprived of security clearance by Atomic Energy Commission. Sen. Joseph McCarthy censured by Senate. Supreme Court decision in *Brown* v. *Topeka Board of Education* holds "separate but equal" standard to be unconstitutional, ends legal racial segregation of education.

1955   Bus boycott organized in Montgomery, Alabama.

1956   Eisenhower reelected, defeating Adlai Stevenson for second time.

1957   Eisenhower sends federal marshals and troops to enforce school integration in Little Rock, Ark. Congress passes Civil Rights Act of 1957. Southern Christian Leadership Conference organized by Dr. Martin Luther King, Jr.

1958   Eisenhower sends U.S. marines to Lebanon.

1959   Alaska and Hawaii admitted.

1960   Congress passes Civil Rights Act of 1960. Student Nonviolent Coordinating Committee (SNCC) founded. U-2 spy plane shot down over Soviet Union, leading to cancellation of Paris summit meetings. Democrat John F. Kennedy elected President, defeating Vice-President Richard M. Nixon.

1961   Freedom riders protest racial segregation in Southern bus systems. Kennedy permits invasion of Cuba by exile forces at Bay of Pigs. 23rd Amendment allows District of Columbia to vote in presidential elections.

1962   Supreme Court decision in *Engel* v. *Vitale* bans prayer in public schools; decision in *Baker* v. *Carr* establishes "one person, one vote" standard for apportionment. Kennedy orders blockade of Cuba to force removal of Soviet nuclear missiles.

1963   Supreme Court decision in *Gideon* v. *Wainright* declares accused persons must be furnished an attorney. United Farm Workers organized by César Chavez. Poor Peoples' March on Washington. NAACP leader Medgar Evers assassinated in Mississippi. President Kennedy assassinated in Dallas by Lee Harvey Oswald; Lyndon B. Johnson becomes President.

1964   Congress passes Civil Rights Act of 1964, Gulf of Tonkin Resolution, Voting Rights Act, Federal Clean Water Act, Immigration Act of 1965, and Medicare Act. 24th Amendment prohibits poll tax. Johnson reelected, defeating Republican Barry Goldwater.

1965   Malcolm X assassinated. Summer riots in Watts district of Los Angeles. Escalation of Vietnam War.

1966   Congress passes Freedom of Information Act. Supreme Court decision in *Miranda* v. *Arizona* requires persons arrested to be informed of their rights. National Organization of Women founded by Betty Friedan. Black Panthers founded in Oakland, Ca.

1967   25th Amendment allows for appointment of new Vice-President to fill vacant office.

1968   Tet Offensive in Vietnam. Civil Rights Act of 1968 passed by Congress. Martin Luther King, Jr., assassinated in Memphis. American Indian

Movement founded. Republican Richard M. Nixon elected President, defeating Vice-President Hubert H. Humphrey.

1969 Warren Burger becomes Chief Justice. American astronauts Neil Armstrong and E.E. Aldrin walk on the moon. 250,000 march on Washington demanding end to Vietnam War.

1970 National Guard troops fire on students protesting invasion of Cambodia at Kent State University in Ohio, killing four. Congress passes Clean Air Act; Senate repeals Gulf of Tonkin Resolution. Earth Day celebrations held.

1971 Top-secret *Pentagon Papers* on Vietnam policy published in *The New York Times*, and right to publish them is upheld by Supreme Court. Amtrak, national passenger rail system, established with government subsidies. 26th Amendment extends voting rights to citizens who have reached age 18.

1972 Federal Water Pollution Control Act passed by Congress. Burglary attempt at Democratic National Headquarters in Watergate Tower foiled; burglars appear to have links to Nixon reelection campaign. Nixon visits China. Nixon reelected, defeating Democrat George McGovern by 521 to 17 electoral votes.

1973 White House staff members H. R. Haldeman and John Erlichman resign, and John Dean is fired over involvement in Watergate coverup. Vice-President Spiro Agnew resigns and pleads *nolo contendere* to charges of extortion and tax evasion, Oct. 11. Nixon nominates Gerald Ford to be Vice-President. Supreme Court decision in *Roe* v. *Wade* recognizes woman's right to an abortion. War Powers Act passed by Congress over Nixon's veto. U.S. troops leave Vietnam.

1974 Privacy Act and Federal Election Campaign Finance Reform Act passed by Congress. Nixon resigns August 8; Gerald R. Ford becomes President. Nelson Rockefeller appointed Vice-President. Ford issues pardon to Nixon and offers amnesty to Vietnam draft evaders.

1975 Congress passes Education Act.

1976 Democrat Jimmy Carter elected President, defeating Gerald Ford.

1977 Carter pardons Vietnam deserters and draft resisters. Panama Canal Treaties negotiated. Department of Energy created.

1979 Strategic Arms Limitation Treaty (SALT II) signed in June, but not approved by Senate. Department of Education created. In November, Iranian extremists occupy American embassy in Teheran, holding 52 diplomats and others hostage. In December, Soviet troops occupy Afghanistan to support faltering Communist government.

1980 Congress passes Alaska National Interest Lands Conservation Act. Chrysler Corporation gets $1.5 billion in loan guarantees in government bailout. Republican Ronald Reagan elected President, defeating Carter by 489 to 49 electoral votes.

1981 Hostages in Iran freed the day Carter leaves office. President Reagan shot by John Hinckley, Jr., but recovers. Congress passes Economic Recovery Tax Act.

1983 U.S. forces invade Grenada to secure pro-American government. Forces committed to Beirut, Lebanon, to assist U.N. peacekeeping; 241 marines killed by terrorist bombing.

1984   Income Tax Reform Act passed by Congress. Reagan reelected President, defeating Democrat Walter Mondale, 525 to 13 electoral votes.

1985   Congress passes Gramm-Rudman-Hollings Act, requiring balanced budget by 1991. Summit meeting between Reagan and Soviet leader Mikhail Gorbachev in Geneva.

1986   Reagan attends summit with Gorbachev in Reykjavik. National Security Council staff Oliver North, John Poindexter, and Robert McFarland secretly and illegally sell anti-aircraft missiles and parts to Iran to gain the release of hostages held in Lebanon, and they divert money from the sales to the Contra rebels opposing the socialist Sandinista government in Nicaragua. Congress passes Federal Clean Water Act (vetoed) and Income Tax Reform Act. Justice William Rehnquist becomes Chief Justice.

1987   Federal Clean Water Act passed by Congress over Reagan's veto. Summit with Gorbachev in Washington. Intermediate Nuclear Forces Treaty signed. Wall Street crash on Oct. 19.

1988   Reagan visits Moscow. Vice-President George Bush elected President, defeating Democrat Michael Dukakis with slogan "Read my lips: no new taxes."

1989   Congress creates Resolution Trust Corporation to handle S&L bailout. Bush sends U.S. forces to invade Panama and capture Gen. Manuel Noriega, who is wanted on federal drug charges.

1990   Congress passes Americans with Disabilities Act.

1991   UN forces, including American troops, expel Iraqi army from Kuwait in Operation Desert Storm.

1992   27th Amendment bars Congressional pay raises from taking effect until after a new election. Democrat Bill Clinton elected President, defeating incumbent George Bush and independent Ross Perot.

1993   Family Leave Act; North American Free Trade Agreement (NAFTA) ratified by Congress.

1994   Crime Bill passed by Congress. Military junta ousted from Haiti and elected President restored to power in a peaceful invasion by American troops.

Appendix C

NOTABLE AMERICANS

Addams, Jane (1860–1935) social worker who founded Hull House in Chicago, one of the first settlement houses to serve as a community center to help the poor and work for social reform.

Anthony, Susan B. (1820–1906) leader of the women's suffrage movement; formed the National Woman Suffrage Association to agitate to gain the right to vote for women.

Astor, John Jacob (1763–1848) German-born immigrant who came to America in 1783 and made a fortune through fur-trading, the China trade, and New York real estate; the richest American of his time, he left an estate valued at $20 million.

Barton, Clara (1821–1912) Nurse, teacher, and organizer of medical relief for the Union army during the Civil War; organizer and first president of the American Red Cross.

Bell, Alexander Graham (1847–1922) invented the telephone in 1876; improved methods for teaching the deaf.

Brown, John (1800–1859) American abolitionist and fanatic; he led a massacre of proslavery settlers in Kansas in 1856 at Pottawatomie. Funded by extreme abolitionists, he led an armed band that seized the federal arsenal at Harpers Ferry, Virginia, on October 16, 1859, hoping to set off a general revolt of slaves. He was soon captured and convicted of treason and was hanged December 2, 1859.

Bryan, William Jennings (1860–1925) Democratic political leader and orator. Three-time unsuccessful candidate for President of the United States. His famous "cross of gold" speech advocated silver coinage (loose money) to help the interests of farmers and westerners. Resigned from Woodrow Wilson's cabinet, where he was Secretary of State, in 1916. Prosecuted the Scopes trial in Tennessee in 1925.

Bush, George (1924–) 41st President, from 1989–1993; was Vice-President under Ronald Reagan, a member of the House of Representatives, United Nations ambassador, and director of the C.I.A.; organized the international coalition that invaded Iraq in 1991 to force it to withdraw from Kuwait in the Persian Gulf War.

Calhoun, John C. (1782–1850) statesman and philosopher who served as Vice-President under John Quincy Adams and Andrew Jackson; defended the interests of the South by promoting the concept of states' rights to nullify federal legislation.

Carnegie, Andrew (1835–1913) immigrant from Scotland who rose from poverty to become a major industrialist producing steel and controlling mines and railroads; became a major philanthropist who used his wealth to fund 2800 libraries and establish the Carnegie Endowment for International Peace.

Carson, Rachel (1907–1964) biologist and author of many books on natural science; *Silent Spring* alerted the nation about the dangers to the environment from the use of pesticides in agriculture.

Carter, Jimmy (James Earl) (1924–) 39th President, from 1977–1981; signed treaties giving Panama eventual control of the Panama Canal; negotiated the Camp David Accords that brought peace between Israel and Egypt, and promoted an energy policy; after leaving office, became a leading advocate of human rights and programs to help the working poor.

Clay, Henry (1777–1852) leader in the House of Representatives and then of the Senate and frequent candidate for President; strong supporter of westward expansion of the United States; known as the Great Compromiser for his influence during times of national crisis.

Clinton, Bill (William) (1946–) 42nd President, elected in 1992 on a program of commitments to economic recovery and a national health care system; encouraged Arabs and Israelis to establish Palestinian self-rule.

Cooper, James Fenimore (1789–1851) first major novelist to write about frontier life; *The Deerslayer, The Last of the Mohicans*, and *The Pathfinder* created a glamorized myth of the frontier and showed the conflict between wilderness life and encroaching civilization.

Crockett, Davy (1786–1836) frontiersman and U.S. Congressman from Tennessee (1827–31 and 1833–35). He joined forces fighting for Texas independence from Mexico and died at the Alamo in 1836.

Davis, Jefferson (1808–1889) West Point graduate and officer in the Black Hawk and Mexican wars. Democratic congressman and senator from Mississippi; Secretary of War under Franklin Pierce. First and only President of the Confederate States of America (1861–65). Captured, charged with treason, and imprisoned; released on bail in 1867 and never tried.

Debs, Eugene V. (1855–1926) Railroad union organizer and socialist; imprisoned for his part in Pullman strike of 1894. Five-time socialist candidate for President of the United States (1900, 1904, 1908, 1912, 1920). Opposed U.S. participation in World War I and was imprisoned under the Espionage Act. Pardoned and released in 1921 by President Harding.

Dix, Dorothea (1802–1887) social reformer who brought about improvement in the treatment of inmates in insane asylums.

Douglass, Frederick (1817–1895) Leading 19th-century African-American abolitionist and Republican party organizer. Escaped from slavery in Maryland and became speaker for abolition in the North and England. Founded and edited newspaper *The North Star* (1847) and assisted runaway slaves on the Underground Railroad. Helped enlist black regiments in the Civil War and served as federal marshall of the District of Columbia and as consul general to Haiti.

DuBois, W.E.B. (1868–1963) African American civil rights leader and author who supported aggressive action to gain full civil, economic, and political equality for African Americans; cofounder of the National Association for the Advancement of Colored People (NAACP).

Edison, Thomas (1847–1931) productive genius in applying scientific principles to practical use; invented the light bulb, phonograph, and motion picture projector; developed a complete system for generating and distributing electricity in communities.

Edwards, Jonathan (1703–1758) The most influential American theologian and philosopher of the 18th century. A leader in the religious revival of the 1740s, known as the Great Awakening. Congregational minister in Northampton, Mass., and later president of the College of New Jersey (now Princeton University).

Emerson, Ralph Waldo (1803–1892) Leading American writer, lecturer, essayist, and philosopher of the 19th century. One of the founders of transcendentalism, a philosophical and spiritual movement based on nature and inspiration.

Ford, Henry (1863–1947) industrialist who used assembly-line techniques to build the first inexpensive, mass-produced automobiles; the Model T and Model A Fords revolutionized communities and transportation by making automobiles affordable for the middle and working class.

Franklin, Benjamin (1706–1790) statesman, printer, scientist, inventor, and writer; experimented with electricity; was a delegate to the Albany Congress, a leader of the Continental Congress, and a member of the Committee that wrote the Declaration of Independence; served as ambassador to France during the Revolutionary War; was an influential member of the convention that drafted the Constitution in 1787.

Friedan, Betty (1921–) social reformer and feminist; author of *The Feminine Mystique*, a book that began the women's liberation movement; founder of The National Organization for Women (NOW).

Garrison, William Lloyd (1805–1879) Leading New England abolitionist who advocated separation from the South. Founder and editor of *The Liberator* (1831) and a fiery and controversial speaker.

Garvey, Marcus (1887–1940) Jamaican organizer and business entrepreneur who brought his "Back to Africa" movement and United Negro Improvement Association to the United States in 1916. He was eventually convicted of mail fraud, pardoned by President Coolidge, and deported.

George, Henry (1839–1897) American reformer famous for his book *Progress and Poverty* and his theory of the single tax.

Gompers, Samuel (1850–1924) founder and first president of the American Federation of Labor; supported efforts of organized labor to concentrate on improvement in wages and working conditions instead of political action; became a leading spokesman for the labor movement.

Hamilton, Alexander (1755–1804) Born on the island of Nevis, he attended Columbia College in New York, joined the Continental Army during the American Revolution, and served as an aide to Washington. After the war, he became a lawyer and politician, attended the Constitutional Convention in 1787, and coauthored *The Federalist* (with James Madison and John Jay) in 1788. He served as Secretary of the Treasury under Washington, organized the first Bank of the United States, and promoted the increase of central government power. A leading Federalist, after Washington's retirement he feuded with John Adams, paving the way for victory by the Jeffersonians in 1800. A dispute with Aaron Burr led to a duel in 1804 in which Hamilton was fatally wounded.

Hearst, William Randolph (1863–1951) Wealthy newspaper and magazine publisher known for his many examples of "yellow journalism." Member of Congress from New York (1903–07).

Holmes, Oliver Wendell, Jr. (1841–1935) Harvard graduate and Civil War veteran, son of Dr. Oliver Wendell Holmes, the author. He taught at Harvard law school, served on the Massachusetts Supreme Court, and was appointed to the U.S. Supreme Court in 1902 by President Roosevelt. He wrote many famous court opinions, including that in *Schenck* v. *United States* setting forth the "clear and present danger" standard.

Houston, Sam (1793–1863) Congressman and governor of Tennessee, he moved to Texas and commanded the army that secured independence from Mexico. Served as president of the Republic of Texas and as a senator and its governor after it was admitted to the United States. As governor, he opposed secession in 1861, but was removed from office.

Jackson, Andrew (1767–1845)   7th President and first President from a state other than the original thirteen colonies; symbolized and supported the westward movement of the United States and growing democratization of politics; ended the eastern domination of politics.

Jackson, Helen Hunt (1830–1885)   writer whose book, *A Century of Dishonor*, chronicled the government mistreatment of Native Americans and encouraged reform in federal Indian policy.

Jay, John (1745–1829)   born in New York City, he represented New York in the First and Second Continental Congress, over which he presided; served as Secretary of Foreign Affairs and Chief Justice of the United States; negotiated the Jay Treaty with England in 1795, settling key financial and diplomatic issues.

Jefferson, Thomas (1743–1826)   3rd President, from 1801–1809, author of the Declaration of Independence and ambassador to France during the Constitutional Convention; as first Secretary of State under George Washington, opposed federalist policies of Alexander Hamilton; bought Louisiana Territory from France despite belief in strict construction of the Constitution.

Johnson, Lyndon (1908–1973)   36th President who, as Vice-President, succeeded John F. Kennedy following the assassination; reelected in 1964 and supported civil rights legislation and an extensive "Great Society" program to help the poor; supported growing U.S. involvement in the war in Vietnam; declined to run again in 1968 following growing public opposition to the war.

Keller, Helen Adams (1880–1968)   lost her sight and hearing before she was two as a result of a serious brain illness; grew up wild until the age of seven when a special education teacher, Anne Sullivan, taught her to read and communicate with her fingers; eventually graduated with honors from Radcliff College and served as a model for the handicapped.

Kennedy, John F. (1917–1963)   35th President, elected in 1960 with a program of social and economic reforms, some of which were enacted after his assassination in 1963; supported the failed Bay of Pigs invasion to force Castro from power in Cuba, but succeeded in using the threat of force to convince the Soviet Union to remove missiles from Cuba.

Key, Francis Scott (1779–1843)   a Washington, D.C. lawyer; write the words of *The Star-Spangled Banner* during the War of 1812; his inspiration for the anthem came as he witnessed the British bombardment of Fort McHenry in Baltimore harbor.

King, Martin Luther, Jr. (1929–1968)   African American minister and civil rights leader who encouraged civil disobedience to oppose segregation laws in the South; most widely known and respected leader in the struggle for political and economic equality for African Americans; awarded the Nobel Peace Prize in 1964; his birthday has become a national holiday.

Lee, Robert E. (1807–1870)   West Point graduate, Mexican War veteran, and career army officer; declined Lincoln's offer to command U.S. Army in 1861 and accepted appointment to command Virginia forces and later the Confederate army; outnumbered and undersupplied, he surrendered to Grant at Appomattox, April 9, 1865, ending major fighting in the Civil War.

Lewis, John L. (1880–1969) labor leader who, as head of the mine workers union, sought to unionize unskilled industrial workers who were not eligible for membership in the trade-union-oriented American Federation of Labor; organized the Congress of Industrial Organization (C.I.O.) to greatly expand the membership and influence of organized labor.

Lewis, Sinclair (1885–1951) novelist who satirized the values and styles of middle-class American life in *Main Street* and *Babbit*; also satirized the medical profession in *Arrowsmith* and religious revivalism in *Elmer Gantry*.

Lincoln, Abraham (1809–1865) 16th President, whose election in 1860 triggered the secession of southern states; preserved the Union by using military force; issued the Emancipation Proclamation to include abolition of slavery as a goal of the Civil War; his speeches expressed the agony of war and sought to heal the wounds of the republic.

MacArthur, Douglas (1880–1964) American general who commanded the war in the Pacific against Japan during World War II, governed Japan after the war as it developed a representative form of government, and led allied forces during the Korean War until removed by President Truman for publicly opposing government policy.

Madison, James (1751–1836) 4th President; was a leader in the convention in 1787 to draft a new Constitution and supported ratification by writing many of the *Federalist Papers*; served as Secretary of State for Jefferson supporting embargo policies that later contributed to the War of 1812, which took place during his administration.

Mann, Horace (1796–1859) American educator and reformer who revolutionized public school organization and teaching.

Marshall, George Catlett (1880–1959) a graduate of the Virginia Military Institute (UMI) he served with the U.S. Army in France during World War I and was the chief strategiest of the West in World War II; architect of the Marshall Plan for the rehabilitation of Western Europe (1947).

Marshall, John (1755–1835) Chief Justice of the Supreme Court for 34 years and supporter of many important decisions which established judicial review and expanded federal influence by a loose interpretation of the Constitution.

Marshall, Thurgood (1908–1993) first African American member of the Supreme Court following a distinguished career as an attorney for the NAACP; successfully argued before the Supreme Court against school segregation in *Brown* v. *Topeka Board of Education*.

McCarthy, Joseph (1908–1957) senator who gained national attention in 1950 by accusations that the U.S. State Department was infiltrated by communists; his name became associated with unverified and unjustified charges of subversion and an anti-communist national hysteria that led to the dismissal and resignation of government employees; his excesses ended when he was censured by the Senate.

McKinley, William (1843–1901) 25th President who supported industrialists, protective tariffs, and U.S. imperialism; supported the annexation of Hawaii and the Open-Door Policy; the Spanish-American War was fought during his administration.

Monroe, James (1758–1831) 5th President whose name is associated with the doctrine that became a cornerstone of American foreign policy for the Western Hemisphere; supported the Missouri Compromise, which resolved differences of slavery in the territories, and the purchase of Florida from Spain.

Morse, Samuel F.B. (1791–1872) successful portrait artist best known for inventing the telegraph that revolutionized communication.

Nader, Ralph (1934–) consumer advocate whose book, *Unsafe at Any Speed*, accused the automobile industry of emphasizing speed and style over safety and economy; instrumental in pressuring Congress to adopt automobile safety standards; formed other consumer groups attacking irresponsible actions of business and encouraging regulation to protect consumers.

Nixon, Richard (1913–1994) 37th President, elected in 1968 with a commitment to end the war in Vietnam; U.S. troops were withdrawn in 1973 after the war was first expanded into Cambodia and air attacks on North Vietnam increased; opened relations with communist China and improved relations with the Soviet Union; resigned in 1974 under the threat of impeachment following the Watergate scandal.

O'Connor, Sandra Day (1930–) first woman appointed to the U.S. Supreme Court in 1981 by Ronald Reagan.

Owens, Jesse (1913–1980) African American athlete (sprinter, long jumper) who won four gold medals at the 1936 Munich Olympics, spoiling Hitler's claims of Aryan superiority.

Paine, Thomas (1737–1809) political theorist and writer of the widely read pamphlet *Common Sense*, which argued that the colonies should be independent of England; other writings encouraged the patriot cause during the Revolutionary War; he later went to France to support the French Revolution.

Patton, George (1885–1945) American cavalry, tank, and army commander who led Allied forces in North Africa, Sicily, and France in World War II.

Reagan, Ronald (1911–) 40th President, elected in 1980 after a career in motion pictures and serving as governor of California; advocated a balanced budget, but brought about a large increase in the budget deficit and national debt by supporting supply-side economics and making tax reductions while greatly increasing military spending; responded to changes in the Soviet Union by negotiating mutual reductions in nuclear missiles.

Rockefeller, John D. (1839–1937) industrialist and philanthropist who became wealthy by organizing the Standard Oil Company, crushing competitors, and extracting rebates from railroads; funded foundations to sponsor research in medicine, education, and natural and social sciences.

Roosevelt, Eleanor (1884–1962) humanitarian and writer; as the wife of Franklin Roosevelt became active in promoting women's causes, civil rights for minorities, and help for the poor and unemployed; lectured throughout the nation and reported conditions and public opinion to her husband; following the President's death, she served as a delegate to the United Nations and supporter of the Declaration of Human Rights.

Roosevelt, Franklin D. (1882–1945) 32nd President, elected to four terms beginning in 1932 with a commitment called the New Deal to use the resources of government to fight the Great Depression; led the nation during World War II.

Roosevelt, Theodore (1858–1919) 26th President, who succeeded as Vice-President following the assassination of McKinley in 1901; opposed business monopolies, supported consumer legislation, promoted conservation of natural resources, and expanded U.S. influence in the Caribbean; ran for President unsuccessfully in 1912 after a term out of office as the candidate of the Bull Moose Party.

Sinclair, Upton (1878–1968) novelist best known for *The Jungle*, an exposé of the filthy and degrading conditions in the meatpacking industry that led to national legislation regulating food production; one of a number of muckrakers who attacked business practices.

Sitting Bull (1834–1890) Sioux leader at Little Big Horn, where Custer's forces were wiped out in 1876. Later retreated to Canada but returned and surrendered in 1881. Active in agitation for Indian rights, he was arrested and shot by guards in 1890.

Stanton, Elizabeth Cady (1815–1902) American crusader for abolition, temperance, education, and women's rights. With Lucretia Mott, she organized first women's rights convention in 1848. She worked closely with Susan B. Anthony and served as the first president of the National Women's Suffrage Association (1890–92).

Stowe, Harriet Beecher (1811–1896) novelist whose book, *Uncle Tom's Cabin*, was an immensely popular attack upon slavery that gained many supporters for the cause of abolition in the North and in Europe.

Tarbell, Ida (1857–1944) a muckraker whose book, *History of the Standard Oil Company*, chronicled the abuses of the company and led to a court case that caused the breakup of the monopoly.

Thoreau, Henry David (1817–1862) author and naturalist who influenced American thought by his individualism and opposition to conformity and materialism; *Walden*, his most famous book, described his solitary coexistence with nature; his support of civil disobedience to protest injustices of authority had influence within and beyond the United States.

Truman, Harry (1884–1972) 33rd President, who as Vice-President succeeded upon the death of Franklin Roosevelt in 1945; led the United States during the postwar period and developed the policies opposing the Soviet Union during the cold war; opposed North Korean aggression in the Korean War.

Tubman, Harriet (c.1820–1913) abolitionist and escaped slave who conducted hundreds of slaves to freedom though the "underground railroad" during the 1850s.

Twain, Mark (1835–1910) (Samuel Clemens) author, humorist, commentator on American life and values; portrayed 19th century American life in *Adventures of Huckleberry Finn* and *The Adventures of Tom Sawyer*; other books of social criticism, fairy tales, and travel showed the breadth of his literary talents.

Warren, Earl (1891–1974) Chief Justice of the Supreme Court for 16 years beginning in 1953; led an activist court whose decisions showed regard for civil rights and civil liberties; wrote the unanimous decision declaring school segregation unconstitutional and supported decisions requiring legislative reapportionment and protecting defendants from police abuses.

Washington, Booker T. (1856–1915) born a slave, he gained an education and established the Tuskegee Institute in Alabama to provide technical education for African Americans; believed that African Americans should work to achieve economic improvement before striving for social and political equality.

Washington, George (1732–1799) First President, elected by unanimous vote of the electoral college after serving as commander of the Continental Army during the Revolutionary War and president of the Constitutional Convention; steered the new nation with a steady hand, asserted federal authority, mediated among his able cabinet members, established wise precedents, and avoided involvement in conflicts stemming from the French Revolution.

Webster, Daniel (1782–1852) Congressman from New Hampshire (1813–17) and Massachusetts (1823–27), Senator from Massachusetts (1827–41), and Secretary of State (1841–43 and 1850–52). One of the greatest orators of his day and a strong advocate of national union. He lost many former admirers when he supported the Compromise of 1850 and its Fugitive Slave Law, which he defended as necessary to preserve the Union.

Whitney, Eli (1765–1825) graduate of Yale College (1792); invented the cotton gin (engine) for cleaning picked cotton; this made slaves far more valuable and virtually ended the drive for emancipation in the South.

Wilson, Woodrow (1856–1924) 28th President, who promoted progressive legislation curbing monopolies, supporting labor, and establishing the Federal Reserve System; led the nation during World War I and the peace negotiations after the war, but was disappointed by the Senate's failure to ratify the Treaty of Versailles and bring the United States into the League of Nations.

QUOTATIONS

"No free man shall be detained or imprisoned, dispossessed, outlawed, exiled, or destroyed in any way, except by the lawful judgment of his peers or by the law of the land."

Magna Carta, 1215

◆

"God helps them that help themselves."

Benjamin Franklin, 1736

◆

"Taxation without representation is tyranny."

James Otis, 1763

◆

"That the king can do no wrong is a necessary and fundamental principle of the English constitution."

Sir William Blackstone, 1765

◆

"By uniting we stand, by dividing we fall."

John Dickinson, *Liberty Song*, 1768

◆

"There never was a good war or a bad peace."

Benjamin Franklin, 1773

◆

"The God who gave us life, gave us liberty at the same time."

Thomas Jefferson, 1774

◆

"A government of laws, and not of men."

John Adams, 1774

◆

"I am not a Virginian, but an American."

Patrick Henry, Continental Congress, 1774

◆

"Don't fire until you see the whites of their eyes."

Israel Putnam, 1775

"Is life so dear or peace so sweet as to be purchased at the price of chains and slavery? I know not what course others may take, but as for me, give me liberty or give me death."

Patrick Henry, Virginia House of Delegates, 1775

"In the name of the great Jehovah and the Continental Congress!"

Ethan Allen demanding the surrender of Fort Ticonderoga, 1775

"Government, even in its best state, is but a necessary evil; in its worst state, an intolerable one."

Thomas Paine, *Common Sense*, 1776

"Yes, we must all hang together, or most assuredly we shall all hang separately."

Benjamin Franklin at the signing of the Declaration of Independence, 1776

"I only regret that I have but one life to lose for my country."

Nathan Hale on the gallows, New York City, 1776

"These are the times that try men's souls."

Thomas Paine, *The Crisis*, 1776

"I have not yet begun to fight."

John Paul Jones aboard the *Bonhomme Richard*, 1779

"A national debt, if it is not excessive, will be to us a national blessing."

Alexander Hamilton, 1781

"Am I not a man and a brother?"

Josiah Wedgeworth, seal of the London Anti-Slavery Society, 1787

"There shall be neither slavery nor involuntary servitude in the said territory."

Northwest Ordinance, 1787

"The tree of liberty must be refreshed from time to time with the blood of patriots and tyrants. It is its natural manure."

Thomas Jefferson, 1787

"Every individual of the community at large has an equal right to the protection of government."

Alexander Hamilton,
Constitutional Convention, 1787

"To be prepared for war is one of the most effectual means of preserving peace."

George Washington, 1790

"The republican is the only form of government which is not eternally at open or secret war with the rights of mankind."

Thomas Jefferson, 1790

"'Tis our true policy to steer clear of permanent alliances with any portion of the foreign world."

George Washington, *Farewell Address*, 1796

"Millions for defense but not a cent for tribute."

Robert G. Harper, 1798

"A citizen, first in war, first in peace, and first in the hearts of his countrymen."

Henry ("Light-Horse Harry") Lee
on Washington, Congress, 1799

"We are all Republicans; we are all Federalists."

Thomas Jefferson, Inaugural Address, 1801

"It is emphatically the province and duty of the judicial department to say what the law is."

John Marshall, Opinion in *Marbury* v. *Madison*, 1803

"These lands are ours. No one has a right to remove us, because we were the first owners."

Tecumseh, 1810

"Protection and patriotism are reciprocal."

John C. Calhoun, House of Representatives, 1811

"We have met the enemy, and they are ours."
Oliver Hazard Perry, Battle of Lake Erie, 1813

"Oh, say, does that star-spangled banner yet wave
O'er the land of the free and the home of the brave?"

Then conquer we must, when our cause it is just,
And this be our motto, " In God is our trust."
Francis Scott Key, *The Star-Spangled Banner*,
September 14, 1814

"Our country! May she always be in the right; but our country, right or wrong."
Stephen Decatur, 1816

"The power to tax involves the power to destroy."
John Marshall, Opinion in *McCulloch* v. *Maryland*, 1819

"The American continents are henceforth not to be considered as subjects for future colonization by any European powers."
James Monroe, Message to Congress, 1823

"Our sufferings will come to an end, in spite of all the Americans this side of eternity."
David Walker, *Appeal to the Colored
Citizens of the World*, 1829

"Our Federal Union! it must be preserved!"
Andrew Jackson, 1830

"Liberty and Union, now and forever, one and inseparable."
Daniel Webster, 1830

"My country, 'tis of thee, Sweet land of liberty, Of thee I sing:

From every mountainside let freedom ring."
Samuel Francis Smith, *America*, 1831

"Our country is the world—our countrymen are all mankind."
William Lloyd Garrison, *The Liberator*, 1831

"I have done nothing for which an Indian ought to be ashamed. I have fought for my countrymen against white men who came to take away our lands."

Black Hawk, 1832

Black Hawk (1767–1838), chief of the Sauk nation, led his people against the Americans in the Black Hawk War of 1832.

"The politicians of New York see nothing wrong in the rule that to the victor belong the spoils of the enemy."

William Marcy, Senate, 1832

"We first crush people to the earth, and then claim the right of trampling on them forever, because they are prostrate."

Lydia Maria Child, *An Appeal on Behalf of That Class of Americans Called Africans*, 1833

"The women of the South can overthrow this horrible system of oppression and cruelty, licentiousness and wrong. Slavery must be attacked with the whole power of truth and the sword of the spirit."

Angelina Grimké, *Appeal to the Christian Women of the South*, 1836

"Here once the embattled farmers stood, And fired the shot heard round the world."

Ralph Waldo Emerson, *Concord Hymn*, 1837

"We have one country, one Constitution, one destiny."

Daniel Webster, 1837

"Fifty-four forty, or fight!"

William Allen, Senate, 1844

"Our manifest destiny is to overspread the continent allotted by Providence for the free development of our yearly multiplying millions."

John L. O'Sullivan, *Democratic Review*, 1845

"If there is no struggle, there can be no progress."

Frederick Douglass, c. 1845

"I know no South, no North, no East, no West, to which I owe any allegiance. The Union, sir, is my country."

Henry Clay, 1848

"We hold these truths to be self-evident, that all men and women are created equal."

Elizabeth Cady Stanton, Women's Rights Convention, 1848

"Liberty is a spirit sent out from God, and like its great Author, is no respecter of persons. Slavery has prepared you for any emergency. Let it no longer be a debatable question, whether it is better to choose *Liberty* or *death.*

Henry Highland Garnet, *An Address to the Slaves of the United States of America,* 1848

"We are not a Nation, but a Union, a confederacy of equal and sovereign states."

John C. Calhoun, 1849

"It is not desirable to cultivate a respect for the law, so much as for the right."

Henry David Thoreau, *Civil Disobedience,* 1849

"I would rather be right than President."

Henry Clay, 1850

"A democracy—that is a government of all the people, by all the people, for all the people."

Theodore Parker, 1850

"Go West, young man, and grow up with the country."

Horace Greeley, *Hints towards Reforms,* 1850

Newspaper publisher Horace Greeley (1811–1872) supported antislavery, but he later helped raise bail to get Jefferson Davis released from prison.

565

"I owe allegiance to two sovereignties. One is to the sovereignty of this Union, and the other is to the sovereignty of the State of Kentucky.
Henry Clay, Senate, 1850

◆

"The word *liberty* in the mouth of Mr. Webster sounds like the word *love* in the mouth of a courtesan."
Ralph Waldo Emerson, 1851

◆

"Eternal vigilance is the price of liberty."
Wendell Phillips, 1852

◆

"The United States themselves are essentially the greatest poem."
Walt Whitman,
Leaves of Grass, 1855

◆

"Be not deceived. Revolutions do not go backward. The founder of the Democratic party declared that *all* men are created equal."
Abraham Lincoln, 1856

◆

"For more than a century before the Declaration of Independence, the negroes had been regarded as beings of an inferior order who had no rights which a white man was bound to respect."

Roger B. Taney,
Opinion in *Dred Scott* v.
Sandford, 1857

Roger Brooke Taney (1777–1864), American jurist. Chief Justice Taney's decision in *Dred Scott* v. *Sandford* (1857) declared the Missouri Compromise of 1820 unconstitutional and opened up all U.S. territories to the expansion of slavery.

◆

"The principle laid down will enable the people of a slave state to introduce slavery into a free state; it protects the rights of the master and defies the sovereignty of the free state."
John McLean, Dissenting Opinion in
Dred Scott v. *Sandford*, 1857

◆

"The negro is my equal and the equal of Judge Douglas, and the equal of every living man."
Abraham Lincoln,
Debate with Stephen Douglas, 1858

"'A house divided against itself cannot stand.' I believe this government cannot endure permanently half slave and half free."

> Abraham Lincoln, Illinois
> Republican Convention, 1858

◆

"You dare not make war on cotton. Cotton is king."

> James H. Hammond, Senate, 1858

◆

"An irrepressible conflict between opposing and enduring forces."

> William H. Seward, 1858

◆

"I am now quite certain that the crimes of this guilty land will never be purged away but with blood."

> John Brown, last statement, 1859

Abolitionist John Brown (1800–1859) resorted to violence and murder to oppose slavery in "Bloody Kansas"; he was hanged in 1859 for leading an attack on the federal armory at Harpers Ferry, Virginia.

◆

"If McClellan is not using the army, I should like to borrow it for a while."

> Abraham Lincoln, 1862

◆

"No terms except unconditional and immediate surrender can be accepted."

> Ulysses S. Grant at Fort Donelson, 1862

◆

"I am not a politician, and my other habits are good, also."

> Artemus Ward, 1862

◆

"I propose to fight it out on this line if it takes all summer."

> Ulysses S. Grant, 1864

◆

"'Shoot, if you must, this old gray head,
But spare your country's flag,' she said."

> John Greenleaf Whittier, *Barbara Frietchie*, 1864

◆

"Damn the torpedoes—full speed ahead."

> David Farragut, Battle of Mobile Bay, 1864

"I have been forty years a slave and forty years free, and would be here forty years more to have equal rights for all."

Sojourner Truth, 1867

"The Constitution, in all its provisions, looks to an indestructible Union composed of indestructible States."

Salmon P. Chase, Opinion in *Texas* v. *White*, 1868

"Let us have peace."

Ulysses S. Grant, accepting Republican presidential nomination, 1868

"The true Republic: men, their rights, and nothing more; women, their rights, and nothing less."

Susan B. Anthony, *The Revolution*, 1868

"Join the union, girls, and together say *Equal Pay for Equal Work.*"

Susan B. Anthony, *The Revolution*, 1869

"The only good Indians I ever saw were dead."

Gen. Philip H. Sheridan, 1869

"As long as I count the votes, what are you going to do about it?"

William Marcy ("Boss") Tweed, 1871

"The only question left to be settled now is: Are women persons?"

Susan B. Anthony, 1873

"We are an island of Indians in a lake of whites."

Sitting Bull, 1874

"My heart is sick and sad. From where the sun now stands I will fight no more forever."

Chief Joseph at the surrender of the Nez Percé, 1877

Sitting Bull (1837–1890), chief of the Hunkpapa Sioux, developed the tactics that led to Custer's annihilation at the Little Bighorn in 1876.

"He serves his party best who serves his country best."
Rutherford B. Hayes, Inaugural Address, 1877

"All free governments are party governments."
James Garfield, House of Representatives, 1878

"War is hell."
Gen. William Tecumseh Sherman, 1879

"The public be damned."
William H. Vanderbilt, 1882

"If nominated I will not run; if elected I will not serve."
Gen. William Tecumseh Sherman
to the Republican National Convention, 1884

"Your every voter, as surely as your chief magistrate, exercises a public trust."
Grover Cleveland, *Inaugural Address*, March 4, 1885

"A mugwump is a person educated beyond his intellect."
Horace Porter, 1884

"The growth of a large business is merely survival of the fittest."
John D. Rockefeller, c. 1890

"America! America! God shed His grace on thee
And crown thy good with brotherhood from sea to shining sea.

America! America! God mend thine every flaw.
Confirm thy soul in self-control, thy liberty in law."
Katherine Lee Bates, *America the Beautiful*, 1893

"All railway companies shall provide equal but separate accommodations for the white and colored races."
Louisiana statute of 1890,
upheld by the Supreme Court
in *Plessy* v. *Ferguson*, 1896

"Our Constitution is color-blind, and neither knows nor tolerates classes among citizens. In respect of civil rights, all citizens are equal before the law."

> John Marshall Harlan,
> Dissenting Opinion in
> *Plessy* v. *Ferguson*, 1896

"You shall not press down upon the brow of labor this crown of thorns. You shall not crucify mankind upon a cross of gold."

> William Jennings Bryan, Democratic
> National Convention, 1896

"It could probably be shown by facts and figures that there is no distinctly native American criminal class except Congress."

> Mark Twain, 1897

Justice John Marshall Harlan (1833–1911) was the lone dissenting voice on the Supreme Court in the case of *Plessy* v. *Ferguson*, which legalized segregation.

"You furnish the pictures and I'll furnish the war."

> William Randolph Hearst, cable to
> Frederic Remington in Cuba, 1898

"The problem of the twentieth century is the problem of the color line."

> W.E.B. DuBois, Pan-African Conference, London, 1900

"There is a homely adage which runs, 'Speak softly and carry a big stick; you will go far.' If the American nation will speak softly and yet build and keep a thoroughly efficient navy, the Monroe Doctrine will go far."

> Theodore Roosevelt, 1901

"A man who is good enough to shed his blood for his country is good enough to be given a square deal afterwards."

> Theodore Roosevelt, 1903

"Taxes are what we pay for civilized society."

> Oliver Wendell Holmes, Jr., 1904

"Wage workers have an entire right to organize."
Theodore Roosevelt, Message to Congress, 1904

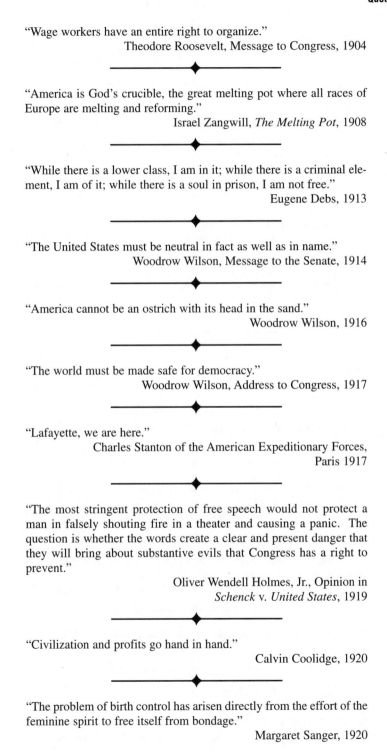

"America is God's crucible, the great melting pot where all races of Europe are melting and reforming."
Israel Zangwill, *The Melting Pot*, 1908

"While there is a lower class, I am in it; while there is a criminal element, I am of it; while there is a soul in prison, I am not free."
Eugene Debs, 1913

"The United States must be neutral in fact as well as in name."
Woodrow Wilson, Message to the Senate, 1914

"America cannot be an ostrich with its head in the sand."
Woodrow Wilson, 1916

"The world must be made safe for democracy."
Woodrow Wilson, Address to Congress, 1917

"Lafayette, we are here."
Charles Stanton of the American Expeditionary Forces,
Paris 1917

"The most stringent protection of free speech would not protect a man in falsely shouting fire in a theater and causing a panic. The question is whether the words create a clear and present danger that they will bring about substantive evils that Congress has a right to prevent."
Oliver Wendell Holmes, Jr., Opinion in
Schenck v. *United States*, 1919

"Civilization and profits go hand in hand."
Calvin Coolidge, 1920

"The problem of birth control has arisen directly from the effort of the feminine spirit to free itself from bondage."
Margaret Sanger, 1920

"When Congress makes a law, it's a joke, and when Congress makes a joke, it's a law."

Will Rogers, 1924

"Fascism is Capitalism plus Murder."

Upton Sinclair, 1924

"The business of America is business."

Calvin Coolidge, 1925

"They hired the money, didn't they?"

Calvin Coolidge, on the European war debts, 1925

"Panic is just like a war: you can talk your way into it, but you've got to fight your way out of it."

Will Rogers, 1929

"I pledge you, I pledge myself, to a new deal for the American people."

Franklin D. Roosevelt, Democratic National Convention, 1932

"The only thing we have to fear is fear itself."

Franklin D. Roosevelt, Inaugural Address, 1933

"In the field of world policy, I would dedicate this nation to the policy of a good neighbor."

Franklin D. Roosevelt, Inaugural Address, 1933

"No business whose existence depends on paying less than living wages to its workers has any right to continue in this country."

Franklin D. Roosevelt, 1933

"I see one-third of a nation ill-housed, ill-clad, and ill-nourished."

Franklin D. Roosevelt, Inaugural Address, 1937

"From the mountains to the prairies,
To the oceans white with foam,
God bless America, My home sweet home!"

Irving Berlin, *God Bless America*, 1938

"The 15th Amendment nullifies sophisticated as well as simple-minded modes of discrimination."

> Felix Frankfurter, Opinion in *Lane* v. *Wilson*, 1939

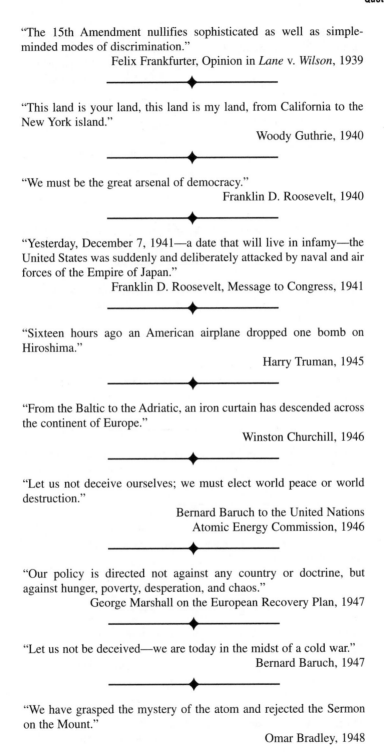

"This land is your land, this land is my land, from California to the New York island."

> Woody Guthrie, 1940

"We must be the great arsenal of democracy."

> Franklin D. Roosevelt, 1940

"Yesterday, December 7, 1941—a date that will live in infamy—the United States was suddenly and deliberately attacked by naval and air forces of the Empire of Japan."

> Franklin D. Roosevelt, Message to Congress, 1941

"Sixteen hours ago an American airplane dropped one bomb on Hiroshima."

> Harry Truman, 1945

"From the Baltic to the Adriatic, an iron curtain has descended across the continent of Europe."

> Winston Churchill, 1946

"Let us not deceive ourselves; we must elect world peace or world destruction."

> Bernard Baruch to the United Nations
> Atomic Energy Commission, 1946

"Our policy is directed not against any country or doctrine, but against hunger, poverty, desperation, and chaos."

> George Marshall on the European Recovery Plan, 1947

"Let us not be deceived—we are today in the midst of a cold war."

> Bernard Baruch, 1947

"We have grasped the mystery of the atom and rejected the Sermon on the Mount."

> Omar Bradley, 1948

"I have here in my hand a list of 205 that were known to the secretary of state as being members of the Communist party and who nevertheless are still working and shaping the policy of the State Department."

Sen. Joseph McCarthy, 1950

◆

"My definition of a free society is a society where it is safe to be unpopular."

Adlai E. Stevenson, 1952

◆

"What's good for the country is good for General Motors, and vice versa."

Charles E. Wilson, Secretary of Defense, to the Senate Armed Services Committee, 1952

◆

"Every gun that is made, every warship launched, every rocket fired, signifies a theft from those who hunger and are not fed, those who are cold and are not clothed."

Dwight D. Eisenhower, 1953

◆

"Local defense must be reinforced by the deterrent of massive retaliatory power."

John Foster Dulles, 1954

◆

"You have a row of dominoes. You knock over the first one, and what will happen to the last one is a certainty—it will go over very quickly."

Dwight D. Eisenhower, press conference, 1954

◆

"We conclude that in the field of public education the doctrine of 'separate but equal' has no place. Separate educational facilities are inherently unequal."

Earl Warren, Opinion in *Brown* v. *Topeka Board of Education*, 1954

◆

"A liberated woman is one who has sex before marriage and a job after."

Gloria Steinem, 1960

◆

"In the councils of government, we must guard against unwarranted influence by the military-industrial complex."

Dwight D. Eisenhower, 1961

"And so, my fellow Americans, ask not what your country can do for you; ask what you can do for your country."
John F. Kennedy, Inaugural Address, 1961

"You won't have Nixon to kick around anymore."
Richard M. Nixon, press conference after
losing California governor's race, 1962

"In a democratic society like ours, relief must come through an aroused popular conscience that sears the conscience of the people's representatives."
Supreme Court decision in *Baker* v. *Carr*, 1962

"The times, they are a-changin'."
Bob Dylan, 1963

"No one has been barred on account of his race from fighting or dying for America—there are no 'white' or 'colored' signs on the foxholes or graveyards of battle."
John F. Kennedy, Message to Congress, 1963

"Injustice anywhere is a threat to justice everywhere."
Martin Luther King, Jr.,
Letter from the Birmingham Jail, 1963

"I have a dream that one day this nation will rise up and live out the true meaning of its creed: We hold these truths to be self-evident, that all men are created equal."
Martin Luther King, Jr., Speech at Washington, 1963

"We have talked long enough in this country about equal rights. It is time to write the next chapter—and to write it in the books of law."
Lyndon B. Johnson, Message to Congress, 1963

"This administration here and now declares unconditional war on poverty in America."
Lyndon B. Johnson, Address to Congress, 1964

"This nation, this generation, in this hour has man's first chance to build a Great Society, a place where the meaning of man's life matches the marvels of man's labor."

        Lyndon B. Johnson, Democratic National Convention, 1964

◆

"We are not fighting for integration, nor are we fighting for separation. We are fighting for recognition as human beings."

        Malcolm X, 1964

◆

"An unconditional right to say what one pleases about public affairs is what I consider to be the minimum guarantee of the First Amendment."

        Hugo Black, Opinion in *New York Times Company* v. *Sullivan*, 1964

◆

"No Viet Cong ever called me 'nigger.'"

        Muhammad Ali, 1966

◆

"I'm tired of feeling rejected by the American people. I'm tired of waking up in the middle of the night worrying about the war."

        Lyndon B. Johnson, 1968

◆

"A spirit of national masochism prevails, encouraged by an effete corps of impudent snobs who characterize themselves as intellectuals."

        Spiro Agnew, 1969

◆

"On public questions there should be 'uninhibited, robust, and wide-open' debate."

        Supreme Court decision in *New York Times Company* v. *United States*, 1971

◆

"People have got to know whether or not their President is a crook. Well, I am not a crook."

        Richard M. Nixon, press conference, 1973

◆

"I believe that government is the problem, not the answer."

        Ronald Reagan, 1976

"Human rights is the soul of our foreign policy, because human rights is the very soul of our sense of nationhood."

Jimmy Carter, 1978

"I think the government ought to stay out of the prayer business."

Jimmy Carter, 1979

"No government has the right to tell its citizens when or whom to love. The only queer people are those who don't love anybody."

Rita Mae Brown, Gay Olympics, San Francisco, 1982

"The current tax code is a daily mugging."

Ronald Reagan, 1985

"Read my lips: No new taxes."

George Bush, Republican National Convention, 1988

"The economy, stupid."

Motto of the Bill Clinton campaign, 1992

ANSWER KEY

UNIT 1

Chapter 1

Exercise Set 1.1

1. D	**4.** B	**7.** C	**10.** C	**13.** A
2. B	**5.** A	**8.** B	**11.** A	**14.** C
3. A	**6.** B	**9.** C	**12.** B	**15.** D

Exercise Set 1.2

1. C	**3.** C	**5.** B	**7.** A	**9.** A
2. D	**4.** C	**6.** B	**8.** C	**10.** C

Exercise Set 1.3

1. D	**3.** B	**5.** C	**7.** A
2. C	**4.** B	**6.** A	**8.** B

Exercise Set 1.4

1. C	**3.** C	**5.** D	**7.** B	**9.** D
2. B	**4.** C	**6.** C	**8.** B	

Chapter Review Questions

1. D	**5.** B	**9.** A	**13.** B	**17.** C
2. B	**6.** C	**10.** D	**14.** B	**18.** B
3. C	**7.** A	**11.** C	**15.** B	**19.** D
4. C	**8.** C	**12.** B	**16.** A	**20.** A

Chapter 2

Exercise Set 1.5

1. C	**3.** A	**5.** C	**7.** D
2. C	**4.** D	**6.** C	

Exercise Set 1.6

1. C	**3.** B	**5.** A	**7.** C
2. B	**4.** D	**6.** D	

Chapter Review Questions

1. B	**3.** C	**5.** C	**7.** C	**9.** A
2. B	**4.** C	**6.** C	**8.** C	**10.** B

UNIT 2

Chapter 1

Exercise Set 2.1
1. D   3. A   5. D
2. B   4. C   6. B

Exercise Set 2.2
1. B   3. D   5. D
2. B   4. A

Exercise Set 2.3
1. D   3. C
2. C   4. D

Exercise Set 2.4
1. D   3. B
2. C   4. A

Chapter Review Questions
1. A   3. D   5. B
2. B   4. C   6. A

Chapter 2

Exercise Set 2.5
1. B   3. A   5. D
2. A   4. C

Exercise Set 2.6.
1. A   3. D
2. A   4. D

Exercise Set 2.7
1. C
2. B
3. D

Exercise Set 2.8
1. A   3. B
2. C   4. A

Exercise Set 2.9

1. C	**3.** A
2. D	**4.** B

Chapter Review Questions

1. D	**3.** D	**5.** C	**7.** A	**9.** D
2. B	**4.** C	**6.** B	**8.** C	**10.** B

Chapter 3

Exercise Set 2.10

1. D	**3.** A
2. B	**4.** A

Exercise Set 2.11

1. B	**3.** C	**5.** C
2. D	**4.** D	**6.** A

Exercise Set 2.12

1. D	**3.** B
2. A	**4.** C

Chapter Review Questions

1. C	**3.** A	**5.** A	**7.** D
2. B	**4.** B	**6.** D	**8.** A

UNIT 3

Chapter 1

Exercise Set 3.1

1. B	**3.** C	**5.** B
2. D	**4.** D	**6.** C

Exercise Set 3.2

1. D	**3.** B
2. D	**4.** A

Chapter Review Questions

1. C	**3.** A	**5.** B	**7.** D
2. C	**4.** D	**6.** C	

Chapter 2

Exercise Set 3.3

1. D	**3.** A
2. C	**4.** A

Exercise Set 3.4

1. C	**3.** D	**5.** D
2. A	**4.** B	**6.** C

Exercise Set 3.5

1. C	**3.** A
2. D	**4.** B

Exercise Set 3.6

1. D	**3.** A
2. B	**4.** C

Exercise Set 3.7

1. C	**3.** B
2. C	**4.** B

Chapter Review Questions

1. A	**3.** D	**5.** C	**7.** B
2. B	**4.** B	**6.** A	

UNIT 4

Chapter 1

Exercise Set 4.1

1. D	**3.** A	**5.** D	**7.** C	**9.** D
2. C	**4.** C	**6.** A	**8.** A	

Exercise Set 4.2

1. A	**3.** C	**5.** B
2. A	**4.** C	**6.** D

Exercise Set 4.3

1. B	**3.** B	**5.** C	**7.** B	**9.** C
2. D	**4.** D	**6.** B	**8.** D	**10.** D

Chapter Review Questions
1. D	**3.** C	**5.** C
2. A	**4.** B	

Chapter 2

Exercise Set 4.4
1. C	**3.** B
2. D	**4.** A

Exercise Set 4.5
1. B	**3.** D	**5.** C
2. B	**4.** A	**6.** D

Exercise Set 4.6
1. B	**3.** A	**5.** D
2. A	**4.** C	**6.** A

Exercise Set 4.7
1. C	**3.** C
2. A	**4.** B

Chapter Review Questions
1. A	**4.** D	**7.** C
2. C	**5.** C	**8.** A
3. D	**6.** A	**9.** B

UNIT 5

Chapter 1

Exercise Set 5.1
1. A	**3.** B
2. D	**4.** D

Exercise Set 5.2
1. B	**3.** D	**5.** A
2. C	**4.** C	

Exercise Set 5.3
1. A	**3.** B	**5.** D
2. C	**4.** B	

Exercise Set 5.4

1. A	**3.** A	**5.** C
2. B	**4.** D	

Exercise Set 5.5

1. D	**3.** D	**5.** C
2. B	**4.** A	

Chapter Review Questions

1. D	**3.** A	**5.** C
2. C	**4.** C	

Chapter 2

Exercise Set 5.6

1. A	**3.** D	**5.** A
2. C	**4.** D	

Exercise Set 5.7

1. A	**3.** B	**5.** B
2. B	**4.** B	**6.** A

Exercise Set 5.8

1. C	**3.** C
2. A	**4.** C

Chapter Review Questions

1. B	**3.** A	**5.** C	**7.** D
2. A	**4.** D	**6.** B	

UNIT 6

Chapter 1

Exercise Set 6.1

1. D	**3.** A
2. C	**4.** B

Exercise Set 6.2

1. B	**3.** D	**5.** B
2. A	**4.** B	**6.** A

Chapter Review Questions
1. D
2. C
3. A

Chapter 2

Exercise Set 6.3

1. B	3. B	5. A
2. D	4. C	

Exercise Set 6.4
1. C
2. C
3. A

Exercise Set 6.5

1. B	3. A
2. C	4. A

Exercise Set 6.6

1. B	3. B	5. A
2. D	4. C	

Chapter Review Questions

1. C	3. B	5. C
2. D	4. C	

Chapter 3

Exercise Set 6.7

1. C	3. A
2. D	4. B

Exercise Set 6.8

1. B	3. A	5. C
2. D	4. C	

Exercise Set 6.9

1. C	3. B
2. A	4. A

Exercise Set 6.10

1. B	3. B
2. D	4. C

Exercise Set 6.11

1. B	**3.** D	**5.** B	**7.** C
2. C	**4.** D	**6.** A	

Chapter Review Questions

1. C	**3.** C	**5.** D
2. B	**4.** D	**6.** C

Chapter 4

Exercise Set 6.12

1. C	**3.** D	**5.** C
2. B	**4.** B	

Exercise Set 6.13

1. D	**3.** C	**5.** B
2. A	**4.** D	**6.** C

Chapter Review Questions

1. A	**3.** A
2. D	**4.** D

Chapter 5

Exercise Set 6.14

1. C	**3.** D	**5.** A
2. A	**4.** C	**6.** B

Exercise Set 6.15

1. C	**3.** D
2. A	**4.** A

Exercise Set 6.16

1. D	**3.** B	**5.** A
2. D	**4.** C	

Exercise Set 6.17

1. B	**3.** B	**5.** C	**7.** C
2. A	**4.** D	**6.** D	

Chapter Review Questions

1. C	**3.** D	**5.** C
2. A	**4.** B	**6.** A

GLOSSARY OF TERMS

Abolitionists those who supported doing away with (abolishing) the institution of slavery.

Abortion the ending of a pregnancy before a live birth.

Acid rain rain, snow, or sleet containing nitric or sulphuric acid produced from the contamination of the atmosphere by smokestack and automobile emissions. It can damage plants and animals and erode stone and buildings.

Acculturation the modification of a people's culture through adaptation or borrowing from other cultures; the merging of cultures.

Activism belief in direct vigorous action.

Administration the management of government; the body of officials in the executive branch; the term of office of a President.

Advocate 1) to plead a case or support a particular issue; 2) one who pleads such a case or supports an issue.

Affirmative action public policy of incorporating women and racial and ethnic minorities into economic, political, and social institutions; usually applied through legislation or court orders.

Affluent wealthy, well-to-do.

Aggression unprovoked attack or act of violence.

Agrarian relating to agriculture or land.

Airlift supplying a city or region by airplane. In the Berlin Airlift of 1948–1949, the United States and allies flew food and other necessities into West Berlin because the Soviet Union had imposed a blockade on land routes.

Ally a person, party, or country joined with another for a common purpose.

Amendment change or addition made in the Constitution; proposed by Congress or a national convention called by Congress and ratified by state legislatures or special state conventions.

Amnesty a general pardon for political offenses, generally to a large group of individuals.

Anarchist one who believes in the abolition of government or is opposed to organized government.

Anarchy the absence of government; a state of disorder or chaos.

Antifederalists opponents of ratification of the Constitution in 1787 and 1788; opponents of the extension of federal power.

Antitrust relating to the limitation or control of monopolies, trusts, or unfair business combinations.

Apartheid racial segregation, specifically in South Africa.

Appalachia region of the Appalachian Mountains from Alabama to New York and western New England characterized in many parts by poverty and economic underdevelopment.

Appeasement attempts to conciliate an aggressor by making concessions. The policy of appeasement toward Hitler in the 1930s ultimately failed to avoid war.

Appoint to name to an office. A President's major appointments must be confirmed by the Senate.

Apportionment allotment of voting districts as required by law.

Arbitration process of settling a dispute by referring it to a third party; both sides usually agree beforehand to abide by the arbitrator's decision.

Armageddon a vast, final, destructive conflict.

Armistice a truce preliminary to a peace treaty.

Articles of Confederation the charter of the first national government of the United States; in effect from 1781 until replaced by the Constitution in 1789.

Assembly a gathering or body of representatives, usually of a state or locality.

Assimilation process of being absorbed into a group or culture.

Atlantic Charter document issued in 1941 by President Franklin Roosevelt and Prime Minister Winston Churchill outlining the mutual wartime goals of England and the United States and their principles for assuring peace after the war.

Backlash strong negative reaction to a law or political event.

Balance of power policy aimed at securing peace by maintaining approximate military equality among countries or blocs.

Balanced budget plan for government taxes and spending in which expenses do not exceed income.

Belligerent a participant in a war.

Bicameral legislature lawmaking body made up of two houses or chambers.

Big business group of large profit-making corporations.

Big stick policy willingness to use military power to influence foreign affairs. It derives from Theodore Roosevelt's saying, "Walk softly, but carry a big stick."

Bill of Rights first ten amendments to the Constitution, adopted in 1791.

Bipartisan involving the cooperation of two political parties.

Birth control artificial or natural means of avoiding pregnancy.

Black codes a series of laws that sought to control and regulate the conduct of freed slaves during and after the Reconstruction period in the Southern states. Generally, they denied blacks their basic civil rights.

Bloc a group of countries or voters with similar political views.

Bolsheviks radical socialists and communists under the leadership of Lenin and Trotsky who came to power following the Russian Revolution in 1917.

Bonus a government payment to war veterans usually based on length of service.

Boom period of economic expansion.

Boston Massacre in 1770 five colonists were killed in Boston when British soldiers fired on a crowd throwing rocks and snowballs; the soldiers were tried and acquitted of murder.

Boston Tea Party incident in Boston, December 16, 1773, when colonists dressed as Indians forced their way aboard merchant ships in the harbor and threw overboard their cargoes of tea so that recently imposed British taxes on it could not be collected.

Bourgeoisie economic and social class between the aristocracy, or the very wealthy class, and the working class (the proletariat); the commercial or professional class; the middle class.

Boycott to join together in refusing to deal with or buy from a party in order to compel negotiation or concessions.

Brain trust experts without official positions who served as advisers to President Franklin Roosevelt.

Brinkmanship pushing a dangerous situation to the limit before stopping.

Brown power phrase describing attempts by Hispanic Americans to use their growing numbers to improve their political and economic standing.

Budget financial plan for income and spending.

Budget deficit the amount by which a government's expenses exceed its revenue or income.

Bureaucracy administrative officials of government.

Cabinet the advisers to the President who also manage the principal executive departments of the U.S. government. The Cabinet is not mentioned in the Constitution, but has grown over time from custom and practice.

Camp David Accords agreements reached in 1978 between President Sadat of Egypt and Prime Minister Begin of Israel, negotiated by President Carter at the presidential retreat in Camp David, MD. The accords evolved into a peace treaty between Israel and Egypt in 1979, providing for Egypt's official

ɔn of Israel and Israel's with-
ɔm the Sinai Peninsula.

.) the seat or main location of a
ernment; 2) money invested or
used to return a profit.

Capitalism economic system in which
the means of production and distribution are privately owned and operated
for profit.

Capital punishment death sentence
imposed by a court.

Capitol buidling in which state or federal legislature assembles.

Carpetbaggers Notherners who went to
the South during the Reconstruction
period to participate in and profit from
its political reorganization.

Caucus a closed meeting of a political
party.

Censorship preventing the publication of
written material or the showing of a
film, television program, or play
because the government or a segment
of society finds it objectionable.

Census a counting of the inhabitants of a
region.

Central Powers In World War I, Germany, Austro-Hungary, and their allies.

Centralized with power or authority concentrated in a central organization.

Charter written document establishing
the rules under which an organization
will operate; an organization's constitution.

Checks and balances division of powers
among the three branches of the federal government so that each branch
may limit actions and power of the
others. *See also* Separation of powers.

Chicanos Americans of Mexican origin
or descent.

Citizen person entitled by birth or naturalization, to the rights and protection
provided by the state or nation.

Civil relating to the state, politics, or
government.

Civil disobedience refusal to obey a law
in order to draw attention to its unfairness or undesirability.

Civil liberties *see* Civil rights.

Civil rights the liberties and privileges of
citizens, especially those guaranteed in
the Bill of Rights.

Civil Service system for filling government jobs through impartial and nonpolitical means, such as standardized
exams. Begun by the federal government in the 1880s.

Civilian a person who is not a member of
the armed forces; pertaining to matters
outside the military.

Clandestine performed secretly.

Clear and present danger standard established by the Supreme Court for determining when the right of free speech
may be limited or denied—"when
there is a clear and present danger that
they will bring about the substantive
evils that [the government] has a right
to prevent."

Coalition temporary alliance of groups
or factions.

Coinage money made of metal; sometimes called hard money.

Cold war a conflict between nations short
of actual military conflict; the political,
diplomatic, economic, and strategic
competition between the United States
and the Soviet Union from 1946 until
1991.

Collective bargaining method by which
workers negotiate as a group with their
employer through their union representatives.

Collective security agreement among a
group of nations to help each other
maintain their safety and territory;
usually by agreeing that an attack by a
foreign power upon one nation will be
considered an attack upon all.

Colonialism national policy based on
control over dependent areas or
colonies.

Colony a territory ruled or administered
by a distant nation, usually for the benefit of the ruling nation.

Commerce the exchange or buying and
selling of goods; business.

Commerce among the states business carried on across state lines, which Congress is given power to regulate by Article I, Section 8, of the Constitution.

Committee a group of people appointed or delegated for a particular purpose.

Commodities common economic goods, such as agricultural products, that are bought and sold.

Common law body of law formed over time by accumulation of precedents and prior decisions, as opposed to laws enacted by legislative bodies.

Common Sense a pamphlet by Thomas Paine that helped rally public support for the Revolutionary War.

Commonwealth an organization of independent states; official designation (instead of state) of KY, MA, PA, and VA in the United States.

Communiqué official bulletin, statement, or other communication.

Communism political philosophy advocating collective ownership of property and the means of production and the abolition of the capitalist economic system.

Compact theory of union doctrine held by many states' rights supporters that the Union was a voluntary compact among the states and that states had the right to leave the Union in the same manner they had chosen to enter it.

Compromise a settlement in which each side makes concessions.

Concession something yielded or given up, often in exchange for something else.

Confederate States the eleven Southern states that seceded or officially withdrew from the Union in 1860 and 1861 to form an independent nation called the Confederate States of America. Their withdrawal was not recognized by the federal government or the remaining states. They were defeated in the Civil War and reabsorbed into the Union.

Congress the legislative branch of the federal government; composed of the Senate and the House of Representatives.

Conscription compulsory enrollment into the armed forces; forced military service; draft.

Consensus general agreement.

Conservation careful management and protection, especially of natural resources.

Conservative reluctant or resistant to change; favoring traditional views and values; one belonging to a conservative party or political group.

Constituents the citizens represented by an elected public official; group of supporters.

Constitution the basic charter of the U.S. government, effective since 1789; it was written by the Constitutional Convention in 1787, ratified by the states 1787–1788, and put into effect in 1789.

Constitutionalism belief that government is limited by legal and political restraints and accountable to the governed.

Constitutional Convention gathering of delegates from the thirteen states in 1787 in Philadelphia for the purpose of revising the Articles of Confederation; instead, they drafted an entirely new Constitution that was adopted in 1788 and put into effect in 1789.

Constitutional Republicanism elected government limited by legally defined guidelines.

Consumerism protection of the interests and rights of consumers against false advertising or faulty or dangerous products.

Containment policy adopted by the Western democracies after World War II to prevent the further expansion of communism and the Soviet Union.

Continental Congress 1) any of several assemblies of delegates from the American colonies before the Revolution to promote cooperation on various issues; 2) the national legislative body under the Articles of Confederation (1781–1788).

Convention a meeting of political delegates.

Conventional traditional or ordinary; in military affairs, it refers to forces or measures other than nuclear weapons.

Cooperative a corporation owned collectively by members who share in the profits and benefits. Cooperatives were first developed by farmers in the late 19th century to avoid high prices charged by middlemen for grain storage, transportation, and farm supplies.

Corollary a proposition that follows a previous one, which it modifies or enlarges, such as the Roosevelt Corollary to the Monroe Doctrine.

Corporation an organization legally empowered to act as one person, including the ability to borrow and lend money, make contracts, own property, and engage in business.

Corruption illegal or improper practices; abuses of authority, especially in connection with bribery or theft.

Coup an overturning; a coup d'état is the overthrow of a government.

Craft union labor union made up of workers with the same skill or craft, such as carpenters or electricians.

Credibility grounds for being believed or trusted.

Crédit Mobilier railroad construction company that cheated on government contracts and bribed Congressmen during the late 1860s.

Creditor nation a nation that exports more than it imports, so that it is owed money by other nations.

Cultural pluralism the acceptance and encouragement of multiple ethnic, religious, and racial groups within one society; respect for ethnic diversity.

Culture the beliefs, social forms, and accumulated knowledge of a group, race, or people.

Currency money in circulation, especially paper money.

Darwinism 1) the theories of biologist Charles Darwin, who explained the evolution of species by natural selection; 2) social theories loosely based on Darwin's work and arguing that "the survival of the fittest" meant that government should not protect the weak from exploitation by the strong.

Debasement a reduction of value.

Debtor nation a nation that imports more than it exports and so owes money to other nations.

Declaration of Independence document passed and signed by the Continental Congress, effective July 4, 1776, declaring the United States an independent and sovereign nation.

Defense spending government spending for military armaments, equipment, and personnel.

Delegate a representative chosen to act for a group or another person.

Demilitarized zone area where no military equipment or personnel may be deployed.

Demobilize to discharge from military service.

Democratic party political party that evolved out of the Democratic Republicans around 1820.

Democratic Republicans political party formed around 1800 by Jefferson, Madison, and others opposed to the Federalists.

Demographic relating to the statistical study of human populations.

Depression an economic downturn, especially one characterized by high unemployment.

Desegregation the ending of segregation, which is the separation of whites and blacks.

Despot a sovereign or authority without legal restraints; an absolute monarch; tyrant.

Détente relaxation of strained relations or tensions.

Diplomacy the practice of conducting

relations between countries by negotiations rather than force.

Direct election election in which votes are cast by the people themselves rather than by their representatives.

Directive order issued by a high authority calling for specific action.

Disarmament giving up or reducing armed forces.

Discrimination partiality, prejudice, or distinctions in treatment; the denial of rights and advantages to minority groups.

Disenfranchise to take away the right to vote.

Dissenting opinion written statement by a member of a court disagreeing with the court's decision.

Distribution of wealth statistical measure of how the property or wealth of a nation is divided among its population.

Dollar diplomacy use of American political and military power abroad (usually in Latin America) to promote or advance the interests of American businesses.

Domestic having to do with the internal affairs of a country.

Domino theory belief in the 1950s and 1960s that the fall of one nation to communism would lead to the fall of neighboring nations.

Draft *see* **Conscription.**

Due process of law doctrine that government's power cannot be used against an individual except as prescribed by established law. Applied to the state governments by the 14th Amendment.

Ecological concerning the relationship between living things and the environment.

Economy the total system for business, production, consumption, and investment in a country.

Eisenhower Doctrine statement made in 1957 by President Eisenhower that the United States would provide military and economic aid—and direct military intervention, if necessary—to nations of the Middle East if they were threatened by communist aggression.

Elastic clause part of the Constitution (Article I, Section 8) that gives the federal government the right to make laws "necessary and proper" to carry out its specific powers and functions; it has sometimes been used to expand the powers of the federal government; also known as the "necessary and proper clause."

Election process of choosing officers by vote.

Electoral college means of electing President and Vice-President established by the Constitution and subsequent amendments; voters in each state choose "electors" who later meet to elect the President and Vice-President. Electors were originally free to vote for any candidate they chose, but they are currently pledged to vote for specific candidates. The number of electors from each state is equal to the number of Representatives and Senators from that state.

Emancipation the act of setting free; freeing from restraint or, especially, slavery.

Emancipation Proclamation issued by President Lincoln in 1863, it declared free the slaves in the Southern states in rebellion but did not affect slaves held in states loyal to the Union, such as Maryland, Kentucky, or Missouri.

Embargo prohibition of commerce with a nation or region, usually to apply pressure or force concessions.

Emigrate to leave one country or region to settle in another.

Encroachment step-by-step interference with the rights or possessions of others.

Endorsement approval or recommendation.

Enjoin to legally forbid or prohibit, usually by court order or injunction.

Enlightenment era during the 17th and 18th centuries when reason replaced religion as guide to politics, philosophy, and government.

Environmentalists persons concerned about the quality of air, water, and land and the protection of natural resources, "green" space, and plant and animal species.

Envoy a messenger or representative.

Equal protection principle that all people or classes of persons be treated the same under the law.

Equality condition of having the same rights, privileges, and advantages as all other citizens.

Escalate to increase the extent, level, or volume.

Espionage the act or practice of spying.

Ethnic belonging to a particular group identified by nationality or national origin and culture or customs.

Ethnocentric believing that one's own ethnic group is superior to others.

Evacuate to remove to a safer area.

Evolution change over time; an adjustment in the existing order.

Executive person or office having administrative and managerial functions; in government, the branch responsible for carrying out the laws and for the conduct of national affairs; it includes the President and Cabinet and the departments under their jurisdiction.

Executive privilege principle that an executive (such as the President) should not divulge certain sensitive or protected information.

Expansionism policy of adding to a country's territory, usually by seizing land from other nations.

Exploitation wrongful or unethical use of someone or something for one's own benefit.

Extraterritoriality right of a resident of a foreign country to be tried in the judicial system of his or her home country.

Fascism political philosophy advocating totalitarian government power, intense nationalism, and military expansionism. Mussolini's Fascist party governed Italy from the 1920s through World War II.

Far East the nations on the Pacific coast of Asia.

Favorable balance of trade exporting or selling more goods than are imported or bought.

Federal relating to the central national government created by the Constitution.

Federal Housing Administration federal agency established in 1934 to insure mortgages and set construction standards.

Federal Reserve Note Currency or paper money issued by the Federal Reserve System and representing a promissory obligation of the federal government. Federal Reserve Notes replaced the older gold and silver certificates, which were backed by or based upon specific reserves of gold and silver.

Federal Reserve System federal agency created by Congress in 1913 to regulate the banking system. Federal Reserve banks in 12 districts supervise banking operations, lend money to banks, and issue currency; a Federal Reserve Commission sets and regulates interest rates.

Federalism system of government in which powers are divided between a central authority and local subdivisions.

Federalists advocates of adopting the Constitution in 1787–1788 and of more powerful central government during the period 1789–1820. Many Federalists later joined the Whig party.

Feminism movement advocating equal rights and privileges for women, including economic, political, legal, and social status.

Filibuster use of delaying tactics, such as unlimited debate in one or both houses of Congress, to prevent action on a legislative proposal.

Fiscal having to do with government revenues, expenditures, and budgets.

Fission splitting or breaking up; nuclear fission refers to the splitting of an atomic nucleus to release a vast quantity of energy.

Foreclosure the act of a lender's taking possession of mortgaged property from a borrower who is unable to make the required payments.

Foreign aid assistance in the form of money or goods supplied to a foreign country.

Foreign policy a nation's policy in dealing with other nations.

Fourteen Points President Wilson's plan for international peace presented to Congress on January 22, 1918.

Franchise the right to vote; suffrage.

Free enterprise the freedom of private businesses to operate without undue government interference.

Free trade the freedom to exchange goods with other countries, especially without tariffs.

Freedman a freed slave, usually referring to a former slave freed by the Thirteenth Amendment.

Freedom of religion right of citizens to hold and practice religious beliefs without government interference.

Freedom of speech right of citizens to say or write their views without regulation or reprisal from government; restricted in some cases, *see* Clear and present danger.

Freedom of the press right of publishers to print material without prior approval by government; *see* Prior restraint.

Freedom riders civil rights advocates who traveled the South on buses to promote the desegregation of public facilities.

Free-Soil party political party before the Civil War opposed to the extension of slavery and the admission of slave states.

Frontier border region between two distinct areas, especially (in America) between settled and unsettled territory. In European usage, a frontier is the border between two countries.

Fugitive Slave Law federal law passed in 1850 that required Northern states to return escaped slaves to their owners in the South. It was widely opposed by a variety of legal and extra-legal means.

Fundamental rights *see* Natural rights.

Gerrymandering drawing the boundaries of election districts to insure the victory of one party or faction by including or excluding neighborhoods of a particular ethnic or social class.

Global relating to the world as a whole; international; worldwide.

Good Neighbor Policy policy first announced by President Franklin Roosevelt to promote friendly relations with all Latin American nations.

Government the institutions and people responsible for the conduct of public affairs.

Great Compromise agreement in the Constitutional Convention of 1787 to have two houses of Congress, one (the Senate) to represent the states equally and the other (the House of Representatives) to represent the people proportionately. Also known as the Connecticut Compromise.

Great Depression period from the stock market crash of 1929 until the start of World War II during which industrial production declined and unemployment rose to over one fourth of the labor force.

Great Society collective name for various social programs of President Lyndon Johnson, including the so-called War on Poverty and programs for job-training, subsidized housing, and free medical care for the poor and aged.

Green revolution the increase in agricultural crop yields brought about by the use of machinery, fertilizers, pesticides, and improved seeds.

Guerilla an active participant in a war who is not a member of the regular armed forces; a kind of warfare characterized by sabotage, harassment, and hit-and-run tactics.

Habeas corpus a writ or legal order directed to an official holding a person in custody, commanding the official to produce the person in court, show cause why the person has been confined, and prove that the person has not been deprived of liberty without due process of law.

Harlem Renaissance a movement among black writers, artists, and musicians centered in Harlem, New York City, during the 1920s.

Head Start educational aid to preschool children from disadvantaged homes.

Hessians hired soldiers from the district of Hesse in Germany, employed by the British before and during the Revolutionary War.

Heterogeneous composed of unlike parts; a society made up of different races, nationalities, or ethnic groups.

Holocaust since World War II, it refers to the genocidal murders of six million European Jews by the Nazis.

Home front during a war, the area of a nation's domestic and civilian affairs.

Homestead Act passed by Congress in 1862, it gave 160 acres of Western land to any head of a family who agreed to cultivate it for five years; it encouraged the rapid settlement of the West by giving immigrants and Easterners free land.

Homogeneous made up of similar elements; a society consisting primarily of the same race, nationality, or ethnic group.

Hot line direct telephone link, especially between the White House and the Kremlin, always ready for instant communication.

House of Representatives the half of Congress composed of representatives allotted among the states according to their population.

Immigration moving into a country where one is not a native to become a permanent resident.

Impeach to bring formal charges against a public official for misconduct. The House of Representatives has the power to impeach federal officials, and the trial is held by the Senate.

Imperialism the practice of forming and maintaining an empire; possession of foreign territories or colonies for the benefit of the home country; the policy of seeking to dominate economically, politically, or militarily weaker areas of the world.

Implementation means of accomplishing or carrying out a plan or program.

Import quota a limit on the amount of a commodity that can be brought into the country.

Inauguration a ceremonial beginning, especially the installing of an official at the beginning of a term.

Incumbent person currently serving in political office.

Indians European term for the native inhabitants of the Americas; it was based on the mistaken belief that the continents were part of Asia or India.

Indictment a legal action to charge someone with a crime.

Individualism doctrine that the rights and interests of individual persons are the most important source of values.

Industrialization economic transformation of society by the development of large industries, machine production, factories, and an urban work force.

Industrial Revolution the transformation from an agricultural society to one based upon large-scale mechanized production and factory organization. It began in Europe (especially England) in the late 18th century and in America in the early 19th century.

Infiltration gradual entrance or buildup with the intent of taking control.

Inflation general and continuing rise in the price of goods, often due to the relative increase of available money and credit.

Initiative process for the direct involvement of voters in the making of laws; by gathering enough signatures on a petition, a group can force a legislature to consider a proposal or require it to be placed on the ballot for public vote.

Injunction order issued by a court directing someone to do or refrain from doing some specific act.

Installment buying practice of buying a product through regular monthly or weekly payments; failure to pay gives the seller the right to repossess the product.

Insurgency an uprising or revolt against a government, short of actual war.

Integration bringing together or making as one; unification; applied especially to blacks and whites.

Interdependent depending on one another, such as nations that rely on each other's trade.

Internal improvements roads, canals, and other means to assist transportation and commerce. In the first half of the 19th century, debate concerned who should fund internal improvements—the states or the federal government.

Internationalism policy of cooperation among nations.

Internment the detainment and isolation of ethnic groups for purposes of national security (such as Japanese Americans during World War II); this is now widely held to have been unconstitutional.

Interposition an argument that the states could legitimately object to acts of Congress if those acts exceeded Congress's legitimate authority. Interposition fell short of Nullification.

Interstate taking place across state lines; involving the citizens of more than one state.

Interstate Commerce Commission established by Congress in 1887 to regulate railroad rates and prevent abuses by railroads; it was later expanded to have jurisdiction over other forms of transportation.

Intervention interference in the affairs of another country, including the use of force.

Intolerable Acts series of acts of Parliament directed against the American colonies and intended to assert British authority and increase revenues from the colonies.

Invalidate to make null and void; to destroy the existence or effectiveness of, as, for example, a law.

Iran-Contra Affair an illegal conspiracy by officials of the Reagan administration to provide funding for the anti-communist Contra rebels in Nicaragua by secretly selling missiles to Iran and diverting the money to the Nicaraguans.

Iron Curtain the series of fortified borders separating Western Europe from Soviet-dominated Eastern Europe; the term was made popular by Winston Churchill.

Isolationism policy of keeping a nation apart from alliances or other political relations with foreign nations.

Jim Crow laws laws enforcing segregation or control of blacks in such a way as to make them unequal.

Joint resolution a legislative act that is the same in both houses of Congress.

Judicial activism developing social policy through court decisions instead of through legislative action, often in response to changing values and circumstances.

Judicial nationalism term used to describe the Supreme Court under the leadership of John Marshall, when its decisions consolidated the power of the federal government by centralizing responsibility for commerce, contracts, and finance.

Judicial restraint the preference of a court to avoid upsetting existing law or practice.

Judicial review power of the Supreme Court to void acts of Congress that are found to violate the Constitution.

Judiciary the branch of government that interprets the law and tries cases; the system of courts.

Jurisdiction authority of a court to interpret and apply the law; in general, the area of authority of a government.

Knights of Labor early labor union, formed in 1869.

Kremlin complex of government offices in Moscow; the center of government of Russia and the former Soviet Union.

Ku Klux Klan secret organization founded in 1866 to intimidate freed slaves and keep them in conditions of servitude through threats and acts of violence; it later developed into a nativist organization opposed to Jews, Catholics, and immigrants, as well as African Americans.

Laissez-faire doctrine opposing government regulation of economic matters beyond what is necessary to maintain property rights and enforce contracts. *Laissez-faire* is French for "let alone" or "let be."

Lame duck an official who has not been reelected and is serving out the remainder of a term.

League of Nations International organization of countries formed after World War I to promote world peace. It was supported by President Wilson, but the Senate refused to allow the United States to join. After World War II it was replaced by the United Nations.

Legislature a body of persons elected to make laws for a nation or state; a congress or parliament.

Levy to place and collect a tax; to draft persons for military service.

Liberal advocating political or social views that emphasize civil rights, democratic reforms, and the use of government to promote social progress.

Liberty freedom.

Life expectancy statistical estimate of the average lifespan of a particular population.

Limited government *see* Constitutionalism.

Line-item veto power of an executive to veto specific provisions of a bill without vetoing the entire bill that contains them. The President does not have line-item veto power.

Lobbying actions by private citizens or organizations seeking to influence (by legal means) the decisions of a legislature or executive department of government.

Loose construction, loose interpretation reading of the Constitution that allows broad use of the elastic clause and implied powers.

Louisiana Purchase the purchase from France by the United States in 1803 for $15 million of the Louisiana Territory, stretching from New Orleans west to the Rocky Mountains, more than doubling the size of the United States.

Loyalists American colonists who remained loyal to England during the American Revolution; also known as Tories.

Magna Carta agreement signed by King John I of England in 1215, granting certain rights (including trial by jury and habeas corpus) to the barons who had taken him prisoner.

Majority number greater than one half of the votes cast (simple majority); a "two-thirds majority" requires at least two thirds of the votes cast.

Malaise vague sense of unhappiness or discomfort.

Manifest destiny belief, held by many Americans in the 19th century, that the United States was destined to control the continent between the Atlantic and Pacific Oceans.

Market economy an economic system in which decisions about production and pricing are based on the actions of buyers and sellers in the marketplace; usually associated with capitalism.

Marshall Plan the program of U.S. aid to Europe following World War II to help those nations recover from the extensive damage to their cities, industries, and transportation.

Materialism valuing economic or material things more than spiritual or intellectual interests.

Media the instruments of mass communication, such as television, radio, and newspapers.

Mediator person who solves differences between two parties. Both sides do not usually agree beforehand to accept the decisions of the mediator, as they usually do with an arbitrator.

Mercantilism the economic policies of European nations from the 15th century until the Industrial Revolution, based on mercantile (commercial, trading) activities and characterized by the acquisition of colonies and the establishment of a favorable balance of trade. The American colonies were established under the mercantile system.

Middle class the members of a society having a socio-economic position between the very wealthy and the poor.

Migration the movement of people from one place to another.

Militancy aggressive opposition.

Militaristic characterized by military discipline and aggressiveness.

Military-industrial complex the combined power of the Defense Department and the industries that supply it with equipment. The phrase was popularized by Eisenhower, who claimed that it worked for unnecessary increases in armaments.

Militia part-time soldiers who do not belong to the regular armed forces.

Minority the portion of a group less than one half; an ethnic or racial group that is smaller than the dominant group and may be subjected to discrimination.

Missouri Compromise an agreement in 1820 between Congressional advocates and opponents of the extension of slavery that preserved sectional balance. It included the simultaneous admission of the slave state Missouri and the free state Maine and the prohibition of slavery in the northern parts of the Louisiana Purchase.

Monopoly the exclusive control or ownership of an industry by a single person or company.

Monroe Doctrine policy announced in 1823, during the presidency of James Monroe, that the United States would oppose European attempts to extend their control of the Western Hemisphere. It became and remains a basic principle of American foreign policy.

Moratorium agreement to postpone payment of a debt or other obligation.

Mortgage legal instrument specifying payments to be made on a loan for the purchase of property. Failure to make payments gives the mortgager the legal right to repossess the property.

Muckraker journalists in the late 19th and early 20th centuries who reported on political or commercial corruption.

Multinational involving more than two nations.

Municipality a city or local political unit.

Munitions armaments and ammunition used in warfare.

Nationalism 1) sense of pride in one's country; 2) extreme devotion to national interests.

National Labor Relations Board federal agency established in 1935 to enforce laws against unfair labor practices.

National Origins Act laws passed in 1921, 1924, and 1929 that limited immigration into the United States and established quotas for nations based on the number of persons from those nations living in the United States according to an earlier census. It was regarded as discriminatory because it favored immigrants from Western Europe.

Native one who is connected with a place by birth; an original inhabitant as distinguished from immigrants or visitors.

Native Americans descendants of the original inhabitants of the Americas.

Nativism in the United States, the policy of favoring native-born Americans and opposing immigrants.

Naturalization the process of conferring citizenship upon an immigrant.

Natural rights rights or liberties to which one is entitled as a human being, as distinguished from those that are created by laws or governments.

Necessary and proper clause portion of the Constitution granting Congress power to "make all Laws which shall be necessary and proper for carrying into Execution" its other powers.

Neutrality policy of not helping either side in a war.

Neutrality Acts laws passed in 1935 and 1937 to avoid U.S. involvement in a war in Europe; they placed an embargo on arms sales to any nation engaged in war.

New Deal name adopted by President Franklin Roosevelt for the reforms and social programs instituted by his administration, beginning in 1933.

New Freedom program of President Wilson to regulate banking and currency to influence the direction of the economy and to support stronger antitrust legislation.

New Nationalism program of President Theodore Roosevelt during his unsuccessful campaign for the presidency in 1912. It promised greater government supervision of the economy to balance the power of big business.

Nineteenth Amendment granted suffrage (the right to vote) to women; enacted in 1920.

Nomination proposal of a candidate for an office.

Nonintervention policy of not becoming involved in the affairs of other nations.

Nonpartisan not based on party interests or bias.

Nonsectarian not affiliated with any religious group.

Nonviolence principle that all violence is to be avoided; the use of peaceful means for political ends.

Normalcy the state of being normal; the term was applied to the era of the 1920s, following the disruptions of World War I.

North Atlantic Treaty Organization (NATO) collective security military alliance formed in 1949 by the United States, Canada, and nations of Western Europe to oppose the threat posed by the Soviet Union and Warsaw Pact nations to Europe.

Northwest Territory federal administrative district west of the Allegheny Mountains, north of the Ohio River, south of the Great Lakes, and east of the Mississippi River, including the present states of Ohio, Indiana, Michigan, Illinois, and Wisconsin, and part of Minnesota. The Territory was organized by the Continental Congress in 1787 from lands claimed by several eastern states.

Nullification argument or doctrine claiming that states could refuse to abide by acts of Congress if the states felt Congress had exceeded its enumerated powers. Used by states' rights advocates; championed by John C. Calhoun of South Carolina.

Nuremberg Tribunal international military court held in Nuremberg, Germany, in 1945–46; top Nazi leaders were tried and convicted of crimes against humanity and violations of international law.

Open-Door policy an attempt by the United States in 1899 to preserve trade interests in China by asking European nations to respect the territorial integrity of China and to permit free access to ports they held in Asia.

Ordinance a law or regulation, usually of a local municipality.

Organized labor workers represented by labor unions.

Original jurisdiction the first court with authority to consider and decide a case, as opposed to appellate jurisdiction.

Overproduction production of a commodity in excess of the demand for it; it usually results in falling prices.

Parity government support of prices for agricultural products to insure that farm income keeps pace with income in other economic sectors.

Parliament the legislative body of Great Britain, consisting of the House of Commons and the House of Lords.

Partition division of a country into two or more separate parts.

Peace Corps U.S. government agency formed by President Kennedy in 1961; it sought to assist developing countries by sending American volunteers to teach and provide technical assistance.

Penal having to do with punishment; liable to be punished.

Pentagon headquarters of the U.S. armed forces, near Washington, D.C.

Per capita the average per person for a particular population, as in per capita income.

Perjury making a false statement under oath.

Philanthropy literally, the love of mankind; desire to help humankind, usually through gifts or endowments to charitable institutions.

Picketing method of demonstration by workers or political groups, usually taking place at the employer or the offices of the opposition; it includes notifying the public of the unfairness of the employer with signs and conversation.

Plea bargaining pleading guilty to a lesser charge in order to avoid standing trial for a more serious one.

Pluralistic type of society in which diverse ethnic, racial, and national groups coexist while maintaining their own cultural heritage.

Plurality a number of votes greater than any other candidate but less than a majority of all the votes cast.

Pocket veto an automatic veto that occurs if the President does not sign a bill passed by Congress during the last ten days of its session.

Pogrom organized, officially encouraged persecution or massacre of a group.

Political machine combination of party and political officials who maintain themselves in office, sometimes through corrupt means.

Politics the practice of government; the art of winning control of public affairs.

Poll tax 1) a tax paid to register or vote in elections (prohibited under the Twenty-Fourth Amendment). 2) a per-person or per-capita tax, not based on income or employment.

Popular sovereignty 1) doctrine in democratic forms of government that power ultimately derives from the people and that the consent of the governed is exercised through the vote; 2) in the years before the Civil War, a political position advocating that the legality of slavery in the western territories be decided by popular vote of the inhabitants; it was ridiculed by its opponents as "squatter sovereignty."

Populism movement that began in agricultural areas in the late 19th century seeking government regulation to curb excesses and exploitation by big business.

Power of the purse the power to authorize revenues and spending; in the federal government, Congress holds the power of the purse.

Pragmatism belief in a practical (rather than an ethical or theoretical) approach to problems and affairs.

Preamble introductory part, especially

the opening of the Constitution, which begins "We the people...."

Precedence the right to be first or have more authority.

Precedent rule or decision that serves as a guide for future actions or decisions; attorneys look for precedents to support their arguments when presenting a case in court.

Prejudice a preconceived opinion or judgment, usually negative, not based on fact.

Preside to act as chairman.

President the chief executive officer of the federal government.

Press the news gathering and publishing industry, including television, radio, magazines, and newspapers.

Price supports government measures to maintain the price of a commodity at an artificially set level.

Prior restraint the prohibition of publication of an article, book, or story by a court order before the material is disclosed to the public. Permissible only in cases of obscenity or of "clear and present danger."

Primary election election in which members of a political party choose their candidates for the coming general elections.

Processing tax a tax on industries that convert raw materials into finished goods, such as cotton into cloth.

Progressive Era the period roughly from 1900 to 1920, marked by political, economic, and social reform movements.

Progressive tax a tax that is higher for the wealthy than for the poor, such as income tax.

Progressivism a broad reform movement during the late 19th and early 20th centuries that sought to remedy the worst effects of industrialism and urbanization by imposing governmental controls on big business, improving social justice, and increasing direct democratic participation in politics.

Prohibition period from the enactment of the 18th Amendment in 1919 until its repeal by the 21st Amendment in 1933, during which the manufacture, sale, import, export, and transportation of alcoholic beverages was illegal.

Proletariat the industrial working class, who sell their labor and do not own the means of production.

Propaganda promotion of particular ideas and doctrines.

Protective tariff tax on imported goods intended to protect the interests of internal or domestic industries by raising the price of imports.

Protectorate an area under the control and protection of a country that does not have full sovereignty over it.

Proviso clause in a document or statute making some condition or provision.

Quarantine isolation of a person or country, usually to prevent spread of communicable diseases.

Quartering forcibly housing soldiers in private residences.

Quota a maximum limit; a share or portion assigned to a group.

Racism belief that some races are inherently superior to others.

Radical, Radicalism favoring extreme and fundamental changes.

Ratification formal legal approval and adoption.

Raw materials products or resources not yet manufactured into their final state, as many agricultural products, lumber, or ores.

Rearmament rebuilding of a nation's armed forces, often with new and better weapons.

Recall political reform procedure for removing a public official from office before the end of a term by popular vote; it is usually initiated by a petition.

Reconstruction period from 1865 through 1876, when the Southern states were occupied by federal troops and under the direct control of the national government.

Red Scare fears about the danger of communist subversion or invasion; especially after World War II, "Red Scare" tactics were used by Senator Joseph McCarthy and others for political purposes.

Referendum a proposal submitted to a popular vote before putting it into effect.

Refinance to change the terms of a mortgage or loan to make it easier for the borrower to make the payments.

Reform to improve or change, especially a social institution.

Regulatory enforcing the rules or laws.

Rehabilitation restoration to a former or better condition.

Relocation the movement (sometimes by force) of a group of people to a new place.

Reparations payments imposed on nations defeated in war to help the victors recover the costs of war.

Repercussion a widespread or indirect effect of an act.

Representative 1) a delegate or agent of another person or group of people; 2) a federal legislator; 3) a type of government by persons chosen from among the governed, usually by election.

Republican party political party formed in the 1840s, opposed to the extension of slavery; Lincoln was the first Republican elected President (in 1860).

Reserved powers powers not specifically granted to Congress or the federal government under the Constitution, and so held to be reserved to the states.

Restraint of trade language used in the Sherman Antitrust Act (1890) to describe combinations and activities of groups (businesses, labor unions) that were prohibited under the Act.

Retaliatory done in response to an attack or aggression; strong enough to deter an attack.

Revenue the income of governments from taxation, tariffs, fees, and other activities.

Reverse discrimination prejudice or bias against a class or person for the purpose of correcting discrimination against another class or person.

Revolution rapid change, often accompanied by violence.

Right to counsel entitlement of an accused person to have an attorney present during questioning or trial.

Rights individual liberties protected by the state or federal constitutions.

Rights of Englishmen an expression of the American colonists during their struggle with England; they claimed to want only the same liberties and privileges enjoyed by British subjects in England, as established by Magna Carta, common law, and the English Bill of Rights, including habeas corpus, trial by jury, and representation in Parliament.

Rights of the accused include the 5th Amendment guarantee against self-incrimination and the right to counsel; also known as "Miranda rights," after the Supreme Court decision in the case of *Miranda* v. *Arizona* (1966).

Roaring Twenties the 1920s, during which the United States returned to "normalcy" after World War I, with rapid economic expansion, changed social values, high spending for consumer goods, and the popularization of the automobile, radio, and motion pictures.

Roosevelt Corollary supplement to the Monroe Doctrine asserted by President Theodore Roosevelt, who claimed the right of the United States to exercise international police power in the Western Hemisphere and to intervene in the affairs of Latin American nations.

"Rule of Reason" term used by the Supreme Court in its decision in the case of *Standard Oil Co.* v. *United States* (1911), which held that only "bad" trusts were illegal.

Ruling an official decision.

Salutary neglect phrase describing the belief that the American colonies benefited from lack of interest in their affairs by the British government during the period before 1763.

Sanctuary place of refuge or protection.

Satellite state a nation controlled by a more powerful nation.

Scopes trial the trial of John T. Scopes in Dayton, Tennessee, in 1925 for violating a state law prohibiting the teaching of Darwinian evolution. The highly publicized trial featured William Jennings Bryan as prosecutor and Clarence Darrow for the defense. Scopes was found guilty and fined $100.

Search and seizure police power to look for and hold evidence in the investigation and prosecution of a crime; evidence from unreasonable searches or searches without probable cause may be excluded from a trial.

Secession withdrawal of a member from a political group; withdrawal of a state from the Union.

Second-class citizenship condition of having fewer or inferior rights and privileges.

Sectionalism development of internal divisions based on geographic and economic alliances; rivalry between different areas of the country.

Securities and Exchange Commission federal agency established in 1934 to regulate the stock market and to prevent the abuses practiced during the 1920s that led to the stock market crash of 1929.

Security safety; freedom from danger.

Sedition the act of stirring up rebellion against a government.

Segregation the isolation or separation of one group from another, usually applied to keeping whites and blacks apart.

Senate the part of the federal legislature made up of two members from each state.

Separate but equal legal doctrine established by the Supreme Court in the case of *Plessy* v. *Ferguson* (1896) that separate accommodations for blacks and whites did not violate the Fourteenth Amendment if the accommodations were of equal quality. Overruled by the later Supreme Court decision in *Brown* v. *Board of Education* (1954).

Separation of church and state doctrine that government may not restrict the free exercise of religious beliefs nor support any religious group or principle.

Separation of powers doctrine that liberty of the people is best assured by the division of government into separate branches. *See also* Checks and balances.

Sexual harassment policy or practice of compelling female employees to submit to the sexual advances of male superiors or to endure verbal or physical harassment, in violation of the Civil Rights Act of 1964.

Sharecroppers tenant farmers who leased and cultivated pieces of land in exchange for a percentage of the crop.

Shays' Rebellion armed insurrection in western Massachusetts in the fall of 1786 led by Captain Daniel Shays and others in protest against economic policies and foreclosures of farms for failure to pay taxes. It was suppressed by the state militia, but it had a significant effect on the framing of the Constitution the following summer.

Sherman Antitrust Act passed in 1890 declaring combinations in restraint of trade to be illegal; it was passed to maintain competition in private industry and to correct abuses of companies that had gained monopoly power.

Sit-in action of protesters in occupying a public place to force concessions; especially by civil rights advocates seeking desegregation of public facilities.

Slavery system of holding persons against their will for involuntary servitude; in a system of "chattel slavery" the person held could be bought or sold as property. Slavery in the United States was abolished by the Thirteenth Amendment.

Smokestack industries heavy industries that burn large amounts of fossil fuels, such as steel-making or auto manufacturing.

Social contract the implied agreement among individuals in a community or between the people and their rulers.

Socialism political philosophy advocating ownership and operation of the means of production (such as land, mines, factories) by society as a collective whole, with all members sharing in the work and benefits. Socialist economic systems usually include government ownership and operation of industries.

Social mobility movement up or down the class scale within a society.

Social Security Act passed in 1935 to provide an income for persons who are disabled or aged and for families without a wage earner; it has become the basic means of support for retired persons who lack private pensions from employers.

Social welfare organized services for helping disadvantaged people.

Sovereign holding supreme authority.

Sovereignty the ultimate power and authority to make laws, either directly or through representatives; in a democracy, sovereignty lies in the people.

Space satellite an object in space that orbits a planet or other body.

Special interest group or industry that seeks to influence government for its own benefit.

Speculation taking extreme risks in business or investing in hopes of earning large profits.

Spoils system system wherein government positions and offices are awarded to political supporters on the basis of party loyalty or service rather than qualification or merit; based on the

saying "To the victor go the spoils"; the system was replaced to some extent by the Civil Service, beginning in the 1880s.

Stamp Act enacted by Parliament in 1765, it required a tax stamp on all printed and legal documents. It was soon repealed after American resistance.

Star-Spangled Banner the name by which the flag of the United States is known.

Statehood condition of being a state and a full member of the United States; for example, Hawaii achieved statehood in 1959.

States' rights group of doctrines holding that the states retained the power to overrule, oppose, or withdraw from the federal government if they chose.

Stock market crash a rapid fall in the price of stocks. The great crash of 1929 was caused by overspeculation that increased stock prices far above their true value; prices started to fall when knowledgeable investors began to sell their shares; that forced speculators, who had invested with borrowed money, to sell as well, and the combined rush to sell caused a panic, which drove prices even lower.

Stocks certificates showing shares of ownership in a corporation.

Strict construction doctrine that the Constitution limits governmental powers to those explicitly stated; contrast with Loose construction.

Strike work stoppage by labor in an attempt to force the employer to make concessions.

Subjugation the act of bringing under control.

Subpoena official written order commanding a person to appear in court or to produce specific items.

Subsidiary in business, a company that is controlled by another company.

Subterranean below the surface of the earth.

Subversion the undermining, overthrowing, or destroying of an established institution, such as government.

Suffrage the right to vote.

Supremacy the highest power or authority.

Supremacy clause portion of the Constitution declaring it "the supreme law of the land" and overriding any state or local laws in conflict with it.

Supreme Court the highest court in the federal judicial branch.

Surcharge an extra charge.

Synthetic artificially produced or made by combinations of chemicals.

Tariff taxes on imports into a country to collect revenues or to protect domestic industries.

Teapot Dome federal oil reserve in Wyoming that was secretly and illegally leased to a financial backer of President Harding.

Technology applied science used in production.

Temperance moderation in the consumption of alcoholic beverages; a movement supporting governmental measures to curb alcohol consumption.

Tennessee Valley Authority federal public works project established in 1933 that constructed dams and reengineered waterways to control flooding and generate electricity in seven Southern states.

Tenure the act or right of holding an office.

Third parties political parties existing at various times in the United States other than the two predominant political parties.

Third World the group of nations, especially in Asia and Africa, that were not aligned with either the Communist bloc or the Western democracies.

Three-fifths clause clause in the Constitution saying that three fifths of the number of persons held as slaves be included in calculating representation in Congress, even though those persons were not citizens and were not entitled to vote. Superceded by the Fourteenth Amendment.

Tories supporters of British rule during the Revolutionary War; also known as Loyalists. In England, and in Canada, the Tory party generally supported the king or conservative interests.

Totalitarian characterized by the government's having total control over the lives of citizens.

Town meeting meeting of the citizens of a town as a legislative body.

Trade deficit the amount by which imports exceed exports; how much is owed to other nations.

Trade gap difference in amount between imports and exports.

Treason acts that intentionally endanger the security or sovereignty of one's own nation; waging war against one's country or giving aid to its enemies.

Triangular trade pattern of commerce pursued in the late 18th and early 19th centuries by New England merchants who carried sugar and molasses from the West Indies to New England, rum and manufactured goods from New England to Africa, and slaves from Africa to the West Indies.

Truman Doctrine policy announced by President Truman in 1947, stating that the United States would provide military and economic aid to nations threatened by subversion or invasion; it was established specifically to assist Greece and Turkey, which were threatened with communist takeover.

Trust a combination of companies or industries established to reduce competition and increase profits.

Turnout the number of eligible voters who participate in an election.

Tyranny absolute and arbitrary power without legal restraints.

Unconditional surrender total surrender without exceptions or conditions; the phrase was made popular by Ulysses S. Grant.

Unconstitutional prohibited by or in opposition to the principles of the Constitution.

Underclass class of the permanently poor.

Unemployment being out of work; government compensation to people who have lost their jobs.

Unicameral of a legislature, having only one house or chamber.

Union 1) the political combination of the states; 2) the northern and border states that opposed secession during the Civil War; 3) an organization of workers seeking collective bargaining with their employer.

United Nations an organization of over 150 nations formed in 1945 to deal with international disputes and threats to world peace.

Universal suffrage the right of all citizens to vote, regardless of sex, race, or economic status.

Unwritten Constitution governmental practices and institutions not specifically set down in the Constitution but based upon custom and practice.

Urbanization the growth of cities and the increasing concentration of population in them.

Utilities companies that furnish electric power, water, gas, or other services without competition and are regulated by law.

Utopian advocating impossibly idealistic or impractical forms of government or society.

Versailles Treaty peace treaty signed in 1919 between Germany and the Allies; it required Germany to give up its colonies, pay substantial reparations, and surrender territory to France, Poland, and Czechoslovakia.

Veto action by an executive official preventing the enactment of a legislative act. A veto by the President can be overridden by a two-thirds majority of Congress. *See* Pocket veto.

VISTA Volunteers in Service to America, a program of President Johnson's 1964 Economic Opportunity Act.

War on Poverty President Johnson's domestic programs for social renovation, including the VISTA, Job Corps, and Head Start programs and the establishing of the Department of Housing and Urban Development.

War Powers Act law passed in 1973 to limit the power of the President to use armed forces in combat without the authorization of Congress; it was adopted in response to the Vietnam War, in which millions of armed forces were sent to Vietnam without a declaration of war.

Watergate hotel in Washington, D.C., where the national Democratic party headquarters were burglarized in 1972 by operatives of the Republican Committee to Reelect the President (Nixon). Attempts by the staff of the White House to cover up their links to the burglars eventually led to a widespread scandal and the resignation of President Nixon.

Whigs in the United States from around 1800 until the Civil War, a political party opposed to the Jeffersonian Republicans and Jacksonian Democrats. Many of its supporters later joined the Republican party. In England, the Whig party generally opposed the extension of the king's power and supported the predominance of Parliament.

Whiskey Rebellion armed insurrection in 1792 by settlers in western Pennsylvania and Virginia protesting federal excise tax on distilled spirits (whiskey). Suppressed by federal troops under Washington, who pardoned most of the participants.

Work ethic belief in the value and moral good of productive labor.

Yalta Agreements agreements reached between Roosevelt, Churchill, and Stalin at Yalta in February 1945, regarding the organization of postwar Europe in anticipation of the defeat of Germany. The agreements divided Germany and Berlin into temporary zones of occupation and established the basis for the United Nations.

Yellow journalism irresponsible, sensational, or misleading reporting of news.

REGENTS EXAMINATION

Part I (55 credits)

Answer all 47 questions in this part.

Directions (1–47): For each statement or question, write on the separate answer sheet the *number* of the word or expression that, of those given, best completes the statement or answers the question.

1 The United States Constitution has been more successful than the Articles of Confederation were because the Constitution is more effective in

1 providing for the admission of new states
2 setting up a two-house legislature
3 making a federal system work well
4 establishing an army and a navy

2 Which aspect of United States government was most influenced by 18th-century Enlightenment philosophy?

1 Three-fifths Compromise
2 the Federal court system
3 the original provision for selection of Senators
4 separation of powers

3 The United States Supreme Court under Chief Justice John Marshall established the precedent that the Court has the power to

1 guarantee civil rights
2 declare a law of Congress unconstitutional
3 reduce the delegated powers of Congress
4 apply the principle of executive privilege

4 The elastic clause of the United States Constitution allows for

1 adaptability of congressional power
2 expansion of Presidential powers
3 judicial review
4 expansion of States rights

5 In the United States Constitution as it was originally written, the methods of selecting the President and Federal judges provide evidence that the framers of the Constitution

1 were strong believers in direct democracy
2 believed the executive branch should hold the greatest power
3 did not fully trust voters to make good decisions
4 wished to deny the states any role in selecting Federal officials

6 Which action is the best example of checks and balances?

1 President Ronald Reagan ordering a military attack on Libya
2 the Supreme Court ruling that President Richard Nixon must surrender the Watergate tapes
3 the 26th amendment giving 18-year-old citizens the right to vote
4 the House of Representatives voting to censure one of its members

7 One impact of the electoral college system on the election process is that this system encourages candidates to

1 concentrate their major campaign efforts in the most populous states
2 focus most of their attention on influencing Members of the House of Representatives
3 find ways to persuade electors to cast their ballots for them rather than for the opposing candidates
4 campaign in each of the 50 states

8 The United States Constitution requires that revenue bills begin in the House of Representatives instead of in the Senate. This provision was included because the House of Representatives

1 has more experts on finance and can best decide how money should be spent
2 has sole control over the banking system
3 is usually controlled by lawmakers who can raise popular support for spending programs
4 is more directly accountable to the voters

9 Sectional rivalries during the period from 1820 to 1860 centered mainly around the issues of

1 foreign policy, the abolition of slavery, and the currency system
2 States rights, the extension of slavery, and tariffs
3 tariffs, the currency system, and trust regulation
4 conservation, foreign policy, and women's suffrage

10 In the late 1800s, which action led to an increase in violations of the rights of African Americans?

1 addition of the 13th, 14th, and 15th amendments to the Federal Constitution
2 integration of public facilities such as restaurants and restrooms
3 passage of Jim Crow legislation by some Southern states
4 start of affirmative action programs by the Federal Government

11 Booker T. Washington and W.E.B. DuBois differed in their approach to equality for African Americans mainly in regard to the

1 speed with which African Americans could expect integration and social change to occur
2 use of violence to achieve their goals
3 importance of voting rights and education
4 necessity of African Americans to help themselves

12 United States interest in overseas expansion in the late 19th century was based mainly on the desire to

1 achieve greater cultural diversity
2 attain new sources of raw materials and new markets
3 spread Christianity to Latin America and the Philippines
4 acquire new lands to ease population pressures at home

13 In the late 19th and early 20th centuries, farmers generally supported

1 less government interference with business
2 nationalization of major industries
3 cheap money policies to raise prices
4 government-sponsored communes

14 In the late 1800s, the outcome of most strikes showed that labor unions

1 successfully used violence to solve labor problems
2 had government support to improve working conditions
3 benefited both workers and management in their efforts to unionize
4 lacked popular and political support

15 Which development was most likely the cause of the other three?

1 growth of urban centers
2 growth of industrialization
3 increase in the middle class
4 increase in agricultural production

16 In the United States, the Federal Reserve System tries to encourage economic stability and growth by

1 controlling the availability of money and credit
2 guarding against securities and exchange abuses
3 regulating the flow of imports
4 controlling wages and prices

17 In the United States, a basic assumption of a progressive tax is that

1 each American should pay an equal share of the tax burden
2 each family is entitled to a minimum standard of living
3 people with higher incomes should pay a greater percentage of their income in taxes
4 ownership of property is the best indicator of a citizen's ability to pay

18 Many of the reforms of the Populist and Progressive parties were not adopted until after these parties ceased to exist. Which is the best explanation for this fact?

1 The reform ideas were not well thought out or well organized.
2 These parties were minority parties and did not reflect the views of the majority at the time.
3 Government could not provide the money necessary to fund these reforms.
4 Business and industry took strong measures to improve their practices without government regulation.

19 Cartoons by Thomas Nast and books such as Upton Sinclair's *The Jungle* illustrate how the arts in the United States

1 created demands for reform in society
2 were just beginning to reach mass audiences
3 generally centered on themes from nature
4 still lagged behind European standards

20 A primary objective of President Theodore Roosevelt was to

1 promote industrial expansion abroad
2 support the rights of African Americans in the segregated South
3 reform the schools of the nation
4 awaken public interest in conservation efforts

21 Abolitionists conservationists, and civil rights advocates have generally promoted

1 government ownership of business and economic equality for all citizens
2 increased participation of the Federal Government in solving social problems
3 withdrawal of United States troops from foreign nations
4 the use of violence to achieve social justice

22 In *Schenck* v. *United States*, the Supreme Court decided that a "clear and present danger" to the United States permitted

1 the expansion of Presidential power in time of peace
2 the establishment of a peacetime draft
3 restrictions of first amendment rights
4 limitations on the voting rights of minorities

23 A major feature of the immigration legislation of the 1920s is that this legislation

1 gave preference to immigrants from northern and western Europe
2 encouraged Asians to migrate to the United States
3 provided equal quotas for all nations
4 restricted immigration from countries that were enemies of the United States in World War I

24 Domestic legislation under President Theodore Roosevelt's Square Deal was similar to domestic legislation under President Franklin D. Roosevelt's New Deal in that both

1 attempted to apply laissez-faire theories to the United States economy
2 were based on the belief that the Federal Government has some responsibility for the general welfare of the people
3 stressed the responsibility of individuals for their own economic well-being
4 advocated government ownership of industry

25 Which feature of the economic boom of the 1920s contributed most to the stock market crash of 1929?

1 increased use of the automobile
2 growth of the entertainment industry
3 use of new energy sources
4 speculation in real estate and other investments

26 What was the primary focus of United States foreign policy in the decade after World War I?

1 to defend the principle of freedom of the seas
2 to reduce United States commitments to other nations
3 to contain the spread of communism in Eastern Europe
4 to fulfill collective security agreements with Western European nations

27 Which fundamental economic problem of farmers did New Deal policies attempt to solve?

1 overproduction
2 scarcity of fertile land
3 shortage of labor
4 lack of transportation facilities

Base your answer to question 28 on the graph below and on your knowledge of social studies.

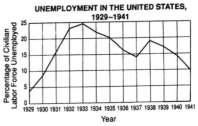

UNEMPLOYMENT IN THE UNITED STATES, 1929–1941

Source: U.S. Dept. of Labor

28 Which statement is best supported by the information in the graph?

1 The New Deal had no effect in reducing unemployment.
2 Unemployment reached its peak within a year after the stock market crash.
3 Unemployment was a major issue in the Presidential election of 1932.
4 Increased production in the early stages of World War II had little effect on unemployment.

Base your answer to question 29 on the cartoon below and on your knowledge of social studies.

Some Day They'll Come Crawling Back to Her

Source: Joseph Parrish. The Tribune (Chicago), 1949.
(adapted)

29 The cartoon is most critical of the United States policy of

1 involvement in international affairs
2 reliance on the political party system
3 continued isolationism
4 dependency on foreign nations

30 "There are too many foreigners and undesirables coming into the United States. Let's pull up the ladder."
This statement best illustrates the concept of
1 populism
2 social mobility
3 nativism
4 reverse discrimination

31 "The seeds of World War II were sown earlier in the 20th century."
Which statement does this quotation most strongly support?
1 United States involvement in Europe after World War I created an atmosphere of mistrust.
2 The United States was not successful in stopping Soviet expansion by peaceful means.
3 The European democracies encouraged Adolf Hitler to rearm Germany.
4 The World War I peace settlement created bitterness and resentment.

Base your answers to questions 32 and 33 on the graphs below and on your knowledge of social studies.

Federal Spending—1957 and 1987

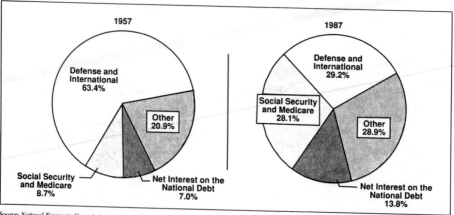

Source: National Economic Commission.
(adapted)

32 Based on the information in the graphs, a valid conclusion is that between 1957 and 1987
1 Federal spending priorities changed significantly
2 the amount of income taxes paid by the average wage earner increased dramatically
3 the size of the workforce decreased
4 the Federal Government succeeded in collecting and spending its revenue more efficiently

33 The change in interest on the national debt between 1957 and 1987 is an indication that the United States has
1 become a creditor nation
2 increased its borrowing
3 developed a new source of income
4 adopted an austerity spending program

34 The World War II experience of Japanese-American citizens is evidence that
1 individual liberties may be threatened by the perceived need for national security
2 constitutional rights are upheld equally in peacetime and in wartime
3 Presidents should regard the national interest as more important than human rights
4 minorities are generally unwilling to help in a war effort

35 The North Atlantic Treaty Organization (NATO) and the Truman Doctrine were attempts to carry out a United States foreign policy of
1 brinksmanship   3 appeasement
2 containment   4 neutrality

36 "Wilson Orders Controls on U.S. Industry To Fight War Against Germany"
"FDR OK's Destroyer Deal with England To Fight Sub Threat"
"Truman Orders Airlift of Supplies to Berlin"

Which generalization about governmental power in the United States is supported by these headlines?
1 Important Presidential decisions usually follow the results of public opinion polls.
2 Presidential actions during international crises have increased executive power.
3 Foreign policy is ultimately determined by Congress' power to allocate funds.
4 Presidential power to act in wartime cannot be exercised without bipartisan support.

37 The Supreme Court under Chief Justice Earl Warren had a major impact on the United States in that this Court

1 became involved in foreign affairs by reviewing the constitutionality of treaties
2 weakened the judiciary by refusing to deal with controversial issues
3 supported the idea that states could nullify acts of Congress
4 followed a policy of judicial activism, leading to broad changes in American society

38 After 58 years, the Supreme Court reversed the decision in *Plessy* v. *Ferguson* (1896) and declared that

1 accused persons must be read their rights at the time of arrest
2 free speech does not extend to shouting "Fire!" in a crowded theater
3 the doctrine of separate but equal" is unconstitutional
4 prayer in public schools is unconstitutional

39 The purpose of President Richard Nixon's diplomatic initiatives toward China in 1972 was to

1 end the United States relationship with the government of Taiwan
2 establish military bases on Chinese territory
3 eliminate Communist rule in China
4 counteract growing Soviet power and influence in Asia

40 Today, the stated goal of the Federal Government policy toward Native American Indians is

1 tribal self-government and economic development
2 the end of reservations
3 assimilation and the end of their traditional values
4 resettlement into urban areas and industrial jobs

41 Which demographic trend has occurred in the United States during the past 10 years?

1 The average age of the population has decreased.
2 The birthrate has rapidly increased.
3 Life expectancy has decreased.
4 The proportion of the population over age 65 has grown.

Base your answer to question 42 on the cartoon below and on your knowledge of social studies.

APPARENTLY THEY'D JUST ACHIEVED TOTAL DISARMAMENT AND THEN SOME HOLE IN THE OZONE LAYER GOT THEM...

NO NUKES

Laxman/Times of India/New Delhi

42 The main idea of this cartoon is that

1 the world will not be able to recover from a nuclear war
2 global pollution may be just as deadly as nuclear warfare
3 science and technology must be regulated by the government
4 efforts to achieve global disarmament are doomed to failure

43 During the 20th century, a major change in agriculture in the United States has been

1 an increase in the number of large-scale farming enterprises
2 an increase in the percentage of families engaged in farming
3 a decrease in overall food production
4 a decrease in per capita productivity

44 In the United States today, legal rights specifically guaranteed to women have resulted primarily from

1 the historic influence of France on United States affairs
2 laws adopted during the colonial period
3 the provisions of the original Constitution
4 many years of political and social activism

45 The practice of gerrymandering is intended to
  1 strengthen the power of a particular party
  2 reduce the number of voters
  3 affect only the Senate and the House of Representatives
  4 reduce the size of the electoral college

46 Political parties, judicial review, and lobbying are similar in that all
  1 became part of the government through constitutional amendments
  2 are examples of direct democracy
  3 illustrate the division of powers established in the Constitution
  4 are aspects of the unwritten Constitution

47 Which Presidential action was perceived as a threat to the system of checks and balances?
  1 George Washington's appointments to his Cabinet
  2 Abraham Lincoln's issuance of the Emancipation Proclamation
  3 Franklin D. Roosevelt's plan to increase the size of the Supreme Court
  4 Ronald Reagan's supply-side economic proposals

Answers to the following questions are to be written on paper provided by the school.

Students Please Note:

In developing your answers to Parts II and III, be sure to

(1) include specific factual information and evidence whenever possible
(2) keep to the questions asked; do not go off on tangents
(3) avoid overgeneralizations or sweeping statements without sufficient proof; do not overstate your case
(4) keep these general definitions in mind:
  (a) <u>discuss</u> means "to make observations about something using facts, reasoning, and argument; to present in some detail"
  (b) <u>describe</u> means "to illustrate something in words or tell about it"
  (c) <u>show</u> means "to point out; to set forth clearly a position or idea by stating it and giving data which support it"
  (d) <u>explain</u> means "to make plain or understandable; to give reasons for or causes of; to show the logical development or relationships of"

Part II

ANSWER ONE QUESTION FROM THIS PART. [15]

1 The Constitutional Convention of 1787 used compromise to address conflicts over major issues facing the new nation. Some of these issues are listed below.

Issues
Representation
States rights
Slavery
Tariffs
Civil liberties
Taxation

Choose *three* of the issues listed and for *each* one chosen:

• Describe a conflict that arose over the issue at the Constitutional Convention
• Explain how that issue was resolved through the use of compromise [5,5,5]

2 Civil rights for Americans have been guaranteed by the United States Constitution, court decisions, and legislation. In practice, some groups still do not enjoy the full benefits of their civil rights. Some of these groups are listed below.

Groups
Women
African Americans
Immigrants
Homosexuals
Native American Indians
Persons with disabilities

Choose *three* of the groups listed and for *each* one chosen:

• Discuss a specific problem this group is facing today in attempting to exercise their civil rights
• Describe a specific government action that has attempted to resolve the problem [5,5,5]

Part III

ANSWER TWO QUESTIONS FROM THIS PART. [15]

3 In the 1800s, the emergence of big business organizations brought about major changes in the United States.
 a Describe *two* economic conditions or historical trends in the United States in the 1800s that led to the development of big business. [6]
 b Describe *one* positive and *one* negative change brought about by the growth of big business. [6]
 c State *one* specific governmental response to the *negative* change discussed in part *b*. [3]

4 The United States has become involved in armed conflict for various reasons. Some of these conflicts are listed below.

Conflicts
Spanish-American War
World War I
World War II
Korean War
Vietnam conflict
Persian Gulf War

Choose *three* of the armed conflicts listed and for *each* one chosen:

- Discuss *one* specific political *or* economic *or* social reason for United States involvement in the conflict
- Describe *one* political *or* economic *or* social impact on the United States that resulted from its involvement in the conflict [5,5,5]

5 Changing historical conditions have led to the development of specific inventions. These inventions have had a lasting impact on American society.

Inventions
Cotton gin—1793
Steamboat—1807
Sewing machine—1846
Telephone— 1876
Television—20th century
Computer—20th century

Choose *three* inventions from the list above and for *each* one chosen:

- Describe historical conditions that led to the development of the invention
- Discuss *two* effects of these inventions on American society [5,5,5]

6 Listed below are several reform movements that have affected the United States.

Reform Movements
Abolitionism
Labor unionism
Populism
Progressivism
Environmentalism
Consumerism

Choose *three* of the reform movements listed and for *each* one chosen:

- Discuss a condition that created the need for reform
- Identify a specific reform proposed by the movement
- Discuss the extent to which this reform affected American society [5,5,5]

7 The themes and issues in the works of individual writers, artists, and musicians have had an impact on American society. Several individuals are listed below according to category.

Writers:	James Fenimore Cooper
	Henry David Thoreau
	Theodore Dreiser
	Langston Hughes
	Jack Kerouac
	Betty Friedan
Visual Artists:	Matthew Brady
	Frederick Remington
	Norman Rockwell
	Ansel Adams
	Grandma Moses
	Andy Warhol
Musicians:	Scott Joplin
	Duke Ellington
	Aaron Copland
	Elvis Presley
	Bob Dylan
	John Denver

Choose *one* individual from *each* category and for *each* individual chosen:

- Identify a specific theme or issue that is a focus of the individual's work
- Discuss how the individual's treatment of the theme or issue had an impact on American society [5,5,5]

REGENTS EXAMINATION

Part I (55 credits)

Answer all 48 questions in this part.

Directions (1–48): For each statement or question, write on the separate answer sheet the *number* of the word or expression that, of those given, best completes the statement or answers the question.

1 Which feature of the United States system of government is the most essential aspect of democracy?

1 judicial supremacy
2 a bicameral legislature
3 a powerful executive
4 freedom of choice

2 One reason for the importance of the Federalist Papers in United States history is that these writings

1 helped persuade some states to ratify the United States Constitution
2 convinced the colonists to rebel against Great Britain
3 presented the first legal arguments in favor of retaining slavery
4 outlined plans for the geographic expansion of the United States

3 Which provision of the United States Constitution has been most significant in broadening the powers of the Federal Government?

1 "All bills for raising revenue shall originate in the House of Representatives. . . ."
2 "The Congress shall have power . . . to make all laws which shall be necessary and proper for carrying into execution the foregoing powers, ..."
3 "The Senate shall have the sole power to try all impeachments . . . When the President of the United States is tried, the Chief Justice shall preside; . . ."
4 "Each house shall be the judge of the elections, returns, and qualifications of its own members, and a majority of each shall constitute a quorum to do business; . . . ."

4 Which headline is the best example of the application of the system of checks and balances?

1 "President Truman Fires General MacArthur"
2 "Senate To Debate Abortion Funding Bill"
3 "Supreme Court Nominee Rejected by Senate"
4 "House of Representatives Votes To Discipline Its Own Member"

5 In the United States, only the Federal Government has the power to

1 pass laws
2 borrow money
3 tax
4 make treaties

6 When John Marshall was Chief Justice, the Supreme Court's interpretations of the Constitution gave power to the

1 Congress to override a Presidential veto
2 Supreme Court to declare acts of Congress and state laws unconstitutional
3 House of Representatives to impeach the President
4 President to veto a bill

7 In the decisions made in *Miranda v. Arizona* and *Gideon v. Wainwright*, the United States Supreme Court has

1 supported a strict interpretation of the Constitution
2 allowed the states to define due process
3 expanded the rights of the accused
4 extended Federal protection of voting rights

8 The tariff issue of 1828, the secession of the Southern states in the 1860s, and school desegregation in the 1950's dealt with the constitutional issue of

1 the federal-state relationship
2 popular sovereignty
3 checks and balances
4 representation in Congress

9 The passage of the 13th, 14th, and 15th amendments in the period following the Civil War showed that

1 the states had increased their power at the expense of the Federal Government
2 segregation would no longer be allowed in the United States
3 Federal powers could be expanded to protect the rights of minorities
4 the political and economic rights of women were protected

10 Which event was the immediate cause of the secession of several Southern states from the Union in 1860?

1 the Dred Scott decision, which declared that all prior compromises on the extension of slavery into the territories were unconstitutional
2 the Missouri Compromise, which kept an even balance between the number of free and slave states
3 the raid on the Federal arsenal at Harper's Ferry, which was led by the militant abolitionist John Brown
4 the election of President Abraham Lincoln, who opposed the spread of slavery into the territories

11 A major result of the Reconstruction period was that

1 the former Confederate states were restored to full membership in the Union
2 most African Americans were able to take advantage of education at colleges and universities
3 the two-party political system became stronger in the South
4 sectional differences and the idea of States rights disappeared

12 In United States society in the late 19th century, the increase in cultural pluralism can be attributed to

1 an established religion and the use of the English language
2 the rise of nativism and the Ku Klux Klan
3 the establishment of the reservation system for Native Americans
4 different immigration patterns and industrialization

13 In the United States, corporations became the dominant form of business organization in the late 19th century mainly because

1 government regulated their development
2 industries needed large amounts of capital
3 proprietorships became too complex to run
4 large numbers of jobs were needed for the immigrants

14 The major purpose of the Sherman Antitrust Act was to

1 promote free competition in the marketplace
2 stop the growth of corporations
3 increase management's power over labor
4 disband large corporations

15 In the United States, which development was a result of the other three?

1 unsanitary working conditions in factories
2 unequal distribution of profits between management and workers
3 formation of labor unions
4 12-hour workday

16 Which is an accurate statement about the labor union movement in the United States?

1 Unions frequently support lockouts and open shops to secure their goals.
2 In the last decade, large labor unions have changed the focus of their demands from increased wages and fringe benefits to a focus on job security.
3 Unions are more powerful today than they have ever been.
4 Membership in unions has steadily increased over the past 10 years.

17 The Supreme Court decision in *Plessy v. Ferguson* (1896) had a major impact on United States history because the decision

1 eliminated the power of the states in the area of civil rights
2 abolished the equal protection clause of the Federal Constitution
3 provided a constitutional basis for segregation laws
4 extended African-American voting rights

18 After the Civil War, Native Americans were relocated to reservations primarily because

1 the Federal Government wanted to preserve tribal cultures
2 the Native Americans had violated most of their treaties with the Federal Government
3 most of the tribal chiefs requested government protection from white settlers
4 settlers, ranchers, and prospectors wanted their tribal lands

19 During the late 1800s, which group in American society most strongly supported the Greenback and Populist parties?

1 industrial workers
2 farmers
3 women
4 consumers

20 The primary contribution of the muckrakers in the late 1800s and early 1900s was to

1 promote the ideals of rugged individualism and laissez faire
2 lobby the Federal Government to open more free land to western settlement
3 expose corruption and negligence on the part of big business and government
4 encourage public support for the building of the Panama Canal

21 Which justification has Congress frequently used for raising United States tariff rates?

1 protecting the jobs of American workers
2 helping American manufacturers to export products
3 increasing the variety and quality of goods available to Americans
4 punishing American industries for their low productivity

22 Automobiles, radio, motion pictures, and television are technological advances of the 20th century. These inventions affect American life because they

1 are less popular than had been anticipated
2 tend to standardize American culture
3 have little impact on traditional lifestyles and values
4 are generally too expensive for ordinary working people

23 In the early 1900's, a common belief held by most Progressives was that

1 deficit spending was essential to raise capital needed for reforms
2 Federal ownership of industry was necessary to correct society's problems
3 a return to a weak central government would encourage business leaders to eliminate abuses
4 legislation could help solve social and economic problems

24 Which statement most accurately summarizes United States policies toward Latin American nations during the late 19th and early 20th centuries?

1 As sovereign nations, Latin American countries were never occupied by the United States.
2 Emigration from Latin American nations was encouraged.
3 The United States protected its interests in Latin American countries with military and diplomatic actions.
4 The United States discouraged American investment in Latin American nations.

25 The purpose of the Open Door policy was to

1 encourage European nations to increase their investments in Asian nations
2 announce a change in United States policy toward immigration from Asia
3 improve trading opportunities in China for United States businesses
4 urge China to lower its protective tariffs

26 One long-term result of the industrialization of the United States has been

1 an improvement in the standard of living for many Americans
2 sharp increases in the prices of manufactured goods
3 a decline in the importance of education
4 the disappearance of class and social distinctions

27 In the 1920s, the belief in never-ending prosperity helped to promote

1 a renewal of interest in handmade goods
2 strict enforcement of governmental financial regulations
3 massive government efforts to increase the incomes of farmers
4 heavy increases in stock speculation

28 Which statement expresses the New Deal philosophy about the role of government?

1 In a capitalist economy, the main duty of the government is to protect business profits.
2 Government should control the prices of goods and services.
3 Government must become involved in the economy to benefit the people.
4 Balancing the budget is more important than creating jobs.

29 President Franklin D. Roosevelt's controversy with the Supreme Court was a result of

1 the requirement that all judges must retire at age 70
2 his belief that the Court was too liberal in its interpretations
3 the Court's unwillingness to accept difficult cases
4 the Court's opposition to several New Deal laws

30 During the late 1930s, which factor most influenced the United States to change its policies of isolationism and neutrality?

1 concern about the aggressive behavior of Germany, Italy, and Japan
2 need to prevent the spread of communism by the Soviet Union
3 desire to strengthen the League of Nations
4 need to protect vital sources of oil in the Middle East

31 During World War I and World War II, the domestic policies of the United States Government led to

1 increased imports
2 increased economic controls
3 greater consumer spending
4 reduced interest rates

32 Which title would be the most appropriate heading for the list below?

I. _____

    A. Suspension of Habeas Corpus
    B. Espionage and Sedition Acts
    C. Internment of Japanese Americans

1 Problems of Immigration
2 Wartime Constitutional Issues
3 Preparations for War
4 United States Foreign Policy

33 The United States became the "arsenal of democracy" in the early 1940s because the United States

1 possessed the economic resources to produce massive amounts of war material
2 introduced a series of strict draft laws
3 had established strong alliances with other countries during the 1920s and the early 1930s
4 relied on the nation's strong tradition of militarism

34 The Truman Doctrine and the Berlin Airlift were examples of the United States foreign policy of

1 colonialism   3 nonalignment
2 détente   4 containment

35 The circumstances surrounding the Red Scare after World War I and the blacklisting of certain actors and writers during the McCarthy Era show that

1 even in a society guided by constitutional rights, mass hysteria can effectively deny people due process of law
2 no matter what influenced the times, the United States has consistently applied the guarantees of the Bill of Rights
3 demands of minorities for racial equality have been increasingly ignored in the 20th century
4 the courts are rarely influenced by public fears and political events

36 A major effect of the rapid technological changes since 1945 has been

1 decreased economic competition between producer nations
2 a growing degree of isolationism
3 greater interdependence in the international marketplace
4 a reduction of the influence of democratic nations in world affairs

37 A major goal of President Lyndon Johnson's Great Society was to

1 make the states rather than the Federal Government responsible for supporting social programs
2 reduce ethnic tensions in society by severely limiting immigration
3 reform society through expanded government social welfare programs
4 give priority to an increase in benefits for Vietnam War veterans

38 Which is a valid conclusion based on the history of third-party movements in the United States?

1 Third parties usually capture large numbers of electoral votes.
2 Third-party ideas that were once considered extreme can become mainstream.
3 Third parties frequently become one of the two major parties.
4 Single-issue parties tend to dominate United States politics.

Base your answer to question 39 on the cartoon below and on your knowledge of social studies.

A Good Time for Reflection

Source: Library of Congress

39 The cartoon was encouraging the American public to

1 exercise caution regarding involvement in European conflicts
2 demand repayment of World War II debts owed by European nations
3 support countries resisting Communist aggression
4 provide food to Eastern Europe

40 Which action in United States history is an example of civil disobedience?

1 The National Association for the Advancement of Colored People (NAACP) filed suit against the state of Kansas for violating the constitutional rights of students in public schools.
2 The Congress of Racial Equality (CORE) supported efforts to have the courts order the desegregation of buses and trains in the South.
3 The Southern Christian Leadership Conference (SCLC) organized a boycott in Montgomery, Alabama, until transportation facilities were integrated.
4 In Montgomery, Alabama, Rosa Parks refused to give up her seat on a bus to a white man.

41 As a result of the experience in the Vietnam War, Congress attempted to

1 increase the number of men drafted into the military
2 take a larger role in shaping foreign policy
3 recall nearly all United States troops stationed overseas
4 force the President to increase aid to Southeast Asia

42 The resolution of the Watergate affair was significant because it reinforced the idea that in the United States the

1 Government is based on the rule of law, not on the rule of an individual
2 Chief Executive has nearly unlimited powers
3 Congress is not effective in dealing with a constitutional crisis
4 Supreme Court is afraid to make decisions involving the Presidency

43 The fundamental problem facing United States farmers since the end of World War II has been

1 the disappearance of fertile farmland
2 overproduction of agricultural goods
3 a steady rise in prices of agricultural products
4 a shortage of modern farm equipment

44 A major reason for the ending of the Cold War Era was that

1 the Soviet Union was seriously weakened by internal conflict and economic difficulties
2 the United States and the Soviet Union were unable to destroy one another
3 the Berlin Wall fell and Germany was reunited
4 a recession forced the United States to cut military spending

45 Membership in the United Nations demonstrates the United States commitment to a policy of

1 containment   3 global cooperation
2 neutrality   4 isolationism

46 Under current Federal laws, Americans with disabilities must be

1 placed in federally funded institutions near their homes
2 guaranteed access to public transportation and facilities
3 educated and supported by their families without governmental help
4 educated only until they complete the eighth grade

47 Which problem did immigrants to the United States face in both the 19th and 20th centuries?

1 Few jobs were available for them.
2 They had difficulty investing wealth brought from their homeland.
3 They were frequently discriminated against.
4 Their arrival led to a shortage of consumer product.

Base your answer to question 48 on the cartoon below and on your knowledge of social studies.

Friday, February 9, 1990

48 The main idea of the cartoon is that the United States economy is

1 decreasing its emphasis on energy conservation
2 expanding its demand for blue-collar workers
3 providing for the retraining of unemployed auto workers
4 experiencing a decline in the number of industrial jobs

Answers to the following questions are to be written on paper provided by the school.

Students Please Note:

In developing your answers to Parts II and III, be sure to

(1) include specific factual information and evidence whenever possible
(2) keep to the questions asked; do not go off on tangents
(3) avoid overgeneralizations or sweeping statements without sufficient proof; do not overstate your case
(4) keep these general definitions in mind:
  (a) _discuss_ means "to make observations about something using facts, reasoning, and argument; to present in some detail"
  (b) _describe_ means "to illustrate something in words or tell about it"
  (c) _show_ means "to point out; to set forth clearly a position or idea by stating it and giving data which support it"
  (d) _explain_ means "to make plain or understandable; to give reasons for or causes of; to show the logical development or relationships of"

Part II

ANSWER ONE QUESTION FROM THIS PART. [15]

1 Several aspects of the United States Presidential election process have been criticized. Some of these aspects are listed below.

Aspects of the Presidential Election Process
Electoral college
National conventions
Primary elections
Campaign funding
Party platform
Role of the media

Select _three_ of the aspects from the list and for _each_ one selected:

- Describe a criticism that was made about the aspect in any past Presidential election [Cite specific historical information to illustrate that criticism.]
- State _one_ solution that was adopted _or_ has been proposed to deal with that criticism of the Presidential election process [5,5,5]

2 Historically, the operations of Congress have been influenced by a number of factors. Some of these factors are listed below.

Factors That Have Influenced Congress
The committee system
Seniority
Political parties
Public opinion
Lobbying
The media

Select _three_ of the factors listed and for _each_ one selected:

- Explain how that factor influences how Congress operates
- Using a specific historical example, show how that factor has influenced an action of Congress [5,5,5]

Part III

ANSWER TWO QUESTIONS FROM THIS PART. [30]

3 The United States Government has followed different policies toward immigration during various time periods.

Time Periods
Prior to 1880
1880 to 1920
1920 to 1965
1965 to 1990
1990 to today

Choose _three_ of the time periods listed and for _each_ period chosen:
- Describe an immigration policy of the United States Government that was characteristic of that time period

- Explain why the United States followed this policy during the time period [5,5,5]

4 Geographic and climatic features of North America have had significant impacts on the development of the United States.

Identify _three_ different geographic and/or climatic features of North America. For _each_ one identified, describe _one_ economic and _one_ political impact that the feature has had on the development of the United States [5,5,5]

5 The cartoon below refers to the United States since the end of World War II (1945).

DO YOU THINK WE'RE STRETCHING IT A BIT THIN...?

U.S.   FOREIGN COMMITMENTS

Eldon Pletcher, Times-Picayune. Rothco.
(adapted)

a Using specific elements of the cartoon, identify an issue raised by the cartoonist. [3]
b Identify *two* different situations involving the United States that have occurred since the end of World War II (1945) in which this issue was raised. Show how the issue applied to *each* situation. [4,4]
c Discuss the extent to which the issue raised in the cartoon is valid today. [4]

6 The years 1991 through 1995 commemorate the 50th anniversary of United States involvement in World War II. That involvement had a lasting impact on areas of American life. Some of these areas of American life are listed below.

Areas of American Life
Population patterns or trends
Role of women
Science and technology
Status of African Americans
Education

Select *three* of the areas of American life listed and for *each* one selected:

- Show how United States involvement in World War II brought about change in that area of life
- Discuss how that area of life has continued to change since the end of World War II [5,5,5]

7 Excerpts from five songs are provided below. Each excerpt is paired with a time period.

a Select *three* of the excerpts provided. Describe how conditions in the United States during the indicated time period are reflected in the theme of the excerpt [4,4,4]
b Select any *one* excerpt provided. Explain how that excerpt reflects *or does not* reflect conditions in the United States today. [3]

Excerpt 1—1787–1865
When Israel was in Egypt's land;
Let my people go,
Oppressed so hard they could not stand,
Let my people go.

No more shall they in bondage toil;
Let my people go,
Let them come out with Egypt's spoil,
Let my people go.
Traditional Spiritual

Excerpt 2—1910–1920
. . . So prepare,
Say a prayer,
Send the word, send the word to beware
We'll be over,
We're coming over,
And we won't come back till it's over over there.
George M. Cohan, c 1917

Excerpt 3—1920–1940
They used to tell me I was building a dream,
And so I followed the mob.
When there was earth to plough or guns to bear,
I was always there, right there on the job,
They used to tell me I was building a dream,
With peace and glory ahead.
Why should I be standing in line just waiting for bread?

Once I built a railroad, made it run,
Made it race against time.
Once I built a railroad. Now it's done.
Brother, can you spare a dime?
Once I built a tower to the sun,
Brick and rivet and lime.
Once I built a tower. Now it's done.
Brother can you spare a dime?....
E.Y. Harburg, c 1932

Excerpt 4—1960–1975
Come mothers and fathers,
Throughout the land
And don't criticize
What you can't understand.
Your sons and your daughters
Are beyond your command
Your old road is
Rapidly agin'.
Please get out of the new one
If you can't lend your hand
For the times they are a-changing.
Bob Dylan, c 1963

Excerpt 5—1980–1990
What's the matter with the crowd I'm seeing?
"Don't you know that they're out of touch?"
Should I try to be a straight 'A' student?
"If you are then you think too much.
Don't you know about the new fashion honey?
All you need are looks and a whole lotta money." . . .
Billy Joel, c 1980

REGENTS EXAMINATION

Part I (55 credits)

Answer all 47 questions in this part.

Directions (1–47): For each statement or question, write on the separate answer sheet the *number* of the word or expression that, of those given, best completes the statement or answers the question.

1 In the 1780s, many Americans distrusted a strong central government. This distrust is best shown by the

1 lack of debate over the ratification of the United States Constitution
2 plan of government set up by the Articles of Confederation
3 development of a Federal court system
4 constitutional provision for a strong President

2 "We hold these truths to be self-evident: That all men are created equal; that they are endowed by their creator with certain unalienable rights; that among these are life, liberty, and the pursuit of happiness; . . ."

This quotation is evidence that some of the basic ideas in the Declaration of Independence were

1 imitations of the principles underlying most European governments of the 1700s
2 adaptations of the laws of Spanish colonial governments in North America
3 adoptions of rules used by the Holy Roman Empire
4 reflections of the philosophies of the European Enlightenment

3 The authors of the United States Constitution believed that the voice of the people should be heard frequently. Which part of the Government was instituted to respond most directly to the will of the people?

1 Senate
2 House of Representatives
3 Supreme Court
4 Presidency

4 In the United States, the use of implied powers, the amending process, and Supreme Court interpretations have resulted in

1 a general loss of individual rights
2 a strengthening of the principle of separation of powers
3 the Constitution being adapted to fit changing times
4 the limiting of Presidential power in domestic affairs

5 Which quotation from the United States Constitution provides for a federal system of government?

1 "He shall have power . . . with the advice and consent of the Senate, ... and ... shall appoint . . ."
2 "Every bill . . . shall, before it becomes a law, be presented to the President of the United States; . . ."
3 "The powers not delegated to the United States . . . are reserved to the states . . ."
4 "Full faith and credit shall be given in each state to the public acts, records, and judicial proceedings of every other state."

6 The system of checks and balances is best illustrated by the power of

1 the President to veto a bill passed by Congress
2 Congress to censure one of its members
3 a governor to send the National Guard to stop a riot
4 state and Federal governments to levy and collect taxes

7 Which Presidential action is an example of the unwritten constitution?

1 appointing Justices to the Supreme Court
2 granting pardons for Federal crimes
3 submitting a treaty to the Senate for ratification
4 consulting with the Cabinet

8 A lasting impact of the United States Supreme Court under Chief Justice John Marshall is that the Court's decisions

1 extended the Bill of Rights to enslaved persons
2 expanded the power of the Federal Government
3 restricted the authority of Congress
4 promoted the views of the President

9 The major role of political parties in the United States is to

1 protect the American public from corrupt public officials
2 insure that free and honest elections are held
3 nominate candidates for public office and conduct campaigns
4 meet constitutional requirements for choosing the President

10 Adherence to a strict interpretation of the Constitution would have prevented President Thomas Jefferson from

1 making the Louisiana Purchase
2 writing "State of the Union" messages
3 receiving ambassadors
4 commissioning military offficers

11 Which argument did President Abraham Lincoln use against the secession of the Southern States?

1 Slavery was not profitable.
2 The government was a union of people and not of states.
3 The Southern States did not permit their people to vote on secession.
4 As the Commander in Chief, he had the duty to defend the United States against foreign invasion.

12 Which statement best summarizes the beliefs of Booker T. Washington?

1 The best solution for African Americans was to return to Africa.
2 Social equality for African Americans would be easier to achieve than legal rights.
3 The way to dissolve the barriers of segregation and bring about an end to Jim Crow laws was by active, violent resistance.
4 The most immediate means for African Americans to achieve equality was to expand their opportunities for vocational education.

13 In the period from 1865 to 1900, the United States Government aided the development of the West by

1 maintaining free and unlimited coinage of silver
2 offering low-interest loans to businesses
3 granting land to railroad companies
4 providing price supports for farm products

14 In the period from 1860 to 1890, which experience was shared by most Native Americans living in western states?

1 They maintained control of their traditional lands.
2 They benefited economically from government policy.
3 They became farmers and small business owners.
4 They were forced to live on reservations.

15 At times, the United States Government has passed protective tariffs to

1 encourage foreign trade
2 help the nation's manufacturers
3 reduce the cost of consumer goods
4 improve the quality of goods

16 In the United States, the main purpose of antitrust legislation is to

1 protect the environment
2 increase competition in business
3 encourage the growth of monopolies
4 strengthen the rights of workers

17 At the turn of the century, why did most immigrants to the United States settle in cities?

1 Jobs were readily available.
2 Government relief programs required immigrants to settle in cities.
3 Labor union leaders encouraged unrestricted immigration.
4 Immigrants were not permitted to buy farmland.

18 Prior to 1890, United States businesses made few foreign investments mainly because

1 state governments discouraged foreign investments
2 foreign investments were prohibited by Congress
3 foreign nations did not accept investments from United States businesses
4 investment opportunities were better in the United States

19 The United States Federal Reserve System was established to

1 provide loans to industrialists
2 end the Great Depression
3 provide for a balanced budget
4 regulate the money supply

20 The Federal Trade Commission, the Interstate Commerce Commission, and the Federal Communications Commission are similar in that each

1 represents the interests of big business
2 is specifically provided for in the United States Constitution
3 has the power to formulate and enforce regulations
4 must get approval from the states to carry out national laws

21 Which conclusion can be drawn about the impact of the Populist and the Progressive parties on the United States?

1 Some third-party goals eventually become planks in the platforms of the major parties.
2 The United States has steadily moved from a two-party system to a multiparty system.
3 Religious ideals have most often motivated people to splinter away from major parties.
4 An increasing number of citizens have grown weary of party politics and fail to vote in elections.

22 Which statement best describes President Theodore Roosevelt's foreign policy position toward Latin America in the early 1900s?

1 The United States should reduce its involvement in Latin American affairs.
2 The Monroe Doctrine permits the United States to intervene actively in the affairs of Latin American nations.
3 Latin American nations should form an organization to help them achieve political and economic stability.
4 The United States should give large amounts of financial aid to help the poor of Latin America.

23 The Republican Presidents of the 1920s generally followed a foreign policy based on

1 collective security   3 noninvolvement
2 brinkmanship   4 militarism

24 A significant cause of the Great Depression of the 1930s was that

1 some banking policies were unsound and had led to the overexpansion of credit
2 a decrease in protective tariffs had opened American business to competition from abroad
3 a wave of violent strikes had paralyzed the major industries
4 consumer goods were relatively inexpensive

25 After World War I, why did American farmers fail to share in the general economic growth of the United States?

1 Many immigrants were settling in the west and competing with the farmers.
2 The Federal Government reduced the number of acres on which farmers could grow subsidized crops.
3 Farmers could not produce enough to keep up with demand.
4 Overproduction and competition caused falling prices.

26 In the 1930s, the enactment of New Deal programs demonstrated a belief that

1 corporations were best left to operate without government interference
2 state governments should give up control over commerce inside their states
3 the Federal Government must concern itself with the people's economic well-being
4 the United States Constitution was not relevant to 20th-century life

27 Critics charged that President Franklin D. Roosevelt's plan to increase the number of Supreme Court Justices was clearly in conflict with

1 the Supreme Court's practice of judicial restraint
2 the constitutional principle of checks and balances
3 attempts of Congress to limit judicial responsibilities
4 efforts to restrict the number of terms a President could serve

28 Which New Deal program was chiefly designed to correct abuses in the stock market?

1 Federal Emergency Relief Act
2 Civilian Conservation Corps
3 Works Progress Administration
4 Securities and Exchange Commission

29 The Fourteen Points and the Atlantic Charter were both

1 statements of post-war goals for establishing world peace
2 plans of victorious nations to divide conquered territories
3 military strategies for defeating enemy nations
4 agreements between nations to eliminate further development of weapons

30 The Truman Doctrine and the Marshall Plan represented attempts by the United States to deal with the

1 national debt
2 spread of communism
3 President's political opposition
4 arms race

31 A similarity between the Red Scare of the 1920s and McCarthyism in the 1950s was that during each period

1 thousands of American citizens were expelled from the United States
2 the Communist Party gained many members in the United States
3 many government employees were convicted of giving secrets to the Soviet Union
4 the civil liberties of American citizens were threatened

32 A major cause of the growth of state and Federal highway systems after World War II was the

1 increased use of mass transit systems
2 growing prosperity of inner-city areas
3 rapid development of suburbs
4 return of city dwellers to farm areas

33 President Theodore Roosevelt's Square Deal and President Lyndon Johnson's Great Society were similar in that both

1 returned control of social welfare programs to the states
2 relied on individual initiative to improve the economy
3 were supported by Congress over the objections of the majority of state governments
4 increased the role of the Federal Government in dealing with social and economic problems

34 Which idea is illustrated by the Supreme Court cases *Schenck v. United States* and *Korematsu v. United States*?

1 The free speech rights of Communists have often been violated.
2 During wartime, limitations on civil rights have been upheld by judicial action.
3 The rights of protestors have been preserved even in times of national stress.
4 Economic interests of foreign nations are frequently upheld in United States courts.

35 Both the Bay of Pigs invasion of Cuba (1961) and the invasion of Panama (1989) are examples of United States attempts to

1 eliminate unfriendly governments geographically close to the United States
2 cultivate good relations with Latin American nations
3 stop the drug trade
4 end the cold war

The speakers below are discussing foreign policies that the United States has followed at various times. Base your answers to questions 36 through 38 on their statements and on your knowledge of social studies.

Speaker A: Steer clear of permanent alliances with any portion of the foreign world.

Speaker B: The United States will give economic aid to needy countries anywhere in the world, but will not provide military aid.

Speaker C: The United States must prevent the growth of communism.

Speaker D: The United States can take over other countries to help them become more like us.

36 Which speakers would most likely support a United States foreign policy of intervention?

(1) *A* and *B*   (3) *C* and *D*
(2) *A* and *C*   (4) *B* and *D*

37 The Korean conflict and the Vietnam conflict were attempts to carry out the foreign policy described by Speaker

(1) *A*   (3) *C* .
(2) *B*   (4) *D*

38 Which speaker states a policy most similar to the foreign policy advice given by President George Washington in his Farewell Address?

(1) *A*   (3) *C*
(2) *B*   (4) *D*

39 Which trend has reflected the increasing pluralism in United States society in recent years?

1 a decrease in immigration from Latin America
2 growing demands for unskilled labor
3 new efforts by public schools to teach about ethnic heritages
4 failure of Congress to approve appointments of women and minority groups to Federal courts

Base your answer to question 40 on the cartoon below and on your knowledge of social studies.

Herblock, 11/12/67

40 What is the main idea of the cartoon?

1 The sale of foreign-made goods in the United States has little effect on economic conditions in the United States.
2 Placing quotas on imports ultimately harms rather than helps the United States economy.
3 mport quotas have been successful in improving the United States balance of trade.
4 Most foreign nations support free trade.

41 In situations where the President is suspected of wrong doing, such as the Watergate scandal, the official role of the House of Representatives is to

1 investigate and bring charges against the President
2 conduct the impeachment trial
3 provide attorneys to defend the President
4 determine the punishment if the President is convicted

42 The goal of current Federal Government policies toward Native Americans is to

1 make Native Americans more dependent on the Federal Government
2 give the states more control over Native American affairs
3 eliminate tribal ties and customs
4 give Native Americans more control over their own affairs

43 Which factor has made the strongest contribution to the development of religious freedom in the United States?

1 Most citizens have shared the same religious beliefs.
2 Religious groups have remained politically unified.
3 School prayer has been ruled constitutional by the Supreme Court.
4 Guarantees in the Constitution have encouraged religious expression and toleration.

44 Which statement best summarizes economic conditions in the United States since the end of World War II?

1 The economy has been in a depression for most of the period.
2 The United States has had the world's highest unemployment rate.
3 The United States has come to depend more heavily on imports to meet its economic needs.
4 The legal minimum wage has steadily declined.

45 In the United States, most new jobs created during the 1980s were jobs that

1 were classified as managerial
2 provided services rather than produced goods
3 depended on heavy manufacturing
4 were farm related

Base your answer to question 46 on the cartoon below and on your knowledge of social studies.

46 The main idea of the cartoon is that
    1 regulation of the savings-and-loan industry is more important than campaign reform is
    2 some problems cannot be solved by congressional action
    3 Congress cannot agree on spending priorities
    4 members of Congress sometimes avoid legislative actions that might limit their political careers

Base your answer to question 47 on the cartoon below and on your knowledge of social studies.

Source: New York Times

47 The main problem illustrated in the cartoon is
    1 the budget deficit
    2 the failure of American education
    3 overpopulation
    4 the generation gap

625

Answers to the following questions are to be written on paper provided by the school.

Students Please Note:

In developing your answers to Parts II and III, be sure to

(1) include specific factual information and evidence whenever possible
(2) keep to the questions asked; do not go off on tangents
(3) avoid overgeneralizations or sweeping statements without sufficient proof; do not overstate your case
(4) keep these general definitions in mind:
  (a) <u>discuss</u> means "to make observations about something using facts, reasoning, and argument; to present in some detail"
  (b) <u>describe</u> means "to illustrate something in words or tell about it"
  (c) <u>show</u> means "to point out; to set forth clearly a position or idea by stating it and giving data which support it"
  (d) <u>explain</u> means "to make plain or understandable; to give reasons for or causes of; to show the logical development or relationships of"

Part II

ANSWER ONE QUESTION FROM THIS PART. [15]

1 Since the ratification of the Bill of Rights (1791), most of the amendments to the United States Constitution have been added to achieve the goals listed below.

Goals
Extending voting rights
Expanding civil liberties
Improving governmental function

- For *each* goal listed, use a different amendment added since the ratification of the Bill of Rights and describe *one* specific change that was brought about by that amendment [You do not have to indicate the number of the amendments that you discuss.]
- Discuss the historical conditions that led to the adoption of the amendment [5.5.5]

2 United States Presidents have used the power of their office to address a number of national and international issues. Each issue in the list below is paired with a specific President who addressed that issue.

Issues/Presidents
Reconstruction/Andrew Johnson
Environmental destruction/Theodore Roosevelt
Isolationism/Woodrow Wilson
Civil rights violations/Lyndon Johnson
Arab-Israeli tensions/Jimmy Carter
International aggression/George Bush

Choose *three* pairs from the list and for *each* one chosen:

- Describe conditions that led to the issue faced by the President
- Discuss how the President exercised a power of his office to deal with the issue
- Evaluate the success of the President's response in dealing with the issue [5.5.5]

Part III

ANSWER TWO QUESTIONS FROM THIS PART. [30]

3 Works of literature have pointed out the need for reform in United States society. Such reforms have occurred as a result of government action, business initiative, and social pressures.

Literary Works
Uncle Tom's Cabin—Harriet Beecher Stowe
History of the Standard Oil Company—Ida Tarbell
The Grapes of Wrath—John Steinbeck
The Feminine Mystique—Betty Friedan
The Autobiography of Malcolm X—Malcolm X and Alex Haley
Unsafe at Any Speed—Ralph Nader
Silent Spring—Rachel Carson
Bury My Heart at Wounded Knee—Dee Brown

Choose *three* of the listed works and for *each* one chosen:

- Describe the societal problem addressed by the work
- Identify a reform that came about as a response to the problem
- Evaluate the success of that reform in addressing the societal problem [5,5,5]

4 Economic conditions within the United States are affected by many domestic and international factors. Listed below are some of the factors that have had an impact on the economic well-being of the United States.

Factors
Rise of big business (1865–1900)
Rise of labor unions (1900–1940)
Military spending (1910–1950)
Mass production of consumer goods (1920s)
Energy crisis (1970s)
Federal budget deficits (1961–today)

Choose *three* of these factors and for *each* one chosen:

- Identify an economic cause of that factor during the indicated time period
- Discuss one positive effect *and* one negative effect of that factor on the United States economy [5,5,5]

626

5 In the United States, attitudes toward immigration have affected immigration legislation.

Immigration Laws
Chinese Exclusion Act (1882)
National Origins Act (1924)
McCarran-Walter Immigration Act (1952)
Immigration Act of 1965
Immigration Act of 1990

a Choose *two* laws from the list and for *each* one chosen, identify the basic intent of the legislation. Explain how attitudes in the United States led to the passage of the legislation. [5,5]
b Describe *two* ways that United States culture has been enriched by immigration. [5]

6 The United States has pursued a variety of foreign policies to advance its vital interests. Some of these policies are listed below.

Foreign Policies
Neutrality
Manifest destiny
Imperialism
Collective security
Détente
Regional cooperation

Choose *three* of the foreign policies listed and for *each* one chosen:

- Identify a specific period when the United States pursued that policy and describe a specific goal of the policy
- Discuss why that goal was considered vital to the interests of the United States
- Discuss a specific action taken by the United States in pursuit of that goal [5,5,5]

7 Developments in United States history frequently have had an impact on various groups in the nation. Each development in the list below is paired with a group it affected.

Developments/Groups Affected
Granger movement/farmers
World War II/women
Television/politicians
Great Society/the poor
Vietnam War/youth
Medicare/the elderly
Computers/workers

Choose *three* pairs from the list. For each one chosen, discuss *two* significant ways the development affected the group. [5,5,5]

REGENTS EXAMINATION

Part I (55 credits)

Answer all 47 questions in this part.

Directions (1–47): For each statement or question, write on the separate answer sheet the *number* of the word or expression that, of those given, best completes the statement or answers the question.

1 In the Colonial Era, developments such as the New England town meetings and the establishment of the Virginia House of Burgesses represented
1 colonial attempts to build a strong national government
2 efforts by the British to strengthen their control over the colonies
3 steps in the growth of representative democracy
4 early social reform movements

2 According to the Declaration of Independence, the people have the right to alter or abolish a government if that government
1 is a limited monarchy
2 violates natural rights
3 becomes involved in entangling alliances
4 favors one religion over another

3 During the debates over the ratification of the United States Constitution, Federalists and Anti-Federalists disagreed most strongly over the
1 division of powers between the national and state governments
2 provision for admitting new states to the Union
3 distribution of power between the Senate and the House of Representatives
4 method of amending the Constitution

4 Which constitutional provision was intended to give the people the most influence over the Federal Government?
1 President's duty to give Congress information about the state of the Union
2 electoral college system for choosing the President
3 direct election of members of the House of Representatives for two-year terms
4 process for proposing and ratifying amendments to the Constitution

5 One similarity between the United States Constitution and the New York State Constitution is that both
1 provide methods for dealing with foreign powers
2 authorize the coinage of money
3 establish rules for public education
4 separate the branches of government

6 The 14th amendment provides that no "state [shall] deprive any person of life, liberty, or property, without due process of law; nor deny to any person within its jurisdiction the equal protection of the laws." A direct result of this amendment was that
1 the process of amending the Constitution became slower and more complex
2 the guarantees in the Bill of Rights were applied to state actions
3 every citizen gained an absolute right to freedom of speech and assembly
4 the power of the Federal Government was sharply reduced

7 When John Marshall was Chief Justice, United States Supreme Court decisions tended to strengthen the power of
1 the National Government
2 state and local governments
3 labor unions
4 trusts and monopolies

8 An example of the unwritten constitution in the United States is the
1 sharing of power by the national and state governments
2 development of the political party system
3 separation of powers among the three branches of government
4 guarantees of due process of law

Base your answer to question 9 on this excerpt from a newspaper article and on your knowledge of social studies.

WASHINGTON, Dec 4 -- Supporters of limits on Congressional terms gathered in the nation's capital today, ...

Limiting the number of years that members of Congress could serve to 12 years -- six terms for House members and two terms for senators -- would force more competition into the system. . . supporters of term limits said this year's elections, with a 96 percent re-election rate in the House, showed how hard it was for even an angry electorate to defeat incumbents.

-- The New York Times, December 1990

9 The major reason for increased support for the change discussed in the article is the public's belief that
1 most current members of Congress have taken bribes
2 the President's political party should have a majority in Congress
3 political disputes in Congress would be reduced
4 the democratic process would be strengthened

10 Alexander Hamilton's argument that the government has the power to create a National Bank is based on which part of the Constitution?
1 the Preamble
2 the elastic clause
3 guarantees to the States
4 the Bill of Rights

11 The legal basis for the United States purchase of the Louisiana Territory was the
1 power granted to the President to make treaties
2 President's power as Commander in Chief
3 authority of Congress to declare war
4 Senate's duty to approve the appointment of ambassadors

12 The reason for ending the importation of enslaved persons to the United States after 1807 was the
1 success of the American colonial revolution against Britain
2 rapid industrialization of the South
3 replacement of slave labor by immigrant workers from eastern Europe
4 passage of legislation that forbids the practice

13 After the passage of the 13th, 14th, and 15th amendments, African Americans continued to experience political and economic oppression mainly because
1 the amendments were not intended to solve their problems
2 many African Americans distrusted the Federal Government
3 Southern legislatures enacted Jim Crow laws
4 poor communications kept people from learning about their legal rights

Base your answers to questions 14 and 15 on the speakers' statements and on your knowledge of social studies.

Speaker A: "The business of America is business, and we would be wise to remember that."

Speaker B: "Government ownership of business is superior to private enterprise."

Speaker C: "Strict government regulation of business practices is a means to insure the public good."

Speaker D: "Only through personal effort can wealth and success be achieved."

14 Which speaker best expresses the main idea of rugged individualism?
(1) A   (3) C
(2) B   (4) D

15 Which speaker would most likely have supported the ideas of the Progressive movement?
(1) A   (3) C
(2) B   (4) D

16 Which term best describes United States economic policy during the era of the rise of big business (1865–1900)?
1 laissez-faire capitalism
2 mercantilism
3 Marxism
4 welfare-state capitalism

17 Which statement best describes the status of the labor union movement in the United States in 1900?
1 Most of the labor force was organized into unions.
2 Government and business opposition had destroyed the labor union movement.
3 Unions were still struggling to gain public acceptance.
4 Unions had won the right to strike and bargain collectively.

18 The purpose of the Interstate Commerce Act (1887), the Sherman Antitrust Act (1890), and the Clayton Antitrust Act (1914) was to
1 eliminate unfair business practices
2 reduce imports from foreign nations
3 reduce the power of the unions
4 increase the power of local governments

19 Why did the United States follow a policy of unrestricted immigration for Europeans during most of the 1800's?
1 Business and industry depended on the foreign capital brought by immigrants.
2 The American economy needed many unskilled workers.
3 Most Americans desired a more diversified culture.
4 The United States wanted to help European nations by taking in their surplus population.

20 In the early 20th century, muckrakers were able to influence American society mainly through their
1 frequent acts of civil disobedience
2 activities as government officials
3 publication of articles and books
4 control over factories

21 The initiative, referendum, recall, and direct primary are all intended to
1 make the President more responsive to the wishes of Congress
2 reduce the influence of the media on elections
3 give political parties more control of the electoral process
4 increase participation in government by citizens

22 The main reason the United States developed the Open Door policy was to
1 allow the United States to expand its trade with China
2 demonstrate the positive features of democracy to Chinese leaders
3 aid the Chinese Nationalists in their struggle with the Chinese Communists
4 encourage Chinese workers to come to the United States

23 President Theodore Roosevelt's policies toward Latin America were evidence of his belief in
1 noninvolvement in world affairs
2 intervention when American business interests were threatened
3 the sovereign rights of all nations
4 the need for European interference in the Western Hemisphere

24 The "clear and present danger" ruling in the Supreme Court case *Schenck* v. *United States* (1919) confirmed the idea that
1 prayer in public schools is unconstitutional
2 racism in the United States is illegal
3 interstate commerce can be regulated by state governments
4 constitutional rights are not absolute

25 A major reason for the isolationist trend in the United States following World War I was
1 a desire to continue the reforms of the Progressives
2 the public's desire to end most trade with other nations
3 the failure of the United States to gain new territory
4 a disillusionment over the failure to achieve United States goals in the postwar world

26 Which events best support the image of the 1920's as a decade of nativist sentiment?
1 the passage of the National Origins Act and the rise of the Ku Klux Klan
2 the Scopes trial and the passage of women's suffrage
3 the Washington Naval Conference and the Kellogg-Briand Pact
4 the growth of the auto industry and the Teapot Dome affair

Base your answers to questions 27 and 28 on the statements below and on your knowledge of social studies.

Statement A: The best way to economic recovery is to subsidize industry so that it will hire more workers and expand production.

Statement B: If jobs are not available, the government must create jobs for those who are unemployed.

Statement C: According to human nature, the most talented people will always come out on top.

Statement D: Our government is responsible for the nation's economic well-being.

27 Which statement is closest to the philosophy of Social Darwinism?
(1) A   (3) C
(2) B   (4) D

28 Which statements most strongly support the actions of President Franklin D. Roosevelt?
(1) A and C   (3) C and D
(2) B and C   (4) B and D

630

29 Which action best illustrates the policy of isolationism followed by the United States before it entered World War II?

1 signing of a collective security pact with Latin American nations
2 passage of neutrality legislation forbidding arms sales to warring nations
3 embargo on the sale of gasoline and steel to Japan
4 President Franklin D. Roosevelt's exchange of American destroyers for British naval and air bases

30 Deficit spending by the Federal Government as a means of reviving the economy is based on the idea that

1 purchasing power will increase and economic growth will be stimulated
2 only the National Government can operate businesses efficiently
3 the National Government should turn its revenue over to the states
4 lower interest rates will encourage investment

31 President Harry Truman justified using atomic bombs on Japan in 1945 on the grounds that the

1 world was ready for a demonstration of nuclear power
2 Axis powers deserved total destruction
3 early ending of the war would save many lives
4 American public demanded that the bombs be used

32 Which precedent was established by the Nuremberg war crimes trials?

1 National leaders can be held responsible for crimes against humanity.
2 Only individuals who actually commit murder during a war can be guilty of a crime.
3 Defeated nations cannot be forced to pay reparations.
4 Defeated nations can be occupied by the victors.

33 In the years just after World War II, the United States attempted to prevent the spread of communism in Europe mainly by

1 taking over the governments of several Western European nations
2 increasing opportunities for political refugees to settle in the United States
3 holding a series of summit meetings with leaders of the Soviet Union
4 establishing policies of economic and military aid for European nations

34 Throughout United States history, the most important aim of the country's foreign policy has been

1 participation in international organizations
2 advancement of national self-interest
3 containment of communism
4 development of military alliances

Base your answers to questions 35 and 36 on the graph below and on your knowledge of social studies.

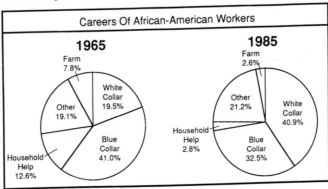

Sources: U.S. Bureau of the Census; U.S. Labor Dept.

35 Which statement is best supported by the data in the graph?

1 African Americans are increasingly entering white-collar occupations.
2 Professional opportunities for African Americans were as limited in 1985 as they were in 1965.
3 An increasing percentage of African Americans are unemployed.
4 The United States economy has little need for skilled African-American workers.

36 Which factor best explains the situation shown in the graph?

1 an increase in imports of consumer goods from foreign nations
2 an increase in the wages of agricultural and household service workers
3 an increase in educational opportunities combined with affirmative action programs
4 a growing refusal by blue-collar employers to hire African Americans

631

37 Under Chief Justice Earl Warren, the Supreme Court was considered "activist" because of its
1 reluctance to overturn state laws
2 insistence on restricting freedom of speech to spoken words
3 expansion of individual rights in criminal cases
4 refusal to reconsider the issues of the *Plessy* v. *Ferguson* case

38 When necessary to achieve justice, which method did Martin Luther King, Jr., urge his followers to employ?
1 using violence to bring about political change
2 engaging in civil disobedience
3 leaving any community in which racism is practiced
4 demanding that Congress pay reparations to African Americans

39 In 1988, Congress voted to pay $20,000 to each of the surviving Americans of Japanese descent who were interned during World War II because
1 the danger of war with Japan no longer existed
2 all of the interned Japanese Americans eventually became American citizens
3 the World Court ordered the United States to pay reparations
4 many Americans believed the internment was unjust and unnecessary

40 A common characteristic of third political parties in the United States is that they
1 tend to focus on one person or one issue
2 come into existence only during periods of corruption
3 have dealt mainly with foreign policy issues
4 have frequently forced Congress to decide Presidential elections

41 The major political parties in the United States obtain most of their national campaign funds from
1 the personal fortunes of the candidates
2 state and local taxes
3 funds appropriated by Congress
4 the contributions of individuals and special interest groups

42 The main significance of the Watergate affair was that it
1 led to the impeachment and conviction of President Richard Nixon
2 showed that the laws of the United States are superior to the actions of a President
3 was the first time a President had disagreed with Congress
4 proved that Presidential powers are unlimited

43 "The great rule of conduct for us in regard to foreign nations is, in extending our commercial relations, to have with them as little political connection as possible."

This quotation supports a foreign policy of
1 imperialism　　　　3 neutrality
2 appeasement　　　 4 economic sanctions

44 The Korean War and the Persian Gulf War were similar in that both
1 represented United Nations efforts to assist nations in repelling aggressors
2 involved unilateral military action by the United States
3 were military defeats for the United Nations
4 brought about lasting solutions to problems in each region

45 Raising import duties on foreign manufactured goods is an example of
1 technological competition
2 supporting free trade
3 lowering inflation
4 economic protectionism

46 The growth of modern technology has resulted in
1 a decrease in the population of the world
2 increasing interdependence among nations
3 a growing need for unskilled labor
4 a sharp decline in the need for oil and coal

Base your answer to question 47 on the cartoon below and on your knowledge of social studies.

47 What is the main idea of the cartoon?
  1 Native Americans and Europeans showed a great willingness to share knowledge at their first contact.
  2 Spanish colonization in the Americas preceded British colonization.
  3 American society has failed to recognize the achievements of Native Americans.
  4 The pluralistic heritage of the United States began to receive approval early in the nation's history.

Answers to the following questions are to be written on paper provided by the school.

Students Please Note:

In developing your answers to Parts II and III, be sure to
  (1) include specific factual information and evidence whenever possible
  (2) keep to the questions asked; do not go off on tangents
  (3) avoid overgeneralizations or sweeping statements without sufficient proof; do not overstate your case
  (4) keep these general definitions in mind:
    (a) discuss means "to make observations about something using facts, reasoning, and argument; to present in some detail"
    (b) describe means "to illustrate something in words or tell about it"
    (c) show means "to point out; to set forth clearly a position or idea by stating it and giving data which support it"
    (d) explain means "to make plain or understandable; to give reasons for or causes of; to show the logical development or relationships of"

Part II

ANSWER ONE QUESTION FROM THIS PART.   [15]

1 In United States history, the system of checks and balances has operated to limit or to strengthen the powers of the branches of the Federal Government.

Examples of Checks and Balances

Judicial review
Impeachment process
Presidential appointment of Supreme Court Justices
Presidential veto
Presidential war powers
Treaty ratification

Choose *three* of the examples listed and for *each* one chosen:

- Describe its use during a specific historical conflict between two branches of the Federal Government
- Explain how one branch of government either lost or gained power as a result of this conflict   [5,5,5]

2 Many disputes have been brought before the United States Supreme Court. Below are listed Supreme Court cases and the constitutional issue involved in each case.

Cases — Issues

McCulloch v. *Maryland* (1819) — federalism
Dred Scott v. *Sanford* (1857) — property rights
Plessy v. *Ferguson* (1896) — civil rights
Korematsu v. *United States* (1944) — Presidential power
Engel v. *Vitale* (1962) — freedom of religion
Miranda v. *Arizona* (1966) — due process
Roe v. *Wade* (1973) — right to privacy

Choose *three* cases from the list. For *each* one chosen:

- Show how the constitutional issue listed was involved in the case
- State the Supreme Court's decision in the case
- Discuss an impact of the decision on United States history   [5,5,5]

Part III

ANSWER TWO QUESTIONS FROM THIS PART.   [30]

3 Throughout United States history, opportunities of some groups of people have been limited.

Groups

Hispanics or Haitians
Native Americans
Senior citizens
Persons with disabilities
One religious group of your choice
[Identify the group.]

Choose *three* of the groups listed. For *each* one chosen:

- Show how the opportunities of that group have been limited at some time in United States history [Be sure to include specific historical information in your answer.]
- Describe *one* way that government has attempted to improve the opportunities of that group   [5,5,5]

4 National controversy has frequently occurred in United States history.

National Controversies

Writing of the United States Constitution
Westward expansion
Annexation of the Philippines
Restriction of immigration
Containment of communism in Southeast Asia
National health care policy

Choose *three* of the controversies listed and for *each* one chosen:

* Describe the historical background of the controversy
* Explain the differences of opinion held by two opposing sides regarding the controversy   [5,5,5]

5 Prominent individuals in United States history who have held differing views on the same issue are paired in the list below.

Individuals

Thomas Jefferson — Alexander Hamilton
Theodore Roosevelt — John D. Rockefeller
Booker T. Washington — W.E.B. DuBois
Woodrow Wilson — Henry Cabot Lodge
Herbert Hoover — Franklin D. Roosevelt
Lyndon B. Johnson — Ronald Reagan

Select *three* of the pairs of individuals. For *each* one chosen, identify one issue about which they had differing views. Discuss the point of view held by each individual concerning the issue. Be sure to include specific historical information in your answer.   [5,5,5]

6 Reform movements have sought to solve many problems in American society.

Reform Movements

Radical Republicans during Reconstruction
Populism
Progressivism
Women's movement
Prohibition movement
Civil rights movement after World War II

Choose *three* of the reform movements and for *each* one chosen:

* Describe a problem the movement attempted to solve
* Discuss the extent to which the movement was successful in solving the problem   [5,5,5]

7 The Great Depression was the most severe economic depression in the history of the United States.

a Describe *two* causes of the Great Depression in the United States.   [6]

b Show how each of *three* New Deal programs attempted to remedy problems that arose during the Great Depression.   [9]

ANSWERS TO REGENTS EXAMINATIONS

JANUARY 1993
PART ONE

1. 3	13. 3	25. 4	37. 4
2. 4	14. 4	26. 2	38. 3
3. 2	15. 2	27. 1	39. 4
4. 1	16. 1	28. 3	40. 1
5. 3	17. 3	29. 1	41. 4
6. 2	18. 2	30. 3	42. 2
7. 1	19. 1	31. 4	43. 1
8. 4	20. 4	32. 1	44. 4
9. 2	21. 2	33. 2	45. 1
10. 3	22. 3	34. 1	46. 4
11. 1	23. 1	35. 2	47. 3
12. 2	24. 2	36. 2	

JUNE 1993
PART ONE

1. 4	13. 2	25. 3	37. 3
2. 1	14. 1	26. 1	38. 2
3. 2	15. 3	27. 4	39. 1
4. 3	16. 2	28. 3	40. 4
5. 4	17. 3	29. 4	41. 2
6. 2	18. 4	30. 1	42. 1
7. 3	19. 2	31. 2	43. 2
8. 1	20. 3	32. 2	44. 1
9. 3	21. 1	33. 1	45. 3
10. 4	22. 2	34. 4	46. 2
11. 1	23. 4	35. 1	47. 3
12. 4	24. 3	36. 3	48. 4

ANSWERS TO REGENTS EXAMINATIONS

JANUARY 1994
PART ONE

1. 2	14. 4	27. 2	39. 3
2. 4	15. 2	28. 4	40. 2
3. 2	16. 2	29. 1	41. 1
4. 3	17. 1	30. 2	42. 4
5. 3	18. 4	31. 4	43. 4
6. 1	19. 4	32. 3	44. 3
7. 4	20. 3	33. 4	45. 2
8. 2	21. 1	34. 2	46. 4
9. 3	22. 2	35. 1	47. 1
10. 1	23. 3	36. 3 (*or C and D*)	
11. 2	24. 1	37. 3 (*or C*)	
12. 4	25. 4	38. 1 (*or A*)	
13. 3	26. 3		

JUNE 1994
PART ONE

1. 3	13. 3	25. 4	36. 3
2. 2	14. 4 (*or D*)	26. 1	37. 3
3. 1	15. 3 (*or C*)	27. 3 (*or C*)	38. 2
4. 3	16. 1	28. 4 (*or B and D*)	39. 4
5. 4	17. 3		40. 1
6. 2	18. 1	29. 2	41. 4
7. 1	19. 2	30. 1	42. 2
8. 2	20. 3	31. 3	43. 3
9. 4	21. 4	32. 1	44. 1
10. 2	22. 1	33. 4	45. 4
11. 1	23. 2	34. 2	46. 2
12. 4	24. 4	35. 1	47. 3

INDEX